Barbara Orser
Ryerson Polytechnic
University
979·5000 (6734)

New Venture Experience

Karl H. Vesper
University of Washington

VECTOR BOOKS

Seattle, Washington 98105

New Venture Experience

© Karl H. Vesper 1994

Suggestions, permission requests and other inquiries can be addressed to the author, Karl H. Vesper, School of Business, University of Washington, Seattle, Washington 98195. Fax (206) 685 9392.

Cases in this book have been made possible by entrepreneurs, businesses and other organizations which may wish to remain anonymous by having names, quantities and other identifying details disguised. Basic relationships within the cases, however, are maintained. Cases are prepared as a basis for class discussion rather than to illustrate either effective or ineffective handling of business situations.

Typesetting: Kathleen Dufour, LaserWorks
Cover Design: April Ryan
Printed in the United States of America
by RR Donnelley & Sons Company

Library of Congress Cataloging-in-Publication Data

Library of Congress Catalog Card Number: 93-85209

ISBN 1-884021-00-X

To

W. Ed McMullan,
*a most creative and supportive
scholar and
entrepreneur*

Preface

This book represents over a decade of work in developing, testing and refining text, cases and exercises to aid learning about entrepreneurship. It is in some ways novel, and a few minutes spent in scanning some special features may make it easier and more effective to use.

This preface begins with suggestions especially for students, followed by comments for instructors and others.

Comment to the Student

Please take a few minutes to scan through the book and notice its design. Some special features to notice include the following:

1. Three main parts comprise the book: text with exercises, cases and appendix. The front of the book contains the text and exercises, grouped into 10 chapters. Following that come the cases, which are numbered and listed in alphabetical order. Finally, there is an appendix of venture plan excerpts at the back.

2. The table of contents has the same three parts. The first lists chapters of the text and notes the location of case questions at the end of each chapter. The instructor may or may not follow the same chapter sequence as the book and may or may not choose to link cases to the particular chapters that suggest assignment questions for them. A given case may link equally well to any of several chapters. The second part of the table of contents lists the cases and briefly notes the type of product or service each concerns. The third part lists the types of excerpts from venture plans that comprise the appendix.

3. Each of the 10 chapters is subdivided into two or three subchapters. This allows the instructor to link topics and arrange the reading schedule with greater flexibility by assigning various combinations of chapters and/or subchapters, possibly coupled with outside readings.

4. Several types of questions and assignment statements appear in the book. At the end of each subchapter are: (1) exercise questions, (2) venture history questions, and (3) questions for developing a business plan. Which ones are appropriate depends upon what cases and what projects have been assigned. There should be no presumption that the questions are either comprehensive or in the best

order for any particular assignment. It all depends. Part of the student's job is to figure out what questions should be asked, perhaps using those in the book if they are helpful as prompts, but not mechanically attempting to plow through them from beginning to end. None of these questions is intended to substitute for thought.

5. Unique to this book are "Application" questions embedded in the body of the text itself, as opposed to those that might appear at the ends of chapters or cases. These crop out in fine print in the left hand margin of the page and cut into the text at points where it may be helpful to stop and think about how the text section just read may apply to either an assigned case or a venture project. Please take a brief look at them now. The instructor may choose to assign particular application questions by noting the pages on which they appear, or simply may ask the class to decide which questions should be considered and why for a particular case or project.

6. Venture plan examples appear in part or in whole at various points in the book. You may find it helpful early in the term to flip quickly through the text and cases spotting these examples for ideas about how to design a venture plan. Appendix 1 at the back of the book presents a collection of excerpts from various venture plans which illustrate the variety of elements a plan may include. These excerpts, however, are not offered as models. Every business plan calls for its own fresh design. Many of the excerpts can be criticized and improved upon. They are intended to stimulate ideas, not imitation. The same is true of venture plans that appear in the cases. An introduction at the front of Appendix 1 suggests further ways of considering the business plan excerpts.

7. The text is designed to stand alone or to be complemented by companion texts or lectures. It is comprehensive in coverage but limited in depth of detail. Any number of companion books or articles may be chosen as suitable complements. Two books in particular that fit as complements are *New Venture Strategies* and *New Venture Mechanics* by the author. The pertinent complementary chapters of these two are noted as supplementary readings at the end of each chapter in this book.

The overall theme of this book in treating the subject of entrepreneurship is **application**. Both the text and cases are intended to help the reader learn information that applies usefully to the task of creating or acquiring a business. The text gives information that applies to cases, field projects and actual ventures. The cases give illustrations of application of text information and also give information that elaborates the text. As you read the book, your emphasis should be on using the information, not just learning it, to become more resourceful in following a business career, whether as an independent venturer or as part of a team developing an enterprise.

The instructor may indicate what to read first: assigned text, non-assigned text, assigned or non-assigned cases, or case questions. Or that may be left for each student to decide individually. The rule should be to do whatever works best. This book is not a mathematical treatise or a novel that should be read from front to back. A better reading strategy may be to jump around among topics, taking whatever is useful for getting the assignment done.

Comment to the Instructor

It can help greatly to have students read the above and examine the design of the book in class, as soon as they have copies. Several text features should be noted.

The text is comprised of chapters containing subchapters, rather than simply a large number of chapters. Intended advantages of this new arrangement include flexibility and convenience for the instructor. Having subchapters allows a total of 23 separate subchapters for assignment. Grouping them into chapters, however, clusters the number down to 10. From the learner's point of view this leaves only 10 main chapters to remember, which is much easier than 23. Yet the subchapters are clustered by related topics so the learner may remember all 23, as well.

An instructor may assign a given chapter, which carries with it all the subchapters on that topic automatically. Alternatively partial chapters can be assigned through selection of subchapters. Assigning one chapter per week fits a quarter term nicely. To fit a semester, subchapters can be selected to increase the number of assignments.

Another feature of the book is the embedding of "Application" questions in the body of the text. These are intended to help students stop and think about the meaning of the text by relating it to its application. From the instructor's point of view, the presence of these questions within the text makes assignments easier to focus and specify. They link the text to cases and projects as the instructor or the student chooses. Students should know, after the brief introduction suggested here, what an instructor means by assigning "the Application question on page 4" or "the second Application question on page 25 ." It will be helpful for clarity to describe during the first or second class meeting such an example in class.

It is not essential to follow the topics of this book in the same sequence as the table of contents. All subchapters end with exercise questions that could be used as starting points. Regardless of the sequence it should be possible, as the term progresses, to explore issues of earlier cases again in later cases, so that as the term proceeds, readers can continually practice and reinforce skills and knowledge learned earlier. Among those skills should be virtuosity in foreseeing problems that lie ahead during venture development, identifying alternative ways of dealing with venture problems and capability to treat them quickly. This should help on a later "real" venture by leaving free more time and processing capacity to treat idiosyncrasies of real ventures that cannot be foreseen in school.

There are some things school can give to a person interested in pursuing entrepreneurship, and other things it cannot very effectively give. This book offers readers an acquaintance with the kinds of adventures entrepreneurs encounter in quest of independent business, the kinds of problems they face and some ways of grappling with those problems. It can't tell an individual what specific venture opportunities lie ahead for him or her, and it can't give specialized skills and knowledge that a particular venture as distinguished from all other ventures will require. Those generally must come from life beyond school. Cases illustrate only a tiny fraction of the variety.

All cases and characters in the book are real and no attempt has been made to distort them, except for the disguising of names and locations in three of the cases. The cases were not selected to glamorize entrepreneurship or convey any particular image other than what it is. They were, however, selected to cover different stages and different types of problems, and some attempt was made to focus upon entrepreneurs who were either in or not far beyond their university experience so students could more readily identify with their circumstances.

Acknowledgments

I would like to thank many who have been particularly helpful in the process of developing this book. Those who permitted cases to be written on their ventures contributed not only information but more importantly time—usually when pressing demands of the enterprises made that difficult for them to spare.

Several people also helped writing the cases. They include Joe Crosswhite, who not only skillfully wrote, but also drew illustrations for many of the cases, Bill Gartner, who helped develop the John Morse case, Bob Mighell, who wrote the case on himself, and Nancy Tieken, who helped in finding leads for many of the cases as well as in writing several of them. Innumerable students at several institutions contributed by participating in the testing and refining as well as adding ideas and examples.

Institutional support for much of the case writing was provided by Babson College under the leadership of President Ralph Sorenson during my year there in the Babson Professorship. Some of the cases begun at Babson were later developed further by the Harvard Business School with the understanding that freedom to adapt and use them would be shared by both schools. The Foster and Shane cases particularly were handled in this way.

Several reviewers added helpful suggestions for the book. These included Ray Bagby, Alan Carsrud, Bartlett Finney, Bill Gartner, Charles Hofer, Don Huffmire, Ed McMullan, Dennis Ray, Harriet Stevenson, Sherman Timmins and Warren Weber. In addition, there were several others whose reviews were given to me anonymously. My hope is that they will identify themselves so they can be recognized with thanks in a future edition.

Crucial help in editing and formatting was provided by several people. Copy editing was done by Ratna Anagol, Philippa Brunsman, Patricia Peyton and Karen Vesper. April Ryan helped greatly with the cover design and graphics in some of the cases. Kathleen Dufour of Seattle's LaserWorks worked heroically, patiently and most constructively on the formatting. Joan Vesper contributed to all parts, writing, editing, designing and making sure things were as right as we could make them.

Finally, vital encouragement to pull this collection together and make it available was provided by all of the above and by the New Venture Development group at the University of Calgary.

Even with all that help, there is undoubtedly room for further substantial improvement. Any comments or suggestions from readers will be most welcome.

Karl H. Vesper
Seattle, Washington

Contents

Part 1 Text

Part 2 Cases

Appendix 1 Venture Plan Excerpts

Chapter 1

Introduction

❑ *SUBCHAPTER 1A - The Entrepreneur's Job*

The path to entrepreneurship, self-employment, owning and managing a business, can begin at any time by happenstance or by design.

Two young men, one a business school graduate and the other thinking about applying to graduate business school, have developed a financing proposal to start a store that will rent microcomputer time. How good is their plan? If they get the money will their venture be likely to succeed?

❖ ❖ ❖

Two women, one a lawyer and the other a beautician, have designed what they believe to be a better backpack for a mother to carry her baby. Both have some acquaintance with business, but neither has previously been involved in manufacturing and selling a product. How should they start?

❖ ❖ ❖

A recent business school graduate employed by a boat builder has been asked by his employer if he would like to buy the business. How should he respond and why?

No situation is a "typical" jumping off place for becoming an entrepreneur. As these three examples illustrate, many starting points are possible. Each of these three is described further in cases that appear later in this book. Examples throughout the book will illustrate even more variety.

What does it take to become a successful entrepreneur? It is hard to think of a single statement in reply that is not either complex or incomplete.

Is the answer "a million dollars to capitalize a new business?" With that amount, a would-be entrepreneur could hire a lawyer to form a corporation, rent an office, take out an advertisement in the Yellow Pages, and put up a sign saying "inventions wanted, capital available." Meanwhile, most of the money could be invested to earn interest which would finance the office until a "hit product" came in. Then the capital could be invested to produce and sell the invention. If such an invention did not turn up, then the money could simply be left invested, the profits would continue, and the venture could be called a success, all thanks to one key ingredient, capital.

The catch, of course, is that the return on investment is not likely to be great enough to justify putting up the money. If part of the return is drained off to operate the office, then the remaining income would be less than the investor could gain by simply investing all the money and not letting part be used for the office. The hope that a sufficiently promising invention will come in to justify the cash drain of the office is hard to support, although advertisements are certain to attract some inventions.

An office was set up with $1 million from the National Science Foundation to provide only services, not including capital, for inventors. It operated at the University of Oregon for five years and succeeded in drawing as many as 3,000 invention submissions per year. But out of that huge number none proved profitable enough even to replenish the office expenses, let alone provide a capital gain.

Venture capitalists, those who operate firms whose business is simply to invest in start-ups and small firms, have better success. But they start with much more than $1 million in capital, they don't try to be entrepreneurs, and they don't invest in inventions. They invest most often in businesses that are already ongoing and much less frequently at the inception stage of ventures that entrepreneurs want to start.

Historically, the returns derived by venture capitalists have ranged widely, both over time and among firms as well as among investments. Less successful venture capitalists have tended to be those with smaller funding who pursue investment activity only part time. With a smaller volume of money to work with, they aren't as well known, and don't attract as many deals of higher quality and larger size. Thus, they are less able to justify hiring complementary expert help or to spend as much time on making deals and assisting with problems and opportunities of the venture as it develops. Even less well set up to make venture investments are individual investors. Yet, both individual investors and small venture capital firms are sometimes very successful, though their results are usually a private matter.[1]

Some of the larger venture capital firms, such as Heizer Corporation, have become public companies and have gained excellent returns on the capital they invested. Examples of ventures that have paid off well for some of them have included Apple, Compaq, Conner, Digital Equipment, Intel, and Microsoft. Most of the big successes have been in high technology fields such as microelectronics and biotechnology. But some have been in more prosaic activities such as broadcasting and discount retailing. Average rates of return for the more successful venture capital firms have ranged upwards from 26 percent per year.[2]

---

[1]Arthur Lipper III , *Venture's Guide to Investing in Private Companies* (New York: Dow Jones-Irwin, 1984).

[2]William Bygrave and others, "Rates of Return of Venture Capital Investing: A Study of 131 Funds," in *Frontiers of Entrepreneurship Research, 1988*, eds. Bruce A. Kirchhoff and others (Wellesley, Mass.: Babson Center for Entrepreneurial Studies, 1988), p. 275.

So another answer to the question of what it takes to become a successful entrepreneur might be "whatever those start-ups have that major venture capitalists would invest in." But this answer too has its inadequacies. One is that not all companies venture capitalists invest in are successful. About 20 percent fail entirely. Roughly another 60 percent become investments the capitalists are sorry they made, either because although the ventures in which the money was invested survive, their profits are too low, or because although profitable the ventures cannot be sold and the capitalists are stuck with their capital tied up. For the remaining 20 percent of their investments to make up for shortcomings of the less satisfactory 80 percent, the few real winners must generate very large profits indeed. It is at that top 20 percent of winners that the venture capitalists must aim.

To do so, venture capitalists impose criteria such as favorable reviews by other investor colleagues of a written business plan that includes convincing information about market potential, financial forecasts, and actions steps to start the venture. These financial forecasts must indicate a high probability that the company will allow the venture capitalists to earn returns of 30 percent or more per year on a minimum investment of about $1 million with the prospect that they will be able to cash out within about five years. Other criteria that venture capitalists impose are verification of technical feasibility by expert consultants, and demonstration that the venture is headed by a team possessing both proven track records in relevant activity and balance among the different functional areas of the business.

The odds of satisfying such criteria are slim. Consequently, very few venture proposals submitted are funded by venture capitalists (around 1 percent or less on average). Out of one-half million or so businesses per year started in the U.S. only a microscopically small fraction receive such support. Almost no ventures, whether successful or not, meet the venture capitalists' standards. Venture capital criteria may be fine, but they are not the only measure of what a venture requires to be successful.

So what is required to succeed with a venture that is less ambitious than venture capitalists aim for but still worthwhile? As a starting point, how about simply having a good idea for a business? A good idea might be one that defines a product or service that prospective customers can be expected to desire.

But, of course, that alone is not enough. The customers must also be able to pay for that product or service, and they must want it more than something else they could buy with the same money. The price they are willing to pay must be high enough to pay the entrepreneur for producing and delivering it with something left over for profit. Moreover, there must be enough customers in total so that their payments not only cover costs and give profit to the venture, but do so over a long enough period of time to produce a return on the venture investment.

Thus, inevitably, the requirements that must be satisfied to create a successful venture become complex. Furthermore, the (1) good idea and (2) customers must be coupled with (3) production capability on the entrepreneur's part. If he or she does not possess that capability personally, then others must be recruited or hired to help with the task. Setting up operations and recruiting such needed help often requires financing, both to set up the venture and to live on while it is getting started. The financing will not likely come from venture capitalists, since they finance only an extremely small percentage of the venture population. But it has to come from somewhere, probably personal and family savings of the entrepreneur and any cofounders.

The idea has to be implemented, and beyond that the venture that carries it out must be able to withstand competitors who come up with the same business idea, possibly as a result of seeing the venture or possibly by independent discovery of their own. If the idea can be patented or protected in some way it may be possible to exclude competitors. But usually before much time elapses substitutes are introduced, and competition grows stronger.

Application *What will it take for the venture ideas in the assigned case to be carried to success?*

Game Theory And Entrepreneurship

Analyzing the complex set of requirements noted above can make creation of a new venture seem almost impossible. But it is not. Every year hundreds of thousands of new firms are started in the U.S. and a large fraction of them manage to keep going, albeit at a small size and relatively low level of profit.

What simplifies the task of the entrepreneur is cooperation from other people who have something to gain by his or her success. The purpose of an entrepreneur is to create a new real-life business game in which all the players can win. Those players may include employees, who get new jobs, suppliers, who get a new customer, investors, who share the profits, lenders, who draw interest from the venture, and various levels of government that extract taxes from it. Because they, like the entrepreneur, believe they have something to win from the game, they agree to participate in transactions with the entrepreneur that help set up the game in which the venture forms a core.

Games in general can be divided into two types, zero sum and non zero sum. It is crucial to recognize that what an entrepreneur must set up is the second type. Game theorists use the term "core" to describe that part of a game, within the rules of a game, that allows all the players to win. One player may win more than another one, and the activity of the game is what determines what the split will be. But no player only loses. It is in the interest of the entrepreneur to recognize just what kind of core is being created. When the entrepreneur attempts to set up a new game in the form of a venture he or she must arrange an option to be in the core for all the needed players, such as customers, suppliers, financers, and governmental agencies. Beyond that, the entrepreneur must enable those desired players to recognize that the core is there so that they will choose to join it.[3]

Application *Whose cooperation will be most needed to enable the entrepreneur and/or venture in the assigned case to succeed? What should that person get out of it?*

There have been relatively few systematic investigations of what it feels like to be involved in setting up or in playing a new venture game. One study of 2,994 independent start-ups by Cooper et al.,[4] reported that although 39 percent of the responding founders said they would make major changes in the way they went about forming their businesses, 82 percent would still do it even given current knowledge. The largest fraction (43 percent) said their level of satisfaction in business was about as expected, while 21 percent said it was higher and 32 percent said it was lower. These responses, it should be noted, came from those entrepreneurs in the sample whose businesses were still in operation one to three years after start-up. No study has reported on how entrepreneurs whose ventures did not survive felt about what they had done. Anecdotally, they rarely seem to report that they regret having ventured, even if the venture failed.

Those who are employed in their own ventures, even struggling ones, often say they would never again work for a company owned by others if they could help it. Along the course of getting started entrepreneurs tell anecdotally of being:

- terrified by problems of maintaining positive cash flow

- thrilled by profit generating events

- frustrated by government paperwork

- angered by feeling cheated in working with landlords, employees or suppliers

- infuriated by legal machinations, and the expense of legal help

- anxious in dealing with lenders and investors

---

[3]One way of viewing the economy is as consisting of two parts, free and forced. In the free economy people choose for themselves how to spend their time and money (which can be viewed as saved time). In the forced economy people's time and/or money is confiscated through taxes or other measures and spent by others, usually governmental agencies. It is usually not within an entrepreneur's power to harness the power to manipulate the forced economy. Hence, he or she can only operate in the free economy where players have the option of playing the game or not as they choose.

[4]Arnold C. Cooper and others, *New Business In America* (Washington, D.C.: The NFIB Foundation, 1990), p. 62.

- gratified by winning over customers

- satisfied by making their own decisions about what to sell, how to price, which equipment to buy, when to take vacations, where to set up new operations, how to arrange the shop, whom to hire, and how to answer the question "what kind of work do you do?"

The price of such a privilege can be high. If the venture fails, the entrepreneur may lose everything. Statistically, start-ups seem to fail at a rate of roughly 10 percent per year. Even if the firm survives, the pay may not be very high. In the Cooper et al. study only 2.9 percent of the entrepreneurs responding three years after start-up reported taking over $75,000 per year out of their businesses, while 27.8 percent reported taking out less than $10,000.[5]

They also reported that the hours were long. Table 1-1 following shows a comparison of CEO work hours reported by the Cooper study, which includes mostly very small firms, with those of very high growth firms of the *Inc.* 500, all of which were five or more years old.[6] In both cases the largest fraction appeared to require between 60 and 70 hours per week on the business. Over a third of entrepreneurs in the Cooper study reported that in addition to their own time other family members gave 10 or more hours to the business per week for no pay.[7]

Table 1-1 Entrepreneurs' Work Weeks (Hours)

Number of Hours per Week	Percent of Entrepreneurs in	
	NFIB firms	*Inc.* 500 firms
Under 50 hours	23%	15%
50 - 59	23	26
60 - 69	28	32
70 - 79	13	13
Over 80	12	3
N/A	1	11
Total	100%	100%

Ventures come in many forms, and the experiences of creating them are varied as well. Entrepreneurs themselves are unique and often unusual individuals, so that how they feel about their experiences in venturing is bound to span a wide spectrum.

---

[5]Ibid.
[6]"Notebook," *Inc.,* September 1990, p. 27.
[7]Cooper and others, *New Business In America,* p. 16.

Ventures sometimes start part time and shift to full time, and sometimes develop the other way around. Some begin from necessity such as unemployment and others as a result of requests for help or even offers of financing. Many arise from frustration with another job, sometimes because the entrepreneur's "better idea" is rejected by higher management. It is rare for a substantial enterprise to emerge directly from an entrepreneurship course or to be started by a graduate immediately following school, but occasionally that too happens.

Application   *What work hours and income level would you predict the entrepreneur in the assigned case will have to live with to get this venture going, and how will those estimates change over the first 36 months of start-up?*

Economic benefits to the entrepreneur from venturing can be vastly higher than those from a job on an established company's payroll, but on the average they are probably lower. Success stories in the press and television tend to play up the most exceptionally successful entrepreneurs such as Michael Dell, Bill Gates, Steve Jobs, and Scott McNealy who have become worth many millions at early ages by starting enterprises that prospered and grew rapidly. Most new enterprises, however, never grow beyond four or five employees. They exact very long hours of hard work, particularly from their owners, pay below average salaries and wages, provide less actual vacation, pay for less in the way of life and health insurance, and offer fewer other fringe benefits such as training programs, gym facilities and recreational activities. Company-paid travel for business purposes is non-taxable in both large and small companies, but the Internal Revenue Service is much more likely to quarrel with it if done by the owner of a small company than by an employee of a big company.

Failure rates for new ventures, as noted above at roughly 10 percent per year, are not as high as has been commonly supposed. A popular estimate for years was that 80 percent of new firms fail in the first five years. More recent studies indicate that only around 50 percent do so, and the rate depends greatly on line of business.[8] In fields such as high technology manufacturing, for instance, some researchers have found all but about 20 percent still in business after five years. Moreover, even the 20 percent they could not find still in business may not necessarily have failed. They may have been sold, had their names changed or simply have been closed down without failure by owners choosing to pursue other ventures instead. The odds of losing a job in self employment are probably not much higher than losing one in an established firm.

At the same time, although most new firms never grow large, some do and some achieve very high profitability. The supreme example may be Microsoft, which in less than 20 years achieved a total valuation rivaling that of General

---

[8]Karl H. Vesper, *New Venture Strategies* (Englewood Cliffs: Prentice-Hall, 1990), p. 32.

Motors, made millionaires out of nearly a thousand of its employees and multibillionaires out of its two founders, Gates and Allen.

High profits are possible when a venture enjoys a monopoly position on some product, service, location, talent, name brand or the like that makes it difficult for others to compete against it on price. The monopoly in Microsoft's case was its ownership of the DOS operating system used on roughly three-fourths of all microcomputers. This ownership constituted a barrier to entry and price cutting by any competitors. The list of possible barriers that inhibit competitors from encroaching includes the following:

- **"First mover" advantages** by being original or possibly even by being quick to copy in a new territory.

- **Patents or secrets** on products and/or processes. Some patents and secrets protect more powerfully than others and allow correspondingly higher profits.

- **Special know-how** possessed by the entrepreneur or loyal employees of the venture.

- **Licenses** with the state which exclude competitors. Physicians, lawyers, and veterinarians are protected by licensing requirements that cost great amounts of preparation to satisfy. Barbers and real estate agents are also protected, but by less demanding licensing requirements and hence their margins are lowered.

- **Capitalization** Banks must meet minimum capitalization levels by law to do business. In manufacturing, capital may be needed to pay for expensive tooling. To gain economies of large scale in manufacturing, capital may be needed for long production runs. To take advantage of a fad, or to gain market share ahead of competitors, cash may be needed in advance to pay for advertising.

- **Staying power** One major hurdle for many new firms is simply lasting long enough to build sales momentum in the market. Advertising usually has to be repeated several times to take effect. New stores and services usually take time to build a clientele and/or traffic. A radio station needs time to let listeners know what it offers, listeners need time to acquire habits of tuning in to it, and so forth.

- **Special status and relationships with customers** Obtaining certification as a supplier of parts for airplanes, railroads or even home furnaces can be an expensive and difficult process. But having attained such certification, a venture may enjoy margin protection that preserves healthy profits and at the same time reduces the effort needed to obtain repeat sales from the certifying customer. Of course, the owner still needs to make sure production is up to specification, delivery times are adhered to and prices do not become so high as to provoke customers to take the trouble to seek out and certify other sources.

- **Special relationships with suppliers** Leases on prime locations, exclusive distribution agreements and personal connections with key suppliers can help to varying degrees and for varying lengths of time. Such relationships may or may not be backed up with formal written agreements.

Application   *How would you expect the odds of success for the venture/entrepreneur in the assigned case will compare to the average and why? What can the entrepreneur most effectively do to raise his or her odds?*

But most ventures aren't launched with heavy shielding to protect their margins from competitive attack. Instead they offer services such as eat-out dining, printing and maintenance help for homes and autos where it is relatively easy for competitors to enter the field. Some people enter ventures out of inability to obtain other employment. Some enter out of preference for the independence that self employment offers. Many accept a financial sacrifice for the sake of liberty, independence or opportunity to implement an idea rejected at work. Steve Mariotti, who left a large company to start his own venture and later won numerous awards for teaching disadvantaged youths in the Bronx to become legitimate entrepreneurs, described his path to venturing as follows:

After I graduated from the University of Michigan's business school in 1977, I got an offer from Ford Motor Company to be a financial analyst. I walked into the best conceivable job a young MBA can get – incredible responsibility and I got to see how a big company was run. But after two and a half years I lost the job in an internal power struggle, so I moved to New York City and started an import-export business.

When I came out of Ford, I was very bruised and real bitter. I had been in this hierarchy and I was on the bottom of it: I was a grade 7 and Henry Ford was a grade 27. I felt constant anxiety. I would go into work and they could pretty much do whatever they wanted with me. There'd be this guy down the hall in this big office, and he'd be a grade 17. He'd have control of my life: if he was going to send me to Australia, I was going to go.

But the minute I went into business for myself — and I really didn't know that much about it — I felt equal to Henry Ford psychologically. I felt like, well, I'm president of this company, and he's president of a company. I just don't have as much capital as he does, and I don't really care. But the effect it had on my own psyche was enormous, marked and immediate.[9]

---

[9] "Steve Mariotti," *Inc.*, April 1989, p. 66.

Another issue of *Inc.* reported in 1990 that one out of eight people held a secret desire to start a business. Among executive and professional women 19 percent were planning to go into business for themselves and another 19 percent were considering doing so.[10]

Why Study Entrepreneurship?

The proposition that studying about entrepreneurship might help make someone more likely to succeed as an entrepreneur is often challenged with "can entrepreneurship really be learned?" Evidence that such study can be helpful is to date mostly anecdotal. Those who have taught the subject occasionally hear former students say "that entrepreneurship course certainly helped me in starting my business." But who can say whether they are representative or only exceptional?

A survey of 600 business major alumni of Babson College who had graduated six to 10 years earlier found that participation in entrepreneurship courses tended to correlate with later owning a business. Half had taken one or more entrepreneurship courses in college and the other half had not. In the half that had not, the survey found that 17 percent had a business, which illustrates the unsurprising fact that study of entrepreneurship is certainly not prerequisite for becoming a successful entrepreneur.

However, the other half of the sample displayed some contrasts. Among those who had taken an undergraduate entrepreneurship course, 27 percent were found to be owning a business six to 10 years following graduation. Among those who had taken an entrepreneurship course at MBA level, 34 percent now owned a business. Thirty in the sample had taken both an undergraduate and a graduate entrepreneurship course, and over 50 percent of this group was found to to be owning a business. That certainly does not prove that courses caused alumni to become self-employed. Perhaps those who as students were already oriented toward starting businesses were simply more likely to choose entrepreneurship courses. But at least the courses didn't dissuade them.

Study of entrepreneurship may or may not be significantly helpful for those bent upon venture start-up. Others who may want to learn about the subject include:

- Some who might work with entrepreneurs in other capacities such as bankers, consultants, suppliers, partners or employees.

- Some who would like to consider entrepreneurship as a career path and might find that knowledge about the subject helpful in deciding whether to pursue it or not.

---

[10]"Notebook," *Inc.*, July 1990, p. 20.

- Some who were planning on another career initially but would like to understand more about entrepreneurship as a possible alternative for later career change.

- Some who regard it as an interesting aspect of business and want to expand their knowledge for the satisfaction of learning.

Entrepreneurship Knowledge

The role of formal study is ambiguous in entrepreneurship as well as in other business fields. Some people learn to be journalists without going to journalism school and artists without going to art school, others learn business without going to business school. Bing Crosby became a skilled musician without learning formalities of music, Abraham Lincoln became highly literate without class instruction. William Lear was a prolific inventor and entrepreneur without college training. Most business people, regardless of their success levels, haven't attended business schools. Countries like Japan and Germany became industrially successful without business schools, though more recently they have been adding them. And most entrepreneurs start companies without having taken courses in entrepreneurship.

Application   *What knowledge would most help the entrepreneur in the assigned case and how could it best be obtained?*

Supplementary Reading

New Venture Strategies Chapter 1. (Vesper, K.H., Prentice-Hall, 1990)

Exercises

1. **Student Information Sheet** On one side of a sheet of paper please provide the following information:

   - Name, address and phone
   - Major, if any, and expected graduation date
   - Nature of present job, if any
   - Nature of prior work experience, if any
   - Nature of any company you have started before
   - Rank order of reasons for taking this course:
     - Want to own and operate a full time business
     - Want to own and operate a part time business
     - Want to invest in start-up firm(s)
     - Want to work with entrepreneurs

- Curious about what venturing is like
- Want to obtain one more career alternative
- Other
  - Do you already have a venture idea you want to develop?
  - List three questions you would like to learn answers for in this course.

2. **Entrepreneurial "Truths"** List a few generalizations you think could be made about entrepreneurship (e.g., entrepreneurs are born, not made, ventures are usually high risk, etc.). Be prepared to comment on your list in class. Occasionally during the term, reconsider your reactions to this list.

Longer Term Exercises

3. **Entrepreneurial Variety** Using such library references as magazines, business sections of newspapers, autobiographies of entrepreneurs and other books on entrepreneurship, develop some lists with examples which show how different types of entrepreneurs, ventures, "venture creation games" and players in those games can be alternatively classified. Discuss the extent to which a would-be entrepreneur either could or should want to choose certain positions in these classifications over others.

4. **Entrepreneurial Career Assessment** Ask two or more entrepreneurs how the net increase (or decrease) in wealth per year which they gained from their ventures has compared to what they would probably have made by holding down "regular" jobs. Also ask how they believe any fringe benefits would have differed. Finally, explore how the answers might depend on other factors such as line of business, industry maturity at time of entry, stage in life when venturing was undertaken, what they did or did not know about venturing at the outset, most important decisions made, "luck" and other dimensions you or the entrepreneurs think might have important bearing.

5. **Venture History Report** Develop a written history of the creation of a company begun five or fewer years ago through interviews with its founders and initial backers. Begin by making a list of questions to ask. Then, if you wish, look at the list of suggested questions at the end of each chapter in this book to extend your list. It is not expected that all these questions should be answered in the history or that there are not others which might be more appropriate. It is important to choose for development those aspects that are most important and instructive. The way to do it best is through a series of short visits spread over time as the term progresses, not all at once, and to interview more than one person involved in the start-up. It will likely help the process if on each visit the entrepreneur or other participant receives a summary of what has been developed thus far on the history.

6. **Team Topic Presentation** For one of the chapter topics in this book prepare with your team a 15-minute oral presentation, drawing upon information from your venture histories. Create this presentation, not by repeating the text or by drawing upon other written works, but rather out of information from the experiences of the entrepreneur(s) you are studying.

7. **Venture Idea Search** Take 10 minutes to list on a sheet of paper as many ideas for new ventures as possible. Then each week for eight weeks add to the list the best additional venture idea you can think of. Turn these sheets in weekly to the instructor so copies can be shared and discussed with other members of the class. (If an idea is simply too good to share, then share the next best one.)

8. **Contact Development** Each week contact at least five people you have not talked to before and seek from each some information that might be helpful to you in developing a venture. Turn in to the instructor each week a list of their names, addresses and phone numbers.

9. **Venture Development Portfolio** Compile specimens of your (individual or team) creative efforts in pursuing venture ideas. Include a table of contents with page numbers. Include as chapters whichever of the following you did during the term:

   a. Venture ideas generated
   b. Checkout screening work done on venture ideas
   c. Venture plan developed
   d. Feedback received, and by whom, on venture plan submitted for review
   e. Business results obtained if the venture was actually attempted
   f. Tasks to be performed for further improvement of venture or venture plan

Your Venture Plan

1. As a way of anticipating what should go into a venture plan, imagine yourself in the position of someone with savings who is being asked by an entrepreneur to invest in a start-up.

   a. What information would you want to see in a plan to assess it for investment?
   b. Where would you expect the entrepreneur might be able to obtain such information?

Team Venture Options

As a team of not more than five members choose one of the following options for developing a written venture plan to be turned in at the end of the term.

Venture Project Option I

Plan a very high profit potential start-up, such as one that aims at achieving $5 million or more in sales by year five and/or an ROI of 30 percent or more on an investment of $300,000 or more. If this option is chosen, the report should include:

   a. A one to three page (maximum) executive summary.
   b. A detailed plan for the venture, including financial forecasts and explanation of the assumptions and details behind them.
   c. A description of reactions to the plan obtained from some person(s) who would be key to proceeding with the venture. They could be a venture capitalist, banker, technical expert, customer, supplier, etc.

Venture Project Option II

Start and operate a small venture with the aim of producing a profit during the term plus prepare a plan for taking it to a higher level of operation in the future. If this option is chosen, the report should include:

a. A venture history of the enterprise in detail, including a copy of the preliminary plan, a breakdown of time spent on it and the result.

b. An analysis of the economics of how the venture turned out based upon its financial statements.

c. A projection of strategic alternatives illustrating what further could be done to build upon the venture in the future, backed up by evidence from the initial experimental operation.

Venture Project Option III

If the team fails to find a venture that will work for one of the above two assignments, then it is to turn in a venture search report which includes:

a. A log of the search process, including person-hours spent, broken down into sufficient detail such that no single entry accounts for more than two person-hours. The dates of these activities should also be specified. This should be the sort of breakdown that you would want a consulting firm to give you if you hired it with your own money to seek a viable venture idea and paid it hourly for the work.

b. A list of all the venture ideas considered in a table that includes the date each occurred, the date it was abandoned and a brief statement as to why.

c. Partial written plans for the ideas that were pursued farthest before being abandoned. These partial plans should indicate which venture plan questions were answered, which were not and why.

Venture Project Option IV

Assist a local entrepreneur off campus who wants help in starting a business. Prepare a consulting report of your activities and results. There should be at least two copies of the report, one for the instructor and one given to the entrepreneur. It should concern creation of a new, for-profit independent venture that is not yet operating. The report should include as appendices:

a. A written statement of work to be performed signed by the consulting student(s) and read by the entrepreneur turned in by no later than the third week of class and appended to the final report.

b. A history of the entrepreneur(s) and venture up to the point where you entered.

c. An analysis of what the venture could become and how.

d. A tabulation of time costs of your effort and results produced. The detail on this breakdown should be of the type you would use if it were a bill to be given the client charging on an hourly basis (such as you might want to see if you were paying for the time).

Venture Project Option V

Prepare a written deal for purchase of an ongoing local business. This report should include:

a. A full description of what is to be bought and for what price and terms. This could take the form of a purchase contract which buyer and seller would sign.

b. An analysis of the business explaining the rationale behind the price and terms.

c. A plan for the future of the business following takeover, including appropriate financial projections and the reasoning behind them.

d. An analysis of the search and negotiation experience including a breakdown of the hours spent and on what, as well as a description of how you would do an acquisition search and negotiation differently if you were to do it again in the future.

Some teams may wish to begin development of more than one alternative project as a basis for deciding which has most promise. Turning in partial development of several projects which were terminated after finding their feasibility was not high enough to warrant full follow-through is acceptable. Whatever is turned in will count toward credit for effort.

❏ *SUBCHAPTER 1B - Thinking Through Ventures*

Certainly some kinds of knowledge are crucial to venturing, and that knowledge must either be learned by the entrepreneur or be provided by others who help create the venture. It can be divided into four types: (1) general business knowledge, (2) general entrepreneurship knowledge, (3) opportunity-specific knowledge and (4) venture-specific knowledge. Each of these is worth examining more closely to see why it is needed and how it can be obtained.

General business knowledge includes conventional business functional area subjects: marketing, finance, operations, "people" topics, business law, accounting, and the like. It may also include management or research and development, engineering and other subjects that work on product and service improvement frontiers. Each of these subjects, although typically taught with an orientation toward established businesses, applies also to start-ups. An entrepreneur with prior knowledge of methods used in market research for established firms may be better equipped to check out the likelihood of customer acceptance for a new product or service to be offered by a venture. One with knowledge of accounting should be better able to prepare records and financial statements that a banker or investor will find reassuring in making a decision to advance money to the start-up, and so forth.

Problems in each of the business functional areas are bound to arise as the company gets started. The entrepreneur's responses will presumably be based on common sense, prior work experience, possibly formal study of business and counsel from others. How effective the "answers" must be to make the venture succeed will depend upon how strong the venture's profit margin and strategic position are relative to competitors. A high margin enjoyed by a monopoly product or service, such as one protected by patents or licenses, can compensate for substantial mismanagement. Without such protection, however, managerial error can easily lead to failure. Moreover, even with such protection it is likely that the degree of success will be higher if the business side of the venture is more competently performed. Learning the facts and methods of business may help raise the level of competence with which the business side of the venture is performed.

This learning can be undertaken at two different times: either before the venture is begun or after. Most entrepreneurs become involved in a start-up through some sequence of unanticipated events, find a need for certain know-how, sometimes through calamity, and then seek it, often through trial and more error than they would like.

The "catch" in this learn-only-when-needed approach is that (1) to a person without such knowledge the need for it may not be apparent, and (2) when the knowledge becomes acutely needed there may not be enough time available to seek it out. Countless other tasks and decisions may simultaneously be clamoring for attention. Developing the product or service, working out deals with customers and suppliers, arranging facilities and production, obtaining permissions from government agencies, setting up records for taxes and many other chores also require acquisition of special knowledge. If at least some of the necessary knowledge can be acquired in advance the bustle of start-up activities may go more smoothly.

Application   *How much general business knowledge of what type(s) will the entrepreneur in the assigned case most need, and how might it best be obtained?*

General entrepreneurship knowledge includes more specialized information within each of the functional business areas that is more applicable to start-up ventures in particular. For instance, in the area of finance the entrepreneur can learn about various sources of capital used for funding ventures by reading about them in Chapter 4 of this book or in many other books and articles on the subject. They treat such subjects as what sources exist, what types of ventures use them, what kinds of terms are struck in making deals, how well venture funds perform, how venture capitalists participate beyond putting up money, how the procedures of banks differ from those of investors and many other topics associated with raising start-up capital.

Alternatively, an entrepreneur can wait until there is need for capital, and then go looking for it, usually by asking people and proceeding from one referral to another until he or she either gets the capital or gives up. Acquisition of entrepreneurial know-how on an "as needed" basis can and often does work, although the acquisition process will take time, and also may consume mental processing capacity that could be used for other tasks of getting the business started: setting up shop, arranging for supplies, making advertising decisions, seeking out needed employees, and so forth.

Entrepreneurship knowledge can include simply awareness of what venturing is like. Most entrepreneurs learn this by doing, but study in advance can add insight. David Birch, an MIT professor who started his own consulting company, commented as follows:

> *I was starting in 1983, and I'd studied histories of 12 million companies. I knew it would take me 8 or 10 years to build the kind of business I wanted to build. I knew it wouldn't happen fast, that I wasn't going to get rich in a couple of years. I also knew that I wouldn't be able to grow in a straight line. I knew there'd be plateaus, dips, and bobs— that it would be erratic—and I was prepared for it. I knew I'd have to work 12 to 14 hours a day. I'd talked to a whole bunch of people and I knew what they went through.*
>
> *Profitability is not really a problem—cash is always the problem. They're very different. In my kind of company, profitability goes all over the place and is really quite manipulatable. If you want to grow, you expense every dollar you've got and keep it working in the company. Cash flow is a constant issue if you don't go for large outside financing, which we've chosen not to do. You've got a fixed*

payroll. Everything on the expense side is fixed, and everything on the revenue side is variable. Somebody gets sick and doesn't pay up on his receivable, or a salesperson gets lazy and doesn't sell for a couple months. All of a sudden your cash flow goes to hell. You find yourself constantly managing cash flow. It's a major issue.[11]

Application   *What will likely be the importance of general entrepreneurship knowledge to the entrepreneur in the assigned case and why?*

Opportunity-specific knowledge, the third type, is that which is possessed by a person who knows the opportunity is there but does not necessarily know how to take advantage of it. Inventors often consider themselves to be in this situation. Sometimes they are right. For example, Chester Carlson was repeatedly stymied when he sought to commercialize his process which later became known as Xerography. Sometimes inventors are wrong, thinking they have winning innovations when they really don't. But Carlson clearly was right. If anything, the opportunity was in his case vastly greater than he or anyone else anticipated.

Application   *What opportunity-specific knowledge has the entrepreneur in the assigned case possessed, where did it come from and how important is it to get more?*

Venture-specific knowledge, the fourth category, includes further information that those who have opportunity-specific knowledge require in order to capitalize on their ideas. To illustrate, if the entrepreneur believes there is a potentially viable market for a new radio station and wants to start one to exploit that opportunity, he or she will need information about how to obtain an FCC license. Some of that information can be read in books and government literature. But much of the essential venture-specific information is too specialized for publication. For instance:

- What frequencies are available in a particular transmitting site?

- What real estate is available to use for a station location? How much does it cost? Who owns it? What do they want?

- Who are the potential listeners and what might they be interested in hearing?

- What do competing stations of the area offer and what do they leave out?

- What should the shows be for this particular circumstance, how will they be acquired, from whom, and at what cost?

---

[11]"Coming of Age," *Inc.*, April 1989, p. 38.

- Where can equipment be obtained? What will it cost? Who can operate it and how can their services be obtained?

- What is the best month to begin operations, and what hours are best to be on the air?

- How much financing will be needed, when and where will it come from, and on what terms?

- What will be the operating expenses of this station, at this site, and with this particular format?

- Who will buy air time for advertising, what type and at what prices?

Three ways to obtain knowledge helpful in answering questions like these are (1) to take a job in such a business and learn it as an insider, (2) to undertake a start-up of the venture and learn what is required step by step, or (3) to develop a business plan for the venture through study and investigation. Each of these three approaches has its strengths and shortcomings. The one best suited to school is usually the third, developing a venture plan, although sometimes for simple ventures the others are also possible.

Any of these three approaches should add both general business knowledge and general entrepreneurship knowledge, as well as venture-specific knowledge needed by the entrepreneur. Probably the higher the level of such knowledge, the greater the odds of success. Almost certainly the most important knowledge will be that which is *opportunity-specific* and/or *venture-specific*. Unfortunately, however, these two are usually by far the least teachable in school and usually little described in books or periodicals. Possibly they can be learned in advance of the venture through work experience or deliberate investigation. But often it is not clear in advance what all must be learned. The need for these types of knowledge is idiosyncratic to individual person, time and circumstance.

Application   *What venture-specific knowledge will the entrepreneur in the assigned case most need and why? How can it best be obtained?*

Learning Through Venture Planning

A would-be entrepreneur may wonder, "Once you have an idea for a venture, where do you start?" A good first step may be to sketch out a venture plan on paper. This can begin with (1) a brief description of what the product or service is, (2) what it will do for the customer, (3) what it will cost to produce, (4) why customers might be expected to buy it and (5) how much they will probably be willing to pay. These notes may only represent guesses. Much more work may be needed to treat these and other topics of importance, as will be discussed later in chapters on idea screening and venture plans. But brief notes can form a suitable beginning.

Eventually, the venture will have to demonstrate that it can make money, so another early step is to guess whether that is possible by making some rough calculations. What is the break-even sales volume (fixed costs per month divided by sales price per unit minus variable costs per unit)? Does that rate of selling seem reasonably possible? How much capital will be needed to get started? What level of return on investment or how short a payback period will the venture likely produce? If the venture idea seems to hold up under such tests, then more investigation and possibly action will be appropriate. If not, it's time to modify or drop the idea to seek a better one.

Perspectives from which to view the idea include those of (1) resource provider and (2) operator as well as (3) owner. Even if all three are embodied in one person it will be a good idea to consider them separately. Will this business adequately pay back any investor? Who will be capable of performing the venture and will they want to? Will this business be worth the time, cost and trouble if it succeeds? Is the risk that it will fail worth taking?

Writing a business plan may not answer these questions as surely as might be wished, but it is usually a low cost, low risk starting point. Both in and after graduation from school, preparing and critiquing business plans can be an effective learning exercise. For a real venture, although most start without formal written plans, the plan can serve as a helpful guide as well as a device for persuading people to advance capital.

Most business plans cover the same general topics, but there is no standard format, as can be seen by comparing plans of different ventures. For a starting point, however, here is one possible outline:

Table of Contents Include page numbers of important sections, including appendices.

Executive Summary In one or two pages hit the main points of the plan with specific figures and facts. This summary should not be vague just because it is short, and it should include the main "punch lines" of the plan.

Company Description The description should tell what the venture will make and sell. (Sketches and diagrams may be helpful.) It should state what benefits customers will receive and how, as well as what the distinctive competence and hoped for sustainable competitive advantage(s) of the company will be.

Sales Tell who will buy from this venture and why, how many will do so, how much they will pay and why, how the selling will be done, by whom and on what timetable. If possible present specific evidence that people will buy, such as market research data or letters of intent.

Competition Describe other choices customers currently have for obtaining such a product or service and how those choices can be expected to change. What companies offer such choices, what their competitive advantages are now and how those will likely change in the future should be stated.

Technology Tell how well-proven the venture's product or service and the venture's ability to produce it are. What else will be done to keep its performance up with or ahead of the times? What sorts of legal protection, such as patents, will be available and when?

Operations Say who will produce the output of the venture and how the venture's production capability will compare to that of competitors. What, if any, special location and facilities will be required, and at what cost and timing? (Flow and Gantt charts may help.)

Financial Aspects Include pro forma income statements, along with balance sheets and a cash flow forecast which breaks down figures monthly for two years and annually for three with footnotes explaining assumptions and important details behind the figures. The plan should indicate how and when any lenders or investors recover their cash.

Team Provide data on founders' capabilities that will be critical to success of the venture, what their task-relevant training and experiences are, and what their stakes in the venture will be.

Appendices Present details behind the body sections in order to keep the body down to about 20 to 30 pages of main facts and exhibits plus the summary and table of contents. Financial statements, resumes, market research details, copies of patents, letters of intent and such can appear here.

Application   *What should the outline of a written plan for the venture in the assigned case be, down to first and second level headings?*

Although venture plans can be written and helpful at any time, most are prepared part way along in a venture when some kind of a start has been made and more money is needed. The entrepreneur and any partners will have used personal savings to make a prototype, open a shop or otherwise get the venture partly going. They will see the cash supply running out and seek more, either from a bank or other investors. Financers will welcome any accomplishments of the venture to date that indicate it has been moving toward success. The entrepreneur(s) will prepare a cash flow forecast to show in dollars and cents how that will happen. Those dollars and cents imply occurrence of other events which also must be described to show there is a basis for believing the figures. Hence other supporting information such as market data, resumes showing prior accomplishments of the venture's founders, diagrams showing how the venture's product or service will work and will compare to competitors, and whatever else is important to the venture's success should be included in the plan.

For prospective partners or key employees the written plan can clarify parts they should play to bring about profits. For the entrepreneur and any others who participate in preparing the plan, that activity itself should help in anticipating problems, working out in advance ways of heading them off as well as discovering ways to improve and refine the venture sooner rather than later. As the venture moves along, the plan can serve as a basis for coordinating activities and checking progress.

The test of a plan ultimately will be how well it serves the venture. It is not possible to assess that in advance. But adopting the viewpoint of those who might read the plan for alternative purposes, such as the parties mentioned above, and asking how well it is likely to serve each purpose can provide an assessment. That assessment can be used for revising and improving the plan. Is more information needed? Are priorities clear? Have the points of greatest potential vulnerability been given thorough treatment? Have facts supporting them been included? Is the plan logical? Does it read well? Is it made easy to read by inclusion of an introductory paragraph explaining organization of the presentation, and by keeping the text compact through relegating details to appendices?

Three overall questions in evaluating a plan are (1) how viable is the venture concept itself, (2) how well suited are the founders for carrying out that concept against prospective competitors, and (3) how effective is the plan for its main purposes? The best way to cross-check answers to these questions, short of starting the venture and seeing what happens, is to ask other knowledgeable people to read and comment on it. Experienced business people are usually the best reviewers.

Application   *What elements in a plan for this venture will be the most (1) critical, (2) troublesome, and (3) "grunt work" to develop?*

Thought Modes

Reviewing and writing business plans calls for exercising several modes of thought, each of which at certain times may be most important and all of which should work together. Five such thought modes are (1) Absorptive, (2) Analytic, (3) Divergent, (4) Projective and (5) Prescriptive.

1. Knowledge-Absorption Mode

The absorptive mode of thought involves acquisition of the four types of knowledge described earlier. General entrepreneurship knowledge includes both facts (e.g. patents are good for 17 years) and routine skills (e.g. how to develop a cash flow spreadsheet) as well as beliefs, rules of thumb, lore and myths about entrepreneuring (e.g. some entrepreneurs seem to be born, others made). Levels of venture-specific knowledge include information about the firm, the economic environment it operates in, how such a business performs its functions, and details of particular people, technologies, and so forth. These facts may have to be sought out through information gathering.

An important part of the absorptive process is perception and discernment. When one potential entrepreneur spots an opportunity there are usually other people who also could do so but for some reason fail to. Practice in looking consciously for venture ideas may help develop this capability. For absorption of routine skills, such as mentally going through a checklist in order to evaluate venture alternatives, or developing cash flow projections, practice can improve performance.

Study of written cases and business plans developed by others can provide practice in some kinds of routine skills, such as thinking through a venture proposition from the perspectives of different players. A strength of studying cases is that many can be examined in a fairly short period, since they are ready at hand and self contained. Their weakness is that they don't allow interrogation or practice in searching for additional information to explore alternatives more fully.

Preparing new venture plans, as opposed to studying cases, limits the number of ventures that can be explored. However, it does allow practice in searching for needed information. Seeking out references and making "cold calls" to get it can add both facts and valuable skills. Much of entrepreneurship is information gathering.

Application   *What is the difference between the factual knowledge possessed by the entrepreneur in the assigned case and that which would be needed to succeed with the venture? In what different ways could/should the gap be filled?*

2. Analytic Mode

The analytic thought mode can take several forms, including *discovery* of relationships between causes and effects, *diagnosis* of problems, *quantification* of important variables, *graphical depiction* of relationships and *logical exposition*.

At any stage in the process of venture creation, from advance preparation and savings accumulation, to opportunity recognition, planning, resource application, start-up, operation and eventually disposition of the enterprise, there are threats, problems and opportunities to be discovered and dealt with. Often these can be brought to the surface by asking the following diagnostic questions:

- What issues does this venture face now and what issues seem to be coming up on the horizon?

- What is at the base of these issues? What are the forces which cause them? What is the evidence? How do those forces work?

To follow up these questions of diagnosis are others which help formulate answers to them, including the following:

- What is the order of priority of these issues?

- What are alternatives for dealing with them?

- What are pros and cons of those alternatives?

- What consequently should be done?

Application   *How should the above questions be answered for this particular case?*

Areas of issue in venturing often include: gaining cooperation from customers, suppliers and financers, trading off benefits versus costs, striking compromises among conflicting preferences, choosing among alternative sequences and allocating time among conflicting demands for it. Some questions that raise issues in start-up are: (1) Is the apparent start-up opportunity attractive? (2) What strategy should be followed to exploit it? (3) How much money will be needed? (4) How should the entrepreneur(s) raise it? (5) Would debt or equity be better? (6) If equity, how should it be split? (7) What other terms of the relationship should partners work out? (8) When should other employment or alternatives to pursuing this venture be dropped?

Application of information from the absorptive mode will certainly be appropriate in the analytic mode. Sometimes that information will already be available, as when the assignment is to review another's business plan or analyze a case study. Other times, as in real life venturing, it is most appropriate to seek out decision making information from publications, interviews and/ or experiments. Subtleties and underlying implications need to be surfaced. Deciding what questions to ask is an important part of this phase, as is correct logic.

For each issue there will be alternative potential solutions, and for each of those solutions there will be pros and cons. Sometimes the pros and cons can only be weighed logically and other times they can be quantified with such tools as break-even, discounted cash flow and probabilistic expected value analysis. These standard mathematical routines are crucial for measuring the extent or degree of critically important quantities such as amount of cash needed, cash available at specific times, and rate of return on investment.

Graphical depiction of quantities and relationships is a powerful tool for both analysis and communication. It is typically underutilized in venture plans. Graphs, histograms and pie charts all can help in thinking through a venture and so should be used. Other graphical tools not limited to quantities, such as decision trees, flow charts, schematics, perspectives, machine drawings, freehand sketches, models and photographs also should be brought into the analysis wherever they can help clarify thinking.

Risks in these analytic thought modes include overlooking issues, misdiagnosing causes and effects, making incorrect applications of systematic techniques or jumping to conclusions without applying such techniques at all. Such "impulse management" may be appropriate if the decision is inconsequential or if there is insufficient time for analysis. It may also be useful as a "first cut." A sense of priority should be brought to bear here. Where the consequences are great, the best analytical tools available should be carefully applied. Skill in applying them comes with practice.

Application   *What alternative computations could be performed with the numbers and/or possible estimates in the assigned case, and what do they show both quantitatively and graphically?*

3. Divergent Mode

The thought modes discussed thus far concern making the right decision from among options identified. The divergent mode, in contrast, seeks out additional options beyond those identified. The earliest stage for applying it may be in searching for a venture idea. Most entrepreneurs turn out to have been lucky enough to have the venture idea come upon them without having to search for it. But leaving opportunity discovery completely to chance probably reduces the odds of accomplishing successful entrepreneurship.

A central question in divergent searching is: What else should be considered? The main risk in applying the other modes is that the wrong alternative will be chosen. The risk in divergent thinking is that of failing to discover a better alternative. All the modes should help reinforce each other. Therefore, one precaution in divergent thinking is to perform information gathering and analysis energetically and thoroughly. Examining an issue ever more closely should reveal more and more ways of treating it.

The other precaution is to think imaginatively about additional possible opportunities, ways of exploiting them and solutions to problems. One question to explore quantitatively, for instance, is "what is the *maximum* reasonable upside potential" of a venture. Others are "how could this be done better," "what are the opportunity implications of possible future scenarios," and "what other possibilities exist for solving problems?" The more answers, the better. The more practical the answers, the better yet.

Application   *What issue in the assigned case most urgently calls for some creative thinking and what are 10 (or 20) possible answers for it?*

4. Projective Mode

Whether viewed as envisaging, forecasting, or generating scenarios or chains of action and reaction, the essence of venture planning is to foresee sequences of events, their interactions, their consequences and their implications into the future. Hence a thought mode that deals in projecting future business scenarios is probably required more in entrepreneurship than in other business activities. Developing business plans is the logical way to develop skill in the projective thought mode.

Application   *How should the following questions be answered for this particular case?*

Questions which elicit the projective thought mode include:

- What will this venture look like once it is operating?

- How will that pattern be different at alternative points in future time?

- Who will be doing what? What customers will be buying what, and why? How will people in the company be serving them?

- What sequences of actions will be required to get those activities underway?

- What milestones will indicate successful accomplishment, when will they occur, and how will they be discerned?

- What could go wrong with the venture scenario, and what alternative paths of action could be taken in such event? What further events and scenarios might then ensue? Here a decision tree could explode. Hence a return to analytic thought modes through consideration of priorities may be needed.

Diagrammatic and quantitative tools for mapping out these chains of events include those mentioned above: decision trees, flow, PERT and Gantt charts with dates on them, financial forecasts, and possibly drawings or sketches of products, facilities and activities. The projective mode calls for visual thinking, and to the extent it can be expressed on paper it can enhance a business plan.

5. Prescriptive Mode

The prescriptive thought mode should crystallize the venture concept in a depiction which links the specifics of a goal and a definite plan of action for achieving it. It can take such forms as written description, a list of steps with statements of who, how, when and at what cost. It can include graphical depiction, a slogan, motto or combinations of such things. In contrast to the projective mode, which is speculative, the prescriptive mode is definite. It draws upon the other modes and concludes with targets and individual assignments. Some of the prescribed action will be contingent on other events in the venture plan coming true, such as capital becoming available or customers responding favorably to the product or service concept, but the action will be definite.

This final mode should produce coherence from the information, analysis, speculation and projections which are generated in the other modes. In venture planning, how well these modes are applied and also how effectively the result is presented are both important. Vastly more important, however, is effective action, regardless of the venture plan.

Application　　*Depict on a transparency three alternative crystallization schemes for characterizing this particular venture now and in the future?*

Standard Questions for Cases

When thinking about potential ventures it is always possible to come up with reasons for rejecting them. The objective, however, is to figure out how to make the most of opportunities, not just to dismiss them. Some questions that should be considered in connection with all the cases in this book include the following:

1. **Upside Potential** What is the most that could be made of this venture?

2. **Venture Fit** What could this particular entrepreneur gain by proceeding with the venture and how might that compare with what some other person might gain from it?

3. **Downside Risk** What will be lost if this venture is pursued but does not succeed, and how can that loss be controlled?

4. **Action** What, based upon analysis of these and any other appropriate questions for this case, should the entrepreneur(s) do in this situation and why?

Application　　*How should the above questions be answered for the chosen case?*

Supplementary Reading

New Venture Strategies Chapter 3. (Vesper, K.H., Prentice-Hall, 1990)
New Venture Mechanics Chapter 10. (Vesper, K. H., Prentice-Hall, 1993)

Your Venture Plan

1. Sketch a "hindsight plan" (what the start-up sequence must have been) for an existing business similar to one you might be interested in starting. Estimate the role of venture-specific knowledge required and how it might be obtained (Absorptive/Analytic thought mode). What events in the company's creation would a plan most likely have anticipated best and which ones least well? What impacts might such planning have had on development of the venture itself?

Your Venture History

The following are some questions that may help in ferreting out the history of the venture you are studying. For any particular venture, however, different questions may at times be more appropriate.

1. What was the background and "prior mental programming" or "task-relevant experience" of the entrepreneur in the venture whose history you are investigating?

2. How much prior knowledge, of the three types mentioned in this chapter, did the entrepreneur have and what else was most necessary to learn for accomplishing the venture?

Exercises

1. **Thought Mode Assessment** List the thought modes in rank order as to how you think you compare to most other people (starting with the one on which you are strongest relative to other people. Come to class prepared to discuss how someone might seek out others to build a team that would collectively be as well-balanced as possible on thought mode strengths.

2. **Thought Mode Consequences** For each of the thought modes list one or more mistakes that failure of that mode might lead to in a venture, and one or more competitive business successes that might result if that mode were particularly well exercised. Be prepared to comment on your conclusions, and also on the relative premium you would place on performing each mode well in starting a venture. Also be prepared to comment on how a career might change each of the modes in relative strength and what a person could do to strengthen them.

Case Questions: Dow, Luhrs

General Case Questions

1. What, in order of priority, are the issues in the assigned case? What are the main alternatives for dealing with those of top priority? What are pros and cons of the alternatives?

2. What kind of enterprise could this venture become?

3. What would be required to make it that?

4. How well suited to the task are the entrepreneurs?

5. What are the downside risks?

6. What should the entrepreneurs do and why?

Dow Case Questions

1. What are the price and terms at which buying the business should be attractive to Cliff?

2. Explain the likelihood that the business should be worth more to someone other than Cliff.

3. Judging from Cliff's experience what could a person do to increase chances of encountering a buyout opportunity like this?

Luhrs and Williams Case Questions

1. What else needs to be done to make this venture a success?

2. What changes in the business plan should do most to make this venture appealing to a potential investor?

3. How have the capabilities of the entrepreneurs in this venture to succeed with it changed over time, and what events caused those changes?

Chapter 2

Ideas

❏ SUBCHAPTER 2A - Searching Methods

"How can I find a good new venture idea?" Usually, effective answers to this question either come easily or not at all. For most entrepreneurs the ideas, in hindsight, apparently came by themselves, unanticipated, often somewhat by surprise. They arose seemingly unbidden—from work, hobbies, acquaintances and everyday observations—as the result of unforeseen events.

Trying to force the process by *deliberately* looking for ideas is a much harder way to find good ones. But if simply waiting and hoping for coincidence is not enough, there may be no choice except to search. Some methods for doing that will be described in this chapter, following a look at historical experience.

From hindsight, it seems that there have been many new business opportunities which could have been found earlier if only someone had searched for them. Federal Express could have been done earlier. Collecting and selling replacement parts for antique houses, which turned out to be the basis of a successful mail order enterprise, could also have been done earlier. The shipping container industry and discount securities brokerage came from still other ideas that waited for someone to discover them.

How could other people have made those discoveries by deliberate searching? What knowledge would they have needed? What searching strategy would have done most to increase their odds of discovering opportunities? Could those same strategies be useful for discovering other opportunities that are as yet undiscovered, lying in wait now to be found and exploited? What could an individual adopt as a search procedure to find a venture idea? This chapter will explore those questions.

How Entrepreneurs Find Ideas

Considering the importance of business ideas in new ventures, it seems surprising that where original venture concepts come from has not been given much systematic study. From informal review of case histories on start-ups written by students at the University of Washington, it appears that the most common source is prior employment (e.g., the employer fails to follow through on a business opportunity and an employee leaves to pursue it independently), followed by hobbies, and then other sources such as social encounters, in that order. When systematic venture searching turns up in the histories, it is usually linked to acquisition as a mode of entry, rather than start-up of a new firm.

A 1988 study by Koller[12] of 82 entrepreneurs randomly selected from the Yellow Pages found that most entrepreneurs:

- Recognized, rather than sought out, business opportunities.

- Learned of opportunities from someone else (business associates, relatives and social contacts, in that order)

- And found them in fields where they had work experience. (Especially frequent was the response that they were attracted to the opportunity because it offered a chance to apply their prior training.)

Koller also found that 33 percent had entered via takeover rather than start-up. His study did not discuss how their opportunity discovery patterns differed, if at all, from those of new company founders.

A very different sample is that of the *Inc.* 500 fastest growing companies. A 1989 survey by the magazine asked the founders of those companies where they first got their venture ideas. Most (43 percent) said their ideas came from work. As can be seen in Table 2-1 below, the other categories of idea sources could overlap, either with this category (e.g., "saw an unfilled niche") or with others, such as hobbies, which was credited with only 3 percent of the ideas. The author, John Case, summarized:

> More common than the out of the blue inspirations were the explicable ones, the ideas that caught their creators by surprise, but in retrospect seem pretty logical.... The mythology of entrepreneurship celebrates such serendipity, propagating an image of the lone company-inventor suddenly flashing on the idea of a lifetime—and sometimes it happens that way.
>
> Typically, though, the idea for a fast-growing business appears in much more pedestrian fashion. The structure of a marketplace shifts, maybe ever so slightly. A new niche opens up. And all at once people... who may never have expected to become entrepreneurs, are out on their own and amazed by their own success.[13]

---

[12]Roland H. Koller, "On the Source of Entrepreneurial Ideas," in *Frontiers of Entrepreneurship Research, 1988,* eds. Bruce A. Kirchhoff and others (Wellesley, Mass.: Babson Center for Entrepreneurial Studies, 1988), p. 194.

[13]John Case, "The Origins of Entrepreneurship," *Inc.,* June 1989, p. 54.

Table 2-1 Where Inc. 500 Founders Got Venture Ideas

Source	Percent
Got idea while working in same industry	43%
Got idea from hobby or avocational interest	16
Saw someone else try, figured I could do better	15
Saw unfilled niche in consumer marketplace	11
Did systematic search for business opportunities	7
Can't really explain it	5
Total	100%

Finally, in another quite different sampling of members of the National Federation of Independent Businesses, a survey by Cooper et al. asked owners of 2,994 firms the question: "Where did you get the idea to go into this kind of business?" Again, the most frequent answer was "prior job," which accounted for 43 percent. Second most frequent, accounting for 18 percent, was a hobby or personal interest. Next came chance events (10 percent) and suggestions by others (8 percent). Interestingly enough, this was closely followed by "education/courses." Also interesting was the fact that those firms which did not survive the first year drew upon the same sources with about the same frequency, as seen in the Table 2-2, which was derived from the figures of Cooper et al.

Table 2-2 Where NFIB Founders Got Venture Ideas[14]

Idea Sources	For percent of Firms Found to Be			
	Discontinued	Sold	Surviving	Total Sample
Prior Job	42%	38%	43%	43%
Hobby/Personal Interest	18	16	18	18
Chance Event	10	13	10	10
Someone Suggested It	9	12	7	8
Education/Courses	6	3	6	6
Family Business	5	5	6	6
Activities of Friends/Relatives	6	6	5	5
Other	4	7	5	5
Total	100%	100%	100%	100%

Idea Generation

---

[14]Arnold C. Cooper and others, *New Business In America* (Washington, D.C.: The NFIB Foundation, 1990).

An investigation by Teach, Schwartz and Tarpley[15] of relationships between idea sources and subsequent venture performance in software firms found some indication that firms founded on "accidentally" discovered venture ideas which had not been subjected to formal screening or planning tended to break even faster and double their break-even sales faster than firms whose founders used more formal techniques of search and planning. Apparently, the founders of "non-formal" firms were also more able to manage with their own funds as opposed to using others' money. This may indicate that it is better to win by luck than effort. However, later it appeared that total sales levels for the different groups were essentially the same.

Application   *How much does it matter where the entrepreneur in the assigned case discovered the idea for the venture?*

Limitations of the statistics in studies to date include: (1) they don't say much about connections between idea sources and just how the ideas come about, and (2) there is no indication of how they may apply in any individual case. To learn more about these questions, a closer look at the following examples may help.

Prior Job

When Louis Krouse suggested to his employer, the NYNEX telephone company, that it consider the idea of arranging for lower income utility customers without checking accounts to pay their bills someplace besides utility offices, which are scarce, and banks, which lose money on such transactions, NYNEX told him to investigate further. An experimental project in Albany worked, but NYNEX decided not to carry it further and instead suggested that Krouse pursue it himself.

Quitting his job, Krouse formed National Payments Network, Inc. (NPN) to collect for companies such as NYNEX for 50 cents per payment (less than banks charge.) He then persuaded retail stores, such as Seven-Eleven, for about 10 cents per payment to allow customers to pay through them. From the stores' standpoint this helps draw customers. In each store a point of sale terminal transmits payment to a central computer, which in turn arranges electronic funds transfer from the stores to the utilities. Founded in 1986, NPN was processing over $2 billion by 1988.[16]

---

[15]Richard D. Teach, Robert G. Schwartz, and Fred A. Tarpley, "The Recognition and Exploitation of Opportunity in the Software Industry," in *Frontiers of Entrepreneurship Research 1989*, eds. Robert H. Brockhaus, Sr. and others (Wellesley, Mass.: Babson Center for Entrepreneurial Studies, 1989), p. 383.

[16]"The Emerging Entrepreneur," *Inc.*, January 1990, p.59.

Recreation

In 1989 Scott Griffiths formed a baseball team at his advertising agency, named it the Rhino Chasers, and had the name emblazoned on T-shirts and hats. He also made up labels with the name and pasted them on bottles of beer for post-game parties. People began asking where they could obtain that brand of beer. Griffiths sought out a local micro brewery to manufacture the product and within a year was shipping 800 cases per month.[17]

Chance Event

Tom Stemberg had worked 12 years in the supermarket industry, starting as a management trainee with Star Market and rising to head of sales and merchandising. He then became division president of another supermarket chain, Edwards-Finast, where he developed a warehouse food business, but then had a falling out with higher management and was fired.

With a year's severance pay he was looking for a job and potential start-up ideas when he visited a discount warehouse in Langhorne, Pennsylvania, for an employment interview. In the store he noticed that the office supplies section was a shambles: empty boxes, torn packages and goods spilled on the floor. He concluded that "this merchandise was moving very fast." Checking with industry analysts, he found that only 100 items in office supply sections accounted for up to 7 percent of the volume in such stores.

He now envisaged a chain of discount stores selling just office supplies. Instead of buying from the half dozen major wholesalers who sold such supplies to retail stores, he would buy from manufacturers and sell direct as did Toys 'R Us. Rather than continuing his job search, he next wrote a business plan and took it to potential venture capital sources. The result was that "dozens of offers poured in." One venture capitalist commented that Stemberg "wasn't proposing just a chain of stores, but an entirely new retailing category. That really catches your attention. It slaps you in the face with the idea that this could be big." The deal chosen included $4 million in the first round and $31 million in three later rounds.

The first Staples store opened on the outskirts of Boston in 1986. Not until 1989 did the company report a profit. But then it was $858,000 on $24.8 million in sales. In April of that year the company raised another $62 million through public offering.[18]

These three examples illustrate only part of the wide range of ways new venture opportunities and ideas are discovered. In each, the role of past experience and unforeseen events can be seen. Also, in each case the opportunity was available for discovery by others. Only in the third example does it appear that the entrepreneur was actively searching, but even there the discovery came by surprise.

---

[17] "Where Packaging Is Job One," *Inc.*, June 1990, p.30.
[18] Stephen D. Solomon, "Born To Be Big," *Inc.*, June 1989, p.94.

Application How many other people should have been in as good a position to discover the idea for this venture as the entrepreneur in the assigned case? Where might they be found?

Discovery Questions

Although would-be entrepreneurs usually don't discover ideas by a deliberate searching strategy (except when pursuing acquisitions of ongoing firms), it is nevertheless possible to impute to their discoveries some implicit searching patterns. These are illustrated by the following questions.

Search

Venture ideas may be prompted by search questions which put the mind into a mode where it might be presumed to try different combinations and to seek answers which may turn out to be product and service ideas. This searching process may well operate subconsciously. Evidence that it happened might be presumed to appear when the mind pushes an idea forward to a conscious level. Search questions might include:

1. ___ What is bothering me? a.___ What might relieve that bother?

2. ___ What else might I like to have?

3. ___What is a.___a situation where something is missing, or b.___ what else might anyone else like to have? (that I might be able to provide)

4. ___What is a.___ missing in a certain situation or b.___ bothering anyone else? c.___ What might satisfy that need?

5. ___ How could this be made or be done differently than it is now?

6. ___ How could this be made or be done better than it is now?

7. ___ What could I make or do with this a.___ resource or b.___ situation that I might want?

8. ___ What could I make or do with this? (that anyone else might want)

9. ___ What do I have the capability to make or provide for a.___ this situation or b.___ others, that might satisfy the want?

10. ___ How can I follow the family tradition?

11. ___ How can I do what I like doing?

Encounter

Another mode of idea prompting may occur from encounter with (1) someone else's idea, (2) a customer request or (3) some other event. Questions by which this process might produce a business idea include:

12. ___ Somebody has asked me to provide them with something. a.___Is it something I could provide?

13. ___ Has this a.__ event, b.__ development or c.__ circumstance change, created an opportunity I could seize?

14. ___ That seems to be done badly a.___ Could there be a way to do it better? (Or b.___ could I do it better?)

15. ___ People went for this same thing elsewhere. a.___ Could I play some role in providing it to a broader market?

16. ___ People went for something like (though not exactly the same as) this elsewhere. a.___ Could I play some role in providing it to a broader market?

17. ___ This seems like a straightforward advance on what is working now. a.___ Could I play a role in providing it to a broader market?

18. ___ I like this thing I encountered by accident. a.___ Could I play a role in providing it to a broader market?

Evaluation

Evaluative reactions to a prompted idea might be:

19. ___ Could I do this job I have on my own instead of as an employee?

20. ___ I wonder if other people might like this idea. a.___ If I were they, would I like it?

21. ___ I like the idea. I'll make one for me. If I like it, maybe others will too. a.___ I wonder if others might like this.

22. ___ Somebody has asked me to provide them with something. a.___If this person whom I have encountered wants it, might others too?

23. ___ People went for this elsewhere. a.___ Might they here too?

24. ___ People went for something like this elsewhere. a.___ Might they here too?

25. ___ Should I take over this enterprise a.___ found through search, or b.___as a result of encountering a seller's initiative.

26. ___ Will doing this give me greater satisfaction than what I'm doing now?

Action Decisions

Decisions to take action might take such forms as:

27. ___ I think people will want this. a.___ So I'll offer it, b.___ and see if they go for it, or c.___and I'm sure it will succeed.

28. ___ I like this, so I suppose others will. I'll offer it.

29. ___ This seems like a straightforward advance on what works now. So I will carry it out a.___ because I believe it will work, or b.___ to see how it will work.

Application   *Which idea discovery questions might do most to help reveal possible improvements in the entrepreneur's most promising venture idea so far? How could those be pursued?*

Innovation Inevitability

Each new venture is an innovation. It, like a person, is individual. Though perhaps very similar in some ways to some other enterprises, it will always have differences. Even if the venture is a franchise that follows all the formats and procedures of the parent firm, the address and immediate surroundings, phone number, employee(s) and combinations of customers will still be different. If the venture is independent rather than a franchise, then its product or service, ways of doing things, logo, decor, hours and prices will be individualized. The success of the venture may be determined by such differences.

Mental Blocks to Departure

Departure can be regarded as having two components: divergence and direction. Hence, generation of an innovative idea as a mental goal can be divided into two tasks. One is to depart from the beaten path. The other is to direct that departure in an effective way. Each of these two tasks has its own set of obstacles to be overcome. And for each of these obstacles there are techniques that might be applied as part of a deliberate search strategy in a divergent mode of thinking.

Obstacles to the first task, that of departing from what is customary, include the following "blocks":[19]

1. **Perceptual Blocks**

   a. Failing to notice clues to opportunity at all.

---

[19]Developed based upon James L. Adams, "Individual and Small Group Creativity," *Engineering Education*, 63, November 1972.

b. Difficulty viewing it from different perspectives.

c. Delimiting the opportunity too closely or too conventionally.

d. Seeing only what you expect to see or think others expect you to see.

e. Saturation: perceptual numbness.

f. Failing to use all sensory inputs available.

2. **Emotional Blocks**

a. Lack of challenge or interest in a new opportunity.

b. Excess zeal, tunnel vision, insufficient patience to see ways of exploiting it.

c. Fear of failure and/or risk.

d. Intolerance of ambiguity; obsession with security, order.

e. Preference for judging rather than seeking ideas.

f. Inability to relax, incubate after strong effort on idea search.

3. **Cultural Blocks**

a. Disdain for fantasy, reflection, idea playfulness, humor.

b. Belief that reason, logic, numbers is superior to feeling, intuition, pleasure.

c. Thinking that tradition is preferable to change.

d. Feeling that analytic thinking is the truly correct way to contemplate business.

e. Accepting that taboos are taboo.

4. **Imagination Blocks**

a. Fear of subconscious thinking.

b. Inhibition about some areas of imagination.

c. Compulsions such as worry, order, activity.

d. Confusion between reality and fantasy.

5. **Environmental Blocks**

a. Distrust of others who might help.

b. Distractions.

c. Unavailability of supporting elements.

d. Discouraging responses of other people to ideas (devil's advocates).

e. Too much else to do and disinclination to rearrange priorities.

6. **Intellectual Blocks**

a. Lack of information or incorrect information.

b. Ineffective application of formal idea-generating techniques.

c. Misperception of the situation.

d. Intimidating or distracting weakness of formal skills such as break-even or cash flow analysis.

7. **Expressive Blocks**

a. Lack of facility in writing, speaking, drawing, or constructing prototypes.

Working from a list such as this, a creatively inclined reader should readily be able to generate a companion list of antidotes for coping with each of the blocks.

Application   *If the entrepreneur in the assigned case fails to find a most promising way to improve on the venture idea(s) presently in view, which mental block will most likely be the reason, and what might be done about it?*

Findings about Creativity

Those who have studied processes for seeking good ideas have found, through controlled experimentation, the following:

1. There is no correlation between IQ and creativity in the normal range. IQ generally correlates with school ability.[20] But it is possible to be low in IQ and very successful in business or high in IQ and unsuccessful as an entrepreneur.

2. Deliberate practice in idea generation can raise idea generation rates of individuals.[21]

3. Effects of such practice do persist with time, although they also decay if not maintained.[22]

---

[20]John P. Guilford, *The Nature of Human Intelligence* (New York, N.Y.: McGraw-Hill, 1967), p.170.
[21]Sidney J. Parnes and H. F. Harding, *A Source Book For Creative Thinking* (New York: Charles Scribner's Sons, 1962), p.357.
[22]Ibid. P. 360.

4. Suspending judgment and deliberately withholding criticism (no matter how weird the idea seems) increases idea output.[23]

5. Quantity of ideas tends to beget quality.[24]

6. Seeking cleverness in ideas tends to beget fewer, but more clever ideas.[25]

7. Better ideas tend to come later in idea-generating sessions. Best ideas may come days, weeks or longer after deliberate idea generating efforts.[26]

8. Many heads produce more good ideas than one person alone. But sometimes the best ideas come from individuals operating alone.

Clearly, there are contradictions in some of these patterns, and individuals must impose judgments to strike compromises between such things as freedom versus focus and search versus evaluation. However, there do seem to be similarities in mental sequences through which outstanding ideas have been discovered in a variety of fields, including entrepreneurship. Identifiable phases in the creative process seem to be:[27]

1. **Preparation** in which the searcher acquires knowledge and skills, most often through work or hobbies, related to the venture opportunity to be discovered.

2. **Searching**, which may involve periods when the individual wants to find new directions of activity and reflects about the possibilities for doing so. Looking back later, a person who discovered a successful venture idea may recollect, "I always wanted to have my own business, but I needed...."

3. **Frustration** arises when the opportunity or better idea does not crop up when desired. Consequently, the searcher stops reflecting and moves on to other things.

4. **Incubation** takes place subconsciously while the individual is engaged in mundane activities (such as showering or commuting) quite unrelated to searching.

5. **Discovery** occurs quite unexpectedly, perhaps as the result of an external event or change in circumstances, or possibly from revelation inside the seeker's mind.

---

[23]Guilford, *Human Intelligence*, p.330.
[24]Parnes, *Creative Thinking*, p. 190.
[25]Guilford, *Human Intelligence*, p. 330.
[26]Parnes, *Creative Thinking*, p. 190.
[27]Calvin Taylor and Frank Birron, Scientific Creativity (New York: Wiley, 1963), P. 355.

Tactics for Departure

To help in idea generation, those who have studied and practiced creative proficiency have generated many suggestions, including the following:

1. Try different ways of looking and thinking about venture opportunities.

2. Work at being prolific in ideas about both what the opportunities are and how they might be exploited.

3. Seek leads from other people, not necessarily opportunities per se, but clues such as problems or unmet needs that might lead to them. Potential sources of leads include business and personal contacts, trade shows, government and private technology licensing offices. Making new contacts and asking for help lead to other contacts.

4. Don't be discouraged by others' negative views. Devil's advocates are plentiful. Experts in the past have predicted impossibility for gas turbines, atomic power, FM radios, and powered flight.

5. Avoid stating negative views until you have generated possible solutions for obstacles. Then offer the solutions rather than problems. (This alone will make you much rarer than devil's advocates and hence higher in market value.)

6. Set quotas and deadlines for identifying potential opportunities, but be open to opportunities that may come later from incubation.

7. When going to bed command your mind either to dream about possible needs or to find solutions to them.

8. Resist the temptation to accept ideas that come early or ideas that meet primarily your own needs. Reach for solutions that might be useful to others able to pay for them.

9. Use idea-generating tricks such as:

   • Brainstorming with formal rules, such as not criticizing, piggybacking ideas and seeking quantity

   • Elaborating on ideas that emerge

   • Considering multiple consequences of possible future events or changes

   • Rearranging, reversing, expanding, shrinking combining or altering ideas

   • Fantasizing, developing scenarios

   • Listing attributes, criteria and possible characteristics of alternative approaches in parallel columns, then randomly connecting items from column to column

- Identifying with a situation or object and imagine what that would be like or what might make it better

- Developing analogies between different circumstances, times or aspects of nature

10. Reach beyond the ordinary in seeking opportunities or ways of exploiting them. If you don't reach as far as ideas that make you laugh, you are being too conservative.

11. Discuss with others what you would like to find in the way of business opportunities. Learn what their aspirations are and whether you could work together.

12. Critique an existing product or service. List ways of improving on it that you might be able to sell.

Application *In rank order, which five departure tactics would be most likely to lead to improvement on the venture idea(s) presently seen by the entrepreneur(s) in the assigned case? Should those tactics be applied?*

Supplementary Reading

New Venture Strategies Chapter 5. (Vesper, K.H., Prentice-Hall, 1990)
New Venture Mechanics Chapter 1. (Vesper, K. H., Prentice-Hall, 1993)

Your Venture Plan

1. Apply tactics for departure described in this chapter to expand your search for a viable business idea or to develop improvements for a chosen idea.

2. Keep a log of your search and occasionally note which approaches seem to be more effective for you and why.

Your Venture History

1. Investigate the chain of thoughts through which the entrepreneur discovered the idea for his or her business. Using the list in the "Discovery Questions" section above, and adding any other questions if needed, number in sequence the implicit series of mental questions that the entrepreneur seems to have gone through in discovering the venture idea(s).

2. Insofar as possible, list and/or describe the ideas that were passed up or rejected in favor of the one which the entrepreneur chose to pursue. Did anyone else pursue those ideas and demonstrate their level of viability?

3. Who else could have pursued the idea the entrepreneur chose? How did their positions for doing so compare?

Exercises

1. Venture Idea Search: Please refer to description in Exercise 7, Subchapter 1A, page 1-13.

2. Interview one or more entrepreneurs and inquire about how they came upon their venture ideas. Carry out question #1 under Your Venture History above. Compare the patterns and comment on the similarities and differences.

3. Set up an idea notebook for collecting potential business ideas. On the first page make a list of approaches to try. On the second page (more if needed) make a timetable for exploring those ideas. On succeeding pages keep a diary of approaches tried. At the end, list what seem to be the best ideas in rank order and briefly describe steps for pursuing each of the top three. Make an assessment of how well the schedule fit the task, how much time per idea each of the approaches cost, which approach was most effective and why. Describe what would be the best approach to follow if the task were to be taken further.

4. Which of the tricks for generating ideas noted in the section of this chapter on Tactics for Departure do you think would be most effective for generating ideas in a one-hour period? Try two and compare results. Alternatively, try one, first alone, and then with one or more other people.

5. Read the example of Tom Stemberg again. Did this opportunity discovery have to be a chance event? Test your answer by visiting one or more stores and looking for potential opportunities by studying the store, the customers and what goes on. Perhaps in a brief effort no truly viable opportunity will appear. But which can you identify that is closest to viable? What would be the product or service? What, from your observation and possibly an interview or two, would be the makeup of a typical target customer?

6. Study three stores or other lines of business you can readily observe in action. Determine which you could come closest to competing with by analyzing how effectively they do their work and how their performance could be improved.

7. Interview two entrepreneurs and ascertain as well as you can what sequence each used in terms of the venture idea Discovery Questions of this chapter. Discuss the similarities and differences, and the degree to which there was any possible choice of sequence open to the individuals involved.

❏ SUBCHAPTER 2B - Imposing Direction

The main emphasis in the techniques described above is to break free of present practices and enter new mental territory. That by itself leaves out the all-important need to discover not just a new idea, but one that usefully exploits a profitable opportunity. Ideas, per se, are limitless in number, and almost all those "off the beaten path" are useless. It is the rare ones with value that must be found, and this imposes a need for direction on the search.

Role of Information

To pay off, mental departure in quest of opportunity must be guided by knowledge of some sort. That knowledge may come from work or hobbies, as indicated earlier. Or it may come from school. Engineers are taught, for example, that nobody has ever found a way to make a perpetual motion machine, and also what the physical laws are that make this so. Hence, they don't waste time on ideas that violate those laws. Information about a new technology that does work can also be a helpful guide. With it, a would-be entrepreneur can go searching for the market that wants something that technology can do. Thus, one type of information helpful for guidance in searching is knowledge about what is not technologically possible as well as what is.

A second helpful type of information concerns what a market is likely to want. With a potential market desire in mind a would-be entrepreneur can go searching for a profitable way to satisfy it. Obtaining useful entrepreneurial information of either type and recognizing the value of that information are both necessary tasks. Either task may or may not come easily, depending on circumstance and mental programming. Information about what markets want can come through observing what goes on naturally, asking questions of other people, or conducting formal market research. In the following example recognition of the magnitude of an opportunity did not occur until after the venture had begun.

> Once he had put so much work into rebuilding the Altair, though, Millard thought he might just as well try to sell his version of the small computer. He called his adaptation the IMSAI 8080, and placed a one-inch ad announcing its availability in *Popular Electronics*.
> What happened next? "You ought to picture this," Millard told us. "I mean, here are five people – two of whom are myself and my wife – in this little place in San Leandro. And we're just trying to survive, okay? The mailman came in with the mail sack. We got 3,500 responses to our ad—our little one-inch ad."[28]

---

[28]Robert Levering, Michael Katz, and Milton Moskowitz, *The Computer Entrepreneurs* (New York: New American Library, 1984), p.351.

The information that came from experiments like Millard's in turn prompted other entrepreneurs to perceive the existence of opportunity. This was illustrated by the subsequent start-up of Osborne Computer. Adam Osborne recalled that he was able to predict sales of his own company, thanks to his observation of what had been going on in the new microcomputer industry, as follows.

> *Taking into account the one-month slip, my original plan proved remarkably realistic. As anticipated, we were able to sell everything we could build. For dealers the Osborne I was a "cash cow."*[29]

Osborne's decision to build the Osborne I which led initially to success was based on knowledge he obtained as a writer about the computer industry. For technical work of the actual design, however, he needed further knowledge he did not possess, and so he hired it. In the longer term, Osborne made decisions less effective than those of competitors, and his venture went bankrupt. Those competitors who succeeded in the longer term probably possessed better information and sometimes made blind choices that turned out to be luckier than Osborne's.

Application   *What facts should form the main boundaries within which "wild" alternatives for the assigned case venture should be selected?*

Opportunity Causes

Understanding what kinds of forces give rise to opportunity may also help guide idea search by giving the mind awareness of patterns that work. So when, in the course of life, such patterns happen to be encountered the would-be entrepreneur will be more likely to recognize them.

Discussions of the future are not hard to find in books and magazines. It is well known that the population is aging, tastes change, technology introduces new capabilities, resources are under increasing demands, pollution is a mounting problem, new markets and sources of supply are opening in former communist countries and third-world countries. The supply of information has been growing at an increasing rate and thereby introducing needs for better ways of handling and communicating it. Advances in telecommunications and computers are helping make that possible, and in the process of doing so they are creating new markets for services, software and hardware.

It is not easy to find start-up ideas that were discovered by a general awareness of these trends. Entrepreneurs don't report, for instance, that they

---

[29]Adam Osborne and John Dvorak, *Hypergrowth* (New York: Avon, 1985), p.33.

noticed the rising cost of health care and suddenly realized what kind of company to start based on that general information alone, or even based on that information plus brainstorming or focus-grouping. But at the same time, those who have taken advantage of such trends were usually aware of them as at least part of the knowledge base from which they discovered opportunity. Awareness of what is going on certainly can be useful in the idea search process.

Application   *What caused the main opportunity that the entrepreneur in the assigned case aims to exploit to come into existence and when?*

Alternative Strategies

Another set of patterns to assimilate that may help later in recognizing opportunity includes the different alternative strategies new ventures can follow. One set of strategic patterns proposed in *New Venture Strategies*[30] includes the following:

- **New Product or Service** A study of 8,000 innovations revealed that small companies produced more of them than did large firms (55 percent vs. 45 percent), but often the start-ups with innovations were performed by people who gained their know-how from big firms.[31]

- **Parallel Competition** The most common strategic approach among new ventures is to do what others do, but a bit better, without being radically different.

- **Buying a Franchise** This strategy requires no ingenuity. It does call for care in selecting the franchisor, and it takes money to buy the franchise. Profits are usually reduced by royalty requirements, and freedom is restricted by the franchise contract.

- **Geographic Transfer** When a new business idea catches on in one locale it usually appears before long in others as well. Looking for new businesses that seem suitable for such transfer and then copying them in new regions is a feasible approach.

- **Exploiting Supply Shortage** Discovery that something is in short supply may come unbidden or it may be pursued by asking people, such as purchasing agents, what they are having trouble getting. Then the entrepreneurial task is to find a way to supply it.

---

[30]Karl H. Vesper, *New Venture Strategies*, revised edition (Englewood Cliffs, N.J.: Prentice-Hall, 1990).
[31]John Case, "Sources of Innovation," *Inc.*, June 1989, p. 29.

- **Exploiting Unused Resources** These too may be discovered by accident. Mineral prospectors go looking for them, but they know just what they want to find and geologically where they are most likely to occur. Analogies in business are not easy to find.

- **Parent Company Sponsorship** This too requires credibility, usually borne of a track record plus a history of working with the parent company.

- **Government Sponsorship** The Federal Government's 400 laboratories are under mandate to work at transferring technology to small firms. What kinds of help the government gives, either as a customer or as a financing source for start-ups, shifts with time and political pressures. [32]

- **Acquiring a Going Concern** Of all the strategies for entering business, this one lends itself most readily to systematic searching. To find a good buy, however, can be difficult, and establishing credibility with the seller can be also.

Application   *Which of the above strategies apply to the entrepreneur in the assigned case's main venture idea and to what extent?*

Individual Specifics

Awareness of such precedent patterns may help. But the most important information for guiding an opportunity search is not about general types of opportunities, causes, strategies or idea sources. Rather, it is very specific information about particular individuals, technologies and circumstances. This information generally cannot be learned from publications but instead must come from encounters by the to-be entrepreneur with other individual people and events in the course of life.

Note in each of the following what role was played by prior information and by information that happened to be gained just prior to getting the business idea. It may be helpful to classify information according to when it was obtained relative to the date of start-up.

> In 1981 Mark Swislow, a part-time MBA student, received a suggestion from a friend that he look into the possibility of producing dust covers for microcomputers to satisfy a marketing course assignment to select a market niche and research it. He and his friend rented a computer show booth and encountered enough interest in not-yet-made covers that they set up shop to make and sell them. By 1989 their company, Computer Coverup, Inc., employed 50 people.[33]

[32]*Inc.*, October 1990, p. 26.
[33]Martha E. Mangelsdorf, "Making the Grade," *Inc.*, January 1989, p. 20.

❖ ❖ ❖

Michael Dell acquired knowledge about microcomputers from hanging around computer stores as a boy. One thing that caught his attention was the large markup. "Let's say," he said, "that you buy a computer from a retail store, and you pay $4,000. The retailer sends $2,500 of that back to the manufacturer and keeps $1,500. The question I asked myself was: What was the retailer doing to earn his $1,500? Was he adding $1,500 of value to that machine for me, a knowledgeable computer buyer? The answer was no."

This inspired Dell to start selling computers. To make his product, he bought stripped-down IBM's and to them added options purchased from other suppliers. At first he sold through direct response advertisements, then through telemarketing, and finally through a sales force as well. At age 19 he entered the industry (in 1984), after competition had already squeezed many other entrants out. He not only survived this competition as a newcomer entering late, but he built a company which by 1989 had sales of over a quarter billion dollars.[34]

❖ ❖ ❖

The first clue that there might be an opportunity in "designer" toilet partitions came to actor, Greg Braendel via his cousin, Adrian Emck, who had designed them for an English company, Thrislington Sales, Ltd. Emck wanted to develop sales of the product in the U.S. and asked Braendel for help. Braendel discussed the idea with a U.S. architecture firm, then with the help of Thrislington's managing director, Brian Moore, went looking for a U.S. company to make them. After several discouraging responses in late 1989, according to Inc., Braendel and Moore were sitting on the patio outside Braendel's Hollywood home. "Brian," said Braendel, "why don't I just manufacture the damn things myself?" "Bloody 'ell," he remembered Moore saying, "why not?" Braendel consequently formed a company, negotiated for rights from Thrislington, which already had all the manufacturing business it could handle abroad, and began organizing a team to enter business.[35]

❖ ❖ ❖

For Ken Girouard the information leading to a start-up began to flow after he made something on impulse. He recalled, "I had to make a birthday gift for a friend of mine, so I took a pair of sandals and sewed a big plastic banana and lemon on top of them. I really don't know why. Somebody saw them and asked me to make her five pairs for gifts. Then a stylist saw those, and she asked for three pairs and put them on an extra in a new James Bond movie. Then someone told me I should take them to this boutique the next time I was

---

[34]Tom Richman, "The Entrepreneur of the Year," Inc., January 1990, p.43. Also, Joel Kotkin, "The Innovation Upstarts," Inc, January 1989, p.70.
[35]John Case, "With A Little Help From His Friends," Inc., April 1989, p.132.

in New York City. I did, and they encouraged me to add big grapes and plastic flowers. They advised me to go to a trade show, which I did. Even though I didn't have a booth, I came back with 3,000 orders. I upgraded them to higher-quality sandals in neon colors, and I started packaging them in green mesh bags. I called them Fruit Flops. The detail can't be automated. I tried paying the local Girl Scouts to make them for me. What a nightmare. They had no concentration. 'This is stupid,' they kept saying. But in the first six months I have sold $18,000 worth of these - everywhere from St. Martin to Saudi Arabia to Chicago. I now have 14 reps. I had no idea there would be any demand for this, and I think it's hysterical."[36]

❖ ❖ ❖

The first information leading directly to Steve Bedowitz's business idea came from study of a market he undertook as partner in an advertising agency that was hired by a home siding wholesaler. From market data he observed that "siding was a $3 billion-a-year industry, and the biggest company I could find did $8 million. I said to myself, 'wait a minute.'" He and a partner invested $3,000 in 1979 to form Amre, Inc. and worked to avoid weaknesses of the existing small firms in the industry. They opened a storefront to avoid a "fly-by-night" image, obtained a Sears franchise to establish credibility, bought the best materials, followed a "tell the truth" policy and utilized computers to maximize efficiency. By 1989 they became the biggest company in the industry, with sales of over $250 million.[37]

In each of these examples it is clear that discovery of the venture idea and shaping it for implementation were influenced by both of the following two kinds of knowledge: first, knowledge that the entrepreneur had acquired along the way starting long before the idea discovery; second, knowledge that the entrepreneur came upon directly before the discovery which both facilitated and triggered the discovery. Sometimes the entrepreneurs took initiatives that gained them the information. Other information came to them apparently unbidden. Greater appreciation of how possession and acquisition of information help in idea discovery may be developed by applying the following questions to examples like those above.

1. What role did information play in these ideas coming to these people?

2. What did these people do to bring about their having effective information?

3. What could they or anyone else have done to influence the likelihood of receiving that information?

4. How else could the same idea have been found by the same person, or someone else, without the same information?

---

[36]"The Year in Start-Ups," *Inc.*, November 1989, p.75.
[37]Edward O. Welles, "Tin Men," *Inc.*, October 1990, p.66.

5. Who else probably had the information but did not benefit from using it to discover the idea?

6. Who else could have done the start-up better?

Application   *What would answers to the above questions be for this particular case entrepreneur's main venture idea?*

Something these examples illustrate is that discovery of venture ideas is not a matter of randomly looking around. Each venture is highly specific, as is each individual entrepreneur, and the information needed for idea discovery is similarly special. General looking may build habits that increase the odds of an individual picking up on ideas others might overlook. But the discovery probably will not occur immediately upon application of a search. More likely, persistence over time will be needed until fortunate coincidence adds the needed final element(s) of discovery.

Managing the Search

In summary, it appears that there are some controllable factors which can be influential, albeit not rigidly governing, in an idea-searching process.

- **Attitudes** that rate opportunity discovery as important and that affirm the searcher's capacity to be creative can be cultivated.

- **Knowledge** about the nature of new business opportunities and ways of exploiting them can be acquired, and relevant skills can be practiced.

- **Circumstances** such as choice of associates, contacts, employment, and geographical region where start-up happens more often can be sought.

- **Methods** of generating venture ideas, such as formal creativity exercises, can be applied at will.

- **Persistent effort** is a strengthening ingredient that can be deliberately brought to bear and — at least in some cases, such as Staples, Inc. — seems to make an important difference. Downstream from start-up it may be even more important in the fine tuning needed to prevail against competitors.

Application   *Which of the above five elements appears to be most appropriate to the entrepreneur in the assigned case for finding and shaping an effective venture idea?*

The discovery of a promising venture idea, whether through techniques such as these or through unsought serendipity, is only a starting point for further exploration. The idea may be good, but not good enough. Or it may be good enough, but only for someone other than the person who discovered it, someone in a better position to exploit it. Consequently, beyond the goal of the activities described here, which is to produce promising ideas for ventures, lies the next goal, which is to check those ideas out for commercial viability and for fit with the particular entrepreneur(s). How to perform this checkout will be taken up in the next chapter and continue through others that follow.

Supplementary Reading

New Venture Strategies Chapters 7 and 8. (Vesper, K.H., Prentice-Hall, 1990)

Your Venture Plan

1. Describe briefly the extent of departure from the competition that your venture idea represents. Also describe alterations that could be made to extend or reduce that departure.

Your Venture History

1. What developments gave rise to the opportunity that the entrepreneur exploited?

2. To what extent would those developments have permitted someone to exploit that opportunity either sooner or later than the entrepreneur did?

3. What elements of the situation helped to center the entrepreneur on an appropriate direction relative to the status quo and not diverge too widely?

Exercises

1. In 200 words or less, describe how someone can find a good venture idea, other than by luck.

2. How can opportunity causes and alternative strategies be used to generate ideas for new ventures? Illustrate with some examples of your own.

3. Apply the questions about information in the section on Individual Specifics to examples described in that section and/or other examples.

4. Introduce yourself to one or more people who might have either (1) needs that are unmet which a new venture might serve, or (2) technical capability to create a new product or service as the basis for a venture. Describe briefly in writing the opportunity(s) you discovered by this process and what would be required for exploitation.

Case Questions: Blanco, Knight, Morse

General Case Questions

1. Discuss the extent to which one or more venture opportunities appear to exist in the assigned case, why, and what sort of venture might best exploit them.

2. What companies or individuals should be best positioned to take advantage of those opportunities and how?

3. What is your assessment of the idea discovery method(s) used thus far by the entrepreneur(s) in the assigned case?

4. What criteria would you propose that the entrepreneur(s) in the assigned case should use for selecting which business idea(s) to pursue from among possible ideas discovered?

5. What business ideas can you think of that the entrepreneur(s) in the assigned case did not think of but might do well to consider?

Blanco Case Questions

1. Would Professor Blanco's way of finding product ideas be likely to follow a "typical" sequence of implicit questions? If so, what would that sequence be? If not, what would most likely determine the sequence for any particular idea discovery?

2. What kinds of ideas does Professor Blanco seem to be better equipped than most people to find? What does it take to become so equipped? How worthwhile does such capability as his seem to be?

3. What actions by Ernesto Blanco might further enhance his capability to discover ideas that could form the basis for a successful business start-up?

Knight Brothers Case Questions

1. How should the market that the Knight brothers aim to serve be defined? What are the alternative ways of serving that market?

2. What, in the way of new technological capability, are the Knight brothers hoping to capitalize on in starting a venture? What applications might they be able to capitalize on that they have not incorporated in their plan?

3. How would you rank the aspects of venture opportunity that the Knight brothers have incorporated in their plan, and how would you rank those potential aspects of venture opportunity, given the technology they have chosen, that they have left out of their plan?

4. If the Knight brothers wanted to look for a venture idea better than the one they have, how could they best go about it?

Morse Case Questions

1. In the John Morse case we find someone attempting to discover good business ideas through systematic searching procedures. Before reading about his procedures think about how to go about such a search. Then read through Morse's experience and evaluate his approach.

    - Was there a better way for him to proceed at any point, and if so, how?
    - Where should he go at the end of the case?
    - Has he come up with too many ideas or too few?
    - Rank order the viability of ideas discovered so far.
    - Which of his ideas are best and why?
    - Did they seem to come earlier in the search, or later?
    - What should John Morse have learned from this process?
    - How might the "right" approach for someone else be the same or different?
    - To what extent does the nature or quality of ideas discovered so far in the case seem to be dependent on the timing of their discovery?

Chapter 3

Screening

❏ *SUBCHAPTER 3A - Physical Feasibility and Market Fit*

Ideas generated by any process, whether a systematic search or simply reaction to chance encounters, will generate far more ideas than can be explored in detail. Giving some direction to the discovery process, as discussed in the last chapter, can help winnow the possibilities. Cursory reflection will be the most attention that can be paid to nearly all the ideas. It may eliminate them all, leaving the search to continue in quest of more. Or it may highlight a few that deserve more serious attention. For those, more intensive and methodical examination, which can help with both selection and refinement of ideas worth significant time, effort and possibly dollar investment, is appropriate. This chapter will describe methods for that more detailed examination, concentrating on four aspects. The first subchapter will consider tests for feasibility and market fit. The second subchapter will treat financial feasibility and fit between the venture idea and the individual(s) who might found a venture to exploit it.

Evaluation Questions

Checklists for evaluating venture ideas can readily be generated. In detail they must depend on the particular venture, but some general questions include the following:

- What kind of business can this venture become in the short run and the long run?

- Why does the opportunity for this venture exist? Are the causes of the opportunity likely to last long enough for the venture to become profitable?

- Who will be the first customer and why can that person be expected to buy? How many more people will buy and why?

- What will make it possible for this company to withstand competition if it comes?

- Who else seems to be in as good or a better position to accomplish this venture, what are they likely to do, and what can be done about it?

- What, in rank order, are the three most critical assumptions upon which success of this venture is projected? What can be done to test those assumptions, and what can be done to make sure they come true?

- What is the upside profit potential of the business if things go as well as can reasonably be hoped? How does that compare to the prospects if things only go fairly well?

- What is the likely downside loss if things go unfavorably?

- What has to happen for break-even to occur? For cash flow to become positive?

- How sensitive are these projections to variations in key assumptions underlying them?

Application   *What would be the answers to the most important of these questions above for this particular case?*

Answers to these questions should be developed in sufficient detail that the same set would not fit another business. They should be true, not simply made up to support a prejudged conclusion either to go ahead with the business or to brush it aside. Likely the answers will be mixed, some favoring termination and others favoring acceptance of the venture idea. So judgment must be made about which route to follow.

Maintaining balance in this analytical process can be difficult. Some analysis may be important, but over analysis is wasteful, and success is produced only by action. More important than making the best decisions is to follow through on them effectively. Part of the evaluation should address how to make the decisions work out even if assumptions underlying them prove invalid, or they turn out to be not the best decisions that could have been made. To keep balance between over- versus under-analysis it can be helpful to consult with other knowledgeable people.

Evaluation of ideas can be viewed as a spiraling process. A possibility is glimpsed, either because of happenstance or search. The impression is tested, either against prior knowledge or through acquisition of additional knowledge. Checkout reveals new facets of the possibility which may be problems or opportunities or both. Possible ways of responding to these are sought and assessed. Thus the search continues until either it no longer appears worthwhile or an action plan for the venture emerges.

All this may happen in the mind, either over time or through a flash of inspiration. Some evaluation may be conscious, but much is bound to be subconscious. If the start-up steps are low cost, the easiest way to test a business idea may be simply to go ahead and implement it. Usually, however, there is justification for some systematic screening first.

Seek Out Weak Spots for Priority

Ideas are easy to come up with. To economize time in screening, attack first those questions most crucial to success of an idea, even if they are harder to answer or face. Almost all product or service ideas are no good, particularly as originally perceived. To find one that is viable requires passing up those that are not and probably reshaping one that is partially all right. A learning process is required both to refine the idea and to test it.

Allocation of time in this process must repeatedly be adjusted between such tasks as:

1. Looking for strong points of a venture idea to build on and ways to do the building.

2. Looking for weak points and either finding ways to fix them or dropping the venture idea.

3. Searching out and gathering information to help with the above tasks.

4. Searching for a better venture idea.

5. Turning to some other task and leaving the current one temporarily to the subconscious.

Application *In what order should the entrepreneur in the assigned case proceed through the above five actions after the end of the assigned case?*

One way to economize time in evaluating an idea is first to seek out the most worrisome aspects and work on those. Which aspects are most likely to be weak will vary from one venture idea to another. Here are some possibilities:

1. Though the product or service of the prospective venture might be valuable, it is not physically feasible, and/or development would cost too much.

2. Some people might like to have what the venture would produce, but either there would not be enough of them, or they would be too hard to find and sell to, or they would not be willing to pay enough to yield a profit for the venture.

3. The venture would likely make some profit, but not enough to justify the investment required.

4. The return on investment would probably be attractive initially, but competitors in more advantageous positions would likely enter and shrink it prematurely.

5. Such a venture could prosper adequately, but it doesn't fit this particular entrepreneur well enough.

Application   *How would the above five possibilities rank in likelihood for the venture in the assigned case?*

Generating alternative future scenarios both of the company and of the competitive arena in which it will operate will give a basis for this assessment. Each scenario should characterize what the company might be like in one, two or five years including such aspects as:

- What it sells and to whom
- For how much individually and in total
- Using what appeals
- Against what competitors
- With what market share
- Providing it how
- With how many employees
- Owned how
- Aiming to achieve what next
- Thanks to what competitive advantages

Two or three such future "portraits of success" which contrast fairly sharply from each other can be formulated. Then the steps necessary to bring each about can be considered as well as the risks, costs and benefits of arriving at these alternative outcomes. This can serve as a basis for deciding which strategy offers most promise initially. All this should help with the decisions of whether to proceed with the venture and if so, how best.

Application   *What would be three alternative "Portraits of Success" for the venture(s) in the assigned case(s)?*

Another approach, making successively deeper penetrations in setting priority, is to:

1. Quickly guess the answer to "what is the most vulnerable aspect of this business idea?"

2. List five general aspects, and for each list in rank order the most vulnerable points: physical practicability, marketability, financial attractiveness, entrepreneur fit and competitiveness.

3. For these five aspects in any order perform a more detailed analysis.

Application   What would be the priority of concerns for the entrepreneur(s) in the assigned case(s)?

For most ideas mental reflection will be enough to conclude rejection. Others that cannot be easily rejected will raise the need for more information to make a decision. The search for this information may itself uncover still better ideas.

Test Physical Practicability

Questions of physical feasibility include whether the venture is legally permissible, whether it can be made to work within reasonable development costs and whether the prospective founder can muster the capability to perform it.

Legal permission for most ventures is not a problem. As much as entrepreneurs condemn problems of dealing with the government, it generally presents little barrier to their getting started. In some fields there are legal monopolies, such as postal delivery to mailboxes and fields where licenses exclude competitors, such as medicine, barbering, law, broadcasting and so forth. In others there are controls over effluents, noise and safety. Zoning sometimes restricts location of businesses. But for the great majority of start-ups such restrictions are not important. It is after the business has started that governmental difficulties of reporting, taxation, inspections and ordinances become more serious.

Demonstration that the product or service can actually be produced and will work can often be accomplished with pencil and paper analysis. For a product a prototype may be needed. For a service, sketches and practice demonstrations will often do.

Testing of physical feasibility must not only show that the product or service can be produced, but also must assure that it can be done well enough. Among *Inc.* 500 firms 88 percent of founders, according to a survey by the magazine, attributed their success to exceptional execution of an ordinary idea, while only 12 percent said they succeeded because of an unusual or extraordinary idea. [38]

[38]John Case, "The Origins of Entrepreneurship," *Inc.*, June 1989, p. 54.

In another study of 2,994 firms Cooper et. al.[39] reported that odds of survival were on the average not higher among firms that claimed a "reputation for quality" as part of their strategy. However, firms which attributed more than 40 percent of their strategy to better service and those which said 40 percent or more was focused on providing previously unavailable products or services did have higher odds of survival. Emphasis on lower prices, or on serving customer groups previously poorly or not at all served, was associated with higher failure rates.

What this seems to suggest is that high quality of the product or service as perceived by customers is a main key to raising odds of success (at least, on average). Hence, in evaluating plans for the venture a most important question is not just whether the product or service physically will be able to work, but also how an extraordinarily high quality in its level of performance will physically be brought about.

Kinds of excellence in performance that seem to distinguish winners in the *Inc.* 500 are illustrated by some examples such as the following.

> Tom Tjelmeland, who had worked on construction sites since age 14, entered a most prosaic line of work, roof repair, by concentrating on commercial customers and doing enough small things better than competitors so his firm would get the orders without need to give quotes. His tactics included clean white trucks and white uniformed workers in an industry notorious for the opposite. Use of computers gave him clearer awareness of costs in order to control them and facilitated reminders to customers about roof inspections. Careful sleuthing of competitors' performance in neighboring markets revealed which would be easiest to expand into. Questionnaire follow-ups of both jobs the company won and those it lost helped show why. Adding a 24-hour emergency service staffed by workers with cellular phones improved responsiveness. Numerous experiments with other ways of marketing and controlling helped identify which ones worked best. All these activities helped set the company apart from competitors and propel it to *Inc.* 500 membership.[40]

❖ ❖ ❖

> James Ake built a six-employee bottle filling machine company to 100 employees in six years by emphasizing speed of delivery to customers. He guaranteed delivery in 10 days. By devising control systems for ordering, manufacturing, shipping and installing to cope with such difficulties as running with almost no backlog, by training, motivating and compensating employees for flexibility and speed, and by managing inventory to allow fast production he was able to achieve to make good on that guarantee.[41] He also offered to subtract air fare for a visit to his plant if a customer bought. "If we can con-

[39]Arnold C. Cooper and others, *New Business In America* (Washington, D.C.: The NFIB Foundation, 1990), p. 8.
[40]Joshua Hyatt, "Out of the Ordinary," *Inc.*, December 1990, p. 110.
[41]John Case, "The Time Machine," *Inc.*, June 1990, p. 48.

vince a customer to visit our place, we'll make the sale about 90 percent of the time....When they see this company has meat on its bones and will be here to service the equipment, it means a lot."[42]

❖ ❖ ❖

In September, 1990, *Inc.* reported that Direct Tire near Boston was offering its tires for $60 to $120 each while the Goodyear store down the street was charging $50 to $100. And yet Direct Tire was also selling far more tires, despite the price differential. Willingness to provide fast service, having seven loaner cars available, making good on tires that go bad, even after 30,000 miles, seem to be part of the explanation, according to the article's author, Paul B. Brown.[43] Noting that the shop's owner, Barry Steinberg, has been in the business for 42 years, Brown observes a combination of many refinements that set his firm apart from competitors. "State-of-the-art equipment not only lets Steinberg offer better service, but it helps him attract the best technicians. For the same reason, he pays technicians 15 percent to 25 percent over the industry average.... Steinberg takes care to order the right magazines for the waiting room and to provide fresh coffee."

Part of what these examples illustrate is that the key to physical feasibility need not have anything to do with technological breakthroughs or esoteric schooling. None of these apparently success-producing actions seems particularly exotic or difficult to accomplish compared to the start-up feats of some companies that clone genes or design microchip testers. Rather, it appears that these firms are winning by doing ordinary physical things extraordinarily well. In hindsight, the ability to perform them may seem straightforward common sense, something many entrepreneurs should be able to do. And yet the competitors of these firms apparently don't learn how to reach the same level of competence. A prospective founder should consider just how well his or her venture will be able to perform ordinary functions relative to its competitors.

Successively deeper penetrations in testing physical practicability could include the following:

1. Imagine trying to implement the idea, and guess what could interfere with making the product, having it work, or operating it at a competitively superior level of performance.

2. Develop a written scenario and sketches that show how the product or service will be produced and delivered, noting any impediments, legal, physical or capability-wise for carrying it through, and how this will be done with excellence.

3. Solicit "expert" reviews of whatever seem to be the most critical items on the above list.

---

[42]"On the floor sales," *Inc.*, August 1990, p.108.
[43]Paul B. Brown, "The Real Cost of Customer Service," *Inc.*, September 1990, p. 49.

4. Make a physical prototype, if the venture will make a new product, and use it to see what happens. If the venture will introduce a service, try performing it, and see how well it can be done.

Application   *What tasks should be performed to check out the physical and legal feasibility of the assigned case venture?*

Check Market Fit

Anything that can be foreseen about customer reactions to the venture's product or service helps in screening and refining the venture idea. Some of this foreseeing can be done by imagination with information a would-be entrepreneur already possesses, possibly to eliminate an idea or possibly to improve upon it. If the entrepreneur previously worked in the industry and knows the customers personally, then information already known may confirm the venture idea and shape it to fit the market. Some ventures even start with customers already in line to buy their products and services. In such a case more market information may eventually be needed to capitalize on future changes in the market, but for inception of such a venture existing information may well be sufficient.

Without some sort of prior confirmation of market fit, however, there will likely be need to gather information about the hoped-for market in order both to establish its existence and to shape the venture to fit it well. Such information may be any combination of data from the following:

- **Prior studies** of the market or related markets by other companies, government agencies or entrepreneurs.

- **Polls** of population samples believed to typify customers. Mail questionnaires, advertisements incorporating feedback mechanisms such as mail-in responses, phone interviews and/or personal interviews may be used.

- **Negotiations** with prospective customers to solicit orders and determine whether they will actually buy.

In analyzing the prospective market to estimate sales and design market strategy some familiar marketing "buzz word" concepts such as "target customers," "segmentation," "nichemanship," "positioning," "price-performance relationships," "comparison grids," and "relative market share" can be very helpful and should be considered, perhaps examined extensively, before giving the idea a "thumbs up" on market fit. Briefly, some aspects to look at for each of these concepts are as follows:

- **Target Customers** What can be said in detail about the first person who will say "I'll buy" when the venture opens for business?

What pattern of logic and emotion in that person's mind will trigger the buying decision? How much of a "close call" will that buying decision be? What can be said about the next few who will buy and about the first one who will give a repeat order? What aspects in design and operation of the venture will affect this process and how?

- **Segmentation** How many customers like those targeted are there? What are the features common to them that distinguish them from other groups of customers somewhat similar but not targeted by the company? What about the venture will enable it to sell one segment if not the other? What might be required for expansion of sales to other segments later?

- **Nichemanship** Within its targeted segment what fraction of the potential customers can the venture hope to capture and how? How is that fraction or sub-segment different from the larger group, and how will the company tune to it in particular? How will it beat out competitors who also target on that particular niche?

- **Positioning** How will the venture's product or service compare to those of competitors in terms of line breadth, quality, price, follow-up and other features customers in the market seem likely to care about? Who is qualified to make that comparison? What evidence can be used to test the extent to which customers will see it that way?

- **Price/Performance** In assessing physical feasibility there must have been assumptions about properties of the product or service that would most appeal to customers. What were they? What evidence is there that customers agree with the assumptions? How much will it cost to provide the appeals that matter most? What must be charged to provide them? Are the features worth enough to customers? Could more be added to justify a higher price or others of less importance to customers be removed to permit a lower price? To explore such relationships it may be helpful to plot curves of price versus various performance dimensions, and of expected price elasticity.

- **Comparison Grids** Like graphs, grids are another way to explore relationships between variables that can be traded off in fitting the venture's product or service to its chosen market. One straightforward grid approach is to list along one axis such things as competitors' predicted offerings and along the other axis features (such as price, appearance, convenience, durability, reliability, performance, service quality, speed of delivery, etc.) of the product or service. Articles comparing products in such magazines as *Consumer Reports* or *Infoworld* illustrate application of such grids, and also provide some alternative ways of rating the products in cells of the grids to generate an overall rating for each that allows easy comparison.

- **Relative Market Share** It is well known that a large market share relative to competitors tends to produce higher profitability due to economies of scale. Hence an important prediction to arrive at from analysis of market fit is just what share the new venture can hope to capture relative to whomever its largest two or three competitors will be. To arrive at a prediction a starting point can be to estimate present market shares from industry interviews and observation, then forecast venture sales, and finally guess how competitors' shares may change from their present values.

Application   *Which of the above marketing concepts are most important to the assigned case venture, and how do they apply? Please create one or more transparencies illustrating how they fit.*

In summary, some successively deeper penetrations of analysis in checking market fit could include:

a. Imagine who might want to buy the product or service of the new venture. Describe why they would buy it instead of whatever else they buy now or will be able to buy from others.

b. Talk to some people who fit the above scenario and ask for their reactions to it.

c. Segment the market into reasonably homogeneous groups and conduct a more formal market survey by mail, telephone or personal interview.

d. Ask for an order.

Application   *How could market feasibility of the assigned case venture best be assessed, using methods such as those four above?*

To say there should be some "market research" to determine what people will buy, moreover, is not enough. The entrepreneur must figure out very specifically what market information to obtain, how much to spend on it, how soon to get it and how to get it. The prospective customers, whoever they happen to be, may not be able to appreciate what the venture proposes to offer. For example, Xerox, microcomputers and pocket calculators all proved to have wildly different markets than any future customer or entrepreneur foresaw.

Supplementary Reading

New Venture Strategies Chapter 2. (Vesper, K.H., Prentice-Hall, 1990)

New Venture Mechanics Chapter 2. (Vesper, K. H., Prentice-Hall, 1993)

Your Venture Plan

1. Rank the questions and techniques described thus far in this chapter in their order of likely effectiveness for testing and shaping your main venture idea. In the time available to you, apply them, starting from the top of your priority list down.

2. Make a comparison grid listing features of your product or service versus its competition at two contrasting time points in the projected development of your venture.

Your Venture History

1. Make a comparison grid for the product or service of the venture versus its competitors.

2. Which checkout procedures, including those of this chapter and any others that may apply, were used in making decisions about proceeding with the venture?

3. How did the strengths and weaknesses of the venture compare to its competitors at two contrasting time points in its development?

Exercises

1. Write out a "portrait of success" or future scenario of some venture idea that seems promising. Do this on one page, and on a second page list the things that could prevent that scenario from occurring. On a third page describe what could be done to solve those problems, weigh the main pros and cons of the idea and state whether it is worth pursuing further.

2. Prepare a comparison grid for a venture idea that includes numerical ratings multiplied by weightings for each cell to produce overall comparative product scores across the bottom totalling the cells in each column.

3. Study, as best you can in the time available, three different local firms. Estimate the profitability of each and formulate a comparison grid to explain differences in their relative profitabilities. Comment on the extent to which you consider them successful.

❏ SUBCHAPTER 3B - Financial and Founder Fit

Compute Financial Attractiveness

To test the financial attractiveness of a venture idea in terms of two critical dimensions, investment and profitability, there are at least five approaches. Investment includes money and other resources that must be put up to make the venture go, as well as unpaid effort the founders put into it. If these are small enough, then the *first* approach for testing viability of a venture idea can be simply starting it up and seeing what happens.

If a larger investment is required, then profit and elapsed time are probably worth computing. There are still shortcuts that may be worth taking to avoid bogging down in long analysis of an idea that may not work. The *second* approach is to consider profitability of comparable businesses. If that is high, then there is reason to hope that the venture's profitability will also be high.

A *third* approach is to look at the margin percentage and guess how much the venture can earn. If the venture will manufacture something, one rough rule of thumb, for instance, is that it should wholesale its product for at least twice the cost of labor plus material. (Jobs and Wozniak sold their first computers to the Byte Shop for twice the cost of parts, not including labor.) If the venture makes a product and it is to be sold at retail, then probably the margin will have to be doubled again to provide for advertising, sales and distribution.

However, such rules of thumb are very rough, often don't fit a particular industry, and are typically on the low side anyway. If the venture is a store, for instance, the critical number is not margin percentage but rather margin in total dollars per month. The question is often how adequately that margin will cover rent, utilities and help.

A *fourth* approach, and the next step beyond margin estimation, is to compute break-even sales level. This is done by adding up fixed costs of the venture, such as rent, wages, utilities, advertising and other more or less fixed costs and dividing by the number of cents per sales dollar left after paying variable costs on each unit sold. If the venture does not seem certain to exceed that roughly estimated break-even sales volume, then it probably will not succeed. It's easy to be too optimistic in such forecasts. For instance, the impact of competitor moves on sales is hard to foresee and so may be neglected while at the same time some items of cost are almost certain to be missed. Thus profits may look higher than they should.

A *fifth* approach, if the idea still seems to hold up, is to generate a financial statement forecast for specific time periods such as monthly for the first year or two and annually for another two or three years beyond that. Estimation begins with an income statement "top line" projecting sales volume over time, derived from analysis of the market fit as discussed in the preceding section. The validity of that top line can be cross checked by such steps as:

- Making global estimates of overall sales by year for the first two to five years and comparing them to those of other similar types of businesses.

- Making detailed lists of customers, market segments, geographic regions and sales channels, and estimating how much sales will flow to each.

- Setting out a spread sheet and estimating by month the actions that will be taken to produce sales, the orders that will be received in units, customers, transactions or the like, then listing for each month the amount of sales each of these will produce, and finally how much money each month will be collected from these sales.

From these sales estimates should flow consequences in terms of expenditures needed for selling, production and delivery of the venture's product or service. Easiest to generate will probably be the profit and loss statement, on which cost of sales may introduce complications by having different levels at different volumes.

Balance sheet forecasting comes next. Some items, such as fixed assets and necessary cash balance may be easy to estimate. If the venture will have inventory, accounts payable and/or accounts receivable those can be scaled in terms of "days on hand" as percentages of sales. Some possible "for instances" are:

- If receivables will on average take one month to collect, then the balance sheet figure for that will be one month's sales. (Watch out for seasonality.)

- If creditors will require payment within one month on average, and if purchased materials amount to about one-third of the venture's selling price, then payables will be about one-third of one month's sales.

- If inventory will turn on average six times per year: (in other words, two months' supply of it will be on hand), then the balance sheet figure will equal two months' cost of goods sold. If the company's gross margin is 50 percent, then the figure for inventory will be half of two months' sales revenue, which is one month's sales revenue.

Another short cut approach for estimating both balance sheet and income statement figures is to obtain statements of a comparable company and "adjust" the figures in those statements to fit expectations of the new venture. Sources of "look alike" company statements include the ratios published by

Robert Morris Associates and those published by Dun and Bradstreet as well as possibly the annual reports of selected companies that might be available through publications, personal connections or trade associations.

Cash flow figures are usually most important. These may be complicated by things hard to estimate in both income statements and balance sheets: cost/volume shifts, seasonal sales variations, lags in collections, and both leads and lags in payments required. Using a microcomputer spread sheet such as Microsoft Excel or Lotus 1-2-3 can help greatly, but thought will still be needed to work out calculation formulas, and judgment will be required for estimating figures.

Once complete, the cash flow and balance sheet figures will show investments required, while the income statements will show profit levels. The profits can then be divided by investments to compute return on investment (ROI). Venture capitalists typically require rates on the order of 30 percent per year and more. Other investors may accept less, but almost surely will want a return well above 10 percent to 15 percent for a start-up venture. This return, moreover, should be generated on a scale of investment that justifies the time and worry needed to work out and live with the venture deal.

Of personal interest to the founder, of course, is the level of compensation it can provide him or her as well as what he or she must do to earn it. Is the return on a copy center, bicycle manufacturing or software company enough to live on? It depends on the individual venture. Some can pay nothing and eventually fail, while others grow and prosper thanks to powerful competitive advantages devised by their entrepreneurs.

How income and compensation will vary with changes in key assumptions must also be considered. With spreadsheet microcomputer programs it is relatively easy to vary the assumptions and see what happens to net cash flow and profits. In what month will the worst cash demand occur, and how much cash will be needed to get through it? How much worse will the need be if hoped for events, such as collections from customers are either below expectations or arrive later than anticipated? What is the downside worst case? How much will be lost if the venture fails, how much will be recoverable and how hard will it be to recover any salvage value? Such a sensitivity analysis should be prepared in the form of alternative financial scenarios to check both the downside risk as well as the upside potential of the venture.

Odds of success range fairly dramatically among industries according to a number of studies performed over the years.[44] For instance, according to a 1988 study of the statistics on 3.6 million firms by Phillips and Kirchhoff, the overall survival percentage of start-ups was 40 percent for six years. The figures ranged from 35 percent for construction and 38 percent for retail firms to 44 percent for wholesaling and 47 percent for manufacturing firms.[45] Most re-

---

[44]Karl H. Vesper, *New Venture Strategies*, revised edition (Englewood Cliffs, N.J.: Prentice-Hall, 1990), p. 32.

cently, Cooper et al. reported that 77 percent of new businesses formed in the U.S. during the mid-1980s survived three or more years, and another 4 percent were sold to new owners.

Also of interest to founders may be forms of compensation other than those that are purely financial. What will be learned from trying the venture? How much fun will it be? What are the odds that it might lead to other attractive opportunities? Starting a venture is like entering an avenue down whose sidestreets lie contacts, adventures and opportunities that cannot be discovered any other way than by proceeding. Just what constitutes success and how to gauge it is a question that each prospective founder must answer individually.

In summary, successively deeper penetrations in computing financial attractiveness for checking out venture ideas include to:

1. Estimate gross profit margin percentage and compare it to norms for the industry.

2. Estimate fixed and variable costs and compute a break even.

3. Project financial statements based on typical figures for the industry and assess whether those figures can be achieved by the venture.

4. Project financial statements for the venture based upon a buildup of sales and cost figures.

5. Add to the above financial statements a cash flow forecast.

6. Show the above financial statements and cash flow forecast to other knowledgeable people and request that they provide a critique or, better yet, an investment or loan.

Application   *Which of the above six methods for assessing financial attractiveness of the assigned case venture are most appropriate, and what does their application show?*

Assess Founder(s)' Fit

A winning opportunity for one potential founder may be not at all a winner for another. Statistically, some lines of business have clearly higher odds of start-up survival than others. The study of 2,994 start-ups by Cooper et al. reported that although most were in retailing (46 percent) or non-professional services (19 percent), those were the areas where firms were least likely to

---

45Bruce D. Phillips and Bruce A. Kirchhoff, "An Analysis of New Firm Survival and Growth," Babson Entrepreneurship Conference, Calgary, 1988. A more recent study by Kirchhoff cited in The *Christian Science Monitor* (May 7, 1993) states that no more than 18 percent of all start-ups fail in the first eight years, while 28 percent voluntarily terminate without losses to the creditors. The remaining 54 percent survive either with their original or new owners.

grow or even survive. Three-year survival rates were 73 percent in retail and 75 percent in non-professional services, compared to 85 percent in professional services, 83 percent in financial services and 82 percent in manufacturing. Another study of a half million start-ups between 1978 and 1982 by Birch[46] found that the start-up area with the highest average survival rate was in veterinary services. Those with the highest average rates of growth were banks.

Who can do ventures such as veterinary clinics and banks best, or even at all, is not a matter of entrepreneurial virtue, character, general business savvy or knowledge of start-up "technology." Rather, it is mainly determined by such qualifications as credentials, training, experience, contacts and reputation. A study of 100 automation start-ups by Chambers, Hart and Denison, reported that "previous start-up managerial experience of the founders is not as predominant a feature of high performing firms as previously believed."[47] Another by Hills and Welsh reported that highest incidence of success factors among 150 small business award winners were in "knowledge of product," "knowledge of market," and "knowledge of industry."[48]

Clearly that does not rule out other possibilities for a would-be entrepreneur. The findings are only on average. There are great successes in virtually all lines of work, even hamburgers, as McDonald's and many other food stores illustrate. Moreover, an entrepreneur who lacks the know-how or connections, to start a bank for instance, may be able to recruit those capabilities in partners.

But these patterns of success do highlight the fact that technical capability can be an important if not all-important factor in pursuing venture success. As noted earlier, it is not enough to be able simply to perform the work of the business. Venturing often requires that it be performed exceptionally well. If the entrepreneur possesses the technical capability, there will still be question as to whether it is good enough. Or if expert help is to be recruited through partners, there will remain the question of just what skills, talent and experience the recruiting entrepreneur brings to the enterprise.

Successively deeper penetrations in assessing the fit of founder could include:

1. Contemplating the question "how well would it fit me to work on this venture idea?"

2. Making lists on paper of (a) capabilities needed to implement the venture idea and (b) personal prior experience, qualifications and resources.

---

[46]David L. Birch, "The Truth About Startups," *Inc.*, January 1988, p. 14.

[47]Brian R. Chambers, Stuart L. Hart, and Daniel R. Denison, "Founding Team Experiences and New Firm Performance," in *Frontiers of Entrepreneurship Research, 1988*, eds. Bruce A. Kirchhoff and others (Wellesley, Mass.: Babson Center for Entrepreneurial Studies, 1988), p. 117.

[48]Gerald E. Hills, and Harold P. Welsch, "High Growth Entrepreneurial Ventures," in *Frontiers of Entrepreneurship Research, 1988*, eds. Bruce A. Kirchhoff and others (Wellesley, Mass.: Babson Center for Entrepreneurial Studies, 1988), p. 496.

Compare the two lists. What complementary talents might it be wise to recruit?

3. Making a third list which includes other people who might be interested in competing with the venture. How do their qualifications compare? What might it take to recruit complementary talents to make a "bullet-proof" venture team?

4. Asking one or more other suitably qualified people to comment on the comparisons made in the above lists.

Application   *Which of the above six methods for assessing founders' fit with the assigned case venture are most appropriate and what does their application show?*

If the answers to these preliminary questions are less than encouraging, there may be ways to modify them by recruiting other partners or by acquiring needed capability through study or work experience. This will test another important issue, namely how strong is the entrepreneur's preference for that particular type of enterprise.

Forecast Competitors' Moves

The importance of competitors can be viewed in the following way. Before the new venture starts, its competitors are getting all the customer orders. If too large a fraction of those orders continue going to competitors after it starts, the venture will fail. The typical competitors of new businesses, according to a study of 2,994 start-ups by Cooper et al., are other small firms. However, a substantial minority, 25 percent, of entrepreneurs in their second year of operations said their primary competitors were more than five times larger. Beyond inception the entrepreneurs expected that the number of their competitors would grow, and two years later they continued to hold that view.[49]

A starting point for competitor analysis is to make a grid which contrasts features of the venture's product or service with those of its competitors. These can range on a spectrum from very direct in competing for customers' money to very indirect. This may explain why 23 percent of the entrepreneurs in the Cooper study were unable to name their primary competitor. The direct competitor for a new hamburger stand may be a nearby fast food franchise. The competition could also include to some degree fancier restaurants, home cooking and even diet programs. The question to consider is, where will a customer spend the same dollar if the venture does not exist or if it does not function

---

[49]Arnold C. Cooper and others, *New Business In America* (Washington, D.C.: The NFIB Foundation, 1990), p. 9.

quite well enough to win that dollar?

Future tense is also important in answering this question. Comparing what the venture plans to offer with what competitors currently offer is a good starting point. More important, however, is the comparison with what competitors will be offering in the future when the venture actually starts, and how their offerings will change after the venture becomes a factor in the marketplace. Awareness of how competitors have responded before to new entrants or other changes in the market may give clues as to how they will adjust in the future. The entrepreneur then needs to think for competitors. What will they do if they are smart? Are they likely to be that smart and to do what they logically should?

Historical evidence suggests that on average market share is a powerful determinant of profitability. Market share in turn seems to be driven by product or service quality and by value (roughly, performance divided by price) as perceived by customers. Therefore a good starting point in analysis of competition is to write down specifically how high the quality and value of competitors' offerings are relative to each other. To that description can be added what the quality and value of the venture's offering will be. A grid or matrix display such as those of *Consumer Reports* and other product magazines will be an effective choice for this.

Other aspects of competitive position may include such things as talents, know-how, location, ideas, reputation, contacts, financial resources, special production equipment or unique elements of the venture's strategy and of the policies through which the venture will be implemented. Dedication level and the willingness to work extra hours per dollar of income can also make an important difference.

After such factors have been assessed, likely changes in competitors' and the venture's performances can be estimated, which should then provide a good basis for assessing prospects of venture success. To forecast competitors' moves probably requires looking first at where they are today, then asking what would be smart for them to do tomorrow. Should they have full lines or does it matter? Will they add offerings to match the venture? Should they cut price to match it? Should they be working on next generation designs now that will leapfrog what the venture introduces in the way of a product or service? What can or might competitors do about any legal protections the start-up might have such as contracts, leases, patents, trademarks or copyrights? Might they sue the venture on such grounds? It's easier to get into a venture than it is to get out, particularly if the venture gets into trouble, and the time to anticipate troublesome eventualities is before taking the plunge.

Successively deeper penetrations in analyzing competitors' moves could therefore include:

1. Guessing what they will do by imagining different scenarios and judging which would make most sense.

2. Writing out grids that compare them in such aspects as price, quality, features, market share, breadth of line, rate of growth, apparent ambitions and strategy, and competitive advantages now and again in the future versus the contemplated new venture.

3. Investing more time and money in gathering the above information.

4. Obtaining reactions to the above grids from one or more suitably knowledgeable people.

Application   *Which of the above four methods for analyzing competitors' moves against the assigned case venture are most appropriate, and what does their application show?*

Cross-check Competitive Advantages

Throughout the idea testing process assumptions will inevitably be made about the venture's competitive advantages and those of the particular entrepreneur(s) for creating that particular venture. At some point these assumptions should be audited explicitly. Questions to consider in this process include the following:

1. What was the entrepreneur's prior task-relevant experience?

2. What factors will govern the profit-generating potential of this venture? Which of the following can it be expected to possess which will give it an advantage over existing and potential competitors?

- License
- Patent
- Lease
- Known brand
- Known personalities
- Invisibility
- High risk activity
- Secret methods
- Resource ownership
- Capital access
- Advertising power
- Political power
- Personal connections
- Skill level
- Rare knowledge/skill
- Personal charisma

- Exceptional intellectual power
- Exceptional energy level
- Habit patterns among constituents and contacts

Presumably, the levels of each of these will start at one point, then change in the future. Similarly, their levels of importance to the venture's prosperity will also change. Part of assessing the venture idea, shaping it and reshaping it additionally in the future must depend on how these levels can be expected to change over time. Hence, they should be forecasted for different future points in time as part of the assessment and planning processes.

Application   *What does application of the above two questions for cross-checking competitive advantages of the assigned case venture idea show and how?*

Accept, Refine, Table or Reject

How much analysis is enough? Each of the above sections ends with questions which may be partially or more fully answered. Having cycled once through the facets of analysis listed above, presumably some more deeply than others based on considerations of priority, the would-be entrepreneur faces a question of whether to drop the venture idea or to continue the analysis with still deeper study of one of the facets. Possibly the first round of analysis has suggested ways to modify the venture concept calling for another round to examine viability of the changed idea. If the idea still holds up, likely the next step will be to obtain information for testing and developing it further.

Successively deeper penetrations in deciding whether to improve further or drop could include:

1. Accept this idea and move ahead to implement it.

2. Keep checking further aspects of this idea in successively greater depth to reach a verdict.

3. Table this idea for now. Work on other ideas and maybe come back to this one later.

4. Reject this one and concentrate all processing capacity on either pursuing other ideas already found or seeking out still more ideas to check.

Application   *Which of the above four alternative actions with respect to the proposed venture concept in the assigned case should be taken and why?*

Supplementary Reading

New Venture Strategies Chapter 6. (Vesper, K.H., Prentice-Hall, 1990)

Your Venture Plan

1. Prepare a five-minute report describing what has been accomplished on your venture plan to date. Begin with description of the current status and then tell about different aspects in terms of what has been accomplished.

2. Apply screening questions of this chapter to rank the 10 most promising venture ideas considered along the way in arriving at your venture plan. Indicate where you put highest priority in screening and how you controlled the depth of investigation to fit the time available for this task. Rank the ideas in some sort of systematic way, and indicate what action you think is called for next in your venture development project.

3. Copy the list of possible competitive advantages from this chapter, and rate the prospects of your venture versus those of competitors on each of them at three different future time points.

4. Make a prototype in some form of your top ranked idea.

5. Do some sort of market testing of your most promising idea by talking to at least one other person about it.

6. Make pro forma financials and a cash flow forecast monthly for the first two years of implementing your most promising venture idea so far.

Your Venture History

1. Which techniques described in this chapter seemed to have been used by the entrepreneur, which were not, and why?

2. How far off were expectations of the entrepreneur from the way the venture actually developed and why?

3. What responses did competitors make to the start-up? Which were foreseen by the entrepreneur and which were not?

4. What comparison grid of the venture versus its competitors does the entrepreneur foresee downstream in time?

Exercises

1. This chapter contains many questions to use in assessing venture ideas. For each of three ideas identify the page and line for 10 different questions that would be best to start with in performing evaluation. Indicate the rank order of priority of those questions for each idea. Be prepared to comment on how the patterns of questions selected differ for each of the three ideas. Also be prepared to com-

ment on how it would be best to go about developing answers for those top priority questions.

2. Apply the evaluation questions of this chapter, in order of their importance to the particular venture, to one or more of your own venture ideas.

Case Questions: Ingersoll, Osborne, Shane

General Case Questions

1. Do the elements of a potentially viable start-up opportunity exist in the situation described by the assigned case? Explain why or why not.

2. As best you can with the information provided in the assigned case, lay out at least one action plan for starting a business in this situation, estimate the upside potential and downside risk (both amount and likelihood) of loss.

3. How well suited is the entrepreneur(s) in the assigned case to compete with others who might start a similar venture?

4. How well suited to the start-up contemplated in the assigned case would be one or more entrepreneurs who were encountered in previously studied cases?

5. If a prospectus were written to invite investment in this potential venture, what factors of promise should it describe to possible investors and what factors of risk should a Securities and Exchange Commission official want to see listed for a public offering circular?

Ingersoll Case Questions

1. What would the entrepreneur in this case have to gain, potentially, by attempting it? Please include analysis of the financial aspects.

2. How much would have to be risked to get that gain? How do the expected benefits and risks compare?

Osborne Case Questions

1. What is your assessment of the feasibility of carrying forward the venture proposed in this case? Please include consideration of legal, ethical and political aspects, in addition to those of finance, marketing and other business aspects.

2. As a prospective investor, what changes in Osborne's plan would you most like to see?

Shane Case Questions

1. Without looking ahead at the Shane (B) case, prepare at least one page of a questionnaire for Michael Shane's market survey. On it include what you would consider to be the most crucial questions, selected from a presumably larger list of questions, to be answered.

2. Postulate hypothetical answer patterns to the above key questions. Explain the action implications for Michael if in fact those patterns did emerge from the survey.

3. The Shane case in fact took place many years ago. How would the prospect and the task of starting a company such as Michael was contemplating be similar and how would it be different today? Could it be done now? If so, who could do it best?

Shane (B) Case Questions

1. What implications appear in results of the market survey regarding (a) whether Michael Shane should go ahead with start-up of a distributorship, and (b) what the strategy and design of the venture should be if he does go ahead with it?

2. In hindsight, how effective was the survey in pointing up future directions of opportunity in the microcomputer business? What questions, if asked by the survey, might have been more revealing to a person in Michael's position?

3. What should be the role of formal market research in creating new ventures, as you see it?

Formal Plans

❏ *SUBCHAPTER 4A - Plan Elements*

Writing a venture plan is the easiest part of creating a venture, and sometimes the least necessary. What makes a venture work is effective action by the founder(s) and others whose help they need. If planning inspires that action, it is helpful. If planning does not lead to that action, the planning process may still have been educational. But then the education must have utility or the planning will have wasted time.

Planning does not have to be done in written form to be useful. In their study of 2,994 new ventures,Cooper et al. found that 43 percent of the founders seriously contemplated business entry for a "long time" before taking action and 14 percent said they had thought someday they might do so. Undoubtedly some of these, particularly among the 43 percent, formally planned. Another 13 percent said they entered business simply because it was the best alternative available and 28 percent reported that the opportunity simply came along and they jumped into it.[50] It seems less likely that these last two groups formally planned. From this and much anecdotal evidence it appears that most businesses start without formal planning and even more without *written* formal plans.

Cooper et al. go on to point out that most firms start very small, 90 percent with less than 10 employees and over half with two or less.[51] This and other studies have also found that most firms stay small, under five employees. It might be supposed that these firms are therefore simple enough for owners to keep any planning in mind while at the same time keeping their enterprises flexible enough to respond to events quickly without much need for anticipation.

---

[50] Arnold C. Cooper and others, *New Business In America* (Washington, D.C.: The NFIB Foundation, 1990), p. 18.
[51] Ibid., p. 5.

Purposes for Plans

Some very successful entrepreneurs, however, believe strongly in formal planning. For instance, Steve Bostic, who built his start-up to top performer on the 1987 *Inc.* 500 list before selling it to Eastman Kodak for a reported $45 million commented about his experience as follows:

> *I m saying it has to be planned. You have to take your vision, think it through, and turn it into a consistent strategy. And then you have to get it on paper. That s key. I maintain that if you can t put your vision on paper, you can never do it in the real world.*

When asked about the many companies that succeed without such planning, he continued:

> *You re talking about companies that are one-man shows. Yes, if you re guiding the ship out front and pulling everybody else along, you don t need to write it down. But if you want to be able to walk out of the room and have life continue in an orderly way, you d better put your vision and your plan on paper.*[52]

Although, most businesses start without formal business plans, some do develop them before starting and many develop them if they start to grow. Some ways a plan can be used include the following:

- As an exercise for learning about entrepreneurship.
- As a test of reasoning about the venture design.
- As a scenario against which founders can test their "fit."
- As a device for obtaining counsel from others.
- As a portrait of the venture as a basis for improving its design.
- As a touchstone for guidance, should events become hectic.
- To obtain a bank loan.
- To help in thinking a start-up idea through.
- To obtain credit from a supplier.
- To obtain capital from an investor.
- To recruit needed partners.
- To recruit key employees.
- To provide guidelines to work from for founders and employees.
- To convince a wanted customer that the venture will deliver.
- To anticipate long lead times required for some action.
- To set up benchmarks for tracking performance.

Application *How should the above purposes for a venture plan in the assigned case venture be ranked and why? How might that affect the design of the plan?*

---

[52] "Thriving on Order," *Inc.*, December 1989, p. 48.

The contents of the plan and how it is structured may vary depending on its main purpose. The majority of plans are written to help in attempting to raise money. This puts emphasis on financial projections in the plan. A banker will be particularly interested in debt coverage and support for a repayment schedule. An investor may be more interested in sales growth, profits and the backup information that supports claims about those dimensions of performance. Prospective employees, however, might be more interested in organization and staffing plans.

Matters of Priority

The place to begin a formal plan, unless another one occurs and looks better, is to brainstorm and write out answers to screening questions that were discussed in the preceding chapter. That will automatically provide key portions of a venture plan. The financial forecasts needed for screening will form a core, since much of the purpose of a plan is simply to explain in more detail just what will cause the estimates for sales and expenses to come true. Hence the writing process can start by setting forth the pro forma financial statements and then working back from them. They will help guide description of the product or service (categories of sales), who will buy how much of it (sales figures), what labor, materials and other expenditures will have to be in order to produce and deliver it (expenses), what physical items the company will need on hand to perform that work (assets) and where the financing (liabilities) will come from to obtain them.

Important General Qualities

Although venture plans can be fancy, there is no need for them to be. Some ventures have raised millions in start-up capital with very simple plans. Sophisticated investors can look past flashiness to assess whether the founders and their venture have credibility, or at least they like to believe they can. If the venture is basically flawed, the remedy should be to redesign or abandon it, not waste effort on gimmicks to make it look good. Founders should also not assume that if they simply plan well enough, they can make any venture work. Validity, realism, truthfulness and full disclosure of worrisome as well as encouraging factors are elements to reach for in creating a plan.

What To Present First

The purposes of the plan and nature of the venture should determine what it first describes. If the market is relatively apparent, as for something that will lengthen life or safety, then it may be best to start with description of the product or service, showing how the venture will be able to improve on what is now available in the marketplace. If the market is not so apparent, then the starting point may be to show readers what kind of need exists, how that was determined and what characteristics of it demonstrate that it can be profitable for the venture.

These are by no means the only two possibilities, as was suggested in the preceding chapter on screening. The objective is to start by letting readers know as directly as possible just what the venture will deliver, what the most outstanding virtue of the venture is and upon what basis that virtue rests. Maybe the basis is some unarguably unusual and powerful talent on the management team, unique property rights to an invention or a location. It could also be a lucrative contract or access to endorsement by some party whose word is likely to be strongly influential with important customers.

Organization of the Rest

In general, the organization of a venture plan should attempt to present more important aspects ahead of those less important, as a newspaper article does. If the reader needs an explanation to understand an important point, then possibly the explanation should come first. If only some readers, not all, will need the explanation, then it can be placed in an appendix at the back, with reference in the text as to where it can be found.

The list of topics to be covered is fairly predictable, although there can be striking differences in sequences, as appropriate to the individual ventures. A sample sequence of topics was presented earlier in Chapter 1. A variety of other arrangements taken from various plans appears in the first section of Appendix I illustrating venture plans.

Application   *Develop two contrasting venture plan outlines for the assigned case venture. Explain the pros and cons of each.*

Some Elements to Include

There are two main parts to the plan, the body and the appendices. The body should typically be no longer than about 20 to 30 pages. The purpose of appendices, which appear at the back, is to allow a reader to go through the plan without having to tackle all the details. The body might contain a summary of market research findings and simplified financial statements. But the details, such as copies of questionnaires used in the market research or more extended financial statements and footnotes explaining the figures, should be relegated to appendices. Within the body of the plan some of the main elements to include are as follows. Some are also illustrated by examples in Appendix I.

Opening

1. **Tables of contents** vary in order of topics. A common feature they share, however, is the listing of page numbers for both sections of the plan: the body and the appendices. A deficiency which makes some plans harder to read is that their tables of contents lack any page numbers or list page numbers for the text only, not the appendices.

    Among the example tables of contents in Appendix I, the longest happens to come from a company that proposed to make ground-effect (hovercraft, air cushion) boats. It did not get funding despite a very well written plan. The reason for rejection was that when the financing was being sought, oil prices shot up dramatically, venture capital available shrank and money became difficult or impossible for any venture to obtain.

    The briefest table of contents example in the appendix here is from a disk drive maker, Priam, which became very successful. That venture's success may not necessarily have been because of its plan, which like its table of contents was very simple and short.[53] But the founder who led the company to success was a staunch advocate of systematic planning.

2. An **executive summary** which follows the table of contents in a venture plan should be an abbreviated version of the overall plan so a reader can catch the main features of a venture in one page, if possible. Making it brief, however, does not mean it should be vague. Wherever possible, specific facts and figures, such as the internal rate of return (IRR) should be given. Introducing specifics need not add much, if any, length. This page is extremely important in approaching any prospective professional backers who are accustomed to reading many plans. If it does not hold their attention, they will not read further and the rest of the plan will be wasted.

3. Following the one page summary, the plan should open with **one summary paragraph** which briefly indicates (1) what the venture will sell, (2) what the principal competitive advantage of the venture is expected to be, (3) what the venture will need to be able to accomplish that, (4) what sequence of presentation the rest of the plan will follow and, (5) why that sequence. A vital function this paragraph should perform is to let the reader know the line of reasoning by which the remainder of the plan is organized and how it is laid out.

Application   *Write a new Executive Summary page and an introductory paragraph of a plan for the assigned case venture.*

---

[53]A copy of the full plan can be seen in Karl H. Vesper, *New Venture Mechanics* (Englewood Cliffs, N.J.: Prentice-Hall, 1993), Appendix B.

4. **Risk factors** may or may not be listed in a section under that title. In principle, a business plan should be designed with maximum realism, and in real life risk is a part of the picture. In contrast to a legal brief or an advertisement, whose purpose is to bias a reader by loading all the arguments only on one side, a venture plan should be balanced. An unbalanced presentation makes the reader and the writer antagonists rather than the collaborators they should be. Grouping risk factors into one section is sometimes an efficient way to introduce this balance. The facts on which those factors are based may speak adequately for themselves. Alternatively, risk factors may be pointed out at those points in the plan where important assumptions are made.

Description of Product or Service

Another task the front section of the plan must do in both the introductory or executive summary and the plan's opening paragraph is let the reader know just what the venture will offer potential customers. Usually this can be done briefly at the outset and then be further elaborated later in the body of the plan.

5. **Product (or service)** refers to what the company will sell. A section in the body of the plan should state clearly what the important features of the product or service are, what stage of development they are currently in, what will be needed to develop them further and how the venture can be expected to do that as well as or better than anyone else. For readers who may be expert in the venture's technology a few facts may suffice. For other readers there may be need for an appendix that will enable them to educate themselves about it.

Each of the excerpts shown in Appendix I of this book illustrates a different mode of describing products and services. The first uses words, while the second uses both words and a table. The latter happens to come from the venture plan of Storage Technology, a venture which received its funding, got started, became successful and went public. Some years later the company got into trouble and collapsed for reasons that would be hard to link to its original plan.

Other description excerpts in Appendix I use graphical depiction: one a flow chart, one an artist's rendering and the third an amateur's sketch. Although not elegant, the sketch displaying a booth for selling Christmas trees at very high prices in Japanese department stores does let a reader easily comprehend how it will look and how it will work. Pictures can truly be worth thousands of words and most business plans would be better if they used more graphics.

Application   *Write on one side of one page as full a description of the product or service in the assigned case as you can.*

Market Analysis

The market arena and how it works encompasses the next five sections. Illustrative excerpts appear in Appendix I of this book.

6. **Competitive analyses** should certainly have been part of the idea screening process, and it was suggested earlier that grids, matrices and tables can be particularly helpful in that process. Examples of such tables appear regularly in product-centered magazines such as *Consumer Reports, Infoworld, Motor Trend,* and *Motor Cyclist.*

Application   *Develop a competitive grid for the product or service of the assigned case, fill in the boxes insofar as possible and describe how information to fill the others might be sought by the entrepreneur.*

7. **Market research methodology** can take many forms, including library search, questionnaires, interviews, test marketing, and focus groups. Market claims for a venture should, wherever possible, be based on factual information from such sources. In school it may be appropriate only to design and pilot test a market research investigation in a way much more limited than would be called for by "the real thing." An appendix in the plan should show clearly how this study was performed, including sample questionnaires and protocols, if any were used.

Application   *Sketch out the design of a market research study to evaluate the selling power of the assigned case s product or service.*

8. **Market research data** should also be presented in an appendix. Excerpts in the appendix to this discussion illustrate use of both verbal description and tabular forms. The data need not be massive, particularly in a school study. Some data, however meager, are better than none, provided they are factual. The data should be accompanied by enough discussion to indicate clearly how they were analyzed.

9. **Market plan elements** may be simple or complex. Tabulating sales and where they will come from for a market plan can help the writer consider alternatives more thoroughly. Writing out tends to highlight any incompleteness. Noticing empty cells is a prompt to search for options that might fill them. If none are found, cells can still be left blank without diminishing value of the tabulation. The blanks can stimulate

searching by readers, who also may be able to suggest more alternatives to formulate a better marketing strategy.

10. **Sales projections** will probably come directly from notes made during idea checkout. The text of the venture plan should contain at least a summary, perhaps in graphical form. One in the form of a histogram and one as a table appear among the appendix excerpts here. The table goes a step farther to present three sales projections; optimistic: pessimistic and most likely. Such an array forms the basis for better financial projections which follow from the sales forecasts.

Application   *Describe two different ways that sales projections could be developed for the assigned case venture by its entrepreneur. Produce a hypothetical set of figures with each.*

Operations

11. **PERT and Gantt charts** are useful tools for planning the sequence of important actions in getting a venture started and for communicating them to others. Also helpful can be a time line with important milestones. Those milestones should include in particular any key accomplishments upon which additional outside funding might appropriately be contingent. Examples shown in Appendix I of this book illustrate only a small amount of the variety possible in formatting such charts.

Application   *Prepare a Gantt Chart and a PERT Chart for development of some aspect of the assigned case venture. Assess the advantages and disadvantages of each.*

12. **Organization charts,** both before and after the venture actually starts, should show clearly who will be the main leader and how other key members of the venture's workforce will be positioned in the power structure.[54] Somewhere in the plan there should also be indication of how ownership will be divided and a list of any key outside advisors. This should include, as soon as they have been chosen, names of any law and accounting firms that will be retained.

Application   *Draw two organization charts for the venture, one for a very early stage and another for later after break-even. Comment on when and how the change should be accomplished.*

---

[54]A two-stage organization chart example from a venture plan appears in Karl H. Vesper, *New Venture Mechanics* (Englewood Cliffs, N.J.: Prentice-Hall, 1993), pp. 338 - 339.

13. **Resumes** are not included among the appendix examples, but appear in some of the cases, such as those of Handel and Glassman. Their inclusion in a venture plan should be completely straightforward. Of particular importance in them should be those aspects of prior experience that show (1) relevance to the job tasks of this particular venture and (2) evidence of accomplishment in prior challenging projects where something new had to be created under difficult circumstances.

Spending Plans

14. **Applications of funds** will be a matter of considerable interest to whomever puts up money for a venture. Presumably some applications, such as advertising or administrative costs, will be unrecoverable in the event the venture terminates. Others, such as capital equipment, inventory or development that results in patents, may continue to have value that will reduce potential losses.

15. **Cost breakdowns** must be made as part of forecasting both cash needs and profitability. The more that major elements of the costs can be subdivided and explained or backed up with references, the more convincing the forecasts become. How much effort to apply to this versus other elements of a forecast, such as sales, is a matter of judgment. One option is to give brief treatment to costs in the "first cut" of a plan but to include with it a brief discussion of how the figures would be further refined if more time were available to work on them.

Application   *List the largest purchases that the assigned case venture will have to make, and describe for each how best the amount of cash outlay required for it can be forecasted.*

Pricing Considerations

Price considerations should be given explicit attention from several perspectives in the venture plan.

16. **Pricing rationale** does not rest solely upon costs. But certainly the relationship between price and costs must be examined, including the way that costs are likely to vary with volume.

17. **Price/volume curves** can be important in formulating competitive strategy. Whichever company is able to move more quickly to lower costs, either by economies of scale or other ingenuity, can enjoy a pricing advantage. Competitors' prices, how they have changed in the past and what competitors might be able to do about them in the future should be explained.

Application   *How, in very specific terms, should the entrepreneur in the assigned case set the price initially for the product or service, and how should it change over time?*

Financial Analysis

Financial analysis includes five different aspects. Each was called for in checking out the venture idea. All that should be required for the venture plan is to copy that analysis over with refinements of the calculations and explanations so that readers will understand how they were done. The text of the plan should include key summary elements of this analysis, with details relegated to backup appendices.

18. **Break-even analysis** Two approaches are available for this analysis, numerical and graphical. The advantage of a numerical approach, dividing fixed costs by unit contribution, is speed and simplicity. The advantage of a graphical approach, which can most accurately be done by using figures from a pro forma income projection, is that it can take into account non-linearity and should be more accurate. It may also be quicker and easier for a reader to absorb. Two different dimensions desirable for the horizontal axis are (1) sales volume and (3) target date.

Application   *To the extent possible compute a new and contrasting break-even analysis for the assigned case venture.*

19. **Pro forma financial projections** are the heart of most business plans. Generating them for a new venture offers an excellent chance to apply anything learned in prior studies of finance and accounting as well as to learn more about them in the forecasting process. These projections form the heart of a venture plan and set forth what the founders will have as goals in creating the new enterprise. It is helpful to include in the plan at least three different forecasts, one optimistic, one pessimistic and one most likely. Explanations of the rationale behind each should appear in footnotes that follow the statements.

Application   *To the extent possible prepare a new and contrasting pro forma income statement and balance sheet for the assigned case venture, monthly for the first six months and quarterly thereafter up to six months beyond break-even.*

20. **Cash flow projections** Notwithstanding the importance of pro forma financial statements for setting goals, it is cash flow that the venture will have to live by. The shortcut approach in creating cash flow projections is to add back non-cash charges to changes in the balance sheet. Much more useful, since non-cash charges don't actually tell where cash is com-

ing from or going, is to list all the actual cash inflows, outflows and their sources by month.

Application   *To the extent possible prepare a cash flow forecast for the first year of the assigned case venture monthly for the first six months and quarterly thereafter up to six months beyond break-even. Explain which of the underlying assumptions are most worrisome and why.*

21.   **Footnotes to the forecasts** Numbers in the financial projections have no meaning unless a reader believes them. Explaining the causes of the numbers will help strengthen such belief. Factual bases and important assumptions behind the numbers should be clearly stated and distinguished from each other. In a very early "first cut" plan, such as might be prepared as part of a one-term course in school, it may not be possible to have strong substantiation for the numbers. In that case, it is still important to say how they were arrived at, even though a fair amount of imagination may have been involved. Beyond that, the plan can be strengthened by describing what specific action might be taken to strengthen the reliability of the numbers further, if more time were available.

22.   **Return on investment (ROI) analysis**   The long run test of a venture may include many aspects. Survival and satisfaction of founders, employees, and customers are some. From a financial standpoint, the main test will probably be return on money invested in the enterprise. An important aspect of this return will be the internal rate of return that the venture earns on assets entrusted to it. If this is strong, then the investors' return is likely to be strong also. Not illustrated in the appendix sample here is just how the return on investment was calculated. Although straightforward, those calculations too should appear in an actual plan.

Application   *Compute ROI for the assigned case venture over its first five years and explain the assumptions to which that figure is most sensitive.*

Venture plan excerpts in Appendix I illustrate graphical and textual features worth considering. Not everything desirable in a plan is illustrated, however, and some specimens in Appendix I may not be important to a particular plan. Sketches of products are included, but not photos, which if available might be better, even if they were only photos of models. Also not illustrated are any number of aspects that would presumably be developed in the text of a plan and perhaps illustrated with tables or charts. How the venture's market would be segmented and how target customers in each segment would be profiled, for instance, is an aspect that should not be neglected.

Supplementary Reading

New Venture Strategies Chapter 4. (Vesper, K.H., Prentice-Hall, 1990)
New Venture Mechanics Chapter 10. (Vesper, K. H., Prentice-Hall, 1993)

Your Venture Plan

1. Write the two most critical sections of a plan for your venture. Add a note that explains why they are most critical and how you would carry them further, given more time and resources.

2. List features which you could incorporate in your plan to make it unusually distinctive and interesting without compromising technical quality. Consider Appendix I examples in this process.

3. For a future point in time when your venture should be able to apply for a bank loan, prepare a bank loan proposal.

Your Venture History

1. What form did the entrepreneur's mental anticipation of future events in the venture take? What were expected to be the highest priority elements and most crucial assumptions? In hindsight which ones actually turned out to be?

2. Was there a written plan, and if so what was its nature, how was it used, and what functions did it turn out to serve?

3. If there was no written plan or if it was not much used, how were the functions suggested in this chapter for a plan accomplished?

Exercises

1. Write a cover letter for submission of a written plan based on one of your business ideas to a professional venture capitalist.

2. Prepare pro forma financial statements and a cash flow statement for one or more venture ideas of your own.

3. Interview three or more entrepreneurs, and describe in as much detail as you can just how planning was handled during start-up of their companies.

4. Critique the excerpted examples from venture plans in Appendix I

   a. Which seems to be the most exceptionally well done and in what way(s)?
   b. Illustrate how some of the quantitative exhibits might be made more graphical.
   c. Which seems to fall the farthest short of its potential? Why do you suppose it is that way? What actions would be required to improve it? Illustrate, if possible.
   d. Discuss how the format of some examples might depend upon the nature of the product or service.
   e. Discuss which of the approaches illustrated would apply to your venture plan.

❏ *SUBCHAPTER 4B - Evaluation of Venture Plans*

What a venture plan reader wants to see in a plan depends on who the reader is. What audience(s) it was written for can be stated along with its purpose for that audience at the front of the plan. How such choices should affect contents of the plan will be discussed in this section.

Regardless the choice of audience, however, two aspects of the plan are important. One is what the plan can truthfully say about the venture. The second is how effectively the plan communicates that information. In "real business" the first of these is what people care about. But if the second of these is not adequately done, they may not be able to assess the first. So both aspects can matter and must be attended to. If the venture is inherently unattractive, then in the business world it is not worth planning. If it is attractive, then the plan must help it move forward or else the planning is a waste.

In school the purpose of plan writing is mainly to learn. The best way to accomplish that learning may be to aim for a viable venture with the plan. The odds are that the venture itself, particularly in the "first cut" form that time in school allows, will not be truly viable. The aim of the plan should be both to design the venture as close to viability as time and resources permit, and to make the most of what the venture allows. The plan should be done well enough that if the venture concept itself were viable and the information at hand were adequate, then the plan could be followed to create it.

That purpose, as noted earlier, can take different forms for different possible participants in the venture, including the following:

- Bank loan officer
- Supplier
- Prospective customer
- Prospective investor
- Potential partner
- Potential key employee
- Employees later on
- Founders later on
- Adviser to the founders

To some degree all these audiences will care about central issues such as viability, profit potential, downside risk, likely life cycle time and potential areas for dispute and for improvement. Beyond that, however, different audiences will care about different details. Two important audiences for the plans of most entrepreneurs are potential lenders, such as banks, and potential investors. Investors include mainly individuals and venture capital firms. Of likely importance to students is yet another audience, the instructor, who is presumably neither a potential lender nor investor, but who may choose to take the perspective of either or both in addition to that of teacher. Each of these three audiences will be considered here in more detail.

Application   *Rank the importance of the above nine potential audiences for a plan written by the entrepreneur in the assigned case.*

What Bankers Look For

Most venture plans are written to raise money, and the source most common to businesses beyond founders' savings is bank borrowing. A banker's first concern has to be recovery of the loan. This is because banks are limited on the upside to a fixed interest rate controlled by usury laws, while on the downside they can lose everything. Moreover, most of the money banks lend is not their own. Rather, it is entrusted to them by depositers who expect to be able to withdraw it any time they choose.

Consequently, questions a banker will have in reviewing a venture plan loan proposal include:

- How reliable is this borrower? What has the person done before? What indication is there that he or she can be counted upon to repay?

- What will be done with the money? To what extent will it be put into things that can be sold versus non-recoverable expenditures? How sure is it to generate profit?

- What is the repayment schedule? How reliable are the sources from which repayment is supposed to come? Will the venture's customers be good credit risks?

- What collateral will there be to insure repayment of the loan? How much equity capital coverage is there on top of the proposed debt money? Will the venture's debt/equity ratio be conservative for its type of business? (Comparison to Dun and Bradstreet or Robert Morris Associates ratios?) Will there be salable equipment or inventory? Will there be a guarantor who can be depended upon? Should the entrepreneur personally guarantee it?

- How gratifying will it be to handle this loan? Will it be hard or easy to set up? Will the venture's control system provide timely and accurate financial reports? Will the entrepreneur be easy to get information from and keep the banker up to date, especially if problems crop up?

Beyond these questions, the banker will be interested to know what the odds are that by lending to this particular enterprise, he or she will be gaining the loyalty of a customer with a future of growing prosperity.

Application   *As a banker, what would be your answers to the above questions for the venture plan in the assigned case?*

What Investors Look For

With prospective investors the likelihood of profit growth is relatively more important than it is with bankers. The power and durability of the venture's competitive edge relative to those of future competitors is central to this. What the venture aims to become, and alternative future visions indicating the possibilities it has, will be particularly interesting parts of the plan. Indication of whatever special capabilities the venture's founders may have that will enable them to prevail over problems of getting started and surviving competitor responses will also be of high interest. Some key questions are likely to be:

- How catchy does the basic idea of this venture seem? Is it likely to be worthwhile to read this plan?

- How much time and money will it cost to check out this proposal thoroughly? Will that be worthwhile?

- What benefit will the venture offer to customers and at what cost compared to other things they might buy instead? Will the cost/benefit performance be sufficient to persuade buyers to switch to a new and unproven supplier? What assurance is there that the venture's technology will not soon be bypassed or surpassed?

- What segments of which markets will the venture seek to dominate and how? How big can they be expected to become? Upon what concrete information from which specific sources do these claims rest?

- Who will make the sales and how? What evidence is there so far to assure they will happen?

- What competitors will the venture be up against, and what will be its relative strengths and weaknesses both initially and later? According to whom or what sources and by what logic?

- What is the present stage of development of the venture's product or service? What testing has been performed, and what are the quantitative dimensions of performance? How fast can competitors catch up? Are any patents held by either the venture or its competitors?

- How will production be accomplished, and what will assure that it will match or exceed competitors in both quality and cost? What investment will be required for this? How much of that investment will be recoverable if the venture folds, and how?

- What levels of gross margin, net profit and return on investment are projected for the venture, and what is the basis for believing they can come true?

- How much money can the venture put to good use at what points in time, and what will it be spent on? What accomplishments will signal the arrival of those points?

- How financially committed are the founders personally?

- When and how should it be possible for the investors to cash in on this investment?

A convenience for investors will be inclusion of the name, address, phone and, if available, fax number of the founder to be contacted regarding any aspects of the plan. To maintain control of copies left with investors for review, it is appropriate to limit the quantity of copies prepared and number them clearly. As will be further discussed, a legal risk of public offering can arise if too many copies, more than one or possibly two dozen, are released.

Application   *As a prospective investor, what would be your answers to the above questions for the venture plan in the assigned case?*

Style

Some other elements to include are, as noted earlier, a one page executive summary, a table of contents with page numbers, and descriptive sections putting main points first plus appendices with supporting details.

Experts who have reviewed hundreds of venture proposals point out that plans which are too sketchy or sloppy will discourage potential investors from struggling to discern what they mean, and also reflect adversely on the competence and craftsmanship of founders who submit them. Plans that are too long, elaborate, complex or fancy may be rejected if they seem to reflect a misapplication of priority from substance to form. A balance between these extremes that is clean, clear, easy and interesting to read, should be sought. That still leaves room for creativity in written presentation, as experts Stanley Rich and David Gumpert have pointed out.

Of all the hundreds of business plans that have been submitted to the MIT Enterprise Forum, one stands out as so exemplary in its format that it can serve as a model plan. This plan was like other plans in that it contained text on each right-hand sheet through the book; what distinguished it from other plans was that each page was summarized on the left hand page. That is, each left-hand page left blank in other plans contained sets of bulleted highlight phrases, so that it was possible to read the summarized version of the entire business plan in somewhat under ten minutes!

Those of us who reviewed the plan all felt that we had seen the ultimate in business plans. Each of us approached it the same way: We read the summary through, from cover to cover, to gain an overview of the company s objectives and approaches to achieving them. Once our appetites were sufficiently whetted, we then read the detailed document. This business plan truly turned into a book we couldn t put down until we had read through to the last page in one sitting![55]

What Instructors Look For

School assignments to prepare business plans usually have a different primary purpose, namely learning. Giving this top priority tends to rearrange what is called for somewhat. Some possible differences are the following:

- Requirements for the venture to be able to show near-certain loan repayment and/or high profitability potential can no longer be imposed. Finding such deals is too much a "long shot" for a school requirement.

- Expectation that such tasks as prototype construction or market research be done to a professionally adequate level in the limited time available for homework is unrealistic. Such time-consuming tasks must be shortcut and compromised.

Instead, some things an instructor may look for that a banker or investor would not be particularly interested in could include the following:

- Evidence of good digging (e.g., pavement pounding). For many students it will be a new and therefore educational experience to approach strangers to obtain needed venture-specific information.

- Effective application of all thought modes described in Chapter 1 of this text. Most people have a natural bias toward using some thought modes to the exclusion of others. School should stretch the mind by pushing it to exercise underutilized capacities.

---

[55]Stanley R. Rich, and David E. Gumpert, *Business Plans that Win $$$* (New York: Harper & Row, 1985), p. 41.

- Good writing. Other things being equal, a better written plan should be more successful in "real life" than a poorly written one. Usually in real ventures other things are not equal and the importance of those outweighs elegance in writing. In school those other things cannot be required as important, but writing well can. If a plan is written by a team, then a particularly challenging part of the writing will be to have the plan sections well coordinated with each other. Doing this requires that enough time be reserved at term end for accomplishing the coordination. Last minute combination of plan sections is not the way to win.

Application   *If you were the instructor in a course where the assigned case plan was submitted, what grade would you give it and why?*

Some Things to Avoid

Some other things to avoid in plan writing, whether for school or for the real thing, are the following:

- Length for its own sake. It is easy to bulk up a plan with magazine articles about the industry and various kinds of literature or, even worse, with simple verbosity. No reader is likely to welcome that.

- Irrelevant information. If there is a shortage of information on something important to the venture there may be a temptation to make up for it by including information on something else that happens to be conveniently available even though irrelevant. Such compensation does not help.

- Duplication of references readily available elsewhere. It may be appropriate to excerpt sections selectively. However, references available in a library should simply be footnoted.

- Adulation of venture or its founders (e.g. "Our excellent product and highly talented management group..."). Such judgments as whether the founding team is competent and virtuous, whether the venture is highly likely to succeed and whether its product or service will be wonderful should be left to the reader. What will help the reader arrive at those judgments are facts the plan should include.

- Directly imitating another plan or adopting a "canned" format. Not letting the design of the plan follow from the logic of the individual venture introduces risks of mismatch in priorities, illogical reasoning, apparent imitation and shallow thinking.

- Reliance on the written document alone. For a venture plan to be accepted, there will have to be personal meetings between the writer and the reviewer.

Oral Presentation

The way to make the most of a personal presentation is to rehearse it ahead of time in front of one or more sympathetic but knowledgeable and critical audiences. If there is a time limit, then those rehearsals should be timed and practiced until they fit within the limit. The natural temptation will be to try packing too much into the available time and to do it by talking faster. That will simply lose the listener.

To keep the talk both slow and within the time limit, one device is to use some graphical displays. They should not be too complex to comprehend, but they can still compress more information into less time.

Another device is to have ready some backup presentations of subsections which present more details. These can be held in reserve and brought forth in response to questions or requests for more detail that the listener may raise.

Finally, of course, the listener can be given access to more details in a copy of the written plan either before or after the oral presentation, as he or she prefers.

Application   *If you were going to make a 10-minute oral presentation of the assigned case venture plan, what highlights would you pull out to present and how would you organize the talk? What graphics would you use?*

Supplementary Reading

New Venture Mechanics Chapter 10 and Appendices A and B. (Vesper, K. H., Prentice-Hall, 1993)

Your Venture Plan

1. Prepare alternative graphical aids for your business plan. Develop a rating scheme to evaluate them and select the most effective ones for inclusion in your final plan.

2. Perform a dress rehearsal of a venture plan presentation, complete with visual aids. Time it with a stopwatch and stay within 10 minutes total. Role play a question and answer session with questions as tough as possible.

Your Venture History

1. If the entrepreneur had a plan, what audiences was it aimed at and for what purposes? What was their reaction to it?

2. If there was no written plan, what audience does the entrepreneur think such a document might most have helped influence?

Exercises

1. For each of the elements noted above as important to (a) bankers and (b) investors, indicate specific evidence that could most helpfully be incorporated in a business plan and how it might be obtained.

2. Bankers, investors and instructors are three potential plan readers discussed above. Name three others, describe how their interests in a venture plan might be different, and how those differences might change how a plan should be shaped to fit their particular interests.

3. Interview a banker or investor who has received business plans, and write a description of the procedure that person typically used for reviewing proposals. Describe the implications of your findings for someone who wants to write such a proposal.

Case Questions: Foster, Hammoude, Thompson, Appendix

General Case Questions

1. Critique the business plan in the assigned case and describe actions that should be taken to improve upon it. List the presumed use(s) of the plan upon which your critique is predicated.

2. As a prospective investor, how would you value (negative numbers are allowable) the venture described in the assigned case and why? What sort of terms could you put into a deal to make it more appealing, and how should the entrepreneur react to those terms?

3. What should be done next by whom in the assigned case to move the venture forward and why?

Foster Case Questions

1. What is your forecast of the numbers Bill Foster proposes to generate for his plan?

---

2. What is your assessment of the method Bill has been using to develop his business plan?

3. What is your assessment of Bill's venture and his plan?

Hammoude Case Questions

1. What is your assessment of Andrew Hammoude's plan so far? If you were there, what might you be able to do to help him make it better?

2. Based on the work he has on plan development, what share of ownership or amount of pay from the other entrepreneurs would you say Andrew deserves as of the time of the case?

3. What should Andrew do over the next three months and why?

4. What should be the prospects for obtaining formal venture capital for ImageSystems?

5. What sort of amounts, timing and terms should a venture capital deal for this company include, assuming venture capital is the route to take?

Thompson Case Questions

1. For each of the different audiences it might most appropriately be given to, what are the criteria against which Greg should design a venture plan?

2. As best you can with the information available in the case, sketch out a plan aimed at satisfying the above criteria. Include specifics insofar as possible.

3. Putting yourself in the position of one or more of the people to whom Greg might submit his plan, describe the information you would expect Greg to include in the plan and tell how you would expect him to go about obtaining it.

Venture Plan Appendix Questions

1. Look over Appendix 1, Venture Plan Excerpts, at the back of the book. Select what you consider to be the four best done and the four least well done examples it includes. Be prepared to explain why.

2. For each of the four least well-done examples prepare an improved revision and be prepared to display it in class.

3. For further explanation of the Venture Plan Excerpts and more questions for analysis, please refer to the first page of Appendix 1.

Chapter 5

Financing

❑ SUBCHAPTER 5A - Inception Capital

Overview

To an entrepreneur who wonders how to raise it, capital often appears to be the main key to moving forward with a venture. In fact, the real key is evidence that the venture can justify capital with an appropriate positive cash flow. Capital represents social permission to use the physical resources and efforts of others in the economy to produce something new. That permission may be inherited, won in a lottery, or earned through work and savings. It can also be acquired on the basis of a convincing track record, persuasive argument, business plan or combinations of such factors.

Since start-up money may not be as readily available as a would-be entrepreneur might hope when contemplating a venture, he or she should consider alternative financing scenarios. Four possibilities are: (1) the money becomes available as planned, (2) the money available is less than planned, (3) the money is not available as soon as projected, and (4) other elements of the venture plan do not occur as projected, affecting both the amount of money needed and the difficulty of obtaining it.

Some Patterns

The range of styles and methods entrepreneurs use for financing ventures includes extensive variety, and any "typical" examples are bound to fall short of full representation. Here, however, is some illustration of the spectrum.

The **True Independent** starts with savings. Nobody else's permission is needed to apply resources for starting the business. Possibly there is some use of personal credit, as by running up bills on credit cards or borrowing at the bank against personal assets. But commercial loan funds or trade credit are not usually part of the initial picture. If they become available it will probably be later, after the business is going and creditworthy in its own right.

As a **variant**, the entrepreneur may have another job or an employed spouse for support while getting started. The Cooper et al. study of 2,994 firms[56] found that 8 percent of the entrepreneurs held other full-time jobs during the first year of start-up, while 7 percent held part-time jobs and another 4 percent held irregular jobs. Thirty-five percent of the entrepreneurs had a spouse who was employed full-time outside the start-up, and another 11 percent had a spouse employed part-time outside.

About half the ventures drew upon services of unpaid family members during start-up. When they did, it was one member in half the cases, two in about a third and three or more in the remainder. In about a third of the cases the typical time given by those members was less than 10 hours per week and in another third it was 40 or more hours per week. Thus, family member "sweat equity" contributions are significant in many start-ups.

The **Enticing Deal Seller** hasn't adequate savings to start alone or as a family unit. Instead, the venture concept is so apparently attractive and/or the individual is so persuasive that other private investors put up the money. They may be family, friends or individuals met through business contacts such as stock brokers, other professionals and other entrepreneurs. Their investment may be based on hard-headed business analysis, emotion or both. An enticing deal, for instance, might be stock in the company or a royalty in exchange for the personal guarantee of a loan at the bank. This could offer an infinite rate of return to the guarantor while restricting leverage of the borrower. However, the venture does not get to keep the money, and the guarantor could lose the amount of the loan.

The **Partner** extends personal savings by joining forces with others, either Independents or Deal Sellers, to undertake the venture as a mutual effort. Family members of partners may also become involved, as with the True Independent.

The **Founding Team Creator** extends the partner concept further, ideally recruiting complementary talents to produce a balanced top management. The team may be dedicated to objectives other than ambitious profits, in which case the start-up financial resources will be limited to personal savings of the team members and those of their families and friends. The enterprise might be a capital-intensive investment, such as a plant, possibly with prospects of employing the team, or of yielding capital gains. Alternatively, the venture may be some sort of cooperative enterprise with idealistic aims.

The **Very-High-Profit-Idea Team Creator** justifies the high cost of multiple members by aiming to start a business with very high total profit potential. This potential is based upon such competitive advantages as exceptional talents on the team, powerful patent protection or other major barriers to competitive entry, combined with a market of high growth potential. The prospect of selling out within a few years may justify interest by venture capitalists who work as independents or in corporate venture divisions and make a pro-

---

[56]Arnold C. Cooper and others, *New Business In America* (Washington, D.C.: The NFIB Foundation, 1990), p. 16.

fession of investing the pools of money they manage in high-growth smaller companies and start-up ventures. Alternatively, if the "big idea" of the venture appears to have enough economic promise and the team has sufficiently impressive credentials, the venture may even be able to obtain its starting capital from a public stock offering.

Application   *Which of the above financing styles could the entrepreneur(s) in the assigned case use? Which makes most sense and why?*

The very first seed capital for almost all start-up ventures begins with income from another job or personal savings of the entrepreneur and his or her partners, family, friends and possibly employees. Then, as the venture becomes more fully formed, it may be able to obtain financial help from suppliers and possibly customers and banks. Individual investors are always a possibility, as are venture capitalists. Generally, however, venture capitalists take interest only in situations where there seems to be a large upside potential, on the order of a 30 percent return on investment (ROI) on an investment large enough to make it worthwhile spending time on the deal. As investment professionals they have offices, staff and other overhead to maintain, and this overhead as well as their salaries and profits for the investors must be paid for by adequately lucrative deals. Moreover, since some of their deals lose entirely, they must seek winners big enough to cover those losses as well.

Deal Elements

When it is possible to obtain capital from others, the terms are usually formulated according to "the golden rule" (the person with the gold makes the rules). But it can be helpful for the entrepreneur (1) to know something about deal possibilities in order to help the process, (2) to know what particular kinds of ventures different capital sources prefer to invest in and what they can provide for their investees, and (3) to consider any venture proposition from the money-provider's point of view. Elements that may come into play for making deals include the following:

1. **Stock Investment** Raising money through stock sales conveys ownership to those who provide financing. Consequently, a question frequently asked by entrepreneurs who are considering this financing approach is how much ownership must be yielded by founders for a given amount of money. The answer to this question is always, "it depends." The basis will likely be what level of return on investment is generated for the investor. The academically customary way of computing return on investment (ROI) is by dividing the annual profit by the amount invested to get a return percentage. Venture capitalists, however, more often speak in terms of multiples, such as getting back three to five times the invest-

ment in three to five years, rather than return percentages. Who has how much control is sometimes an important issue to be negotiated. Terms may also be incorporated in the deal to provide that the better the company does, the smaller the ownership fraction investors will be entitled to.

2. **Borrowing Cash** When and how a loan to the venture will be repaid and what interest rate it will carry are two immediate considerations. But there are others. Terms may allow conversion of the debt into equity at the lender's discretion. They may also provide that lenders can step in and take control if certain performance levels or ratios set forth in the venture plan are not maintained. Having someone guarantee a loan can sometimes be a way of borrowing where otherwise it would be impossible to do so. One catch is that the entrepreneur will then have to pay something to the guarantor on top of the customary costs of the loan itself.

3. **Other Forms of Debt** Instead of conventional borrowing, loans may take the form of trade credit from suppliers, advance payment by customers, or temporary use of others' plant and equipment. Rental involving leasing or installment purchase can be viewed as forms of debt. It is sometimes possible to borrow equipment or people's efforts directly. The indebtedness in such cases may be formal or informal. One entrepreneur recalled such an experience.

This other entrepreneur had really helped me out. I told him so, and said I hoped some day I could pay him back. He told me other people had helped him when he was getting started, and said that if I wanted to return the favor he would prefer that I pass it along to someone else rather than to him.

4. **Payment by the Entrepreneur** Compensation for the use of capital can take the form of share ownership in the company, options to buy shares, royalties based on sales or profits, interest or other cash payments including consulting fees, agreements by the entrepreneur's company to do business with or favors for those who make the capital available, or possible tax shelter advantages for them.

5. **Splitting Off Assets** An investor may put up money for real estate against a mortgage and lease that property to the venture, or may advance cash for advertising in return for a royalty on sales, or may buy stock in the venture as part of an employment package. The potential variety of deals involving "I'll give you this in exchange for that" is endless. This type of deal also carries a limitless variety of possible problems. Thinking ahead about implications and what could go wrong is a necessary part of rationally approaching such deals. Consideration of the deal by both parties from both parties' points of view is also needed.

Entrepreneurs often commandeer resources they don't have title to. In addition to borrowing, they sometimes barter and sometimes presume. Doing favors is part of entrepreneurship, both giving and receiving. Author George Gilder has pointed out that the entrepreneur begins by a charitable act, putting forth effort and resources before receiving anything back in order to make a venture happen.[57] Other times entrepreneurs receive favors from sympathizers, including other entrepreneurs who wish them well, and community supporters who appreciate what ventures add to the store of available jobs, goods and services. Effort, initiative, imagination, vision and persuasion can be important forms of currency for obtaining use of other people's effort and resources.

Application   *Which of the above financing mechanisms, in rank order, should be most appropriate for the needs of the assigned case venture in its early stages?*

Maintaining Control

The "golden rule" mentioned above entitles those who put money into a venture to take some rights of control in return. This may take the form of written rules the company must follow, such as not to make any investments over a certain amount without permission, not to pay more than a certain amount to executives, to submit specified financial information on a certain timetable, to maintain certain balance sheet and income statement ratios, or to employ certain people in specified capacities. Control can also take the form of continuing interaction between investors and managers of the venture.

It is natural for an entrepreneur not to want to share control. There is plenty to worry about in creating the venture without having to consider how investors feel about it. There is plenty for the entrepreneur to do without having to take time out for interacting with investors. To the entrepreneur, sharing control can mean danger of distraction, interference and wasted time.

It is also easy to see why an investor would want elements of control. Incentive to be careful with the money would be higher if it were the entrepreneur's own. To make up for this limitation the person with the money attaches strings. It is possible to structure the arrangement such that the strings take hold only if the venture is falling too far short of its forecast.

Investors and lenders more experienced in dealing with ventures really don't want control. It can lead to interference that handicaps the venture and possibly destroys the enthusiasm and motivation of its creators. It is the founders, after all, who are most expert about the venture. Lenders and investors don't know how to create it or run it as well as they do. It may be wise for them to have some strings on the venture, but they should leave them loose

---

[57] George Gilder, *The Spirit Of Enterprise* (New York: Simon and Schuster, 1984).

as much as possible, stepping in only if the venture seems to be heading disastrously off track.

The entrepreneur should seek investors based upon their prior experience and reputations. In arranging a deal both sides should consider possible future problems, what will best motivate the founders and what sorts of deviations from course should trigger investor or lender action in the best interests of both their money and the venture.

Retaining Ownership

Division of ownership raises issues similar to those of control. Taking too much away from entrepreneurs can reduce their incentives. Taking too little can limit the investor to inadequate returns considering the risk. In the end, division of ownership must be negotiated, and the investor usually has the upper hand. The entrepreneur may have some of the following choices:

- Taking a "bigger piece of a small pie or a smaller piece of a bigger one"

- Keeping ownership by assuming the risk of borrowing, or giving up some ownership in return for someone else sharing the risk

- Seeking more capital at early inception, even though that makes it more expensive. The alternative is to begin with less capital and wait until the venture grows to where it needs more. Seeking it then, however, may take time away from the many demanding tasks of building the venture, a sacrifice that may be serious or even fatal to the venture's continued development.

There are no standard formulas for choosing among such alternatives. They must be negotiated by each entrepreneur for each individual venture, with careful thought about the alternative scenarios that can follow.

Pitfalls

The ultimate evidence of error in venturing is a shortage of cash. Either too little came in, or it went out too fast or both. The general pitfall of venture financing is to run out of cash. Ways this can come about include:

- Failing to foresee needs adequately
- Lacking good financial controls
- Waiting too long to seek capital
- Underestimating effort required to raise capital
- Pursuing capital sources that don't fit the venture

- Selling stock to an investor who has inadequate capability to help further
- Asking for money without adequate advance preparation
- Selling equity when debt will do
- Taking on too much debt
- Agreeing to a misunderstood deal
- Losing credibility by failing to meet commitments
- Paying too much for capital
- Getting too many shareholders too soon
- Misapplying the capital

Application   *How would you rank the likelihood of the above pitfalls happening to the assigned case venture and why?*

The importance of watching cash was emphasized by Harvey Quadracci, who created a printing company with 1990 sales of $375 million.

> *Nobody understands what cash flow is unless they ve lived by it. The experience changes you permanently. I have a telephone in planes, trains, cars and bedrooms because I have a phobia. I break out into a cold sweat if I m away from a phone. It goes back to those days when I was always calling to ask, Did the check come in the morning? OK, release those other checks.* [58]

The discipline of handling money with maximal efficiency is one many entrepreneurs learn out of necessity and one which can give their ventures an advantage over older competitors long beyond start-up.

Minimizing Needs

For each of the above pitfalls it is fairly easy to think of one or more preventative actions. The starting point is to prepare financial forecasts which show how much cash will be needed when, and where it should come from. Both the cash needs of the founders personally and those of the venture should be forecasted. Each of these forecasts will be based upon assumptions which could be incorrect in various ways. Consequently for every likely variation in the assumptions, the impact upon cash needs should be explored. Most optimistic, most pessimistic and most likely forecasts would be three in particular to explore.

The first step in developing these forecasts is to make lists of things on which money will have to be spent. Naturally, some cash will be needed for

---

[58]"Going For Broke," *Inc.*, September 1990, p. 35.

the entrepreneur to live on while starting the venture. Some items for the venture activities include:

- travel, meals and correspondence with helpful contacts
- lawyer fees
- construction of a prototype
- design of a logo
- costs of preparing advertisements
- costs of running advertisements
- fabrication of tooling
- rental deposits
- initial inventory
- office equipment
- production equipment
- license fees
- phone, fax and mail expenses

Application *What items should the above expense list include for the assigned case venture, and how would the items rank order in terms of amount?*

This list must be developed as fully as possible, and it might be helpful to rank order the items according to total expenditure for the first year. Despite an entrepreneur's conscientious effort to be complete, there will almost certainly be omissions. How will taxes be handled? What if a supplier wants payment in advance or a customer wants (or simply takes) extended credit? What if a supplier raises a price or tacks on some charge for service, COD, or late payment? Was insurance included? What if something breaks or is stolen? What will be done while waiting to replace it? What if there is a lawsuit over something? What if a personal emergency requiring cash arises for the entrepreneur at home? It is altogether too easy to see the need for start-up cash and at the same time to underestimate how great it will be.

Spreading these expenditures out month by month and adding them up will forecast the cash flowing out, which can be cumulated month by month to show a worst case of how much money must be raised in one way or another by the venture. This amount may come from investors, lenders or customers. Assumptions about which of those people will provide how much cash to the company at what points in time must be made with care. What alternative actions can be taken if one or another of them either reneges or simply delays payment?

Pitfalls in forecasting the cash needs are easy to imagine, and some are suggested above. They can also include:

- Failing to list something for which cash will be needed.
- Underestimating how much something will cost.
- Falsely assuming suppliers will extend credit.
- Underestimating how much inventory will accumulate.
- Assuming customers will pay sooner than they will.
- Assuming nobody will make an error handling cash.
- Expecting loans will be processed quickly.
- Expecting investors will pay in promptly.

Application   *How would you rank order the likelihood of the above possible pitfalls happening to the assigned case venture, and upon what factors would the ranking depend?*

The amount of cash needed to start a business obviously will range widely from one venture to another. Amdahl Computer started with $17 million. Apple Computer started with less than $1,000. Some indication of the spread among other fast-growth start-ups appears in a survey of the 500 fastest growing small companies listed by *Inc.* magazine as its "*Inc.* 500." Results of this survey are listed in Table 5-1 below: [59]

Table 5-1 Levels of Start-Up Capital in Inc. 500 Firms

Start-Up Capital Needed	Percent of Firms
less than $10,000	34%
$10,000 - $49,000	35
$50,000 - $99,000	12
$100,000 - $249,999	10
$250,000 or more	9
Total	100%

The National Federation of Independent Business (NFIB) firms surveyed by Cooper et al. are probably more representative than the "*Inc.* 500" of the overall business population, yet they yielded a comparable pattern, as shown in Table 5-2:[60]

---

[59]John Case, "The Origins of Entrepreneurship," *Inc.*, June 1989, p. 62.
[60]Cooper and others, *New Business in America*, p. 28.

Table 5-2 Levels of Start-up Capital Among NFIB Firms

Start-Up Capital Needed	Percent of Firms
less than $10,000	32%
$10,000 - $50,000	41
$50,000 - $100,000	15
$100,000 - $250,000	8
$250,000 or more	4
Total	100%

The similarity of these patterns seems remarkable considering the difference in longer term performance. The *Inc.* sample of the 500 firms out of all U.S. industry that have grown the most over the past five years, is a very thin layer of top performers. These data seem to indicate that in terms of start-up capital most top performers begin with much the same level of resources as "typical" start-ups.

Application   *Which of the financing amount categories above would the assigned case venture fit into, and how did you arrive at that estimation?*

Ways to reduce the amount of cash needed for start-up are virtually endless. Actions an entrepreneur can choose for doing so include:

- Make do without (dining room table for desk?)
- Buy, don't make (use subcontractors)
- Make, don't buy (homemade production equipment?)
- Barter, don't pay cash (free samples for help?)
- Buy used, not new (any auctions of other firms?)
- Buy cheap (hire students, GIs off hours, homemakers)
- Lease, don't buy (copy machine, computer, space, etc.)
- Lease, don't hire (temporary help)

The catch with such approaches is that they usually extract tradeoffs in terms of quality, dependability, speed or the entrepreneur's time. Sometimes less immediate cash outlay requires paying a higher total price, as in the case of leasing equipment. Thus, cash conservation may impose profit sacrifices, while raising cash may require sacrificing ownership, control or both.

Application   *Which of the above cash-saving measures should the entrepreneur in the assigned case adopt and what tradeoffs would be required to do so?*

Compromise is not always costly. Harvey Quadracci, quoted above, recalled how in earlier days his company enhanced sales by giving customers the impression that it was financially better off than it was.

> *The client would come in and see rolls of paper stacked up but not know that in the middle they were hollow. Or we would have the press printing this one magazine, which had a run of maybe 15,000. The press would print 25,000 an hour. Here comes the client, and we d start the press up and get him to move very quickly because the paper was going through. Then we d get him out into the office, and suddenly the whole plant would shut down. What was that? he would say. Oh, it must be everybody breaking for lunch. It s perception.[61]*

Ken Hendricks, a roofing distributor with sales of $250 million in 1990, described how start-up economies continued even after his company had grown large.

> *We still buy used, but nice, furniture. My desk came from somebody that had gone bankrupt. I ve thought about the tears that had to fall on that desk, and it s something that reminds me every day that I m not going to let this happen to me.[62]*

First Cash Sources

Personal Resources

Savings of the founder, as noted above, are the main source of start-up cash for most ventures. Among *Inc.* 500 companies, for instance, the most important cash source for the entrepreneurs themselves and their families to live on during start-up was personal savings in 43 percent of the companies, support from spouse and other relatives in 12 percent, salary from another job in 17 percent and salary from the start-up in only 20 percent of the cases.[63]

When respondents were asked which sources were most relied upon for capital to start the company, the fraction who nominated each category (some nominated more than one) was as shown in Table 5-3:

---

[61]"Going For Broke," p. 36.
[62]Ibid.
[63]Case, "The Origins of Entrepreneurship," p. 62.

Table 5-3 Start-Up Capital Sources of *Inc.* 500 Firms[64]

Sources of Capital Used	Percent
Own resources	75%
Mortgage of own assets	35
Corporate loan from bank	33
Partner's assets	29
Personal loan from bank	23
Parents or other relative	20

Curiously missing from this list are sources such as informal outside investors, venture capital investors, corporations and public offerings. These sources too are sometimes used in start-ups, although relatively rarely. A later report on the *Inc.* 500 stated that for 56 percent the main source of seed money was personal savings, 40 percent received loans by mortgaging personal assets. Venture capital was used by less than 2 percent of the companies polled. Corporate loans in this later report showed a 41 percent response, compared to the earlier 33 percent above.[65]

The Cooper et al. study of 2,994 firms brought still more sources into the picture, including outside individuals, venture capital firms and suppliers, as can be seen in Table 5-4.

Table 5-4 Start-up Capital Sources of NFIB Firms

Sources of Capital Used	Percent
Personal Savings	74.6%
Banks	45.8
Friends/Relatives	28.7
Other Individuals	7.8
Suppliers/Trade Credit	6.3
Government Guaranteed Loans	3.2
Venture Capital Firms	1.3
Former Owners (Acquisitions)	8.9

---

[64]Ibid., p. 58.
[65]"The Year In Startups," *Inc.*, November 1989, p. 66.

Customer Advances

In some circumstances, customers will advance part of the capital needed to start a business. For research and development work in selected areas, agencies of the federal government will provide grants under its Small Business Innovation Research (SBIR) program.[66] Under this program, federal agencies with research budgets must set aside 1.25 percent of the money in them for grants to companies with under 500 employees.

Grants are given under two phases. The first phase provides up to $50,000 over six months for feasibility analysis of a proposed innovation of interest to one of the 11 federal agencies that are by law required to give such grants. The second phase, contingent on performance under the first, provides up to $500,000 additionally. However, less than 15 percent of first-phase and 40 percent of second-phase proposals were being accepted as of 1989, and the trend was toward the number of proposals growing faster than the available funding.

Contractors frequently receive progress payments on construction projects. Both software and hardware makers in the microcomputer industry have been known to accept orders and advance payments for products to be made in the future. Two contrasting examples of capital coming from customers are the following:

> Pat Sayers founded Nursing Systems International with cash advances from hospitals more than a year before her product, a computerized expert reference system for nurses, existed. She had previously tried selling, as a consultant, a textbook and a slide series, from which she recalled "how tough it really is to reach the market until people are out there saying 'we want it.'" Consequently, when a hospital suggested she develop a system, she asked for payments up front, and received them. In return, she promised the contributors significant discounts on the product. The advances gave her credibility as well as cash that in turn helped her raise the remaining capital needed from other sources.[67]

❖ ❖ ❖

> Bob McCray raised half the $500,000 needed to start manufacturing electrical valve equipment from manufacturer's representatives who wanted to carry the product. Each representative was asked for a loan of $5,000 for every 1 percent of national market territory. In return, McCray promised to give the representative repayment on a short schedule, with interest at 1 percent over prime, plus exclusive territory rights and a discount of 50 percent off list in contrast to the customary 33 percent. McCray observed that "They look at us as more of a partner, which is good. We didn't want to be thought of as just another vendor. I certainly have no trouble getting them on the phone."[68]

---

[66]Mangelsdorf, Martha E., "*Inc.*'s Guide To 'Smart' Money," *Inc.*, August 1989, p. 51. Also, a useful contact is the Small Business Administration's Office of Innovation, (202) 653 6458.
[67] "The Year In Startups," p. 75.
[68]Ibid., p. 71.

Application   *What line of persuasion could be tried by the entrepreneur in the assigned case to obtain customer help in financing, and to what degree would that be worth trying? Please explain.*

Outside Investors

Respondents in the Cooper study reported that 7.2 percent began with outside individual investors and 5.6 percent said they received 40 percent or more of their funding from outside individuals.[69] There may be overlap here between "other individuals" and "former owners," and from inclusion of the latter it appears that both start-ups and acquisitions were lumped together. This may also be true for the *Inc.* sample. And it is possible that the outside investors included some who bought into a public offering.

The variety of people who become informal investors in ventures was shown by Aram from a study of 55 eastern Great Lakes region informal investors.[70] These investors were mostly business owners and managers with a mean age between 40 and 50 who made an average of two risk capital investments every three years. The average investment was just under $50,000. A third of the investments were made within 10 miles of home and three-fourths were within 50 miles. Over 90 percent co-invested with typically four other people. Half of the investments were in start-up firms. Typical target returns on investment were over 35 percent for high technology firms and about 25 percent for others. Those are averages, however, from which individuals may deviate widely. Some entrepreneurs have been lent capital at no interest, for instance, with comments such as, "Somebody helped me when I was starting my business; now I figure it's my turn to put something back."

Foreign investors are a rare source of capital for U.S. ventures so far, but may grow in importance in the future. One three-year-old venture reported to have tapped such sources was headed by a former U.S. assistant secretary for international trade. Likely his government work had conferred special know-how, connections and credentials.[71] Theoretically, foreign sources could also be approached for start-up financing by more "ordinary" entrepreneurs. This has probably happened, but to date little, if any of it, seems to have been reported.

The way to find informal investors is to "ask around" selectively, as there are no published lists. There is a computer matching system at the University of New Hampshire and some other universities. But these keep the names confidential. Some likely people to ask for leads include other entrepreneurs, bankers, stock brokers, real estate brokers, accountants, and attorneys. Each contact can lead to others. The search becomes one of exploring a web of con-

---

[69] Cooper and others, *New Business in America*, p. 29.
[70] John D. Aram, "Attitudes and Behaviors of Informal Investors Toward Early-Stage Investments," *Journal of Business Venturing*, 4, no. 5, (September 1989), p. 333.
[71] Ellyn E. Spragins, "Globetrotting For Dollars," *Inc.*, August 1990, p. 116.

tacts to find the rare one who may happen to fit needs of the venture. Some contacts, such as stock brokers and real estate agents, expect commissions on deals that come from leads they provide. Others, such as bankers, do not. Looking for ways to return favors of anyone in the search can help the process.

The most likely sources of capital for a given enterprise may be those who are in the best position to understand and help the business in other ways besides financing, as illustrated by the experience of Jeffrey and Carolyne Greene.

Greene had, in 1979, designed a humorous doll ("FROYD"), which she attempted to sell to toy makers. They complimented the toy, but declined to invest. At the same time, it seemed to her that toy stores needed new products, but toy makers were too conservative to introduce them. After several years of searching she met Jeffrey, then a venture capitalist, who decided to hire the same market researchers who had tested Cabbage Patch dolls and to have them perform the same tests. The results were strongly positive, but toy makers still would not buy.

So the pair decided to start a business and market the product themselves. They began talking with contract manufacturers and retailers as they developed a business plan to raise capital. They sent out 100 copies of the plan and made presentations to ten investment groups, without success. This first round of rejections was followed by a second. Venture capitalists, it seemed, did not take much interest in toys, particularly since some prominent toy companies, Wonder and Coleco, had just failed.

Next, the two tried cutting the project down and seeking as private investors some of the experts and business people they had encountered in researching and designing the venture. Many of these had complimented the product. Now, when asked to invest in it, they did. Sixteen of them put up the $600,000 being sought, and other investors had to be turned away. "The key," according to author Ellyn E. Spragins, "was approaching individuals whose business expertise give them a special appreciation for marketing or the character-development business. Thus, the company's backers include senior executives in an advertising agency, a consumer products company, and a direct-mail business." [72]

Understanding on the part of potential investors can be enhanced by effective presentation, including data, prototypes, demonstrations, expert testimony, a well-written business plan and a carefully rehearsed presentation, ingredients that appear to have been present in the Greenes' venture.

Application   *From the viewpoint of a private investor, what kind of a deal for financing the assigned case venture might make sense and why? To what extent should such a deal be acceptable to the entrepreneur and why?*

---

[72]Ellyn E. Spragins, "Intelligent Money," *Inc.*, June 1990, p. 106.

Early Debt Sources

Early investors may choose to buy shares, loan the company money, or guarantee a loan in return for some incentive. Other sources of debt initially can be finance companies (to support the purchase of resellable equipment) and special interest organizations, such as community groups that may want to help formation of local companies in order to provide jobs.

Supplementary Reading

New Venture Strategies Chapter 4. (Vesper, K.H., Prentice-Hall, 1990)

New Venture Mechanics Chapter 5. (Vesper, K. H., Prentice-Hall, 1993)

Your Venture Plan

1. Assess the fit of the most promising three alternative sources of capital for your most promising venture idea.

2. Assume the position of each of the three above sources, and formulate terms for extending capital to the venture that would be appropriate from the viewpoint of that source.

Your Venture History

1. What were the resource needs of the company for each of the first 12 months, each of the next four quarters and years after that, however long it has gone?

2. How did the founders go about meeting those resource needs?

Exercises

1. Extend or elaborate the lists of expenses above by examining in detail either what costs were involved in starting an actual business or by planning in detail the needs for starting a specific new business.

2. Ask the owner how the start-up of his or her company was financed and what the problems were.

❏ SUBCHAPTER 5B - Growth Cash

Early Debt

The attractive thing to an entrepreneur about borrowing money, assets, and other people's efforts in creating a business is that it allows retention of ownership. From the lender's viewpoint, however, such financing offers only risk and upside potential limited to the rate of interest. Hence, borrowed money is often hard to get, particularly if the entrepreneur's own resources, as back-up for the loan, or track record, as an assurance of ability to perform the venture, are limited.

Bank Loans

From both the Cooper et al. and *Inc.* survey results described in the preceding chapter, it appears that banks typically play a strong role in the initial financing of companies, as 33 percent and 45 percent, respectively, of entrepreneurs responding to those surveys indicated. Yet often entrepreneurs say they could get no funding from banks in the early stages of start-up. The cliché is that "a bank will loan you money only if you don't need it." Banks don't have loan departments for start-up ventures. However, banks sometimes do make loans to ventures, and they also help ventures with information and other contacts.

Certainly, there is reason for banks to be cautious. First, the money they hold is not their own. It belongs to depositors, who expect to be able to withdraw any or all of it whenever they please. For the bank to have it loaned out to ventures that cannot repay immediately or perhaps at all cannot be allowed. Secondly, banks are severely limited in what they can charge as interest. Thus, while they can lose all, they can't win much. It does not make sense for them to give risky loans.

So why do banks seem to participate in financing so many ventures, according to the surveys? One explanation probably is that a fairly large fraction of the ventures surveyed were not actually start-ups but rather acquisitions that had assets to pledge. A second is that even among start-ups the banks may have lent money not at inception but only after the start-up was running and showing promise of strong solvency. Moreover, some of the entrepreneurs may have had sufficient personal assets to provide guarantees on the loans.

Guarantees can come either from private individuals who have resources to back them up or from the Small Business Administration (SBA) of the federal government. The SBA will guarantee 90 percent of a loan if a bank is willing to risk the other 10 percent. The contact for pursuing this course of action is the bank willing to take that risk. However, even a 10 percent loss is very significant to a bank.

Despite the risks, there are also positive reasons for banks to make loans to start-ups. Banks are in business to "rent" money, and doing so is therefore competitive. Every good customer helps, and founders who are aided by banks in the early days of their ventures often stay loyal to those banks after the ventures have grown and become attractive and profitable borrowers. Banks know this and therefore sometimes will even loan money unsecured to start-up companies. To encourage a banker to help with financing a venture an entrepreneur can:

- Prepare a well-written business plan that makes clear just how much money will be needed (cumulative cash flow forecast with explanatory footnotes), what it will be used for and when and how it will be paid back with interest.

- Seek out an individual bank lending officer who has the authority to make loan decisions, is experienced in loans of the type needed and has a good "personal chemistry" with the type of venture and the founder(s).

The latter task is one that may take some searching. Many entrepreneurs report having been turned down by several banks before finding one that would grant credit. The following entrepreneur recalled the necessity of searching in the right locality to find a bank for financing the purchase of a small business. He had worked out his deal with the seller, and now all that was needed was cash from the bank for a down payment.

> *I made a major error at this point that almost killed the deal. I assumed that my best chance for financing the acquisition was to approach the larger banks in Laurel, the town where the business was located. As a result I didn t go to any local Annapolis banks where friends could get me in the door at the right levels. The banks in and around Laurel wanted nothing to do with me or my deal. I was incredulous. I had assumed that putting the financing together would be a matter of a couple of weeks, at the most.*
>
> *It took six. I was extremely embarrassed to tell people the banks were stringing me along. What was I, some kind of deadbeat?*
>
> *In desperation, I called several friends for help. They got me in to see Annapolis bankers (I didn t know anyone from the local banks because, although I lived in Annapolis, I had worked in Washington since moving to town). They listened. They checked me out. Then I got a yes. Then another yes. Then another, and another. All but one were from strictly local banks. I wasn t a deadbeat after all. In fact, I was able to get pretty good terms.*[73]

These bankers wanted to be sure of the person they were dealing with, which is always an important factor. Other elements that can be influential in getting a bank loan include:

---

[73]Hendrix F.C. Niemann, "Buying a Business," *Inc.*, February 1990, p. 38.

- How debt-heavy the venture will be if it gets the loan.

- What collateral the venture can provide, and how readily cash could be extracted by selling it.

- How solid the customers of the venture are and how certain they are to buy. Having a government or big company contract can make a big difference.

- How fully "loaned-up" versus hungry for loans the bank is.

- How good the bank's recent experience has been with loans like this.

- The extent to which this loan might help relations with other customers, such as perhaps suppliers to the venture.

Application   *What is the best line of persuasion the entrepreneur in the assigned case could attempt to use with a bank to get a loan in light of the above types of considerations that are important to bankers?*

Finding an effective combination of such elements can take considerable homework and searching. The entrepreneur can get a jump on this process by both venture planning and becoming acquainted with prospective bankers in advance of seeking a loan.

Supplier Credit

As noted above in the Cooper et al. data, about 6.3 percent of the time suppliers appear to play an important role in capitalizing start-ups. Like customers, they have a vested interest in what the venture will produce. What they are most likely to extend, however, is credit rather than cash. But most will not do even that for a start-up with no evidence of past performance in paying bills. This can become easy to understand by reading through published lists of bankruptcies. The lists are long, and each represents an individual or company from whom suppliers are unable to recover what they have lent. Consequently, many require COD or even payment in advance by start-up entrepreneurs.

Application   *From which of the suppliers it will need might the assigned case venture most likely get credit soonest, from which latest, and why? How much help, dollar-wise, should that be at which points in time?*

Other Debt Sources

After the company is going, still other debt sources may come into play, such as factoring companies, which buy accounts receivable at a discount for immediate cash. However, such financing is expensive.

Fast Growth Capital

For start-ups that can show convincingly that they are headed for very rapid growth and high profits, there are additional sources of capital. Principally, these are formal venture capital firms, private placements with larger institutions and public stock offerings. None of these would be interested in financing typical small businesses.

Capitalization Stages

Some ventures have sufficiently high margins and low capital intensity to start and sustain high growth without outside capital. Venture capitalists love to invest in those, but may not get the chance since such ventures don't need outside money. Next best are ventures that have profits that are high but not quite high enough to support all their growth. To expand, such ventures must continually "return to the well" for capital. If their growth and profits are strong, there is a high incentive for venture capitalists to invest, because such ventures offer both high rates of return and opportunity to make large enough investments at those high rates to justify substantial effort in checking the ventures out initially, arranging their successive financings and helping their managements as they grow.

Because of this need for repeated successive cash inputs, the financing of high-growth ventures is sometimes described in terms of stages. Pratt's *Guide to Venture Capital Sources* suggests three categories: (1) Early Stage, (2) Expansion Stage, and (3) Acquisition/Buyout financing.[74] Each of these categories in turn can be broken down as follows:

(1) Early Stage

- **Seed capital** is for product development, market research, team formation and planning.

- **Research and development capital** is for similar purposes but set up as a limited partnership permitting tax write-offs against personal income to limited partners.

- **Start-up capital** carries the venture up to but not through first sales.

- **First-stage capital** is for ventures moving into full-scale manufacturing and sales.

---

[74]Jane K. Morris, and Susan Isenstein, *Pratt's Guide to Venture Capital Sources* (Wellesley, Mass.: Venture Economics, 1989), p. 2.

(2) Expansion Stage

- **Second-stage capital** is to cope with expansion of receivables and inventory during early growth.

- **Third-stage** or **"mezzanine" capital** is for major expansion and product development in profitable firms.

- **"Bridge" financing** is short in timing, and applies to companies in transition and possible reorganization for going public.

Application   *Which of the above financing stages might the assigned case venture reasonably hope to reach and by what dates?*

(3) Acquisition/Buyout Financing

- Money may go to a *going firm* for buyout of another

- Money may be provided for *individuals* to undertake a leveraged buyout. In this arrangement, the buyer uses the capital for a down payment and for working capital and then pays off the remainder of the purchase price to the seller out of earnings from the business.

Orders of magnitude for different stages were reported on 25 leading venture capital firms in 1989 by *Venture* as displayed in Table 5-5 below: [75]

Table 5-5   Venture Capital Firm Investments

Type	Deals	Price (millions)
Seed & Start-up	20	$12.6
First Stage	66	27.5
Later Stages	4	12.0
Acquisitions	4	17.5

One implication of these stages is that different sources of money and investors with different types of objectives apply to each of them. A study by Freear and Wetzel[76] sampled 236 firms that had raised outside equity capital at some stage from venture capital firms. Among this group 46 percent had raised capital from other individual non-management investors ("informal in-

---

[75] "Financing," *Venture*, September 1989, p. 19.

[76] John Freear and William E. Wetzel, Jr., "Equity Capital For Entrepreneurs," in *Frontiers of Entrepreneurship Research, 1988*, eds. Robert H.Brockhaus, Sr. and others (Wellesley, Mass.: Babson Center for Entrepreneurial Studies, 1989), p. 230.

vestors"), most often before the venture capital firms contributed. Their suggestion as to a typically most appropriate sequence for raising capital was that first should come personal savings, then informal investors, then formal venture capital and finally public offerings.

Such staging concepts do not apply to most ventures, which typically start small with insider money, grow somewhat using debt and retained earnings but never advance through stages that use outsider equity capital. As could be seen in Table 5-4 presented earlier, Cooper et al. found that less than 8 percent of ventures drew upon outside individual investors, and less than 2 percent used venture capital firms.

Venture Capital Organizations

Formal venture capital organizations are companies set up to manage pools of investment money by investing it in start-ups and small growth-oriented firms. They can be grouped into four categories, knowelege of which can be helpful to an entrepreneur seeking to identify as many as possible of the capital sources potentially appropriate for a particular venture, in order to find the best one. These four categories are:

- **Private Venture Capital Firms** Full-time professionals manage pools of money put up by individuals. Most venture capital firms are private. A few are publicly held. Deals are often structured as limited partnerships in which the firm is a general partner.

- **Small Business Investment Companies (SBICs)** By agreeing to observe certain federal guidelines restricting investments, these firms become qualified to borrow federal money at attractive rates and thereby leverage their investment capital.

- **Corporate Venture Divisions** Similar to the above, but the money comes from a corporation, usually seeking "windows on technology" through investment in smaller firms. Operators of these firms are usually employees of the corporation.

- **Amateur Venture Capital Firms** Sometimes a small group of individuals will pool savings to become venture capitalists as a sideline, hobby, recreational, or social activity.

Lines between these types of firms are not always clear, but distinctions can help highlight some important considerations about where to look for capital. All these investor firms seek exceptionally high rates of return, on the order of 30 percent or more per year average, because they are undertaking high-risk deals. All will also want to become involved in the venture beyond simply putting up the money and walking away with some ownership. Typically, they want one or two seats on the board of directors. Some ask for interest on the money they put in by extending it as interest-bearing debt convertible into stock at their option. Others ask consulting fees and become more actively involved in the venture.

Experienced venture capitalists are typically found in those venture capital organizations that have been in business for several years or that are starting out with large sums of money to invest. In looking at potential investments they usually want a clear idea from the outset about when and how they will be able to cash in on their investment, either by selling the venture off to another firm or taking it public. This may conflict with goals of an entrepreneur who would rather stay with a venture and keep it closely held. Of course, cashing in may also be to the advantage of the entrepreneur, and professional venture capitalists will probably be more competent at accomplishing it.

Corporate venture capital investors often have a goal of drawing upon the venture for technical information to serve R&D goals of the corporation. One way this may come about is through interaction between technical people of the corporation and those of the venture as it develops. Another is through merger of the venture into the corporation at a later point in time. Each of these possibilities can have major implications for those running the venture.

Amateur investors raise another set of implications. For them, involvement with a venture is more likely to be a learning experience. This means they will more often than professionals make mistakes such as interfering too much or too little in the venture, arranging deals with counterproductive terms or giving the venturer inappropriate advice. Their funds are also more likely to be limited, so that when the entrepreneur needs further capitalization they will not be able to help. Worse, they may become fearful and defensive, blame the entrepreneur for creating a predicament and thereby generate more problems for the venture.

It can be awkward to get started with one set of investors and want to change to others. Even within types of venture capital firms there are contrasts in goals. Venture capital professionals sometimes specialize in certain types of industries or investments. Because of such contrasts of goals between investors it can be hard or impossible to get a second firm or group to buy into the deal structure a prior group has established. Thus, the choice of which source to begin with can be crucial to determining longer-term support for the venture.

Seeking the Money

Finding venture capital firms is not nearly as difficult as finding informal investors. Such firms are in business solely to pursue venture investments and are generally known among banks and local stock brokerage firms. SBIC type venture capital firms can be identified by calling the Small Business Administration and asking for a list. Publications, such as Pratt's *Guide To Venture*

Capital Sources mentioned above, not only list venture capital firms but also give their addresses, phone numbers and investment preferences.

Venture capital firms typically receive hundreds of proposals each year and fund only 1 or 2 percent of them. Thus, much of what they do is screen proposals out, looking for the very small fraction of ventures capable of earning returns high enough (1) to pay for the time to find and work out terms with them, (2) to cover losses on those that don't work out and (3) to provide a return on the capital. Roughly 10 percent of those selected turn out to satisfy their hopes. Much as they would wish otherwise, another 10 percent are complete losers and those in between prove somewhat disappointing. For example, even Sevin Rosen Management, a venture capital firm with $1.7 billion in successful public offerings of its investees' stock, including such companies as Lotus and Compaq, found that 10 out of the 45 start-ups it backed failed.[77]

In approaching such firms it can be helpful, if possible, to obtain introductions by recognized sources, such as others who have dealt with those firms or are known to them. References familiar with prior accomplishments of those applying for capital have proven to be an especially effective part of the screening process to find the few winners. It has become a cliché in the industry that "it is better to bet on a grade A team with a grade B proposal than a grade B team with a grade A proposal." Experience has taught venture capitalists that problems with the idea are bound to arise and a grade A team is more likely to recognize them early and find effective ways to succeed in spite of them.

The venture itself, of course, must also appear highly promising. Ideally, it should:

- be able to employ enough money to make the investigation and investment effort worthwhile. Deals under $500,000 probably aren't worth their consideration, although there can be exceptions.

- be able to earn a high rate of return on that capital, on the order of 30 percent per year and higher.

- appear likely to be salable, either to another company or to the public within approximately five years so the investors can cash in.

- be compatible with the kinds of investment interest, expertise and personalities of the venture capitalists.

Venture capitalists usually expect to see a well-thought-out venture plan that was written personally by the founders. If they get past the executive summary, read the rest of the plan and still have interest in the venture they will typically send the plan for selective review to one or more consultants expert in the venture's proposed line of work.

---

[77]"Risky Business," *Inc.* March 1990, p. 31.

Application   *Describe a path of development for the assigned case venture that could conceivably make it eligible for professional venture capital.*

The deal, if they make one, will be proposed by the investors and may include several main provisions, such as:

- debt conditions convertible into equity or debt with warrants,

- a conversion rate that may depend upon performance; better performance by the venture, less equity for the investors,

- interest or consulting fees,

- purchase of "key person" insurance by the venture on certain founders,

- a nominee from the venture capital firm on the venture's board of directors,

- controls on spending or specification of ratio limits, violations of which will allow investors to take charge to mitigate potential downside investment loss.

An important factor with many venture capitalists is the extent to which founders of the venture have committed their personal assets to it. Founders' motivation can be enhanced both by their committing personal assets and by the consequently larger share of ownership and control they receive for doing so. Venture capitalists want their investees to be as highly motivated toward success of the venture as possible.

How much ownership and control venture capitalists will want is often a concern of entrepreneurs who are seeking capital. In fact, as noted in the last chapter, the capitalists don't want either. What they most care about is the return they get on capital, not who owns how much of the venture. Average rates of return on 131 venture funds, according to a study by Bygrave, et al, ranged from 32 percent in 1980 to less than 10 percent in 1985. This varied greatly, however, according to the age and founding date of the fund, some reaching between 40 percent and 50 percent in peak years and others going negative.[78]

---

[78] William Bygrave and others, "Rates of Return of Venture Capital Investing," in *Frontiers of Entrepreneurship Research, 1988*, eds. Bruce A. Kirchhoff and others (Wellesley, Mass.: Babson Center for Entrepreneurial Studies, 1988), p. 275.

Institutional Private Placements

Other institutions with money that sometimes invest in ventures include insurance companies, pension funds, university endowments, community development funds, family trusts, credit unions, foundations and other variations. Some are profit-oriented, while others have other goals, such as social causes, education and economic development. There is no directory for these, so they must be found simply by asking around and general reading.

Locating a private placement through an investment banker may cost around 5 percent for the broker, another 1 percent to 2 percent as a commitment fee to the institution making the loan, and anywhere from $20,000 to $100,000 in legal fees.[79] Because of these high costs, private placements usually tend not to be for small start-ups, but rather for larger ventures probably farther along. Institutional investors judge their credit ranking by such things as:

- industry rankings of market share, growth rate and profitability compared to competitors
- formulas such as those of Standard and Poors or Moody's
- expected profit multiples of interest coverage
- debt-to-equity ratios and evidence of repayment capacity
- credibility evidence such as use of distinguished accounting and law firms.

Public Offerings

Finally, although it rarely happens, there is the alternative of mounting a public offering to raise venture capital. There are two main parts to this approach. The first is to arrange the offering in such a way that it will be legal. Government regulations have been set up at both national and state levels to protect the public from fraudulent securities sales. The second, and often hardest part, is the task of persuading people to buy the offering.

Offering Types

Alternatives for getting past the governmental hurdles to public offerings are the following:

- Rule 504 under Regulation D of the Securities and Exchange Commission deregulates public offerings of under $1 million. State regulations remain, but a standard 49-question form called the U-7 makes those relatively straightforward in an increasing number of states.

[79]Ellyn E. Spragins, "The New Quiet Money," *Inc.*, June 1989, p. 125.

- Full registration with the Securities and Exchange Commission places no limit on offering size. However, it is vastly more expensive and time-consuming to go through this procedure for permission. State approval is also required.

- Intrastate offering permission is for ventures that do business only locally, and where the offering itself is limited to that state. Intrastate offerings are exempt from federal registration, but formal state approval is required.

On simple offerings there is the alternative of hiring a lawyer for help or of performing the work personally by imitating the paperwork of prior applicants. The main tradeoff is between the time a lawyer would take, much less but at a high cost, versus time the entrepreneur would take to complete the process.

One further option may be merger of the venture with the corporate shell of a company that has already gone public, and therefore has the permission, but is no longer in operation. If shares of the shell already have warrants for shareholders to buy more shares attached, these can be used to raise capital after the merger.[80] If the shell already contains capital, that too helps. Beyond that, the shell may do an additional offering, but permission will again be required. The approach can be legally complicated and is not much used by start-ups.

Getting the Money

Persuading people to buy the public offering is the most uncertain part of raising capital by this route. The entrepreneur may attempt to do it personally[81] or may engage a professional broker to do the selling. The broker may operate on a "best efforts" or "firm underwriting" basis. The hard part of the latter route is to persuade a brokerage firm to accept responsibility for guaranteeing the sale. Going through a broker can cost 10 percent or more of the offering. The smaller the offering, the larger the share of it that will have to be paid to accountants, attorneys and brokers.

Application   *Formulate a line of argument to persuade an investor to put up money for the assigned case venture.*

---

[80]Ellyn E. Spragins, "Back-Door IPOs," *Inc.*, September 1989, p. 121.
[81]Ellyn E. Spragins, "Who Needs Wall Street?" *Inc.*, October 1990, p. 159.

Pros and Cons of Going Public

Arguments in favor of public offerings as a way of raising capital for a venture are the following:

- There are a large number of potential investors to go after, and a large amount can be raised without any of them having to invest a great amount.

- The investor pool may become a helpful set of connections for the company.

- It is easier for investors to get their money back out of a publicly-held company, and this may make them more willing to invest.

- Public ownership may make the company more impressive to others with whom it wants to deal.

The following are disadvantages of public offerings for raising venture capitalization:

- Going public can cost a substantial amount of time and/or money.

- The offering may only partly sell, leaving the venture in a lurch.

- More owners gives management more constituents and potential litigants to contend with.

- More owners can make it difficult or impossible for the company to raise equity capital from other sources such as venture capital firms.

- Affairs of the company must be made public, which is a bothersome task and can divulge information helpful to competitors.

Application   *Describe the conditions under which it could conceivably make sense for the assigned case venture eventually to go public, and explain what it would take to reach those conditions.*

Supplementary Reading

New Venture Mechanics Chapter 6. (Vesper, K. H., Prentice-Hall, 1993)

Your Venture Plan

1. Assess fit for the most promising three alternative sources of capital for your most promising venture idea.

2. Assume the position of each of the three above sources, and formulate terms for extending capital to the venture that would be appropriate from the viewpoint of that source.

Your Venture History

1. Describe the actual (of those that exist) and projected (for those not reached yet) funding stages and sources of the venture being examined.

2. By what reasoning were alternative sources of funding rejected?

Exercises

1. Interview a banker and ask what he or she has learned from experience about lending to entrepreneurs.

2. Locate and plot on a map the venture capital firms most likely to fund ventures in your area.

3. Find and interview a small business investor about his or her experiences investing in ventures.

4. Obtain an offering circular, and describe what should be included in each section for a prospective new venture based upon one of the cases studied so far this term. Also comment on what sections might not apply to the new venture and what others should be added.

Case Questions: Foster (B), Handel, Think Tanks, Van Hague

General Case Questions

1. What would be your assessment of this business from an investor's point of view?

2. What price and terms would you reach for on the venture if you were (1) a founder of it and (2) a prospective investor? Please explain your reasoning.

Foster B Case Questions

1. What do you see as Bill's main alternatives for financing, and what plan of action would you recommend he follow for them?

Handel Case Questions

1. What are the alternatives for Dan and his partners to obtain resources needed to get a company going?

2. As a potential investor, what deal and terms would you propose that they should find acceptable?

3. What fallback strategies should the company adopt in what sequence if the hoped-for financing alternatives don't work out?

Think Tanks Case Questions

1. What is your assessment of the proposed offering terms from the perspective of a potential investor?

2. How would you change the proposed deal to make it one that an investor should find acceptable? Also, please describe the nature of the investor you think would be most appropriate.

Van Hague Case Questions

1. Describe three possible source(s) of funding that could be approached for this venture, and be prepared to explain your choices.

2. Describe the method of approach you would recommend for each of the above three possible sources.

3 Prescribe the terms each of those sources should impose if it did decide to provide the funding for Mr. Van Hague.

Chapter 6

Setup

❏ *SUBCHAPTER 6A - Solidifying the Business Idea*

Time Before Start-up

A 1989 survey by *Inc.* magazine of its *Inc.* 500 fastest growing small firms revealed that 26 percent of the companies had, during start-up, taken only "a matter of weeks" to go from idea to beginning operations. For 37 percent the time lapse was "a few months," for 28 percent it was between six months and a year, and for 9 percent it was more than a year.[82] Cooper et al. reported from their contrasting sample of 2,994 start-ups that "Although the majority went through a relatively lengthy planning period prior to business entry, 87 percent reported that the time between their first business expenditure of $500 or more and their first cash receipt (sale) was three months or less. Just 3 percent reported the time to be seven months or more."[83]

Activities during the time between discovering a business idea, planning its exploitation and having a business up and running are required in all functional areas of the business including finance, marketing, accounting, personnel, R&D and operations. This chapter will take up three topics which cut across these conventional business disciplines.

First, ways of firming up the business concept to strengthen and make it better able to prevail against competitors will be considered. Some aspects of this topic are design-centered, such as refinement of the concept through prototyping, testing and development. Others concern protection from competitors. Trademarks, copyrights and patents are legalistic devices for protecting intellectual property such as inventions and designs. Other protection devices are strategic. They include ways of focusing and differentiating in the market, minimizing costs and managing effectively.

Second will be choice of a business legal form, whether proprietorship, partnership or corporation, and things to consider in designing the details of that form. A related topic is that of governmental requirements for establish-

---

[82]John Case, "The Origins of Entrepreneurship," *Inc.*, June 1989, p. 54.
[83]Arnold C. Cooper and others, *New Business In America* (Washington, D.C.: The NFIB Foundation, 1990), p. 5.

ment of the business. Third come tasks of setting up shop, which include choosing a site, arranging to use it, possibly modifying it to fit needs of the business, plus obtaining and installing equipment.

Application   *Develop an explicit list of main tasks to be performed in the next 90 days of the assigned case venture. Rank them as to your estimate of (1) the personal hours they will require from the founder(s) and (2) the number of calendar days that will elapse between when work on them begins and when it will essentially end.*

Firming Up the Business Concept

The next step after thinking of a business idea, weighing whether to work on it, and doing some planning about how to implement it, should be an attempt to make the concept more real in some form. If there is a possibility that the idea is truly novel, then legal protection, such as copyrighting or patenting should be considered, as will be discussed shortly. If the idea is for a product, then some sort of prototype(s) should be made. If it is a service, then sketches and possibly physical models of facilities should be made. In this more concrete form, the concept can then be tested to see how well it works and how it might be improved.

Prototypes

Preparing a prototype in some form, a working model, a mockup or even just drawings and sketches, can help greatly in not only testing feasibility but also improving a new product or service idea. For patenting, a prototype may be essential to demonstrate that the concept will work, and drawings that show how it will work are absolutely required.

One path of refinement, once a prototype is in hand, is to test, critique, modify, retest and thereby improve the design. Another is to let others try it, show it to prospective buyers and receive feedback as part of the testing. If there is concern that the idea might be stolen, then those to whom it is shown should be selected with careful attention to both their reputations for integrity and the incentives they may be subject to. Additionally, they may be asked to sign a non-disclosure agreement in which they promise not to divulge the idea to others or take advantage of it themselves without approval. It may be appropriate to compensate such people for agreeing thus to bind themselves and for their efforts in helping improve the idea.

Professionals accustomed to helping with prototypes include job manufacturing shops, custom plastics molders, industrial designers and testing laboratories. These can readily be located through the Yellow Pages and by asking around. To get the most help from them as economically as possible, it will probably be a good idea for the entrepreneur to attempt prototyping personally first, at least in the form of sketches, dimensions, target specifications and, if possible, physical models. Physical working prototypes can be very powerful not only for determining that a concept is truly workable and for finding ways to improve upon it, but also for persuading potential backers to put up money and even for persuading customers to buy. In the following example a customer's enthusiasm for buying the prototype itself led to a premature sale.

In 1968 a printing press mechanic recently arrived in Seattle and set up a repair shop. He also began development of a new four-color press that would produce greatly improved clarity but cost less than existing machines. He made two prototypes at a cost of $90,000 and began showing them to potential customers. One responded with a high-priced cash offer to buy the prototype itself. The mechanic, seeing how the cash could help him advance his venture, agreed to sell it provided he could set up and service it as well.

The machine was shipped to the customer in California and installed satisfactorily. But some operating problems developed soon after, and when the mechanic went to fix them he found himself blocked in California by a union contract provision allowing only their people to work on it. Union personnel hung a sign on the machine reading "Lost Horizon." Fearing that word of the machine's failure would spread and stymie future sales, the mechanic bought it back.

Application   *Describe the steps and costs required to develop a prototype or working version for test of the product or service in the assigned case.*

Beyond Prototypes

How hard it is to finish a product design, test and refine it adequately shows up frequently in the massively expensive recalls issued by auto manufacturers. Problems beyond the prototyping state also crop up in new ventures, as illustrated by the following examples.

A team of moonlighting Boeing engineers began in September 1970 an on-board weighing system more accurate than those currently on the market for trucks. Twelve months later they had orders for eighteen units at $1,250 each and commenced production. A couple of months later rains began, and the product proved vulnerable to them. Complete redesign had to be undertaken and followed-up with reinstallations that nearly broke the venture. As it turned out, the company's response earned it a reputation for servicing that helped sales later. But management observed that it need not have been nearly so costly had testing been better in the first place.

❖ ❖ ❖

A Canadian micro brewery, needing a package for its product and recognizing the very high cost of packaging machinery, seized the opportunity to rent an unused wrapping machine offered by a kraft paper supplier. Some difficulty was encountered in attempting to print the brewery logo on the kraft paper, but production proceeded anyway. When sales began a more serious problem arose. The package tore too easily, allowing bottles to drop and smash. It took six months to negotiate withdrawal from lease of the machine, locate another to process heavier material, have a designer create a new package and set up to produce it. The entrepreneur commented, "Beware of the easy solution."

❖ ❖ ❖

An enterprise set up to produce an instrument for guiding road graders accurately found, after selling a number of units, that a key component bought from an outside supplier to conserve capital, contained an inherent design deficiency not anticipated in the purchase contract which caused it to malfunction in hot climates. At great expense, the supplier contract was re-negotiated to terminate, another supplier was recruited, and with that supplier a complete redesign of the component was undertaken. The venture survived, but at a cost in dollars, customers and reputation, all of which took years to rebuild.

❖ ❖ ❖

In 1974 a design engineer teamed up with a wealthy investor to create and produce a new hand-held electronic tallying device for the wood products industry. Market studies revealed no competitive products but a sales potential in the range of $17.5 million per year. In early 1973 a prototype was demonstrated at a forest products show. No orders resulted, but visitors to the booth showed such enthusiasm that the investor insisted on going ahead with production and sales. The engineer argued that more field testing was needed, and when the two could not agree suggested that the investor set up a separate company for sales and give the original venture a purchase order. This the investor did, which left him with a large inventory he was not able to sell.

Laboratory testing, field testing, "beta" testing with customers, focus group evaluations and limited trial marketing are all techniques that may help shake out bugs before investing in full-scale production.

Application   *Describe the sequence that might be used for effectively testing and refining the product or service in the assigned case.*

Packaging

The importance packaging can have for a new venture was illustrated by Sophia Collier, whose venture began with a new soft drink, SoHo soda. She recalled:

What really made SoHo succeed was when we changed our packaging in 1982. When you re selling a product, the little, tiny billboard that you have is your label, and people are going to see your product and be aware of its label when they re using your product.[84]

In a broad sense whatever physical way the product or service is presented can be regarded as its package. Fast foods have containers. Table-served food has many physical elements to its presentation, including plates, silverware, napkins, table arrangement and so forth. Oil changes include presentation of a checklist of what was done. How these physical elements used in transmitting services to customers are handled can help or detract from selling and should therefore be evaluated relative to competitors and given careful thought, perhaps with professional help.

For a product there are not only questions of eye appeal and convenience. Such questions as how units can be efficiently combined for shipment, how well they will protect the product in shipment, how hard or easy they will be to display, to open and possibly to steal must be considered. Is disposability important? Can the same package easily be modified or adapted to other uses? How much space will it take, and how much will it weigh? How much will it cost? How should it feel? What should the printing look like? Should there be a stand, backboard or other point-of-purchase display to go with it?

An extensive reference on packaging is the *Packaging Supplier Source Guide* published each March by Cahners, 1350 East Touhy Avenue, Des Plaines, Illinois 60018. A reference on point-of-purchase displays is the annual *Illustrated Guide to P.O.P. and Promotion published by* Creative Magazines, Inc., 37 W. 39th St., New York 10018.

Intellectual Property Legal Protection

Because the government wants to encourage people to develop new ideas it has provided legal ways for those who do so to enjoy monopolies on them. Copyrights, patents and trademarks are those legal mechanisms, and each applies to certain categories of ideas. These legal monopolies can be tremendously powerful for creating and sustaining a business in some cases, although in others they are worthless. Hence, an entrepreneur should have some understanding of them. It is also useful to know that they are not the only ways of protecting ideas or gaining monopoly power.

---

[84]J. Donald Weinrauch and Nancy Croft Baker, *The Frugal Marketer* (New York: AMACOM, 1989).

Copyrights

Written materials and works of art can be protected by copyrights, which are issued by the Library of Congress. Under international agreement, moreover, the U.S. protection is automatic in more than 80 other countries as well. The procedure for securing a copyright begins with writing on the "work of art" a "c" with a circle around it (©), followed by the name of the idea's creator and the year in which it is created. If the work is produced and distributed with that mark, it is automatically entitled to the legal protection. Taking the further step of contacting the Library of Congress and registering it, there is a way to assure that the creator of the work has laid claim to copyright protection on that date, in case anyone else should attempt to claim the work as theirs. But it is not necessary, and registration can be applied for any time.

There can, however, be significant disadvantages in waiting. Delay in filing precludes recovery of statutory damages, which can range up to $100,000, and attorney's fees for infringements that occurred prior to registration. The copyright holder can recover only actual damages. Some courts have even barred recovery of statutory damages for infringements that occurred after registration when they judged such infringements to be of the same character as those that occurred prior to registration.

As with virtually anything legal, copyrights have their gray areas where disputes are always going on and never fully settled. Currently, computer software copyrighting is a hot legal battleground. In 1992, for instance, a decision was rendered in favor of a company that had been sued for disassembling copyrighted software for purposes of "reverse-engineering."[85] Another decision was rendered in favor of a company that duplicated a copyrighted piece of software in order to understand it.[86] Navigation in such shifting seas calls for attorneys who specialize in that particular gray area. Nevertheless, copyrighting still begins with the simple imprinting step that does not have to wait for an attorney's help.

Defending such a legal monopoly when someone else infringes on it is where attorneys are most needed and also are most expensive. The copyright itself does not prevent anyone from imitating the original work. Only the action of a court can do that. For the court to act a lawsuit must be filed, a verdict must be rendered and action must be taken to get it implemented. Such a process takes time, work and money. Decisions could go either for or against protection on that particular creation. How much legal expense is justified must continually be decided by whoever is paying for it as the litigation moves forward.

---

[85]Seega Enterprises, Ltd v. Accolade, *Inc.*, 977 F.2nd 1510 (9th Cir. 1992).
[86]*Atari Games Corp v. Nintendo of America, Inc.* , 975 F.2d 832 (Fed. Cir. 1992).

Patents

The steps for getting a patent are different and more complicated than those for copyrighting. Patenting begins with making notes that describe an invention, dating them and having them witnessed by others. This should begin as soon as the inventor thinks he or she is really onto a good new product or process idea and decides to continue pursuing it. Since the date of conception of an idea is especially important, the inventor should consider filing a "disclosure" of it with the Patent Office, which can be done for only $6. This is not the same as applying for a patent, however, and if an application is not filed within two years the disclosure is discarded.

Beyond the witnessed notes, patenting requires proof that the conception can physically work, complicated and lengthy activities of application to the U.S. Patent Office and a two- or three-year wait to learn the verdict. If issued, the patent gives the patent owner a right to sue anyone who violates it. Maybe the suit will prevail, the violator will be ordered by the court to stop the violation, and damages will be awarded. Maybe the suit will not prevail. The patent may be declared invalid by the court. Even if it is valid, the court may decide that the alleged violator is in fact not violating it. If a judgment is rendered in favor of the patent holder, maybe the damages awarded will justify the time, expense and trouble of the lawsuit—or, maybe not. The concept of a patent right is simple, but the game of defending it can be very costly, complex and chancy.

Patents protect products, processes, and living plants, in contrast to copyright-covered writings and works of art. Services, as such, cannot be patented, but software and manuals for services can be protected through copyrighting. Only features of products and processes that are new, different and not obvious for someone who is "skilled in the art" to have discovered them are protectable. Expert "patent examiners" employed by the U.S. Patent Office decide which "claims" in a patent application qualify for that distinction. Waiting for such decisions to be made is an experience taking typically two or more years and involves legal arguing back and forth between the applicant's lawyer and the Patent Office.

As with copyrights, patents only grant rights to sue imitators. Sometimes imitators are able to "design around" the claims of issued patents, and thereby in effect nullify them. Some companies never file for patents, figuring the technology will be obsolete too soon to benefit from them, that courts will not back them up or that the ideas they protect are not sufficiently valuable. Others obtain dozens of patents on ideas that in fact aren't profitable. Occasionally patents prove incredibly powerful, as did those that protected Polaroid's camera from competition by Kodak.

Rules for setting up and keeping a notebook to seek patent protection are described in literature available from the U.S. Government Printing Office and in commercially published works.[87] Rules include that the notebook not have

---

[87]Gary S. Lynn, *From Concept to Market* (New York: Wiley, 1989).

removable pages, each page be dated and signed, the book be witnessed and signed by others, and that pursuit on development of the idea be continuous and diligent. The purpose is to demonstrate that nobody else developed the idea sooner. Checking out that possibility requires searching through prior patents. A search of "prior art" is also needed as part of the patent application process. An inventor can undertake that search personally at one of the patent libraries that are scattered around the country, or can hire a professional to do it.

Whether the expense of searching and, assuming the search indicates patenting is likely feasible, filing for a patent is justified, is one of the judgments that may be called for in pursuing a venture. Costs can run into thousands of dollars, and the costs of defending the patent against infringers can cost tens of thousands or even millions more. This may seem discouraging. But possession of a strong patent can be very powerful in recruiting capital to develop a venture or alternatively in licensing the idea to another company in return for cash and/or a royalty. It can also pay off by protecting the venture's market. Tony Maglica, for example, concluded it had been worthwhile to spend $16 million in lawyers' fees over six years to protect the design of a flashlight around which his company was built.[88]

The life of a patent is limited to 17 years, so there is reason to keep moving on exploiting it and on improving what it protects with additional patentable features that obsolete the original design and extend the protection time further. Projective thinking about how others may foil or supersede a patent was outstandingly exemplifed by John Ryan.

> The co-founder of Macrovision, a Cupertino, California company, Ryan developed and patented an anti-copying system to protect videotapes. Then to foil those who would make devices to circumvent his system he also developed and patented the technology required for circumvention. With this second patent, his company filed 21 infringement suits against would-be makers and sellers of circumvention "black boxes." Four manufacturers of the boxes settled with his company before the suits, three more settled as a result of them and all 12 distributors agreed to stop selling the boxes.[89]

Secrets

Another "catch" with a patent is that when issued it must make public the technology it embodies. That gives competitors opportunity to learn just what is protected and what is not about the idea as a basis for seeking ways to go around it.

---

[88]Paul B. Brown, "Magnificent Obsession," *Inc.*, August 1989, p. 89.
[89]"Defending Anti-copy Rights," *Venture*, September 1989, p. 72.

Sometimes there is an alternative of keeping key aspects of the product or process secret. The formula for Coca Cola is not patented, it is secret (although Mark Pendergrast, author of *For God, Country, and Coca Cola,* Charles Scribner's Sons, 1993, claims he came across the recipe in company archives). Many manufacturing processes that perhaps could be patented are kept secret. How colored adhesive plastic tapes used in graphics are sliced to very thin widths has been kept secret for decades. This has both avoided competitor imitation and saved the substantial costs of searching, filing and defending patents.

With secrets there are still precautions that must be taken, however. Employees should be asked to sign secrecy agreements. Measures should be taken to prevent outsiders from seeing how production is accomplished. And if secrets are stolen, legal action will be needed in addition to proof that such precautions have been taken, in order to collect damages from any secrets that may have been divulged.

Trademarks

A third type of government-granted monopoly, in addition to copyrights and patents, is a trademark. Like patents, a trademark is issued by the U.S. Patent Office, but like a copyright, the trademark of a product (or, in the case of services, a service mark) applies to a visual design or emblem. An ordinary word, like water, cannot be trademarked, but a non-word, like Kodak when it first was used, can. If a word becomes ordinary through use, as "Formica" did, then it cannot have trademark protection. The decision rendered on "Formica," (is it really that ordinary a word?) illustrates how, as usual, there is a gray area surrounding what qualifies for protection. Goods bearing the trademark must be "sold or transported in commerce" to qualify for protection of the mark or, under an important 1989 change in the law, the applicant must have a good-faith intention to so use the goods.

For trademarks issued after 1989 the life of a trademark is 10 years and can be renewed each 10. Trademarks can also be extended from an established product to a new product that conveys the same benefits to a new market (Neutrogena soap to Neutrogena shampoo) or to a new product that conveys new benefits to the same market (Tom's of Maine toothpaste to baking powder).[90] Detailed information about how to apply for trademarks and to renew them is available from the U.S. Government Printing Office and from the Patent Office.

There are international agreements covering copyrights, patents and trademarks. Therefore in applying for them it is advisable to consider filing applications in other countries as well. Individual states have trademark laws that may confer further benefits and consequently also should be considered with aid of an appropriate legal specialist.

---

[90]"Will It Travel?" *Inc.*, April 1990, p. 116.

Application What forms of legal protection should be sought by the entrepreneur in the assigned case for which specific aspects of the product or service?

Out-Competing

Most companies are not able to gain protection of much power from patents, copyrights or secrecy. Trademarks are only as good as what people believe them to represent in terms of product or service quality and value. Consequently, the main mode of protection used has to be competitive performance in producing, pricing, selling and delivering a product or service.

> Donald Beaver invented a better way to soak up industrial fluid leaks. Rather than the current practice of spreading kitty litter on the floor, he proposed using sausage-shaped socks full of absorbent matter which could be laid as more effective barriers and more easily picked up afterward. Calling it a PIG ("Partners In Grime") he patented the product and in 1986 put it on the market. Within three years he gained over 8,000 customers and annual sales of $10 million.
>
> The sales also attracted over 60 imitators. Rather than suing them for their attempts to design around his patent, Beaver adopted improvement tactics, principally in service, to stay ahead. These included:
>
> - Catalog plus telephone plus computer linkup to four warehouses to allow next-morning shipment and three-day or faster delivery on all orders.
> - Twenty-day free trial with invoicing only after a company representative has called and found the customer satisfied. (Result: 95 percent pay up)
> - In case of product failure, replacement of the product within hours, no charge on that purchase and 10 percent off on the next one.
> - Working with customers to make sure the company's products are used as effectively and efficiently as possible.
> - Creation of new products through careful attention to customer problems or requests that existing products don't satisfy.
> - Including in the annual catalog articles on industrial cleanup to help customers learn better ways to accomplish it.
> - Calling each customer twice per year to make sure names are updated and correctly spelled.[91]

Out-competing may begin with a "better" idea or may not. It should aim to include better refinement and execution of the idea. Keeping track of what competitors are up to may also help. Information about them can be obtained legally through a number of means, including talking with suppliers, customers and former employees of the competitors. Their products and services can be bought and examined. Advertising they buy can also be studied with the aid of clipping services ("Clipping Bureaus" in the Yellow Pages) and, if they are public, through their securities disclosures and reports. A yearly list of

---

[91] Rachel Meltzer, "Fending Off The Copycats," *Venture*, February 1989, p. 62.

1,500 sources of information about companies is also available from Washington Researchers Publishing, 2612 P Street N.W., Washington, D.C. 20007.

Application   *What activities should the entrepreneur in the assigned case set in motion to assure that the venture will be competitive in the more distant future and how?*

Supplementary Reading

New Venture Mechanics Chapter 3. (Vesper, K. H., Prentice-Hall, 1993)

Your Venture Plan

1. Sketch a proposed trademark and any other protection methods that might apply to one of your ventures and list in detail the steps and likely timing and costs that would be involved in setting them up. List individuals you contacted for information in carrying out this process. Research what is needed to get a patent.

2. Sketch out designs to allow physical demonstration of your product or service idea in three contrasting forms and/or levels of elaboration. Develop cost projections for each of the three.

3. For each of the alternative ways of protecting business ideas (1) describe the steps required to apply it to your venture, (2) list the pros and cons of doing so, and (3) explain the best approach to follow.

4. Impanel a focus group and search for ways of (1) competing with your planned product or service and (2) improving it to stay ahead of competitors.

Your Venture History

1. How long did it take to go from idea to beginning operations in the venture? Make a time line of events with approximate dates.

2. How did the founders test and refine the venture concept? How much did it cost to do so?

3. What thought was given to protecting the venture concept, and what action was taken on it? How much did that cost?

Exercises

1. Interview a local firm capable of helping develop a prototype. Learn what operating policies it has about working with new ventures, and what have been some experiences from which those policies emerged.

2. Generate a scenario for a beta test of some new product idea.

3. Contact at least two patent lawyers, either locally or long distance. Develop a description of how each specializes within patent law, and what, historically, have been the approximate costs of getting patents through them.

4. Learn the location of the patent library nearest you and how far back its patents go. Who mostly uses it and for what?

5. Obtain a copy of the *Patent Gazette*. Note its date, how many of what types of patents it contains (using whatever classification scheme and sampling procedure you choose), and how long, typically, it took to get them issued. How may claims does a typical patent have?

❑ SUBCHAPTER 6B - Forming the Company

The existence of a business, like that of an individual, takes a variety of forms. Name, reputation, habits, equipment, logo, location and output are all part of it. Several of these forms comprise elements of its existence on paper, which will be the focus of this chapter.

Government Requirements

A simple one-person business may be able to get away without registering with any government agencies, although it will have to report income to federal and possibly state agencies. The federal form is a "Schedule C" which becomes part of the owner's personal income tax filing. Technically, a city business license may be required, but it is simple and inexpensive to obtain, and failure to get it may not be noticed if the business stays small, as in the case of a couple of college students cutting lawns or painting houses on the side.

If the business becomes more visible, however, it will have to observe more registration and reporting requirements at all three levels of government: local, state and federal. Requirements may vary with geographical locale. For Washington State they can include the following:

Local

- City Business License - Easily obtained at City Hall for a nominal fee. Forms will automatically come to the venture for paying a Business and Occupations tax based upon sales.

- County Licenses - For businesses that deal with tobacco, juke boxes, shuffleboard games, etc. additional licenses must be obtained from the county clerk. Forms will then come in the mail for county property and inventory taxes.

- Certificate of Firm Name - Filed with the county clerk.

State

- Certificate of Registration - Filed with the State Department of Revenue. Tax forms will be sent automatically.

- State Licenses - Must be obtained for many specialized activities such as contracting, barbering, practicing law or medicine, operating beauty shops or employment agencies. The State Department of Commerce or Department of Licensing can be contacted for a list.

- Corporate Name Reservations - Obtained and annually renewable from the Secretary of State.

- Employer's Requirements - Needed if the firm is going to employ people other than the owner. These requirements include:

  - Registration and Industrial Rating Number from the State Department of Labor.

  - Employer's Identification Number for Employment Security from the State Employment Security Department.

Federal

- Income Tax Forms for the owner and the business, available from the Internal Revenue Service.

- Employees' Income Tax Withholding, also arranged with Internal Revenue. Banks can help with this. It is an important area where mistakes are easy to make and costly.

- Employees' Social Security requirements, verified by the Social Security Administration.

For particular lines of work other forms of regulation may apply. Mail order is regulated by the Federal Trade Commission, franchising by state agencies, airlines by the Department of Transportation, trucking by the Interstate Commerce Commission, radio and TV broadcasting by the Federal Communications Commission, importing and exporting by the Federal Trade Commission, and so forth. Some agencies, such as the Occupational Health and Safety Administration and the Environmental Protection Agency cut across many lines of work.

Regulations can change any time, and so must always be checked on a current basis. One source of information to begin with is the U.S. Small Business Administration, which can suggest other points of contact. Another is the State Department of Commerce. Best, however, may be to contact other businesses in similar lines of work and ask what government agencies they must deal with. Cross checking with more than one source may also be advisable.

Need for regulatory approval can sometimes completely stymie a company even though it may have a product that would ultimately be approved. How this could happen is illustrated by the reaction of a solid waste manager, John Conaway, to a new foam product developed by a start-up company, Rusmar, for reducing the costs and extending the life of a landfill.

Rusmar looks to have a good product, but here in California the permit process will be a big pitfall. I d be using Rusmar s foam right now if it weren t for the regulatory nightmare. We have a severe capacity crunch. But any time you file for a major operational change here and foam would fit into that category you need new permits from three separate agencies.

It would cost us more then $1 million just to apply for them, given all the monitoring and documentation they require. I can easily see being required to do a very complicated and expensive series of ground water tests and surface/air emission tests. Some of these are fly-emergence tests, where you have to get people to come out and actually count the number of flies that emerge prior to using the foam and then after using it. And even then there s no guarantee we d get approval.[92]

Still, notwithstanding such barriers, new companies do get started by introducing products that must hurdle them. But often they must bring to bear more effort and ingenuity, spend more money and take more time to accomplish start-up than they expected.

Application   *In what sequence should steps be taken to assure compliance with any government requirements you can think of by the assigned case venture?*

Company Name

With millions of companies in business and the U. S. Patent Office registering approximately 25,000 new trademarks per year, it can be a challenge to find an effective name for a new venture. The choice is important because, like picking a location, it can stand in lieu of great expenditures in advertising if done well. Compared to a location choice, it will probably remain with the company longer. Should it indicate what the company does (e.g. Software Arts) or not (e.g. Eveready)? Should it be a word with intrinsic meaning (e.g. Apple) or not (e.g. Kodak)?

There is plenty of room for disagreement. It cost a lot of money to change from Standard Oil to Exxon. The company was big enough that it would have imparted meaning to any word. Univac was a familiar word, as is Honeywell. But did the money spent on creating the name Unisys add to familiarity or image? Who can remember what familiar company names were abandoned to form it?

If a company becomes large it will ultimately make its name familiar. Ford and Hershey were not particularly evocative words by themselves. On the other hand, some names probably do help. Santa Monica, California in the mid-1950s saw the opening of a new soda fountain somewhat off the main thoroughfare, on sixteenth street. The name, Sweet Sixteen, quickly became fa-

---

[92]Jay Finegan, "Down In The Dump," *Inc.*, September 1990, p. 98.

miliar and is still known to a vast majority of old time and former residents who long since forgot other stores' names, although the enterprise itself is no longer there.

However, the name will not make the company. For years, the name Astrodynamics was owned by an electrician on Hollywood Boulevard who did nothing with it except keep the registration current because he thought it had promise. It was not the name of his electrical contracting company. No great company grew out of it. But it could probably have been a better name than most for the right enterprise.

It is important to choose a name that is not already owned by another firm for the territory where the new venture will operate. Once chosen, the name should be registered with the state department of commerce where the company will be operating and possibly with the U.S. Patent Office to tie up national rights. If international rights may one day have value, then ways of registering in foreign countries as well should be sought.

There are consultants who specialize in company names and there are also references on the subject. *Brand Names: Who Owns What* (Facts on File, Inc., 460 Park Avenue South, New York, 10016) lists 15,000 brand names of 750 firms. *The Trademark Register of the United States* (Trademark Register, 300 Washington Square, Washington, D.C. 20036) lists over 600,000 names on file with the U.S. Patent Office. There are also attorneys who specialize in determining the registerability of company names. And there are services which maintain databases on names that an entrepreneur can use to do his or her own searching.

Application   *What would be two likely alternative names for the assigned case venture, and what are the pros and cons of choosing each?*

Legal Entity

Either by initiative or default, some legal form must be chosen for the business. Three choices include proprietorship, partnership and corporation. Within each of these, particularly the latter two, are other choices to be made.

Reasons for choosing one business form over another are easy to identify:

Proprietorship is what the business is if no action is taken to make it something else. It is part of the owner. If the business is sued, the owner is sued. If the owner dies, the assets of the business individually are part of the owner's estate and debts of the business are owed by the owner's estate. In paying federal income taxes the owner uses a "Schedule C - Income From Business or Profession" as part of the 1040 form and any corresponding state income tax form.

If the proprietorship operates under some name other than the owner's it may be referred to as a DBA (doing business as) enterprise. Most states require that such an enterprise be registered with the county government with some sort of certificate of doing business under an assumed name. Federal taxes are paid through use of a "Schedule C" form.

Partnership is what the business becomes if more than one person owns it, but no action is taken to separate it legally from its owners. There need not be any paperwork to have a partnership, just ownership by more than one person. Such an arrangement can be created by such things as more than one person contributing assets, doing the work of the business or withdrawing profits from it. Actions like these may even create a partnership inadvertently.

Unless there is paperwork to the contrary, the state will assume ownership is equal among the partners. Also, any partner in such a case can commit the business to obligations or be sued for debts of the business. These can be reasons for arranging the legal form and ownership of the business in a formal manner using legal help. To formalize a partnership some sort of certificate of partnership may have to be filed with the county clerk.

If a partner dies a partnership automatically terminates. Hence part of the legal task of creating a partnership is to consider what disposition of the business should be made in such event.

Partnership Agreements can specify that partners are not equal and can spell out such things as duration, conditions for partner withdrawal, division of responsibilities, assets, income and so forth. These agreements should be written, signed, notarized and filed with a county or state agency to maximize their enforceability.

Limited partnership (Ltd) is a variation in which liability for obligations of the company are limited for some partners. There must still be a "general partner" whose liability is not limited. The partnership agreement can specify any arrangements about relationships between partners as above. Venture capitalists sometimes set up investment pools as limited partnerships. The capitalists run the partnerships, and get paid, while the limited partners put up most of the money and have certain rights to participate in winnings of the investments but no say so in operations. After a time specified in the paperwork, the partnership is liquidated and investors receive their specified share. They are owed whatever the partnership says they are.

As with a proprietorship, income taxes of the partnership arise as part of each partner's personal income picture.

Incorporation is the path chosen by most companies that grow beyond the one- or two-owner stage. Setting up the business as a corporation separates it technically from the owners in terms of liabilities and taxation. Technically, owners are no longer liable for debts of the business, although lenders may refuse credit unless the owners agree to waive that feature. The corporation files its own tax forms, separate from those of its owners. Choice can be made as to whether it will be taxed at the personal rate (Subchapter S Incorporation) or the corporate rate. For the former some special restrictions apply, which can be learned from the federal Internal Revenue Service. Switching back and forth between types is also restricted. Sometimes a Subchapter S status is desirable, usually at the earliest stage for deducting company losses from personal income. Other times, such as when restrictions such as those on voting apply, it is not. Some other features of a corporation are:

- If owners die or give up their shares in a corporation, it continues. If any partner withdraws ownership from a partnership, the partnership does not automatically continue but rather must be reformulated.

- It is easier to issue, sell and exchange corporate shares than partnership shares. For these conveniences and the liability protection, owners often set up businesses as corporations, despite such disadvantages as requirements for meetings and more paperwork.

- If the corporation is very simple, an owner can set it up personally by purchasing the forms and filing them with the appropriate state agency. Usually, however, there are enough complications to warrant engaging a lawyer who is experienced in the task for help in making sure it is done properly. Hiring a lawyer is similarly advisable in terminating a corporation.

Application   *Which legal form should the assigned case venture have and why?*

The procedure for creating a corporation involves (1) filing articles of incorporation with the appropriate state agency, and (2) depositing at least the minimum paid in capital amount required by the state. The state issues a certificate of incorporation, which means that the corporation now exists. Beyond that are tasks of issuing shares, appointing directors, electing officers, setting up bylaws and commencing business.

The main items of paperwork in this process are (1) the articles of incorporation and (2) the corporate bylaws. What the articles must contain is specified by the state. In Washington State, for instance, the following must be specified:

- The company name and address
- How long the company is to last (e.g. "in perpetuity")
- What its purpose is (e.g. "any legal business")
- What kinds of shares and how many are to be issued
- How many directors it will have
- Names and addresses of the incorporators

Answers to these questions may be simple or complex. For instance, stock issued may be common. Or it may be preferred, voting, or nonvoting, carry all sorts of different rights, and so forth. Simple answers an entrepreneur may be able to provide without help. More complex questions probably require assistance from a suitably specialized lawyer.

At its first directors' meeting the corporation should pass bylaws describing further details of its operating rules, including such things as:

- Where and when directors meetings will be held
- What constitutes a quorum
- Who can vote
- How proxies work
- What powers directors will have
- Directors' tenure terms and replacement
- What officers' jobs there will be
- Who the officers will be
- How corporate records will be handled
- Who can sign checks and contracts
- Issuance and replacement of stock certificates
- How bylaws can be amended

Standard forms for bylaws, as with articles of incorporation, partnership agreements, and business licenses, can be obtained from legal supplies stores and possibly from other entrepreneurs. The entrepreneurs, however, may have to do some hunting for them because once issued they are rarely looked at again during operation of the company.

Application   *What should be the most important provisions in the paperwork setting up the assigned case venture? Formulate some hypothetical examples to illustrate.*

Supplementary Reading
New Venture Mechanics Chapter 4. (Vesper, K. H., Prentice-Hall, 1993)

Your Venture Plan

1. Compile a list of the licenses, permissions, inspections, taxes and any other government requirements that apply to your venture.

2. Choose a company name and perform a quick preliminary check of its legality.

3. Choose a legal form of organization for your venture idea, and explain why it is appropriate. Describe the document on which that legal form should be recorded, and explain the provisions it should include. Tabulate the steps and estimated costs of executing this document.

Your Venture History

1. What paperwork was involved in establishing the enterprise? How much did it cost? Did it provide any instructive experiences?

2. What legal form was adopted for the enterprise, how much did it cost to set up, and how have its provisions mattered?

Exercises

1. Interview operators of two or three contrasting businesses. For each, make a list of the governmental requirements for permissions and for reporting. Which has it worst and why? Which enjoys more protection from competitors due to governmental entry barriers? How have requirements changed over time?

2. Contact government offices and learn what is involved in setting up foreign trade ventures.

❏ SUBCHAPTER 6C - Setting Up Shop

Arranging for Production

Whether to make or buy what the company will sell can be a major issue in setting up shop. How long it will take and how much it will cost to accomplish delivery, as well as how much investment will be required are all questions that should be answered to weigh the alternatives. Other questions include how well quality can be controlled, how much flexibility there will be to change production levels, and possibly to what extent confidential aspects of the operation must be divulged.

In mid-1985 two Canadians decided to collaborate on a product one had developed, a belt-like device with fabric pouches for carrying audio tape cassettes. How fast to move on it was a question. They wondered whether they should seek sales in the forthcoming Christmas season even though most stores had already done their advance ordering. Based on informal research the two saw the product as a gift that would likely be a hit with teenagers. They had heard, however, that competitors were developing similar products. Maybe the pair could slip in ahead of them by acting fast and taking advantage of the fact that stores usually keep a small amount of slack in their Christmas buying schedules for last-minute additions.

Another question was how to accomplish production. The pair lacked both the resources and know-how to set up a production line, which they expected would take too much time to accomplish anyway. The options seemed to be either to drop the Christmas target or seek out a supplier willing to perform a rush order. Among suppliers, the alternatives were either domestic or foreign. Through personal contacts one partner found a supplier in Hong Kong not only willing to do the work, but to do so at a fraction of the cost compared to domestic producers. A deal was struck.

Some Christmas sales were made, but not as many as hoped. The company survived, but not very profitably. The main benefit of this fast action appeared to be education. Lessons the entrepreneurs said they learned from this experience were that:

- Overseas cost savings are eroded by (1) travel costs to arrange the deal, (2) long distance phone costs to keep things moving, (3) air shipping costs to cope with late deliveries, and (4) correction costs of inability to oversee quality.

- Having to spend extra time on production subtracts time from marketing and reduces sales.

- Even with good contacts, effective control of production and quality at producers who are located far away is difficult and sometimes impossible.

- When a distant producer promises delivery immediately it may mean two weeks, and a promise of one month may mean six to seven weeks.

- Plants in the Orient take Christmas orders in February and gear up their plants to deliver by August. Persuading them to reschedule for rush orders, even though they are willing to do small ones, costs extra.

These entrepreneurs concluded that this adventure, despite its problems and disappointments, had been worthwhile because now they had a business going, knew more about the market, were working on new ideas for expanding their product line and had improved both contacts and know-how for doing better next time. Giving more advance thought to possible problems and ways of mitigating them were precautions they would add.

Laying out a value chain which describes each stage in the process of creating and delivering something to the customer, then considering the costs and benefits to the venture of performing versus purchasing the work of each of those stages can be a useful form of analysis. Also laying out a PERT chart depicting steps and their timing for setting up operations of the various stages in production can be helpful. Beyond their usefulness in making decisions about creation of the venture, these two analyses can add to the strength of a written plan describing the venture for other people, such as potential investors.

Application   *What aspects of the assigned case venture s product or service could be produced through purchase from outsiders? Which ones should and which should not?*

Supplies

Ordering supplies may take some careful estimating and decision-making. Larger purchase orders usually yield price breaks from suppliers as well as possibly better service and delivery from them. However, trade credit needed to obtain supplies, which often is at best hard to get on small orders, will probably be even harder to get on larger ones. Hence bigger orders require more start-up capital. They also raise the risk of loss if what is ordered turns out not exactly to fit the venture's need. If the initial inventory is too small, however, and the lead time for ordering is long, there may not be time to restock before what is on hand runs out. Thus forecasting in this area can be an important part of setup decision making. Gaining the cooperation and help of suppliers will be further discussed in a later chapter.

Application   *What should the schedule of purchases by the assigned case venture be, and how should that contrast with its schedule of deliveries?*

Premises

It may be simplest to take the first location found vacant. It may be attractive to choose a location close to home so as to reduce commuting time. There may be appeal in picking whatever site offers the lowest rent or best purchase terms. But these may be the wrong reasons for selecting a particular site for the business.

The law firms retained by major corporations are typically ensconced in high-priced downtown suites with expensive furnishings, spacious conference rooms and up-to-date office equipment. Job machine shops may contain high-technology numerically-controlled machine tools, but most are located in grimy industrial districts with old and/or cheap furniture in the entry office, giveaway calendars on the wall and no furnished waiting room. Both types of premises probably fit equally well the firms they serve. More economy in the law firm office would lose it the kind of customers it wants, and more elegance in the job shop would simply increase expenses without expanding sales, and therefore hurt profits.

Location

For retail stores, eating places and some kinds of services, such as shoe repair, location is a crucial variable. To make intelligent guesses about whether sales volume will cover costs and generate a profit, the following must be weighed against the rent level per frontage foot or per internal square foot:

- target customer profiles
- number of certain customer types within a certain radius
- availability of parking
- level of foot traffic
- kinds of other stores in the vicinity
- regulations about permissible signs

Most of these considerations lend themselves to objective analysis; weighing their importance requires subjective judgment. Advice from other people experienced in similar lines of business may be helpful in making such choices, but only if it is heeded.

When Donald Hauck decided to open a small department store in Montevideo, Minnesota, the first site he chose, which was in the middle of the business district, was "too expensive, we thought." He ignored another retailer who said "Don't be afraid of the rent. If you find the right spot, the rent will take care of itself."

Instead, Hauck took the recommendation of a banker who offered enough credit to open the new store in a building Montgomery Ward had vacated. "That alone should have told us something." Hauck recalled. It was located not centrally but rather "about 40 feet too far north" and had no similar stores near it. But the rent was cheap.

A variety of attempts to attract customers with advertising, promotions, sales, changes in decor and even changes in line failed, and Hauck eventually closed the store. But he drew upon this experience in setting up his next store, a bridal shop. This time he chose a site directly across from a major shopping center with a huge lighted sign. "Almost half our customers find us because of that sign," Hauck observed. "I'll never again make the mistake of being 40 feet too far north." [93]

For another type of business the 40 feet might not have mattered as much as the rent. In the next example, for instance, it was more the nature of the building than where it was located that became decisive.

When a frozen food distributor vacated a cold storage building and moved to a larger one in another part of town, a young man who had been renting a small space in the building to store tree seeds, which he harvested as a part-time job, thought he saw a good opportunity to set up his own cold storage business. The plant was over 50 years old but in good working order, and the rent seemed to him very low. Without much thought he signed a lease.

He then went looking for clients to fill the space but learned that many wanted not just storage space but also services such as processing and packaging in addition to receiving, storage and shipping. He found himself short on both experience and equipment for these. There was no "sharp freeze" capability. The layout included four floors, a very slow elevator, small rooms with many corridors and doors to be navigated, all of which made work slow. The elevator capacity was so limited that each floor needed its own forklift. Low ceilings, small rooms, wooden floors and limited ventilation made the building unsuited to processing lines. Both the loading dock and the approach alley were inadequate to the traffic.

Negative cash flows resulted and prompted him to seek partners. Eventually, he persuaded one to join him in financing legal action to break the lease, move to another plant and begin the business over again, "right" this time, but no longer as sole owner.

The second time around, this entrepreneur knew what to look for from experience he had bought at a high price. Had he done more investigation into what factors were important for a cold storage location to work well he might have done better the first time. Part of such investigation should include not just whether the location is suitable at present, but whether it is likely to remain so. For instance, zoning restrictions could be all right today, but then change. If they did change perhaps a business not within those new rules would be given an exemption to continue under some sort of "grandfather" provision. But if later it needed to expand, the exemption might not apply and the firm might be forced to move.

Application   *What should be the criteria for selection of a location for the assigned case venture and what should their rank order of importance be?*

---

[93]Donald Hauck, "Location, Location, Location!" *Venture*, April 1987, p. 100.

Leases

In addition to any government zoning restrictions, an entrepreneur who chooses to economize capital by renting rather than owning premises must also give forethought to the impact that lease terms can have on a venture. This is illustrated by the following experience.

> Having obtained a $10,000 line of credit to set up an imported smoked meat sandwich booth in a mall, an entrepreneur signed a "standard" lease for the site and built a booth himself with the help of his brother and his wife. When it opened, business started slowly, but then gradually grew. As a complementary activity, the owner started wholesaling meat to a local supermarket chain. Attempts to sell to other markets, however, failed.
>
> Noticing the growth in business at the booth, the building owner allowed three other fast food stores with similar products to start selling, notwithstanding a clause in the lease that the first entrepreneur had understood would forbid such competition. He considered suing but decided that the time and money costs would be too high. Sales growth slowed, but still continued, and net cash flow became strong enough, when coupled with the supermarket wholesaling, to pay an adequate living income plus some accumulation of capital.
>
> Then the building owner closed a deal to put up a new building on the same site and exercised a demolition clause in the lease, which put the sandwich stand out of business. Not seeing a site he considered suitable for another such stand, the sandwich shop owner started looking for partners to raise enough cash to begin a restaurant, even though he realized it would require different practices and skills than did the sandwich stand.

Customarily a "standard" lease has a lot of fine print in addition to "custom" terms of rental amount, timing and conditions for renewal that will be negotiated and written in. It should all be read and considered with care, possibly with the help of a broker friend, an attorney or another entrepreneur. Contingencies to consider may include such things as whether it is possible to sublease; conditions under which the lease can be renewed or broken; what the landlord will provide in the way of security or parking; whether competing enterprises can obtain leases in the same building; what happens if the nature of surrounding businesses changes or too many of them move out; and how flexible the landlord has been in dealing with the leases of other tenants.

Application   *If the assigned case venture were to lease premises, what conditions in the lease should be considered most versus least important?*

Facilities

It was earlier suggested that to minimize start-up cash needs it might be well to lease, not buy; build, not buy; or buy used, not new, in order to save money on equipment. There is no general choice, but at least the alternatives can be considered before making commitments.

On installing equipment there may be choices between doing it personally or hiring professionals. The latter cost more but save time and may do the job better. The following experience of a day care center illustrates how problems can cascade if power wiring is not done correctly:

> A short in the wiring started a fire which ruined $54,000 worth of the day care center's equipment, including refrigerators, microwave ovens, television, video recorder, toys, furniture, books and rugs. Fortunately, nobody was hurt and insurance covered replacement of these items. But business had to stop immediately and customers took their children elsewhere. Until the insurance could be collected there was no income, and rent payments drained the owners' capital.
>
> In this case the owners first persuaded the landlord to let them delay, although not discontinue, rent payments. Local community service agencies were implored for donations to help recovery. Customers were asked to return when rebuilding was accomplished, and enough of them did to allow restart of the business.

In addition to power wiring, some businesses require anticipation of present and future computers and other office equipment. It may be cheaper in the long run simply to set up for all reasonable possibilities by installing several types of wiring, including some for unforeseeable future needs. For example, video requires coaxial cable, whereas telephone, fax, and computers presently use ordinary wires. Data can be sent over regular power lines by use of special adapters[94], but fiber optic cables carry more information and will likely be used more in the future.

Projective thinking—creating scenarios and imagining what might benefit from advance remedies—can be a very useful exercise in making facilities and equipment decisions. How will the shop be laid out? Where are bottlenecks most likely to arise? If the company grows, where will the bind first be felt? What chain of calamities could follow from a breakdown? At what points along a growth curve should the next expansion problem be foreseen and from what clues? How far ahead should action be taken to forestall such problems?

Application   Draw a layout map of the shop in which the assigned case venture should be operating six months after the end of the assigned case.

Insurance

Anticipating what can go wrong should inevitably be combined with

---

[94] Cary Lu, "The Wired Office," *Inc.*, August 1989, p. 129.

thinking about not only how to prevent problems but also how to insure for those that occur anyway. Some types of coverage to be considered include:

- Fire
- Theft
- Key employee's life
- Liability - Product, Directors', Property
- Health
- Disability
- Vehicles - Company's and/or employees'
- Workmen's compensation
- Business interruption
- Accounts receivable

There are ways to save money. Carefully list and review the things that could go wrong, produce accidents and attract lawsuits. Then apply imagination to the task of reducing the risks of each of those things happening. Design of the product, production, warning labels, layout of the plant, instructions to employees, types of equipment used, application of safety guards and warnings, maintenance of the equipment and plant, storage and handling of hazardous materials, alarm systems, fire extinguishing and escape systems, education of salespeople and customers, and plant security are all areas where precautions can be considered.

There are ways to get help on the task. Employees can help reduce accident possibilities. They can also be motivated to take more care of their own health by being required to share costs of health care. Government literature and inspectors can provide useful suggestions. Insurance consultants and company representatives have experience they can share about how to lower risks and costs of coverage. The state workers' compensation bureau can provide information about how to qualify for discounts based on favorable safety experience ratings.

Some ways to reduce costs of the insurance directly are to (1) consider higher deductibles on policies, (2) consider introducing hold-harmless agreements to get around needs for some kinds of liability coverage, and (3) obtain premium quotations from several competing insurance carriers. A way to check on the financial soundness of the carriers themselves is to look at their ratings in *Best's Insurance Reports* at the library.

Application   *What forms of insurance should the assigned case venture buy, and what is the most it should be willing to pay for each?*

Implementing Plans

By the time these actions to start a business are being taken much of the plan writing, if any, may have faded into memory. The start-up process will take on a life of its own, and most decisions will usually follow automatically from obvious choices. It may help occasionally to refer back to plans for assessment of how things are going. It may be necessary to update plans as a way of thinking through major decisions or to apply for further financing. But the main guide to start-up action in entrepreneurship must be action itself.

Application   *Develop a Gantt and/or PERT chart for steps in setting up the assigned case venture. Preferably, use an overhead transparency.*

Supplementary Reading

New Venture Strategies Chapter 4. (Vesper, K.H., Prentice-Hall, 1990)

Your Venture Plan

1. Design an ideal location for your business idea. (Alternative tasks may include performing a community analysis, comparing alternative sites, and interviewing a location consultant.)

2. Find a specific, real location for your venture. Obtain details of the lease and setup requirements. Also learn the cost to buy and to build a suitable shop. Project costs over time, anticipating expansion.

3. Draw a layout of the facility in which your venture will operate, noting the locations and costs of the most important and most expensive assets the facility will house. Explain the rationale behind it.

4. Based on discussions with an insurance broker, list the forms, amounts and estimated costs of insurance and fringe benefit policies that should be used by your venture. Explain how the choices were made and how the dollar figures were obtained.

5. Find another entrepreneur who should have experience with the above in his or her venture. Ask for comments about the specifics you have developed.

Your Venture History

1. Sketch a value chain depicting where the venture fits in at two different time points in its history. Insofar as possible, quantify stages of the chain.

2. On what payment terms were the first supplies delivered to the venture? At what points over the first year did how much credit become available?

3. Describe how location and facilities decisions were initially made. What would have been either better or next-best choices? Which of those were considered?

4. What forms of insurance were taken out when, and at what costs?

Exercises

1. Interview a local commercial real estate agent. Learn of two contrasting properties for sale or rent. List in rank order of appropriateness some types of firms that could start in each. Explain your rankings.

2. By phone or personal visit talk to three or four firms from which a start-up might buy supplies. Ask what lessons each has learned from selling to start-ups. What are consequent lessons for entrepreneurs?

Case Questions: Bailey, Brown, Goldman, Windsurfer

General Case Questions

1. What alternative strategic forms could the venture take that is being contemplated by this entrepreneur? By what sequence of analysis can the best choice be made?

2. Prepare (1) a time line, (2) a Gantt chart, (3) a PERT diagram and (4) a guess at an expense budget for performing setup actions mentioned in this chapter on the venture described in the assigned case.

3. Envisage a hypothetical competitor for this venture. Formulate a plan of action, based upon what you know about this venture, to wipe it out. Describe possible actions that the entrepreneur could take to cope with such an attack.

4. What other issues do you see in the assigned case, how should they be handled and why?

Bailey Case Questions

1. Has Ben Bailey done anything a "typical" business school student could not in creating the company he now operates? Why don't more such students take comparable entrepreneurial action?

2. What can Ben do to make his company less dependent on its chip supplier? Should he?

3. What action steps would it take to create a shop to do what IDC does at present? How would you expect that to change as it develops in the future?

Brown Case Questions

1. How could the physical facilities needed to start a company such as Deaver and Alex are considering best be determined, and how could the advisability of obtaining those by different methods be cross-checked?

2. If Deaver and Alex did get set up to make strollers and for some reason the strollers did not sell well enough, what else could the two possibly do with the productive capacity they would have established?

Goldman Case Questions

1. What actions should Jan and Jude take to get the physical facilities they need? Please rank their options in order of advisability.

2. What can a company like theirs seek to acquire in the way of a proprietary barrier to competitors?

Windsurfer (A) Case Questions

1. What issues are raised in the court decisions of this case?

2. What else, if anything, might Hoyle Schweitzer have done to maximize the protection of his business idea(s)?

3. What requirements for effective patenting are illustrated by the court decisions in this case?

Windsurfer (B) Case Questions

1. What procedures for trademarking are illustrated by this case?

2. What vulnerabilities of trademarking are illustrated by the court decisions in this case?

3. What "lessons" for a prospective entrepreneur are suggested by the Windsurfer (A) and Windsurfer (B) cases?

4. What requirements for effective trademarking are illustrated by the court decisions in this case?

Chapter 7

Help

❏ SUBCHAPTER 7A - Insiders

Cooperation is at the heart of entrepreneurship, much as entrepreneurs value independence and use it to competitive advantage. Serving customers is cooperation to satisfy their needs and preferences. Obtaining permissions, supplies and the efforts of others to make the venture go requires cooperation. Obtaining information to figure out, step by step, the actions required to start and move the venture forward requires cooperative interaction with others who know bits and parts of what an entrepreneur must learn. Earlier chapters explored to some degree how entrepreneurs get help from financing sources, customers and suppliers. This chapter will consider those somewhat further and look also at other help sources such as partners, employees, various types of advisers and institutions. They will be grouped into two categories. Insiders, those who are relatively permanent owners or employees of the business will be the focus of the first subchapter of this chapter. Outsiders, those who may deal with and help the venture, but are primarily employed elsewhere, will be the subject of the second subchapter.

Cooper et al.[95] found among 2,994 National Federation of Independent Business (NFIB) entrepreneurs that those whose ventures were more likely to be surviving than not surviving after three years:

- Were more likely than not to have had full-time partners (30 percent in surviving firms vs. 25 percent in non-surviving firms)

- Started with more employees

- More often said they obtained important help from accountants (47 percent vs. 41 percent), bankers (35 percent vs. 32 percent) and lawyers (20 percent vs. 17 percent)

---

[95]Arnold C. Cooper, William C. Dunkelberg, and Carolyn Y. Woo, "Survival and Failure: A Longitudinal Study," in *Frontiers of Entrepreneurship Research, 1988*, eds. Bruce H, Kirchhoff and others (Wellesley, Mass.: Babson Center for Entrepreneurial Studies, 1988), p. 224.

For founders of the *Inc.* 500 fastest-growing small firms, help on development of business ideas came from the sources listed in Table 7-1.[96]

Table 7-1 Sources of Help on Business Ideas for Inc. 500 Founders

Source	Percent of firms
Potential customers	52%
Spouse	51
Partners	50
Colleagues in the same industry	44
Suppliers	29
Professionals such as lawyers, consultants, etc.	26
Potential backers	19

Need for Complements

Areas where entrepreneurs need help from other people can broadly be grouped into four categories: (1) information, (2) production, (3) resources and (4) sales. Helpers who can contribute in these four areas can be grouped into seven categories: financers, partners, employees, suppliers, advisers, institutions, and channels. There can be overlap among these seven. For instance, partners may also be financers, and employees may help as advisers. Each of the seven categories can also be subdivided. For instance, there are many types of advisers, including professionals such as accountants and lawyers plus informal advisers, such as other entrepreneurs, to whom a founder might turn for advice.

Each category of helper will tend to contribute mainly to one area of need for the venture and will possibly contribute to others secondarily. Table 7-2 illustrates what the patterns might be. Advisers contribute mainly information and financers mainly resources, for instance. Using this table, an entrepreneur might rank either categories of help by type of helper who might be most useful (rank the rows in each column), or type of helper by areas of capability to serve (rank the columns for each row). The point of doing so is to clarify mentally just what help is needed by the venture and who might be able to provide it. Getting the wrong person for a particular need can be expensive, as some entrepreneurs who felt disappointed by partners, for instance, have attested.

---

[96]John Case, "The Origins of Entrepreneurship," *Inc.*, June 1989, p. 54.

Table 7-2 Help Types and Sources

What the Person Can Help with

	Information	*Production*	*Resources*	*Sales*
Financers				
Partners				
Employees				
Advisers				
Institutions				
Channels				

Application   *List for the assigned case venture the types of help the entrepreneur will likely need and where it should come from by filling in the grid in Table 7-2 above.*

Although the help needs of no two ventures are exactly alike, it may be useful to review the history of one start-up and identify the entrance of help at certain important points during its development. The following sequence occurred during the early days of cable television.

In 1962 a to-be entrepreneur began working for his brother helping install TV cable in a major city. The following year, while he was visiting in a suburb of the city which did not yet have cable, he noticed on a friend's set that the reception was poor. Knowing he could help and that money could be made with a cable system, he knocked on the doors of several households in the neighborhood and asked if they might be interested to see whether a cable could improve their reception. The replies encouraged him.

Using his car as collateral, he borrowed $1,000 from a bank, bought some used equipment from a dealer and started, as a sideline to his regular job, setting up a system. Over the next year he installed a cable system for 17 charter subscribers, and brought in enough cash to pay off the bank.

Six months later, in mid-1965, he got a call from city hall in the suburb telling him he needed a city franchise for his cable system. He duly submitted an application and received the franchise without problem. This sequence raised concern in his mind, however, that perhaps he should tell the phone company that he was using its poles. In response, the phone company demanded he obtain a $5,000 bond to cover any possible damages as well as a lease fee.

Concerned about the implications of liability that had been raised, the entrepreneur decided he should reform his cable company as a corporation. He was not sure how to do this, but had noticed the nameplate of an accountant in one building where he had worked. Now he approached this man for assistance. The accountant said he would help in return for some stock and a small salary. He introduced the entrepreneur to a friend of his who was an attorney. For a customary fee he helped with incorporation, registration of a company name, obtaining a bond and setting up a contract with the telephone company in late 1966.

While these arrangements were being made the entrepreneur had heard about another nearby suburban area where some homes had poor reception. He knocked on some doors in the local area to verify this and noted a nearby hill where a reception antenna to serve the area might work. He applied for a franchise at the end of 1967 and a year later had an approval for it.

During the wait for approval, he began seeking sources of cash to build the next system. By now he had concluded that he had picked the wrong accountant, paid more than he should have for help in setting up the company, and made a mistake in sharing stock. Determined not to share more of it, he tried to borrow for the company expansion from several potential financers whom he approached, but they all wanted stock.

He decided to scale back initial capacity in the new antenna system, seek another bank loan and develop the system incrementally. Pledging his personal assets he borrowed $5,000 and began construction. Costs grew faster than revenues, however, payments to suppliers began to slip, and one supplier brought suit in an effort to take over the company. The entrepreneur hired another lawyer to defend him, who discovered that the supplier had not properly registered his own firm with the state and therefore could not demand payment.

By letting this account payable continue to run and issuing more stock shares with which to pay friends and relatives to help him, the entrepreneur completed setup of the new system in early 1968. Revenues now grew, bills were paid, the number of subscribers continued to expand, and the entrepreneur asked a real estate agent to help him find permanent quarters for the company. The company also hired its first full-time employee in addition to the entrepreneur.

Answers to several questions about what an entrepreneur needs to implement a business idea successfully can be explored in this example. What personal characteristics most affected the successfulness of this entrepreneur? What capabilities did this particular entrepreneur possess that another might not for accomplishing this venture? Whom did he talk to when he first discerned his venture idea? To what extent does it appear that he knew "the right people" in advance? What did he not know that others had to guide him on? How did he find them? Why did they render the help? How could he go wrong in getting the help? How could he go wrong in not getting the help? What should he have learned from this experience about acquiring partners?

What could he have studied in advance of encountering his opportunity that might have made him more effective? Would it have made him more likely to prevail if a competitor discovered the same opportunity at the same time? How might the help that another entrepreneur might need with another venture differ from the experience of this man? Information in the next few sections should help broaden the picture.

Partners

Most entrepreneurs (69 percent), according to the findings of Cooper et al.,[97] began their companies without partners. Twenty percent started with one partner, 7 percent with two and the remainder with more. (Apparently some had outside investors whom they do not consider partners, since only 63 percent said they owned 100 percent of the equity.) In subsequent years the fraction with partners increased, but only by a few percentage points.

In the contrasting sample of *Inc.* 500 firms which quickly grew large it appears that owners much more often ended up sharing ownership. A survey of *Inc.* 500 founders revealed in 1989 that the amounts of equity still held by founders and their families by the time their firms reached "500" status was as follows:[98]

39% still held 100%
18% still held 75%-99%
22% still held 50%-75%
21% still held less than 50%

The general theory advanced for sharing ownership is sometimes cast as a claim that "50 percent of a $100 pie is worth more than 100 percent of a $25 pie." From this *Inc.* 500 sample, however, it appears that a fair percentage of entrepreneurs, almost 40 percent, manage to retain 100 percent of some very valuable "pies."

However, a majority did share ownership. Although their reasons for doing so were not reported, they probably included: to raise capital, to recruit a team to give the enterprise special competence enabling extraordinary growth, or as part of a "strategic alliance" with some other company. A study of electronics companies with sales under $100 million reported in the June 1990 issue of *Inc.* found that 71 percent had some sort of strategic alliance, most often for market channels.[99]

The basic reason for sharing ownership should be to provide extraordinary incentive, and the founder(s) must decide to whom the incentives should be given and for what. McMullan, Lischeron and Cunningham have reported[100] that there seems to be a relationship between sharing of ownership and company performance which follows a "J-Curve" pattern, with specific figures as shown in Table 7-3 below. At the left tip of the J, with fairly high performance in terms of sales and employment growth, are companies where all ownership

---

[97] Arnold C. Cooper and others, *New Business In America* (Washington, D.C.: The NFIB Foundation, 1990), p. 5.
[98] John Case, "The Origins of Entrepreneurship," *Inc.*, June 1989, p. 58.
[99] "Hotline," *Inc.*, June 1990, p. 33.
[100] W. Ed McMullan, J. Lischeron, and B. Cunningham, "Building Entrepreneurial Teams: Some Options, Rewards and Barriers," (Working Paper #88-13, presented TIMS/ORSA, Denver, October 1988).

is retained by founders and investors. In the bottom of the J, with lower performance, are companies in which founders and investors shared ownership with key managers and technical people only. At the high end of the J are companies with shared ownership throughout their employee populations. Not reported were either the stage at which ownership sharing expanded or the extent to which sharing was a cause versus an effect of the company growth.

Table 7-3 Company Growth, 1978-83 vs. Ownership Distribution

Ownership	Average Sales Growth	Average Employment Growth
Founders and Financers Only	156.6%	75.8%
Above plus Managers	64.6	20.4
All Above plus Professional/Technical	91.0	125.3
All Above plus Prod'n/Clerical/Other	597.0	312.1

Notwithstanding this apparent endorsement for sharing ownership, there is a view among many entrepreneurs that it is better to go without partners and retain 100 percent of ownership if possible, even if it means that the company will not grow as safely or as large. Although no systematic study has reported on the hindsight judgment of entrepreneurs who had partners, as contrasted with those who did not, it appears anecdotally that it is easier to find entrepreneurs who succeeded but had trouble with partners and who would not want to have them again, than it is to find entrepreneurs who succeeded without partners but wish they had had them.

Sometimes, however, there is no other workable choice but to share ownership, and then the goal must be to find the right partner(s), make the right deal and develop an effective working relationship as the enterprise progresses. A starting point is self-assessment by the entrepreneur coupled with estimation of what the enterprise needs. Questions in this assessment include:

- What tasks must be performed to make this company go? (The answer can be cross-checked by asking founders of similar businesses to review it.)

- What tasks does the founder know how to perform at various levels compared to those with more experience in them? (Both how well the founders can perform them and how long it will take compared to having "pros" carry them out should be considered.)

- On what tasks can the founder recruit help, and at what cost? (Some "asking around" will probably be needed to ferret out answers to this question.)

Application   *What are the best estimates you can give for the assigned case venture to the three questions above?*

Unfortunately, it often turns out that finding answers to these questions does not ensure success for the venture. The venture idea may not be sufficiently worthy. The founder may not "bring to the party" enough that others will want to join in. Or it may not be possible within the time and resources available to locate a good enough combination of co-conspirators to justify proceeding. Still, the attempt to recruit the needed help may be worthwhile either for its educational value and/or because it can lead to discovery of other worthwhile opportunities and contacts.

Selection

Partners may contribute in any of the four areas: information, production, resources and sales. Within each of these, what can the entrepreneur provide at a competitive level and where is help needed? Is the competition weak enough, or the venture simple enough to provide adequate time for acquiring what is needed along the way, or must it be available from the outset? When needed, can it be hired, or must it be bought with ownership?

The following ambitious start-up was undertaken by an entrepreneur who lacked important prior experience, and therefore needed considerable help to get it going.

Greg Braendel, who was introduced earlier in Chapter 2, was described by *Inc.* as "a 44-year old itinerant Hollywood actor."[101] A cousin who worked in England for Thrislingon, a company that made unusually decorative bathroom partitions, visited and persuaded Braendel to help sell them in the U.S. "My idea," Braendel said, "was to find a manufacturer and then sit back and collect my royalties for 10 years or so. Then I could pursue my acting career."

A U.S. partitionmaker whom he approached declined the job but suggested a distributor, who liked the product and in turn introduced Braendel to a manufacturer's representative. A representative of the British producer came to help Braendel find a U.S. manufacturer, but even together the two were unsuccessful in finding one. Then the Briton suggested that Braendel make them himself. Braendel obtained rights from the British maker in return for a royalty on sales and set about forming a company. *Inc.* summed it up as follows.

"Add it up. He was setting out to build a company—something he had never done successfully—in an industry he knew next to nothing about. He would be making a low-tech product that, while distinctive, could easily be copied. To succeed he'd have to line up reps and distributors all over the country, set up and operate at least one factory and ultimately several more, persuade architects and interior designers to gamble on a new and still-untested manufacturer—and do all this before competitors moved in on his turf. Braendel

---

[101]John Case, "With A Little Help From His Friends," *Inc.*, April 1989, p. 132.

figured that he could count on his parents back in Pennsylvania for some seed capital, but he had little money of his own and little notion of how to raise more.

"As for the start-up team he assembled, well, an optimist would say that they made up in enthusiasm what they lacked in relevant experience. Braendel's friend, Jack Dunsmoor, 42, gave up a marketing job at Republic Pictures to become Thrislington's vice president. Dunsmoor's half-brother, Tim Haase, only 26, became manager of production, and a young actor named Bo Rostrom, 27, became marketing coordinator. Jo Strate, 63, a friend who was training director for General Nutrition Center, managed the office and kept track of the cash."

Braendel chose well-known professional firms for help. A prestigious Los Angeles law firm, White and Case, helped with trademark and logo protection plus preparation of a private placement memorandum. Peat Marwick helped with preparation of a business plan, for $14,000, and was expected to help further with setup of a computerized accounting system and possibly executive search. Suppliers also helped. DuPont and Formica both sold materials needed in the partitions and offered to help with cooperative advertising and distribution of literature.

Disappointments also followed. A company engaged to perform assembly let the venture down and Braendel and his partners ended up doing the work themselves. One bank agreed to make a loan, but only against Braendel's personal collateral. Later when his venture was going and sought more working capital it was turned down at that same bank and elsewhere. A venture review panel at an "Entrepreneurial Forum" sponsored by Stanford alumni criticized Braendel and his group for undertaking a line of work in which they had no experience. One venture capitalist commented that "We took a vote of five or six people after the meeting and it was unanimous. They wouldn't get the money they needed, and they wouldn't succeed if they did." Two years into the business, however, sales had risen to $2.7 million annually and the company was still going, with plans for continued expansion.

Whether this venture succeeds in the long run or not, it shows how entrepreneurs find help. They start with whatever acquaintances they have and work through them, and they make "cold calls" on professionals such as lawyers, accountants, bankers and suppliers to find people who can provide the needed help.

Recognizing what to look for and what to avoid in partners and other potential helpers calls for both hard-headed assessment—what have they done before, what do they know, what reputation do they have among those with whom they worked, how much compensation do they want?—and subjective appraisal—is this person enjoyable to work with, does he or she seem enthusiastic and reliable, are we getting along well, do motivations match? If there can be an opportunity to work together before cementing the relationship, that may provide even more helpful information.

Application   *Formulate criteria for seeking and selecting one or more partners to complement the entrepreneur(s) in the assigned case.*

Terms

Striking a deal with a prospective helper or partner has two sides: who should add what, and who should get what? Each of these two sides has its objective and subjective aspects. What should be added can be sorted out in terms of the four categories mentioned above: information, production, resources and sales. These four can be aligned with capabilities of the potential helper to see how good the fit should be. Usually, information is the easiest to come by, while the other three, production, resources and sales, may be both harder to get and more important because they require more serious commitment.

Who should get what can be examined through developing answers in specific terms, quantitatively insofar as possible, to such questions as:

- How much would it cost elsewhere to obtain the same thing?

- How much might the venture be worth if it works out, and what is the probability of its doing that well?

- What is the discounted expected present value of the venture's future cash flow, and hence how much would a specific fraction to be shared with a partner be worth?

- Will the partner get a special tax break, such as being able to deduct expenses of the business from personal income?

- Will the partner enjoy insulation from some problems of the business by having part of it set up separately in such a way that the partner shares only some particularly appealing aspect, such as a tax break? Sometimes, for further illustration, a separate partnership will be set up for sales or for ownership of certain facilities. These may be unencumbered, while another part of the business copes with past losses or other risks.

Thinking about what can go wrong should be part of setting up a deal, not because things necessarily will go wrong, but because they might, and thinking ahead may mitigate or head off problems. Examples of potential difficulties include the following:

Two men formed a machining company. At year-end the wife of one of them took a look at the books to prepare taxes and found that the partner had been making unauthorized withdrawals from the company bank account and attempting to disguise them as supply purchases. The partnership was dissolved.

❖ ❖ ❖

One man had a small manufacturing company. He was approached by a second man who offered to help with sales. As proof of his sales ability, the second man obtained from a potential buyer a letter of intent to buy enough to increase the company's volume five-fold for the year. The two formed a corporation, divided the stock 50/50 and both cosigned a note at the bank to obtain working capital. Sales, however, turned out to be far slower than forecast, and with a large inventory the company began to have trouble paying its bills. Creditors, including the bank, pressed for payment.

The original founder became increasingly unhappy with his sales partner who had not met his promises. When, in addition, the founder learned from the bank that the salesman had sold the company truck to help raise more cash for selling expenses, he was furious. He approached the bank and offered to pay off his half of the bank obligation personally with cash. The banker agreed. Then the founder approached the salesman, said what he had done and offered to pay off all the company's suppliers personally if he could have the inventory. The salesman said it would be a mistake, that things would pick up soon. The founder replied that the only mistake had been their becoming partners. He wrote the salesman's lawyer saying his name could no longer be used in connection with the business. Thereafter, the founder operated as a sole proprietor, sold off the inventory and started expanding the business. His conclusion was that the $15,000 he had lost in this process had been tuition for an educational process about caution in taking on partners.

❖ ❖ ❖

Three partners in a fish farm negotiated with some potential "silent partners" to obtain capital. The understanding of the three partners was that the investors would pay the company in a lump sum to be used for expenses during start-up, and they attempted to include this provision in the investment agreement, which they wrote themselves. Shares were duly issued to the investors, but the latter chose to mete out the cash slowly, which frustrated the founders. The investors claimed that costs of start-up were becoming higher than promised and therefore they were entitled to more ownership. The founders sought legal counsel, and were disappointed to learn that the agreement they had drafted left loopholes which gave the investors the upper hand.

❖ ❖ ❖

Bob Ohlson, one of four partners in a computer cable company, saw the other partners as both lacking in vision as to what their company could become and not pulling their weight. He tried persuading first one partner and later a different one to join with him to take over from the other two. Eventually, however, the other three all aligned against him and offered to buy him out. Ohlson rejected the deal, claiming that both the price and the condition that he sign a promise not to compete were unacceptable. Instead he quietly set about organizing a new company in the same line of business. He recruited key employees to come with him, offering shares of ownership in his new company as part of the inducement. Suddenly one day his partners were surprised to find that he and 18 of their 80 employees had left, including three-fourths of the salespeople. They struggled to recover, however, and by a year and a half later the company had grown to 95 employees. The partner in charge, John Berst, however, felt he had nevertheless lost something. "With Bob Ohlson I bared my soul," he said. "Now, I'm reluctant to totally confide in anyone."

Ohlson's new company had also managed to survive and was now up to 36 employees. Reflecting on his departure from the partnership, he commented, "If I had had enough money, I probably could have cleaned the whole organization out. This was a super move on our part. Obviously, I'm more cynical about personal relationships. At one time I would have considered John Berst my best friend in the whole world. And then he went and stuck a knife in my back." [102]

❖ ❖ ❖

Two doctors formed a clinic. One started feeling progressively more overloaded and wanted to hire a third doctor to get some relief. His partner, however, resisted because he knew doing so would cut into profits. After considerable debate, the two agreed that the new doctor would be hired, but the doctor interested in maintaining profits would take no cut in his draw. The other did take a cut in draw, but only for a while, because with the new doctor business and profits soon increased enough to provide the same draw for both.

The variety of things that can go wrong is endless. Not all problems can be anticipated in setting up a partnership, but some of the possibilities can, including provision for dissolution. One "shoot-out" clause sometimes used to provide for possible breakup says that either partner can buy out the other on the terms he or she offers provided the other has the right first to buy on the same terms and declines to exercise it. Thinking through this possibility and other "what if's" can be helped by talking with others who have gone through the process, such as other entrepreneurs and attorneys with new company formation experience. Also helpful, particularly in negotiating arrangements, is to consider the "what if's" alternatively from each party's point of view before taking a position.

Application   *Formulate terms that the entrepreneur in the assigned case should shoot for in taking on a partner. Be prepared to explain how the prospective partner should respond to those terms.*

Employees

One way around partner problems, if the founder(s) can raise enough capital, is to hire the help needed with cash. Flexibility is high in hiring and firing when a company is very small. If it grows and adds more employees beyond three or four, things become more complex in terms of governmental restric-

---

[102]Edward O. Welles, "Blowup," *Inc.*, May 1989, p. 63.

tions and requirements. At a still larger size, unionization can add further complications. Such consequences of growth are why some entrepreneurs permanently keep their enterprises small.

That is not to say there are no complications. Occupational health and safety (OSHA) rules, both federal and state, still apply. Payroll deductions for taxes and social security must still be made. Premiums for industrial insurance and unemployment compensation must still be paid. And, of course, employees can still sue if they think they have cause and might be able to collect from the venture.

Hiring

One way to avoid such complications can be to hire "temporaries." Rather than paying them directly, the venture can hire their services from other firms that employ them, pay them, take care of their payroll deductions and governmentally-required paperwork. The venture instead simply pays their employer and thereby escapes the complications of putting them on a payroll. Another possibility is to buy services from people who operate as independent contractors, and leave it to them to take care of their own payroll deductions and insurance. Consultants, for example, are hired in this way. Caution is required, however, to remain within the bounds of legality. If the government gets the idea that these people are really employees of the venture who are just masquerading as independent contractors, it will move in to stop the practice and likely impose penalties.

In attempting to attract and recruit desired employees, start-up firms have some obvious handicaps and advantages. Handicaps include:

- relative financial insecurity
- relatively low pay
- limited, if any, fringe benefits
- lack of opportunity to move around within the company
- little or no formal training opportunities
- no association with a "name brand"

To be weighed against these are such advantages as the following:

- a more personal environment
- capability of the company to grow and change faster
- more responsibility and breadth of coverage in work
- opportunity to make a visible difference personally in the fortunes of the company
- opportunity to rise faster as the company expands and perhaps to

share a significant part of the ownership which could become very valuable. A very high percentage of Apple's early workforce became very wealthy, for instance. Microsoft's workforce is said to include upwards of a thousand millionaires.

It is up to the founders to "pitch" these potential advantages effectively, and often their own enthusiasm and excitement during start-up helps them do that. Consequently, start-ups, in spite of their handicaps, sometimes manage to recruit some excellent employees. Another advantage they have is that being small and consequently flexible, they can accommodate unusual people who do not fit well in established firms or simply don't like the regimentation such firms impose in pursuit of efficiency. Homemakers, part-timers, members of the family, military people in off-hours, school teachers during summers, handicapped and retired people can be more readily accommodated by start-ups than by companies whose routines have grown more firmly fixed.

Classified advertisements in the local paper are the customary way to locate recruits. Start-ups sometimes find employees in other ways as well, such as through personal contacts, family and friends. Customary checkout procedures, such as contacting former employers and looking into past performance records, are as appropriate for start-ups as for other employers, even though the time required for those procedures may be harder for founders to come up with due to the many other time demands they face.

Application   *Formulate a staffing plan for the assigned case venture over the next two years, indicating criteria for selection, specifications for training, projected organization charts and estimated costs.*

Pitfalls

Start-ups run into all sorts of problems with employees, just as do other firms. Some examples include the following:

The founder and 65 percent shareholder of a security systems company was out of town inspecting work on a new job when the operations manager, controller and marketing manager, concerned about loose management of the company, approached the company's bank and suggested that the bank tell the founder either to resign or have his loan called. Upon learning of this, the founder contacted his lawyer and the two visited the banker, whom they informed firmly that all relations between the bank and founder were to be kept confidential. They vowed to file suit against the bank for conspiracy if any damage to the company resulted from the bank's meetings with the employees. The employees were given the choice of resigning or being fired and chose the former.

❖ ❖ ❖

The factory of a jacket enterprise burned down. Arson appeared to be the cause, but when the owner appealed to the insurance company for compensation both it and the local fire department indicated they believed management had been behind the fire for the sake of the insurance money. The owner hired a former FBI agent to investigate. This man found, in the fire department records, the notes from a interview with a woman who had been eating in a restaurant near the plant when the fire broke out and had reported seeing a young man enter the restaurant muttering somewhat incoherently about the blaze. An amateur artist, she had also submitted a sketch of him to the fire department. The FBI man showed this sketch to the owner of the jacket enterprise and learned it depicted a former employee. Investigation of the employee's background turned up earlier troubles with the law. Eventually, the employee confessed to setting the fire, the insurance firm paid off and the jacket enterprise continued.

❖ ❖ ❖

The founder of a restaurant said employee stealing was a never-ending problem. Tablecloths, silverware, pots and pans, food and other supplies continually disappeared. He recalled firing one cook who had taken large quantities of food, including whole beef roasts, by putting it in plastic bags, throwing it into the garbage and later retrieving it from the dumpster after hours. The only solution the owner could think of was to be eternally vigilant and accept the fact that some things were bound to go wrong.

These examples illustrate only the tiniest fraction of problems that arise with employees. A new venture at least offers opportunity to start out right with careful employee selection coupled with clear formulation and enforcement of rules. Starting a pattern of careful attention to employee needs and problems can set a positive trend from the beginning, and head off later need to fix dysfunctional habits.

Application   *List, in order of probability, the problems most likely to arise with insiders over the next two years of the assigned case venture and what should be done to forestall or cope with them.*

Supplementary Reading

New Venture Mechanics Chapter 4. (Vesper, K. H., Prentice-Hall, 1993)

Your Venture Plan

1. Assess your strengths and task-relevant experience for carrying through your venture idea. List the areas where complementary talents and capabilities of others might be most helpful.

2. Ask someone else to review and comment on the above assessment. Write a summary of what that person said.

3. Formulate the composition of the best team you think you might be able to recruit to help you start your venture. Describe the incentives you could provide for them to do so and how you would attempt to persuade them to join.

4. Test the incentive system above by writing out a description of it and asking someone else to comment on it.

5. List your prior work and/or hobby experience, and note the functional areas (accounting, production, marketing, etc.) in which you would be best-equipped to contribute during start-up of the venture you are developing a plan for.

6. List the capabilities in co-founders that would be most useful to you for accomplishing such a start-up.

7. List the provisions you think would be most important to include in a partnership agreement or corporate bylaws for your venture.

8. Compile biographies of key people for your venture as they should appear in a venture plan. Be prepared to explain what you chose to include and why.

Your Venture History

1. List the cast of characters and where they came into play in getting the venture started.

   - If it involved partners or investors, what were the deal terms that brought them in?
   - What does a look at the written agreement reveal?
   - Which contacts were first delivered when, and how?

2. How did the entrepreneur:

   - Find, select and recruit employees?
   - Learn about and arrange for legal requirements?
   - Learn about and arrange for fringe benefits?

3. Approximately how much time did this require?

Exercises

1. Obtain the views of three entrepreneurs on the subject of partners. Upon whose experience, those of the entrepreneurs or those of others, are they based? How consistent are they with each other, and what do you conclude?

2. Same as above, but for employees.

3. Assess as potential partners some people you met while sizing up the competition or potential vendors in connection with development of a business plan.

4. Based upon examples you have seen in the readings, class and any field searches thus far, how would you answer the following questions:

- What kinds of help do entrepreneurs need?
- Do creative people need partners because they lack business sense?
- How does an entrepreneur tell if contacts or partners are needed?
- How does an entrepreneur decide what to do personally versus hire others to do?
- How does an entrepreneur choose among potential partners?
- What types of people should be avoided for a venture team?
- How does an entrepreneur get others to help in starting a business?

❏ SUBCHAPTER 7B - Outsiders

Every business, including a start-up, needs help from outsiders, people who have neither ownership nor employment in the company. An entrepreneur can benefit by becoming acquainted with a number of outside help sources and their costs. Government agencies and libraries provide information without fees. Some types of professionals charge directly for their services, lawyers, for instance. Others, such as bankers and insurance agents, provide counsel without charge and get paid for the other services they offer. Still others offer free counsel on a volunteer basis; for instance, retired executives who work with the Small Business Administration and other business people who serve as advisers "pro bono" to small firms.

Whether free or not, all of these help sources cost time to use, and an entrepreneur must weigh the benefits of outside help against both the time and money costs of obtaining them. Most specialists cost money but save time because they know what they are doing and don't have to stop and learn as a newcomer does.

More important than the cost in either money or time is often the quality of contribution that the venture receives. People who have the strongest proof that they can deliver high-quality performance often tend to charge the highest prices. Is the venture really worth enough to justify such an investment? High-priced help may easily be justified if its benefits can be spread across a large operation. But how can a small one justify such costs? And if it can't, what is an entrepreneur to do? Juggling these dilemmas is not impossible. Entrepreneurs do it all the time. It calls for imaginative and energetic management.

Suppliers

Suppliers were discussed in subchapter (6c) of Chapter 6 in connection with setup of the company shop. They have a vested interest in seeing a new venture, that might be a future customer, succeed. Consequently, they are predisposed to help if they can and if it will not cost them too much. Large corporations with well-known names may have both talents and connections of value to the venture. They may be able, for instance, to use the venture in their advertisements to capture favorable interest for themselves, while the venture itself gets free advertising. Useful advice in product development, contacts for other help, provision of samples and extension of credit all may come from suppliers.

Against potential gains from giving help to the venture, suppliers must weigh three possibilities: first, that the venture either will not succeed and therefore not be able to pay the suppliers back at all, second, that it will survive but remain very small and therefore not return the investment made to help it, and third, that after it gets going the venture will shift to other suppliers. It is natural for suppliers to favor their most important customers and to avoid those who lack a proven track record of paying bills. Even with such precautions, suppliers continually absorb bad debts. Bankruptcy filings typically report liabilities in excess of assets, which is an indication of bills that suppliers are unable to collect.

The way to find suppliers is by asking around from one referral to the next until the ones needed turn up. Some places to start in this search process include:

- The Yellow Pages of the phone book
- A manufacturers' directory for the city or state
- *Thomas Register* in the library
- Firms that might use the same type of supplier.

Once a suitable supplier is located, a selling job by the customer (entrepreneur) begins. Quality, delivery time, price and credit terms, if any, must be arranged, and usually the start-up founder is at a disadvantage. Some suppliers are sympathetic to entrepreneurs, but most are not so generous that they will jeopardize either money or other customers to help out. They may require payment C.O.D. or even in advance. They may put other orders ahead and deliver later than promised. They may compromise any prior arrangements, and for that reason the entrepreneur must stay in close touch. This may be difficult with all the other demands to be met during start-up, but it may be necessary to get the needed help.

Application   *List the types of suppliers that will likely be needed by the assigned case venture, indicating which five will likely be the most difficult to deal with and why.*

Professionals

Many different types of specialists are available to help ventures. Most provide information, as opposed to production, resource or sales help. Many also provide introductions to other useful business contacts. Generally the more successful the professional, the better the contacts he or she can provide.

Legal Advice

Conventional wisdom advises entrepreneurs always to put important agreements in writing, read and understand the fine print and hire the most competent lawyers they can find to help with these tasks and keep them out of legal trouble. The law never requires that lawyers be hired, and many entrepreneurs have successfully accomplished their own legal work ranging from filing for incorporation to drawing up contracts, conducting their own trials, handling their own public offering applications and writing their own wills. But the conventional wisdom to hire good legal help persists, with the support of virtually all who have done so. A lawyer costs more money than handling legal work personally, but there is usually a more than offsetting saving in time expenditure and mistake reduction.

What an entrepreneur needs to know about the law is (1) where it generally comes into play, (2) how to go about becoming better-informed in those areas where it is likely to become especially important for the particular business, (3) how to find an appropriate lawyer, and (4) how to use legal services effectively and efficiently.

Lawyers help with:

- legal formation (Should the venture be incorporated, and if so, with what provisions?)

- relationships between owners, employees and others (Will the venture need non-disclosure agreements, union contracts or non-compete agreements? Should it have pension or profit-sharing plans?)

- legal protection of intellectual property (Should the entrepreneur file for a trademark or patent? Should the venture sue for theft of trade secrets?)

- contracts (What should be the wording with suppliers, customers, landlords?)

- lawsuits (Where are the litigation risks greatest and how can they be mitigated?)

- taxes (What are the allowable deductions, what must be paid when and what must be reported when?)

- government permissions and requirements (What records must be kept? What applications and reports must be filed and in what form?)

- issuing securities (What advance preparation is advisable? What can and cannot legally be done, and how are approvals obtained?)

- personal property issues (What estate planning should the founders do? Should they be leasing assets to the company?)

An entrepreneur should attain some knowledge of the meaning of each of these categories and the kinds of issues that might arise within them. Some issues are suggested above in the parentheses, but each issue is complex, and the list is by no means exhaustive. Moreover, the ways of dealing with these issues depend on the individual circumstances. Incorporating as a sole owner can be simple, but with partners it tends to become complicated. Government permission for selling stationery is simple. Opening a foundry is complex in some situations and virtually impossible in others. Some start-ups will never sell shares publicly and need not worry about rules governing that. Others that eventually will should explore whether they need to get started right away with certified accounting audits in order to qualify later, and so forth.

Information about each of these topics is available in libraries, particularly law libraries, which are operated both by law schools and by governmental agencies. The standard reference on law firms is Martindale and Hubbell.[103] Talking with other entrepreneurs in related lines of work or who have faced similar situations, and reading up are two "free" ways to become prepared to answer such questions as:

- Is something legalistic called for?
- Should a lawyer be engaged to help with it?
- Should the lawyer be a generalist or specialist?
- Should a large or small firm be engaged?
- Which firm should be hired?
- What should be bought from it?

Application   *Make a schedule of legal tasks to be done during the next two years of the assigned case venture and, insofar as possible, answer the above questions and formulate a legal expenses budget.*

Answers will vary with the source of the opinion as well as the kind of business situation the entrepreneur faces. For instance, many if not most lawyers will advise engaging them early to help with the decision of how and when they should be used. A lawyer from a large firm will point out that large firms have the advantage of employing many specialists to provide most efficient, informed and up-to-date information on whatever legal assistance the entrepreneur needs.

A lawyer from a smaller firm will counter that the large firm will typically assign top partners to the major accounts and use the small firm as a training ground for younger and less-experienced members of the firm. In contrast the small firm may assign a top (or maybe the only) partner, and where specialists are needed it will refer the entrepreneur to whomever is the best specialist in the business rather than simply to one whom the firm already employs and therefore must utilize.

The big firm may respond that it has more numerous and powerful contacts (but why should it draw upon them for a small venture?) and a better-known name to enhance the venture's image (but it will likely charge

---

[103]*Martindale-Hubbell Law Digest* (New Providence, N.J.: Martindale-Hubbell).

more. Will the extra money be better spent on that or on advertising, quality improvement, employee training or R&D?). Investigation and application of judgment by the entrepreneur are required.

Some feeling for a law firm can be obtained by briefly discussing with it such matters as these before deciding whether to hire it. It is always appropriate for the customer to ask whether the firm thinks it should be hired, how much it will charge and when the "meter" will start running.

According to a study by the Technology Executives Roundtable, 45 percent of high technology entrepreneurs found their lawyers through business acquaintances, and another 15 percent found them through accountants and bankers. Large law firms were the choice of 41 percent and sole practitioners of only 11 percent.[104]

Picking a Bank

Bankers help with:

- raising money
- obtaining credit reports on other companies
- anticipating financial binds
- numerous other services such as payroll processing, foreign exchange, trust management, business contacts as well as services familiar to individual customers

Critical elements in a banking relationship, aside from whether it has expressed willingness to lend money to the venture and on what terms, are which bank officer will handle the venture's account, how much interest that person takes in the venture, how comfortable the entrepreneur is with that particular person and how much weight that person carries within the bank. When a banker says "I'll have to take that up with the loan committee" it is usually not a particularly auspicious sign. When the banker who is dealing with the entrepreneur moves to some other activity in the bank and is replaced by someone else as the venture's contact, it is sometimes the worst possible sign.

Application   *Assume the role of a banker, and comment on the attractiveness of the assigned case venture as a client.*

---

[104]"Hands On," *Inc.*, July 1989, p. 99.

Accounting Help

Accountants work on

- setting up financial reporting and control systems
- evaluating financial performance
- anticipating financial needs
- tax computations and auditing

Cooper et al. found in their survey of National Federation of Independent Business firms that initially bookkeepers were most often considered important sources of counsel (46 percent), followed by bankers (32 percent), other business owners (28 percent) and suppliers (28 percent). Later in the venture's development the accountants were still regarded as high in importance, while bankers were regarded as less so.[105] Bankers are chosen, according to a survey by the Technical Entrepreneurs Roundtable, much the same way as are lawyers, at least by technology entrepreneurs. Most frequently business acquaintances are the source of referral (44 percent), while bankers and lawyers are the source only 18 percent of the time.[106]

Application   *Prepare a forecast of the CPA time needed by the assigned case venture over the next two years, and explain the tasks it presumes.*

Selecting Insurance

Insurance brokers help with:

- many forms of insurance, including fire, theft, liability, directors' liability, auto, key person life coverage, health and accident, and pension plans

- ways of reducing risks (e.g. fire, security and safety systems)

One choice to be made is between an agent who represents a single insurance company and a broker who represents many different ones. Convenience favors the latter when there are different types of insurance to be bought, which is the case in starting a new company. But it is crucial to find a broker who is fully competent. Insurance policies contain many fine points. For instance, suppose the venture has a contract with a customer guaranteeing delivery of products. The plant burns down, and fire insurance covers the loss.

---

[105]Arnold C. Cooper and others, *New Business In America* (Washington, D.C.: The NFIB Foundation, 1990), p. 7.
[106]"Hands On," p. 114.

But the customer sues for damages due to non-delivery of what was promised. Will the insurance cover those too?

Shopping around among several insurance companies by talking to their agents is a way of cross-checking on both coverage and rates. Another way is to hire an insurance consultant who is paid by the hour rather than through a percentage commission, as are agents and brokers. Yet another is to check with other entrepreneurs whose businesses, although not directly competitive with the new venture, are similar enough to require comparable insurance coverage.

Advertising

Advertising agencies help with

- design of brochures, displays, packages, advertisements
- placement of advertisements
- placement of public relations messages

The *Standard Directory of Advertising Agencies* lists all but the smallest. For a start-up company with drastically limited cash, however, the smallest may be preferable, and that must be found locally by "asking around."

Application   *Describe specifically the help an advertising agency might provide for the assigned case venture, and explain whether it should.*

Designing Facilities and Products

Industrial designers help with

- graphics, plus styling of products and packages
- human factors such as ease of use, foolproofness, comfort, safety, and so forth in design

Sophia Collier, who found package design to be so important to her SoHo soda pop start-up, as was mentioned earlier in the first subchapter(6a) of Chapter 6 in connection with product development, tackled the design task first by reading extensively at the library about printing and packaging and then seeking out a professional for help.

She chose a general style, "art deco-ish," then sought out names of designers specializing in that style. One of them, Doug Johnson, expressed interest in the project until she told him she had no money. Then he told her to forget it.

But she persisted, and eventually persuaded him to accept a royalty for his help. "The fact that I kept coming back suggested that I would be as tenacious with other things," she said. "It gave him more faith in me."[107]

Other elements of her advice in addition to persistence included taking the time to learn about printing, the effects it can produce and how to get them most economically, then making the designer a working partner by selecting one who is personally compatible, providing information as completely and early as possible, staying in close touch as the job progresses and paying on time.

All these types of advisers may be able to help in finding other useful contacts. The way to evaluate such advisers is to learn about what they have done before and to talk with other people who have worked with them. This leads naturally to further contacts. As a general rule, smaller companies do better working with smaller professional firms and agencies. That way they represent a relatively larger share of the professionals' business and are more likely to get the attention of top members in the professional firms rather than being relegated to apprentices.

Application   *List the tasks for which professional designing and graphics help will be needed by the assigned case venture over its next year, and estimate the workhours those tasks may require.*

Engaging Consultants

Consultants can be found on virtually any topic. Unfortunately, some will claim expertise on almost any issue, even though they may not have that expertise. Making inquiries with other business people who have bought a particular consulting service is probably the best way to check it out. Some specialize in helping prepare business plans, but those who read the plans usually prefer that they be written by the entrepreneurs who will carry them out.

Other Advisers

In addition to professionals there are numerous other types of ad hoc advisers, including the following:

Networks

The crucial role of business contacts in assisting start-up has long been known, but relatively few systematic studies of it have been undertaken. Part of the difficulty is that the contacts are so varied, and which are most useful is

---

[107]J. Donald Weinrauch and Nancy Croft Baker, *The Frugal Marketer* (New York: AMACOM, 1989).

both unpredictable and idiosyncratic. Many times the most useful contacts are those that were acquired before it could be foreseen either that they would be helpful or how they might help. Hence, business contact building is something worth starting at any time, the earlier the better. Moreover, according to a study by Butler and Hansen, breadth in social networks appeared to expand the set of options open to entrepreneurs for start-ups.[108]

Application   *Describe the kind of contacts network the entrepreneur in the assigned case should seek to develop, and suggest how it might be done.*

Directors

Every corporation must have directors, and this necessity provides a platform for recruiting advisers in that capacity. But a director's motivation is always a key question. Providing help usually requires effort and effort usually calls for compensation. There may be some people who will provide effort gratis to a start-up. Here and there an entrepreneur who has prospered and wants "to give something back" or a retired executive who is more concerned with being active than with compensation may be willing to contribute to the venture without compensation. Most others will require it, either in the form of pay, ownership or possibly expenses to meet at a vacation spot. How to provide enough compensation with meager resources can be a major problem for a start-up wanting help from directors. There may be the alternative of an exchange of free help in return from the entrepreneur, but the entrepreneur may not be able to afford the time.

A second problem concerns directors' legal liability. Insurance can be bought to protect directors against lawsuits in performance of their work. But it is usually expensive, reflecting the fact that the risks are significant. These in turn impose a disincentive for people to become directors.

If a company has great ambitions of growing and perhaps one day going public and can back those ambitions up with a convincing plan, it may be able both to attract prominent directors and use them to bolster its image. However, that rarely seems to happen. Even among the *Inc.* 500 companies, which were selected for their high growth rates, 43 percent were found to have no outside directors.[109] At start-up and among more "ordinary" small firms this

---

[108]John E. Butler and Gary S. Hansen, "Managing Social Network Evolution and Entrepreneurial Benefits," in *Frontiers of Entrepreneurship Research, 1988*, eds. Bruce Kirchhoff, Bruce H. and others (Wellesley, Mass.: Babson Center for Entrepreneurial Studies, 1988), p. 430.
[109]"Hands On," *Inc.*, October 1990, p. 151.

percentage would likely be as great or greater.[110] It appears that those companies that add such directors most often seem to do it out of needs that arise downstream from start-up when they and directors can both offer more to each other. [111]

Application   *List the kind of people the assigned case entrepreneur should recruit as directors or an advisory board. Explain what would be in it for them, and lay out an agenda for their next meeting.*

Shareholders

The founding shareholders may include both working and silent (investing or lending only) partners. Silent partners may or may not live up to that name. Those who are not silent may or may not be helpful in their counsel. If they have put their savings into a start-up and it is struggling, they may become anxious about the risk they have bought and consequently plague the entrepreneur with questions and worries about how the business is coming along, when they will be able to get their money out, and so forth. Seasoned entrepreneurs may be helpful advisers as shareholders in start-ups (as Ross Perot may have been to Steve Jobs at Next), but newcomers are less likely to be. Even the value of professional venture capitalists as advisers is the subject of debate as research on it continues. The general answer seems to be that it depends.[112]

Institutional Help

Recognition that new ventures create jobs and add useful new products and services has inspired institutions of various types to help them.

Associations

Trade Associations can be very helpful providers of information on specific industries. Sources of information about them include The *Encyclopedia of Associations* and the *Directory of the National Trade and Professional Associations*

---

[110]Flynn Bucy and Sam Seaman "Relationship Between Role, Composition and Perceived Benefits of Boards of Directors for Privately Owned Firms," in *Frontiers of Entrepreneurship Research, 1988*, eds. Bruce Kirchhoff, Bruce H. and others (Wellesley, Mass.: Babson Center for Entrepreneurial Studies, 1988), p. 499.

[111]Elizabeth Conlin, "Unlimited Partners," *Inc.*, April 1990, p. 71.

[112]Joseph Rosenstein and others, "Do Venture Capitalists on Boards of Portfolio Companies Add Value Besides Money?" and Harry J. Sapienza and Jeffry A. Timmons, "Launching and Building Entrepreneurial Companies: Do The Venture Capitalists Add Value?" in *Frontiers of Entrepreneurship Research, 1989*, eds. Brockhaus, Robert H., Sr. and others (Wellesley, Mass.: Babson Center for Entrepreneurial Studies), 1989, pp. 216 and 245, respectively.

of the United States. These will likely be available at the downtown library if not the local business school library. The associations themselves gather and share information, providing contacts, newsletters and meetings where members can exchange helpful suggestions and moral support.

Application   *In the library, look at a list of associations and state which one(s) the entrepreneur in the assigned case should consider joining and why.*

Government

Federal Government agencies attempt to favor small firms in making purchases and issuing R&D contracts. The Small Business Administration in particular helps by guaranteeing bank loans to start-ups and small firms. It also offers free consultation services, seminars and literature on many aspects of starting and running small businesses. A telephone call to the nearest SBA office can provide an inventory of services available from the agency. A library source of information is *The Monthly Catalog of U.S. Government Publications*. These can be bought from the Superintendent of Documents, U.S. Government Printing Office, Washington, D.C. 20402.

Three government programs under the Small Business Administration that provide direct assistance to smaller firms are the Small Business Institute Program, in which participating universities assign student consulting teams to work with the company, the Service Corps of Retired Executives (SCORE), in which retired executives donate their services and the Active Corps of Executives (ACE), in which currently active executives do so. None of these programs costs money to the company.

State Governments usually seek to help start-up and small firms through publication of booklets on requirements for setting up a business in the state, and sometimes other services. City governments also try to help in various ways. Both the local chamber of commerce and the state department of commerce are places to call for finding out what help is available. A 401-page overall directory published by the U.S. Small Business Administration is *The States and Small Business: A Directory of Programs and Activities*. Another of 170 pages is the *Directory of Federal and State Business Assistance* which is available from the National Technical Information Service (catalog number PB88-101977).

The pros and cons of drawing upon government programs vary from case to case. Some impose strings, while others do not. Some cost money and others are free. The effectiveness of a given program depends upon the particular government people running it, what their prior experience is, how heavily they are scheduled at the moment, and so forth. So it can pay to investigate, provided not too much time is spent on that task.

Universities

Universities provide extension courses on starting and running businesses. Participating in such a seminar can be a way to meet other entrepreneurs who can help. Some universities also operate Small Business Institute programs in which students provide consulting services to entrepreneurs, as mentioned above, for course credit. Some universities also operate Small Business Development Centers in which professionals are employed to provide free consulting services to small firms.

Places to contact at the university are its office of extension programs and its business school. If the entrepreneur has a particular type of help in mind, such as market research or setting up an accounting system, then contact with the chairperson of the department teaching that subject may also be a good place to start.

Application   *Formulate a consulting assignment that might be suitable for a team of students seeking to help the entrepreneur in the assigned case.*

Incubators

Incubators have been set up in some communities to help companies get started. Some provide cheap rent for a year or two. Many provide ancillary services such as Xerox, phone answering, secretarial and possibly accounting and legal help. If the incubator is affiliated with a university, it may also provide access to use of laboratory facilities and to help from faculty and students. Association with other entrepreneurs using the incubator may help provide useful contacts as well as moral support and mutual problem solving.

The number of incubators, according to the National Business Incubation Association, grew from 55 in 1984 to nearly 400 by 1990,[113] more than 100 of which were linked by electronic mail.[114] The largest fraction of incubators (39 percent) are those affiliated with local government agencies and development agencies. Next (17 percent) are those of universities, followed by centers run for profit (14 percent), according to the above association.[115]

As an indication of performance, one incubator in Chicago, begun with a $1.7 million federal grant, was able to report after nine years of operation that it had served 142 companies with such things as cheap rent, shared services and space, business plan help, group consulting and eventually low-cost loans. Sixteen percent of the clients had failed, and one who had grown to 17 employees commented that "It's a shame not all start-ups have this kind of assistance."[116]

---

[113]Leslie Brokaw, "New Businesses," *Inc.*, May 1990, p. 25.
[114]Martha E. Mangelsdorf, "Hotline," *Inc.*, July 1990, p. 27.
[115]Leslie Brokaw, "New Businesses," *Inc.*, August 1990, p. 21.
[116]Martha E. Mangelsdorf, "*Inc.*'s Guide to 'Smart' Government Money," *Inc.* August 1990, p. 60.

Supplementary Reading

New Venture Strategies Chapter 2. (Vesper, K.H., Prentice-Hall, 1990)
New Venture Mechanics Chapter 4. (Vesper, K. H., Prentice-Hall, 1993)

Your Venture Plan

1. List the professional services that would be needed to implement your plan. Prepare an itemized list, with dates, of the costs of those services and the firms that could be expected to provide them at those costs.

2. Pick a banker, lawyer, accountant and any other professionals to be engaged by the venture you are planning. Explain the rationale of your choice.

Your Venture History

1. On a list of all the help sources noted in this chapter:

   - Which came into play when?
   - How would each rate in helpfulness?
   - How much did each cost?

2. For those of the above that had the most positive or negative impact, what was the chain of events?

Exercises

1. Make a list of as many as possible different types of professionals a start-up might obtain help from. For each, note how the amount of payment is determined. Describe the pros and cons, from the venture's viewpoint, of these incentives and what cautions are consequently advisable.

2. Interview an entrepreneur and find out how he or she took care of each of the tasks listed above under professionals. Which tasks turned out to be most critical, and which did professionals give the most help with and/or cost the most for help on?

3. Find out the cost of directors' liability insurance. Discuss alternative answers to the question of who should want to serve as director in a new venture and why. Discuss implications of your answer from an entrepreneur's perspective.

4. Interview one or more of the following to learn what experiences they have had in working with start-up companies as well as what they have concluded from those experiences. Describe your findings and the implications they should have from an entrepreneur's viewpoint.

   a. Lawyer
   b. Accountant
   c. Insurance broker
   d. Advertising agent
   e. Banker

5. For three of the above professionals, make a list of things that can go wrong if he or she does not do a good job for the venture. Be prepared to comment on how the entrepreneur could detect such problems in time to avoid serious trouble.

6. Locate a venture incubator. Describe what it offers, what it charges and how it compares to conventional commercial real estate as a location for three contrasting types of start-ups.

7. Develop an inventory of the governmental assistance programs for entrepreneurs in your local community. Sort them into those aimed at ongoing small firms versus those that help entrepreneurs during start-up.

Case Questions: Davidov, ImageSystems, Milne, Redman

General Case Questions

1. Formulate, as realistically as you can, a hypothetical competitor grid for the venture described in the assigned case. Discuss recruiting actions that could move the venture to a stronger position on the comparison.

2. How well do capabilities of the entrepreneur in the assigned case align with tasks that must be performed to make the venture a success? What complementary talents should he or she seek and through what specific sequence of actions?

3. Envisage some suitable individuals, in terms of their experience and capabilities, whom the entrepreneur(s) might reasonably be able to attract to this venture situation. Briefly describe each of them. Describe what the principal founder should be willing to give up in order to recruit them. Should they accept such terms?

4. Formulate a set of guidelines for the entrepreneur(s) in the assigned case to follow in hiring (if any) such professionals as you think should be hired to help start the venture.

Davidov Case Questions

1. What is your assessment of the role each of the prospective entrepreneurs in this case could most appropriately play to maximize its chances of success?

2. To what extent would it be advisable for each of them to undertake such a role?

3. If they did undertake the roles prescribed above, what would you recommend concerning the division of ownership and control and concerning compensation from the venture?

4. Considering the above and any other relevant information in the case, what would you recommend that the potential entrepreneurs in this case actually do?

ImageSystems Case Questions

1. What sorts of contingencies should be provided for in the articles of incorporation for a company like Imagesystems? What would be the best procedure for working them out?

2. What vulnerabilities of existing companies is Imagesystems seeking to take advantage of? To what sort of competition might it find itself to be most vulnerable, and what could it do about that?

3. What advice should the company's founders follow and why? What advice should it reject and why?

Milne Case Questions

1. Develop a grid which lays out on one side the names of people in the case who should receive ownership in the venture. Along the other side list what different people can best contribute to the venture.

2. State how ownership and responsibilities should be divided in the venture and explain why.

Redman Case Questions

1. What ethical issues do you see in this case, and how should they be treated?

2. If the prospective entrepreneurs in this case decide to start a firm of their own, how should the responsibilities and ownership be divided and why?

Chapter 8

Start-Up

❏ SUBCHAPTER 8A - Selling

Crucial action steps in getting a venture started are to obtain customer orders, deliver on them, collect payment, and keep repeating that cycle, which may require additional financing if the enterprise grows. In each of these areas — selling, delivery and collecting — problems can lie ahead that are worth worrying about at start-up to ward them off or at least be able to respond effectively when they crop up. The problems may occur immediately, later or both.

Five Pathways To New Venture Sales

The different ways to get sales in an enterprise can be grouped into five categories: (1) responding to customer requests, (2) advertising, (3) opening a store, (4) selling by personally "hitting the road," and (5) paying others to do the selling.

Responding

The first of these, responding to some customer's request, is a way many ventures have begun. The entrepreneur was approached by someone either asking how to obtain something or asking the entrepreneur if he or she could provide it.

ASK Computer was started by Sandra Kurtzig when, as a sales representative for General Electric's computer operation, she was asked by a potential customer for something her employer did not offer. When she informed the customer of this, the customer asked why she did not start a company of her own and provide it. She did.

Sometimes, customer requests are more formally publicized. The *Commerce Business Daily*, for instance, prints notices of things the U.S. government would like to buy. It awards contracts totaling $200 billion per year, and its agencies are encouraged by federal policy to buy from small firms when they can. The Small Business Administration helps police these rules and is a good contact to make for information. Other helpful documents are *The U. S. Government Purchasing and Sales Directory*, and *Doing Business With The Government*. State governments also post notices of things they would like to buy and provide information for those interested in bidding on them.

"Catches" in serving as a government contractor include the possibility that some other contractors may have established relationships with agencies that give them advantages in "competitive" proposals. Other drawbacks include drawn-out approvals, slow payment, and programs coming and going capriciously at the whim of Congress and red tape. The following company apparently encountered grief from a combination of governmental factors.

> Comcraft, an independent young phone installation company, noticed a request for quote in the *Commerce Business Daily* in 1987 for installation of a phone system in an Army Corps of Engineers office. Terms of the government request said the system could be either a "key" system or a more complex "PBX" system. For the latter system, however, approval of the General Services Administration would be needed because a PBX would duplicate to some degree a system already used by the GSA, which owned the building used by the Army.
>
> The company's founder, Dominick Macaluso, Jr., discovered that the Army would save over 75 percent of the charges it was paying for use of GSA lines if he installed a PBX system. He said, "We were told that the Army would get anything it wanted, that it would march four-star generals down if it had to." Concluding that he could give the Army a bargain, a PBX system capability for a key system price, he proposed a PBX. Two Army technical evaluators visited the company, examined its equipment and were "enthralled." Comcraft received official notice that it was the most technically-qualified, lowest-cost vendor.
>
> Before it could celebrate, however, the company received another notice, this time from the GSA, that it had disapproved the proposal. Comcraft began a series of appeals. But the end of the government's fiscal year was approaching, motivating government agencies to spend up their budgets. Hence before the appeal process was complete, another company had been given the contract. Instead of the Army getting its savings, the GSA kept its rental income. The GSA telecommunications chief said, "We had already paid for those lines." Comcraft had no contract and was out approximately $25,000 it had spent pursuing it.[117]

For some markets and lines of business a practical device to facilitate response to customers is use of an 800 telephone number and possibly an answering service. Costs include installation plus any directory listing costs and a rate per call depending on where it comes from. A Boston company selling live lobsters, for instance, found it cost them $200 for installation, $1,500

---

[117]Ellen Forman, "Deal Carefully With Uncle Sam," *Venture*, September 1989, p. 14.

per year for directory listing and roughly $2,000 per month for calls, as compared to twice that amount previously spent on responding to collect calls.

Advertising

A second way to get sales is to advertise. The most obvious starting point for many firms is to buy an advertisement in directories such as the Yellow Pages. Thumbing through a phone book makes it quickly apparent that the advertisements vary in size and content. Each advertiser has made independent decisions about which design will be most effective for what purposes. There are choices to be made about which directories, for which geographical areas, what sizes of advertisements, how many should be listed, under what names and with what contents and graphics. The phone company itself may be of some help, and beyond that an advertising agency may have good advice. Visiting some advertisers and asking what their advertising experiments have taught them can also be informative.

Paid advertisements in newspapers, magazines, radio and television are other avenues of advertising. Yet another is to write articles which papers and magazines will print free as information. Posting notices, passing around flyers, sending sales letters, literature, newsletters, staging free lectures, public relations events or stunts and sending samples through the mail are ways of putting out news of what the venture has to offer. Either starting a catalog or seeking space in another company's catalog is also an option.

- In the heyday of hi-fi, many companies started by advertising do-it-yourself kits for building amplifiers, tuners and such in magazines.

- In the early days of the microcomputer, companies such as MITS, IMS and Osborne rapidly generated large sales through advertisements in magazines.

- Flyers stuck under auto windshield wipers or under the door at home are familiar advertising to most consumers.

- Coupon books can be handed out free to students starting the school year and to homeowners.

Another variation on advertising is the use of public relations techniques to get word out about the venture's product or service. Approaches for doing this include the following:

- Writing technical articles for magazines or journals where the publicity can help, or where the publication can be held up to substantiate the technical validity of what the venture sells. Testing the articles by asking other authorities in the field for critiques can help shape them into forms more likely to be accepted.

- Sending press releases to newspapers, magazines or other media announcing what is new about what the venture is up to. These have to contain elements that would be considered news. Testing and comparing ideas for their content against other published news items can be a way of assessing their likely publication. Brainstorming with sympathizers can help generate ideas for making the releases more catchy or newsworthy.

- Seeking interviews with radio or TV to demonstrate what the venture will offer. Practice on audio or videotape and possibly sending copies of the final tapes to stations may help with invitations. These too should be catchy, with visual displays, specimens, props, demonstrations and possibly participation by the interviewer or audience in order to retain interest.

- Becoming involved in publicity causes, public events and/or stunts to draw attention to the company. Corporate contributions to Public Broadcasting System and National Public Radio programs, local arts and music programs, student contest prizes and charities are one form. The founders of Fratelli's Ice Cream, for instance, chose to cosponsor Fourth-of-July fireworks for local visibility in Seattle.

How much to spend on advertising and publicity is a special problem for a new venture. For advertising expenditures in established companies, there are often rules of thumb, such as 1 to 5 percent of gross sales . In a new venture there may be no sales yet and possibly no appreciable amount of available cash, so the percentage could range from an infinite percent of (no) sales to zero. Yet a new company is usually unknown and therefore may have especially great need for advertising. Since its resources are typically very limited, it needs to find ways of getting the most advertising for the least money. To do that, in addition to seeking free publicity, here are some possibilities:

- Business cards and flyers are inexpensive.

- Homemade newsletters can be more effective than slick advertisements for some markets.

- Many small, inexpensive ads can add up to major impact over time.

- Classified ads are much cheaper than display ads.
- Piggybacking on ads of others can allow cost sharing.
- Suppliers often share advertising costs.
- Off-hours on radio, back corners in trade shows, poor locations for signs and last minute fill-ins are often available at low rates and sometimes work.

- Advertising departments of papers, magazines and radio stations will provide free help in ad design.
- Advance payment may yield discounts.
- It may be possible to pay by bartering rather than with cash.
- Frequent checking to see whom the ads are affecting and how can help cut costs.

Information about advertising costs can be found in publications of the Standard Rate and Data Service, available in many libraries as well as from the service itself, whose address is 3004 Glenview Road, Wilmette, Illinois 60691. It lists, for instance, thousands of cooperative advertising programs available from manufacturers throughout the country. The "bad news" about advertising is that the average American is hit with an estimated 500 advertising messages per day but remembers only 12 of them. How to be remembered on an extremely small advertising budget calls for careful thought and very sharp focus of the message.

"Specialty advertising" involves imprinting a company name on innumerable gift items such as calendars, mugs, clocks, rulers, pencils, pens, knives, paperweights, jewelry, bumper stickers, decals, combs and so forth. Although expensive on a per person basis, such advertising is usually sharply-focused so that the total cost is not so great and the impact is high. One company that gave empty flower pots and followed up with flowers to put in them estimated that its campaign was more effective and cost around $5,000 in contrast to an estimated cost of $20,000 for print advertising or $200,000 for a magazine campaign. An important question to consider, aside from cost, is whether the gift will be more effective as a door opener, a reminder or a memento of thanks after a sale.

Application   *What alternative advertising approaches might most likely help the assigned case venture get its first sales? Illustrate on one or more transparencies. How would their costs probably compare? Which should be used and why?*

Storefront

Easiest to see are ventures that got sales through the third approach, which is to open a store. Important variations on this approach are to set up a display at shows, fairs, malls, and auctioning. Choice of location, methods of display and advertising, selection of inventory, pricing, credit policies and methods of dealing with customers are variables that crucially influence results. For some "name brand" chains there are elements of science in controlling these variables. But the science is never perfect, and for new ventures there is inevitably considerable suspense in first opening the store. For some new stores the customers show up soon. For others it takes time to build up a clientele. The fact that many storefronts change tenants from lease to lease demonstrates that for many stores the clientele never becomes adequate to continue the business.

Aspects to consider with a storefront include not only location and cost, as discussed earlier, but also decor, use of signs and point-of-purchase displays, how much inventory to carry, how best to display it and how to arrange the store layout.

Storefronts can be either stationary or mobile, permanent or temporary. One variation, often used by start-ups to make their existence known, test customer responses to what they offer, study what competitors offer, and recruit sales agents, is to open a booth or rent part of the space in someone else's booth at a fair or a trade show. The cost per lead at a trade show has been estimated at around $100 and the added cost of follow-up to close the sale at roughly another $100, though clearly this would vary depending upon a host of variables (selling handicrafts at a fair certainly costs nothing like that), so that the total cost per sale through that avenue would be roughly $200.[118] A guide to show costs is published annually by the International Exhibitors Association of Annandale, Virginia. These costs include those of the exhibit itself, plus the entry fee, travel, transportation, setup, samples and literature expenses. Other helpful information about shows and their costs is published in *Trade Show Week* (2,000 shows) and *Exhibit Schedule* (10,000 shows).

Things to be mapped out clearly in advance include who will be coming to the show(s) selected, what information will be sent in advance, given out at the show or sent later as followup to show attendees, what information will the venture seek to obtain from attendees, what sales results will the venture seek to accomplish through the show, who will help out (sometimes suppliers and/or local governments will), and how the activity itself will be managed. Innumerable "tips" on making the most of trade shows are available in books and magazines that can be located through such sources as those above or the National Association of Exposition Managers. Another way to learn is simply to attend some shows locally. The State Department of Commerce, Chamber of Commerce or local Convention Bureau can provide information about shows coming up.

Designing a layout and display, whether for a store or a show, is an art form that can be very helpful to sales, if well done. Someone with visual talent and originality may have inspiring ideas for how to do it. Those without such gifts can either study the displays of others and copy what works or ask for help from those with the talent.

Application   *What types of storefronts might be most useful for the assigned case venture and how?*

---

[118] J. Donald Weinrauch and Nancy Croft Baker, *The Frugal Marketer* (New York: AMACOM, 1989).

Personal Selling

"Hitting the road," calling on customers and selling personally is a fourth approach to create sales in a new venture. The first sale in a venture is often made by the entrepreneur personally. After that, if the venture survives and grows, subsequent sales are usually made by others. In personal selling, a particularly important quality is credibility as perceived by the potential buyer, as illustrated by the following example.

In 1974 a young man from the Pacific Northwest with an interest in photography learned of the success that a cousin in Southern California was having in producing and selling wall-sized photographic murals. He decided to set up a firm like his cousin's and installed the necessary photographic equipment in a darkroom to do it. Then he began calling on potential customers, telling them what he could do and asking whether they had favorite photos they would like to have made into decorative murals. Unfortunately, his verbal descriptions were not adequate to obtain orders. Consequently, he prevailed upon his cousin to lend him page-sized photographs illustrating different applications the cousin had made in California. When accompanied by these examples, his sales pitch was successful, orders began to come, and before long he was able to replace his cousin's examples with those of his own.

Developing new contacts in personal selling is hard, but can be very rewarding and may be essential. It calls for self-discipline and initiative. Because time is such a scarce resource for a founder, it is vital to define with care whom to go after, what to seek from them, how much effort to apply in each attempt and how to assess the results in planning each next action. Contact building constantly calls for judgment. Insufficient persistence can render efforts futile. However, too much of it applied on the wrong tack can be even more wasteful.

If there is a "technology" side to what the venture will offer, then one way to explain that technology to prospective customers may be to invite them to seminars where it will be explained. These may be given at trade shows, trade association meetings or advertised directly. It is easy to rent a meeting room in a hotel to present the seminar and to advertise it to prospects through direct mail or newspaper advertisements. The seminar can be without charge or for a fee, depending upon what it offers and how prospects are likely to feel about it. Familiar examples are "personal finance" and "real estate" seminars occasionally advertised in local papers. Usually the person attending such seminars first receives information free and is invited to buy literature, tapes and additional seminars for a price. Seminars for industrial customers are usually less carnival-like.

When Bruce Milne and his partners developed a new software package for accountants he organized a seminar presentation to which he personally invited a small number of professionals. There they were able to learn just how the program worked and what it did for them, as well as to exchange information with each other about their needs, problems and possible solutions. Milne put his message across and received feedback that was helpful both in refining his package and securing customers for it.

❖ ❖ ❖

William Delphos became an expert in low-cost government resources for smaller firms to develop overseas sales when he worked for four years as a White House appointee in foreign investment. To find customers as a consultant on the subject, he spent $1,000 putting together a humorous cartoon slide show, then persuaded an electronics trade association to include it among the programs available to their 21 councils across the country which continually offer various programs to their members. This exposure, he said, gave him both credibility and opportunity to display his expertise to prospective customers for his consulting services. He found it best not to attempt any selling at his seminar but to follow up afterwards with a letter to each participant.[119]

Some other ways of personal selling that particularly lend themselves to sharp focus on selected audiences include the following:

- Sales Letters. Mailing lists can be purchased which include only people who fit particular parameters. Companies with such lists will do the addressing, mailing, more if desired. They can be found in the Yellow Pages. Tips on sales letters can be found in books on business communications and magazines such as *Direct Marketing*. Probably several rounds of letters will be needed to "get through."

- Telephone Selling. Although it is sharply focused market-wise, this approach is expensive in time and money compared to sales letters. Advantages, however, are that it allows progressive interrogation of the people called, and can yield much better information. Information about this approach is available from the American Telemarketing Association, 104 Wilmot Road, Deerfield, Illinois 60015. However, the best way to find what works is to write out a script, follow it and modify it with each call until it "peaks out" in effectiveness. The final version is almost certain to be greatly changed in both contents and performance.

Application   *What types of personal selling should be needed at different stages as the assigned case venture develops?*

---

[119]Ibid.

Paying Others

The fifth approach to selling is to pay others for handling it. Alternatives include hiring salespeople as employees, engaging independent representatives, or selling to "middlemen" such as brokers, wholesalers, catalog houses or retailers. Each of these costs money. *Sales and Marketing Management* estimated the cost of an average sales call at $118 in consumer markets, $162 in service markets and $179 in industrial markets. McGraw-Hill estimated the average overall cost as $230 and added that it takes on the average 5.5 calls to get an order. Costs differ depending not only on what is being sold, but also the type of representative used, what the representative does and, of course, how well the selling effort is managed.

Application   *Prepare for presentation in class a personal selling pitch for the product or service of the assigned case venture.*

With each mode of selling there are tradeoffs to consider. For example, independent representatives must be paid only if they accomplish sales, which eliminates the risk of paying for no performance. Commissions, which are paid as a percentage of sales, range considerably as shown in figures of Table 8-1 below, which were taken from *Sales and Marketing Management* magazine's annual "Survey of Selling Costs."

Table 8-1 Sales Commissions in Different Lines of Business

	Percent of Commission Paid		
Line of Business	High	Average	Low
Advertising	24.2%	16.2%	8.1%
Toys, Novelties	12.8	9.3	5.9
Robotics	12.4	10.3	8.2
Building Supplies	10.7	7.7	4.6
Electronics	10.4	8.5	6.5
Consumer Electrical	6.7	5.6	4.6
Lumber	6.4	5.1	3.7

Application   *If the assigned case venture were to pay others to sell for it on commission, what should the commission percentage be and why?*

In addition to the commission, however, there are costs of samples, literature, communications and training that the venture must pay. Moreover, independent agents typically concentrate on only those sales that are largest or come easiest, which is likely to leave out the product of a new company. Selling through brokers and wholesalers lowers the risk of collection problems, but such middlemen have to be convinced that retailers will buy from them, or they will not carry the line. Similarly, retailers must be convinced that consumers will buy, which may require the venture to spend money on advertising and promotions, and those, if not successful, can cost enough to break the venture. Failure can also occur if the venture is successful in persuading consumers, but the wholesalers and retailers do not stock up fast enough to capitalize while the demand exists.

It is not unusual to sell through a combination of the above approaches. For instance, advertising in the Yellow Pages at least and by other means as well, is widely used in combination with a storefront for retailing. Also common is to start with one means of selling and shift to others over time. Some examples include:

An electronics company sold its first few products personally, then rented a booth at a trade show where it distributed advertising brochures and recruited manufacturers' representatives. Technical articles were written for magazines to get word of the products out further. Ultimately, sales grew to a point where the company began adding its own sales employees in place of the manufacturers' representatives.

❖ ❖ ❖

An olive oil company began packaging and shipping in a garage and selling to wholesalers. Due to zoning restrictions the founders moved their operations to an empty storefront. Passersby started asking to buy directly and the founders changed the storefront to a retail operation and moved packaging and shipping to another rented plant.

❖ ❖ ❖

A bakery producing muffins started by selling retail out the front door but found it could make more by selling wholesale out the back door to restaurants.

❖ ❖ ❖

An ice cream company set out to introduce another brand of premium ice cream, only to conclude that it was too late. Other companies had grown too dominant in that market. Consequently, the company dropped its own brand and shifted its sales efforts to persuade stores to buy its premium product under their brands instead.[120]

---

[120]Paul B. Brown, "When Quality Isn't Everything," *Inc.*, June 1989, p. 119.

Chapter 9

Acquisition

❏ SUBCHAPTER 9A - Prospecting

Many firms outlast management by their founders. Hence opportunities for new owners to acquire those firms eventually arise. Sometimes the acquirers are other corporations which want to invest spare resources or simply to expand their empires. Sometimes the acquirers are investors who see the potential of higher returns in majority ownership of smaller companies. Recent years have seen many venture capital firms follow this path, for investment purposes.[131] Finally, sometimes the acquirers are entrepreneurs. In fact, it appears that about a third of entrepreneurs enter business through takeover, while two-thirds start businesses from scratch.[132] How takeover by an entrepreneur can come about is the focus of this chapter.

To enter a business usually requires physical resources. They can include such things as a shop, equipment and inventory. Resources can be obtained new or used and can include only selected parts of a business or a whole ongoing business: the name, customer lists, procedures, contracts, trademarks and perhaps consulting help from the former owner. Advantages of buying an ongoing concern include:

- **Time** is saved from start-up activities (which are usually much more consuming than expected).

- **Risk** of the unexpected is reduced by existence of a "track record" upon which to evaluate the business. Cooper et al. found for instance, that firms acquired by entrepreneurs were more likely to be still operating after three years than those started fresh (69 percent vs. 63 percent).[133]

---

[131]Natalie T. Taylor and Frederick A. Hooper, Jr., "Entrepreneurial Buyouts - Developments and Trends 1978-1988," in *Frontiers of Entrepreneurship Research, 1989*, eds. Brockhaus, Robert H., Sr. and others (Wellesley, Mass.: Babson Center for Entrepreneurial Studies), 1989, p. 575.

[132] Arnold C. Cooper and others, *New Business In America* (Washington, D.C.: The NFIB Foundation, 1990), p. 5.

[133]Arnold C. Cooper, William C. Dunkelberg, and Carolyn Y. Woo, "Survival and Failure: A Longitudinal Study," in *Frontiers of Entrepreneurship Research, 1988*, eds. Bruce H. Kirchhoff, and others (Wellesley, Mass.: Babson Center for Entrepreneurial Studies, 1988), p. 234.

- **Resource requirements** may be reduced if the seller will advance credit and the buyer can borrow additionally from other lenders against company assets.

- **Procedures and habits** of employees, suppliers and customers, which are costly to set up, are already in place.

Such assets are sometimes bought whole and sometimes in part. Franchisors, for example, offer not a going concern, but such elements as an established brand, procedures and equipment which have been developed, tested and proven, training in how to perform functions of the business, guidance in selecting a location and running the business, and possibly help in financing it.

Application   *To what extent does each of the above advantages of buying outweigh start-up as a way of entering the assigned case venture?*

The discussion that follows here will consider, first, the possibility of acquiring an entire going concern and, second, in subchapter (9b), the halfway alternative of buying a franchise instead.

Search

The acquisition process can be divided into three general stages: (1) finding a company to acquire, (2) evaluating it, (3) negotiating the acquisition and (4) managing the acquisition after the deal. The most difficult and crucial of these is usually the first, to find a company that is an attractive acquisition. Less attractive acquisitions, such as small businesses with profit records that are marginal or worse, that require long, tedious hours of work for low pay and that are prone to failure are easy to find through "business opportunities" sections of newspapers and through commercial real estate brokers.

However, businesses that have a significant proprietary advantage in a brand, a product, or a skilled workforce are much sought after by many buyers. Small manufacturing companies with these characteristics are frequently approached by established firms on the prowl for acquisitions. Owners of such firms frequently enjoy owning them and are not anxious to sell. When they do reach a point of wanting to sell they can fairly easily find interested buyers and typically prefer to sell to those buyers with the greatest resources and/or demonstrated business success record as proof that they will carry on the firm successfully. So for a would-be buyer the biggest problem is to find an attractive firm whose owner is inclined to sell to him or her.

One way acquisitions are found is through employment. An aging owner may want to change lifestyle and therefore sell to a younger employee in his or her company. Or in a larger company, top management may decide to sell off a department or division for one or more of the following reasons:

- The division no longer fits well with the corporation's main thrust or goals.

- The division is losing money and is distracting management attention from higher priority concerns.

- The corporation is short on cash and can increase liquidity by selling something off.

- The employees have seen a way to make the division worth more and are consequently offering a price higher than the corporation feels the division is worth as part of the corporation.

An example of employee buyout as a way of entering business is Leslie Otten, whose venture turned out to be a ski resort.

In his mid-20s, Otten was working for a ski resort in Vermont when his employer dispatched him to manage a small resort it had recently acquired in Maine. "He was stuck in the back of nowhere," his wife Chris observed, "and people paid little attention to him....Every spring he'd say, 'We're outta here,' and we'd write up a new resume. But then he'd stay around to paint the chair lift."

It troubled him that the owners showed no inclination to invest and build the enterprise up further, and around 1976, four years after he had joined the company, Chris recalled, he began talking about what he would do "if this were my place."

By 1980 the resort was losing $240,000 per year on revenues of $541,000, and the owners were open to selling it. "I turned 31 years old," Otten said, "and I was ready for something. You could have put me almost anywhere, into almost any venture." He arranged with the owners to take ownership of the business in exchange for an $840,000 note.

He began by cutting costs, then adopted a strategy that contrasted with other ski resorts by emphasizing the quality of the skiing rather than amenities of the lodge. Financial performance turned around. By 1986 the company's profits were over $1.6 million per year and by 1988 they were over $6 million.[134]

Otten encountered the fortunate coincidence that the company he worked for was one he could acquire. In general, however, such an event is unlikely. For the entrepreneur who decides to pursue an acquisition-entry strategy there may be no other choice except to go looking for an available company. Some possible sources of acquisition leads include the following:

[134]Bill McGowan, "The Turnaround Entrepreneur," *Inc.*, January 1990, p. 53.

- Classified ads in the "business opportunities" sections of both local and national newspapers. In local papers small service firms will predominate, along with "hustles" for making money without knowing much, doing much or investing much, so they will say. Classified advertisements for more substantial types of businesses such as manufacturing companies are more likely to be found in national papers such as the *Wall Street Journal*.

- Business brokers. Usually, these are real estate brokers whose licenses permit them to claim brokerage fees on sales of businesses as well as properties. Typically, however, the business listings are a small or virtually non-existent sideline. Aside from the classified listings, there simply don't tend to be many businesses actively looking for buyers. (If a business for sale was highly attractive, why would the broker not buy instead of sell it?)

- Cold calls. The fact that a business is not looking for a buyer does not mean its owner would not sell it if the price and terms were "right." The owner may be comfortable and not willing to consider anything but an unjustifiably high price. Or possibly the owner will have become unenthused about the business and just not yet reached a point of seeking a buyer. Entrepreneurs have found firms like the latter simply by walking in office doors and asking at one company after another until hitting "pay dirt."

- Other contacts. Besides business brokers, people who might know about firms for sale include:

  - Bank trust officers responsible for custody of companies whose owners have died.
  - Attorneys whose clients want to rearrange their estates.
  - Commercial loan officers who may have loans out to firms in need of new management and funding.
  - Accountants with clients who need management help or want to get out of their firms.
  - Other entrepreneurs who know of colleagues who should want to sell out.

Application   *Which of the above sources should be most likely as a way of finding the assigned case venture as an acquisition for one who had no prior link to it?*

A positive aspect of seeking to buy a business is that the task of finding one lends itself much more to systematic searching than does the opportunity for starting a new one. That is not to say the finding is easy. But the number of possibilities, although large, is at least finite, and they can readily be located, categorized and checked out. The diary of an entrepreneur, Hendrix Niemann, who went searching for an acquisition after losing his job ("If 'resigned' suggests that it was entirely my doing, that's not a fair characterization") included the following comments.[135]

> I started by wading through the ads slowly, one by one ANSWERING/ BEEPER SERVICE ANTIQUE RESTORATION AUTO BODY/PAINT .I had absolutely no idea what I was looking for but I ll know it when I see it. Certain names and/or phone numbers kept popping up. These must be the brokers or agents for the owners.
>
> I had started my first business, a regional magazine, along with my college roommate when I was 24. We ended up being taken over five years later. I started a magazine for someone else .and I had been the CEO of an independent TV news company in Washington.
>
> This time I wanted to do it all myself; no partners, no investors, just me . I d contact all the lawyers, accountants and bankers in Annapolis. Surely they would have a client or friend who wanted to retire. I pictured a friendly man of around 65, getting tired, nobody to turn the company over to, wanting to take care of his longtime employees. Not greedy, doesn t want a lot of money down, a nice long-term payout. I m his salvation, and the company s. A nice little business. Doing a couple million. Doesn t really matter what it is. No retail, of course, but maybe light manufacturing or some kind of distributorship, or a niche service business How tough can it be to find something like this? I ll probably have several to pick from.
>
> Nothing. A dry hole. Dead ends .The time had come to take on the business brokers .I started with the one offering the hospital transcription service. Like many business brokers, he was a realtor who had kind of backed into selling businesses. He had no formal business or accounting background. He came to our appointment armed with a confidentiality agreement and four typed pages about the transcription company. The first three showed revenues and expenses for 1986, 87 and 88. The fourth sheet was a projection for 1989. There was no balance sheet, no customer list, no promotional literature, no written history of the business. He said none of that existed, that he had spent days just pulling together what I held in my hand .
>
> On to the next .He said, I need some venture capital. I happen to be a small investor in a company that s going to make a computer screen that will revolutionize the industry. He told me all about it, for an hour and a half. I asked him if he had any companies for sale that I might be interested in. Not right now. I ll call you. And so it went.

The difficult task of search continued, and eventually Niemann located a lead which worked out through answering a blind classified advertisement in the *Wall Street Journal*, "after 17 business brokers, dozens of blind ads and four months." The advertisement for this company had been placed by a business broker. Other entrepreneurs have found their leads through brokers and meth-

---

[135]Hendrix F.C. Niemann, "Buying a Business," *Inc.*, February 1990, p. 28.

ods which failed previously. No systematic study has been made of which search methods work best for what kinds of entrepreneurs and what kinds of ventures.

Checkout

Once contact with a company whose owner is open to selling is made, the task is to check it out for "fit." This process must work from two viewpoints, that of the owner and that of the buyer. From the owner's perspective, why is this the best buyer available? Unless the buyer is going to pay cash, what is the assurance that he or she will be effective enough as a new owner to assure that the business will survive and make its payments on time? The present owner may be emotionally attached to the company and to its employees. Will this buyer be the best person to take care of them, see that the firm continues and prospers? What evidence is there in the buyer's prior experience to support such a hope?

From the buyer's side a different set of questions applies. Some deal with the current balance sheet. What assets and liabilities will the buyer really get with the business? Other questions deal with future cash flow. Can the company cash inflows meet its needs, plus those of the new owner plus whatever payments are required to carry out terms of the takeover? Depending upon the company, here are somewhat more specific questions to consider:

Assets

- Which assets will be bought as part of the deal and which will not? Will the building stay with the owner? If so what will be the terms of the lease? If those had been the terms previously, how would the company's income statement have looked? If there is a present lease, is it transferable, how long will it run, and are there rights to renew, reassign or sublet? Will it constrain the business?

- Company name, patents, trademarks, licenses, customer and mailing lists, credit records, supplier arrangements, know-how for performing the work, ongoing pattern of employee and customer activities. Are they effective? How assuredly will they be retainable by the buyer? How hard would it be to replicate them? Will the seller or competitors have incentive or be able to undercut them? What is the company's reputation? According to whom?

- Tooling, fixtures, equipment and furniture. To what extent are they in good condition and up to date? How much could they be sold for separately? How much would it cost to replace or upgrade them?

- Inventory and receivables. How much must the company be prepared to carry? Which ones will be transferred in the sale and how? How will they be valued, at what time and by whom?

Liabilities

- Accounts payable. What will they consist of at the time of sale, who will pay them when, and what is the assurance that the seller will follow through on any promises?

- Hidden liabilities. What precautions should be taken, both through inspection and in the purchase agreement, to cover any non-apparent liabilities, such as impending lawsuits, customer claims, outstanding warranties or other obligations of the company? Are all obligations such as time payments, back taxes, and accrued employee holiday pay considered and provided for by written promise of the seller?

- Credit. Does the company have any problems with suppliers that may surface later? How good will credit be under the new owner?

Cash Flow

- How much working capital has the company needed in the past, and how will this change under new ownership? How will the timing of payments to suppliers and collections from customers shift after the sale?

- What will the future pattern of sales most likely be, and what capital will be needed to finance that?

- How will the buyer cover living expenses simultaneously with purchase payments to the seller?

- Have all new costs of recruiting, repairs, modernization, redesign or retraining been included?

Application   *How should the above checkout questions be rank ordered for application to the assigned case venture?*

Perhaps more important than any of the above questions is that of whether any other issue of importance has not been considered. Every business is a special case with unique issues of its own. Possibly, the entrepreneur will think of new questions through careful analysis and development of a plan to make the most of the business. It might be advisable to consult an expert on that particular type of business, such as the operator of a similar but not competing firm. Certainly, it will be advisable to bring in one or more experts on such subjects as law, accounting, appraisal and taxes.

The main indicator of whether a company acquired by an entrepreneur will succeed is most often how well the company was doing before takeover. A company with a well-accepted product or service can be hard to kill, while one without that may be hopeless, regardless how dedicated and intelligent the new management. Copies of the income tax reports filed by the business and/or its owner over recent years can be very helpful for gauging past performance. They may be on the conservative side as regards net profit and salaries, since there is incentive for the owner to minimize taxes by expensing as many things against them as possible. However, if cost of goods sold is computed based upon inventory valuations that were already written down in prior years, then that figure may be an understated cost. Another understated cost may be depreciation if equipment was already written off in prior years.

Prior experience in the business or in a similar line of business may help, but is clearly not a prerequisite for success with an acquisition. Many entrepreneurs who took over firms in lines of work where they had no prior experience have succeeded magnificently. Interestingly, it is not so easy to say the same for companies that acquire other companies.

Valuation

Such analysis of financial records is an important part of determining what price and terms should be suitable for buying a business. If the seller has already proposed a price, there is the choice of whether to haggle over it or to accept the price and negotiate on terms instead. For assessing price, a variety of approaches are possible including:

- Seller's offered price
- Present value discounted future cash flow
- Present value with a control premium[136]
- Multiple of earnings of comparable companies
- Balance sheet book value
- Book value corrected to include goodwill
- Market value indicated by other offers
- Price of similar companies sold
- Replacement cost
- Liquidation value

---

[136]Ellyn E. Spragins, , "Locking Up Good Value," *Inc.*, November 1989, p. 157.

Application   *Insofar as possible, develop a sale price for the assigned case venture using each of the above methods. In light of them all, what would be a fair price?*

An important element to include in assessment of the firm is what salary and other fringe benefits accrue to the buyer. These may, particularly in smaller firms, be much greater than the profits. Whether they or other customary company expenditures have changed recently and thereby affected the apparent profit level can also be important.

In the case of Hendrix Niemann, the business broker, Lauren Finberg, sent him a package of information which included proposed terms of a deal. He recalled:

> *Of greatest importance to me was a two-pager showing how I could purchase the company with 100 percent financing, get the owner his purchase price, service the debt and still take out 75 percent of what I had been earning before.[137]*

Subsequently, however, an item-by-item physical valuation of the assets, coupled with new figures showing decline in earnings lowered the company's estimated worth and cash-generating ability. Niemann continued:

> *When the inventory was complete, it came in at 60 percent of its stated value on the balance sheet and $16,000 less than my accountant s worst-case scenario. We talked about what the company was worth and agreed that with the combination of the ongoing losses for the year, the old receivables and the inventory reductions, it was worth about half the previous year s book value. And that was to be our offer, no more, no less, take it or leave it. Book value. Period. The purchase price had come down a full 50 percent from the amount we had agreed to that July day in the hot, unlit Italian restaurant. The offer was accepted within 24 hours.[138]*

Disappointment in the true value of assets, as opposed to what the seller claims they are worth, is a frequent occurrence among buyers. Another entrepreneur who bought a company which included general-purpose machines recalled a setback even after he had taken the precaution of having a used-equipment dealer give him an appraisal on them.

> *I had bought equipment before based on appraisals. Normally, there would be a statement at the bottom of the dealer s appraisal sheet to the effect that as of this day we will agree to pay X dollars for this equipment. That lets you know that it is really worth the figure they give. But this time I did not notice that the statement was different, and instead it said something to the effect that this is*

---

[137]Niemann, "Buying a Business," p. 38.
[138]Ibid.

our best judgment as to what this equipment is worth. As it turned out, the equipment was actually worth only about 60 percent of the estimate, and I got stuck.

This company buyer also found other problems with the business. Financial statements prepared by his own accountant turned out to contain substantial errors which lowered the value of what he thought he had bought. The company's job costing system was woefully inadequate and had to be revamped. Finally, the head man in the shop, who knew the most about how to run it and had been considered invaluable to the buyer, turned out to have a serious drinking problem and had to be let go. The buyer ultimately was able to keep operating at a profit, but one substantially lower than he had projected.

One way of viewing a prospective venture which may help in valuation is to consider acquisition versus start-up of the same firm, which could avoid many of these "inherited" problems. Could the prospective entrepreneur accomplish such a start-up? How much would it cost and how much time would be required? Answering these questions should help bracket the high end of what could justifiably be paid for the company.

Credibility

The seller is likely to care greatly about two things: First, that he or she is fully paid in accordance with whatever deal is struck for the business, and second, that the business continue in satisfactory condition, maintaining jobs for its employees and carrying on the entity which the seller grew accustomed to regarding as an original proprietary creation, a personal property or both. To feel assured that these will happen, the seller will want the company sold to someone capable and dedicated to accomplishing them.

A record of integrity should clearly be regarded as necessary for the buyer, since that person will, after takeover, be in a position both to "loot" the business and to let purchase payments lapse. A tight contract may be able to mitigate damage from such acts to some degree, but cannot prevent them entirely. If a buyer with integrity cannot be found, the seller would likely be better off either to keep the business or else to liquidate it.

A young man, here referred to as "H," had passed through a series of ventures, one of which had failed and gone into receivership. Subsequently, however, he accomplished a successful acquisition, which was sold and left him with money to invest. With a partner he began looking for possibilities.

The partner inquired at banks about possible firms to buy and came up with several leads. On the way to one of them with H he was describing it as a small distributorship owned by an elderly man and his wife who seemed to be slipping in their capability to run the business and might do well to sell it before anything went seriously wrong with it. He recalled being surprised when

H looked at him with a big smile and said, "Let's see if we can steal it."

Shortly thereafter, the partner received a call from a venture capitalist he knew who said he had heard the partner was looking for deals with H. Did the partner, he asked, know about H's previous business practices? Did he know H had gone through personal bankruptcy for $7,000? No, the partner replied. The capitalist recounted how his firm had invested in a venture run by H, who had bordered on fraud in running it.

"For instance," the capitalist said, "he counted sales early and expenses late. He would have his people put stuff on the loading dock, tally it sold, then take it back into the shop. We lost a couple hundred thousand on our investment in that company, but that isn't what made me angry. It was H's dishonesty.

"I can give you names of other reputable people who will bear me out on this. This guy is a pathological liar. If you get involved with him, you deserve what happens to you and so does whomever you two buy a business from."

After this conversation, the partner quietly stopped looking for acquisitions, made himself hard for H to get hold of and went on to other things, as did H.

Among acceptable potential buyers with unsullied reputations credibility will be determined by further factors such as the following five:

Financial Strength A buyer with savings may be able to make a substantial cash down payment to give substance to the deal. Pledging any personal assets, such as home equity, may help. Even greater help will be co-signature by another individual with substantial assets.

Track Record "What has this person done before that demonstrates he or she can tackle a difficult problem and see it through to a solution despite major obstacles?" This will be a natural question for a seller to ask. Another is "What challenges has this person failed to tackle or tackled and failed to meet?" Asking for references and asking the references for other references are logical ways to seek answers.

Related Experience Having worked in the industry of the acquisition will look especially good, even though acquisitions frequently are made by people without that advantage. More relevant, perhaps, will be prior experience in general management, which demonstrates the buyer's capability to run a business.

Persuasiveness Selling is inescapably an emotional experience, and although it would seem logical to base the deal on more objective factors such as those above, sellers in fact prefer to sell to people they like. Careful study of the business followed by thoughtful planning and forecasting of its future under the prospective buyer, as well as diplomatic handling of the checkout and negotiations, may overcome other weaknesses on the buyer's part.

Seller's Urgency If the seller wants badly to sell and does not have other attractive buyers, that may be the most powerful persuasion of all. Unfortunately for the buyer, such a circumstance is not something the buyer can create. To the extent it can be controlled, the seller has the choice whether to sell or not. Sometimes, sellers postpone selling too long, then get in a hurry to complete it and aren't able to muster the self discipline required to attack the selling task in a systematic and thorough way, which gives the buyer a strong advantage.

Supplementary Reading

New Venture Strategies Chapter 9. (Vesper, K.H., Prentice-Hall, 1990)

Your Venture Plan

1. Describe the elements in your proposed venture that could be obtained by acquiring one or more other existing companies, and estimate the cost of obtaining them through acquisition versus fresh start-up.

2. Assess the options of start-up versus acquisition as a way of entering the venture you have been working on.

Your Venture History

1. What opportunities can be seen in hindsight for the founders of this venture to have bought out an existing company rather than to have started a new one?

2. How could those have been discovered by the founders through a deliberate searching process?

3. How well-qualified as buyers should the founders have seemed from a seller's point of view?

Exercises

1. Interview someone who acquired a firm. Ask how he or she found it and how someone else looking for a firm to buy could best go about finding one.

2. Discuss the appropriateness of a search criterion which says simply, "I'll know it when I see it."

3. Carry out one or more search modes, such as using the "business opportunities" section of the newspaper classified advertisements, contacting a business broker, or cold calling on companies to find a business for sale.

4. Test the theory that "any business is for sale if the price is right" by interviewing the owner(s) of one or more local firms.

5. Draft a list for checking out a prospective acquisition, and apply it as best you can to one or more local firms, whether they are for sale or not.

❏ SUBCHAPTER 9B - Dealing

Negotiation

If the buyer is regarded as highly credible by the seller, negotiating the purchase can be a very short and simple process. As a division officer in a privately held aerospace corporation, Daryl Mitton was well-known to the managers above him when his CEO decided the company should rid itself of Mitton's division.

> *No sooner did he announce that my division was to be sold, than he suggested that I buy it. We came to an agreement on terms of the sale in very short order. I would buy the hard assets at book value. His firm would loan the total amount for the purchase of these assets, with the loan secured by the assets and repayable over five years. I would purchase the existing inventories for cash, payable in 90 days. His firm would supply headquarters support services for up to 90 days at cost.[139]*

It was to Mitton's advantage in working out his deal that the company knew him, and he was intimately familiar with the division he was buying from having worked in it.

In contrast, Hendrix Niemann had no prior knowledge of his acquisition, and the path to agreement on a deal was correspondingly bumpier. His deal to buy the company had almost foundered repeatedly: on down valuing of assets, finding hidden liabilities, learning that key employees were set to leave, running into trouble with banks trying to obtain financing, and at the last minute further problems with the seller's attorney. The deal had been on the attorney's desk two weeks before closing. But it received no attention, drew no suggestions for changes and provoked no objections until Niemann went to the bank, obtained the down payment check, on which interest immediately began accruing, and arrived at his attorney's office, where Lauren Finberg, the broker, was already waiting to close the deal with the seller, Peter Klosky and Peter's lawyer. As Niemann described it:

> *Peter and his attorney were late. When they did arrive, they wanted to rewrite the whole deal. Better for Peter s taxes this way. We re not changing any amounts, just the way it s paid out. And, by the way, we re not satisfied with the collateral you re using to secure the note to Mr. Klosky. Did we neglect to mention that before? Well, it doesn t really matter if we settle today, does it?[140]*

---

[139]Daryl C. Mitton, "The Anatomy of A High Leverage Buyout," in *Frontiers of Entrepreneurship Research, 1984,* eds. John A. Hornaday and others (Wellesley Mass.: Babson Center for Entrepreneurial Studies, 1984), p. 414.

[140] Hendrix F.C. Niemann, "Buying a Business," *Inc.,* February 1990, p. 38.

Niemann and his attorney refused to yield, gambling that the seller would give in. He did, and the deal went through. Had it not, there would likely have been further protracted negotiations, more legal expenses and in the end, perhaps no deal at all, just the search for another job.

Application   *List and rank the strengths and weaknesses in bargaining positions of buyer and seller in the assigned case.*

Deals

There are two principal dimensions to deals, the price and the terms. Usually, a seller will have a price clearly in mind and some ideas about kinds of terms that will be acceptable or desirable. A possibility, for instance, might be:

Price $500,000

For Going concern, name, tooling, equipment, customer list and records, plus inventory valued at $200,000, to be verified by mutual physical count at time of deal; price to be adjusted according to any discrepancy. Seller will keep company bank account and receivables. Seller also agrees to pay all payables outstanding at time of purchase. Buyer assumes the existing lease.

Down Payment 30 percent at time of closing.

Terms Balance to be paid over five years with interest at 2 percent over prime on unpaid balance.

In this deal the buyer must come up with a down payment and working capital except for inventory. Possibly this can be borrowed at the bank, which would make it a completely leveraged buyout. Personal savings may still have to be used by the buyer to live on until the company generates enough cash to meet payroll, plus debt payments plus salary for the buyer. Savings may also be needed for coping with unwanted surprises—a machine breaks down, a theft occurs, some supplier wants advance payment, legal fees of the deal are higher than expected, and so forth.

Variations on such deals are endless. Making part of the purchase price a consulting contract to the seller, for instance, makes that part tax-deductible to the business, although not to the seller. If the seller claims the company has higher earning potential than the buyer believes, then perhaps part of the price should be in the form of a royalty on sales for a specified period of time based upon the seller's claim. Or to lower the price, perhaps the seller may keep some furniture or some general-purpose equipment of the company which is not immediately needed for production. To make the deal more secure to the seller, possibly the buyer will agree not to take any cash out of the company personally, living on income provided by a spouse perhaps, until a certain percentage of the outstanding debt is repaid. Or perhaps the buyer's promise to pay can be backed up by a cosigner, who in turn may take a percentage interest in the company or a royalty on sales.

The shop itself, if the company owns it, may be included in the deal, or the seller may sell all the assets except real estate and lease the shop to the buyer. Leasing can lower the purchase price and let the seller retain an income stream from rent. In such a case, of course, the buyer needs to add to the cash outflow, rental costs which may not have appeared there historically. Many other details must be considered as well, such as:

- What assets of the business guarantee any note the seller may be accepting? Must other loans to the company be subordinated?

- Should the seller sign a non-competition agreement, and if so, for what activities, time and geographical area?

- Is every single asset to be transferred listed in the agreement?

- How about shares of any stock, articles of incorporation and minutes of shareholders' meetings?

- Is there certification that shareholders have duly authorized the sale?

- What does the seller guarantee about outstanding liabilities, claims or lawsuits against the company?

- Does the seller have partners, and if so, are they signing too?

- Exactly when does the buyer take over what? Are there any protections for the seller to cover things the buyer might do after sale?

- What are the buyer's longer-term aims for the firm? Are there any constraints on how the buyer can dispose of assets or the business?

Application   *What would be answers to the above questions insofar as possible for the assigned case venture?*

Signing the deal will complete the third of four big tests involved in business entry via acquisition. The first is to find an acceptable company to buy, as discussed in the preceding subchapter (9a). Second is to demonstrate credibility to the seller, as mentioned earlier in this subchapter. Third is the deal, and fourth the transition to new management. It is at this fourth stage that many acquisition deals, particularly when the acquirer is a larger corporation, falter and ultimately fail. Corporation managements tend to perform heavy-handed acts, such as changing the name of the acquisition, imposing new internal systems and new managers, showing disregard for methods that have traditionally worked well for the acquired company and disrespect for its employees. These kinds of measures add confusion and drive out key employees who have other options so that the acquired company, even though it may be able to draw on greater financial strength from its new parent, becomes weaker and ultimately gets sold again or possibly even closed down.

Application   *What deal terms, in order of importance, should (a) the seller and (b) the buyer seek to obtain in the assigned case?*

Although systematic statistics are limited, entrepreneurs appear to fare much better with their acquisitions than do corporations.[141] They are dependent on existing employees and know it, consequently treating them with care and respect for their views and interests. Because they are typically risking everything they own and will earn for the foreseeable future, they simply must find ways to make their acquisitions work out, and usually they do.

Franchising as a Compromise

An alternative which combines some elements of taking a job, starting a new company and taking over one already going is to buy a franchise. In their study of 2,994 small firms, Cooper et al. reported that this option often played a role.

One quarter (26 percent) began operations with some type of franchise, though just 12 percent reported that at least three-quarters of their sales came from franchised goods or services. The latter 12 percent corresponds to the number who operated under a franchise name (11 percent). No relationship existed between the possession of a franchise or operation under a franchise name and survival. However, a negative relationship existed between the percent of franchised sales and growth.[142]

It was estimated in 1989 that there were over 3,000 franchise chains in the U.S. operating over 500,000 outlets.[143] Restaurants were estimated in 1990 to account for 102,000 outlets, gas stations 112,000 and business aids and services 67,000, with the latter having grown 21 percent since 1988.[144]

Many franchises are simply dealerships (e.g. a Ford dealership). Others are so-called "format franchises" wherein some company with a proven operating formula, such as McDonald's, sells (1) rights for use of that formula, plus (2) training, (3) special equipment, (4) help in choosing a location, (5) periodic review and guidance on performance, plus (6) advertising and (7) use of the brand in return for an up-front franchise fee and/or a royalty on sales.

Claimed advantages of starting with a franchise are that the entrepreneur need not look farther to find a business idea, need not invest time in puzzling

---

[141]Robert B. Brown, John E. Butler, and Karl H. Vesper, "Performance After Acquisition: The Role of Entrepreneurs," in *Frontiers of Entrepreneurship Research, 1989*, eds. Brockhaus, Robert H., Sr. and others (Wellesley, Mass.: Babson Center for Entrepreneurial Studies), 1989, p. 575.
[142]Arnold C. Cooper and others, *New Business In America* (Washington, D.C.: The NFIB Foundation, 1990), p. 5.
[143]Carol Steinberg, "The Right Deal," *Venture*, June/July 1989, p. 53.
[144]Leslie Brokaw, "New Businesses," *Inc.*, May 1990, p. 25.

out a plan for the business and learning how to pick a location, and may not have to search for financing, which the franchisor company may conveniently provide. There are also claims that odds of failing are lower, since the formula has already been proven to work at other locations. Doubt about the latter claim, at least, has appeared in the study of 2,994 firms by Cooper et al., which found no relationship between possession of a franchise or operation under a franchise name and survival three years after start-up.[145] Undoubtedly, survival of some franchises is much more probable than others.

Of more significant interest to the prospective franchisee should be the level of profitability. Cooper et al. did find that franchise-based start-ups grew faster than independents. However, profitability assessment must take into account (1) the amount invested in shop, equipment and inventory, (2) the cost of the franchise fee, and (3) the impact on profits of any royalty fees. After subtracting those, discounting for a suitable return on the investment in the business, and taking into account the hours worked, the income to the franchisee may not be very attractive. It will probably cost more to start a franchise than to buy or start a comparable business, and the profits, after royalties, may well be less with a franchise. Certainly, the freedom to manage will be less.

Some indication of franchise costs can be seen in the following examples:[146]

- CelluLand (cellular phone stores) - Fee $25,000, royalty 5 percent, plus store cost $80,000 to $250,000

- Papyrus (greeting card stores) - Fee $29,500, royalty 6 percent, plus store cost $70,000 to $150,000

- Valvoline (auto oil change) - Fee $35,000, royalty 6 percent, plus store cost $55,000 to $100,000

Net income is generally not reported, but varies widely with volume and how the owner chooses to allocate expenses. The projected income statement for a new pizza franchise was reported by *Inc.*[147] (See Table 9-1.)

Of the $325,000 investment required, it was projected that $75,000 would be for equipment, $13,000 for a point-of-sale system, and $135,000 for the modular building to house the store. Experts in similar industries polled by the magazine were divided about whether the concept, fast window-pickup pizza, would succeed. Most said no.

---

[145]Cooper and others, *New Business In America*, p. 5.
[146]Echo M. Garrett, "Ten Franchises on a Fast Track," *Venture*, March 1989, p. 21.
[147]Joshua Hyatt, "The Next Big Thing," *Inc.*, July 1990, p. 44.

Table 9-1 Sales and Expense Projections for a Proposed New Pizza Franchise

Sales		$520,000
Expenses		
Food Purchases	140,400	
Other Costs of Goods	36,400	
Labor and Benefits	145,600	
Royalty	20,800	
Advertising	26,000	
Land Rent	25,000	
Utilities	15,000	
Delivery Expenses	6,500	
Miscellaneous	28,900	
Depreciation	43,642	
Total Expenses		488,242
Net Profit Before Tax		$31,758

Very important beyond financial considerations is the extent to which the entrepreneur will find the work of franchisee satisfying. A franchise typically places very significant restrictions on flexibility in managing. What products or services to offer, how to make them, how much to charge, how to advertise, what decor to have in the store and how to run operations may all be tightly controlled by the franchisor, leaving the franchisee feeling more like a middle manager or shop worker than an entrepreneur. Perceptions vary among franchisees, however, and some see their work as more entrepreneurial than others.[148]

Because of abuses in the past, laws have been developed to curb and control franchisors, and these vary from state to state. Consequently, it is advisable to engage a lawyer who specializes in franchises and has extensive experience in the state where the entrepreneur's business is to be located. Checking with other franchisees who have bought from the same franchisor and perhaps with some of their employees is another obvious precaution to take before buying. The Chamber of Commerce, the Better Business Bureau and banking connections may also be able to add helpful information to that which will be provided by the franchisor.

Some pitfalls that others have run into in dealing with franchisors in the past have included:

---

[148]Cecilia M. Falbe, Ajith Kumar and Thomas C. Dandridge, "Industry and Firm Influences on Entrepreneurial Behavior Among Franchisees," in *Frontiers of Entrepreneurship Research, 1989*, eds. Brockhaus, Robert H., Sr. and others (Wellesley, Mass.: Babson Center for Entrepreneurial Studies), 1989, p. 559.

- Formats that may sound good but don't really work
- Promises of training that are not fulfilled
- Fees and charges by franchisors that eliminate franchisee profits
- Franchisees becoming stuck with unsalable inventory from the franchisor
- Promises of advertising that are not fulfilled
- High-pressure selling that does not allow the prospective franchisee to evaluate sensibly
- Failure to reveal negative aspects of the franchise firm's past performance
- Failure by the franchisee to appreciate just what it will be like to work "for" the franchisor
- Failure by the franchisee to obtain input from other franchisees and a qualified franchise lawyer before signing the franchisor's contract

Checklists for evaluating franchisors and their franchises are readily available in books about franchising and from governmental agencies such as the Small Business Administration. Many of the problems that might arise, however, are difficult to anticipate either with or without a list. One entrepreneur, who later became highly successful in building a company, American Photo Group, which he sold to Eastman Kodak for an estimated $45 million, recalled his first business as a franchisee.

> I had a Burger Chef franchise when I was 21. It was terrible. I was thrown into two weeks of training at a hamburger school, and I didn t understand anything. I worked seven days a week, 12 to 15 hours a day. I took off one afternoon for my wife s uncle s funeral. I didn t know what was going on. I couldn t tell day from night for seven months. I must have been one of the worst managers Burger Chef ever had. But I had so many things go wrong. We were in a shopping center that was under construction, and there was a big economic crisis. Interest rates shot through the roof. So they stopped building the shopping center and shut down the road in front of us. The whole thing was a disaster. My father-in-law helped finance the deal, and we lost everything he put into it $70,000.[149]

Franchises can be acquired second-hand as going concerns, just as can independent businesses. The fact that the franchise may be well-known and that the unit for sale may have records of its past performance does not assure that the buyer is getting full value for the purchase price.

---

[149]"Thriving On Order," *Inc.*, December 1989, p. 47.

A 41-year-old Seattle man had worked independently in home remodeling and operating his own auto generator repair shop. Through an acquaintance he learned of a transmission repair shop for sale operating under a well-known franchise. Records indicated that the present owner had been able to draw an income from the business which the prospective buyer found attractive.

Several days after taking over, he was told by the employees that they had been promised raises and would quit if they did not receive them. Not knowing how he would replace them, the buyer agreed, and found his labor costs were now 70 percent of revenues instead of 60 percent. Shortly after that he found that many people who needed transmissions repaired were poorly prepared to pay cash for the work, and as a result his cash flow squeezed ever more tightly.

Total sales were also disappointingly below what they had been under the previous owner. Discussing this with workers in the shop, the buyer was told that prior management had seen to it that virtually every car brought into the shop for inspection was found to need expensive repairs urgently, regardless of its condition. Such a procedure had not occurred to the buyer, who prided himself on honest business practices.

Finally, order processing in the shop, he found, was sloppy. Estimates were lost, there was no way to trace labor costs on jobs, transmission parts could not be found, and it was impossible to reconcile the company checkbook. To correct these problems, the buyer started a job-numbering system to trace labor and parts costs, hired a part-time bookkeeper to reconcile accounts, negotiated with a finance company to provide cash with which customers could pay for work, and raised prices to cover his increased labor costs.

Sales, however, continued to lag, and the buyer consequently resold the business at a loss, took a job elsewhere and struggled to collect from the new buyer, who soon had trouble making payments due on the shop.

Thus this entrepreneur shifted from one strategy to a second. The first was to operate as a franchisee. The second was to buy and resell a franchise. The latter strategy, although not profitable for him, is one that can be successful. The other two most likely ways to make substantial profits on franchises are either to find a successful business formula and sell it by becoming a franchisor or to acquire multiples of franchises, if possible in the early days of a to-be-successful franchise, before the price of it has gone up.[150]

Although the average individual franchisee may make a meager income and relatively low return on investment in exchange for long hours of hard work, the top layer of most successful franchisees appear to enjoy sales on the order of 30 percent and more above average and profits still higher. The secrets of such performance appear to lie in straightforward application of good management disciplines, careful attention to many fine details and, above all,

---

[150]Jeannie Ralston, "Franchisees Who Think Big," *Venture*, March 1989, p. 55.

finding ways to motivate employees in providing exceptional service to customers.[151]

Application   *What would be the pros and cons of buying whatever franchise might make most sense, as opposed to buying the assigned case venture, for the entrepreneur in the assigned case?*

Supplementary Reading

New Venture Strategies Chapter 10. (Vesper, K.H., Prentice-Hall, 1990)

Your Venture Plan

1. Describe what you expect would be the margin of negotiation for the needed elements of your enterprise through acquisition of one or more existing firms, and describe a strategy you might use for striking the best possible bargain.

2. As an acquisition for some other person whom you specify, assess the value your venture should have at points six months, one year and two years down the path of start-up.

3. Describe your expected bargaining position for selling your venture at three contrasting states projected by the plan of its future.

Your Venture History

1. What selling price and terms would it be reasonable for the founders to ask for the venture at two contrasting stages in its development?

2. Who would have been a good buyer at each of these stages, and how could a seller have gone about deliberately searching for such a person?

3. In hindsight, what does the founder(s) conclude about the advisability of start-up versus acquisition as a way of entering independent business?

Exercises

1. Discuss with the owner of a local business what characteristics a "person most logical to buy" that business would have. Rank those characteristics in order of (a) importance to the seller, and (b) likely effect of the bargaining strength of the buyer.

2. Interview someone who bought a business, and learn about how the terms were arrived at. Also learn about competing buyers, either real or potential at the time, and evaluate their relative bargaining strengths and what they could do about those strengths.

---

[151] Curtis Hartman, "The Best-Managed Franchises In America," *Inc.*, October 1989, p. 68.

3. Study one or more local firms both by observation and by reading whatever you can find about that type of business. Determine an estimated selling price for the business, and explain how you arrived at that price.

4. Draft a list of criteria for checking out a prospective franchise, obtain information about an available franchise by following up a business opportunities advertisement, and apply the checklist to evaluate it.

Case Questions: Allen, Hoppe, Logan, Mills

General Case Questions

1. As best you can estimate the financial capacity of the entrepreneur involved, what sort of price and terms in a buyout should this person seek?

2. Assess the attractiveness of the entrepreneur in the assigned case as a business buyer from an owner's point of view. Describe the sort of terms you would recommend an owner seek in selling to such a person.

3. Rank the entrepreneurs studied thus far in the assigned cases, including this one, as potential company buyers. Explain the reasons for your ranking.

4. What should the entrepreneur(s) do at the end of the assigned case and why?

Allen, Logan and Mills Case Questions

1. Who would be the ideal person to buy this business, from the seller's point of view? How could such a person be sought? How does the proposed buyer match that profile? How could the proposed buyer best improve the fit?

2. Formulate, as realistically as you can, a hypothetical competitor grid for the venture described in this case. Discuss actions that could move the venture to a stronger position in the comparison.

3. Assess the alignment between the skills and abilities of these two prospective entrepreneurs and what the venture will require.

4. By what sequence of actions could they maximize their potential win from this venture opportunity?

5. What deal should they offer the prospective seller it they want to give this venture a try?

6. If they do buy the business, in what ways would you expect their work experience to be different than it is now?

Hoppe Case Questions

1. Is Michael an appropriate person to be seeking a venture to buy? What are the pros and cons, and how do they balance out?

2. Assuming the answer to the first question is "yes," what would be the best way for him to go about finding the "right" company to acquire?

3. What have been the most and the least effective aspects of his approach so far?

Chapter 10

Careering

❏ SUBCHAPTER 10A - New Business Entry

How to succeed as an entrepreneur is not much a matter of magic. Coincidence sometimes plays an important role, as in other activities. Anyone can choose to start a business, and those who do are apparently much like other people. In hindsight, prior related work experience often seems particularly important. Founders tend to be more highly educated than the average, but the amount of education does not seem to correlate with success. However, many entrepreneurs continue to pursue training, particularly that which is job-specific, rather than concerned with business in general. They draw important assistance from contacts. Personal savings help increase power and choice. Spotting opportunity and performing competently are highly important in entrepreneurship as they are in other occupations. Rendering service at an attractive price to others is here, as elsewhere, the basic justification for being paid.

To the degree that any professional can exercise a monopoly, higher pay can result. But with an independent venture, the entrepreneur may be able to delineate this proprietary edge more sharply than in a job and thereby garner more profit from it. That doesn't necessarily indicate anything special about the person, just the vehicle of employment. Acquiring a professional edge and choosing company creation to capitalize on it have traditionally come largely from unplanned evolution for most entrepreneurs. The extent to which future generations will use information about that evolution to develop entrepreneurial careers more systematically remains to be seen.

Those Who Become Entrepreneurs

Over two-thirds of new ventures are in relatively easy-to-enter lines of business, namely retailing and services. But higher success rates are experienced in other lines such as manufacturing and professions.[152] Prior work experience, including at least some in a supervisory position, provides much

---

[152]David L. Birch, "The Truth About Startups," *Inc.*, January 1988, p. 14.

of the qualification to perform these start-ups. Over three-fourths of start-ups are done by men. Those whose ventures survive are usually married, and many (40 percent of male founders and 64 percent of female founders) have working spouses.

Founders' Ages

Frequency distributions of the ages at which entrepreneurs start businesses usually find the maximum point somewhere between 30 and 40 years of age, most often about halfway. Cooper et al. found that start-ups most frequently occurred in the five-year interval between ages 30 to 34 (21 percent).[153] Ronstadt found a similar result among Babson College graduates, with 31 percent in this five-year age band.[154] This pattern parallels the age distribution of the general population and so seems unsurprising.

It may also be that at earlier ages the entrepreneur has not yet learned enough about some kind of business to be able to compete against other companies that are already established. Before that age, a would-be entrepreneur may not have enough savings to live on while setting up the business, nor enough contacts or credibility to gain support from others. At ages beyond this 30-to-40-year range, the potential entrepreneur may be less likely to start for other reasons. He or she may have reached a point of income and success in some other occupation that makes it hard for the probable expected payoff of a start-up to measure up. Time commitments and financial responsibilities to family may have become greater. The amount that can be lost in terms of savings will likely be greater. Thus the incentives for venturing will have become lower and the risks higher, making entrepreneurship relatively less attractive.

But these are only generalities. Individual cases range widely. Some entrepreneurs start very young, the founders of Apple and Microsoft being examples. Others start much older than the typical, though it is hard to think of any examples whose success was even remotely as great as those two. How such patterns work has not been much studied.

Kinds of Entrepreneurs to Become

There are many possible schemes for displaying alternative types of entrepreneurial jobs. One is by industry in which the start-up is performed. The

---

[153]Arnold C. Cooper and others, *New Business In America* (Washington, D.C.: The NFIB Foundation, 1990), p. 2.

[154]Robert Ronstadt, "The Decision <u>Not</u> To Become An Entrepreneur," in *Frontiers of Entrepreneurship Research 1983*, Eds. John A. Hornaday, Jeffry A. Timmons, and Karl H. Vesper (Wellesley: Babson Center for Entrepreneurial Studies, 1983), p. 202.

sample of 2,994 start-ups studied by Cooper et al.[155] was dominated greatly by retailing and services, as shown in Table 10-1.

Table 10-1 Start-ups By Line Of Industry

Business	Percent of start-ups
Retailing	46%
Services	19
Manufacturing	8
Construction	7
Professions	5
Finance	5
Wholesale	4
Other	6
Total	100%

Within each of these categories further breakdowns into virtually unlimited subdivisions can be made, as the Yellow Pages and *Thomas Register* or any manufacturers' directory readily illustrate. Thinking about them might stimulate ideas about kinds of acquisitions to consider or jobs to look for, but not likely kinds of start-ups to undertake. In order to glimpse a useable start-up opportunity, however, a would-be entrepreneur will likely need much more close-up vision than such categorization allows.

Entry strategy can also be used to classify entrepreneurial jobs, according to interviews with 106 entrepreneurs conducted by Gartner et al.[156] The six "archetypes" thus identified were:

Escaping to New Work A secretary and a speech therapist taught themselves something about pet stores by studying some, running one for a couple of days, renting a site, buying stock and opening the doors.

Deal Making The inventor of a novelty product personally developed sales channels, subcontracted manufacturing and created a firm to coordinate these functions.

Providing Expertise A specialist in compensation left his job, incorporated, and recruited clients from his former employer.

Buyout A long-time bicycle enthusiast retired from the military, bought an existing shop and improved its performance.

---

[155] Cooper and others, *New Business In America*, p. 15.
[156] William B. Gartner, Terence R. Mitchell, and Karl H. Vesper, "A Taxonomy of New Business Ventures," *Journal of Business Venturing*, 4 (no. 3), May 1989, p. 169.

Aggressive Service An investment banker incorporated, set up his own office to provide an innovative service, recruited the needed contacts and expanded his service to other parts of the country.

Methodical Organizing An MBA frustrated by life as a corporate employee formulated criteria for an industry to start in, assembled customer focus groups to scan that industry, discovered a weak product and set up to introduce an improved design.

Application   *Which of Gartner s archetypes most closely fit the assigned case entrepreneur, and what sort of knowledge and skills in general would those types most require?*

For each of these and other such types it is possible to consider examples and assess just what would be required to compete with such a person. That may help a would-be entrepreneur decide what kinds of start-ups to avoid, which to pursue further and what complements to seek, either through more learning or by recruiting partners.

Success Patterns

Cooper et al. reported from their study of 2,994 NFIB entrepreneurs averaged across all types[157] that some controllable characteristics of those whose start-ups were more likely to be surviving after three years than not surviving included that entrepreneurs with surviving ventures:

- Were more likely to be college graduates (27 percent vs. 18 percent)
- Were on average slightly older (36.4 vs. 35.4 years) athough founder age and firm growth were not correlated
- Had held fewer full-time jobs (4.2 vs. 4.9 average)
- Were less likely to have a goal of organization building (28 percent vs. 35 percent)
- Started with more capital
- Were less likely to have continued to hold other jobs
- Were more likely to have started with similar products and services (32 percent vs. 27 percent), similar customers (31 percent vs. 24 percent) or similar suppliers (31 percent vs. 25 percent) to those of their prior work
- Were more likely not to be in retailing (44 percent vs. 53 percent)

---

[157] Arnold C. Cooper, William C. Dunkelberg, and Carolyn Y. Woo, "Survival and Failure: A Longitudinal Study," in *Frontiers of Entrepreneurship Research, 1988*, eds. Bruce H. Kirchhoff, and others (Wellesley, Mass.: Babson Center for Entrepreneurial Studies, 1988), p. 225.

- Were more likely to have a goal of not working for others (19 percent vs. 15 percent)
- But were less likely to have left prior jobs out of dissatisfaction (24 percent vs. 29 percent).

Application   *How well does the assigned case entrepreneur align with the statistical success patterns listed above?*

These authors reported the rate of discontinuance overall in new firms was about 11 percent per year, as contrasted with a figure of 10 percent by others (Reynolds and Tauzell) and higher than 11 percent by still others (Shapero). *Not* correlated with success were levels of prior management experience, prior business ownership, sources of initial funding, number of hours worked per week (the average was 56 to 57 hours), having come from a business versus non-business background, having taken business courses, or having parents who owned businesses.

The folklore that successful entrepreneurs tend to come from parents who were self employed does not fit *Inc.* 500 founders, in two-thirds of the cases. The theory that entrepreneurs who become most successful usually had businesses when they were children was also not true almost two-thirds (63 percent) of the time for *Inc.* 500 entrepreneurs. Nearly three-fourths (72 percent) said they acquired the main skills they needed as company builders during adulthood, not childhood. Prior employment was where most learned what they needed for start-up. For 59 percent the company that made the *Inc.* list was the first one they had started, while 41 percent had started another company previously.[158]

Founders' Professional Qualifications

A repeating theme in both the *Inc.* and Cooper et al. studies is the importance of prior work experience in preparation for entrepreneurship. When asked to identify the single most important source of ability to build a company, over two-thirds of the *Inc.* 500 founders cited work or professional experience in an industry. Founders, it appears from the Cooper et al., study, not only tend to start companies that are in the same industries as their prior employment, but also tend to have concentrated their work experience on fewer jobs. In contrast to the general 30-to-34 aged population that averages 6.7 jobs, less than 25 percent of founders had over 6 jobs and almost half (46 percent) had held three or less. Moreover, fewer prior jobs for the founder tended to correlate with higher odds of venture survival.[159]

Reasons that related and concentrated work experience helps are not hard

---

[158]John Case, "The Origins of Entrepreneurship," *Inc.*, June 1989, p. 53.
[159]Cooper and others, *New Business In America*, p. 22.

to imagine. Work puts the would-be entrepreneur in position to examine the frontier of technology, and/or the market and specific customers where opportunity can best be discerned. Work provides practice against standards required to compete and thereby hones excellence. It helps a would-be entrepreneur judge whether he or she truly could compete with an independent venture and adds to self-confidence in making a venture choice. Through work the would-be entrepreneur can acquire contacts vital to operation within the particular industry, and from work should come savings which can help finance the start-up. More founders preferred doing technical or selling work in their venture to managing it (38 percent versus 28 percent). However, the great majority of founders were sufficiently successful in those jobs to reach supervisory positions, which likely developed skills in managing, not just doing the work of the venture.[160]

Emphasis on technical skills showed up in educational backgrounds of the founders studied by Cooper et al. Founders on average progressed farther in education than the general population. For 40 percent of founders, schooling included at least some courses in business. But more dramatic was the finding that 57 percent had courses in vocational or professional training. Moreover, after founding their firms, owners continued to take courses with a focus on industry-specific rather than general business subjects. Curiously, however, although schooling was correlated with likelihood of start-up, it had no correlation with likelihood of survival or growth of the venture.

The apparently strong role of prior work experience in founding ventures adds interest to the study of exceptions. Vast numbers of them must exist, since the correlation is far from perfect. How could someone without such experience start a successful new enterprise? Clearly one way would be to have had avocational rather than vocational experience with the product or service.

> Debbie Fields had no prior start-up experience and no work experience in the pastry business when she opened her first cookie store in Palo Alto. But she had been making cookies since she was a child and was highly skilled at making cookies that other people liked.[161]

❖ ❖ ❖

> Ted Hatfield had no experience in start-up or manufacturing when he decided to make a replica of his great-great grandfather's long rifle and take it to a shooting contest. But he had grown up with guns and taught himself how to repair and rebuild them. When he received orders at the contest for 20 guns he started making them personally in a rented garage and also learning how to make them more efficiently through use of modern machine tools and subcontractor help. Over the next 10 years sales grew to $2.5 million with a backlog of 2,000 guns on order.[162]

---

[160]Ibid., p. 3.
[161]Debbie Fields, and Alan Furst, *One Smart Cookie* (New York: Simon and Shuster, 1987).
[162]Geoffrey W. Norman, "The Real Hatfield," *Inc.*, October 1990, p. 127.

Four other ways to start up in an unfamiliar business with some chance of succeeding are (1) through acquisition of a going concern, (2) by taking on a partner who has the requisite experience, (3) by entering a business that is very simple to operate, such as some forms of retailing (e.g. small shops) and service (e.g. house-painting or housecleaning) or (4) happening to find a new industry where there is not yet any competition and where firms with related skills don't see enough growth to enter (e.g. early days of making surfboards or skateboards).

Application   *How well do the assigned case entrepreneur s professional qualifications fit the assigned case venture and what could best be done to enhance the fit?*

Founders' Personal Attributes

For most, if not all, new business opportunities, it would seem that there must be others whose experience, circumstances and awareness qualify them as well as those entrepreneurs who take advantage of them. Is it simply chance that makes the difference? Or is it the ever so slight distinctions that make no two circumstances identical? Or are there differences in habit, personality or individual motivation that cause some of the qualified candidates and not others to be entrepreneurs?

Studies of psychological attributes have turned out to be inconclusive. Entrepreneurs seem to be much like everyone else after they start companies, and nobody has systematic evidence to show that they were different from others before they started them. Studies to match those who could and did against those who could and did not perform the start-ups have not been conducted. Even if they were, the history of psychological testing suggests that results would be varied and each individual would be left to wonder whether he or she fit the "typical" entrepreneurial pattern or was an exception to it.

There have been attempts to classify types of entrepreneurs according to psychological tests (e.g. craftsmen versus opportunists, for instance), and statistical correlations of significance were reported. However, the study of 4,814 entrepreneurs by Woo, Cooper and Dunkelberg, for instance, found that although at one level such classification might be possible, significant divergencies could exist under similar labels.[163]

So a practical operating rule for a would-be entrepreneur is probably not to worry about whether he or she fits any supposed psychological profile and concentrate instead on whether a venture is worth doing and whether he or she wants to do it.

---

[163] Carolyn Y. Woo, Arnold C. Cooper and William C. Dunkelberg, "Entrepreneurial Typologies: Definitions and Implications," in *Frontiers of Entrepreneurship Research, 1988*, eds. Bruce H. Kirchhoff, and others (Wellesley, Mass.: Babson Center for Entrepreneurial Studies, 1988), p. 173.

Application *How well do the assigned case entrepreneur s personal attributes fit the assigned case venture, and what could best be done to make the most of the fit?*

Career Paths

The variety that is characteristic of entrepreneurship in general is also true of the career paths that lead to, through and from it. Notwithstanding the occasional stories of people who "resolved to become an entrepreneur and make a million before age 30" and did it, most entrepreneurial career paths are steered more by unforeseen events than planning and rarely lead to a million. They do include points of decision, where choices can be made that are consequential, however, so there can be reason to learn something about how they work and where the choices may lead.

Predicting how much choice any particular would-be entrepreneur can expect to have is problematic. Anyone can try venturing. Many can venture and survive at it, though the financial compensation, notwithstanding some big winners, is usually low and the hours are long.

Venture Career Starting Points

Most entrepreneurial careers, like most venture ideas, follow from jobs. The entrepreneur gets an idea on the job and pursues it independently. The entrepreneur gets fired from a job and venturing looks better than another job. The entrepreneur quits a job, looks around for something else to do and decides upon venturing. These are particularly common starting points, but they represent only part of the path list, which includes the following:

- Job to venture
- Unemployment to venture
- School to venture
- Retirement to venture
- Homemaking to venture

Examples of each of these can be read elsewhere[164] but are fairly easy to imagine. The most common path, according to the study of Cooper et al. is from either job or unemployment to venture. Most often, the prior job was in a business with 100 or fewer employees, and that job was left either due to its being discontinued, by being fired or by quitting without plans. Locating the start-up within a radius of 150 miles was another frequent pattern.[165]

---

[164] Karl H. Vesper, *New Venture Strategies,* Revised Edition (Englewood Cliffs: Prentice-Hall, 1990), Chapter 3.
[165] Cooper and others, *New Business In America*, p. 4.

In addition to starting point, other important variables could include extent and nature of prior education and experience, amount of savings and capital available through contacts, technical or market advantages, personal financial responsibilities, health, alternative job openings and personal aspirations.

Finally, there is simply capacity to perceive opportunity. To illustrate, the emergence of commercial applications for biological science suddenly increased the fraction of biologists who embarked on entrepreneurship. Similarly, the emergence of cheap microchips vastly increased the number and percentage of computer designers who took up entrepreneurship, and in turn the wide availability of cheap computers vastly increased the number of computer programmers who saw entrepreneurship as an attractive career. Less obvious was the effect that discovery of oil on Alaska's North Slope had on entrepreneurship. It seems to be only rarely that public employees drop their civil service jobs to become entrepreneurs, but when the pipeline boom generated lucrative opportunities for those in Alaska with arctic know-how, such as how to keep sewers from freezing in an Eskimo village, federal employees of such agencies as the Public Health Service who had been doing such work suddenly left their jobs to start ventures in the private sector. In 28 percent of the sample reported by Cooper et al., the entrepreneurs said their start-up resulted when "a good opportunity came along and I jumped."[166]

Venture Participation Roles

Although entrepreneurship may commonly be regarded as only one role, that of the person who heads a venture, there are, as seen in Chapter 7 on Help, many different ways to participate in a venture, including the following:

Banker Not many become founders, but some do. Some start banks. At one Seattle bank a management advisory group set up to help entrepreneurs spun off to become an independent enterprise.

Accountant Some branch out to start their own accounting firms. Dave Ederer, a "big six" accountant, was asked by one of his clients, a heat treater, to buy his business so he could retire. Ederer did so, then went on both to buy and start other firms.

Other Professionals Consultants to small firms sometimes become best qualified to take them over and do so. Seattle's Tel-Tone, for instance, was taken over by a consultant who had served the company for several years. Lawyers sometimes take shares of start-up stock in return for services. An advertising agent, asked by an inventor to help market his product, ended up forming a team to buy rights and start a company to make and sell it.

---

[166]Ibid.

Venture Capitalist Each venture capital firm is itself a start-up. Usually partners and employees of those firms participate on boards of their investments. It is not uncommon for employees of the venture capital firms to slide over into managerial positions with stock options or ownership in ventures.

Informal Investors To qualify, wealth is required. That wealth can be used to participate in start-up however the investor wishes, if not in one venture, then in another.

Founding Team Member Becoming a part-time team member while keeping another job is possible. Such people are usually picked for what they very specifically contribute in skills, contacts or resources.

Venture Employee If the bargain for ownership is not struck at the time of employment, it is usually hard to get it later unless all employees are included. The finding by Cooper et al., that entrepreneurs most often were previously employees of smaller companies does not indicate how recently-started those companies were.

Scholar Some scholars of entrepreneurship start ventures, most often in consulting. Scholars in engineering and sciences more frequently seem to start proprietary product firms and firms that grow larger.

This is obviously only a sampling of roles in which a would-be entrepreneur might interact with ventures. But they illustrate some of the possibilities.

Application   *How well-suited would the entrepreneur in the assigned case be for each of the above eight roles, in rank order, before the venture versus after?*

Role Sequences

Some would-be entrepreneurs undertake other jobs, not necessarily involved directly with ventures, as intentional preparation for entrepreneurship. The most ambitious study of this pattern was undertaken by Ronstadt, who tracked careers of over 200 Babson College business major graduates. He reported that those who chose a prior career to prepare for entrepreneurship tended to start entrepreneurial careers younger and stay with them longer (over 25 years long) than those who had not thus prepared. Within that group, those who started the other preparatory career younger tended to wait longer to take up the entrepreneurial career.[167] This seems to support the impression

---

[167]Robert Ronstadt, "Does Entrepreneurial Career Path Really Matter?" in *Frontiers of Entrepreneurship Research 1982*, Ed. Karl. H. Vesper (Wellesley: Babson Center for Entrepreneurial Studies, 1982), p. 540.

that time is generally required to prepare for starting a business.

Despite this work by Ronstadt, the career patterns of those who chose jobs deliberately as stepping stones to entrepreneurship have not been much studied. Regrettably, nobody has reported any further follow-up of the early studies by Ronstadt or others like them. It is not known, for instance, how well the various venture participation roles, including that of founder, serve to enhance chances for succeeding as a founder or even which are most likely to lead to becoming a founder.

Start-up Versus a Job

Most people with jobs keep them rather than leave to start their own companies. Much of the reason may be that they are not exposed to entrepreneurial opportunities in their work or don't effectively discern them. Many may not be qualified to compete as entrepreneurs. And for still others the deciding factors may be such advantages of established company employment as:

Higher pay and greater fringe benefits in return for shorter hours and more clearly delimited responsibilities. (The average salary plus bonus of an *Inc.* 500 company CEO in 1989 was only $104,802,[168] not high compared to the top 500 physicians, lawyers and *Fortune* CEO's. Of course, the *Inc.* CEO also likely has ownership value increase as additional compensation.) Ability to move around within the organization if one part of it becomes uncomfortable. Opportunity to learn proven, effective procedures that have been worked out at considerable investment over time. More availability of company training programs. Possible chances to move ahead and be able to apply massive resources to achieve organization goals. Prestige from association with a well-known company name.

Salaries on the average are higher in larger companies, according to U.S. Census Bureau data for 1987. Companies with annual sales over $1 billion paid employees average salaries twice as large ($24,066) as those of companies with sales of less than $1 million per year ($12,870). Interestingly, diversified large companies paid on average 30 percent higher than single-industry companies.

Notwithstanding these advanteges in pay and fringe benefits, entrepreneurs leave jobs in established companies, both large and small, because of other characteristics of those jobs such as as the following:

Too much regimentation and lack of perspective in the confinement of a narrow specialty. Not enough opportunity to move ahead and make more money. Uncertainty over where management will take the company next. Risk of suffering because of the mistake of a boss or of being swept out in a wholesale layoff. Possibly having to move home and family at a big company's whim to one unfamiliar and possibly less attractive geographical location after another. Lack of freedom and encouragement to generate ideas that have promise

---

[168]Bruce G. Posner, "Executive Compensation 1989," *Inc.*, September 1989, p. 74.

or to follow through on new ideas that might have promise. Inability to see the impact of one's own efforts on performance of the organization. Lack of individual recognition for contributions to that performance.

One entrepreneur, Steve Bostic, who had formerly worked in big companies characterized some of the negatives of that experience as follows:

> *You have no control over your own destiny. You can succeed in a big company and still get the axe. That s the ultimate risk. I see it happen all the time with people I know in big corporations. They work their butts off, do a great job and then get thrown out or forced into early retirement. It doesn t matter how high up you go, either. In my own case, the further I moved along in the corporate environment and the higher I got, the more I realized I was not in control. And the situation is even more turbulent now. In the old days, the guard would change and you d realign yourself with the new guy s thoughts. Today the whole division gets sold out, spun out, divorced.[169]*

For many, the path leads first to employment where necessary learning occurs, savings are accrued and contacts are made, and thence to entrepreneurship where those advantages are put to use. Steve Bostic, notwithstanding his criticism of big-company employment, also drew upon it as education for his own start-up.

> *I advise young people to get the corporate education but have a clear plan. Move around. Learn what you need to learn. Then step out of the corporate environment and get into your own enterprise .*
>
> *I was fortunate that my first job after Burger Chef was at American Hospital Supply Corp., where they really teach you to sell. They teach a systematic approach to selling to an entire hospital. We had a 250-man sales force at American. When I left after about five years, I d moved up to the top 10 or 15, not because I was such a great salesman, but because I had learned the process.[170]*

That it can often be important to know the process is emphasized by the large percentage of entrepreneurs who start only businesses they are experienced in. A study by Koller, for instance, reported that 38 percent of the entrepreneurs interviewed said their personal contribution was that of actually producing the product or service of the venture themselves. Only 24 percent had no prior experience in that type of work.[171]

After comparing a sample of 208 practicing entrepreneurs with that of 102

---

[169]Steve Bostic, "Thriving On Order," *Inc.*, December 1989, p. 48.
[170]Ibid., p. 51.
[171]Roland H. Koller, "On the Source of Entrepreneurial Ideas," in *Frontiers of Entrepreneurship Research, 1988*, eds. Bruce H. Kirchhoff, and others (Wellesley, Mass.: Babson Center for Entrepreneurial Studies, 1988), p. 200.

others who seriously considered entrepreneurship but then abandoned the effort, Ronstadt[172] concluded that higher odds of leading a start-up could be achieved by:

- Starting to prepare for venturing sooner in life.

- Being prepared to accept modest, rather than highly ambitious, venture goals initially, or else seeking out major financial backers.

- Seeking partners with suitable industrial experience.

From the findings of a study by Cooper et al., it appears that there is a relationship between at least the last two of these three elements and the size of the start-up. Apparently a larger start size requires better experience and more likely a team.[173]

Application   *List and assess the pros and cons of venturing versus seeking a job at the time of the assigned case for the assigned case entrepreneur.*

Maintaining Mind Set

Navigating alone in the sea of commerce, an entrepreneur may at times find it challenging to maintain the optimism and enthusiasm needed to keep paddling energetically. Books on "positive thought" offer innumerable suggestions for ways to maintain a productive attitude. Established companies provide pep talks, house organ articles, retreats, training programs, picnics and many other mechanisms to maintain morale.

Franchise firms, whose franchisees operate much like lone entrepreneurs in many ways, provide analogous services, with agents who rove the country working with franchisees and providing periodic performance reviews through which franchisees can compare their sales and profits to other periods and industry norms. They also stage annual meetings where vendors display their wares, franchisees meet one another and swap experiences, inspirational speakers lecture to the group, contests are held and prizes are awarded. In local areas, franchisees meet for some of the same activities on a smaller scale.

Analogous services are offered to independent entrepreneurs through all sorts of trade associations. Some specialize by line of business, others by geographical area and others by size of business. The National Federation of Independent Business specializes by type of ownership. Other groups concentrate on "family businesses" or "home-based" businesses.

---

[172]Ronstadt, "The Decision Not To Become An Entrepreneur," p. 192.
[173]Arnold C. Cooper, Carolyn Y. Woo, and William C. Dunkelberg, "Entrepreneurship and the Initital Size of Firms," *Journal of Business Venturing*, 4, no. 5.

From these precedents several alternatives for "staying in tune and in touch" can be seen for independent entrepreneurs:

- Join one or more appropriate associations.
- Contact and become acquainted with several other entrepreneurs in similar situations.
- Enroll in local courses that convene groups of similar interests.
- Read and consider the advice of "positive mental outlook" books.
- Subscribe to industry trade magazines.
- Take breaks from the business occasionally to get recharged at association meetings or other "getaway programs" such as are offered by universities and independent consulting firms.
- Hire experts occasionally to review the business. If possible, recruit free advisers, possibly by exchanging a similar service with them.

Application   *How would you rank order the advisability of the above seven alternative actions for the entrepreneur in the assigned case (a) at the time of the assigned case versus (b) one year after the case, as best you can tell?*

The choice of ways to "recharge" is individual. One entrepreneur said that when things got grim in his business, he found he could always cheer himself up by asking himself how the business would look to him if he no longer owned it and somebody offered to let him have it for free.

Supplementary Reading

New Venture Strategies Chapter 3 and Appendices A and B. (Vesper, K.H., Prentice-Hall, 1990)

Your Venture Plan

1. Describe what you would do next to improve upon your venture plan if there were more time and resources available.

2. Formulate a personal plan by which you could put yourself into a better position than you are now to carry forward the venture described in your venture plan.

Your Venture History

1. What turned out in hindsight to be the most valuable task-relevant prior experiences of the founders?

a. When and how were they acquired?

b. To what extent can they be seen as an intentional self-education experience in preparation for venturing?

2. What personal savings policies and practices did the founders follow prior to start-up? To what extent did or could they have had impact on the start-up?

Exercises

1. List your personal goals, pick an industry, segment it, display the goals, problems of attaining them and possible solutions for those problems in a table or grid. Then describe how the array of alternatives in the grid could be narrowed down to an overall plan of action for achieving the goals.

2. Examine two or more case histories of entrepreneurs. Compare and contrast key elements they drew upon such as know-how, contacts and resources as well as "track records" and "happenstance" for starting new enterprises. Comment on the extent to which (1) either could have started another's venture, (2) either could have deliberately designed a career which would have led to the start-up, or (3) you could plan a career deliberately to culminate in such a start-up.

3. Contacts Network. Map your contact network. Identify gaps. Formulate activity patterns that could be intentionally adopted to render it more likely effective for start-up.

4. Synthesis. Prepare an essay of not more than 1,000 words on how, in general, a person might design a career that will likely lead to successful start-up of a specific type of business.

5. Personal Strategic Plan. Formulate a combined analysis of your preferences, history, present, role requirements, task-relevant prior experience, competencies, and ability to apply each of the entrepreneurial thought modes. Prepare a personal strategic plan by which you could become founder of an ambitious venture based on this analysis.

6. Feedback. Exchange one of the above with someone else, possibly after you apply the assignment as best you can to them and exchange feedback.

7. Franchising. Contact one or more franchisors, and obtain information about what franchising offers. Formulate a career plan designed either (1) to end up in ownership of such a franchise, or (2) to end up starting a firm which will successfully compete with such a franchise. Include discussion of the pros and cons of both approaches.

❏ SUBCHAPTER 10B - Sequels To Entry

The importance of contemplating during start-up what the later evolution and ultimate disposition of a venture will be varies among participants. For the entrepreneur there is plenty to think about in working through the many immediate tasks of start-up without worrying farther ahead. But others may feel differently. Outsiders who put money into the enterprise will likely want to know just how and when they will get it back. Employees may be interested in longer-term career implications. Customers may want assurance that the venture will be there to back up what it sells them. Suppliers will care about being paid and beyond that whether the venture will afford them opportunity for expanded and continuing business transactions. Thus inevitably, founders have to have some concern with where the venture is likely to lead in the longer term if disputes among such stakeholders are to be avoided.

A Southern California entrepreneur founded a company making high-performance electrical equipment such as motors, fans and pumps. He loved designing and working on the equipment, and the company succeeded in gaining a series of contracts first from the defense department and then from commercial aircraft makers. This built sales rapidly, but because the work did not carry high margins the company needed external capital for expansion. Through private placement it raised the capital, but the founder had to give up voting control to outside shareholders. They were interested in return on their investment, while he liked to work on technical advances. If a motor failed in some distant city he would typically catch a flight to go work on it, learn what was wrong and devise improvements in the design.

While he was working on technical problems, other aspects of the company, such as contract completion, cost control and bidding on new work would tend to slacken or drift off target, and before long profits would diminish and sometimes slide into the red. When this happened the investors would become upset and start badgering the founder about sticking to his job as CEO rather than design engineer. He would "get back to business," and profits would come back into line. But only for a while, because then he would relax, delve back into technology and the loss cycle would begin again.

After several years of discomfort with this pattern the outside investors, unable to find anyone whom they felt could replace the founder, reached an agreement with him to sell the company to a larger corporation in which he would continue to operate as division head of his company. He soon left to form another firm, which he kept small so as to retain complete control.

Venture Types

To this entrepreneur the goal of independence and being able to follow his technical enthusiasms was more important than building a large company or maximizing wealth. Other entrepreneurs have both other goals and other constraints on their ability to choose. Many have to take what they can get in the way of a venture and do what they can with it. Some venture types, which they may or may not be able to choose, include the following.

Job Replacement Ventures Some venture because they lose a job, cannot get a job or cannot stand a job. The venture is an escape from unemployment.

Lifestyle Ventures Some entrepreneurs deliberately leave jobs for ventures that may not pay as much, simply because they prefer the independence and like the work better.

High-Pay, Stably-Small Ventures Lack of competition thanks either to occupation of niches unnoticed or too small to attract others or due to entry barriers such as patents, proprietary assets, secrets or special skills enables some ventures to operate with high margins and yet stay small.

High-Growth Ventures Similar advantages to those above coupled with large or growing markets enable some ventures to expand rapidly. The top layer of this group is represented by the *Inc.* 500. Interestingly, its composition changes considerably every year, both in terms of specific firms on the list and in terms of the industries represented among the leaders. The explanation includes elements of science, art and luck.

The odds are that a given entrepreneur will be headed for one of the first three types of firms or some combination of them not involving high growth. Almost all ventures stay smaller than five or six employees. Cooper et al., found that only 37 percent of start-ups added to initial employment in their first three years, only 11 percent added four or more employees while 11 percent, although they survived, actually shrank.[174]

It is a minority of small ventures that yields high earnings and attractive fringe benefits for owners. Most give low pay and security for long hours of work topped by bookkeeping, tax preparation and red tape compliance that cuts into evenings and weekends. But at least it's an honest and truly productive living, not under the thumb of a boss or confined by the regimentation of someone else's organization. That does not mean that ventures give owners as much control over their lives as they expect. Cooper et al. found that whereas 78 percent of founders saw such control as an important motivation, 61 percent later were disappointed in the extent to which they attained it.[175] At the same time, however, 82 percent of those whose businesses survived three years said they would form them again, even though 32 percent said they were disappointed in how well they had done.[176]

---

[174]Arnold C. Cooper and others, *New Business In America* (Washington, D.C.: The NFIB Foundation, 1990), p. 1.
[175]Ibid., p. 12.
[176]Ibid., p. 11.

Application   *How would you distribute the probabilities among the above four venture types as what the assigned case venture might become if it succeeds?*

Growth Venture Life Stages

Whether most founders could continue to manage their ventures if economic forces opened greater growth opportunities for them is usually moot, since their ventures don't grow. But high growth can strike where not expected. A poll of the *Inc.* 500 fastest-growing small firms in America revealed that 50 percent began as "regular but small" businesses and 48 percent began as informal operations in a garage or home. Only 2 percent began with all systems in place for fast growth.[177]

Folklore has it that those who start businesses are usually not suited to running them if they grow. Examples sometimes suggested to bear this out are Steve Jobs of Apple, Adam Osborne of Osborne Computer, William Lear, creator of the Lear Jet and other innovations, and earlier "greats" such as Edison, Steinmetz and Durant. But there are also easy-to-find counter-examples, such as William Hewlett and David Packard of Hewlett-Packard, Donald Douglas of Douglas Aircraft, and Edwin Land of Polaroid. So the folklore is sometimes true and sometimes false.

It appears that when ventures do grow many experience similar problem sequences and stages. Several authors have depicted "typical" sequences, beginning with Buchele's "Key Crises"[178]. To this have been added Steinmetz' "Critical Stages"[179] Thain's "Corporate Stages"[180] and Greiner's "Evolution/ Revolution Stages."[181] A synthesis of those stages, problems and possible actions called for by the founders, if still in charge, includes the following.

1. **Imbalance** The founder's strengths, if not complemented by a well-rounded team, can produce a start-up strong in some areas, such as technical or marketing expertise, for instance, and weak in others such as production or finance. The result can be failure. The most likely remedy is to recruit complements or subcontract in weak areas. The study of start-ups by Cooper et al., found that at the earliest stages in a venture the typical owner personally participates in production of the venture's product or service.

---

[177] John Case, "The Origins of Entrepreneurship," *Inc.*, June 1989, p. 54.

[178] Robert B. Buchele, *Business Policy in Small and Growing Firms* (Scranton, Penn.: Chandler Publishing), 1967.

[179] Lawrence L. Steinmetz, "Critical Stages of Small Business Growth," *Business Horizons*, February 1969, p. 29.

[180] Donald H. Thain, "Stages of Corporate Development," *The Business Quarterly*, Winter 1969, p. 33.

[181] Larry E. Greiner, "Evolution and Revolution as Organizations Grow," *Harvard Business Review*, July-August 1972, p. 37.

2. **Cash Crunch** Development or initial sales come slower than expected and the company runs out of money before it really gets going. Solution: Anticipate with cash flow forecasts, maintain effective records monitoring, and line up potential sources ahead of needs.

3. **Delegation** Mistakes occur because the founder is trying to make all the decisions and can't keep up. Solution: Hire, take as partners or, if time allows, train people to take on parts of the leadership task.

4. **Leadership** Even with delegation from the founder, mistakes again arise with further growth if those to whom responsibilities have been given cannot themselves delegate and develop the leadership capabilities of those organizationally under them. More formal organization structure, control systems, communication channels, training programs, budgeting, work standards and so forth are called for.

5. **Finance** Growth goes beyond what the company can finance internally. Ownership must be shared outside. Privacy must be sacrificed if the company is to grow further.

6. **Prosperity** On one side of the company's growth tightrope lies complacency and on the other lies chaos. This calls for self-criticism, complemented by bottom-up reviews and participation at all organizational levels, help from knowledgeable outside counsel, careful monitoring of performance, forecasting, planning and evaluation.

7. **Bureaucracy** Systems set up to suppress chaos impede flexibility, innovation and eventually productivity. Central authority can't deal well with diversity. The solution is to divisionalize and grant more autonomy to disparate units. Profit centers are created.

8. **Sprawl** The autonomy leads to less coordination among units. Line incompatibilities and uncoordinated resource allocation occur, product lines match less well, and direction becomes unclear. The solution may include some merging of units, more formal planning and review procedures, policy statements from headquarters and coordination sessions between division heads.

9. **Stagnation** The policies, paperwork and meetings created to control sprawl drain off energy and stifle initiative needed to maintain clear thrust. Bureaucracy rises again. Poor financial performance may lead to contention with shareholders as well as infighting that dampens morale and wastes resources.

10. **Vacillation** The cycle of tightening central authority versus decentralizing goes back and forth. Products mature and profits rise, leading to diversification efforts, and perhaps corporate venturing. Those consume capital and the mature products become obsolete, leading to losses, cut-

ting off innovation efforts, retrenching, restructuring, more centralizing, and the cycle begins again.

These stages and solutions are oversimplified characterizations of complex processes. But they give some indication of problems that lie ahead that are worth at least some reflection in advance. For a given entrepreneur they suggest a basis for asking how far down the trail he or she wants to travel, is qualified to be useful or wants to learn "new tricks" in order to become qualified.

Application   *Sketch out a scenario by which the assigned case venture might develop into a large enterprise. At what level of employment might each of the 10 challenges arise? What could the entrepreneur do in advance to prevent or to mitigate it?*

Exits from Ventures

Whether or not the venture survives and grows there is always the option of withdrawing one way or another. Sooner or later founders and venture must part ways. There are several paths by which this can come about.

Departing from Management

The best way to withdraw from management seems to be to plan for retirement and groom a successor. Founders who have been ousted by investors due to business problems often seem to leave with some bitterness, usually blaming others for the problems. Owners who withdraw for personal reasons without preparing for this in advance typically seem to do so either by selling the company at a lower price than they could have received with more careful transition efforts or else replacing themselves with managers who don't work out well, possibly because the founders keep meddling.

Departing from Ownership

The happy ways to relinquish ownership are either to "go public," to sell to another entrepreneur under non-distress conditions or to sell to another company with which the venture is a good fit. When the acquirer is another company whose markets and technologies do not fit well with the acquisition, the odds are that the acquisition will not work out well. If they do fit well but the new management is not sensitive to pitfalls of takeover, the odds, again, are that it will not work out well and the founders' "baby" will be injured.

How owners of 359 firms, over three-fourths of which had sales of less than $14 million, expected to cash out of their enterprises was reported in 1990 by the American Institute of Certified Public Accountants[182] as can be seen in Table 10-2 below:

Table 10-2 Expected "Cash-out" Methods

Method	Percent
Sell to a Large Corporation	26%
Sell to Outside Investors	25
Pass Company Along to Family	22
Sell to Insiders	16
Go Public	3
Liquidate	2
Don't Know or Other	6
Total	100%

Application   *Which of the above departures from the assigned case venture should its entrepreneur aim for if the venture develops successfully?*

In Case of Success

The biggest success stories are those few start-ups whose owners manage to sell ownership on the public market. If the company manages to get its shares listed on a public exchange, the owners can choose when and how much of their interests to sell. Such a listing does not occur unless the company has grown fairly large and has even larger growth prospects in the future. So the total valuation of a company that manages to arrive at this stage has usually grown fantastically from its origins, and the founders are correspondingly well off.

Selling shares publicly, however, does not guarantee listing, and there are many companies with shares fairly widely distributed that are not publicly traded, not easy to make money from and not all that successful. They simply have the restrictions of public ownership and the burden of dealing with many owners without the luxury of easy ownership sale.

Selling the venture to a larger company is another way for entrepreneurs to cash out. By this path the entrepreneur may exchange shares in the venture for shares in the larger company and/or cash and/or a continuing consulting contract. Since acquiring companies often pay high prices for what they buy, this can be a lucrative way to depart from venture ownership. The downside is that acquiring companies on average don't do very well at keeping their acquisitions healthy or happy, and that can leave the founder wealthy but disappointed.

---

[182]*1990 Small Business Report* (New York: American Institute of Certified Public Accountants, 1990). See also *Inc.*, October 1990, p. 152.

Selling to another entrepreneur or team of entrepreneurs is more likely to yield a lower price for the venture but also to have the venture continue to operate more successfully. The selling entrepreneur will probably receive cash, a payout contract, some sort of continuing consulting contract in exchange for ownership of the venture plus an agreement not to start another one that will compete with it.

In Case of Failure

Entrepreneurship requires optimism and founders are usually optimistic. Over two out of three estimate their chances of success at 80 percent or higher, according to the data of Cooper et al.[183] But it is an awkward fact that start-ups sometimes fail. The rate of failure is not as high as often supposed. On the average roughly 10 percent of firms per year are discontinued, some of them presumably for reasons other than failure, but many of them due to failure. When that happens, many people may be let down: the founders, suppliers, investors, customers and lenders. The less they are let down, the better, and it therefore makes sense, though it is not enjoyable, to consider in advance such questions as the following:

1. What, in order of likelihood, are the ways things could go wrong and cause this venture to fail?

2. What might be early warning indicators that one or more of those events is coming?

3. What could be done about such events early enough to minimize the chances of failure?

4. What could be done in advance to minimize the costs of failure, both financial and otherwise?

Application   *How would you answer each of the above four questions for the assigned case venture?*

How to tell when the venture is not working is a function both of how the venture is supposed to work and where it is along the path of development. If there is a written business plan, then one sign of alarm may be that forecasts in the plan are not being achieved. It may be possible, however, for it to appear that progress is on schedule when it is not. If, for instance, the company has produced its goods, sold them and collected from customers, the financial statements may look all right. But customers may be having trouble with the goods that will lead to large returns and/or to collapse of the market. Possibly the deliveries have even laid a basis for lawsuits which will crush the

---

[183]Cooper and others, *New Business In America*, p. 4.

venture. Or the venture may be on track, customers may be happy, and just ahead are as yet unannounced moves of competitors that will obsolete what the venture offers. Many ventures in the microcomputer industry, for instance, were doing fine until IBM and Microsoft introduced the DOS standard and made it dominant in the marketplace, rendering obsolete the operating systems of those other ventures.

Thus, some signs that the venture isn't working may be obvious, as when it can't raise needed capital, recruit key people, obtain supplies or get customers either to buy or to pay for what they bought. Other signs such as technical obsolescence may be harder to discern. But what to look for should be thought through as part of the planning process, so that if the venture is not going to work out, at least the founders can take action as early as possible to minimize the downside losses.

Application   *If the assigned case venture were to develop along a satisfactory projection over the next 12 months, where would it be and what warning signals should the entrepreneur be on the alert for?*

Supplementary Reading

New Venture Strategies Chapters 1 and 3. (Vesper, K.H., Prentice-Hall, 1990)

Your Venture Plan

1. Present your venture plan to someone who could be important in helping it succeed, such as a banker, investor, key employee or important customer or supplier. Take note of the feedback they provide and describe how you would improve on your plan for a "next round" effort at carrying it forward.

2. Describe what you have learned from your work on a venture plan, and tell how you would go at such a plan differently if you had it to do over again.

Your Venture History

1. How did the founder(s) initially envisage the longer-term pattern of development of the venture, how has this vision changed over time and why?

2. How does the rate of increase in personal net worth of the founder(s) compare to what it would be if they sold the venture, invested the proceeds and took jobs?

Exercises

1. Apply question two above, under your venture history, to one or more other ventures besides that of the history.

2. Are there any "most important truths" of entrepreneurship, and if so, what are they?

3. What can be learned about entrepreneurship from studying it versus attempting it?

Case Questions: Glassman, Mighell, Walkuski

General Case Questions

1. Project the reasonably possible highest annual rate of wealth increase this venture could generate for the entrepreneur. State the main assumptions on which this projection is predicated, and comment on the likelihood that they could come true.

2. Assess the qualifications and proclivities of this particular entrepreneur for undertaking the particular type of venture he has in mind.

3. Critique the actual career path to date that the entrepreneur in the assigned case has taken and assess its appropriateness to the particular type of venture he or she is undertaking.

4. Within the realm of what is reasonably likely, design an ideal career path for undertaking the venture this entrepreneur has in mind. To what other types of ventures might such a career path be suited?

5. Develop a projection along which the venture might develop for two or three years. Describe the options for the entrepreneur to get out of it at three points along that path. State which of the options you think would be best and why at each of those three points.

6. Identify the assets, both intangible and tangible, that the entrepreneur has built into the venture as of the time of the assigned case. Specify the dollar value you think each of these two types of assets should have as of the time of the assigned case to:

   a. The entrepreneur.
   b. Two contrasting potential buyers, real or hypothetical.

Glassman Case Questions

1. Assess the role that Debra's personal philosophy has played in her venturing to date.

2. What would be your advice as to the role that her philosophy should play in her future business activities and why?

Mighell Case Questions

1. How would Bob's capabilities for making a go of the venture he is considering compare to yours and why? What could you do to compensate for what you see as his advantages?

Walkuski Case Questions

1. Describe what business school training might be able to add to Joe's capabilities for creating a venture. Assess how important you think such addition(s) would be and what his options would be for obtaining the same capabilities without going to business school.

2. Describe what you think you could add to Joe's prospective venture if you were to become a partner with him. What should he be willing to grant in return?

CASES

Case 1

Terry Allen

Terry Allen was being "courted" to take over a failing business. In January 1980 he had approached the Small Business Investment Corporation (SBIC) of Vermont with an idea of starting a publishing and seminar business on marketing. After he had shown the SBIC managers his resume and told them about his entrepreneurial background, they suggested that he consider taking over a game manufacturer in which the SBIC had invested $35,000.

The manufacturer produced a board game called *All About Town*™, which was somewhat like Monopoly™ except that, instead of real-estate properties, the board depicted retail stores and other business enterprises of an actual city. Each player drew game money bearing the name of a local bank and then embarked on shopping trips around the game board with the objective of using less money and returning "home" sooner than the other players. Local merchants of the real city represented by the game paid to have their names on the board as advertising and were invited to sell the game as dealers. The game producer thus obtained revenues from two sources: merchants who advertised on the game board, and customers who bought the game. The idea had been well received by some merchants, chambers of commerce, and shoppers during the Christmas holiday season, but as yet sales had not been sufficient to cover costs, and the game manufacturer had more debts than it could pay.

The Vermont SBIC managers said they believed Terry was the type of person who could turn the company around, and they encouraged him to develop a proposal for doing so. He was intrigued by the idea, but wondered whether he should take the job. A recent divorce had reduced his personal net worth to near zero. He had subsequently remarried, gaining four children to support in addition to three from his previous marriage. He currently taught marketing at the University of Vermont, and he was working on a doctorate in business at the University of Virginia, which required occasional trips to Charlottesville and a substantial amount of time.

He had also acquired a seat on the Chicago Options Exchange and three days after returning from his honeymoon, he learned that the person representing his seat had lost him $20,000 from speculating. This depleted his cash, but he was still receiving $1,000 per month from a business he'd sold the previous year. He commented on the prospect of taking over the game manufacturer:

> I could develop a game just like that on my own, but it would probably take me a year. So the value of the company to me is in terms of what one year of my time is now worth. I could either try to sell the game in as many cities as possible or sell a franchise in a limited number of locations for, say, $5,000 each and a percentage of the gross sales.
>
> Either way, I would probably farm out the manufacturing and do the selling on my own. It looks like a great opportunity to make money. I just don't know if this is the right time for me to take on another business.

Personal Background

At age 15 Terry had told his family he

was going to attend Harvard Business School and become a millionaire. His early enterprises included a 170-house paper route, a lawn-mowing service that wore out a rented mower in one summer, and a biweekly backyard carnival featuring his collection of 50 pet snakes, which netted him nearly $50 per show. Later, while attending Wesleyan University in Connecticut, he learned that the school bookstore refused to carry paperbacks. He began selling them himself. He also held two jobs while doing his course work plus engaging in social and athletic activities, and he began selling do-it-yourself kits for making paperback books into hardbacks. For the latter, he traveled to New York and secured the New England-area franchise. He borrowed the $2,000 required for inventory from four people whom he hired to sell the kits. Thinking there might also be a market for the kits nationwide in veterans' hospitals, he mounted a direct mail campaign. Overall, he made around $2,000 on the book venture, more than enough, he said, to offset the $1,000 loss he had incurred on stock investments made with his scholarship funds.

Following graduation from Wesleyan in 1961, Terry entered Harvard's MBA program. By his second year there he had started a roommate-matching service for the Boston area and been elected chairman of the Small Business Club. As graduation approached, he said, he felt an "instinctive urge to live in Vermont," and consequently wrote every company with over 40 employees in that state. Among the four job offers that resulted was one he accepted to become assistant to the president of a Rutland-based manufacturer of plywood reels for wire and cable.

He soon left that job because, he said, "I felt that by nature I was more a promoter than a manufacturer." He obtained an insurance broker's license and took over a general insurance agency, which he continued to operate for the next eight years. He

purchased an abandoned schoolhouse and converted it into a 140-bed ski dormitory. His other real estate dealings grew until he averaged $30,000 per year in commissions, owned 21 buildings, and leveraged his cash flow to include $200,000 in personally-signed mortgages. He became a director of the Rutland Cooperative Savings and Loan Association, and after a year on the board was elected president, "in recognition of the fact that I was the only one who bothered to ask questions at board meetings," he recalled.

In 1966 Terry bought a franchised rental store called Taylor Rental Center in Rutland. This acquisition he expanded over a three-year period into a chain of six rental stores in New England and upstate New York, renaming it Green Mountain Rentals. This expansion he began by starting a store from scratch in Glens Falls, then taking over a store through a distress sale in Hamden, Connecticut, and buying a rental business from a retiring proprietor in Manchester, New Hampshire. Finally, he acquired two others, one in West Hartford, Connecticut and one in Barre, Vermont.

Each purchase was structured to fit his financial liquidity at the time of acquisition. Equity investments, secured and unsecured notes, and sale with lease-back of the assets to the company were all part of Terry's financial dealings to build his rental-store business. He worked to smooth out seasonal cycles common to the rental industry by adding snowmobiles and a line of winter party accessories that complemented the peak demand for tools and equipment during summer months. To attract more new homeowners to the stores he used a service called Welcome Wagon, which sent them discount coupons.

However, he soon decided he could perform this advertising service better himself by starting one of his own, which he called Merchant's Welcome Service.

This business sent direct mail to new homeowners, whom he located through local real estate associations and by perusing records in the Registry of Deeds. Terry found that a mailing that cost 9 cents per letter offering a $3 discount coupon averaged a response rate of 10 percent with a typical rental order of $11.25. He then recruited other merchants for inclusion in the mailing, asking a fee of 30 cents per mailed letter and promising that the coupon book would include only products and services that didn't directly compete with each other for a given location.

This business began to grow, but he began to encounter difficulty servicing debt on the rental service and consequently in 1970 he decided to sell it. He managed to find in New York City, a man attracted by the idea of escaping from metropolitan pressures to run a small business in a quieter location who could come up with cash for both the tangible assets and the Green Mountain Rental name.

Terry now concentrated on building up the relatively low-capital-intensity Merchant's Welcome Service. He believed it had greater profit potential and could be expanded geographically. He also developed a derivative venture that used the new homeowners list to produce reports of interest to real estate brokers on property transfers in five different states. By 1976 he had built sales of the Merchant's Welcome Service to 2,000 clients in eleven states, and he decided to sell both it and the real estate report business.

Next, he worked at Harvard Business School for a year as a research associate, writing cases on small business. He decided to pursue a Ph.D. in marketing and enrolled at the University of Virginia at Charlottesville. To supplement his somewhat sporadic income from stock options, he taught business courses at Babson College in Wellesley, about 15 miles from Harvard. He initiated a course in entrepreneurship, which later became a major area of study for the college.

Moving to Virginia to concentrate on his doctoral work, Terry juggled his time between schooling, his commitment at Babson, a consulting contract he obtained in Fort Lauderdale, Florida, his seat on the Chicago Options Exchange and a publishing company he acquired in late 1978. The publishing company produced booklets developed by a university professor on sex education aimed at teenagers from low- and moderate-income households. Terry recalled that he bought the business for the value of its inventory, $17,500, and sold it nine months later in 1979 for $40,000. He observed:

> I found that in nine months, I had a company that had turned a $30,000 profit and had a lot of momentum for future growth. But then it developed that I was about to lose my key employee. Also I didn't really trust the judgment of the professor who had written most of the material and now wanted me to distribute books that I would just as soon avoid. The woman running daily operations was interested in buying me out, and there were some other opportunities in California and Chicago that looked promising. I could have received more for the company, but the $40,000 was a clean and quick way to sever the business relationship before it could turn sour.

His main interests became his seat on the Chicago Options Exchange and what he termed some "minor real estate investments." He said that he went into ventures without worrying about the amounts or sources of capital that might be required to start or acquire them:

> Too many people are preoccupied with raising money. That's the easiest thing to do, in my mind. I've developed what I consider to be a hierarchy of capi-

tal sources which can work for anyone who is looking to get into business. The trick is to go to the right source and cater to that person's main objective.

For some, it's making more money and for others it's ego. For still others, it's the romance of being connected with entrepreneurship. And finally, some consider financial deals a matter of self-preservation. I like to start at the top of my hierarchy and work down; there are fewer guardian angels than strangers or secured lenders, but also there are generally fewer strings attached with their money.

A sketch and brief description of Terry's hierarchy of venture capital sources is reproduced in Exhibit 1.

History of Aladco Corporation

The company Terry was now being invited to buy, Aladco, Inc., had been started in 1976 by an advertising salesman in his early 20s who got the idea while stalled by traffic in a New England town. As he sat in his car it occurred to him that if he had a local town map perhaps he could find a better way around the jam. Then he thought about how local businesses might be used as landmarks on the map, like the properties on a Monopoly™ game board. Maybe, he thought, those businesses could be charged an advertising rate to be listed on the map. And the map could be sold...perhaps as a game if other Monopoly-type elements were added.

He sketched an example freehand, and with nothing more than that managed to sell one city on the idea. Then he used the game produced for that city as a sample to get orders from other cities. Thus Aladco became a business. Its new game, named *All About Town*, was expected by its inventor to be mainly a gift that would sell during the Christmas shopping season.

Area businesses that agreed to partici-

pate each paid a $400 base fee to be depicted on the board or cards. Play money and coupons advertising other enterprises were also part of the package. Participating stores were given exclusive distribution rights for the game in their respective cities. Local chambers of commerce were encouraged to participate to add a sense of legitimacy and serve as a single point of contact for selling advertising spots on the board.

Depending on the chamber's involvement, the game could also make money for that organization. It seemed to Terry that responses from chambers (illustrated in Exhibit 2) and the general public had been positive in many instances. A promotional brochure included testimonials such as the following from people who had purchased the game or received it as a gift:

I loved it. The action was intriguing. I loved the way it was set up.
—*Plymouth, Massachusetts*

We received an All About Town Holyoke (Massachusetts) game for Christmas. I was thrilled. As you can see, we live a long way from our home town and this will be a favorite reminder for us. I'm glad you thought of it.
—*Caruthersville, Maryland*

Through the end of 1979, *All About Town* had been accepted in 19 cities, listed in Exhibit 3, all but two of which were in New England. Participating merchants received a 40-percent discount from the game's retail price of $12.50. They paid for advertising at rates similar to those for small advertisements in the local newspaper, but received visibility in a targeted audience similar to direct mail.

Timing game sales to peak right after the Thanksgiving holiday coincided with a publicity blitz in the local press and other media on an exchange basis. The game would include on its board or pieces television stations, radio stations and newspapers in the city without charge. In exchange, the media organization had to provide an amount of air time or space worth what a retail store would pay for participating in the game.

As further incentive to retail consumers, redeemable coupons were included with each game for such things as discounts on automotive work or free piano lessons. For cities with significant non-English-speaking populations the directions and cards were also printed in other languages. The *All About Town* game as described by Aladco's promotional brochure, excerpts of which appear in Exhibit 4, seemed to offer appeal to any city. Yet the company's cash flow position had been deteriorating. Terry said that by the time the Vermont SBIC discussed it with him the corporation was near bankruptcy.

> *They've just had their phone disconnected, they have no assets to speak of, their inventory is worthless, they've overdrawn their checking account, and they are about $10,000 behind on payroll taxes to the government.*

Financial Information

The distribution of outstanding Aladco stock was as follows:

SBIC of Vermont:	33 1/3%
Single Private Shareholder:	30
Company Management:	25
Other Shareholders:	11 2/3
Total	100%

Terry's impression from talking to the venture capital firm and other shareholders was that they would love to recover the capital they had invested in the firm, and that some of them had hard feelings because things had not worked out as prom-

ised. Terry said the founder had told him the initial deal with the SBIC was to have been that the SBIC would put up $30,000 in return for a third of the stock plus $5,000 as debt. On that basis the founder said he had gone out, solicited orders and made commitments with suppliers for large numbers of games. But at closing its deal the SBIC insisted upon applying the $5,000 for stock and the $30,000 as loan money, terms the founder felt compelled to accept because he was already committed to customers and suppliers. Now, the founder retained only a fourth of the outstanding stock, and in addition he was personally liable to the Internal Revenue Service for $9,000 in unpaid withholding taxes, which he could not pay. He had also been obliged to guarantee personally the $30,000 SBIC loan.

The most recent investor in Aladco had agreed to put approximately $40,000 into the business despite its lack of financial records, but had taken the precaution of having his own accountant review such records as were available and prepare a balance sheet, which appears as Exhibit 5. Cash on hand was $4.96, and Terry said he believed the realizable value of the accounts receivable and other assets listed was little at best or zero at worst. He noted that the company had failed on its promise in some cities to get games delivered before Christmas, and this had caused some retailers to cancel their orders and others to become "stuck" with games that wouldn't sell quickly. Of the five cities signed by the corporation for 1979, according to Terry, only two received their shipments in time for the holiday season. In the other cases, the printers had refused to ship the finished product until they were paid for their services.

Terry explained that the accounts payable items reached back to the previous year (1978). A further problem, not reflected in the financial figures, he said, was that the company had developed a bad reputation among some chambers of commerce that had worked with it in the last year or two. He recalled telephone conversations he had conducted with some of them:

> *I've called up the chamber executive in every city that has had a game. The story I keep getting is that the game is a fantastic idea, people love it, but the supplier has not kept his word. Apparently Aladco has repeatedly run into problems of not fulfilling production schedules, while its sales force has been undependable because of personnel leaving shortly after joining the company.*

Terry was unable to obtain any profit and loss statements for the company. Apparently, financing had been obtained "as needed," and neither the founder nor the SBIC operators had substantial experience in accounting or finance. The company had never prepared operating statements for management purposes, and Terry concluded that excessive expenditures draining off company cash had been one result. He noted that the company rented a rather plush office for $400 per month and the founder, drawing a salary around $35,000 per year, had driven an $11,000 company car which was totaled after three weeks with no insurance coverage. Terry interviewed one of the eight artists whom the company employed full time, and was told that they had gone to great lengths to make work last and to look busy, even though not enough new game orders were coming to keep them occupied. Terry deduced that two full-time artists would have been adequate if careful planning and management had been applied.

Production

Aladco's founder had estimated manufacturing costs at just under $5 per game,

based on figures shown in Exhibit 6. Terry said he thought these figures were probably fairly reliable as estimates for contracting the work out because they were based on actual experience of the company. However, he noted that the college community of Burlington, 12 miles from his home in Hinesburg, Vermont, included art students who could work at home on graphics for the game and its cover, which might allow him to produce the games on his own more cheaply. Checking with a printing-equipment supplier, he learned that equipment for doing much of the printing work himself would cost approximately $10,000. Excerpts of summary financial information for printing and publishing companies appear in Exhibit 7 (from Robert Morris Associates) and Exhibit 8 (from Dun and Bradstreet). Making the parts and assembling them into games would require coordinating a number of steps, from artwork through quality-control checks to ensure that all the right items were in each game box. Each game with all its components, as listed in Exhibit 9, weighed approximately two pounds.

Terry expected the majority of shipments should begin around October and run through mid-November for the Christmas season. He had inquired about renting space in a local Grange hall. Terry commented that a number of people in town had said they had wanted to buy the hall since the Grange had gone out of business eleven years earlier, but had been told that it was not for sale. Terry had difficulty learning just who might have the authority to sell it. Each person he talked to referred him to someone else until he had talked to nearly a dozen people. Finally, however, he established contact with appropriate authorities and worked out terms under which he could lease the hall for four months at $250 per month and then pay an additional $25,000 for full ownership. He commented:

I know the man who owns a business next door to the hall tried to buy it recently but gave up when he couldn't find any interest in selling. If I don't sign the deal now, I'll bet he'd be glad to.

For his workforce, Terry expected he could recruit local young people willing to accept minimum-wage employment on a seasonal basis for assembling the games. He had worked out a per-game cost estimate of his own, based on production and color printing of the box and game board by outside contractors, black-and-white printing done either in-house with the used printing equipment or outside, and assembly done in the Grange hall. His cost estimates appear in Exhibit 10. He thought he could oversee production himself part time, since he expected it would be fairly routine, while he took care of sales and other aspects of the business in addition to his schooling and other activities.

Marketing

The company had used a direct-commission force to sell. It recruited salespeopole through classified advertisements. Each was given a territory, samples and literature, but no expense account. Terry commented:

Apparently they hired anyone who walked in responding to the want ads. And these would not tend to be the world's most high-classed salespeople. Often, they would be salesmen nobody else would hire on a salary basis. One of them would sign on, somehow get himself to a town that didn't have a game, and talk one of the local hotels into trading him lodging for a listing on the game board. Then he'd go to a restaurant and swap advertising for meals, and at a car dealer he would swap for a

car rental. He might not worry too much about how the game turned out, how many games were sold, or whether they were delivered on time. There was always another town to start swapping with.

Terry was considering two marketing alternatives. The first would be to sell franchises to individual chambers of commerce in cities that expressed interest in the game. To check the feasibility of this approach, he drew up a pro forma income statement and disclosure information sheet that could be sent to inquiring communities (Exhibits 11 and 12).

A one-time franchise fee of $5,000 would purchase game rights to a city. The franchisee could have Terry manufacture the games or look for another production source on its own. A franchise would extend five years, with an option to renew or amend the agreement. Terry's pro forma income statement (Exhibit 11) assumed an annual 3 percent royalty payable to Terry, averaging $300 per franchise. Thus, by signing up between 30 and 40 cities, he would gain $150,000 to $200,000 annually from franchise fees. Overhead would consist of telephone, legal expenses and office supplies, with any games manufactured at a unit cost of $6. Whether to promote the game more than once during the five-year period would be up to the franchisee.

How often the game could be repeated in a city was, said Terry, an open question. One chamber official had estimated that the game probably couldn't be done more than once every ten years. However, several merchants who had sold out their games had written to ask whether the program could be repeated the following year.

An alternative to franchising would be to sell the program directly to chambers of commerce and individual local merchants in a city, keying on the advertising benefits possible with the game. With this approach, he said, his goal would be to work from a base of 10 or 15 cities per year, up to 50 or more communities. Depending on the success of the program in a given locality, he figured the game might be repeated once every three to five years. He said he hadn't formulated criteria for choosing participants, but would talk with any reputable person or organization that appeared interested in having his or her community involved.

To do the selling Terry figured he could recruit business students during summer and assign them to visit various cities where they would obtain advertising orders form local merchants, including banks, large department stores, smaller retailers and local media, and solicit orders for shipments of games. The students could choose to sell directly or through commissioned sales representatives whom they would hire themselves. Each salesperson's goal would be to gererate orders for at least 4,000 games, packed 12 to a case. In this way Terry thought he could use advertising revenues to pay for his selling expenses and cover production costs with retail sales of games. He had drafted a possible commission schedule (Exhibit 13) and a price list (Exhibit 14).

It seemed to him that the franchising approach would take less of his time and probably be a safer course to follow. On the other hand, the profit potential from directly selling to as many cities as possible and controlling rights to the game at every stage seemed limitless. He had been told that one of the drawbacks in franchising was that franchisees tended to look for a continuing earning stream, not a single revenue source every few years. Regardless what decision he made about the venture, Terry said he didn't have any cash of his own to invest. His options loss had taken care of that.

Terry noted that there was no direct

competition because the game was unique. However, if the game began to sell well someone else might invest the time and expense to make something similar. One company that concerned him particularly was located in California and sold advertising products exclusively to chambers of commerce. He observed:

> *They spend half a million dollars a year marketing to chambers of commerce, and if and when they decide to focus that kind of money on competing with me, I suppose I'm dead.*

Decision Point

> *My first inclination is to go ahead anyway because I think it's a good way to make some money. Whether the franchise or direct selling approach would be better, I'm not sure yet. Either way, I'd really like to try a business with a manufactured product. I've never really been involved with production from the standpoint of my own business, and I'd like to prove to myself that I can do it.*
>
> *On the other hand, I don't want the business to become a siphon for my time. The whole basis for valuing the company is on the year of my time that it would save me to take over versus trying to replicate the concept.*
>
> *My teaching will continue, and I also want to work on a system I've developed over the past three years to recoup my losses in the market. And, oh yes, there's my dissertation,which I have yet to finish. The people at Virginia are anxious for me to show progress on that, so I'll probably tie up a good deal of my time on doctoral studies in the near term.*
>
> *Whether this game is the best opportunity for me right now, I'm not sure. On paper, it looks tempting, but . . .*

EXHIBIT 1 Terry Allen's Hierarchy of Venture Capital Funding Sources*

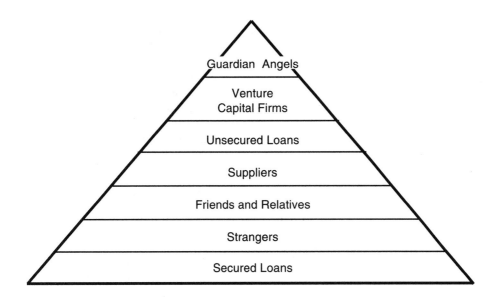

*Terry said that as one progressed from the top of the "pyramid" downward, the frequency of sources in each category increased. At the same time, the number of "strings" attached to the money tends to increase as well. Guardian angels included private individuals willing to finance a venture, based on their confidence in the entrepreneur and business. Venture capital firms offered a ready source of funds, yet were typically geared to business ventures promising high growth rates and rates of return.

Unsecured loans included trade credit or borrowing against personal credit cards, while secured loans were the traditional vehicles used by banks and financial institutions. Terry regarded borrowing money from friends and relatives as "tainted" money, due to the personal relationships involved. Strangers included unexpected sources of capital that might be discovered by the entrepreneur in the course of seeking out financing for his or her business.

EXHIBIT 2 All About Town Comments from Chamber Officials

I checked three chambers before we signed with them. The three chambers all spoke very highly of ALL ABOUT TOWN, and all made from $5,000 to $11,000 for their chamber.

Executive Director
Peru Area Chamber of Commerce
Peru, Indiana

People who see it (the ALL ABOUT TOWN game) love it. The game is very popular. We made about $13,000 on it.

Executive Vice-President
Bangor Area Chamber of Commerce
Bangor, Maine

I have never seen a project approved, by any Board of Directors I ever had, with so much enthusiasm. It's a real winner.

Executive Vice-President
Greater Fall River Chamber of Commerce
Fall River, Mass.

All 4,000 games were sold out in less than two weeks . . .

President
Chamber of Commerce of Greater
Portland, Portland, Maine

I found it to be one of the most unique promotional tools for any community in which I have been involved.

Executive Vice-President
Lake Champlain Regional Chamber of Commerce
Burlington, Vermont

. . . one of the best combination community-promotion and fund-raising projects I have ever seen in our business.

It is a hot item to sell and promote. A chamber will make at least four figures and could make five. We did extremely well.

EXHIBIT 3 All About Town Editions*

Manchester, New Hampshire (1975, 1977)
Concord, New Hampshire (1975)
Keene, New Hampshire (1975, 1977)

Holyoke, Massachusetts (1976)
Nashua, New Hampshire (1976)
Greenfield, Massachusetts (1976)
Springfield, Massachusetts (1976)
Hartford, Conn. (1976)

Worcester, Massachusetts (1977)
Plymouth, Massachusetts (1977, 1979)
Waterville, Maine (1977)

Bangor, Maine (1978)
Augusta, Maine (1978)
Portland, Maine (1978)

Fall River, Massachusetts (1979)
Burlington, Vermont (1979)

Newport, Rhode Island (1980)
Peru, Indiana (1980)
Anniston, Alabama (1980)

* *Earlier years are approximate.*

EXHIBIT 4   Excerpts from Aladco Advertising Brochure

Aladco manufacturing representatives will accumulate local information and use the following presentation to show local business owners the proven benefits and techniques of participating in *All About Town* as an advertiser and as a retailer.

Aladco was incorporated in March of 1976 to develop and market *All About Town*. *All About Town* is a beneficial community project that enables local business people and their chamber of commerce to promote all the good things their city has to offer.

Aladco's PERSONNEL work with each chamber of commerce to personalize the "game of their city" and make it truly "a special edition."

Prearranged PROCEDURE & POLICY allows each business to participate by working with their chamber of commerce and to benefit by the development of a product that reflects PRIDE in their business and in their community.

All About Town is a very profitable, high-volume, retail merchandise item sold exclusively in participating business locations. The game is a unique product that teaches people how to travel from their house, or any place in their city, directly to a business' front door!

The young people of the area enthusiastically identify familiar locations on the game board and the street where they live. *All About Town* is the first item they bring out to show and play with visiting friends and relatives.

The elder, established residents of the area are very proud of the city where they have lived and raised their families. They purchase copies for themselves and their families and send copies to the folks who have moved away.

All About Town games have been sent to almost every part of the world.

The business, professional, and industrial people in a community become involved in the game through their role as local consumers, and their support makes the game of their city possible.

Newcomers and vacationers find the pictorial map of the game board the easiest way to learn how to get around the town. Because customers were carrying game boards in their cars, we now include an extra game board label in each game, folded as a map, for convenience.

Employees take pride in seeing the place where they work pictured on the game board. Retail establishments make money selling the games. The industrial attractiveness of the area is demonstrated by depiction of existing industry. Civic, historic and cultural points are sponsored by participating business and industry. Rehabilitation centers, schools and their faculties endorse the educational value of *All About Town*. Literally . . . "We have something for everyone."

Most people remember details of Monopoly™ over 10 years after they last played it... This shows that "People remember the details of games they've enjoyed for years and years!"

Through the medium of a game, we are teaching people in local communities who the businesses are and what they offer.

EXHIBIT 4 (continued)

And, through the inclusion of valuable, redeemable coupons, *All About Town* will bring identifiable new faces through ththese businesses' doors, proving the value of participating in the game of their city . . .!

Major chains and independent businesses - banks, realtors, clothiers, jewelers, grocery stores, insurance companies, cleaners, theaters have ALL participated on previous editions of *All About Town*.

All About Town's continuing success is demonstrated by letters and editorials from local consumers, folks who have moved away, past participants and teachers.

Newspaper headlines, radio-talk shows, plus television 6 and 11 O'clock coverage stimulates widespread interest in each edition of the game before it is released. A multimedia promotion introducing the game and its retail outlets is coordinated with a press conference announcing the game's availability.

In Portland, Maine, 6,400 copies were sold out in the first 2 1/2 weeks causing the entire promotional campaign to be held off until the spring reprints were available.

It doesn't actually rain money from the sky when *All About Town* is released, but it does generate multiple thousands of dollars that flow back into the edition's community. The greatest profit is made by the participating businesses that sell *All About Town* to the public and keep 40% of the retail price. In Portland, this product generated in excess of $26,000 in retail profits.

The second largest profit is made by the local chamber of commerce for introducing Aladco and *All About Town* to their community, providing the local information that personalized the "game of their city" and distributing the completed game when released. The chamber can expect to net between $6-12,000 from the first printing of *All About Town* on their city.

Business owners, the chamber of commerce and the community profit in image, recognition and dollars and cents, while everyone involved in this game is a winner!

SUMMARY
1. *All About Town* enhances the image of the chamber and the community on business, industrial and consumer levels.
2. Your role includes: introducing Aladco and *All About Town* to your community and members, making appointment calls for Aladco's representative and providing details that personalize the 'game of your city' to make it truly a special edition.
3. Advertising packages range from $400 to $4,000. A minimum of 40 participants or $16,000 is required.
4. Games wholesale are $7.50, including shipping and retail at $12.50. Retailers net 40% or $5.00 per game.
5. The program takes 12 weeks from initiation of sales to release of games.
6. While promoting "all the good things your city has to offer" *All About Town* should generate $5-12K for your organization of its first edition.

EXHIBIT 4 (concluded)

AT NO EXTRA CHARGE CHAMBER RECEIVES:

(1) Logo on box cover, (2) Logo on board, (3) Full, basic participation package, (4) Rules - from cover 2-color ad, (5) Up to 6 free locations chosen by you, (6) Control of design and clients to be approached, <u>NO RISK</u>, (7) Potential future membership levers, (8) Community goodwill and exposure, (9) A means to promote "all the good things" your city has to offer.

CHAMBER COMMUNITY PROFITS

40 businesses participating @$400.00(min.)=$16,000.00	
10% profit to chamber	$1,600.00
4000 games wholesaled @ 7.50 ea. = $30,000.00	
10% of wholesale as distributor profit	3,000.00
Add'l retail margin of $5/game x 400 games	<u>2,000.00</u>
Total of Above	$6,600.00
2% override on gross participation and wholesale	<u>920.00</u>
Net Profit to Chamber	$7,520.00

* * * * * * * * * * * *

50 businesses participating @$600.00(avg.) =	$30,000.00
10% profit to chamber	$3,000.00
5000 games wholesaled @ 7.50 ea. = $37,500.00	
10% of wholesale as distributor profit	3,750.00
Add'l retail margin of $5/game x 500 games	<u>2,500.00</u>
Total of above	$9,250.00
2% override on gross participation and wholesale <u>1,350.00</u>	
Net Profit to Chamber	$10,600.00

COMMUNITY RETAILS PROFIT 5000 GAMES = $25,000.00

EXHIBIT 5   *Aladco Inc. Balance Sheet*

<u>BALANCE SHEET</u>
Period ending 12/31/79
Prepared without audit for management use only

ASSETS

<u>Current Assets</u>
Cash—Bank of New Hampshire		(448.35)
Cash—Depositors Trust		4.96
Accounts Receivable	46,230.07	
Accounts Receivable—Employees	1,756.57	
Inventories	6,286.84	
Deposit	530.00	
Accounts Receivable —Stockholders		<u>11,170.46</u>

Total Current Assets   65,530.55

<u>Property and Equipment</u>
Furniture and Fixtures   7,101.21

<u>Less: Accum. Depreciation</u>
Res. for Dep'n, furn. & fixt   (942.49)

Net Property & Equipment   6,158.72

TOTAL ASSETS: 71,689.27

EXHIBIT 5 (continued)

<u>BALANCE SHEET</u>
Period ending 12/31/79
Prepared without audit for management use only

<u>Current Liabilities</u>

Notes Payable—Shareholders	6,000.00	
Taxes Payable—FICA & W/H	3,995.82	
Account Payable/Production	<u>131,143.49</u>	
Total Current Liabilities		141,139.31

<u>Long Term Debts</u>

Notes Payable—SBIC	29,630.20	
Notes Payable—Comm. Credit	2,073.86	
Notes Payable—Sales Mgr.	6,157.20	
Accrued Commissions	3,487.65	
State Scale Company	<u>38,761.68</u>	
(Secured by receivables)		
Long Term Debt		80,110.59
Total Liabilities		221,249.90

<u>Equity</u>

Capital Stock	23,000.00	
Retained Earnings	(81,333.06)	
Net (Loss) Income	(91,227.57)	
Total Equity	(149,560.63)	
TOTAL LIABILITY AND EQUITY		71,689.27

Note: Assets—Accounts Receivable, Stockholders is uncollectable but has to be shown bringing the Net Loss to $102,398.03.

EXHIBIT 5 (continued)

Accounts Receivable

1.	Hesser College	232.00
2.	Toy City	840.00
3.	Treisman's	504.00
4.	Augusta, Maine	2,572.29
5.	Burlington, Vermont	3,847.16
6.	Peru, Indiana	7,804.68
7.	Anniston, Alabama	22,954.34
8.	Plymouth, Massachusetts	7,455.60
	Total Receivables	$ 46,210.04

Inventory

1.	Plymouth, Massachusetts	500 games @ 4.70	$2,350.00
2.	Manchester, New Hampshire	99 games @ 3.50	346.50
3.	Keene, New Hampshire	39 games @ 4.70	183.30
4.	Augusta, Maine	504 games @ 5.97	3,008.88
5.	Anniston, Alabama	504 covers @ .52	262.08
6.	Anniston, Alabama	1,512 boxes @ .09	136.08
	Total Inventory		$6,286.84

Accounts Payable

American Premium	$42,770.88	Llewellyn Co.	$207.86
Baird & Bartlett	1,036.80	Manchester Oil	517.67
Bay State Box Company	6,818.57	Miles Kendex	417.00
Cook Cover, Inc.	434.86	Mills Industry	200.48
Budget Rent-a-Car	633.88	Moore Center	387.18
Concord Answering Serv	100.00	N.E. Telephone	1,451.09
Concord Electric Co	22.92	N.E. Audio Vis	38.75
Cullity & Kelley	690.87	Poore E.W.	244.00
Domesticare	150.00	Procorp	3,156.26
Easobox Company	9.30	Proj Triangle	1,522.30
Easter Seal Society	894.51	Quick Print	55.46
Eckstrom, Harold	164.50	Royal Press	5,374.61
Fall River Inn	82.44	Ryder Truck	80.85
Fish & Richardson	135.00	Safeguard Bus	266.96
Friend Box Company	1,815.77	Soney Co.	125.00
Granite State Ofc Sys	184.42	Stewart Nelson	212.00
I.B.M.	226.75	Tom-Ray Ofc Supp	120.99
Kelley Services	61.05	Szararz, Inc.	704.71

EXHIBIT 5 (concluded)

Kopy Korner	40,079.64	Tyler Press	7,320.17
Label Art	551.61	U-Haul	135.37
Lafayette Press	9,551.40	United Broadcast	327.00
Longevin & Roberge	800.00	Welcome Aboard	895.00
Little M.G. & Son	51.61	W.F.E.A.	136.00
Subtotal:	107,266.78		$23,876.71
Total Accounts Payable	$131,163.49		

EXHIBIT 6 Aladco Inc. Production Cost Analysis

Production Cost Analysis for Fall River, Massachusetts

Number of Games: 8,454   Date Completed: 10/12/79

	ITEM	AMOUNT	UNIT COST
I.	In-House Art and Production		
	A.Direct Time	$3,694.40	.437
	B.Art Administrative Team	439.61	.052
	C.Art Supplies	997.57	.118
II.	Color Printing (Labels, Maps, Playing Pieces)		
		4,784.96	.566
III.	Small Copy Printing		
	A.Coupons, (Travel Cards, Playing Pieces) 13 sheets		
	B.Money		12 sheets
	C.Rules and Parts List		2 sets
	D.Shopping Lists		2 sets
		13,526.40	1.600
IV.	Small Copy Collating	1,454.09	.172
V.	Boxes (Cover, Laminating, Bottom)	1,935.97	.229
VI.	Mfg Matls/Production	13,526.40	1.600
VII.	Delivery	1,268.10	.150
VIII.	Total	$41,627.50	$4.924

EXHIBIT 7 Selected Averages of Commercial Printing Companies (SIC 2751) (Robert Morris Associates, 1979)

ASSET SIZE	0-250M	250M-1MM	1-10MM	10-50MM	All
ASSETS (%)					
Cash	8.4	7.9	6.3	9.7	7.6
Accts Rec	28.0	30.6	30.1	27.3	29.7
Inventory	13.8	16.2	21.0	19.2	17.3
Other Current	2.7	0.9	1.2	0.3	1.4
Total Current	52.8	55.6	58.6	56.5	56.0
Fixed (net)	39.0	34.8	32.5	36.8	35.3
Intangibles	1.8	2.0	0.2	1.3	1.3
Other Non-Curr	5.5	7.7	8.3	6.5	7.3
Total	100.0	100.0	100.0	100.0	100.0
LIABILITIES					
Notes (Sh Term)	10.3	7.5	7.8	1.5	8.0
Cur Mat LTD	4.3	5.1	3.7	0.8	4.3
Accts Payable	14.1	15.8	15.4	7.3	14.9
Accrued	5.7	7.6	7.6	7.7	7.2
Other Current	3.3	4.1	2.9	2.7	3.4
Total Current	37.6	40.0	37.5	19.9	37.8
LT Debt	24.5	17.6	17.0	14.8	18.9
Other Non Curr.	0.6	1.7	1.8	5.7	1.7
Net Worth	37.3	40.7	43.7	59.5	41.7
Total	100.0	100.0	100.0	100.0	100.0
INCOME DATA					
Net Sales	100.0	100.0	100.0	100.0	100.0
Cost of Sales	59.1	66.6	74.6	67.1	67.6
Gross Profit	40.9	33.4	25.4	32.9	32.4
Operating Exp.	35.2	27.8	18.9	22.3	26.3
Operating Profit	5.8	5.5	6.5	10.6	6.1
Other Exp.	0.8	1.5	0.4	0.3	0.9
Profit Before Tax	5.0	4.1	6.0	10.3	5.2
RATIOS					
Current	1.5	1.5	1.6	2.7	1.6
Quick	1.1	1.1	1.0	1.8	1.1
Sales/Receivables	9.2	7.8	7.1	6.8	7.7
COS/Inventory	13.7	11.0	8.7	6.9	10.3
Sales/WC	14.6	13.0	10.8	5.3	11.6
EBIT/Interest	5.3	5.2	4.4	na	5.2
Fixed/Worth	1.1	0.8	0.7	0.6	0.9
Debt/Worth	1.5	1.5	1.4	0.8	1.5
Sales/Fixed Assets	6.2	7.0	6.3	4.5	6.6
Sales/Total Assets	2.6	2.4	2.0	1.7	2.3
Lease/Sales	2.4	1.8	1.5	na	1.8
Ofcrs Comp/Sales%	6.7	6.4	3.1	na	5.5

EXHIBIT 8 Excerpts From D&B KEY RATIOS, 1979

SALES	SIC 2741 Miscellaneous Publishing				SIC 2751 Commercial Printing, Letterpress				SIC 2752 Commercial Printing, Lithography			
	to 50M	50-2MM	2MM+	Total	to 50M	50-2MM	2MM+	Total	to 50M	50-2MM	2MM+	Total
Curr Assets/Curr Debt	1.60	2.23	3.28	2.27	1.61	2.40	2.34	2.09	1.50	2.22	2.07	1.90
Profit/Sales %	5.76	5.26	5.90	5.65	5.58	5.20	3.94	5.13	5.65	6.35	3.44	4.95
Profit/Net Worth %	28.49	27.26	11.97	31.31	44.08	20.08	15.96	23.16	40.67	23.37	14.70	24.28
Profit/WC %	26.23	48.02	19.63	27.73	45.82	39.37	26.93	36.92	34.71	51.02	27.23	38.74
Sales/Net Worth	5.71	4.81	2.56	3.93	5.47	3.69	3.30	3.92	5.63	4.10	4.16	4.60
Sales/WC	3.66	6.42	4.27	5.73	6.39	6.67	6.11	6.46	6.79	7.82	7.48	7.30
Coll. Period(days)	38	41	54	46	32	41	46	38	32	42	49	39
Sales/Inventory	14.0	25.0	6.5	12.1	26.0	20.8	12.8	20.5	32.6	26.1	14.0	26.9
Fixed Assets/Net W	42.1	39.7	29.3	36.1	93.0	66.3	59.6	72.7	91.0	69.1	69.3	80.1
Current Debt/Net W	65.3	39.3	29.9	35.6	52.2	35.5	40.4	40.4	51.1	40.5	58.1	48.7
Total Debt/Net W	105.8	67.8	37.4	65.6	101.0	55.4	60.2	68.1	93.0	68.3	102.0	82.4
Inventory/WC	21.4	32.8	37.8	32.2	28.9	33.3	46.7	33.6	21.1	28.0	52.9	28.9
Current Debt/Inv.	223.1	209.8	119.2	139.7	225.1	189.3	143.6	196.8	312.7	281.4	177.5	266.0
Funded Debt/WC	31.0	55.1	31.4	42.8	129.2	66.9	40.0	74.4	88.2	69.4	74.3	77.9

EXHIBIT 9   Manufacturing Specifications of All About Town Special Edition

The following materials are included in each game:

Game board label and
  folded map:
  (maps optional)

Size: Approx. 536 sq. inches.
Material: 70# offset litho coated one side.
Printing: 4-color process plus varnish.

Game board:

Size: Same as game board label and map.
Material: 90 pt. chipboard, laminated with label and backing paper.
Cutting: die cut with 6 interlocking pieces.

Casemade gamebox:

Size: approx. 10 1/2 x 13 1/2 x 1 1/4.
Material: 60# chipboard wrapped with 60# offset litho.
Printing: 4-color process.
Includes tray for pieces.

Travel cards:

Size: 12 to each 8 1/2" x 11" page (number of
  pages varies according to number of participants)
  Maximum number of Travel cards: 96.
Material: 110# index or equivalent.
Printing: 1-color on colored stock.

Hazard cards:

Same specifications as travel cards.
Quantity: Three pages per game.

Coupons:

Same specifications as travel cards.
Quantity: Determined by client ads.
Maximum 96. Acknowledged by label on each game.

Shopping lists:

Size: 6 or 8 per 8 1/2" x 11" page.
Quantity: Two pages per game.
Material: 90# index or equivalent.
Printing: 1-color on whit stock.

Rules:

Size: 11" x 17" folded.
Material: 50# litho.
Printing: 1-color on white stock.

Money:

Size: Approx. 4" x 2".
Quantity: 20 each of 5-8 different denominations determined by
  client ads.

Dice:

Size: 3/8" cubic.
Quantity: 2 per game.

Playing pieces:

Minimum of 6 per game, maximum of 12.
Plastic pawns. (Special printed playin pieces are optional.)

Packaging:

Corrugated cardboard cases.
Size: Approx. 14" x 11" x 15".
Quantity: 1 per each, 12 games.
Weight packed: Approx. 38# each.
Note: Games individually shrink-wrappe in plastic before
  packaging.

EXHIBIT 10   Terry Allen's Estimated Manufacturing Costs

(Per Game in 3,000 Unit Quantities)

Fixed Costs:		Costs Per Game
30 line drawings at $10 each = $300		$.100
Cover art = $400		.133
Typesetting, and layout, cards = $600		.200
Game board, layout and paste-up		.200
Color separation - cover = $450		.150
Total Fixed Costs		$.783
Variable Costs:		
Game board (complete diecut) includes printing label		$.880
Gamebox (includes printing label)		.452
Money (5 colors, 20 each)	($.196)	.140
Coupons (3 sheets)	($.113)	.040
Travel cards		
Hazard cards (13 sheets)	($.481)	.242
Shopping lists		
Rules	($.050)	.022
Dice		.036
Plastic stands		.062
Stick-on labels		.030
Printed playing pieces		.100
Packing boxes		.050
Assembly (including double shrink-wrap)		.600
Total Variable	($3.014)	$2.661
Total Cost	($3.797)	$3.444

(Figures in parentheses represent best outside quotation received for printing to be done in-house.)

EXHIBIT 11 Terry Allen's Pro Forma Earnings Statement for Franchisee

Advertising Sales	$30,000
Sales of 4,000 Games @ $7.50	30,000
TOTAL INCOME	$60,000
Cost of Games	$24,000
Initial Franchise Fee	5,000
Continuing Franchise Fee (3% of Advertising Sales)	900
Fee to chamber of commerce (Not mandatory)	3,000
Travel, Office, Postage	1,000
TOTAL EXPENSES	$33,900
NET PROFIT	$26,100

These advertising sales figures are based on the average sales experienced in the last five New England All about Town editions (Augusta, Maine; Bangor, Maine; Portland, Maine; Fall River, Massachusetts; Burlington, Vermont). These figures may be checked by counting the number of advertisers on each game and multiplying by the *All About Town* standard fee schedule of $400 minimum per advertiser.

Sales of 4,000 games at $7.50 each is projected. The actual number of games sold in the above five (5) cities was greater than 6,000 games per city. *All About Town*, Inc is recommending, but not insisting, to franchisees that fewer games be distributed in the future (to help achieve a sold-out situation and build demand for future years).

Cost of games is based on franchisee employing franchisor to manufacture said games. If franchisee elects to have another company manufacture these games, actual costs may be greater or less than $6.00 per game.

CAUTION

These figures are only estimates.

EXHIBIT 12   Disclosure Statement Outline

(Copied from Terry Allen's Worksheet)

<u>Note to Self:</u> The prevailing statute for providing information to prospective franchisees is detailed by FTC regulation, located in 16 CFR 436.1 et. seq., FTC Trade Regulation Rule Concerning Franchising and Business Opportunity Ventures.

General Information

1. Identifying Information as to Franchisor
2. Business Experience of Franchisor's Directors and Executive Officers
3. Business Experience of the Franchisor
4. Litigation History
5. Bankruptcy History

Terms of the Franchise

6. Description of Franchise
7. Initial Funds Required from a Franchisee
8. Recurring Funds Required from a Franchisee
9. Affiliated Persons the Franchisee is Required or Advised to do Business with by the Franchisor
10. Obligations to Purchase
11. Revenues Received by the Franchisor in Consideration of Purchases by a Franchisee
12. Financing Arrangements
13. Restriction of Sales
14. Personal Participation Required of the Franchisee in Operation of the Franchise
15. Termination, Cancellation, and Renewal of the Franchise

Other Conditions Concerning the Franchise Agreement

16. Statistical Information Concerning the Number of Franchises (and Company-owned Outlets)
17. Site Selection
18. Training Programs
19. Public-Figure Involvement in the Franchise
20. Financial Information Concerning the Franchisor

EXHIBIT 13   Commission Policy

All sales persons selling *All About Town* shall be on the following commission schedule:

1st $5,000 cash advertising sales:	15% of cash collected
2nd $5,000 cash advertising sales:	20% of cash collected
Over $10,000 advertising sales:	25% of cash collected
Commission on game sales:	10% of cash collected
Commission on media trade outs:	7% *

If a salesperson is to collect the full 10 percent commission on the sale of games, he/she must also be responsible for delivering the games and picking up the money. If it is not possible for the salesperson to be available to perform these tasks in November when the games are delivered, either he/she may arrange for someone else to do it, or all About Town, Inc. will arrange it. In the event that *All About Town* arranges for delivery and collection of money on game sales, a 5 percent commission will be paid to the original salesperson, and 5 percent will be paid to the person who delivers and picks up the money. Our truck will deliver games to all accounts who order at least 12 cases (1 gross), 144 games. The salesperson is not responsible for collecting these sums, and will be paid full commission as long as the merchant pays upon delivery.

Commissions are payable each Monday on sales made through the previous Friday, as long as all of the art work is included with the contract. Commissions will be held up until art work is sent in.

The first $50 of a salesperson's commissions are held in escrow until the salesperson has terminated with *All About Town*, and then it is paid to him/her upon his/her turning over of all sales materials to the appropriate sales manager.

---

*NOTE: Radio stations may be traded one case of games (12 games) at retail for every $1,000 of trade-outs at regular advertising rates (maximum 24 games).

EXHIBIT 14   All About Town Price List

BASIC PACKAGE $400
1. Shopping List
2. Travel Card
3. Game Board Square (with line drawing or black and white logo)
4. Rules Index Listing
5. Redeemable Coupon (optional)

EACH EXTRA LOCATION INCLUDING ALL ABOVE FEATURES: $350

Billboard: $200
Hazard Card: $100
Outside Rules: $200 (one color in addition to black)*
Inside Rules: $100
Masthead: $300
Denomination of Money: $300
Sponsorship: $200
Additional Travel Card/Shopping List Combo: $200
Additional Color - Travel Card: $200
Additional Color - Game Board Square: $100
Playing Piece: $300

* THE COLOR ON THE ADS WILL BE THE SAME FOR ALL OUTSIDE RULES - THE FIRST ADVERTISER WILL CHOOSE THE COLOR

Ben Bailey

In September 1980, fifteen months after receiving his bachelor's degree in business administration from Babson College, Ben Bailey stood in the office he had recently leased to start a new company, Intelligent Devices Corporation (IDC). The office consisted of two small rooms and housed a desk which doubled as a file cabinet, two chairs, two lab tables on which were arranged a selection of computer parts, wiring tools, and a light table with drawing equipment for laying out computer circuit diagrams. Ben wondered aloud about the setting:

How can two of us handle all this? We've got two lines: a circuit board we designed to be used with a chip kit made by a large chip manufacturing company, and a new computer produced by Onyx Systems, Inc., on which we have distribution rights. I'm designing circuit diagrams, running everything in the office and trying to sell circuit boards and computers while I learn about the industry and look for other opportunities. My partner is a great help when he is available, but that's only part time.

We've got other irons in the fire that could make the workload even bigger. We're short on money, but looking for other partners would require still more time, and so far, the prospects we have encountered have not really worked out. What we want to do here is not just to survive, but to become immensely successful by industry standards as a base for tackling even bigger things. So far, though, we aren't generating cash fast enough to get growing.

Some comments of Ben's about the computer industry, as he saw it, appear in Exhibit 1.

Ben Bailey

Ever since childhood, Ben recalled, he had always had "something going." In elementary school it was model airplanes; during high school it was racing and repairing motorcycles (dirt bikes), or driving fast cars—not always cautiously. He had worked for an aircraft company for a year after high school, but when he saw the difficulties in working his way to the top, he decided to attend college, then seek some experience with a large firm until he could strike out on his own.

At Middlesex Community College, he chose an economics major and considered himself a "pro-capitalism radical," an advocate of complete laissez faire, with the federal government limited to providing only for the national defense, police, and courts. "But no one was teaching that sort of thing," so Ben tried a few business courses, liked them, and applied as a transfer student to Babson College in May of his freshman year. "I don't know why they took me," he admitted. He said he was an indifferent math student whose grades fluctuated erratically between As and Ds in no pattern he was able to identify.

After a summer at Babson, Ben got married and spent the next year running a hotel. Then he returned to Babson in the fall of 1976. Among other courses he took one offered by Professor Justin Whiting on basic computer science, which introduced him to "that incredible toy" and led to a close friendship with Whiting. In his junior year, Ben also took courses from Whiting in Systems Dynamics and in Microprocessors. The latter course dealt with the range of applications for microprocessors and required independent student projects. As his project, Ben chose to assemble a computer, using a kit from Intel Corporation.

Intel was a large, fast-growing manufacturer and marketer of computer hardware and software, based in Texas with over $600 million in revenues during 1979. For sales promotion, its Special Products Group packaged and sold educational component kits to schools and colleges for use in computer science and engineering courses at prices as low as one-fifth of the original cost. They were described as follows in an Intel brochure:

<u>Educational Component Kits</u>

For projects implementing microprocessors, you can select Educational Component Kits from Intel's three main processor families: 16-bit, 8-bit and single chip.

These kits provide fully functional Intel components, with slight cosmetic defects, at significant discounts. The kits are made up of the same components your students will be using when they graduate and begin their careers in computer science or engineering.

Each kit has all the component devices necessary to build up a minimum microcomputer system, including CPU, ROM and RAM. You provide the resistors and capacitors, breadboards and solder. You can readily expand the system, adding components and capabilities to suit your course offerings....

Professor Whiting had bought five of these kits for Babson but discovered that the process of "wire-wrapping" the chips to connect the circuits was far too difficult and time-consuming to be included as part of his course. Four of the kits were still unopened, and Whiting was pleased when Ben took an interest in them. The two men spent much time inserting each chip and other circuit components into the board, then connecting red, white and blue wires to appropriate terminals by twisting or wrapping their ends tightly to the terminals.

But the end result was a dysfunctional tangle of "spaghetti." A picture of such a wire-wrapped board appears in Exhibit 2. While the two men worked, their discussion often turned to finding a quicker way than wire wrapping to hook up the bargain-priced chips. This seemed like a good project, since they suspected that there were many Intel kits collecting dust on classroom shelves; however, they made no effort at first to turn their idea into a business. "Whiting was under the delusion that if an idea was good, everybody was already doing it," Ben remarked.

Another topic of conversation between the two was the computer field in general and the range of machines available. As a result of working for his father during the summer, Ben had been seriously searching the marketplace to find a system best suited to his father's needs. Mr. Bailey, a prominent attorney, held majority stock in several companies throughout the world. He wanted a compact computer capable of providing a variety of management information services, but which was priced lower than the $70,000-and-up mini-computers currently available.

He wanted a computer that could be used both by the various companies to provide internal management information, and by Mr. Bailey to monitor their operations. Ben's search included working in a computer store for a time, going to trade shows, reading industry publications, talking to people in the business, and visiting over 20 showrooms and stores. Ben and Whiting discussed pros and cons of floppy versus rigid disks, telephone accessing, and other technical aspects of the industry. They agreed that there did not seem to be a machine in the $5,000 to $20,000 range with adequate capacity. Ben reflected on these discussions:

We used to hash over what the perfect businessperson's computer should be and what a need the market had for it. To us, nobody in the small end of the market was meeting this need. There was nothing between a microcomputer like an Apple II and a low-end mini like Digital Equipment makes.

During his last two years at Babson, Ben operated several on-campus enterprises. He wrote computer software programs for student businesses on a contractual basis, and made a deal with one student business "whereby I would collect 5 percent of their gross sales if I promised them not to open a competitive service."

Ben graduated from Babson in June 1979 as a quantitative methods major. He "almost" got into the Sloan School of Management at MIT. He had intended to pursue his interest in computers, earn an MBA and go to work for a big computer company. By summer's end, his thinking had changed:

When MIT told me I should re-apply some other time, I began to think seriously about how to get into the computer market immediately.

Ben's View of the Computer Industry

Ben said there was no question in his mind that computers comprised the growth industry of the future. He sketched a rising graph, reproduced in Exhibit 3, to illustrate his point. From his observations of companies now in the field and from his own experiences with computers, he judged that technological advances in the next few decades would continue to outstrip the capacity of the industry to assimilate and apply them. He predicted that in the near future, there would be many more projects to do than people to do them. He described the situation as a "technology gap" and said this view was shared by engineers, salespersons, and market research people he had come to know. Opportunity alone, however, was not the right way to choose a venture, he said.

If I hadn't really loved computers in the first place, I never would have gotten into this. You've got to start with something you're really interested in. I don't think of myself as a little guy; I think of myself as a big guy who doesn't have much cash yet.

Forming a Company

The decision of Ben and Whiting to try developing a company emerged from discussions about how the technology gap might be bridged and how such bridging might be commercially exploited. They felt they worked well as a team, with Ben's ability to learn quickly and his mechanical aptitude complementing Whiting's doctoral training in physics and his understanding of electronics. Each characterized the other as "an idea man," alert to opportunities for new products. "Whiting is the most entrepreneurial person I know," Ben commented. Both were undaunted by the fact that neither had any formal training in designing computer components. With help from the law firm of Ben's father, they completed the paperwork to form Intelligent Devices in August 1979 as a Massachusetts corporation.

Ben escalated his commitment to computers. He attended major trade shows in

New England and California and enrolled in a number of industry-sponsored seminars, which he described as the "best place in the world to meet the people in the business." He also took a job as night guard with a local security company, since both he and IDC needed cash, and night work would leave his days free.

Due to Whiting's teaching commitments at Babson, Whiting did not openly associate himself with the corporation as Ben did. Nevertheless, both shared responsibilities of keeping abreast of the market and working on specific products. "I don't do anything in this business without my partner," said Ben. "I believe John D. Rockefeller's philosophy that if you have a partner, you go to your partner first with new opportunities."

Initial product development efforts of the two were disappointing. It seemed that either they were unable to learn a new technology quickly enough, or they couldn't find a source of supply for a necessary part, or both. One such instance was their experience with Vendex Company. Vendex purchased downloaders for one of their computer systems from a separate manufacturer. Vendex was paying $2,500 on the outside per downloader that Ben and Whiting believed could be made for one-tenth the price. But to make one, they had to teach themselves more skills: specifically, microprocessor interfacing, digital/analog, analog/digital conversion, and technology for storage of digital information on magnetic tapes.

By the time they thought themselves ready to try making a downloader, Vendex had decided to do so internally. Ben remarked:

> That's the way it was. A great opportunity would present itself and one or two key details would kill it. Even so, we were learning more every day, meeting more people and getting ourselves some exposure.

By November of 1979 Ben was seriously considering a career with an established company, since IDC was still without a product.

Developing a Circuit Board for the Intel Chip Kit

One area of potential need Ben and Whiting discussed during their search was how the Intel chip kit could be made easier to assemble and more durable in its assembled form. The most likely solution seemed to be replacing the wire-wrap mounting board with a printed circuit board. On this board the complicated wiring to be formed by wrapping of many tiny wires would be replaced by circuits chemically deposited or "printed" on the boards at the plant. With it the user, instead of having to connect each wire by wrapping its ends to the appropriate terminals, would simply insert a component, such as a chip, and solder its terminals at the appropriate points on the pre-printed circuit of the board.

With this process, assembly would be easier, faster and much less likely to produce errors. The connections produced by soldering to the printed circuit would be permanent and more reliable, and the tangle of tiny wires, prone to possible snagging or rubbing together and shorting, would be eliminated. Exhibit 4 depicts a printed circuit board assembly in contrast to the wire-wrapped assembly in Exhibit 2.

But, Whiting asked, wouldn't Intel be likely to introduce such an improvement anyway? Ben suggested that Whiting call Intel and ask. When Whiting did so, the marketing manager for the Special Products Group told him there were no such plans. It would take a substantial number of hours of design to work out the circuitry, and Intel's engineers were tied up on projects with vastly greater market potential than the chip kits. Would Intel be interested in having IDC develop and sell such a board for them? Yes was the reply. "Whiting could hardly believe that the field was so wide open," Ben commented. "Of course, it cost them nothing to let us try."

During the summer of 1979, Ben and Whiting worked on development of the printed circuit board. First, they had to complete one of the chip circuits in wire-wrap form to become familiar with the circuit and be able to see clearly where the different connections had to be as an aid in visualizing how the printed circuit paths might be routed best. Then they had to lay out the circuit for printing in such a way that the proper connections would be made without any crossed wires. It was a difficult task, and eventually, they decided to hire an electrical engineer to help.

After four months of searching, as they continued to struggle with the design, they located a man who seemed qualified. But he wanted a down payment of $2,000 to design the board. This was more than Ben and Whiting were prepared to pay, so the two continued working alone. Ben said it was slow going, and he was having serious second thoughts on the project. "We didn't know how to do much, but we figured we could learn," Ben reasoned.

Then one afternoon in late November the phone rang. It was Intel informing them it had decided to change the combination of chips in the kit in order to balance the company's overall chip inventory. This meant the existing circuit on which Ben and Whiting were working was obsolete. A new digital circuit for the different combination of chips would have to be designed. Could IDC wire wrap and debug Intel's new circuit within seven days? If so, Intel would authorize IDC to make an Intel-approved printed circuit board and advertise it exclusively in Intel literature, which was sent to 50,000 potential buyers by Intel. The board would be identified as an IDC product suited for use with the Intel chip kit.

Ben and Whiting said yes. Intel shipped the new chips and a diagram of the new circuit in which they were to be used, and the two men went to work. To their dismay, they could not make the wire-wrap circuit work, and found to their surprise that the circuit design diagram itself contained errors. They sought advice, often by making cold telephone calls to people knowledgeable in the field, and this, together with their prior experience in attempting to develop circuits, enabled them to correct the design and deliver it on time. Ben emphasized the importance of their prior efforts on other circuits:

> If the proposal from Intel had come any earlier, we wouldn't have known enough to perform the work.

Whiting explained Ben's reasoning in more detail:

> We're dealing here with digital circuits. In them each component is either on or off, like the ignition key of a car; not one-fourth or half-way on, like the throttle might be. We're not dealing with analog circuits which, like the throttle, allow a range of possibilities. Analog circuits are like radio volume controls, allowing any number of positions between on and off. To design them takes electronic training we don't have. Digital circuits are a matter of logic, and that we can handle.

Now, having made the Intel delivery on time, the two had a working wire-wrap version of the circuit and the prospect of an exclusive market for a printed circuit board version, provided they could design, produce, and deliver one. Ben shelved his thoughts of getting a job, took up a new book on circuit boards, and spent the winter of 1979-1980 learning about how to make them. Using Whiting's knowledge of theory and computer logic, and Ben's patience and dexterity, they worked out the design by trial and error.

Once the wire wrapped version operated properly, Ben had to transform its circuit from the dense mass of wires into a flat sketch where every circuit path lay in the same plane, and no two paths ever crossed. This arrangement then had to be drawn out very precisely, so it could be photographed. Through optical reduction coupled with chemical processes, the circuits were then reproduced on circuit boards at half the drawn size.

Ben sought out suppliers who could take the drawings, apply the appropriate photographic reductions and chemical processing and produce the boards. By having the boards manufactured under subcontract, IDC avoided investing in production facilities. All Ben needed for the design work was a light table (a drawing table with a glass top illuminated from underneath) plus inexpensive tools ($900) and supplies for drawing. The unit cost charged IDC by the supplier was nearly $10 per circuit board. By spring, 1980, IDC had its first product, the printed circuit board, ready for sale.

The two decided to offer complete kits, as well as boards only. IDC kits would include not only the boards and Intel chip kits, but also all the sockets, resistors, capacitors, solder and other parts needed, so customers would not need to buy them separately as they had in the past. IDC bought those other parts from local stores at or close to retail prices, and essentially doubled their purchase costs in setting kit prices.

Another option they decided to offer was fully-assembled boards. The IDC labor required for this assembly was one to two hours, and material costs, besides the circuit board, totaled about $60. The assembly work was essentially quite simple and could be done by unskilled labor at $3.50 per hour. A sales brochure and price list prepared for customers and distributed

with Intel literature are illustrated in Exhibit 5.

Ben said that pricing their products involved looking at comparable market prices for circuit boards and estimating the value of the time they themselves invested in readying the products for sale. Ben pointed out that boards ranged in price from $80 and $250, including the cost of components and tools. The chief variable in price was quality and reliability of the circuitry. Ben explained how they came up with a price for the boards they designed:

> We think that to get anywhere with a start-up, we'd better have incredibly high margins. So we decided that ten times the raw materials cost from the sub-contractor would be a reasonable price. The other parts that go into the kit are priced at twice their cost to us. As for the software, we virtually give that away in some cases—mainly when we've substituted our version as an enhanced package to replace the one that came with the Intel kit.

Adding a Second Line: The Onyx Distributorship

As preparation of the circuit board for market was reaching completion, Ben spotted an opportunity to bring a second line of activity into the company. It was triggered by memory of the search he had conducted earlier to find a suitable computer for his father, a search which he had discontinued during his last year at Babson when he found no such machine on the market. Ben described criteria for the business microcomputer he sought as follows:

> I want a system that can be turned on and left alone; self-contained and reliable. This eliminates all of the hobby microcomputers. It should be "user friendly," easy for the lay person to operate, and accessible by telephone—the

last provision eliminates systems with floppy disks.

The software must have enough capacity for every business need, from which data can be easily removed and stored at a low cost. This apparently doesn't exist; it's an either-or market. Floppy disks are less expensive storage modes, while rigid disks are quicker to access and have greater storage capacity.

I need a good service guarantee, such as 24-hour turn-around that currently exists only for large computers. The system should be accessible to a number of users, yet have protection to prevent unauthorized access to each other's data. Again, these features are found only with large computers. Finally, I need a price tag for the complete system of $15,000 to $25,000.

Ben said this mental check list came to mind while he was browsing in a New York computer store in the spring of 1980. He noticed a new machine made by Onyx Systems, Inc., a small California-based manufacturer. Ben said that the machine seemed to meet his check list and retailed for $14,000. Although impressed by this product, Ben described the way it was being merchandised as "weak":

The store salesman didn't ask the right questions. What a business person wants to know is, what will it do for me and how fast can it be serviced? To a great extent, the user doesn't care about megabytes, CPU types, or what's in the box; he or she just wants it to perform. The store salesman didn't know what it did himself, and had no literature about the machine. And for service, you had to bring the machine back to the store so it could be shipped back to the West Coast—something most businesses won't put up with.

Ben saw this as a potential opportunity for more knowledgeable representatives to sell a good small business computer. The product was there, and he felt it begged to be marketed better. He learned from the salesman that Onyx management had just been through a "shake-up" two weeks before, a situation which Ben knew from his studies at Babson, might be a good time to get a foot in the door. Ben flew to California and told the new management its product was being poorly represented in computer stores. He warned that if they didn't want to lose future sales, including his, they should consider putting him in charge of the New England territory.

He came away with a contract he had largely written himself. For his guarantee to sell and service 100 units per year, including 15 by December 31, 1980, Ben received exclusive rights to sell Onyx systems in the states of Connecticut, Massachusetts, New Hampshire, and Rhode Island. For sales of 50 or more systems to a customer, the order would be given to Onyx directly, and IDC would receive a commission. Onyx was obliged to guarantee delivery of the units within 90 days of receiving an order. Initially, Ben said he would act as his own service representative at the industry rate of $50 per hour. To provide a ready source of spare parts, he decided to stock several Onyx systems, figuring he could also use them in his office to train customers' employees.

Progress and Problems

By September 1980, the circuit boards were beginning to sell and the Onyx contract was in hand, although no customers had yet been lined up to buy computers. Reflecting on the company's situation, Ben outlined what he considered to be problem areas for each of the two main product lines.

Intel Chip Kits

The circuit board for the Intel chip kit (IDC 86) had already generated $15,000 in sales. Though the IDC 86 was producing income, its sales were considerably less than Intel's sales of kits, and Ben felt its value lay more in establishing IDC's credibility with Intel and opening up a parallel distribution network for IDC. How IDC was appearing in Intel's sales literature can be seen in Exhibit 6.

The Intel connection had resulted in two other opportunities for IDC. One was a circuit board for the Intel 1000 series (IDC 1000) targeted for home computers as well as educational kits. Sales projections were for 500 units a month at a retail price of $300. In addition, a third circuit board (AB9009), designed to Intel's specifications, was on the drawing board awaiting Intel's go-ahead. The AB9009 was expected to generate at least 1000 units of sales for a two-to-three-year period at a price of $1,500 per unit in the product evaluation market.

Ben estimated research and development (R&D) costs for the latter two boards at $700 to date. The start-up costs for the AB9009, however, would be considerable: $25,000 for development hardware, three to five person-months of R&D time, $2,000 for the prototyping and $5,000 for inventory. Intel would continue to do all the advertising for the boards; but depending on sales, Ben would probably have to increase his rate of production to keep up with orders. Further, Ben would have to make a long-range decision about what he wanted from his connection with Intel. Would he be content to remain an independent design house, hoping to strike it rich with his tie-in to one of Intel's kits, or should he try to find other tie-in products? In light of Intel's delay in approving the AB9009 board, he was uneasy about the practice of producing for only one company.

But the broad question, it seemed to him, was one of strategy. On the upside,

Intel furnished IDC with a protected market, provided IDC with inside information about new products and took care of advertising. On the downside, IDC had no way, independently, to forecast sales. Intel had estimated that the first circuit board would sell 1,000 units; actual sales had come nowhere close. Intel could decide at the last moment not to make a product for which IDC had designed an accessory. If that happened, IDC had no recourse, no way of recouping its investment. If Intel kits sold, Ben foresaw no problems. But, he wondered, what it they did not?

Onyx Computers

The Onyx marketing plan, according to Ben, had not progressed as fast as hoped, because he and Whiting had spent so much of their time developing circuit boards. To date, Ben had lined up sales of two computers to customers he had contacted directly, and commented that they were a pleasure to represent because or their high performance level and low cost. Since Ben did not have time to search out other prospective buyers, he had offered a friend somewhat more than the standard commission if he could make any sales. Ben was also offering finders' fees ranging from $500 to $1,000 for anyone who could locate a sure buyer. He was unwilling to hire salaried sales persons; he could not afford the fixed salary costs.

Ben was still debating how to sell Onyx other than by direct sales. He was considering the pros and cons of selling them through computer stores versus through retail office equipment stores. Another possibility was to take a booth at the Northeast Computer Show in November, which would cost between $14,000 and $25,000.

He also foresaw that his own time would become too valuable to allow him to be his own repairman and planned to hire a TV repairman to do routine servicing. Since the advent of solid state TV, he believed that repairmen were becoming an endangered species, but that their skills were transferable to computers. Ben summed up the importance he felt that Onyx contributed to his business:

IDC needs profits quickly from Onyx sales for two reasons: first, to generate cash; and second, to steal the competitive edge on good, low priced business computers. IDC needs cash because the new circuit boards haven't generated any yet, and we can't say for sure that they ever will. The timing on Onyx sales is critical, because we have about two years before IBM, Digital Equipment, or Wang respond to our price and cut their own. There's a window for cost-effective little people like Onyx. But is isn't open for very long.

The big manufacturers won't cut prices right away or they'd be competing with themselves on other products they introduced earlier. As long as small companies only nibble at their market, they don't care. Besides, they have their name going for them. A salesperson says, "I'm from IBM" and he or she commands immediate credibility. Who cares if a salesperson says, "I'm from Onyx." Anyway, we've got about two years to reach our customers and sell them these machines. The question is, how do we do it?

Personnel and Staffing

Ben believed that, for IDC, the top priority in staffing was "an electrical engineer, because neither Whiting nor I have that kind of training." He hoped to hire someone right out of college, with high potential and an interest in long-term rewards rather than short-term cash. For this person, Ben realized he would have to match industry wages of $2,000 or more per month. He planned to offer an amount on the low side, plus "...the return on the

person's own projects. And though I don't plan to give away any equity in this company, I would be willing to allow project and royalty payments," Ben added. However, he pointed out that he was reluctant to hire such a person until he had a product for the person to develop, which would recoup the added salary expense.

Ben encountered another personnel problem, which he believed was caused partly by IDC's not yet being able to pay adequate salaries. He had hired a fellow student, Arthur, as controller. Arthur was in his last year at Babson, an accounting major who was willing to work without pay until one of IDC's projects caught on. While Arthur was still in school, he had always managed to find time to prepare IDC's financial statements and billings. Ben insisted upon regular reports regarding the fiscal health of the venture. Arthur worked quickly but made frequent errors.

Ben said that when he suggested that he adopt a system of "self-checking," a technique Ben had learned through painful experience while building circuit prototypes, Arthur took the remark personally. After graduation, Arthur found a job in the accounting department of a large computer company. As he tried to work on IDC's finances in the evenings, it became clear to Arthur that he could not do two demanding jobs at the same time. Arthur resigned, and Ben picked up the financial chores himself with the help of his wife, observing that, "I can run the business with my eyes closed. Babson taught me how to do that, and now it's all background. I know what needs to be done."

Finances

Ben hoped that IDC's low-overhead, high-margin, cost-effective operation would return enough profit by the end of 1980 to make IDC self-sustaining. He did not want to borrow money, except as a last resort, preferring to cover current expenses with current income and "scrounging" to find the least expensive ways of doing R&D work. Ben commented:

> *I want to see what I can do with what I have. When I have a product in my hand I know I can go out and raise money to get it made, but I'm not going to raise money with only a promise to sell. Besides, I couldn't direct a million dollars in resources right know; I haven't had enough experience to manage the power represented by that amount.*

For these reasons, Ben had decided against seeking formal venture capital. He said that he was mildly interested in the possibility of negotiating a deal whereby he would maintain control of his company if he fulfilled specific goals, giving up controlling interest only if he failed to meet his own projections. He had not formalized such financial projections on paper. But in discussion he estimated a current profit and loss statement which appears in Exhibit 7. He rejected the idea of selling the company for capital to start a new one, commenting:

> *It's like a marriage to me. I couldn't bail out on this company. I have so much of myself invested in it that relinquishing controlling interest sounds absurd to me.*

Ben had gone substantially into debt, and his wife had gone back to school. He still owed Babson money, and his charge card had been cut off after he had run it to the limit.

Use of Ben's Time

Ben said that spreading his time over the many projects that IDC was involved in was becoming a task in itself:

> *I never work less than 40 hours a week; usually it's more like 60 hours. I'm in by eight in the morning and work straight through until dinner. Then I have karate lessons; and if I go back to the office after that, it's midnight by the time I get home.*
>
> *I think my expertise is in finding places under Intel's umbrella for new products. On the other hand, I'm a pretty good salesman if I believe in the product, as I do with Onyx. Yet my time can only be stretched so thin, and Whiting is busy with other commitments. How should I allocate my time?*

Additional Projects: Ben's greatest concern was which of the increasing number of development opportunities available to him should be selected. Options he said he preferred were those involving low investment and high margin, which could be totally self-financing once under way. He listed some projects currently being considered:

- To design, assemble and distribute an IDC computer system, to compete in the business market (estimated R&D: $100,000).

- To adapt the Bell Labs UNIX time-sharing system to the Intel system (estimated cost of software licensing from Bell Labs: $25,000).

- To manufacture and sell computers in Latin America (estimated investment of $5,000 before a "go/no-go" decision could be made).

- To design and distribute ancillary computer components.

- To use optical discs and feedback programs to create "universities without walls."

- To use microprocessors to replace the telephone.

Ben's Hopes for IDC

Ben's long-term goals for IDC, he said, were to build and maintain control of a multi-million dollar operation. He did not want stockholders looking over his shoulder, and cited Daniel K. Ludwig's legacy in Brazil as an example of the sort of control he himself would like to have:

> *I need the freedom to take high risks that no Board of Directors would ever allow. I want the right to fail, and failure is bad enough without having to worry about a stockholder's suit.*

He intended to be a pioneer in the computer industry and to become involved in two specific areas: 1) an intelligence amplifying system to hook up the human brain with a computer to speed up thought processes, and 2) a project to people outer space with colonies of humans, which he believed could be done with existing technology.

However, he realized short-term problems had to be dealt with first. He ticked these off as:

- Getting the two in-process Intel circuit boards into production to meet increased demand and deciding how to use the Intel connection further.
- Selling and servicing 100 Onyx systems in the next year.
- Choosing at least one new opportunity in the next few months.
- Maintaining a positive cash flow.
- Attracting additional people to work for IDC, without having the money to pay them yet.
- Deciding how best to allocate his own time when it seemed to him there was already more than he and Whiting could do.

Ben had jotted down a list of some short-term "to do" items. A copy of the list appears in Exhibit 8.

EXHIBIT 1　Ben's Comments on the Computer Industry

During the last 25 years, there have been a whole series of inventions that have dramatically reduced the cost of building computing circuits, and therefore, computers. But surprisingly, there have been few changes in fundamental computer concepts. Thus, with each new technological breakthrough, we have built the same computer as last time, but charged much less for it. And we have built a new, more powerful computer for the old price. This can be illustrated as shown below:

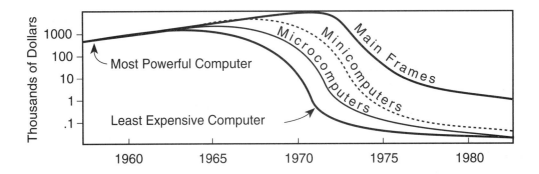

With the huge differences in computer price and performance that appeared during the 1960s, it was inevitable that some product stratification would occur. Around 1965, the most inexpensive computers started to be called minicomputers. More powerful computers, by way of differentiation, were called mainframes.

Price and packaging are really the only differences between mainframes and minis. There is considerable overlap. Mainframes are packaged as business data processing or scientific data processing systems, while minicomputers are sold in a variety of ways, some of which are identical to mainframe computers while others are not.

To some extent, history has repeated itself with the advent of the microcomputer. Around 1975, very low-cost computer products began to appear and were called microcomputers. The prefix "micro" applies to the very small size of the product as compared to a mini. But once again, there is a substantial overlap. The most powerful microcomputers are displacing minicomputers, in the same way that minis were displacing mainframes ten years ago.

The microcomputers are attractive from the standpoint of their small size and relatively low price. This allows them to be used for applications previously considered too expensive to automate. The result is that different marketing techniques are being introduced to capture a part of the business population which heretofore never encountered computers on a daily basis.

EXHIBIT 2   Wire-Wrapped Circuit Board Assembly

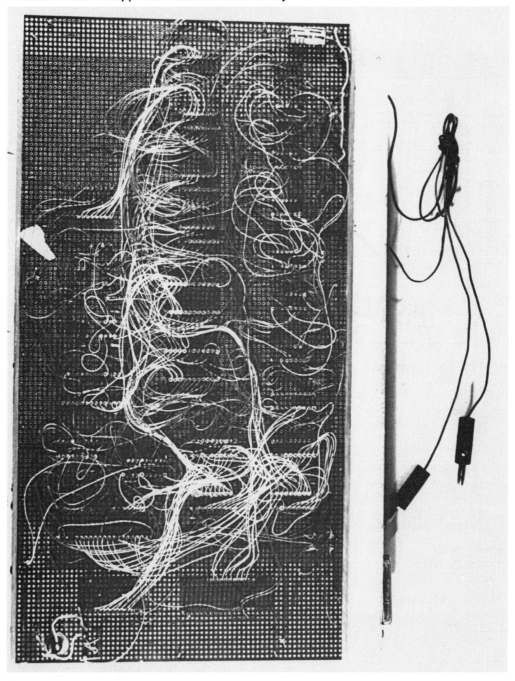

EXHIBIT 3   Ben's Illustration of the Technology Gap

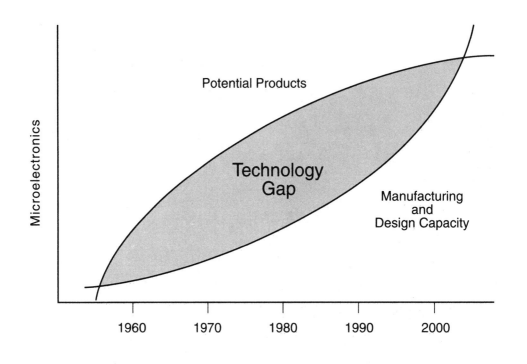

EXHIBIT 4   Printed Circuit Board Assembly

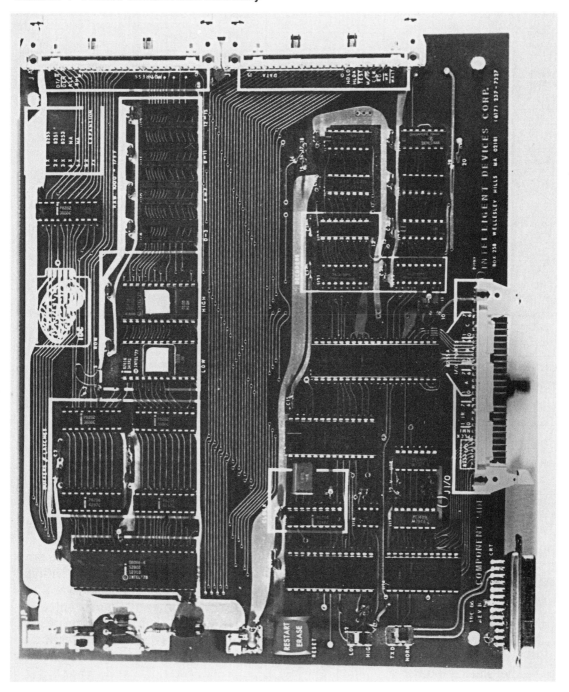

EXHIBIT 5 Listing of Products

EXPERIENCE THE POWER

THE IDC 8086 SINGLE BOARD COMPUTER

A COMPLETE, CLEAN SOLUTION FOR THE
IDC 86 UNIVERSITY KIT!

Intel has executed a major coup by implementing hardware upgrades and special functions for the 8086 via coprocessors. Coprocessing, combined with full machine-language-capable upgradability to the IAPX 286, makes the 8086 family of processors superior to any other processor on the market today. Combine hardware superiority with Intel's total system solution approach to software, and you have an unbeatable teaching tool backed by the company that invented the microprocessor. Intelligent Devices Corporation wants to help you get those Intel University Kits off the shelf and into the classroom quickly and cleanly. With our IDC 86 products, you can have a total 8086 system solution for under $250. So get started today.

EXHIBIT 5   (continued)

IDC 86 KIT SPECIFICATIONS

THE IDC 86 IS AVAILABLE IN SEVERAL CONFIGURATIONS!

IDC 86-b
    The circuit board alone. Kit includes the IDC 86 circuit board and the IDC 86 user's manual/assembly manual.
    The service phone line is <u>not</u> available to purchasers of board-only products, because we have no control over the quality of parts used on the board.

IDC 86-BC
    This is the circuit board and components required to get your ECK-86 up and running right away. All you need to supply is +5 Volts @ 1.5 Amps, an RS232 Terminal and your ECK 86 University Kit.* The IDC 86-BC includes the circuit board, a user's manual, sockets for all IC's, an additional 8282, one RS232 driver, six TTL LS IC's, DB 25 connector, 4 switches, crystal, resistors, diodes, 25 capacitors, and stand-offs.

IDC 86-SBC
    The super single board computer kit includes everything from the IDC 86-BC plus the super options: an 8255A Programmable Peripheral Interface and an 8253 Programmable Interval Timer/Counter, plus the required hardware for mounting the chips.

IDC 86-C1, IDC 86-C2
    The components only. The IDC 86-C1 contains the components from the IDC 86-BC, and the IDC 86-C2 contains the components from the IDC 86-SBC. Both parts kits come with the IDC 86 user's manual. For the convenience of those who thought they could buy the parts cheaper elsewhere. Renews access to the service phone line for those who previously purchased the board only.

ASSEMBLY AND TESTING
    Save the time and trouble of all that soldering! We assemble your kit for you and test to the extent we are able without inserting the parts contained in the ECK 86 University Kit. Includes selecting the jumper options according to our standard configuration via wire wrap pins. Add the prefix 'AT' to the part number of your order. This service is done at an additional charge of $35.00 per kit.

---

*As of July 1980 the ECK 86 contained one 8086, two 8282s, two 8286s, one 8284, two 2616s, four 2114s, one 8259A, and one 8251A. INTELLIGENT DEVICES CORPORATION IS NOT RESPONSIBLE FOR THE CONTENTS OF THE ECK 86. NO ECK 86 PARTS ARE INCLUDED IN OUR KITS.

EXHIBIT 5   (continued)

IDC 86 SOFTWARE SPECIFICATIONS

BOOST YOUR SYSTEMS PERFORMANCE WITH OUR PROVEN SOFTWARE!

IDC 86 SERIAL MONITOR

The IDC 86 Serial Monitor is an interactive design-debugging software tool that greatly enhances the value of your IDC 86 Single Board Computer. Commands available with the IDC 86 Serial Monitor are:

S	Substitute Memory
X	Examine Registers
D	Display Memory
M	Move/Fill Memory Block
I	In Port
O	Out Port
G	Go
N	Single Step

Also available are commands that allow true Host-Target operation so you may develop programs on a Host System and load the compiled hex file directly into the IDC 86 via the serial port. These commands are:

R	Read Hex File
W	Write Hex File

The IDC 86 SERIAL MONITOR comes in two configurations. The IDC 86-SM1 is the serial monitor in a pair of 2716 EPROMs. The IDC 86-SM2 is the serial monitor in either 2716 EPROMs or 2616 ROMs (our option), and you must trade in your 2616 ROMs containing the DEMO 86 monitor that came with your ECK 86 University Kit. In order to qualify for the discount, the 2616s (two of them) you send us must be functional. For further information order the IDC 86 SERIAL MONITOR Manual.

NOTICE

NO SOFTWARE WILL BE SOLD IN ANY FORM WITHOUT THE EXECUTION OF A SOFTWARE LICENSE AGREEMENT. Theft of software is a serious impediment to the development of this industry. Intelligent Devices Corporation will prosecute any violation of our copyright to the full extent of the law.

EXHIBIT 5   (concluded)

Intelligent Devices Corporation

P.O. Box 258 Wellesley Hills, MA 02181 (617) 237-7327

DC 86 PRODUCT LINE ORDER FORM
LY 1980

ITEM	QUANTITY	PRICE	TOTAL
IDC 86-B (Circuit Board Only)	_____	$99.50	$_____
IDC 86-BC (Kit)	_____	$158.95	$_____
AT-IDC 86-BC (Assembled Kit)	_____	$193.95	$_____
IDC 86-SBC (Kit)	_____	$198.45	$_____
AT-IDC 86-SBC (Assembled Kit)	_____	$233.45	$_____
IDC 86-C1 (Parts for IDC 86-BC)	_____	$70.00	$_____
IDC 86-C2 (Parts for IDC 86-SBC)	_____	$110.00	$_____
IDC 86-SM1* (Software)	_____	$95.00	$_____
IDC 86-SM2* (Software)	_____	$77.50	$_____
IDC 86 Manuals	_____	$7.50	$_____
IDC 86-SM Manual	_____	$7.50	$_____
CROSS 86 VAX (Software)	_____	$250.00	$_____
CROSS 86 11/70 (Software)	_____	$200.00	$_____
CROSS 86 BASIC LISTING (Software)	_____	$100.00	$_____
CROSS 86 Manual	_____	$7.50	$_____

*See back.

SUB TOTAL $_____

5% Mass. Tax (Residents) $_____

Shipping, $3.50/<u>Item</u> $_____

TOTAL ORDER $_____

TERMS

Institutional purchase orders are accepted. All personal checks must clear prior to shipping. Intelligent Devices Corporation reserves the right to substitute comparable parts where necessary. We will never substitute a part we have not tested and do not have total confidence in. Delivery is from stock. Due to supplier uncertainties, we cannot guarantee a delivery period. Call for current delivery times. Prices are subject to change without notice.

<u>ORDER STATUS INFORMATION</u>

The order service personnel are available between 8:00 am and 7:00 pm EST. Feel free to call for the status of your order.

Thank you for your interest in our products!

EXHIBIT 6 Excerpts about IDC from an Intel Brochure

TECHNOLOGY EXCHANGE

NOW THERE'S A BOARD FOR THE COMPONENT KIT — THE IDC-86

Some inventive types from Babson College in Massachusetts have collaborated to produce a circuit board for the 8086 Component Kit. The group, called Intelligent Devices Corporation, is currently marketing the IDC-86 board, which uses the same basic circuit as in the circuit diagram supplied

The 8086 Kit, With A New Twist

The main advantage to using the IDC-86 board is that certain adjustments have been made to the basic circuit. These adjustments greatly enhance overall performance. First of all, using the 8286 Octal Bus Transceivers supplied with the kit, the data bus has been buffered. This ensures data stability and gives you more room for on- and off-board expansion.

Second, special circuitry has been added to generate the transmit and receive clock signals to the 8251A USART for baud rate generation. This feature provides selectability from 110 to 2400 baud.

Finally, the RS232 interface has been redesigned to let you operate from a single power supply voltage, ground and +5V, eliminating the need for +12V and -12V.

These three changes not only let you operate from a single power supply, but they have eliminated the need for off-board square wave generators. This keeps both your package size and your total system cost to a minimum.

More Room To Grow

The IDC-86 comes with board space and circuitry for the addition of two expansion options: the 8255A Programmable Peripheral Interface and the 8253 Programmable Internal Timer/Event Counter.

When added to the board, the 8255A Programmable Peripheral Interface lets you expand your communication and control horizons. It has 24 input/output lines, configurable in three different modes for I/O or interrupt-driven I/O. It is also fully programmable.

The 8353 Programmable Interval Timer/Event Counter provides the kind of real-time control you need to make the Component Kit a versatile control computer. When used with the 8259A Interrupt Controller (also supplied with the kit), the 8253 can generate interrupt-driven delays from 0.5 microseconds to over four years without tying up one second of central processor time. It can also be used to drive the transmit and receive clock of the 8251A USART, giving you complete software control over data transmission rates.

It All Adds Up

For more information contact:
Ben Bailey
Intelligent Devices Corporation
P.O. Box 258
Wellesley Hills, MA 02181
(617) 237 7327

EXHIBIT 7 Approximate Income Statement for IDC *

Sales

Computers		$47,000	
Circuit Boards		13,000	
Total Sales			$60,000

Cost of Goods Sold

Computers		35,000	
Circuit Boards		6,000	
Total Cost of Goods Sold			41,000

Gross Profit — 19,000

Expenses

Office Rental ($260/mo)	780	
Telephone, utilities, office overhead ($320/mo)	960	
Salaries:		
Ben ($500/mo)	6,000	
Circuit board assembler	500	
Tax (minimum Massachusetts tax for corporations)	300	
R&D (3 circuit boards)	1,650	
Booth at computer show	14,000	
Incorporation fee	125	
Total Other Expenses		24,295
Profit (loss)		($5,295)

*Prepared by the casewriter from information supplied by Ben. The company had not as yet prepared formal financial statements nor completed tax returns.

EXHIBIT 8   Ben's "To Do" List

Bendrix Lee Bailey
September 1980

In Order of Priority

    DO FOR IDC

Write Letter to Tom Lathrum, RE: the SDK86, by a.m.

Put IDC Books up on System. Ben or John
Put IDC Customer Mailing list up on System.   Gary or John
Send thank you to Williams/Rilatto.

IDC 88 Circuit Board:

Design and test 2716 and 8755 EPROM Programmer.
Build and test cheap Cassette interface.
Interface Micro Com. Cassette drive.
Do wire layout.
Design UPI 41 interface and cable interface.
Adapt Sockets for 8755/8155 both.
Interface 8279 to bus and design socket interconnection.
Design current loop interface to serial channel.
Test 24-volt power supply for EPROM programmer.
Lay out logic area.
Design case for tape drive.
Contact Grayson about keyboard.

IDC 8 Circuit Board
Design it, build it.

DO FOR ONYX
Contact RE office for computer sale.
Contact Jim's friend about sale.
Put ONEI Books up on Accounting System. Ben
Design Booth Dimensions.
Discussion about signs for Onyx Booth.
Call Paul F. Home (603) 526-6327

Ernesto Blanco

Professor Ernesto Blanco sat behind a cluttered desk in his fourth-floor office of the Massachusetts Institute of Technology Mechanical Engineering Department and mused about entrepreneurial ambitions and frustrations.

I'd really like to get a profitable company going. My job here leaves me flexibility to do it. I have technical expertise and experience plus a collection of product ideas and the personal capability to generate more like them—products that perform useful functions effectively. But so far I haven't been able to formulate the right idea combination to make a new company that can operate reliably. But I'm not sure why or what to do about it. For instance, I'm puzzled about why this product doesn't seem to serve as an effective starting point.

He held in his hand a small stainless steel encased sensor roughly the size of a pocket knife. It was connected by electrical cord to a control box about the size of a hardback dictionary. Excerpts depicting the device appear in Exhibit 1. He continued:

What it does is detect faulty needles before they break on commercial fabric knitting machines. Breakage of a knitting needle on one of those machines rapidly generates defective material until the machine is shut down for needle replacement. With this sensor, shutdown happens immediately instead of waiting for an operator to notice and flip the switch off. That can save enough

money to pay for the sensor in as little as six weeks. One factory has been using it successfully for over three years. Several others have run tests and found it performed perfectly. The machine operators and foremen seemed pleased, but for some reason I haven't been able to get more sales and turn it into a going business.

Should I stay with this sensor and try something else to exploit it? Should I drop it and work on some of my other product ideas instead? If so, how? That's what I'd like to figure out. All I know for sure is that my time is limited and I have almost no financial resources, so I can't try many different things at the same time.

Personal Background

Ernesto Blanco was born and raised in Cuba. As a child, he found that repairing his toys was more fun than playing with them, and that making toys of his own design was the most fun of all. When he completed them, he gave them away. "I remember thinking then that my vocation should be making things," he recalled. He earned an engineering degree, with a specialty in machine design, in the early 1950s. In 1956 he became chief engineer in a Cuban textile mill. Shortly thereafter, he was invited to teach machine design at the University of Villanova in Cuba. He worked as a mill consultant in addition to his university commitments, thanks to his former employer, the mill owner, who also sat on the university's board of regents.

In 1960, after Fidel Castro came to power, Professor Blanco came to the

United States and was offered a teaching position at MIT. Again, he combined his academic responsibilities with hands-on engineering assignments. He participated in an MIT project to develop aids for the handicapped. For the MIT Sensory Aid Research Center, he designed and built a motorized Braille display machine prototype that converted characters from tape to a continuous band of raised Braille letters on paper. He also began work on a stair-climbing wheelchair. However, his ideas far exceeded the time and money available to him for developing them to the production stage.

Outside the university, he took on consulting assignments for a wide variety of clients, including some with familiar names such as General Electric, Fairbanks-Morse, Gillette and Polaroid. A frustrating aspect of consulting, he found, was that he was always working his way out of a job as he completed each assignment. He said it would be nice to create a company with proprietary ownership of products that could provide steadier income.

In the late 1960s he began consulting for Compton Mills,* a large corporation devoted in part to producing pile fabrics.** For that company exclusively, he developed and produced a variety of devices that improved both production speed and quality of knitted pile fabrics. Eventually, however, his string of assignments at Compton ended when the company encountered a sales slump in the 1974 recession.

Having foreseen such a possibility, he had sought other ways to earn a living from his engineering ideas. It seemed logical to him to concentrate in the textile industry because his consulting had been greatest there. Taking care not to duplicate products he had designed for Compton, he reviewed undeveloped ideas that had occurred to him over time and listed several that he thought would be particularly interesting to work on. Some of the items from this list appear below, beginning with the Faulty-Needle detector.

1. Needle-Master: A faulty-needle detector.

2. Synchro-Frame: A special web accumulator capable of storing in-process fabric without tension.

3. Cone-Roll Idle-Glider: Simple, inexpensive and effective guide system for rolling fabric. Estimated cost, $230.

4. Magic-Roll: An entirely mechanical linear feedback web guider. It would expand and remove wrinkles from the fabric, while at the same time centering and guiding it within the accuracy of 1/4 inch. A sales price of $2,300 would be well below the electro-mechanical or electronic competition.

5. Octa-Pak: A method of adequately packaging bolts of delicate pile fabrics.

6. Gale-Frame: A device to remove effectively the entrapped water or other liquids from fabrics prior to heat-drying operations.

7. Yarn-Master: A mechanical device for monitoring the tension on yarn.

To illustrate further the nature of these machines, excerpts from a report describing the second one on the list, the Synchro-Frame, appear in Exhibit 2. In contrast to

---

* A disguised name.

**Pile is a fabric such as artificial fur, velours, coat linings, and some rugs, constructed from loops of fiber, cut or uncut. It has a fuzzy surface. Although pile fabric may be woven, the pile referred to here is exclusively knitted. Pile fabric, such as artificial fur or velours, is relatively expensive. Therefore, it provides a cost-justifiable target for quality control devices.

the Synchro-Frame, the Faulty-Needle detector was a smaller item that Professor Blanco could assemble and work on at home. The design concepts he devised for these products were quite different in principle from those he had done for Compton, so he was confident of avoiding any conflict of interest in developing them.

The Knitting Process and the Needle-Master System

In a textile factory, there were two chief ways of converting fiber to fabric, weaving and knitting. Weaving was done on looms that produced flat rectangular sheets of fabric. Knitting was done on knitting machines, which were either circular or flat. Each machine incorporated many hook-shaped needles. On circular-type machines, these needles were mounted on a rotating cylinder. Fiber or yarn was fed to the hooks, and a tube of material was knitted. The material was then flattened and rolled as it came from the machine. Later it was unrolled and cut down one side to make a flat length of fabric.

Pile-knitters were a type of circular-knitting machine. They required rugged needles, all of which had to be changed at least once per month. Even then, needles broke at a rate of four or five a day. As soon as one broke off, a hole in the fabric, which quickly became a run, was produced. This flawed fabric either had to be discarded or sold as seconds. The more expensive the fabric, the greater the expense of such waste.

A typical knitting machine operator was in charge of 10 machines and was responsible for stopping a machine and replacing any broken needle whenever a flaw in the material appeared. Once the machine was shut off, it took the cylinder one rotation to stop completely. On a pile-knitter, this produced about 3/4 of an inch of fabric. Even though the operator might be vigilant, he had 10 machines to watch,

and a yard or more of fabric could easily be knitted before a run was detected. Detection with Blanco's sensor, he said, would take at most one revolution of the machine.

It's entirely possible it will be caught before that, he continued. If the needle breaks right after it passes the center it would have to go all around before it hits again. There is a possibility of detecting not necessarily a defective needle, but one that is worn out. The timing on that is difficult to tell, but it would be before the defect appears. Usually you have to adjust the sensitivity quite high to detect a worn-out needle but it can be done. We really have not tried to sell the idea of detecting the needle before it breaks, because there's only one case in which it works out, and that would be the case of the worn-out hook. No other part of the needle can be detected until it is broken.

Non-pile knitters, either single-knit or double-knit, had many more needles mounted on the rotating cylinder than did pile-knitters. One rotation could produce 10 to 12 inches of fabric. So by the time a flaw was detected and the needle stopped, those machines could produce many wasted yards.

The purpose of Professor Blanco's "Needle-Master" was to sense needles that were weakening or broken and shut the knitting machine down automatically as quickly as possible to minimize production of defective fabric.

The Market for the System

Professor Blanco had sought data on the overall potential market for his "Needle-Master." The Compton pile-knitting operation, with which he was most familiar, utilized over 200 circular pile-knitting machines, each of which cost around $80,000 to $160,000 new.

In 1975, he had met with staff members of *Textile World* magazine, an industry publication. They estimated that there were 70,000 knitting machines in the United States, with perhaps 50,000 in operation. They expected this number would steadily decline. Approximately 20,000 machines produced double-knit fabrics. Another 30,000 did single-knits, and about 3,000 were pile-knitters (also called sliver-knitters). He noted that no recent issues of the magazine had carried advertisements for any sort of Faulty-Needle detectors. He guessed that out of the 50,000 machines in operation approximately 30 percent to 40 percent could economically justify addition of his device. He commented:

> Actually, all the machines could economically justify it, although for some the justification would be weaker because they produce lower cost fabrics. But union regulations require a certain minimum number of operators. That fact, particularly when it combines with the lower value of fabrics on some of the machines, reduces the number that can be justified.

Trade shows in the industry, he believed, were effective showcases for new products. Sales of knitting machinery, he said, were almost exclusively made by direct selling. Normally, a salesman made his "pitch" to the purchasing department. If that department took an interest, the engineering department and the plant managers would test the product for a period of time. If the results were as promised, a decision to buy might be proposed to top management, which would approve or disapprove it. If it were approved, the purchasing department would work out terms for a contract with the salesman. Blanco commented:

> I'm not aware of the extent of an international market, but there probably is one. One of the people that answered an ad I ran in the Wall Street Journal expressed interest in selling the broken needle sensor abroad.

Professor Blanco characterized the U.S. textile industry as "a jungle—almost like a mafia."

> The competition is intense; the largest producer controls only 7 percent of the market, and the two or three companies dominating pile production account for less than 2 percent of the market. The industry has an ethic all its own. Below the top echelon of reputable manufacturers, such as Burlington, DuPont, J.P. Stevens, and maybe Lowenstein, are many, many smaller companies competing furiously. It's like something out of Charles Dickens, and so are the managers. Their mentality is nineteenth century; they resist technology, and efficiency doesn't seem to interest them.
>
> It's a dog-eat-dog industry, except at the very top. One small company will take a loss in order to drive another one out of business. I think if they managed more logically, they would not have to be so devious. But when I said that to one manager, he just looked back and said, "it's more exciting our way." The last company that did not buy said that they wanted to buy new machines and they couldn't afford my product.
>
> Fabric sales have been down for quite a while, although they are supposed to be picking up. The company that has 40 sensors did poorly last year, but their sales seem to be increasing now.

Excerpts from Standard & Poor's 1980 summary of the textile industry appear in Exhibit 3.

Formation of Unitex Corporation

In 1974, Professor Blanco formed a corporation named Unitex with two partners. One was a financial analyst, and the other an old friend and experienced manager with some money to invest. Their stated purpose was to market a variety of mechanical and electro-mechanical devices created by Blanco as development engineer. He wanted Unitex to become a company in which he could apply his expertise in product development to the fullest without worry about client politics, finances and marketing. Thereby, he said, it should return a profit to all the partners. He personally invested $1200 to cover the lawyer's fee, corporate filing, and other small start-up expenses such as stationery and telephone. His partners prepared a prospectus for raising $100,000 to cover costs of prototypes, patents and initial manufacturing.

A lawyer was engaged to search for patented technology on any devices like those Blanco had worked on for Compton. The partners wanted to steer clear of any possible disputes about stealing of ideas. Before long, the president of Compton Mills arranged for a meeting with Professor Blanco, ostensibly to look for new products for his factory. However, Blanco believed it was to discover whether he was using any of Compton's proprietary ideas. Blanco was able to show the president that the design for the Faulty-Needle detector he had made as a consultant for Compton had, Blanco later discovered, been patented in 1932. Also, Blanco determined that the Needle-Master he had designed after leaving Compton was different and freshly patentable. An unpleasant scene ensued, and the president left in bad humor. "I believe he was trying to prohibit

me from making any new products," Blanco commented.

It also became apparent in 1975, he said, that the capital market had dried up, thwarting the plan for a quick, strong start-up. Nonetheless, Professor Blanco and his partners decided to proceed as best they could with limited cash. Although continued patent work on the Needle-Master might cost an estimated $4,000 to $5,000 and take perhaps a year, Blanco and his partners considered it appropriate. The device, he said, was intentionally unsophisticated, and therefore relatively easy to copy. It was electro-mechanical, with one small sensor and few moving parts. Professor Blanco commented:

> *Most technology in the textile industry is relatively unsophisticated. The mechanics are wrench-men. The machines are mechanical and reliable; a few drops of oil from time to time takes care of most maintenance. This is one industry which, as yet, is not suited to electronic modification. In fact, the first company to introduce a faulty needle detector, a German firm named Sick, used electronic technology in the sensor itself, and it was too touchy. Vibrations from other machines set it off; dust got into it. The two other competitive products now on the market have made the same mistake and are not selling at all. Machine operators like my detector better because it is easy to adjust and relatively insensitive to outside disturbances.**
>
> *I figured that if I had a patent, it would give me something to sell. If a big company should try to copy my product, the patent might not prevent them from doing so, but in court I could argue that*

---

* There were no advertisements for any sort of faulty-needle detector in recent issues of Textile World magazine and Professor Blanco commented that "no one is selling any."

they should pay me for rights. Unfortunately, I understand it could cost me over 10 times as much to sue them as it did to get the patent in the first place. I don't know how I could pay for that, even if I were certain to win, which nobody ever is.*

Early Installations

As a backup to his only other sources of income, part-time teaching at MIT, and occasional consulting, Professor Blanco had worked on the needle detector nearly full-time in his basement, experimenting, refining, and testing, "until I had something worth patenting," he recalled. After two units had been installed on a machine and worked flawlessly for a month, he began patent application. One partner then invested $10,000 in the company to pay patenting expenses. Shortly thereafter, he invested another $19,000. Half was as a loan and the other half was for a 30-percent share of the company.

The original Faulty-Needle detector Professor Blanco designed for Compton had, he said, two major problems. First, it was too sensitive. Second, it was difficult to manufacture. He had made it personally by hand because the textile company machine shop had found it nearly impossible to produce. Therefore, his new design after leaving Compton aimed to overcome these difficulties through simplification. It also had a more rugged housing. All but two or three of the units installed three years earlier were still in operation, Professor Blanco commented.

There is little maintenance. We have had about two or three that failed. Possibly one failed and two were mis-

---

* It had recently been reported that fewer than half of suits filed by patentees against infringers were successful, due to a view held by many judges that patents hsould not convey too much monopoly power.

treated. But generally the reliability is very high.

Although the first working prototypes were entirely handmade by Blanco, the partners believed that when more capital was invested, the company could begin to think in terms of delegated production. The partners' hope was to manufacture 1,000 units per year in this manner at a gross cost of $500 per unit. Professor Blanco commented that a complete breakdown of parts cost could be very difficult, since the parts he had used had been bought at different times, and many of them had been worked on by different vendors and assemblers. For the sensor, he expected purchased parts would cost approximately $50. He said he might be able to make them for less if he had the appropriate machinery, but he had neither that nor the space or people to run it.

The electronic module, Blanco said, required outside purchases of approximately $200. Purchase of additional assembly work on it and the sensor might cost another $50, but was something Professor Blanco expected he could handle with his own facilities. All that was needed for assembly, he said, was one desk, a few small tools, a magnifier and two skilled hands. Once installed, the unit required very little maintenance.

He set the selling price for the assembled unit at $1,000. This, he noted, was below the $1,200 to $1,500 other companies had asked for systems that had not worked properly. His system could be expanded to three sensors per electronic module at a price of $300 per additional sensor. He commented on installation as follows:

The first installation, until we train somebody to do that, requires my presence initially. In a plant where I go with the salesperson and install the first unit, the rest of the mechanics—these plants all have maintenance people and so on—

should easily be able to do the job themselves. But so far I've been doing that for free. The last trip cost me $400.

Initial Sales

In 1976, during the time he was working on the Needle-Master prototypes, Professor Blanco had run into a former Compton Mills employee and good friend at a convention in Atlantic City. The man had left Compton the year before Blanco and formed his own consulting firm, Intertex Industries Corporation, but had remained friendly with the president of Compton Mills. Blanco described his invention to the salesman, who immediately expressed an interest in handling sales of the Needle-Master in addition to his consulting work. They agreed to a commission rate of 20 percent on sales.

First, the salesman had arranged for prototype tests in the Compton factory, on the understanding that if the tests were successful, the mill would buy Needle-Masters. Blanco had supervised the installation, working with some of the same mill mechanics whose thoroughness he had admired when he had served on the Compton consulting staff.* The tests, Professor Blanco said, were flawless.

Nevertheless, he decided to refine the needle detector yet again, to make it even more immune to outside vibrations and dust. In effect, this obsoleted his six original prototypes, three of which had now been purchased. He was able to modify both the electronics and the sensor to make them more rugged, and to reinstall the three he had recalled.

It was at this point—with three revamped Needle-Masters operating, an-

other three upgraded prototype units on hand, plus a single handmade prototype of a next generation model—that Unitex received its first multiple order. It was from Compton Mills for six units. Professor Blanco had decided earlier that tooling up for production would be justified if he could get an order for 12 units or more. He informed the salesman, who returned to Compton and got the order raised to that number.

To deliver on the order, Professor Blanco said, he had to do "a lot of wiggling" in dealing with suppliers and toolmakers, to reach understandings on specifications, prices and delivery dates. Assembly was set up in his home and the 12 Needle-Master systems were delivered. Compton then ordered another 24. Blanco recalled:

In fact, Compton could have used detectors on all of their 200 machines, but there are some fabrics on which they are forced to use a certain number of people because of union rules. The Needle-Master could still help there, but you have to pay for so many operators anyway that the justification is not as great on those fabrics as it is on others.

Reassured by the proceeds from these sales to Compton and what he saw as the prospect of more orders, Professor Blanco purchased enough parts and material (gold alloy, stainless steel, etc.) to make another 200 Needle-Masters. By 1978 he had sold over 40 units, all but one for pile knitters, and he had material enough for 200 more. He had also received a U.S. patent (Number 200,026,128) and had applied for patents in France and Germany. His estimate was that the foreign market might be half as large as that in the U.S. However, Unitex was in debt for $6,000 to one supplier who had agreed to wait for payment until the products sold.

Despite his initial success, and even

---

* While at Compton, Professor Blanco had paid a small incentive bonus to the mechanics with whom he had worked, in appreciation for the extra demands he had made on their time. Several of these men were now responsible for monitoring the Needle-Masters.

though the Needle-Master was given an unconditional guarantee of one year, the salesman seemed unable to sell units to any other company. He said there seemed to be a pattern in which the salesman would persuade the purchasing agent and foreman in a mill to take the device for a trial period, usually a month. When the month was up, the customer would agree that the product had worked well but give some excuse not to buy, possibly dissatisfaction with the price or concern about unseen effects on future operation of the machine. Blanco commented:

I know those managers. They consider any money spent on innovations as excessive. As an engineer, I was not prepared for their resistance. The machine operators and people in the shop seemed to like my product, but management just wouldn't go for it.

Following these failed efforts to get customers beyond Compton, Professor Blanco had severed the salesman's exclusive contract.

He agreed that he should no longer be our sole representative but predicted that any other salesman would encounter the same resistance. He may have been trying to justify his poor performance; I did not know.

Product Justification

Professor Blanco commented that there was no other device quite like the Needle-Master and that his own exhaustive pretesting had convinced him that it would work as claimed. Without fail, it would detect a defective needle as soon as the needle passed the sensor, often even before the needle fully broke, which meant within one revolution or less of the knitting machine's producing flawed fabric. Replacement of a needle was then fairly

cheap. The needle itself cost approximately 25 cents to 50 cents, depending upon type. An operator had to be there all the time anyway. Changing a needle would take approximately 10 minutes of operator time, which Professor Blanco said represented approximately $1 worth of labor time.

The cost of material ruined when a needle broke and was not promptly detected was much greater. Professor Blanco had compiled records indicating that when installed on pile knitters, Needle-Masters had typically paid for themselves within four to six weeks. He said the return on investment for these pile knitter installations was 400 percent per year, and even on single-knit machines, the payback was no longer than six months, yielding a savings of $2,000 per year.

Various add-on devices made by other companies for knitting machines seemed to sell all right. One was a retrofit lubrication system that had successfully been added to the majority of existing machines. It consisted of some flexible lubrication lines which were clipped on to the machine and connected to a dispensing box about the size of the Needle-Master electronic control box on the side of the machine. Its cost was also about the same, but it was less complicated to install and machine maintenance people could perform the task on their own. Blanco said the company that sold the lubrication system might be a potential sales channel for Needle-Masters. They had even been quite friendly with his former salesman. "But they didn't buy any," he said. "I think it would be difficult to deal with them without the salesman who seemed to be friends with them."

He commented that new knitting machines coming on the market were much more sophisticated than the majority of existing machines. One made in Germany, called a Moratronix, was almost fully electronically controlled, allowing even the purchasing of programs for automatic knitting of different patterns. The Moratronix machine was very expensive compared to existing machines, costing around $120,000. A full maintenance contract normally came with such a machine.

As yet, these machines did not incorporate any sort of broken needle detectors, let alone a device that would sense all modes of failure and operate as effectively as his. "There is," Professor Blanco said, "simply no other device like it." He thought it would be difficult, if not impossible, for machine makers to add such a device without infringing on his patent. If they did, however, he was not sure what he should do. All other broken needle detectors, he said, had failed commercially.

Some of them were too sophisticated and too sensitive. They required a lot of attention beyond the level of competence of operators. Every machine has one type of broken-latch sensor. It only senses when the latch is broken or sticking. But they cannot detect anything else on the needle. There are four modes of failure in the needle and this system only detects one. Our sensor detects all four.

Professor Blanco's Own Selling Experience

Professor Blanco considered himself more an engineer than a salesman, but he considered the experience of trying to sell constructively educational. He commented:

I have tried to sell the Needle-Master myself to a former client with over 100 machines, all single-knitters. I called him and arranged for the knitting department to see my machine.

When I got there they were expecting me. First, I explained the device to the

mechanics, and then I rolled up my sleeves and got right into the machine with them, like I always do, to demonstrate the installation. I get a lot of dirty suits, especially in the northeast mills. There is dust everywhere, and the noise is terrible.

At any rate, I brought my own mechanic and asked the foreman to assign to me whichever mechanic of theirs would be responsible for the detector. I spent two days with him, installing the device. He was cooperative but asked for a longer trial period, six months. If it worked that long, he said, his boss would buy Needle-Masters for all his knitters.

After five months I called my friend, the foreman. He told me they weren't going to buy. Why? Because the president had decided that the cost was not justified for single-knit material. He said the company was planning to buy a number of pile knitters in the future, and when that time came, they would consider giving me an order. I wrote to the president, asking for the device to be returned. He confirmed the story, even though the Needle-Master System had functioned perfectly. That was typical.

I have had some people who referred me to other companies. The last one I visited tried a Needle-Master for about six months. At the end of the test, which was very successful, it was returned in perfect shape. They claimed that they could not afford to buy because they wanted it for all their machines and that would cost too much!

My impression of the way selling works is that someone in upper management has to make the buying decision. Permission to install the device only for testing can be given by someone who is just in charge of the knitting department, because testing costs them nothing. But when it comes to actually buying, it's a capital investment decision, and that's a very different matter.

That has to be done by upper management, presumably the president or general manager or someone like that who has to decide on the budget.

But why, he wondered, would a top manager not buy the product? Some possibilities he characterized as far-fetched occurred to him but seemed too implausible to take seriously. One was that somehow top managers of different companies might be jointly conspiring to keep their investments down. Another was that his one client might be discrediting the product to maintain exclusive use of a competitive advantage. Or maybe the union of textile workers, for some reason, opposed the consequences of his improvement regardless of the benefit to individuals involved. These unions were, he said, regarded by many managers as extremely strong and troublesome.

Several other observations puzzled him. One was that no one seemed interested in the possible economy of buying more than one unit per control box, even though each box was capable of handling three. He remarked:

The price of the box and the sensor together is $1,000, but additional sensors cost only $300. Possibly on a pile-knitter, the manager feels the savings in fabric would not justify the extra sensor, but for flat-knits—with many more needles—three or four inches of material could be saved with three equally-spaced sensors mounted on the cylinder.

A second puzzling thing was a statement by one manager that he did not believe the device was cost-justifiable at all for use on "flat fabric" machines. Instead, the manager said it would be better to invest in more pile knitting machines to increase production. Blanco continued:

If I put myself in the position of a

manager, I would be reluctant to accept that a larger capital investment in production machines would be better than a smaller capital investment in getting more good product from existing equipment. He was surprised that manufacturers were not more concerned about increasing the percentage of flawless fabric. Sometimes they don't seem to mind producing seconds.

Further Marketing Efforts

Until last year, I was reluctant to make a big splash with this product. Failure of other producers' Faulty-Needle detectors had given such gadgets a bad reputation, so I have been very cautious in testing mine, both in the laboratory and in the mill. I don't want to put a device on the market that won't be quite what the user would like. I want it to be sought after by potential users. That would indicate that it was doing what it was intended to. Then I would be ready to bring it to the large companies. Now, I have the feeling that maybe there is something else, something interfering with sales that has nothing to do with performance of the device itself.

What to do about it, I just don't know. I would be willing to try almost anything. If I had a personal contact in a big fabric company, I would go there at once and try to sell the device or rent it, or even sell the entire idea. If I had money, I would be willing to try an advertisement in Textile World *at more than $2,000 for a full page. I would be willing to set up a booth at a trade show at even higher cost than that. But I no longer have the capital, and for now the least expensive and most effective way of marketing seems to be direct selling. Of course, I would welcome publication of an article in* Textile World *to tell what my product can do for the industry, but*

I have no experience in public relations.

I did try one small advertisement. I put an ad in the Wall Street Journal, *with a caption reading "New Revolutionary Textile Product." Ten people replied. Some were textile machinery manufacturers representatives. Three of them were textile manufacturers. Two of them were in general marketing organizations and said things like "We'll find you your market for a fee of $2,500, and you don't have to pay until we have sold more than $2,500 worth of your product," which of course is crazy.*

One who replied was a manufacturer of needles. This is very interesting. A maker of needles could offer my product to broaden his service to the industry. He could sell it as something that would allow the operator to replace a worn-out needle before it broke and caused a run in the fabric. But I have not had time to reply, and I'm not sure just what arrangement I should go after or how.

I would be happy to have a salesman look at the potential for European markets. I feel quite certain that information about our products has become known there. Possibly, theirs is a more receptive situation.

In this country, though, I'm becoming discouraged. Aside from that newspaper advertisement, I also sent out a letter (a copy of which appears in Exhibit 4) on our company to over 60 contacts. Not one has replied. I wonder what motivates potential consumers for this product and how to persuade them to buy it. It's hard for me to understand the thinking of managers in the textile industry. Maybe I'm too emotionally involved.

Six letters have come from manufacturers' representatives asking about it and my terms of sale. But the only personal contact I had was this salesman who is not selling. I didn't make any other contacts.

Other Possibilities

Professor Blanco had thought at length about the role of the inventor/engineer in American society, observing:

I see three groups of people: producers, predators, and observers. A small number of producers work, often in isolation, to find solutions for specific problems. Predators, which include politicians and managers, swarm like sharks when they spot an idea that can be exploited, and look first to maximizing their own profits. The observers are the passive consumers. We have a need for all three, but the strength of our economy depends ultimately on the producers.

Yet, this country seems to have lost the will to make a nurturing climate for struggling innovators. We are science-heavy, management-heavy, and engineering-lean. We are not teaching our students the importance of engineering. The concept of application, of making something work, is not esteemed. We spend money on research, but of what use is science if you cannot put it to work? Yes, a microprocessor is a marvel of a brain, but what good is a brain in a glass? One must devise a way to make it perform, to give it a body.

This is why I feel a great obligation to my students, and why I share with them many of the devices which I have invented but have neither time nor money to bring to the marketplace.

I believe strongly in what I do as a mechanical engineer. Any device, no matter how sophisticated, always has two points of physical interface—two contacts with the physical world, two mechanical connections. First, someone must start it. And second, it must deliver something of use to that person. At each of these two junctures, a mechanical device is needed. A switch must ac-

tivate the machine and thereby the results, whether a display of Braille characters or the shutdown of a knitting machine with a faulty needle. This function must be made available in a way useful to the person for whom the machine is designed.

I accept existing technology, taking whatever is available in solid state electronics, or whatever, and I design mechanically a way for it to perform a certain task. I begin with a simple concept and work to make it simpler. My constraints are the budget, the capabilities of the user, and the amount of time allotted.

But I need an organization to exploit my ideas and give me a reasonable rate of return. The ingredients for commercial success remain a mystery to me. In my work so far, I have not had to make the decisions about what to design; the circumstances controlled the choice.

I also believe that if I have done much work on a project I should finish it, even if the market for it is not there immediately. Later it will be ready when its time comes. Possibly I am wrong in these matters. Often I feel I am putting much in and getting very little out. I am a maker, not a seller.

At this moment, the Needle-Master is nearest to commercial success. But another design I've invested much time and thought in is a micro-solenoid Braille display cell. When I returned to MIT in 1977, Professor Mann asked if I intended to return to my work with the Braille displayer. He had information about a proposal for a compact reading machine for use by blind telephone operators and others whose needs were not met by the new '"talking books." I gave him drawings for a new machine that utilized new technology in solenoids, enabling the machine to be very small and energy-efficient.

At his suggestion, I applied to the National Science Foundation for a preliminary grant of $25,000. (A summary of the final report on Phase I of the micro-solenoid operated Braille display appears in Exhibit 5.) With this money, I developed a single Braille display letter unit, capable of fitting into standard letter and line spacings and electronically controlled from a magnetic tape cassette. This unit is very small, the size of my little finger, and the surface to be touched is only four-tenths to one-fourth of an inch. When I had finished this unit, I was asked by NSF (National Science Foundation, a federal research grant agency) to apply for a Phase II grant. This grant would be in the neighborhood of $250,000. With that we might be able to develop an entire page of refreshable Braille no larger than a book, utilizing perhaps 3,000 units. It is very ambitious. This type of NSF program to give grants for new product development only started about a year ago. There may have been a half dozen companies created by it so far.

I have been told there are approximately 300,000 blind people in the United States. Between the totally blind and the legally blind, there are probably quite a few more than that. Some of the legally blind may not need the instrument, and not all blind people read Braille. So I would guess there might be a potential market of around 100,000 users.

A third possibility is a page-turner for music books. In 1976, my sister who plays the violin was frustrated at having to stop to adjust her score, and asked me if I could make her a machine to do it that she could actuate with her foot. I thought it could be done, and made a model out of wood. It worked, and for $150 I had one manufactured. Then I got busy and forgot about it. One aspect that still needs to be perfected is the mechanism for holding the page in place *once it is turned.*

The market for it would be very hard for me to estimate. It would consist of a certain percentage of paralyzed people, and I don't really know how many there are. It might also be used by some musical performers, and maybe even some orchestras. If I had to make a guess, I'd suppose maybe there might be a market in total for about a thousand per year, but I don't know.

I am also still very interested in the problem of designing a stair-climbing wheel-chair. I have engaged my students in that project as well, and they find it very challenging.

As I see it, I have responsibilities both to my students and to the investors in Unitex. This means I must continue teaching, and in addition produce a product that will provide a return on investment, one which our corporate charter would tolerate. Also I must find time to apply for the Phase II NSF grant; I've worked too hard on that Braille machine to abandon it now.

I cannot imagine why people see progress as inevitable. In truth, it requires very hard work. But there are only so many hours in a day and there are so many possible things to work on. Where should I start?

EXHIBIT 1 Excerpt from the Needle-Master Brochure

Finally...
A Reliable Faulty Needle Stop Motion System

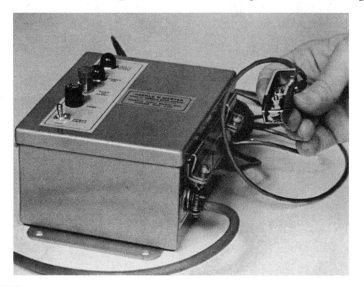

DESCRIPTION

The Needle-Master System was designed to eliminate wasted yardage caused by unnoticed defective needles. Savings in direct cost of this wasted material should pay for the system in a matter of weeks.

All common needle defects... broken hooks, broken latches, sticky latches, broken butts, and even worn-out hooks... are instantly detected without error.

The heart of the system is the uniquely designed sensor probe. Unlike other designs, the Needle-Master probe is a reliable electro-mechanical unit that "feels" each needle as it hurries by. Since the sensor probe actually touches the needles, false signals are eliminated. Needle vibration and ordinary misalignments have no effect on sensor performance.

Each and every needle is individually inspected for shape, position, and quality while the machine is in operation.

The sensor units are compact and exceedingly sturdy. They are precision machined out of stainless and tool steels, sealed, and lubricated for long service life. They are maintenance free, and are easily cleaned with a blast of shop air during routine machine cleaning.

Up to three sensors are monitored by the Needle-Master electronic module. Controls are heavy-duty industrial units designed to operate in the "fail safe" mode. Any damage to the system, such as a broken connection, will cause the machine to stop, thereby preventing a temporary loss of protection.

A green light on the control panel indicates normal machine operation. When a needle defect is detected, the machine is immediately stopped and a bright red alarm light alerts the operator.

EXHIBIT 1 (concluded)

TOP VIEW

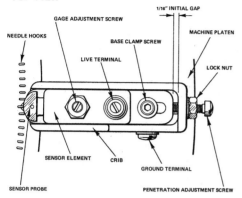

SIDE VIEW

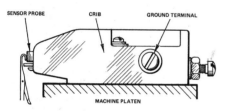

THE SENSOR UNIT

The Sensor Unit consists of two parts, the Sensor Element and the Crib. The Crib protects the Sensor Element from accidental damage during machine operation or maintenance, while at the same time it provides a rigid base for adjusting the Sensor Element in relation to the needles. The Crib is attached to the machine platen by means of a bolt and a dowel pin, becoming part of the ground electrical connection.

INSTALLATION

The Gage Adjustment Screw on top of the Sensor Element is factory set for the needle gage specified and should not be tampered with.

The installed height of the sensor in relation to the needles is shown in the side view above. Height can be adjusted by using shims if necessary. Needle hooks should be at mid-height of Sensor Probe face. Prior to installation there should be an Initial Gap of 1/16 inch between the Sensor Element base plate and the rear wall of the Crib, as shown in top view.

The Sensor Unit should be installed perpendicular to the needle line, with the Sensor Probe just touching the needle hooks. The Base Clamp Screw and the Lock Nut should then be loosened and the Penetration Adjustment Screw turned inwardly until the needles are slightly pushed to insure that they all slide across the face of the Probe. Needle deflection should be about 1/3 of hook depth. That will serve to stabilize the needles and insure reliable sensing action.

The Base Clamp Screw and the Lock Nut should then be tightened, the electric leads connected to the sensor terminals as indicated, and the installation checked by running it with a needle with a broken hook placed at several locations on the cylinder.

Shown above is the proper installation of electrical leads to sensor terminals. The long red lead goes to the Live Terminal, and the short black one goes to ground at the Crib.

EXHIBIT 2   Excerpts from Synchro-Frame Description of Tensionless Festooner Web Accumulator

This machine is a special web accumulator capable of storing in-process fabric without tension. The machine consists of a floor-mounted modular frame holding at its top a series of power driven rolls over which the fabric is automatically festooned. The system differs from standard web accumulators in that the stored fabric is conveyed by the rolls across the unit as in a power conveyer without being subjected to tensions of any kind. All the rolls supporting the fabric are powered by a novel drive system called Synchro-drive, which insures that each roll turns at exactly the proper speed so that all the festooned loops are formed with the same length throughout, whether the machine is being loaded or unloaded. The input and output of the machine are independently driven by SYNCHRONOUS motor systems under proportional control from sensing rolls at each end.

Through the sensing rolls, the machine adapts automatically to any input or output speed from 0 to 120 yards per minute in any direction. The fabric can be fed into the machine from either end, or from both ends simultaneously at any rate or taken out at any rate from either or both ends, but the loops remain tensionless and of equal length whether they may be going up or down during the operation. The machine behaves like a tensionless "fabric tank" that receives fabric from the preceding machine and delivers it to the following one, or else stores it, in accordance to the speed requirements of the production line.

Machine capacity can be tailored to customers' requirements. The 400-foot capacity model measures 12 feet high by 7 feet wide and 8 feet in length. In one actual line installation, the machine also monitored electrically the speed of line operation. As a result, production was increased by 12 percent through the resulting improvement in synchronization.

When operating with very unstable fabrics it is recommended that a stabilizing frame be installed to guide the fabric loops along the machine. The stabilizing frame consists of an extremely light assembly of thin-wall aluminum rolls fitted with plastic cone guiders that keep all the hanging loops in line during operation.

This machine is almost essential when processing very delicate pile fabrics which are frequently damaged if dumped into scrays. The space required for the installation of the machine is comparable, if not smaller, than that required by a scray.

The price of this machine will vary according to capacity. The 400 foot unit, including all electrical controls and the stabilizing frame, is tentatively priced at $26,000.

EXHIBIT 3   Excerpts from Standard and Poor's 1980 Textile Industry Summary

Expansion of capacity has been limited in recent years to a few growing markets, such as denim and corduroy. This is because the major thrust of the industry has been toward increasing manufacturing efficiency, a policy that is likely to persist over the intermediate term. Spending will be largely for advanced types of equipment that can lower costs and fortify trade positions in specific areas, both domestically and abroad. The below-average return on investment in the industry, the high cost of new equipment and excess capacity in some areas will tend to work against further additions to capacity. Furthermore, substantial expenditures are still required to meet environmental standards, which will tend to reduce available funds.

Capacity utilization for the industry peaked at some 85.6 percent during the closing months of 1979, according to McGraw-Hill...a slight gain from 85.1 percent in 1978, while 1977's average or 82.3 percent was up from the 1975 low of 77.5 percent.... Accurate data on industry capacity cannot be calculated, partly because of the broadly diversified equipment in place and the ability to shift machine output from one product to another with variable running speeds.

The significant rise in imports of textiles during the 1970s attests to the increase in world output and capacity, which have been excessive for many years. Studies indicate that the number of looms in developing nations has been increasing, while in industrialized nations it has been declining.

Textile manufacturers are expected to remain steady purchasers of equipment that offers the potential for improving productivity, as well as product quality and productive versatility.

The speed of processing all fabrics is expected to increase in the 1980s, aided by improvement in fiber quality and in manufacturing processes. The textile plant of the 1990s will require one-third fewer workers to operate, according to the Institute of Textile Technology, but the cost for a 40,000 spindle mill could rise to $140 million, on top of an estimated 400-percent increase during the 1970s.

Capital investments per employee in a new textile plant was placed at $250,000 to $300,000 in early 1980. About 20 years earlier, the cost per employee needed for a new, integrated textile mill was placed at about $50,000.

Some new machines have a production potential as much as 50 percent greater than their predecessors.... Demand for single-knit machines was strong during the latter part of 1979, partly because of the great variety of effects possible on these machines and market strength in single jersey fabrics from apparel manufacturers. Most in demand were machines that specialize in super-fine jacquard effects, raised and brushed surfaces, inlay patterns, and such things as sculptured terry/velour, all of which help to satisfy the stylistic demands of the consumer. New machines are also faster, have a much wider diameter, and an increased number of feeds to compound production rates. Growth is expected in terry, velour, and pile fabrics.

Shifts in fabrication methods are likely to continue over the longer term as a result of changes in the types of equipment and in market demands. The cost of new equipment is likely to continue to rise with technological advances, but these high prices will have to be justified by lower production cost per unit of output.

EXHIBIT 4 Sales Letter

TO OUR PROSPECTIVE CUSTOMERS

Gentlemen:

As you are well aware, industrial operations are often affected by technical problems such as high maintenance costs, unsatisfactory efficiency, or the need for equipment for special applications not available from conventional suppliers. Not even the best plant engineer can be expected to tackle successfully those problems requiring extensive technical analysis while discharging his supervisory duties adequately. At times, outside assistance becomes essential.

Our staff, composed of experienced engineers and technical specialists selected from a variety of textile and research fields, can be of invaluable assistance to your operations. Several of our key personnel have been, and some still are, connected with the academic and research communities, thereby bringing into our corporation a wealth of knowledge not common in the textile field.

In addition to the above mentioned services our manufacturing facilities are equipped to handle any desired machine improvements, including the design and fabrication of equipment for special purposes. In other instances our existing components, such as low cost web guiders, expanders and tension controls could solve many nagging problems.

Let us know your desires and your problems, whether large or small. A visit from one of our engineering executives can be arranged at your convenience. He will listen to your staff, analyze your needs, and make recommendations on how to improve your operations.

We look forward to being of assistance to you in the near future.

Sincerely,

Ernesto, E. Blanco, P.E.
President

EXHIBIT 5   NSF Report Summary (Award amount, $25,000)

The objective of this project was to investigate all critical parameters involved in a concept of a Braille display letter unit capable to fit into standard letter and line spacings while being electrically controlled from a magnetic tape cassette.

All the initial objectives have been accomplished or exceeded. A prototype model based on the research findings has been built and tested successfully. The prototype comprises 140 components enclosed in a metallic shell the size of the little finger. It is capable of very fast cycling rates and provides a "feel" most identical to that of "hard copy" embossed Braille.

Vertically-moving Braille stimulators are driven by six micro-solenoids, embodying a combination of leakage-flux and tapered-plunger principles and providing ideal force-stroke characteristics with minimal power consumption. Once energized, the stimulators remain in the display mode without drawing power, held by tiny latches that "jam" the solenoid stems and resist finger forces until released by either an electric or a mechanical signal.

The implications of this research for the blind are obvious. This unit makes it possible to display refreshable Braille in multiple lines at standard spacing in scientific instruments, computer readouts, word processing output systems, the TSPS blind telephone operator's system, etc.

Further research leading to the manufacture of a full-page text display surface under the command of a magnetic tape cassette will constitute the subject of a proposal under a PHASE II of this program.

The work that remains consists of the research and optimization of manufacturing parameters so that the ultimate commercial price be kept as low as possible. Despite some reasonable efforts to consider manufacturing approaches at this time, it is unrealistic to expect that at this early stage those matters would be given sufficient attention. The fields of conceptual and manufacturing research are too far detached to be taken into account simultaneously. In fact, serious attention to manufacturing at this stage could be detrimental to conceptual research by imposing excessive geometric and analytical constraints.

Case 4

Deaver Brown

In October 1970 Deaver Brown faced what he regarded as a major decision. He and his partner, Alex Goodwin, could either go ahead in an attempt to start a business producing collapsible baby strollers or they could continue looking for better opportunities. A sketch of a European stroller design that had given them the idea appears in Exhibit 1.

Deaver said that pressing ahead with the stroller idea would be risky. First, the two would be giving up very promising positions in their respective professions. Deaver was earning $25,000 a year as a product manager for General Foods, and Alex was making $14,000 as a lawyer in the U.S. Justice Department's Antitrust Division. Second, conversations with persons who made and sold strollers led the two to regard the product as part of a "dead-end" industry, whose buyers were suspicious of anything "new or different." Since their idea was based on a stroller that would fold up, much like an umbrella, Deaver suspected that potential buyers might be reluctant to purchase such a novelty. Moreover, if there really were a market for such a device, quite possibly some other company established in the baby products, carts, or tubing products business was already moving ahead with development of it. Finally, there was always the possibility that other more profitable ideas for a business awaited discovery by the two.

Countering the risks were a number of considerations which Deaver listed: the prototype had been well received by people on the street who were shown the product. Annual sales of strollers in the United States totaled an estimated $30 mil-lion which, it seemed to him, should make the market small enough for a start-up to enter. Since he thought the industry was mature and not prone to new products, perhaps an innovation such as theirs could provide the competitive edge they needed to succeed in a start-up. Deaver commented:

If you're going to be in a horse race, be in one with slow horses so that you stand a chance of winning.

The two had spent over 200 hours researching various industries that they thought might be appealing for a business venture. The stroller had received most of their attention during the last few months, and they had talked with people in their spare time about market potential. To test their ability to sell the product to retail stores, Deaver and Alex rented a booth at a juvenile furniture products trade show—where manufacturers, suppliers and retailers got together to line up their business for the peak consumer season in the spring. After the first day of the show Deaver observed:

We've spent the past year looking for a way to start a business. We've talked to department store buyers, people on the street who were pushing strollers, suppliers, and just about everyone else we can think of that might have an interest in our product. What we've found is that this is a very stodgy market, from the manufacturer down to the retail outlet. Distribution would really be tough, and we'd need to contract out produc-

tion and work with dozens of suppliers.

At the same time, I think the collapsible stroller idea is a good one, and the consumers we've shown it to think that the lighter weight and convenience of being able to fold it is great. Now that we've tried participating in a trade show with it, I think it's time we made a "go/no-go" decision. Sooner or later, you need to quit agonizing and testing and put your chips on that table, or else pull out of the game so you can play something else.

Personal Background

Alex Goodwin and Deaver Brown had known each other since high school in Rochester, New York. When reminiscing in 1969 about the "good times" they used to have together, they decided to see if they could develop an idea for a business into a full-time pursuit. Alex had worked in Washington, D.C., since graduating from law school at Columbia University in 1968. Deaver attended Harvard, majoring in American History and Literature as an undergraduate, and receiving his MBA from the Harvard Business School the same year Alex graduated from Columbia. Deaver said they both had good jobs, yet neither was comfortable working for a large organization where they couldn't readily see the impact of their efforts.

Deaver recalled that he had pursued a number of sideline ventures while growing up, including a profitable stint as a Fuller Brush salesman. His interest in entrepreneurship led him to enroll in a new ventures course while at Harvard. He talked about what happened:

The course had nothing to do with the little ventures that I had tried before then. So I decided that they must be right, and I must be wrong. I did badly in the course, which was largely just about finance; always had the wrong an-

swers. The experience convinced me I wasn't cut out to run my own business, so I'd better get a job with a large corporation if I wanted to gain some practical skills. General Foods offered me a position where I would be able to have some profit-and-loss responsibility, which I felt would be healthy. So I packed my bags and went to White Plains, New York.

He spent three months in sales training, going from store to store and showing buyers a variety of products offered by General Foods. His sales results led to rapid promotions, first to district manager calling on retail chains, and then to product manager. Deaver recalled that he liked the selling part of the job, a task considered "the dregs" by many of his business school classmates. He added that as he continued to be promoted, his job became less of a "street salesman" and more like a staff assistant reporting to middle and upper management.

Deaver said that his temperament wasn't like that of his management peers at General Foods who seemed to enjoy the glamour of being considered a manager and involved with a Fortune 500 firm:

As a student of American History, management's attitude seems to me like the old British problem of having a prejudice against trade and great respect for lawyers, doctors and the professions. Sometimes I felt like I was dying a slow death by job boredom.

Searching for an Entry Point in the Market

During 1969 and 1970 Alex and Deaver spent part of their time researching markets that might suit them as fledgling entrepreneurs. Deaver described their search as one of conceptualizing. Typically, they would be sitting in a room, staring at the walls and ceiling, and talking about what trends or needs seemed apparent in the market. When they came across a seemingly promising business idea they would go talk with someone in a related line of business and also look up government statistics on the particular industry. Deaver recalled one such search:

One area we were interested in was the fireplace market. Our feeling was that the country was entering the 1970s as a period of consolidation and nostalgia under the Nixon Administration. Nostalgia brought to mind fireplaces and New England. We figured there would be growth in the fireplace market and also some opportunities for innovation. So, I went to a store, found out what was new in the market and got a feel for consumer buying habits by talking to the salesmen.

Alex worked in Washington, D.C., so it was easy for him to look up patents and see what was being developed in the industry. We put the information together and tracked down a couple of owners of patents that looked particularly interesting to us. You've got to realize that a lot of patents never turn into a salable product, so there was some interest by the patent owners about producing the product. We never came to any agreement on the worth of the patents and have put the idea on the back burner for now.

Another market the two had examined was what Deaver termed the "re-education" of business professionals. He speculated that business men and women needed to review the basic skills of selling, production, marketing, and writing from time to time, and that translated into a need for a service. After looking under "education services" in the Yellow Pages, he called up a few people in the trade to seek their advice. It seemed to him, he said, that continuing education received a lot of lip service but not much action.

For the education scheme to work, some third party would be needed to pay the tuition costs. Corporations that might sponsor the fees, the two entrepreneurs found, either wanted to see immediate results or were already conducting their own in-house training programs. Deaver added that existing services were too technical and tended to over-promise results to students and businesses alike. The trick, he pointed out, would be to get sponsorship from enough medium-sized organizations to justify development of solid curricula and hire qualified instructors.

In addition to talking with persons in the industries they thought promising, Deaver and Alex looked up statistical data to get an idea of market size and potential growth trends. For instance, the U.S. Census of Manufacturing provided details on heating stoves for the home and for juvenile products such as strollers. Excerpts of typical data they found appear in Exhibits 2 and 3.

While the two men used a deliberate approach to focus on services or products, they also sometimes "tripped onto products," like the stroller, as Deaver described it.

Last Spring, Alex was visiting London with his family. They were walking through Picadilly Circus and didn't know what to do with the baby, so Alex went into a department store and bought a stroller. It folded up like an umbrella and people would try to buy the stroller from him everywhere they traveled in Europe; some offered him as much as $200. So when he came back home, he said, "You're not going to believe this. We've been looking around for a product, and I've finally found this juvenile vehicle market—we can make a stroller that works like this one."

Alex explained that there were patents on the design and folding concepts of the British-made stroller. He added that a successful patent defense would likely extend only to the design, since the concept of folding a product had been widely used in many types of products. No product like the European stroller, depicted in Exhibit 1, was currently available in the U.S., so far as Deaver and Alex had been able to learn.

Structure of the Juvenile Vehicle Products Industry

Contemplating the stroller as a possible entry wedge for a venture, the two proceeded to explore what type of industry the stroller was in and who the major "actors" were. First, they talked with manufacturers or suppliers of available strollers and visited department stores to look at displays. Deaver explained that most of the firms had started shortly after World War II, when many men returning from the service found it difficult to get work and viewed the "baby boom" as a growth industry to get involved in. Presently, the largest manufacturer did eight million dollars in sales each year. While statistical data placed strollers in the toys and sporting goods industry, whose statistics appear in Exhibit 2, Deaver said he thought competition would likely come from manufacturers of juvenile furniture.

Both of those industries were populated, it seemed to Deaver, by small, fragmented competitors whose rates of both growth and new product introduction were low. Total shipments for furniture were estimated at $200 million, with the vehicle industry (excluding bicycles) at close to $80 million. Similar figures for strollers were estimated at $16.3 million based on wholesale shipments, F.O.B., during 1967. Of the 45 firms producing children's vehicles, 22 employed less than 10 workers. Eighty percent of stroller shipments were from companies that relied on

that product as their major product. By comparison with similar industries aimed at children, the value added and market potential was considerably less for strollers (see Exhibit 3). Deaver commented:

> *The competition seems to be a hodge-podge of small sleepy companies who haven't offered anything new to the market since they first started business. And since both the primary and secondary markets are present, it's not a matter of building a market for strollers and then convincing people that they should buy from us. The market for strollers is there and people on the street have told us they like our product. On the other hand, it looks like we're in a very stodgy market, from the manufacturer down to the retail outlet. So introducing something new might be hard.*

Deaver expected the fact that another manufacturer in Great Britain was making a similar type of stroller meant that competition could exist almost from the start. The opportunity to become a low-cost producer would depend partly on the response of existing stroller companies to their new product line and partly the extent with which cost savings could be significant for this type of production. He said companies in the juvenile furniture industry were also threats, since they had established lines of distribution. Deaver noted that relatively low technology and lack of patent protection facilitated competitive entry.

Both of the partners felt that the collapsible stroller's convenience should fit well with increased mobility and use of space which young adults enjoyed. With the leading edge of the baby boom from World War II now 23 years old, and the number of births in the United States expected to increase in the coming decade or two, the stroller market might be perceived by some firms as a growth opportunity, which could encourage other companies to enter competition. Deaver said that any such conclusions drawn by a large corporation could spell trouble for their venture, since economies of scale tended to favor large firms over smaller ones:

> *I was at General Foods long enough to learn that a little company doesn't stand a chance if they are trying to compete directly with a giant. They simply don't have the resources to draw upon, the cash flow, talent, and ability to weather short-term losses that big companies get from support by other product lines.*

One option that the two had considered was to have another product in addition to the stroller. Deaver explained that they had thought of a backpack that would be used to carry children and have an added feature of doubling as a stand-alone chair. This would be accomplished by use of a "U" shaped aluminum support that would keep the pack upright and make it easier to load and unload the child. However he noted that only 150,000 baby packs were sold each year, which might be too small a market to help much. Moreover by starting a company that offered two products instead of one, they would be spreading themselves thinner.

Attracting Interest to the Collapsible Stroller

For guidance regarding design and production, Deaver had turned to an engineering friend, Jim Sloan, who agreed to accept a 10 percent interest in the venture as compensation. Deaver had also started calling machine shops around the country trying to find one able both to make a prototype and to deliver high volume production runs. He said that after talking to "zillions" of people and investigating 200 to 300 companies, the search was nar-

rowed to two machine shops: one in Alabama and one in Rochester, New York. His experience with General Foods convinced him that upstate New York was a good test market, since the demographics were similar to the national average. A second advantage he pointed to was that the location was near his present home in New York City and, having grown up in Rochester, he knew that the area had excellent tool making capabilities. The shop owner agreed to produce the prototype, which was completed during the summer of 1970.

Deaver and Alex then took the prototype and went to various stores to solicit interest from buyers—however, the stores showed disappointingly little interest. However, when the partners would stop people on the street to demonstrate how light the stroller was and how it folded, it seemed to Deaver that nearly everyone thought it was a good product. He explained how product quality was important to any business venture the two might attempt:

> *There are three categories of products: Those that will never work, those that are great, and those in the middle. Firms like General Foods will have people try a product and they'll say "...it's OK, pretty good," and that will be sufficient. Most products that come to the market are marginal; they're neither good nor bad.*
>
> *When a really good product is tested, like General Foods did with Cool Whip, people respond enthusiastically: "Yea! It's super!" You can tell pretty early if you've got a good or marginal product.*
>
> *Consumers we've shown the strollers to seem to indicate it is really a good product. But unfortunately trade buyers and retail customers are two different things. Most of the trade buyers have been telling us that our product stinks.*

The buyers, he said, had rejected the

stroller "out of hand" claiming that strength and durability were the primary selling features for strollers, with price close behind. They told the two that lighter weight and the collapsible feature were not enough to offset the higher price ($24.97 retail versus $20.00 for conventional strollers on the market) or the fact that they were an unknown entity in a well established industry; Deaver and Alex hadn't even settled on a name for the company yet. People in the industry had told Deaver that retailers typically received 40 percent off of list price and manufacturers representatives typically received a commission of around 5 to 7 percent of the wholesale price.

Production

From experience in creating a dozen prototypes, Deaver said it could be foreseen that tasks needed to produce strollers would fall into three main areas: materials and equipment, cost control, and people. Making the stroller would require that some parts be made by specialty companies, examples being injection molded plastic parts, and plating work. Items like wheels might be bought standard or fabricated from custom parts. Much of the work would involve simply assembling parts, with the frame, wheels and seat being three main components.

He explained that he had recently taken a mechanical engineering course on line balancing at Columbia University, which gave him some practical skills he felt could be applied to optimizing output. His engineering friend, Jim Sloan, told Deaver that he would be willing to help out in a start-up "crunch" period, but couldn't devote too much time due to his regular work as a research specialist for a local electronics firm. Deaver noted tasks that would be required to transform the raw materials listed in Exhibit 4 into a completed product:

Frame Assembly

1. Cut, bend and drill holes in the aluminum tube.

2. Cut, drill holes and hinge the rear metal support.

3. Cut the front support and bend to attach.

4. Assemble the aluminum frame through inserting v-nuts, bolts, rivets, and plastic fittings.

5. Finish the open ends of the aluminum and cover with plastic plugs.

6. Cut, bend and attach the plastic handles to the frame.

Wheel Assembly

1. Assemble each front and rear wheel, using the hub and axle, hubcap, rubber tire, and vertical attachment to fit with the aluminum frame.

2. Cut, bend, and insert the metal rod braking device in the rear wheel.

Seat Assembly

1. Cut, sew, and laminate the fabric to make the seat.

2. Cut, sew, and attach the fabric seat belt to the seat.

3. Attach the plastic rings to the seat belt as a buckling device.

4. Attach the seat to the aluminum frame of the stroller.

Packaging

1. Fold the stroller to fit within a packing case.

2. Include the instructional literature and replacement parts, if any, with the stroller(s) in the packing case.

3. Seal the case shut with tape and/or staples. (Assumes packing case is

complete, having been cut, assembled and screened to include any artwork promoting the stroller.)

He pointed out that each of these tasks could probably be broken down into more detailed sub-tasks. Whether a group of people would be responsible for part or all of the assembly for a single stroller was a question he had not yet answered. He expected the various parts would have to be arranged along the production line to keep the process moving. Space would have to be provided for inventory and to make sure that a particular order didn't get mixed up with another one. Deaver also listed areas of concern and issues in production that he supposed would arise if he and Alex decided to try making strollers on their own. This list appears in Exhibit 5.

Performing the manufacturing after purchasing parts and subassemblies was only one option Deaver and Alex had looked into. Another would be to purchase and provide all materials and then have an outside manufacturer transform them into strollers. They found that to obtain some of the materials, such as rivets produced to the specific size required, they would have to order amounts sufficient to produce a large number of units. On other materials they would have to order large amounts to obtain substantial quantity discounts to keep costs down. They estimated they would need around $100,000 worth of materials to commence production, plus another $25,000 worth of custom tooling to fabricate the parts.

The best price they had been able to obtain on assembly work was $3.51 per unit from a local manufacturer. Another manufacturer located in Alabama would do the work for a few cents less, but it seemed to them preferable to keep the work near home if possible. The local manufacturer had engaged his lawyer to write up a contract for producing the units at $3.51 each,

and Deaver noted that it did not require purchase of any minimum number of units, which he expected would be to his advantage. The contract also provided that the manufacturer could experience as much as 1 percent scrap wastage of the material. Deaver wondered whether that might not be a bit low.

I figure it is to our advantage to have the lawyer for the other side draw up the contract," Deaver commented. "Some people say you should always have your own do it, since your own lawyer is more likely to look out for your interests. But I also understand that if the contract is ever taken to litigation, the court will take note of which side wrote it up.

He guessed that legal fees to pursue a patent, plus accounting fees might cost around $2,000 per month for the first year or two.

In addition to the assembly work an additional cost per unit of $4.49 was expected for the raw materials and parts which would be purchased from other suppliers and subcontractors for delivery to the manufacturer performing the assembly work. Deaver estimated that returns, allowances and freight might add up to perhaps another dollar per unit, although it was difficult to be sure he had thought of everything and estimated it correctly.

Deaver and Alex had personal savings plus friends and relatives from whom they expected they might be able to obtain personal loans to muster up to around $50,000 cash for start-up. Beyond that they expected they might need trade credit and bank loans against such collateral as their company might have. To curb capital needs, Deaver had weighed the possibility of operating out of his home as against renting an office. He calculated that the former would be cheaper (Exhibit 6), but he expected that prospective creditors or investors might be more favorably impressed by the more businesslike appearance of the later. (Some industry financial ratios appear in Exhibit 7.)

Although they thought it might be preferable to use an outside manufacturer for assembly work, Deaver and Alex were not fully convinced. Deaver said that a major concern for him was how fast the contractor could make strollers, even under the best of conditions. He had only been in the man's plant once and didn't know if the current employees would be sufficient to turn out as many as 100 strollers each day. If more workers, space, or equipment were required, the $8.00 cost might have to be renegotiated lest the contractor be forced to work on a thinner margin or perhaps at break-even. Deaver went on to state that any time that he and Jim Sloan spent at the production facility would be time lost for purposes of other activities important to the venture. Deaver commented on his visit to the proposed manufacturer's plant.

The place is an absolute zoo—packing cases at the front of the assembly line, things like that. It's not so easy to take the work to another contractor. I've talked with nearly all of them already and none would give us the time or price we need to be competitive. To think that someone else will do a better job might be wishful thinking. So if we get into production problems with the guy, then will we be worse off than doing it ourselves? Should we have a contingency plan, at what point should it activate, and what should it be?

Trade Show Selling Attempt

In fall 1970 Deaver and Alex took some prototypes of the stroller to a juvenile furniture industry trade show in New York City, where Deaver had arranged to share another company's booth for $100. This show was expected to be the last trade

event before the peak selling season, and major retailers and wholesalers were in attendance. Also, the two expected there would be many manufacturers representatives present seeking new lines to carry in the various parts of the country from which they came.

During the first day of the trade show, Deaver and Alex demonstrated their product for people who passed by the booth and received essentially the same types of responses they had encountered earlier when going from store to store. As a result, they decided that they needed to try some harder selling tactics or the show would also turn out to be a failure for them. The second day they deliberately became more aggressive in "buttonholing" people who were passing by the booth. They also got hold of some friends and had them push strollers around outside the building posing as satisfied customers. Whenever things would grow quiet at the booth, Deaver or Alex or both would push prototypes around inside the building, going to other booths and display areas to attract attention to their product. Deaver commented that this unorthodox approach drew some wrath from other companies at the show. He described his "pitch" as follows:

We've shamed people into agreeing they would order from us by saying that if they don't give us an order, they're going to put us out of business. We don't have anything to lose, and we've got some prospective orders dribbling in —ten or so at a time.

I tell them that this is the only chance that they'll get to be able to give their customers something new over last year—they owe the consumer a choice. Their reply? 'It's lousy, it isn't strong enough, it's too expensive.' So I say, "You're probably right. But what if you're wrong? Can you afford to be wrong?"

By the end of the second day, notwithstanding the unpopularity they had earned among some of the other companies displaying at the show, Deaver and Alex had managed to persuade prospective customers to accept some 200 strollers if they were to start producing them. They had also met several manufacturers representatives who said they would be interested in carrying the product in various territories of the country. All the prospective orders they received were in small lots, however, and none had come from any major department store chains. This was an important concern in Deaver's view, because such chains had the capability of moving large numbers of products. They could provide the kind of volume Deaver considered essential to economical operation.

Deaver remarked that the biases of buyers he met at the show regarding consumer preferences in a stroller were much harder to change than he had expectecd. He added that overcoming this bias would be critical if they decided to go ahead with the venture. Otherwise, they would never reach the volume of sales needed to recover their costs or hold any prospects for growth.

A potential selling approach that Deaver and Alex were designing, but had not yet tried, was to display strollers by hanging them folded on a metal rack, much like clothes hanging in a rectangular display rack. Deaver said that eight strollers could be packed in two square feet of selling space. He didn't know how responsive buyers would be to this merchandising approach; the annual reports he had read boasted of "quality displays." But financial data were shown only for the corporation as a whole, not specific product lines. Exhibit 8 presents information Deaver had gathered on major retail chains.

Advertising was another front on which Deaver expected they would need to move. An advertisement in *American Baby*, a magazine distributed to approximately 1 million homes each month would cost around $800 per month, while advertisements in a couple of relevant trade magazines might cost around $250 per month each. "These would be small ads," Deaver observed, "but that is all anybody uses. It seems to be basically a rather chintzy industry."

At the New York trade show Deaver had been able to arrange to display prototypes at low cost by sharing the booth of another company. Later shows might, he expected, cost substantially more, possibly 10 or more times as much, especially if they had to travel to Chicago or Los Angeles to attend them. Preparation and mailing of brochures to potentially interested stores he guessed might cost another $500 to $2,000, depending upon quality of the brochures and the extent of the mailing.

Choosing the Next Step

As he contemplated the complexities and hurdles facing the venture, Deaver wondered whether its basic strategy was viable at all. The number of orders they could gather from the show seemed likely to be far below what break-even would require. Even if they were able to enter the market, there would be little to prevent others with more resources from following suit. It seemed quite possible that there might be litigation from the British stroller manufacturer. It might very well, he thought, decide to test its patent claims and sell extensively in the United States. Deaver reflected on their current situation in trying to get production issues settled and determine if they, or competitors, stood the best chance of successfully marketing this stroller. He commented:

> *What are the implications of starting a business in a dead-end industry? What does it take to make it work? Can we erect a sufficient competitive barrier*

to withstand competition in the future? And if we can, does that come from having the product, control over production, or establishing superior channels of distribution? Is the nature of the juvenile products industry one that will change from dormant and mature to a growth industry again and if so, how could we tell when that will that occur?

Maybe there are other companies that are better suited to breaking the retail bias and fragmentation that now exists. But if we're as close as anybody else, we just might be on the verge of having a very successful business.

If they decided to "go" with the venture, Deaver explained that he and Alex would quit their jobs for a time to work on the business. He admitted that they had invested a lot of thought and time in this industry, but cautioned that the investment was a sunk cost. He summed up their position in deciding whether to proceed or abandon the idea for the collapsible stroller:

Both the primary and secondary markets are present. So it's not a matter of building a market for strollers before we can try to convince people that they should buy from us.

If we're going to make this business work, I suppose we need to tailor our sales pitch to the store buyers and not worry about the consumer. Consumers will benefit from the fact that the stroller works.

I don't know what the secret is of selling to the retailers . . . maybe that can't even be done. If not, I suppose we had better drop this idea right now and look for another industry to get into. Like I told some buyers today: "Being wrong is unaffordable."

EXHIBIT 1   Sketch of British-made Stroller

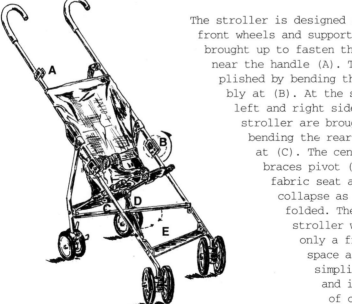

The stroller is designed so that the front wheels and supports can be brought up to fasten the metal arm near the handle (A). This is accomplished by bending the frame assembly at (B). At the same time, the left and right sides of the stroller are brought together by bending the rear support upward at (C). The center connecting braces pivot (D) while the fabric seat and leg rest (E) collapse as the stroller is folded. The result is a stroller which takes only a fraction of the space as before, simplifying storage and improving ease of carriage.

EXHIBIT 2 **Sales of Possibly Related Products**

INSTRUMENTS AND PARTS: TOYS AND SPORTING GOODS
Quantity and Value of Shipments by All Producers

Product Code	Product	Quantity (million units)	Value ($1,000)	Quantity (million $)	Value (million $)
943 —	Children's vehicles, except bicycles, Total	(X)	99.6	(X)	82.7
943 11	Baby Carriages, including combination carriage-strollers	320	8.2	329	7.4
943 15	Strollers	1,454	16.3	1,023	12.8
943 21	Baby walkers	978	3.3	612	4.4
943 33	Children's pedal driven automobiles & tractors	1,019	9.7	1,055	9.8
943 43	Velocipedes (3-wheeled) and tricycles; including chain-driven tricycles	3,271	23.7	3,113	20.8
943 61	Children's wagons (coaster express, and others)	(X)	(X)	2,562	8.6
943 71	Sleds	1,186	4.9	1,271	5.3
943 81	Parts for children's vehicles sold separately	(X)	1.6	(X)	2.2
943 98	Other children's vehicles, including scooters, sidewalk cycles, 3-wheel play cars, etc.	(X)	28.5	(X)	9.9
944 —	Children's vehicles, except bicycles	(X)	2.8	(X)	(X)
944 02	Children's vehicles, except bicycles (For companies with less than 10 employees)	(X)	0.6	(X)	1.9

EXHIBIT 3 Ratios on Possibly Related Companies

ITEM	Games & Toys (SIC 3941)	Dolls (SIC 5942)	Children's Vehicles, except bicycles (SIC 3941)
Primary Product Specialization Ratio	.88	.90	.81
Coverage Ratio	.96	.70	.61
Establishments' Total...............................	684	340	45
with 1 to 19 employees	354	202	22
with 20 to 99 employees	221	112	11
with 100 employees or more	109	26	12
All employees, average for years	55.1	11.9	3.7
Payroll for year, all employees million $264.9	40.4	19.4	
Production workers:			
Average for year 1,000	46.1	10.7	3.1
March.. "	36.3	8.3	3.0
May .... "	43.1	10.3	3.2
August .... "	51.4	12.1	3.1
November .... "	53.6	11.8	3.0
Man-hours ....millions	86.6	10.0	6.4
January-March .... "	16.9	3.5	1.6
April-June .... "	20.5	4.5	1.7
July-September .... "	23.9	5.2	1.6
October-December .... "	25.4	5.1	1.6
Wages ....millions	178.0	34.3	13.9
Cost of materials, etc., Total.................. "	490.6	80.0	40.9
Materials, parts, containers .... "			
etc., consumed .... "	427.9	69.9	35.9
Cost of resales................................ "	39.3	6.0	2.9
Fuels consumed .... "	2.0	.2	.2
Purchased electricity .... "	5.8	-	.4
Contract work .... "	15.7	5.8	1.5
Value of shipments, including ..			
resale .... "	1113.5	362.0	78.7
Value of resales .... "	27.2	7.2	3.5
Value added by manufacturer .... "	614.3	62.6	38.7
Manufacturer's Inventories .... "			
Beginning of year, total .... "	169.4	17.2	12.5
Finished product .... "	78.5	7.7	4.0
Work in process .... "	29.0	2.8	3.0
Materials, supplies, fuel, etc., ... "	61.9	3.7	5.6
End of year, total .... "	159.4	16.4	15.9
Finished product .... "	69.9	8.3	4.1
Work in process .... "	29.0	2.8	3.8
Materials, supplies, fuel, etc., ... "	60.5	5.8	6.0
Expenditures for Plant and Equipment,			
total .... "	35.5	2.6	3.6
New Plant and Equipment, total .. "	39.9	2.4	3.5
New Structure and Additions			
to plant .... "	12.5	.3	1.7
New Machinery and Equipment "	21.4	2.7	1.9
Used Plant and Equipment .... "	1.7	.2	(2)

EXHIBIT 4   List of Supplies Needed for the Stroller

Aluminum tubing	Back aluminum hinge piece
Fabric for the seat	Front wheel enclosures
Denim	Plastic loops for seat belt
Nylons	Washers
Plastic handle grips	Plastic covers for wheels
Fabric strip	Glue
Wheels (straight and swivel)	Wheel lubricant
Rubber for the wheels	Fabric laminate
Plastic plug ends	L shaped fasteners
Plastic fastener	Packing box
Plastic joints	Staples
Wheel axles	
Fastening bolts	Printing
Thread	Instruction sheet
Braking device	Packing material
Front foot rest	Stationery
Screws	Sewing needles
Rivets	Invoice forms

<u>Note</u>: In some cases, Deaver expected to develop second source of materials so as not to be in a production delay situation. Depending on a final agreement to be worked out with the contracting manufacturer, other hand tools relating to the production of the stroller might be required.

EXHIBIT 5 Anticipated Production Issues if Brought In House

I.   AREAS OF CONCERN

A.   <u>Materials and Equipment</u>
- Order entry
- Production planning
- Product specification
    1. Performance
    2. Dimensions
    3. Style
    4. Delivery dates
- Purchasing
- Inventory control
- Factory layout and location
- Make or buy decisions
- Fixed assets
- Quality control
- Retail applications

B.   <u>Cost Control</u>

C.   <u>People</u>
- Plant Mmnager
- Supervisors
- Factory and clerical workers

II.   ISSUES TO BE DECIDED

A.   Method for quality control
B.   Set-up for production line
C.   Space set aside and positioning for parts and inventory
D.   Definition of tasks and sub-tasks
E.   Record keeping system to monitor production times
F.   Decisions on second sourcing
G.   Decisions on cross training of workers
H.   Methods of shipment
I.   Packaging and display models for retail outlets
J.   Invoicing for payment and tie-in completion of order
K.   Assignment and number of people for each task, group of tasks
L.   Seasonal and shift scheduling
M.   Level of inventory to be maintained
N.   Planning for production capacity expansion
O.   Assignment of costs
P.   Pricing changes from productivity improvements

EXHIBIT 6   Projected Offices Expense: Home vs. Traditional

Comparative Monthly Costs

Expense	Office at Home	Traditional Office
Rent	$0	$400
Part-Time Helper	50	500
Phone	2,000	2,200
Office Equipment	0	100
Miscellaneous	50	200
Total	$2,100	$3,400

Exhibit 7   Excerpt from Troy's Manual of Ratios, 1966

Toys, Amusement, Sporting and Athletic Goods (SIC 394)

Sales Volume Record of Total Industry		Year Sales ($Billion)	1958 1.0	1963 1.6	1964 1.8	

	Asset Size Ratios, 1964	Under 500	500 to 2,499	2,500 to 9,999	10,000 to 49,999	50,000 and over	Total Industry
	% of Sales						
1	Cost of Sales	74.6	74.5	71.7	70.8	64.8	71.8
2	Executive Salaries	4.9	2.6	1.8	1.0	0.4	2.2
3	Rent	1.7	1.3	0.7	1.0	1.3	1.2
4	Repairs	0.3	0.6	0.6	0.9	0.7	0.6
5	Bad Debts	0.6	0.5	0.5	0.5	9.3	1.6
6	Interest	0.7	0.9	0.8	1.4	9.9	2.1
7	Taxes	2.7	2.4	2.6	2.5	4.5	2.8
8	Contributions	na	na	0.1	0.2	0.2	0.1
9	Depreciation	1.6	1.3	2.2	1.6	1.8	1.7
10	Advertising	1.4	2.2	2.9	5.2	2.0	3.0
11	Benefits	0.5	0.4	1.1	0.7	1.0	0.7
12	P.A.T.	1.9	2.1	3.8	5.2	3.2	
	Ratios						
13	Current	1.5	1.8	2.2	2.1	1.6	1.8
14	Quick	0.8	0.9	1.1	1.0	1.5	1.2
15	Sales/W.C.	8.5	6.0	4.0	4.7	1.2	3.7
16	Sales/Net Worth	6.5	4.4	2.6	3.4	1.2	3.0
17	Inv. Turns	na	na	na	na	na	3.4
18	Liab/Net Worth	2.1	1.1	0.8	1.0	2.3	1.5
	Factors						
19	C.L/Net Worth	152.3	91.0	56.0	65.6	160.1	105.5
20	Inv/C.L.	50.0	49.6	49.0	53.8	10.0	32.7
21	Income/Net Worth	12.6	9.3	9.9	12.8	6.2	9.6
22	Ernings/Income	94.0	91.1	80.5	85.0	54.8	79.9

EXHIBIT 8 Selected Information from Major Retail Chains

<u>Sears</u>

Net Sales	$9,251,000,000
Net Income	$ 470,000,000
Total Number of stores	827
Total Amount of gross floor space (s.f.)	89,600,000

Credit sales comprised one-half of total sales, with 20 million credit customers at year end. Revenues from catalogue orders, direct mail, finance charges, and repair services accounted for 25 percent of net sales. Over 10,000 domestic suppliers are used by 48 buying departments, divided into 805 product groupings (the largest grouping accounts for less than five percent of net sales).

<u>Woolworth's</u> (1970)

Net Sales	$2,507,375,000
Net Income	$76,000,000
Total Number of Stores	3,656
Total Amount of Gross floor space (s.f.)	59,000,000

(over 95% are Woolworth or Woolco Department Stores)

<u>Macy's</u> (1970)

Net Sales	$ 955,976,000
Net Income	$ 20,660,000
Total Number of Stores	61
Total Amount of Gross floor space (s.f.)	14,740,000

<u>Dayton Hudson</u> (1970)

Net Sales	$ 965,400,000
Net Income	$ 19,000,000
Total Number of Stores	see below
Total Amount of Gross floor space (s.f.)	see below

	No. of Stores	Total s.f. of space
Full Line Department Stores	17	7,875,000
Low Margin Discount Stores	25	3,417,000
Specialty Stores	291	not available
Jewelry Stores	204	not available

EXHIBIT 8 (concluded)

FIVE YEAR OPERATIONS SUMMARY

	1970	1969	1968	1967	1966
Penney stores - full line					
Number of stores	240	208	176	141	108
Net selling space (mill. sq. ft.)	19.4	16.5	13.7	10.4	7.4
Sales ($ millions)	1,628.1	1,327.0	1,002.0	661.2	477.7
Sales per square foot ($)	92.97	90.76	85.53	79.13	78.86
Penney stores - soft line					
Number of stores	1,407	1,438	1,476	1,517	1,548
Net selling space (mill. sq. ft.)	18.1	18.4	19.0	19.4	19.5
Sales (millions)	2,119.3	2,156.1	2,105.7	2,105.7	2,042.4
Sales per square foot ($)	115.75	115.22	110.10	105.51	105.03
Catalog					
Number of sales centers	1,019	944	660	637	565
Number of distribution centers	2	2	1	1	1
Distribution space (mill. sq. ft.)	4.1	4.1	2.0	2.0	2.0
Sales-mail order ($ millions)	70.0	61.9	57.7	52.5	40.8
The Treasury stores					
Number of stores	13	10	10	6	5
Net selling space (mill. sq. ft.)	1.5	1.2	1.2	0.7	0.5
Sales ($ millions)	146.2	127.5	85.3	54.1	48.9
Sales per square foot ($)	113.15	107.96	96.83	97.53	92.27
Drug stores					
Number of stores	189	171	157	148	138
Net selling space (mill. sq. ft.)	1.0	.9	.8	.7	.7
Sales ($ millions)	98.0	83.5	71.9	62.8	86.39
Supermarkets					
Number of supermarkets	23	20	17	16	13
Net selling space (mill. sq. ft.)	.3	.3	.2	.2	.2
Sales ($ millions)	88.4	72.4	56.6	45.7	37.8
Sales per square foot ($)	294.98	298.68	259.70	255.27	261.24
European operations					
Number of stores	92	95			
Net selling space (mill. sq. ft.)	1.2	1.2			
Sales ($ millions)	203.8	84.2*	NA	NA	NA
Sales per square foot ($)	119.11	49.26			

Catalog merchandise sold through stores is included in the sales of those stores. Drug and supermarket sales through Penney and Treasury stores are included in the sales of the latter divisions. Food sales by European operations are included in that division's sales. The statistics shown above for drug stores and supermarkets are exclusive of their operations in Penney and Treasury stores.

Reclassification of several stores in 1973 resulted in a net increase of two full line stores and a net decline of two soft line stores. Sales per square foot includes only those stores in operation for the full year.

* Reflects sales of Sarma, S.A. from July 31, 1969, date of purchase.

Case 5

Matthew Clark and Steve Wilson

I guess the essential decision is how fast do we grow? Too fast takes too much money and we may fall on our face. If we grow too slowly, we may lose the market. Our first burst of growth will determine whether we make or break in this venture.

Steve Wilson leaned back on his chair in April 1981 and talked about the electronics venture he and three Harvard College classmates had started 16 months earlier. Their product was a device for analog-to-digital conversion enabling Apple II microcomputers, which ran on the CPM operating system, to process data from laboratory sensors that measured such properties as temperature, light and pressure. A description of its application appears in Exhibit 1.

Steve and his friend Matthew Clark were working full time to fill the 10 orders they had received for their product since placing their first advertisement the previous May. They had borrowed cash from family and friends, rented space in an old warehouse in East Cambridge, and started production while still pursuing their bachelor's degrees in liberal arts. To locate suppliers and subcontractors who could help them get shipments moving, they had started with the advice of friends and frequent use of the Yellow Pages. Financial records consisted of a running list, kept in a ledger, of expenses from the time the business was started in January. A summary of this list appears in Exhibit 2.

Now, Steve remarked, they needed to map out a complete strategy for the venture. He said that writing a business plan might be the best way to sort out many issues facing them. These included financing, marketing, hiring employees to build the instruments, designing an organizational structure that fit with their personal goals for the venture, choosing advisers for legal and accounting assistance, and providing a way to measure their progress for the next 12 to 18 months.

It was hard, they said, to find time for all these tasks. They were behind on filling orders, and constant interruptions prevented the two from production work on a full-time basis. Steve commented:

Maybe it's been a mistake not to explore the administrative and financial aspects more than we have. We need to spend more time on those issues. It's just that we've been trying to get the products done and sent to our customers so we'll have some money flowing into the business.

Origins of the Business Idea

Steve Wilson had been interested in electronics for most of his 21 years. He had learned about it as a teenager by assembling and repairing stereos and other home equipment, as well as from self-study of basic engineering principles. After graduating in 1977 from public high school in Concord, Massachusetts, he enrolled as a science and engineering major at Harvard. Within a few months, however, he withdrew, having discovered that he liked "fiddling around" with hardware better than theoretical study. He recalled:

I was very discouraged after the first

semester and knew by the end of my freshman year that I should switch my major to liberal arts. I was never happier with any decision than I was with that one. But since engineering had always been a passion with me, I wanted to continue dabbling in it. So, I sought jobs that required engineering skills and began working in the school's biology lab to automate an experiment they had been working on. It let me do some engineering design work and served as a balance to my studies in anthropology and sociology.

Steve's job involved an experiment concerning the concept of "biological clocks" in plants and animals. Lab technicians conducted the experiment, which sometimes lasted days or weeks, and resulted in hundreds of thousands of measurements printed on graph paper by a recording machine. Variations in the plotted line on the paper (similar to printouts of earthquake tremors on a seismograph) were then measured by hand and recorded in a journal for later study. The work was tedious, slow, and prone to errors in transcribing the data.

The lab wanted to eliminate manual recording of data and use a microcomputer to collect, store and interpret the information. The trouble was that microcomputers could not translate waved lines on a graph into digital information to process it. A device was needed to change the analog measurements (i.e., a continuous stream of varying voltages or currents from sensors that measured properties such as temperature, pressure, light, or wave frequency) to exact digital signals (i.e., decimal equivalents). This sort of translation was being done for larger minicomputers but required equipment that typically cost $10,000 or more. In addition, the translation required expensive on-line computer time for instantaneous collection and ma-

nipulation of the data. These costs, coupled with advances in technology, now made it attractive for the school to try introducing a peripheral device that might allow a desk-top computer, such as the Apple II, to collect and process experimental data. Not much earlier, Steve said, such a step would have been impossible.

Tackling the job, Steve managed to develop circuitry that worked for one experiment. The lab director then asked him to make additional units for other similar experiments. These, as Steve's paper in Exhibit I pointed out, could save considerable amounts of time and money while improving the accuracy of data. As more units were requested, made, and put to use, he began to think there might be commercial applications for the device, and that he could capitalize on them by starting his own business.

By this time, Steve was in his junior year at Harvard and had just met a classmate who was majoring in psychology, Matthew Clark. The two struck up a friendship and began talking about starting a business to manufacture instruments like those Steve had designed for the biology department. Matthew, who had some experience in commercial art, suggested that Steve work on engineering and product development while he did marketing and administrative tasks. As they chatted about the idea with friends, two others also expressed interest in working on the venture. These were Mike Fridkin, an economics major, who knew how to write microcomputer software, and Steve Brand, who was studying history and sociology.

Steve and Matthew continued to talk about the idea. They listed what it would cost to incorporate, buy stationery and get a minimal supply of parts for developing circuit boards. In early May 1980, they decided to name the business "Data Acquisition Systems," and set up shop in the basement of Matthew's Cambridge home.

Although a commercial prototype wasn't yet developed, they placed a small advertisement in *Microcomputing Magazine* to test for interest in such a product. Steve remarked that the laboratory models had given him confidence that they could complete the necessary design work and drawings by May 28. "Besides," he added, "everyone in the computer business announces their products before they're ready for delivery."

Developing a Prototype

That advertisement, plus another small one in *Byte*, drew more than 2,500 inquiries from across the US and Canada, which the partners considered very encouraging. Steve and Matthew worked on their business between classes and answered calls from scientists inquiring about their product. By the end of May, they had received five orders. Unfortunately, work on the prototypes progressed much more slowly than they anticipated. Not only was the design work complex, but Steve said, a number of other issues relating to the business took their time away from developing the product. Finding suitable office space was one example he cited.

> When the semester was over, we found our present space in this warehouse and spent a lot of time fixing it up. Other people argued with us that this was an odd priority to begin with; that we should just continue to work out of a garage until we had a product finished. But we felt it was important to have a more professional environment to work in and to present the image of an established business. So the first part of the summer was spent getting the office in order.

A typical sequence for developing many new products, Steve had been told, was to build a prototype and then measure its performance to determine the specifications. Then, after some small refinements, the finished product would be advertised in hopes that a waiting market for a device with those specifications would appear. In his own case, however, Steve had developed the specifications first, to fit his laboratory assignment. Then he had modified those specifications based upon telephone conversations with scientists responding to the ad. The modifications turned out to be substantial and required more development work than he had expected.

His design used a modular arrangement that allowed users to "plug in" modules to provide different functions or expand capacity for different data collection efforts. Steve explained that this feature would also allow him to keep up with technological advances in computers by continuously developing upgrade modules that could be shipped to customers to ward off product obsolescence. Thus, while the housing of a unit would not change, users could install new modules to keep the inner workings up to date.

Designing circuitry for the modules also took more time than anticipated. Steve recounted how, with Matthew's assistance, he learned as he went in developing the prototype instrument :

> Laying out all the printed circuit work was something we thought would take about a week. In fact, it took about two months. We knew nothing about how to make printed circuit boards and couldn't find anything written on the subject to help us. It's just sort of a skill that you pick up. We had some materials to work with and a friend of a friend who manufactured prototype boards. We spent days and nights working on the design and it wasn't until August that prototype boards came back based on design work we had done.

While waiting for the circuit boards, the

two talked with friends and called possible suppliers to find other parts needed for the instrument. They would leaf through the Yellow Pages, then telephone machinists and silk-screen printers about prices and willingness to do the work. Four subcontractors were lined up in addition to the person making the circuit boards. First was a machinist to provide the metal cases that housed the electronic parts, second was a company making printed circuit boards; third was a painter to finish the case panels and fourth was a silk-screening company to do lettering for the front of the instrument. Matthew explained how they chose among alternative suppliers.

We just went around and talked with a lot of them, got bids in an informal way, and chose in part by how we felt we'd be able to get along with the individual on a continuing basis. We've been pleased with the results for the most part. The only one we're thinking of changing is the machinist, for the sake of lowering our costs.

When they had received the circuit boards from the subcontractor in August, the two began assembling a prototype. Once complete, it was tested and, to Steve's dismay, didn't work as expected. He explained that the problem "didn't make any sense." He rechecked the connections and reviewed the logic he had used in designing the modules, but test output still showed erroneous data. After a month of troubleshooting, Steve discovered the problem: a short in the cable connecting the instrument with the host Apple II computer. They had tried to build all the cable connections on their own, even though they lacked some tools to do the job properly, and this had been painfully instructive:

The lesson was that we should never try to do something we aren't properly

equipped to do. You're tempted to try the work as a way to cut costs when, in fact, you end up spending more time and money than if the task had been subcontracted in the first place.

As the venture entered its sixth month, there still was no finished product to ship to customers. Steve had taken a year off from school to work on the business full time. The other three had continued their final year of undergraduate work, with Matthew juggling both the business and school work on as close to a full-time basis for both as he could.

Cash needs were met through an initial payment of $1,000 each from Steve and Matthew and through loans from family and friends. By the end of October, the two had spent between $10,000 and $15,000 on rent, materials, sub-contracting costs, telephone, advertising and related expenses. No salaries had been paid, and customers had been told that they would receive finished products shortly after the prototype had been fully tested and documented.

By mid-November, a prototype was finally completed and tested successfully against the specifications Steve had written the previous summer. To celebrate, the two invited personal friends and others who had helped on the project to a product introduction party. Local computer distributors were also invited, one of whom turned out to be the area distributor for Apple. Steve and Matthew reached an agreement with him that he would serve as their distributor and would buy at least five instruments each month. He would be entitled to whatever price discount was customary and would help advertise the product in addition to making direct sales efforts. Steve added that there was nothing written in the way of an agreement. "We just shook on it."

A flyer, excerpts from which appear in Exhibit 3, was prepared describing the product for advertising purposes.

From Prototype to Business

When product shipments started in January 1981, Steve said, the venture entered a new phase wherein a number of tasks the two had ignored while developing the prototype would soon have to be faced, despite an intensifying shortage of time. Initial customer reaction to the product seemed favorable, but the two agreed that they would need a much larger customer base before they would be comfortable about long-range prospects for the venture.

They estimated that they currently spent about 40 percent of their business time on product development or assembly, and the other 60 percent talking with customers over the phone, calling suppliers, or listening to sales representatives who came by the office to tell them of computer-related products and advances in the field. Steve explained that they had been able to reduce one source of frustration by working with sales representatives as a way to purchase parts and products components.

> *We never knew this—that it paid just to establish friendly contacts with sales representatives whose task it is to bridge the purchasing gap. They've helped us enormously in the past few months. Another thing we found is that sales reps who aren't with a particular company tend to be less helpful. They're less informed about the product, lack dedication to the company they represent, and, in our opinion, don't speak for the company —just themselves.*

Production

Steve estimated that each instrument took approximately 10 hours to assemble and test. He expected that production time could eventually be reduced to eight hours for each unit. Per-unit costs consisted of the following: $70 for the metal case and painting of the panels; $90 for the printed circuit board; $3 for the silk-screen lettering; and between $500 and $525 for the other components such as wire, cable, switches, buses, and electronic equipment. Labor costs for assembly averaged an estimated $100. Parts costs are listed in Exhibit 4.

Receipt of metal cases was expected to take between four and five weeks. To date, Steve and Matthew had ordered only once with the subcontractor, and delivery had been made approximately one month later. They believed six weeks should be allowed for the printed circuit boards, while silk-screening could be done on very short notice.

Most of the engineering was done by Steve, although Matthew had acquired enough skills by helping with the prototype to assist in assembly of the product. They set a goal for delivery time at between "off the shelf" and three weeks. Current quotes to customers were between six and eight weeks for delivery of an instrument. The two also wanted to build up a stock of replacement components for quick service, but had not yet been able to do so because of a lack of cash and the demand by some suppliers for a certified check or cash upon delivery. Matthew remarked that only a few suppliers allowed them terms of net 30, but he was working to increase their number. "The worst part," he said, "is the time needed to fill out all the forms they send us."

Steve was still doing product development on additional modules that could be plugged into the instrument. He commented on his progress up through March of 1981:

> *We've finished four of the ten modules, which sounds like we're only 40 percent complete. Since the main development was in the prototype and chassis design, I would say that we're closer to 80 percent complete. The drawings*

are nearly finished, so we hope engineering can be wrapped up by the middle of summer.

The standard unit consisted of five modules, each with five channels available for receiving data and two channels for output. Six slots were incorporated to allow a user to plug in additional modules as desired. Matthew pointed out that this feature was the product's primary strength, since the expansion capability provided a wide range of possible applications and made it easy to incorporate state-of-the-art technology.

For adequate production space, the two expected they would require a new location in the next 12 months. They preferred to remain in Boston or Cambridge and not move to suburbs as had many high technology firms. They also discussed a need for appropriate personnel to assist with hardware and software development. Mike Fridkin was writing software part time, while Steve Brand helped on a variety of tasks. Both planned to enter graduate school in the fall, Mike as a law student at Harvard and Steve as an overseas student in the social sciences.

Marketing

Advertising costs had been assumed by the distributor as part of an informal agreement worked out in late 1980. Steve and Matthew expressed some dissatisfaction with the distributor's performance, noting that the one or two advertisements he had placed to date hadn't even mentioned their product except in reference to peripheral products available to augment the Apple line of computers. The distributor frequently referred inquiries directly to them instead of calling up on his own to learn more about the product. As a result, Steve guessed they spent an average of an hour and a half on the telephone for each sale made. This could be in the form of one

call or up to six conversations with the same person, answering specific questions about the instrument's performance. Steve added that they hadn't had much success in telling the distributor to respond to customer queries directly. They hoped the owner's manual which was expected back from the printer in the next week or two, would solve the problem and also help the distributor to promote their product and company name.

Steve estimated that 80 percent of those who called about the product had heard of it through the distributor, while 10 percent had seen the instrument in a customer's office or lab and 10 percent had seen the early versions Steve designed for Harvard. Those who learned of the product through the distributor had to be referred back to him if they wanted to purchase a unit. Others could buy direct from Steve and Matthew. Steve said the percentage of people who inquired after seeing the instrument in use by a present customer was increasing, and he expected this trend would continue.

As of March 31, 1981, seven Standard Systems had been sold, at a cost of $1,500 each. The sales had been made in recent months, and 15 orders remained outstanding for similar units. The distributor had yet to purchase any units from the company. Total revenues for the company to date were $10,500.

Current wholesale and retail prices for the instrument were set at $1,300 and $1,650 respectively. The 27-percent discount allowed to the distributor was contingent on provision of advertising support. Steve explained that if they resumed advertising on their own, or worked out a marketing relationship with a manufacturer such as Apple, they would attempt to lower the discount, although he wasn't sure what figure would provide them with sufficient margin and still meet competitor's prices. A tentative price list appears as Exhibit 5.

The competition consisted either of other small manufacturers who relied on printed circuit boards to be inserted into the host computer or, in a couple of situations, a separate peripheral unit. Steve considered these products were inferior, both in performance and ease of use, to those of Data Acquisition Systems. Not only did they lack the feature of modular design, but he questioned whether competitors would be able to provide complete documentation and follow-through support to customers. Service and reliability were becoming two of the most sought-after features for computer-related products, according to Steve, who reasoned that because many people were not used to working with microcomputers, service would be essential in building a customer base and product loyalty.

One problem Matthew said had to be overcome was getting Data Acquisition Systems' name out before the public. He believed the company's size and obscurity were hampering efforts to attract sales, and he doubted that many prospective customers knew their product existed. That was where the instrument's compatibility with the Apple Computer could prove valuable. He commented:

> The people at Apple know that peripheral equipment which is compatible will help increase their sales, and they've taken some small companies "under their wing" in terms of promotion and support. There's one company I know of that was as small as we were six years ago. It got to talking with Apple and the firm has grown incredibly fast since then.

Matthew said that although he and Steve hadn't talked directly with any people at Apple thus far, they hoped to do so in the next six months, to determine whether Apple might be willing to help promote the Data Acquisition Systems' present and future products.

Finance

Through the third quarter ending in January 1981, the venture had spent most of the $10,000 in loans provided by relatives and friends in addition to $2,000 capital paid in by Matthew and Steve. Terms for repayment had been set up on an individual basis spread over the next two years. Interest ranged from zero to 10 percent, and only two of the loans had written repayment schedules—most were verbal assurances to repay. Steve mentioned that he and Matthew wanted to begin as soon as possible repaying those who had helped the venture get started.

To date, no financial statements existed for the company. Neither Steve nor Matthew had spent much time recapping expenditures until the past month (see Exhibit 2). Steve said they were trying to figure out their current monthly overhead rate and how it should affect pricing. Both had limited acquaintance with business administration—Matthew had taken an introductory financial accounting course the previous semester, but found it confusing.

Banking relationships had consisted only of setting up an account at a nearby bank. The partners had avoided talking with loan officers because they figured that a business such as theirs wouldn't be able to get a loan until revenues were coming in regularly. "The only way we could get a bank loan now," Steve suggested, "was if one of our parents co-signed a personal note. That's something we would rather not do, so we simply haven't talked with any bankers so far."

Steve and Matthew had discussed the possibility of raising money through venture capital or private stock offerings, but their need for legal advice and mistrust of venture capitalists had deterred them.

They thought they might explore those directions further, however, some time in the next 12 to 18 months. Steve explained that he and Matthew wanted to retain control over the business as much as possible. He regarded financial negotiations as "painful," and added that he would probably consult a family friend involved in the financial community who had offered his assistance. Several investors had approached the two with offers of financial backing. Steve commented:

> We've had venture capitalists come in and we are simply terrified, not knowing what they want out of the deal. About three or four months ago, two very preppy looking types came in. They were in their mid 30s, talked and acted very slick, and started leaving information about themselves and sample prospectuses. They were in the building because some other man was trying to talk them into renovating the place. The landlord had told them about us and when they walked in, they were very interested, seeing that we were working off the coattails of Apple. Through deliberate negligence on our part, we wrote that relationship off; venture capital is something we don't want to get into quite yet.

Administrative Concerns

Steve mentioned personnel as another problem area. Addition of an employee would not only allow the partners more time for paperwork and administrative tasks that had been put off, but would also enable them to build instruments faster. Other demands on their time had slowed production until only one instrument was being produced every two weeks. Steve and Matthew decided to look for students who enjoyed a variety of tasks, had a basic understanding of electronics and were willing to work part time or full time. This would allow the partners to maintain flexibility in scheduling and avoid problems they said might occur if they hired a person much older than themselves Steve commented:

> We would look first and foremost for people who are good with their hands and enjoy assembling things. We'd also pay attention to getting people with diverse talents, versatile people who enjoy a variety of tasks. We figure that because there are so many universities around, the resource pool we have to draw on here in the Boston area is immense.

With the expected loss of Steve Brand and Mike by fall, Steve Wilson said engineering talent would be another area of need. He mentioned that he wanted to avoid the controls and hierarchical structure common to most businesses and instead emphasise creativity and independence to attract and keep talented programmers, analysts and engineers. He saw high turnover and lack of company loyalty as the norm for high technology firms. "But whether we will be able to overcome that when other companies haven't," he added, "I'm not sure."

Regular salaries, the partners expected, would be paid to any employees hired full time. They estimated that industry rates for software and hardware development personnel with little or no experience were between $20,000 and $30,000 per year. With benefits and overhead, the cost of hiring an engineer experienced in the electronic industry they thought would be between $50,000 and $75,000 per year. Steve explained that in contrast they had only begun paying themselves any type of salary within the last two months. He recalled how the four divided their first "paycheck" at the end of February:

> It's not regular or large enough to

call a salary; "stipend" would be a better word. We divided $300 four ways for about 150 hours of work, so the hourly rate was close to $2. We developed an elaborate system to split the money. Two-thirds was distributed according to the number of hours each put into the business during February. The remaining third we divided equally as compensation for all of the unpaid work and commitment to the venture.

Steve and Matthew talked about other administrative tasks they either handled piecemeal or took care of as best they could. If a legal issue arose and seemed to need attention, one of them might spend most of the day at the Harvard Law Library or talking to a friend to find out what should be done. Matthew recalled, for example, researching import-export regulations to learn what might be involved in trading overseas.

Aside from discounts allowed to the distributors, selling and administrative costs were estimated to be running between $300 and $400 per month. This included rent, utilities, typewriter rental, office supplies, and any ads that the company might place directly. Salary costs were not included. Steve explained that any payment of compensation was a matter of examining expenses at the end of the month and seeing if any money was left for salaries. "It's not a very sophisticated method," he admitted, "but it has worked for us so far."

Whether the product should be patented was another question that concerned the two. Matthew recalled that they had considered filing for a patent, but lacked the $3,000 to $5,000 he estimated an attorney would charge. He had discovered that, under patent law, a company had one year from the time it first advertised a product to file a patent application on it. This meant that he and Steve had one month left in which to find a lawyer and complete

the writing and filing of the necessary documents. Otherwise, they would forfeit rights for patent protection of their present design. Matthew went on to explain that to have any lasting value, the patent should be as "global" as possible in terms of protecting the design and possibly even the process, commenting:

It takes some incredibly extensive research of existing patents plus good writing, and that's why you go for the best patent attorney you can find. It also means spending a lot of money which we don't have right now.

Steve and Matthew said that within the coming year, they would like their company to reach a position where it had completed development of the first product, was shipping products regularly, occupied a new office in Boston or Cambridge, and employed around 10 workers full time. Steve added that his plans for completing school were "somewhat hazy, perhaps in the next year, but definitely within the next three." Matthew would be finished by June and able to devote his attention to the business with fewer distractions. They had thought about recruiting advisors, and explained that they would probably rely on personal friends or friends of the family for legal and financial assistance.

Both mentioned name exposure as being very important in "getting the jump" on competition and building a base for steady orders. Steve said that among the many issues and tasks awaiting them in the next 12 months, an overriding concern was to search out and retain qualified personnel.

We've found that a lot of pretending goes on initially in starting a company like this. You have to convince yourself that you are not just students fooling around. It takes a couple of months to stop laughing when you answer the phone with your company name. But if we are going to succeed in the long run, we will have to do a lot more. I think we will have to bring in very talented engineers and build a reputation for techni- *cal excellence. The prospect of hiring people is exciting. But it's also very scary, because we are going to have to come up with enough money on a regular basis to meet a payroll.*

EXHIBIT 1 Excerpt from "Personal Computers in the Scientific Laboratory" by Steven F. Wilson

THE SMALL COMPUTER IN THE RESEARCH LABORATORY

The value of a small computer in the research laboratory has long been appreciated, not solely for computational tasks, but for automated data acquisition and experimental control as well. In such applications, the computer directs the complex experimental procedure, collects scientific data in real-time from all types of transducers and instrumentation, and then reduces, analyzes, and periodically stores this information on magnetic disk. Later, the researcher may review and graphically represent the derived data on an interactive CRT terminal. Sections of special interest can be automatically highlighted and expanded, critical points probed, and parallel sequences contrasted. For a permanent record, these results can be plotted on an X-Y recorder or printed in tabular form, all on command.

But the computer alone is inadequate for such a task. Analog conversion hardware is required for the processor to meet the analog environment on its own terms. Physical parameters are measured with any conventional transducer—thermocouples, strain gauges, photo multiplier tubes, a multiplexed analog-to-digital converter, all under computer control. Tens or even hundreds of thousands of conversions per second at up to 16 bits accuracy can be achieved. Further, with appropriate algorithms and hardware, the computer can generate any type of analog signal—from precision DC reference voltages to complex high-frequency wave forms. The full circle back to the analog environment is achieved.

The versatile minicomputer of the 1960s demonstrated well the merits of such a system, for all the experimental sciences—and medical applications as well—but at a high cost. At $10,000 or more, many laboratories found such instrumentation beyond their means. In addition to the high cost of sophisticated analog conversation circuitry, this expense derives from the unusual demands placed on the CPU by real-time tasks. Significantly, even the least expensive minicomputers proved too costly when dedicated to a single experimental task. Real-time data acquisition is largely incompatible with time-shared systems, as the input/output task cannot be delayed: timing is dictated by external experimental constraints.

The advent of the microcomputer coupled with that of the new integrated analog conversion technology has brought about a drastic reduction in system costs with only minimal loss of capabilities. As a result, the implementation of compact and highly versatile computer-based data acquisition systems is now possible at a cost of under $3,000. The introduction of such systems promises to have a rapid and profound effect on the methods of experimental research in the 1980s.

EXHIBIT 1 (concluded)

LEVELS OF IMPLEMENTATION

We justify such a forecast by pointing to the dramatic effect such equipment will have on the resources of the scientist. Previously, the researcher faced a two-fold limitation. First, technological limitations in analog instrumentation severely curtailed the number of discrete observations retrievable from the study of short-lived phenomena. If, for example, a scientist had only a chart recorder or an oscilloscope at his disposal, its response time would severely limit his ability to closely study the kinetics of a chemical reaction or the characteristics of a single neuronal impulse. Second, long-term experiments were limited by the expense, tedium, and potential for error implicit in the technique of manual data transcription. In either case the paucity of experimental data reduces the strength of theoretical conclusions.

Computerized data acquisition, by contrast, provides an abundance of data—in a short-term experiment perhaps tens or even thousands of observations per second, and in long-term studies an essentially unlimited number of error-free data points. Even more significant, the power of statistical analysis is for the first time fully at the service of the scientist.

A RESEARCH APPLICATION

At the Biological Laboratories at Harvard University, several APPLE II computers and early versions of the DAS-5 have been in use for over a year for biophysical measurements in the laboratory of Professor J.W. Hastings. One application involves the study of organisms omitting light according to a circadian rhythm, a kind of biological clock with an approximate periodicity of 24 hours. This phenomenon is the single-celled equivalent of the phenomenon we experience most notably in the discomfort of "jet-lag," the readjustment of our own biological time-keeping mechanism to an environment that is newly out of sync with our own clock. It appears that virtually all species exhibit this behavior. The aim of the researcher is to investigate the nature of this timekeeper, and to discover means of controlling it. Typical experiments have involved the subjection of the cells to variations in temperature, light exposure, and chemical environment, and the monitoring of the biological clock for several days. Because the week long experiment must be regarded many times under different conditions, the computer proved an invaluable addition.

Before the computer was implemented, measurements were made by placing vials containing the appropriate culture of luminescent cells before a photo tube and recording light emission over long periods on a chart recorder. The analysis of these paper records proved tedious, because the recorded light intensity was found to be composed of two components, a continuous low-level glow, and randomly spaced bright flashes which last 0.1 to 1.0 second each. Quantitative analysis of these flashes was not feasible from chart records, but it was clear that they did not share the periodicity of the glow. Previously, it was necessary to discern the glow level from the sporadic intensity of the flashes by inspection of the chart records with a straight edge. The analysis of the data produced by a single six-day experiment required that someone measure the height of some 8,000 pen deflections, each corresponding to the glow of one vial at a given moment, and then transfer by hand these values to a data table or directly to graph. Fortunately, the computerized data acquisition system permitted this task to be accomplished in a real-time statistical algorithm. This software technique sacrifices information about the kinetics of the individual flashes but efficiently determines the integrated light level from each of the two sources—flash and glow. Thirty or more samples of the organism undergo varied chemical treatment by the researcher and are then placed in a mechanical turntable. A motor driven photo multiplier carriage passes sequentially, under computer control, from one vial to the next. The entire sample-holding structure has provisions for a temperature-controlled circulation water bath.

Exhibit 2 Tabulation of Expenditures

	Feb Thru May	June	July	Aug	Sept	Oct	Nov	Dec	Jan	Feb	Total
Office Remodel, Improve	0.00	839.60	41.50	16.53	24.95	10.01	0.00	0.00	16.80	31.91	981.30
Office Supplies, Computer	1.16	8.19	63.74	0.00	0.00	0.00	24.76	7.54	26.88	20.70	152.97
Tools, Equipment	0.00	1,642.25	367.75	28.88	0.00	0.00	0.00	13.99	19.82	0.00	2,072.69
Electronic Parts, Hardware	0.00	0.00	239.24	243.51	116.22	178.43	2,105.09	1,103.08	1,647.87	598.38	6,231.82
Telephone Charges	0.00	82.57	102.68	98.68	0.00	46.88	87.89	82.34	90.64	127.00	718.68
Rent, 3d Street	0.00	150.00	150.00	150.00	150.00	150.00	150.00	150.00	150.00	150.00	1,350.00
Utilities	0.00	0.00	16.86	0.00	0.00	0.00	0.00	0.00	0.00	0.00	16.86
Insurance	0.00	0.00	0.00	0.00	0.00	75.00	0.00	97.00	0.00	0.00	172.00
Legal, Incorporation	144.00	0.00	0.00	0.00	0.00	0.00	0.00	0.00	0.00	0.00	144.00
Post Office, UPS, etc.	53.50	0.00	157.17	52.00	36.24	8.00	18.45	44.57	50.00	28.00	447.93
Copy, Offset	86.58	0.00	123.97	154.47	0.00	215.64	121.99	123.32	0.00	25.61	851.58
Graphic Arts Supplies	33.18	0.00	50.82	19.68	0.00	11.24	38.05	0.00	23.96	20.63	197.56
Selectric Typewriter	50.00	0.00	0.00	0.00	0.00	63.00	0.00	378.00	0.00	0.00	491.00
Advertising	98.50	0.00	0.00	0.00	0.00	0.00	300.00	50.00	0.00	50.00	498.50
Publ, Books	0.00	15.98	23.29	15.11	0.00	0.00	0.00	0.00	0.00	0.00	54.38
Expense Account	0.00	0.00	0.00	0.00	0.00	22.74	490.00	0.00	0.00	15.50	528.24
Wages, Stipends	0.00	0.00	0.00	0.00	0.00	0.00	0.00	300.00	50.00	750.00	1,100.00
Subcontracts	0.00	0.00	0.00	0.00	0.00	0.00	0.00	3,364.90	1,780.61	104.00	5,249.51
Total	466.92	2,738.59	1,337.02	778.86	327.41	780.94	3,336.23	5,714.74	3,856.58	1,921.73	21,259.02

EXHIBIT 3 Excerpts from Advertising Flyer

das

DATA ACQUISITION SYSTEMS, INC.   CAMBRIDGE, MASSACHUSETTS

DATA ACQUISITION SYSTEMS, INC.

Data Acquisition Systems: A manufacturer of state-of-the-art precision analog conversion instrumentation engineered to meet the exacting requirements of science, medicine, and industry. DAS anticipates the rapid implementation of low cost conversion and control systems for distributed processing in diverse applications around the world.

THE MODEL 5 ANALOG INPUT/OUTPUT SYSTEM

The Model Five Analog I/O System. It's the extraordinary new analog subsystem from DAS. For the first time, a microcomputer-based system can meet your most exacting specifications of performance and reliability. The power and precision of computerized data acquisition were previously available only to the minority of specialists who could afford the expensive minicomputers and their costly data acquisition peripherals. With the DAS-5 and the APPLE II microcomputer, you have a powerful, universal data acquisition package that offers the combination of speed, accuracy, and flexibility of systems costing five times more.

In the laboratory, the DAS-5 is a remarkable new research tool for automatic data acquisition, analysis, and display, as well as for experimental automation and control.

In industry, the DAS-5 permits cost-effective, reliable implementation of localized process control.

CONDITIONING, CONVERSION, AND CONTROL

All in one package. With the DAS-5, you create a total link to the analog environment. The system is modular and fully expandable. A full family of modules for conditioning, conversion, and control allow you to tailor your system to the task at hand. And you pay only for the capabilities you need. The DAS-5:

*Up to 256 extra single-ended inputs, or 128 differential, all in the same chassis *Up to 8 precision 12 or 16-bit D/A outputs with switch-selectable voltage and current ranges *Up to 16 channels of 4-20 milliamp Current Loop Outputs   *1.5 microsecond 12-bit A/D *Programmable Gain Amplification   *Direct Memory Access Controller under development

Best of all, the system is ready to go.

EXHIBIT 4 Estimated Parts Costs

das

DATA ACQUISITION SYSTEMS, INC.   (617) 491 5051

March 30, 1981

"Parts" = cost of parts in module described, including subcontracting, but not including labor; "New" = new prices as listed on price list; "Margin-Dir" = the margin of profit on direct sales to customers over the parts cost expressed as a percentage; "Dist-Price" = the price of the same parts when sold to a dealer or representative; "D-Marg" = the margin of the distributor, assuming he or she sells at the same price as our direct sales; expressed as a percentage above 100 percent, the price he or she paid at the Distributor prices; "Marg-Dist" = the margin of profit over the price of parts on sales made at the distributor's discounted prices.

	PART $	NEW $	MARGIN DIR %	DIST-PRICE	D-MARG %	MARG-DIST %
Standard System	700.00	1,650	236	1,340	27	186
Case, Power, w/Front'	301.24	450	144	375	20	124
System Controller	28.14	190	675	145	31	515
Analog Input Card	79.72	330	414	250	32	314
ATC (Prot)	91.42	345	377	265	30	314
A/D	137.47	400	291	295	36	215
5 A/D	342.48	650	190	525	240	153
Single-Ended	53.55	244	373	150	33	180
Single-Ended (Prot)	65.25	215	330	165	30	253
Differential A	151.62	350	231	275	27	181
Differential A (Prot)	163.32	365	223	240	26	178
Differential B	165.62	370	223	290	28	195
Differential B (Prot)	177.32	385	217	305	26	26
Transducers (4-CH)						
2-Bit D/A	71.46	260	364	190	37	266
6-Bit D/A, 15 LIN						
6-Bit D/A,16 LIN						
20 MA	221.83	450	203	375	20	169
P Dig I/O	37.78	90	232	65	38	168
Niv. Dig. I/O Proc						
Apple Int	22.83	60	263	50	20	219

EXHIBIT 5 Tentative Price List Effective March 25, 1981

das

DATA ACQUISITION SYSTEMS, INC.   (617) 491 5051

DAS - 5 Analog Input/Output System

Description	DAS Retail	Distrbtr.
Standard Series, for the APPLE Computer	1,650.00	1,300.00
System Controller Module	190.00	145.00
Analog Input Module, Standard Inputs	330.00	250.00
Analog Input Module, Protected Inputs	345.00	265.00
Successive Approximations A/D Converter Module	400.00	295.00
Very High Speed A/D Converter Module	650.00	525.00
Input Expansion Module (Single Ended)	200.00	150.00
Input Expansion Module, Protected Inputs	215.00	165.00
Input Expansion Module with Differential Inputs, High Accuracy Standard Inputs	350.00	275.00
Input Expansion Module with Differential Inputs, High Accuracy Protected Inputs	365.00	290.00
Input Expansion Module with Differential Inputs, High Speed Standard Inputs	370.00	290.00
Input Expansion Module with Differential Inputs, High Speed Protected Inputs	385.00	305.00
Low Level Input Module for Transducers	*	*
12 Bit Precision Digital to Analog Converter Module	260.00	190.00
16 Bit Precision D/A Converter Module, 15 Bit Linearity	*	*
16 Bit Precision D/A Converter Module, 16 Bit Linearity	*	*
Dual Channel Current Loop Output Module	450.00	375.00
General Purpose Digital Input/Output Module	90.00	65.00
Universal Digital I/O Processor Module	*	*
Case and Power Supply, Full Front Panel	450.00	375.00
Case and Power Supply, OEM Front Panel	*	*
Apple Computer Interface Card and Cable	60.00	50.00

* Contact Data Acquisition Systems for prices on these parts.

Notes:

1. Software package and complete documentation covering all areas of system operation and implementation are included in all system purchases.

2. The Standard System, described in the Specifications Sheet, includes Modules 1,2,3 and two of #8, standard case with front panel and power supply (DAS-5-CPF), interface card for the APPLE computer (DAS-5-AI), software package, and complete documentation.

3. System configurations other than the Standard System may be constructed to suit your analog requirements by adding more modules at the above prices to the Standard System, or should all the elements contained in the Standard System not be required, by purchasing the DAS-5-CPF chassis and any combination of modules form the list above. Consult the guidelines under "Module Selections" in the Specifications Sheet, page 6. The APPLE interface card is included free of charge in all system purchases.

4. Quantity discount information is available upon request.

5. Consult our distributors or the factory for delivery information.

6. APPLE is a trademark of the APPLE Computer Company.

Case 6

Dataword

In January 1980 Bruce Milne and Lauri Chandler gave notice to their employer, Alpine Data Systems, that they were resigning. Working initially from the den in Bruce's house, they incorporated their venture as Dataword, Inc. on February 22. A third partner, Brian Duthie, joined in the formation, but still remained on the job at Alpine, reluctant to leave because of concern about risks in the new enterprise coupled with the prospect that his family responsibilities would shortly increase with arrival of a new child.

The business plan was not formally reduced to writing at this point, but Bruce was working on it in anticipation that they would need to raise cash beyond the initial $27,000 they could muster from savings and family members. They reasoned that to generate short-term sustaining income the three would continue selling minicomputers with third-party software while working on the side to develop a new software product, which they would bundle with Altos microcomputers to sell as accounting systems for accountants. Bruce would work on lining up suppliers and customers. Brian would develop the new software, and Lauri would run the office. All three would also work on selling the existing minicomputer systems and on consulting, Bruce in accounting systems, Lauri in word processing and Brian on programming.

Because they aimed eventually to provide systems for both accounting and word processing, they chose the name Dataword for their company. In fact, however, they knew they would have to choose initially between the two software packages, accounting versus word processing, for development. Lauri favored word processing because that was her field of familiarity. The other two partners favored accounting, because they had seen what they believed were weaknesses in the market leader of that field, which would give them particularly strong competitive advantages. Accounting was chosen for the initial thrust.

The income-generating strategy did not work as well as they had hoped. They did manage to sell some minicomputer systems as planned, deriving momentum from some leads that came their way as they left Alpine and from their ability to point out that they had proven track records with these established systems. However, a problem all along had been that such major systems invariably required extensive installation and service follow-up work as customers learned to operate them. This took a great deal of the founders' time, and although Brian finally was persuaded in March 1980 to leave Alpine and join the venture full-time, it was still difficult to work on the new software, perform enough consulting and selling to pay the bills and try to line up suppliers and customers for the new microcomputer system all at the same time.

Bruce was able to operate with no salary because of his wife's job, but the other two could not, and there were other expenses of operating the office. It was necessary to add other employees, a part-time secretary and a part-time programmer. Two offices were rented, one in which Brian could concentrate on programming and the other for Bruce's and Lauri's selling and consulting work.

To cope with these expenses as their initial capital dwindled, Bruce undertook to raise more seed capital. From three individuals he raised $10,000 each. One was the proprietor of a cheesecake manufacturing company, a former customer of Bruce's at Alpine who had become a personal friend. The second was an attorney whom Bruce had long tried without success to sell Alpine products, who had also become a friend. The third was a former competitor who had reaped substantial financial gains when his employer, in which he held a share of ownership, had gone public. He too had become a personal friend of Bruce's. The contributions of these investors brought the total capitalization of Dataword to $57,000.

With expenses exceeding revenues by about $10,000 per month Bruce could foresee that something would have to be done soon as fall approached. Although it was not clear that the new software would be ready, he began making arrangements to hold a seminar for accounting firms at which the new system would be displayed and sales orders to buy it would be solicited. This, Bruce observed, would be the first time, so far as he knew, that seminar selling had been applied to microcomputer systems.

The new software was, in fact, not fully complete as the day of the seminar arrived. But there would be enough to display what its capabilities would be. Bruce decided to keep the seminar on schedule. There would, he figured, be a month or two of leeway after taking orders, during which the Altos computers would have to be obtained and delivered to customers, and during that time Brian could put on the finishing touches.

At least, that is what the Dataword founders hoped. Bruce knew they would have reached the limits of their solvency by the time of the seminar. There would still be about $27,000 cash in the bank, but the company would have unpaid bills of approximately the same amount. Brian and Lauri were aware of the cash balance, but not the accounts payable amount. Bruce did not think it would help to have them worrying about financial problems in addition to their other job responsibilities.

But it seemed clear to Bruce that they absolutely had to get orders at that seminar. He had been working on terms of a limited partnership offering which he believed might bring in another $50,000 if they could get orders on books to substantiate that the company had a future. If they could not get the orders, however, it looked to him like they would not be able to raise more capital. In that case he expected they would have to use their cash to pay existing bills and Dataword would be finished.

The seminar was held as scheduled, presenting the new microcomputer accounting system with Brian's developing software package, "Datawrite," and went off as planned. Several accounting companies showed up, asked questions and seemed satisfied that the new system offered a much more economical system, around $25,000 compared to over three times that for other systems, to meet their needs.

The only problem seemed to be that they would not be willing to place orders unless Bruce could answer one more question for them. "We have bought new systems before only to end up with a mess of new problems in getting them to work," they said. "How do we know we will be able to rely on the performance of this new system you want us to order from you?"

Case 7

Ray Davidov and Ken Vorhies

We've circled around this thing a number of times. I'd like some good advice about what strategy to follow. What sequence of steps would be best to get me from where I am to where I want to be? Where I want to be, of course, is successful in entrepreneurship.

Ken Vorhies was reflecting on the work he and Ray Davidov had done to explore the possibility of starting a company in July of 1980. The idea of doing so had grown out of acquaintance with two mechanical engineering professors at the University of Washington who had discovered a need for protective covers on lights attached to road signs of the state's interstate highway system. If a firm order for light covers were to come from the Washington Department of Highways, they believed they could fill it. But where would that lead?

Ken, who had enrolled in a doctoral program at UCLA, planned to return there in the fall to continue his studies, and one of the two professors was about to go on leave to the east coast. Ray had, in his words, "mixed feelings about making light covers," but also was excited that they might have a competitive edge with a product that could potentially be marketed nationwide. Both he and Ken saw a potential for this product, since Washington was one of 50 possible customer states. Apparently there were no existing manufacturers of the type of shield desired by the Highway Department's District Office in Yakima, where incidents of vandalism had originally stimulated interest in one.

Personal Backgrounds

Ken Vorhies had received his bachelor of science degree in biology in 1974 from the University of Washington, where he subsequently earned an MBA. During college he had helped organize a glider soaring club, spent six months at the University of Oslo in Norway studying Norwegian, formed the University of Washington Tae Kwon Do Club (a martial art), helped organize an orienteering club (wilderness/running) and learned to fly aircraft. Currently, he worked as both a teaching and research assistant at the University of Washington in the areas of management and small business. He had, since receiving his MBA in 1976, taught courses in business and industrial engineering. In 1979 he enrolled in the Doctoral Program of the UCLA School of Management. The following summer he returned to Seattle for vacation and to work on potential business ventures. He felt that while doctoral studies would require a great deal of effort and concentration, the flexibility time-wise might allow him to pursue a venture opportunity for awhile, if the situation arose. He commented:

I think entrepreneurship is the only way to make a substantial amount of money and enjoy the process of doing it. My feeling is, that unless some day I get involved with a venture, my life will somehow be incomplete.

Ray Davidov's experience included prior business ventures. After starting college in 1965, he had dropped out in 1969 as a political activist during the Vietnam War. With partners, he became involved in a candle-making venture which, though profitable, he left following the departure of first one partner and then another. In the nine years between enrolling in the university and graduating, he organized an art gallery, which was not profitable, and managed several types of businesses including a night club, a tavern and a record store. For the last five of those years, he worked for a theatrical booking agent—an activity he characterized as a dead-end. "The owner had his two sons working there," he said, "and I couldn't see how I was ever going to get anywhere. So I quit and went back to school."

While pursuing a bachelor of arts degree in business at the University of Washington, Ray managed an apartment building to pay his way. Following graduation in 1979, he became coordinator of the school's Small Business Institute, a program that arranged for student projects to help provide technical assistance to small businesses. His main function was to match businesses that wanted consulting help with classes where such projects fit. Like Ken, Ray felt that the idea of entrepreneurship was attractive. "I was raised in an atmosphere where independent business was admired," he said, "and I think the only way I could enjoy working is where I am in charge."

Discovering a Need and Possible Product

While enrolled at the University of Washington, Ken and Ray became acquainted with two mechanical engineering professors who occasionally explored companies in the Seattle area that might offer good opportunities for investment or acquisition. While investigating a plastic-forming company for sale, they learned of possible interest by the State Highway department in plastic covers to protect lights

being vandalized in the Yakima area, east of the Cascade mountains.

Many highway overpasses in the state had large signs informing motorists of road exits, distances to cities ahead or services available at the nearest town. Typically, these signs were illuminated at night by lamps with bulbs covered by large glass lenses. Maintenance personnel found that occasionally people would walk out on the overpass above a sign and drop rocks on the lights, smashing lenses and the bulbs, and scattering glass on the roadway below. A replacement lens cost only $12, but the special trip by maintenance personnel to replace it cost several times that much. Further damage risked by cars below from running over the broken glass was also potentially very expensive.

Highway Department engineers had called the lamp manufacturer to see if the firm made protective shields for the lights, and were told no such item was available. The engineers then called a plastic company to see if they might be interested in making such a shield. The engineers were told that the breadbox shape needed was not compatible with the extrusion company's production process. It was at this point that the professors learned of the need and decided to try making a prototype on their own, reasoning that if the product proved successful, it might be the basis for developing a company. This first product might become an industrial foothold that could be extended to other business opportunities—whether in lighting, plastics or other problem-solving products.

One of the professors called the Yakima district of the Highway Department to see if there might be interest in a prototype. The district engineer said yes, and the professors proceeded to make a test shield. They bought some sheets of polycarbonate, a particularly tough, transparent plastic from a local industrial plastics distributor whom they located through the Yellow Pages. They experimented with ways of heating and bending it, something that the plastics extruder had told them could not be effectively done. They did find a way to do so, however, and made a shield to fit over the light lens, as shown in Exhibit 1. They took it to Yakima for Highway Department personnel to evaluate. One of the professors recalled what ensued when he assembled the shield on a dismounted light in the repair shop to show how it fitted over the lens.

> The district engineer asked a shop worker to go find a rock. The guy came back with one the size of a cannonball. The engineer frowned at it and said, "no, I mean a rock; a _real_ rock." The crew man went back out and brought back a boulder about the size of a soccer ball. They set up a ladder about 10 or 12 feet high, laid a light under it on the concrete floor with a shield mounted on it, pushed that boulder up to the top and then let it drop on the light.
>
> Well, of course that boulder shattered the shield, the lens, the light and the metal light housing; everything was smashed. We didn't think that was a fair test. So we made another shield that was thicker and invited them to pound on it with hammers all they wanted. That one survived.

The district engineer then wrote one the professors indicating that the Highway Department would be interested in ordering up to 100 shields for testing in the field. The professors now found themselves with the prospect of an order for a product that no other firm made. However, neither had enough free time to follow-up with the Highway Department and pursue the venture. One had just been appointed to become department chairman in the Engineering School beginning in the fall of 1980, while the other was about to begin a leave of absence to teach at a small college on the East Coast for a year. Consequently,

they invited Ray and Ken to take over the project while they shifted to advisory and possibly financing roles for turning it into a business venture.

Technology of the Shields

The prototype shields were made from a type of plastic sheet known as polycarbonate. This material, introduced about 20 years earlier by General Electric, had found wide acceptance in a variety of industrial, commercial and consumer product applications. Beer pitchers, houseware, medical equipment, automobile parts, doors, windows, protective eyewear, motorcycle fairings, component parts for printers, copiers and solar collectors were but some of the ways in which polycarbonate had found a "home" in the marketplace. "Vandal proof" school and bus stop windows were a particularly common application.

Major advantages of the material were its high impact strength, ability to withstand a wide range of temperatures (from $-60°$ to $270°$ F), capacity to be shaped and molded, and favorable performance in withstanding transmission of ultraviolet light. Major producers included General Electric (under the trade name Lexan), Rohm and Haas Company (Tuffak) and Mobay Chemical (Merlon). Other firms made additives that could be put in with the resin to improve particular characteristics that a user might desire, such as thermal stability.

From a piece of flat polycarbonate sheet of about two square feet, a pattern was cut and drilled as depicted in Exhibit 2. The piece was then bent, where the dotted lines are shown in Exhibit 2, to form the breadbox shape that would fit over the lamp lens. The lamp's glass lens was retained beneath this shield, to help diffuse the light rays, insulate the plastic from heat generated by the bulb, and protect the plastic somewhat from ultraviolet rays which tended to degrade it and cause it to yellow.

Shields made from one-eighth inch polycarbonate could be bent while cold but would not withstand high enough impact, as had been learned from the first prototype tested in Yakima. A one-fourth inch thickness was needed, but bending such thick material cold was unsatisfactory because the bend would show hairline splinter cracks or even break. Plastic welding the ends together didn't work for polycarbonate. Adhesives were available, but the professors doubted that gluing flat pieces together would work.

To be bent, the sheet had to be heated selectively along the fold lines. The professors were told by one plastics fabricator that it could not be done properly. They tried a propane torch for heating and bending but found they could not form corners sharply or uniformly. After further puzzling over the problem, one of the professors thought of trying to uncoil a stove burner to make a long, thin heater. Contacting a stove repair shop, they obtained several of the discarded burners, which are made of a material called "calrod," and bent them out straight by hand. Then they connected one to an electricity source. Happily, they found it still got hot.

Considerable experimentation and practice were still required, however, to bend satisfactory corners in the polycarbonate. Temperature control to bend a flat sheet of polycarbonate was more important than with other types of plastic, such as Plexiglas; too cool and it would not be a permanent bend; too hot and the sheet would bubble, forcing the entire piece to be scrapped. Trial and error finally produced an acceptable shape. When finished, the shield could withstand severe blows without cracking or breaking. The first shield took nearly two hours to make, while the second one and one-half hours.

Production required a table saw and drill in addition to the calrod elements.

The calrod was held within one inch of the polycarbonate one and one-half minutes for the longer bends and two minutes for the side bends. Cooling required 15 seconds for each bend. The table saw could cut through the one-quarter inch sheet at a rate between 6 and 12 inches per second. Next, metal strips were cut to connect the lamp base and the shield on each side, with holes drilled through the metal and polycarbonate, and pop rivets inserted to secure the shield to the lamp. For small quantities of polycarbonate, cost of material was $7 per square foot.

Although the prototypes had been made from flat sheets, a process called rotational molding was also used in the industry to manufacture hollow-shaped objects. The advantages were in reduced scrap, uniform quality and speed in a low-volume production run. However, inquiries by one of the professors indicated that a mold would cost up to $50,000. The raw material used in rotational molding differed by being in powdered form, which had to be heated under pressure with other additives.

Exploring the Possibility of a Venture

When one of the professors asked if they might be interested in attempting a venture beginning with the light shields, Ken and Ray decided to seek additional information that would help them evaluate the prospect. The most economical approach seemed to be for each to explore a different part of the problem. Ken chose to look for a subcontractor to make the shields. He called four companies listed under "plastic forming" in the Yellow Pages and asked if they would be interested in a polycarbonate sheet-bending job to make outside light fixture covers.

His impressions were that "nobody was too anxious to mess with polycarbonate." Two of the companies had no experience forming it. A third said he had some experience with the material, but not in bending it. The fourth was a supplier of polycarbonate sheet who said he would supply and bend it to Ken's specifications. The prospective subcontractor mentioned that he would need the prototype for a couple of days and added that a new adhesive was on the market which he thought could be used to glue polycarbonate. He said only one firm, Sheffield Plastics, Inc. of Sheffield, Massachusetts, handled this type of glue. Ken called Sheffield and learned that the firm knew nothing about any special glue for polycarbonate. Rather, they used an adhesive common in the industry, methylene chloride.

At the end of the phone conversation, the man on the other end asked what the name of Ken's company was. Ken replied that there was no company as of yet, but that they were working on putting one together. To Ken's surprise, the man told him to call when it was formed, since it might be possible for Sheffield to set the company up as a distributor for their plastics in the Pacific Northwest. Sheffield's closest distributor at present was in Southern California. Ken took note of the fact that in large quantities such as a distributor might order, one-fourth inch polycarbonate sheet sold for around $3-4 per square foot. He also learned that Sheffield Plastics was experienced in plastic forming using rotational molding techniques.

Meanwhile, Ray had been attempting to determine what type of market existed for the shields. First, he called the district engineer in Yakima to see if the Highway Department was still interested in buying them. While he had done nothing with the project since the first of the year, the engineer was still interested and was waiting for a price quote for the 75-100 shields he would be willing to try.

Ray got the impression that time delays and budget considerations, which could sometimes be a factor in dealing with the state, would not be a problem with this order because of its urgency. He was still unsure about the extent of need for the product, however, since the district office in Yakima was not certain how widespread the vandalism was. Recalling a conversation with the workers in Yakima, one of the professors summed up the Highway Department's thoughts on how many cover shields might be needed:

> We don't know, maybe a thousand. And that's only in our territory. There are a lot of adjacent territories, and we don't know how many have situations like this with this kind of problem . . . but the breakage is driving us crazy.

The Washington Highway Department was divided into six districts, which covered the state's 39 counties. In addition to Yakima, district offices were located in Seattle, Wenatchee, Tumwater, Vancouver and Spokane. The Department was responsible for maintenance of state and federal highways, which included approximately 1,200 miles of interstate and limited-access highways. The Yakima District covered the southeast part of the state and took in much of interstate highways 90 and 82. This district was also one of the hardest hit when the Mt. St. Helens volcano erupted in May 1980.

Ray tried obtaining further information about the extent of need from the Washington State Highway Department headquarters in Olympia, but after three calls, had been unable to locate the head of the Maintenance Division. He then called the District Office head in Seattle, who said he was unfamiliar with the problem of light breakage but had heard that it did occur in outlying parts of the state.

A related aspect in determining market potential, Ray said, was information about the performance of the Holophane lamps used on the interstate system. A 1976 study by the Materials Division of the State Highway Department had examined the life of Holophane lamps, which might allow Ken and Ray another ingredient in determining the cost savings possible from use of the protective shields. Ray was aware of the study but had not yet seen the report.

When they asked what form orders for the shields would take, the two were told that local and state governments were occasionally encouraged to make preferential contracts with small businesses. In 1977, the Washington Legislature passed a law permitting the Commissioner of Highways to set up regulations that would waive certain paperwork and bond requirements for small business contractors who worked on highway projects. A maximum contract limit of $25,000 had been established, but neither Ken nor Ray knew the current status of these regulations.

Potential Competition

Ray and Ken were unsure what competition, if any, might exist in making protective shields similar to their design. He called the manufacturer of Holophane lamps, Johns-Manville Corporation, which was the leader among the three or four principal suppliers of outdoor lighting fixtures used in commercial and industrial settings. While Johns-Manville did make plastic covers for one particular light fixture model, it was not the one used to illuminate the road signs. Furthermore, it was being considered for elimination from the product line.

One of the professors knew that the city of Seattle had experienced similar problems with vandalism of street lights in parts of the city. Recalling the city's experience, he said:

> They have some areas they call half-hour areas or two-hour areas. That

means you put a light up and it lasts a half hour.

To solve this problem, the city had contracted for installation of protective globes which were teardrop-shaped and substituted for the glass lamp. Since the globes had been installed, there had been no breakage. Ray's impression was that the company that made the globes for the city, a general plastics-molding company, did so as a "one-shot" deal, rather than as a company aiming to pursue vandal-proof light covers as a line of business.

Ease of entry for other entrepreneurs who might view the shields as a profitable venture was another concern of Ken and Ray's. One of the professors commented that they could apply for a patent, but he doubted its viability.

> You can always apply for a so-called design patent, which is different from a utility patent. A design patent applies to the physical configuration in an aesthetic sense, but offers you very little protection. Anyone else can just add a dimple or some other little shape change and get around your design patent.

To Ken and Ray it seemed unlikely that any of the polycarbonate makers would become competitors. General Electric's plastics division, for instance, only manufactured flat sheet in polycarbonate. Ray had written the firm to get technical specifications on the properties of the material but had yet to receive it. During his phone conversation with the firm, he did learn that a form of polycarbonate had been developed that was less sensitive to ultraviolet light than earlier types. This, he thought, might make it feasible to manufacture light shields which would substitute for the glass lamp rather than be fitted over the light.

Possible Strategies

By June, Ken and Ray still had unanswered questions they thought might be important. For instance, the company that told Ken it would be willing to subcontract the order for up to 100 shields had initially responded with a price quote of $3.78 per shield. As Ken put it:

> I told them that there had to be a mistake because that wouldn't even cover their raw material costs. They came back with a quote for one, two and one hundred covers . . . $100 for one, $200 for two and $2,000 for one hundred.

From this initial mistake and his telephone conversations with the firm, Ken got the impression that the company was "a little flaky." He still believed that it would be possible to use them for the initial order, and Ray had said he was relying on Ken's judgment in this matter.

Ken and Ray also said they would be willing to invest time doing "grunt work" to make the shields themselves if the situation called for it. They admitted that the prospect of making "light covers forever" was not very appealing. What did excite them was that this order might be an opening that would give them a competitive edge on a regional or even national basis. Ken commented:

> Mainly we see this as an entry wedge. If we can generate some goodwill through our initial orders, maybe we can bootstrap ourselves to a larger customer base.

Both imagined ways a business might be extended. Ken had seen a bicycle parked one day that had a plastic fairing, much like a motorcycle windshield. Ray commented that "anyone who uses outdoor lighting could to some degree be a potential customer of ours."

One strategy they thought of would be to take the profits from the initial order and invest the money for re-orders or other products to solve problems that other companies don't want to handle. However, they questioned whether the one order was enough to start with. Ray commented:

> One order's not going to mean anything. But if I start getting some positive feedback from more market research, then I think we should form a company and do it.

Ray expected that they could rely on a commercial freight service, such as United Parcel Service, to ship the shields to Yakima when production was completed. He and Ken were still uncertain of what price to quote the Highway Department for making the shields. They knew that without a high enough margin, moving ahead with production wasn't worth their while. Ray felt that if they did sign a contract with the State Highway Department, they should not sit still during a test period but should proceed to work on other orders. If the Yakima order worked out well, he expected it would allow them to point to the shields' good performance as evidence of quality and workmanship, which would be helpful in obtaining further orders.

Ray said further orders would be necessary if the venture were to move ahead, but thought their most pressing need was for some "good market research." One possibility he thought of in this area was a U.S. Department of Commerce program he had recently learned about known as WITS (Worldwide Information and Trade System). In an attempt to encourage exports, the Commerce Department had developed a data base that persons could access in Seattle and other major U.S. cities. The database contained listings of distributors operating overseas, the types of products they were interested in exporting and unmet needs of foreign customers.

Ken said the most immediate need was to develop some engineering specifications to assure quality control if the order was confirmed and they continued with the project. He wondered about his current usefulness in the venture and said:

> *If we decide that my role in this is nonexistent, that's okay. I'd be happy to do anything if it makes economic sense. I can also see that by being in California, I'd have the chance to explore the market there and assist the project in attracting customers.*

The four had not fully discussed what role the professors would have in the venture if they proceeded. It appeared that by fall one of the four would be in Massachusetts, one would be in California, leaving Ray plus one professor in Seattle. They also had not discussed whether it would be best to set up as a corporation or some type of partnership. Like many states, Washington had provisions for establishing a corporation, full partnership or limited partnership. Ken believed that they should avoid setting up as a corporation at first since "they're a lot harder to get out of." They hadn't talked with any lawyers about such issues as this or legal aspects of contracting. They expected that most people they did business with would have boilerplate contracts that they could use to sign agreements for making shields or other products.

Finding money for start-up didn't appear to be a problem for Ken and Ray. The professors had indicated a willingness to invest in the venture, subject to learning just how much it would require, possibly in the form of a personal loan to Ray. Additional financing for the venture, if it began to grow substantially, hadn't been discussed—nor had possible lines of credit with banks or venture capital sources been explored.

Other individuals Ken and Ray had talked with about the venture had raised various questions. These ranged from the possibility of going to the Small Business Administration for assistance, speculating what would happen if the signs were placed on the side of the highway rather than beneath underpasses, or if different shaped light fixtures were used to replace the Holophane lamps.

The Current Situation

Meanwhile, a letter from the state had arrived (Exhibit 3) expressing interest in the cover and suggesting that a proposal for more covers be submitted. By July 1980, the four potential venturers had decided that they needed to determine what, if anything, they should do about starting a company. They knew that funding for the Small Business Institute that Ray coordinated had been cut for the coming year, and that Ken still planned on returning to UCLA in the fall.

Ken believed that for their venture to be successful, they would have to concentrate on products and services no established companies wanted to bother with. As a small firm, Ken felt that the competitive edge lay in their ability to solve problems, specializing in areas in which their backgrounds could provide needed expertise. On competing with large companies Ken commented:

> *They could come in and "blow us out of the water" with larger volume and economies of scale.*

Ray concluded:

> *I pretty much agree with everything Ken has said. What I'd like to know is whether we're wasting our time or not, and what would be the best way for each of us to move ahead with the project.*

EXHIBIT 1 Light Fixture

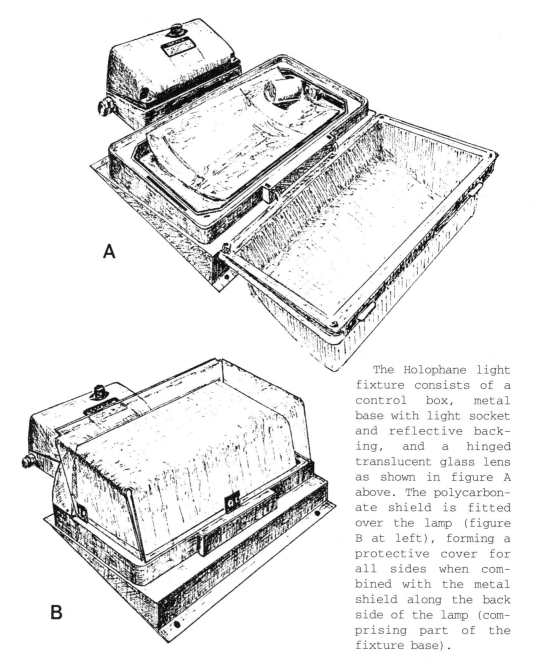

A

B

The Holophane light fixture consists of a control box, metal base with light socket and reflective backing, and a hinged translucent glass lens as shown in figure A above. The polycarbonate shield is fitted over the lamp (figure B at left), forming a protective cover for all sides when combined with the metal shield along the back side of the lamp (comprising part of the fixture base).

EXHIBIT 1 (concluded)

The polycarbonate plastic shield fits over the translucent glass lamp lens as shown below. The metal clips allow the shield to be secured to the fixture base forming protection from the top and three of the four sides. A metal shield fits along the back of the lamp (partially in view) to protect the remaining side of the lamp.

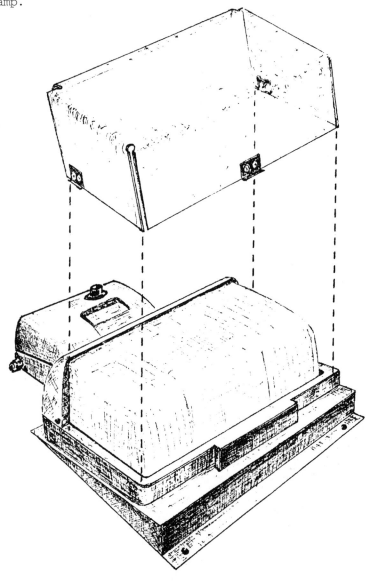

EXHIBIT 2 Shield Fabrication

The shield is cut from a rectangular piece of polycarbonate in the outline indicated by the heavy lines above. This is done after four holes have been drilled as shown, with bends then made along the dashed lines. The result is a breadbox shape which is fitted over the lamp and fastened to the base by metal clips, attached to the polycarbonate with two rivets each (shown at right) and indicated above by the pair of drill holes on each of the three ends.

Drawing above approximately $\frac{1}{2}$ scale. Drawing at right not drawn to scale.

EXHIBIT 3 Letter from State

STATE OF
WASHINGTON

Dixy Lee Ray
Governor

DEPARTMENT OF TRANSPORTATION

Office of District Administrator
2809 N. Main St., Union Gap
P. O. Box 52, Yakima, Washington 98907

Mr. Howard Merchant
Univ. of Wash.
Mechanical Engr. Dept.
Mail Stop FU-10
Seattle, Wa. 98195

Dear Mr. Merchant:

The enclosed sign light cover appears adequate for our
intended use.

I stepped into the midst of your negotiations with John
Murray and have had to sort out bits and pieces of information regarding this matter from several sources. I believe
I finally have the background on this and, hopefully, we can
proceed with the project as planned.

Please spec out the cover and provide me with the information.
The approximate anticipated price would also be helpful.
Initially, we plan to install 75-100 covers, providing the
funding can be arranged.

I apologize for the delay in getting this project on track,
and look forward to working with you to our mutual benefit.

Very truly yours,

Jerry A. Daniels, P.E.
District Traffic Engineer.

Case 8

Cliff Dow and Steve Shaper

In June 1990, four months after receiving his MBA degree from New Hampshire University, Cliff Dow was contemplating with his wife and with another couple whether to drop his job hunting plans and instead buy a store selling classical guitars in Portland, Maine. He knew he was on the "short list" of a major national consulting firm which had said it would notify him with the next month whether it would hire him. He expected the consulting work would be able to pay him more than working in the store, but the job was not certain to materialize. The store, however, had just been put up for sale by its owner, and both Cliff and his prospective partner, Steve Shaper, expected it might sell soon, as the owner said there were already several buyers who said they were seeking financing and expected to make offers within the next week or two.

The Company

Classicraft Guitars was a 15-year-old store in the old section of Portland, which in recent years had been transformed into a chic shopping and tourist area. The first owners of the store had been practicing musicians who had developed it as a sideline and, according to Cliff, given it a good reputation as a source of high-quality instruments with a non-commercial atmosphere. In the back of the store, they had installed several soundproof rooms where they and others gave lessons in classical guitar playing.

Over time, however, the owners found there were conflicts between their occupation as musicians and the work of tending the store, and three years earlier they had sold it to a second owner. The buyer was a guitar maker, who rearranged part of the store into a work area where he both built and repaired instruments. He too, Cliff said, maintained a reputation for handling high-quality instruments and the store was known to have the largest selection of exclusively classic guitars in New England north of Boston. However, this owner had found himself in conflict between his instrument building work and that of tending store, and after three years decided to sell the store and confine his activities solely to manufacturing.

The store at this time utilized about 1,100 square feet on the ground floor of a four story building. It included an entry area approximately 15 feet wide, which opened off a side street near the main thoroughfare in Old Portland. Guitars were displayed in front windows about four feet wide on either side of the front door. Inside, there were guitars hanging along the wall on one side, and on the other side, a display of sheet music, records and instrument cases. At the back was a mahogany office desk with a computer terminal on top and a doorway leading farther back to a hallway with more guitars on the walls, a locked display case with the most expensive instruments costing up to $3,000 and two soundproofed practice rooms where two experienced teachers, one of whom was an initial founder of the store, gave guitar lessons.

Steve Shaper

Steve and Cliff had been friends since

working together as retail clerks for a sporting goods store. Steve spent some time in the service following high school, then went on to the University of Maine, where he received both his undergraduate degree and a Ph.D. in English. He then took a faculty position and became a professor of English. He had also been a serious student of classical guitar, taking lessons for many years and playing mainly for personal satisfaction. This avocation he shared with Cliff. The two also shared enthusiasm for long-distance running.

Steve's wife, Sharon, had studied business administration at Portland State and then gone on to become a C.P.A. with the Bangor office of a major national accounting firm. The couple did not have any children, but expected they would in the future.

Cliff Dow

Cliff had gone to the University of New Hampshire following high school. Initially he majored in engineering, but after his sophomore year, he transferred to business administration because it appeared to him that engineering offered "too much dull grind and not enough life. My Dad was an engineer," he said, "and frankly, it didn't look like all that much fun as a career."

Following graduation in 1979, Cliff took a series of jobs in retailing. The same year, he married his wife, Chris, whom he had met at the university through a common interest in running. In retailing he also gravitated toward athletics and worked mainly in sporting goods stores. Chris too went into retailing, starting as a clerk in a women's clothing store. By the time Cliff decided to go back to business school for an MBA degree, Chris had risen to upper management in a chain with 200 stores, over which she had responsibility.

Cliff, however, said he had grown tired of retailing and did not see attractive opportunity for further advancement. He de-

cided to major in finance and international business. On the side he had become interested in Japanese. As part of his degree program, he had completed a summer internship with a firm in Japan. He commented:

As fate would have it, the Japanese company happened to be in retailing. So there I was again, back where I didn't want to be. But it was a good experience anyway.

Cliff also developed an interest in entrepreneurship, and even went so far as to extend his graduation by one quarter in order to take the university's entrepreneurship course. As a project for the course he developed a plan for a venture. He recalled:

It was—you guessed it—a retail store. My concept was to start a store in sporting goods, which was something I had lots of experience in. It would differ from most sporting goods stores by offering a wider variety of products, lessons, tours and other sports-related services. It would aim to be the sporting goods superstore of them all. But when I tried to analyze it objectively I could not find a competitive advantage that really seemed likely to work against competitors who could readily imitate anything I came up with, and who would have the resources, skills and established position to do it as well or better.

I learned a lot in the course about how businesses get started. I had developed confidence in some aspects of venturing, but not in my ability to spot a truly workable venture idea or to finance one even if I did find it. At the end I felt frustrated that I had not actually been able to extract from it a truly viable competitive entry wedge. I had wanted the instructor to give me one. But what I found was that by the end of the course, I had developed a plan for a business idea that was not really workable and that I could not finance even if it was.

Worst of all, it seemed that the task of finding an effective entry wedge was still all up to me. It seemed as though all I could do was keep looking and try to be receptive to opportunity if and when it arose without being able to make it happen. So I really didn't see much likelihood of becoming involved with a venture in the foreseeable future, and I put aside the idea of becoming an entrepreneur.

Following graduation Cliff interviewed for jobs in several areas, particularly product management and management consulting. A major national accounting firm had shown serious interest in him as a potential recruit for its consulting activities. Several interviews followed, and the firm had told him that he was likely to receive an offer, but not for a month or two while the firm firmed up its overall staffing plans.

Shop For Sale

It was during this interlude that he noticed in a classical guitar magazine the advertisement for sale of Classicraft. He had started learning to play the guitar since before elementary school, and his interest in playing had continued ever since. Classicraft was a familiar place to him for buying instruments and music, and he shared the opinion of other classical guitarists that the store was tops in its geographical area for high-quality classical instruments.

He mentioned the advertisement to Steve Shaper and asked whether Steve might have any interest in pursuing it. As they talked, the idea seemed unlikely to

work out. They estimated that the cost of a store like Classicraft would probably be in the range of $100,000 or so. That would be substantially beyond what they could pay without borrowing, and both doubted they would be able to get a loan to buy a business anyway. Cliff said:

We decided it couldn't hurt to approach the store owner and ask how much he wanted. We were surprised when he gave us a figure right off the bat. Then, when the figure turned out to be $30,000 we were even more surprised, and I had to work hard at suppressing delight. That is the kind of figure we can finance personally from savings.

Records of the store were minimal, consisting of a check ledger for expenses and a general ledger for keeping track of sales. The owner had also made available his tax filings for the preceding two years, copies of which appear in Exhibits 1 and 2. He was proposing to sell all the inventory, fixtures and furniture but retain his guitar building tools. The inventory consisted of finished guitars, sheet music and small items such as strings, picks, stands and cases, which he estimated were worth $19,000. The furniture and fixtures he said were worth approximately $5,000. As a total price, he told Cliff and Steve he wanted $30,000.

Two teachers each paid $150 per month for use of the practice rooms. Lesson charges were typically $25 per hour, of which the store received $2. Steve noted that one had been an initial founder of the store, and was very well known and respected in the local music community. He also taught in the music department of the university as well as at a local school of the arts.

Cliff and Steve had examined the store and made an asset list of their own. Based upon estimated purchase costs of inventory and estimated depreciated value of furniture and fixtures they reached an estimated total for the list of $18,592, as shown in Exhibit 3. Cliff noted that based upon his prior retailing experience, it seemed to him that the inventory turnover rate of some items was low and characteristic, at the values they had given it, of "dead stock." Based on historical figures he had projected turnover rates by category as shown in Exhibit 4. He concluded:

> *There should be a turnover rate of at least 2.5 on any category, and on some it looks like the store is doing half that.*

Cliff further commented that, although the present owner was a knowledgeable and pleasant person, he did not seem to be operating all that effectively.

> *He is very low key and doesn't seem to use suggestion selling at all. At the same time, the store could seem intimidating to visitors. The guitars are not labeled, and they are tied down in a way that makes it hard to take them off the wall so they can be played. The owner doesn't really encourage people to play them, maybe because he's afraid they might get scratched, or because he is preoccupied with making and fixing instruments. Or maybe he just doesn't think people want to play them or would be more likely to buy them if it were easier to do so.*
>
> *The way he has sheet music and records stacked in milk crates isn't very orderly, and the workshop area creates dust that leaves the overall level of cleanliness lower than you could wish for. The store seems to me to be entirely out of some items that sell best, probably because the owner has had to make hard*

choices between taking income and investing in inventory. There aren't any CD's at all in the stock or any electronic instruments or equipment like amplifiers.

Need for a Decision

> *The question is whether we should do it and if so what terms and conditions we should propose to the owner. For me, it would mean dropping the possible job opportunity, which I expect might pay somewhere between $40,000 and $60,000 per year. There is no way Steve is going to quit his teaching job and move himself and his wife to Portland to run the store.*
>
> *He said he and his wife are willing to put up half the money if Chris and I put up the other half. But then, who takes responsibility for the store? Chris and I can get by on her income, but we definitely plan on expanding our family in the near future, and that will both require money and deflect her activities away from earning it. If I take on the store, that will plunk me right back into—there it goes again—retailing, though I must admit I really like the store, the guitars and other people who are interested in them.*
>
> *Steve and I figure we have enough interest in this possibility that we should figure out what steps would best be involved in going ahead with it before we decide whether to do that or to drop it. He tells me that, after all, I'm the one who studied business and should be able to spell out all the considerations, contingencies, best plan, pros and cons of going ahead. If we don't move on this thing fast and in the right way, it seems to us very likely that someone else will. So there I am. What should I say?*

EXHIBIT 1   Classicraft Tax Filing for 1988

SCHEDULE C
(Form 1040)

Department of the Treasury
Internal Revenue Service   (3)

Profit or Loss From Business
(Sole Proprietorship)
Partnerships, Joint Ventures, Etc., Must File Form 1065.
▶ Attach to Form 1040, Form 1041, or Form 1041S.   ▶ See Instructions for Schedule C (Form 1040).

OMB No. 1545-0074
1988
Attachment
Sequence No. **09**

Name of proprietor

Randolph Price
Business: Retail Sales - Classical Guitars and Accesories
Principal Business Code: 4333
Business Name and Address: Classicraft Guitars,
41 Lundy Lane, Portland, ME   04102

E   Method(s) used to value closing inventory:
   (1) ☒ Cost   (2) ☐ Lower of cost or market   (3) ☐ Other (attach explanation)
F   Accounting method: (1) ☐ Cash   (2) ☒ Accrual   (3) ☐ Other (specify) ▶ ....

	Yes	No
G Was there any change in determining quantities, costs, or valuations between opening and closing inventory? (If "Yes," attach explanation.)		x
H Are you deducting expenses for business use of your home? (If "Yes," see Instructions for limitations.)		Y
I Did you "materially participate" in the operation of this business during 1988? (If "No," see Instructions for limitations on losses.)	x	

J   If this schedule includes a loss, credit, deduction, income, or other tax benefit relating to a tax shelter required to be registered, check here. ▶ ☐
   If you check this box, you MUST attach **Form 8271**.

Part I   Income

1a Gross receipts or sales	1a	90,462	53
b Less: Returns and allowances	1b	1,800	00
c Subtract line 1b from line 1a. Enter the result here	1c	88,662	53
2 Cost of goods sold and/or operations (from Part III, line 8)	2	48,186	54
3 Subtract line 2 from line 1c and enter the gross profit here	3	40,475	99
4 Other income (including windfall profit tax credit or refund received in 1988)	4		
5 Add lines 3 and 4. This is the gross income ▶	5	40,475	99

Part II   Deductions

6 Advertising	6	650	74	23 Repairs	23		51	22
7 Bad debts from sales or services (see Instructions)	7			24 Supplies (not included in Part III)	24		305	50
				25 Taxes	25	1	398	11
8 Bank service charges	8	591	74	26 Travel, meals, and entertainment:				
9 Car and truck expenses	9			a Travel	26a			
10 Commissions	10			b Meals and entertainment		88	00	
11 Depletion	11			c Enter 20% of line 26b subject to limitations (see Instructions)				
12 Depreciation and section 179 deduction from Form 4562 (not included in Part III)	12	2,694	91					
13 Dues and publications	13	133	90	d Subtract line 26c from 26b	26d		88	00
14 Employee benefit programs	14			27 Utilities and telephone	27		3029	95
15 Freight (not included in Part III)	15	522	23	28a Wages				
16 Insurance	16	647	27	b Jobs credit				
17 Interest:				c Subtract line 28b from 28a	28c			
a Mortgage (paid to banks, etc.)	17a			29 Other expenses (list type and amount):				
b Other	17b	3,878	27	Contributions......10.00				
18 Laundry and cleaning	18			License/Permits.105.00				
19 Legal and professional services	19	295	00	Security System..462.00				
20 Office expense	20	271	11	Training/Education..945.00				
21 Pension and profit-sharing plans	21							
22 Rent on business property	22	10,625	00		29	1	522	00

30 Add amounts in columns for lines 6 through 29. These are the total deductions ▶	30	26,704	95
31 Net profit or (loss). Subtract line 30 from line 5. If a profit, enter here and on Form 1040, line 12, and on Schedule SE, line 2. If a loss, you MUST go on to line 32. (Fiduciaries, see instructions.)	31	13,771	04

32 If you have a loss, you MUST check the box that describes your investment in this activity (see Instructions)
   32a ☐ All investment is at risk.
   32b ☐ Some investment is not at risk.
   If you checked 32a, enter the loss on Form 1040, line 12, and Schedule SE, line 2. If you checked 32b, you MUST attach Form 6198.

For Paperwork Reduction Act Notice, see Form 1040 Instructions.   Schedule C (Form 1040) 1988

EXHIBIT 2   Classicraft Tax Filing for 1989

SCHEDULE C
(Form 1040)

Department of the Treasury
Internal Revenue Service   (3)

Profit or Loss From Business
(Sole Proprietorship)
Partnerships, Joint Ventures, Etc., Must File Form 1065.
▶ Attach to Form 1040 or Form 1041.   ▶ See Instructions for Schedule C (Form 1040).

OMB No 1545-0074

1989
Attachment
Sequence No. 09

Name of proprietor

Randolph Price
Business: Retail Sales - Classical Guitars and Accesories
Principal Business Code: 4333
Business Name and Address: Classicraft Guitars,
*   41 Lundy Lane, Portland, ME 04102*

E Method(s) used to value closing inventory: (1) ☑ Cost   (2) ☐ Lower of cost or market   (3) ☐ Other (attach explanation)   (4) ☐ Does not apply (if checked, skip line G)

F Accounting method: (1) ☐ Cash   (2) ☑ Accrual   (3) ☐ Other (specify) ▶ ....

	Yes	No
G Was there any change in determining quantities, costs, or valuations between opening and closing inventory? (If "Yes," attach explanation.)		X
H Are you deducting expenses for business use of your home? (If "Yes," see Instructions for limitations.)		X
I Did you "materially participate" in the operation of this business during 1989? (If "No," see Instructions for limitations on losses.)	X	

J If this schedule includes a loss, credit, deduction, income, or other tax benefit relating to a tax shelter required to be registered, check here . ▶ ☐ If you checked this box, you MUST attach Form 8271.

Part I   Income

1	Gross receipts or sales	1	92,046 71
2	Returns and allowances	2	250 00
3	Subtract line 2 from line 1. Enter the result here	3	91,796 71
4	Cost of goods sold and/or operations (from line 39 on page 2)	4	52,686 64
5	Subtract line 4 from line 3 and enter the **gross profit** here	5	39,110 07
6	Other income, including Federal and state gasoline or fuel tax credit or refund (see Instructions)	6	42 13
7	Add lines 5 and 6. This is your **gross income** ▶	7	39,152 20

Part II   Expenses

8	Advertising	8	2872 16	22 Repairs	22	18 92
9	Bad debts from sales or services (see Instructions)	9		23 Supplies (not included in Part III)	23	202 13
10	Car and truck expenses	10		24 Taxes	24	737 69
11	Commissions	11		25 Travel, meals, and entertainment:		
12	Depletion	12		a Travel	25a	
13	Depreciation and section 179 deduction from **Form 4562** (not included in Part III)	13	2824 63	b Meals and entertainment		120 50
				c Enter 20% of line 25b subject to limitations (see Instructions)		24 10
14	Employee benefit programs (other than on line 20)	14		d Subtract line 25c from line 25b	25d	96 40
15	Freight (not included in Part III)	15	353 09	26 Utilities (see Instructions)	26	1547 04
16	Insurance (other than health)	16	622 44	27 Wages (less jobs credit)	27	
17	Interest:			28 Other expenses (list type and amount):		
a	Mortgage (paid to banks, etc.)	17a		*Security System 462.00*		
b	Other	17b	4033 76	*Training/Education 500*		
18	Legal and professional services	18	1295 00	....		
19	Office expense	19	1211 56	....		
20	Pension and profit-sharing plans	20		....		
21	Rent or lease:			....		
a	Machinery and equipment	21a		....		
b	Other business property	21b	10,975 00	....	28	

29	Add amounts in columns for lines 8 through 28. These are your **total expenses** ▶	29	27,256 82
30	**Net profit or (loss).** Subtract line 29 from line 7. If a profit, enter here and on Form 1040, line 12, and on Schedule SE, line 2. If a loss, you MUST go on to line 31. (Fiduciaries, see Instructions.)	30	11,895 38

31 If you have a loss, you MUST check the box that describes your investment in this activity (see Instructions). If you checked 31a, enter the loss on Form 1040, line 12, and Schedule SE, line 2. If you checked 31b, you MUST attach Form 6198

31a ☐ All investment is at risk.
31b ☐ Some investment is not at risk.

For Paperwork Reduction Act Notice, see Form 1040 Instructions.

Schedule C (Form 1040) 1989

Exhibit 3   Tally of Classicraft Assets By Cliff & Steve as of October 11, 1990 (dollars)

Inventory	Value	Furnishings	Value	Fixtures	Value	Depreciables	Value
		Velvet wall	128	Carpet	234	Fixtures	3,232
Guitars		Posters	81	Floor tile	204	Furnishings	3,051
Carlos 080	400	Flwrs & vase	51	Slide window	51	Total	6,283
Granini 1/4	70	Seashell	8	Slide door	127	(Acc depn)	-2,255
Granini 3/4	73	3 humidifiers	170	Track lights	595	Book Value	4,028
Castilla 3/4	40	Desk chair	68	Adj light fixt	18		
4 F Saez 4A	572	Teak desk	213	Wood doors	20		
P Saez 6A	153	Large fan	25	Wood beam	34	**Assets**	
P Saez 8A	168	Small fan	17	Paneling	82	Inventory	14,596
Artensano 20	137	2 metal chairs	34	Plaster board	51	Book F&F	4,028
Tak C1325	255	2 wood chairs	26	Access. shelf	26	New items	328
Dauphin 535	467	Wood stool	21	Record shelf	10	Total	18,952
Hirade 7	620	Bulletin board	13	Bath shelf	13		
Hirade 8	660	Oak displ case	510	Mirror	4		
Hirade 10	1,050	Small oak case	34	Guitar cabinet	213		
Osterby 17	1,800	Oak shelf	191	Alarm system	359		
Total	6,465	Coffee table	17	Storage cab	213		
		Lamp	51	Book display	127		
Cases		Orientl rugs 2	213	Door alarm	17		
7 GC 318	105	Carpet pieces	4	Hanging sign	510		
GC 316	14	Clock radios 2	26	Wall sign	128		
Used	25	Trunk	42	Door handles	106		
SLM	58	Kitch appli.	42	Front window	90		
AT	65	Humidity gage	13	Total	3,232		
2 ATB Blk	138	File boxes	60				
2 ATB Brn	146	Plastic crates	37				
Total	551	Waste baskets	14	**New items (Expensed)**			
Lights & dec.	51	Floor light	15				
Other (est)		Extension cords	13	Large fan	31		
Accessories	830	Display guitar	38	Small fan	16		
Records	450	Interior signs	64	Folding chairs 4	35		
Music, Books	5,400	Sndwch sgns 2	723	Couch	130		
Strings	900	Fire exting.	34	Phone	56		
Total	7,580	Cash box	4	Calculator	45		
Card table	15	Total	328	Total	3,051		

EXHIBIT 4　Classicraft Turnover Computed by Cliff

	Guitars	Strings	Access.	Books	Records
1990 Proj. Sales	59,235	5,185	3,886	8286	474
CGS %	56	41	56	68	58
1990 CGS	33,172	2,126	2,176	5,634	275
Inventory @ Book	7,016	900	830	5,400	450
Inv. Turnover	4.73	2.36	2.62	1.04	0.61

Case 9

Gerry Erickson

The approach of summer 1980 found Dr. Gerry Erickson working to develop a strategy that would allow him to become a successful entrepreneur. It had been over two years since he and a friend had started Infometrix, a computer software and consulting firm that specialized in solving complex statistical problems. A profile prepared by the company appears as Exhibit 1.

During this time Gerry handled a number of problems, from promoting the company's existence to generating a sufficient cash flow that would help make the venture a commercial success. For the past six months he had been working full time on the venture while his two colleagues were occupied with other responsibilities. Now, Gerry said, he was nearing a decision on reallocation of his efforts, and he wanted to strike an appropriate balance between selling proprietary software Infometrix had developed and consulting. He figured he could work on Infometrix either full time, or just evenings and weekends as his two partners did. Either way, he wondered how best to use his time to move the venture ahead, knowing that the firm had little money to work with.

Personal Backgrounds and Startup

Gerry Erickson held degrees in both physics and business administration from the University of Washington. After completing a physics Ph.D. in 1971, he joined a small consulting firm that did mostly government contract work, as "consulting scientist." He remained there while enroll-

ing to pursue his MBA and then left in the spring of 1977 to concentrate full time on completing the degree.

He also consulted for various organizations during this period and often found himself working on problems at the University's computer center. One night while working on computer modeling of pollution problems, he overheard two other men discussing some work they were doing for the Air Pollution Control District in Los Angeles. As Gerry recalled:

It was about 2 a.m. and all of a sudden I hear these guys talking about air pollution. That piqued my interest so I walked over to introduce myself. One of them was a professor from the University of California at San Diego who had come to Seattle to work on a project with a chemistry professor here. I told him the Environmental Protection Agency (EPA) was interested in doing some studies on air pollution in the Pacific Northwest, gave him a contact to phone and figured that was it.

Soon after, however, Gerry received an invitation from the California professor to collaborate in a proposal to the EPA (Environmental Protection Agency) as someone familiar with the local area. The third person to work on the study would be the professor's colleague at the University of Washington, Dr. Bruce Kowalski. Gerry thus became acquainted with Bruce, and although the EPA study was never funded, the two developed a close friendship that led to their partnership in forming Infometrix during early 1978.

Bruce Kowalski had been on the University of Washington faculty since 1973. His research efforts centered on the use of statistical measurements applied to problems in chemistry and the natural sciences. During this time, Bruce worked on ways to recognize patterns in scientific data, which typical statistical methods were unable to do. He became involved in a project to refine such techniques (known as applied pattern recognition) by developing a computer software package called ARTHUR.

The later success of ARTHUR in problem solving was evident to Bruce as more and more scientists began using programs it contained. ARTHUR had been developed using government funds and was available to the public at no charge. Bruce continued to work on further applications and specific analytical chemistry programs before teaming up with Gerry to form Infometrix. Bruce also wanted to see a company, like Infometrix, able to assist those groups that had contacted him with problems that didn't fit into the academic process. Although valid problems, they typically were forms that had been generally solved, and so were unsuited for pioneering research that could be the basis of a graduate student's thesis. Bruce felt that by helping to start Infometrix and providing guidance and consulting expertise to the company, he would be aiding the wider community that had the problems he couldn't tackle without detracting from his academic responsibilities.

Gerry described what he believed to be Infometrix's competitive advantage with its skill in ARTHUR and consulting capabilities as follows:

> *In a way, the software is kind of like a tool bag for a plumber, with all sorts of different tools he can use. The assumption of knowing about the distribution of the data is one you can toss out the window when using these statistical packages. They're designed to deal with messier problems where you have fewer observations, a large number of variables and no knowledge about distribution of the data.*
>
> *There's almost no competition because we're on a frontier. There are maybe two competitors I can think of, one in California and one on the East Coast, and Bruce and I think we have the edge on them.*

Forming the Business

To start, the two turned to an attorney Bruce knew to incorporate the company. Both felt that the advantages of limited liability were worth the added costs of incorporating and that by doing so under Subchapter S of the federal tax code, they could still enjoy the advantages of a partnership. They decided to keep expenses down as much as possible. Gerry recalled:

> *The financing that we've needed has been minimal. We started the company on about $2,000. Bruce and I actually kicked in about $500 each. Five hundred dollars of that went into legal expenses of getting the company incorporated. The rest of it went into original artwork, forms, business cards, stationery... things like that.*

The two were able to put the business venture in "the black" immediately by providing consulting services. Even so, the level of business was such that Bruce worked on the venture part time while still at the University. Gerry had to combine different contract activities to provide an income of $19,000 during 1979, the first full year of the venture. Gerry reflected on the sources of his income for that year:

> *Twelve thousand of that came via a consulting contract with a chemical company's New Venture Department. I spent the last 18 months working one-*

third of my time for NVD in technology searching. That meant traveling up and down the West Coast talking with venture capital firms, banks, universities— looking for people who had new business concepts or new technologies that might be of interest to the company.

Gerry added that the remaining $7,000 came half from air pollution consulting and half from Infometrix. If he were willing to work in industry and leave the Seattle area (he did not prefer to move), he expected that his salary would be in the $30,000 range.

By the end of 1979, a third partner, Clemens Jochum, joined Gerry and Bruce to work on developing proprietary software that the firm could market and sell. Clemens was working under Bruce at the University of Washington in a research group in the Chemistry Department. Gerry continued to keep the books and take care of many business tasks for the firm.

Our offices are in my basement. We do our own reports, letters, and bookkeeping. I can type 30-40 words per minute with a mistake here and there. Written material that occasionally has to be more correct we take to a professional typing service.

Developing Proprietary Software

Gerry's opinion was that if Infometrix were to grow and prosper to the point he wanted, they would have to develop a standard product to sell. For this reason he believed the need to develop proprietary software was an important part of the business.

Our current thrust is based partly on consulting. That was a reasonable beginning, but in the back of my mind, I've known you never get rich if you're constrained to selling your time to someone else. What will make or break a company is when you've got a standard product you can pull off the shelf. Then when someone says, "Yeah, I'd like five of those," you just wrap them up and send them off.

You do a lot of front-end work, but once you've got that product developed, you can essentially pump it out the door. You're not constrained by the time you put in. For example, if a doctor or lawyer puts in 80 hours a week, he gets more than if he puts in 60 hours a week. For our company to do only consulting, it's the same thing.

Gerry and Bruce decided that their software would focus initially on the area of applied pattern recognition. By mid-1980 these proprietary packages had been completed and were ready for sale. These programs were designed to solve problems in the natural and social sciences, providing advantages other statistical packages currently available did not have. All the packages were written in Fortran. The partners admitted that other computer languages would be easier to use, but Fortran was still dominant because of its familiarity to practitioners and its compatiblity with powerful mainfraimes. As Clemens put it, "people just don't want to bother with learning another computer language."

A final selling point, according to Gerry, was that the programs were "small" enough to be adapted to the very popular mini- and small business computers that were being sold. He estimated that their programs would be developed so that about a third of the total could be used in business-related applications.

Protecting the programs from being illegally copied had been a matter of concern to Gerry from the beginning. His views on the use of licensing agreements or copyrighting had changed after drawing up an initial agreement that customers would be asked to sign:

> *We spent about $1,200 in legal fees to develop a licensing agreement that was fairly watertight. I bounced that agreement off two people and both of them said, "Well that's great, but if I had that agreement come to me through the mail I wouldn't buy your programs." This was simply because no one is willing to put their name on a bottom line to an agreement that has a penalty clause like the one we had.* (A copy of this agreement appears as Exhibit 2.)

Gerry said that such an agreement was probably not needed. He pointed out that the entire industry suffered when theft of software occurred, and people were improving security measures to prevent abuse. "Besides," he added, "the academic community would know easily if a program were stolen, since questions of how research results were obtained usually come up." He also questioned the value of copyrighting programs:

> *It's so easy to modify a few lines of code, by just calling the variables different names, that I don't think it's much protection. And besides, a copyright is expensive. I think it would cost something like $2,000 to get one of our programs copyrighted.*

Financing the Company's Operation and Growth

"A long-term goal," Gerry said, "would be to reach an employment level of 30 employees, half professionals, within 10 years." He thought that a mix of consulting and software activity might be the best strategy to meet this goal, since he regarded them "like pants and suspenders—one supports the other."

He saw no immediate need for outside capital. Infometrix was currently debt-free,

with controlling interest split between himself and Bruce. Future financing could come from operations. During the most recent quarter (see Exhibit 3), Infometrix had realized about $900 in income from revenues of $6,000. These profit and loss figures were on a cash basis. Compensation was paid only for consulting work, with software development work done with the expectation of future sales providing an eventual return. Typing expenses were for professional help in preparing materials for mailings.

Pricing rates for consulting were based on a number of considerations, including provision of sufficient funds to finance the venture for the near term. The rates (see Exhibit 4) ranged downward as the length of contract increased, with computer, travel and non-salary expenses listed at cost. To set rates, each partner decided how much he wanted to earn per day (judging from what he could command in industry on salary), allowing for the fact that in consulting, not all days would be occupied. A 50-percent markup was then added to cover overhead and profit. Thus, a one-week contract would range from $500/day for Dr. Kowalski down to $125/day for any hourly-paid research assistance they thought would be needed. A per diem of $50/day was included for meals and lodging if travel was required. By comparison, the federal government allowed its employees $50 to $75 per day for travel per diem.

For pricing software, Gerry started by assuming a feasible "life" of five years before a set of programs became obsolete. A desired rate of return between 12-15 percent was used to reach a present value for each of the programs shown on Exhibit 5. His rationale in establishing a different lease rate for academic institutions was that this seemed to be a traditional business practice. The discount ranged from 30.4 percent for the Protein Phylogeny program up to 41.8 percent for the UVFA program. The latter program was still in the process of being documented for a user manual.

Gerry had explored prices other firms were charging for programs of approximately the same level of complexity. In his opinion, Infometrix was price-competitive, whether leased or purchased outright:

The programs are reasonably priced to the point where, if someone were to try developing a similar program, they would spend a lot more than they would otherwise by purchasing from Infometrix.

The front-end costs required in developing the software, and the fact that funds were being obtained solely from consulting, meant that a significant amount of time was being invested by the three without any immediate compensation. Gerry explained that as incentive for spending time on software, some of the future cash flows would go to those working on it. Clemens, for instance, had spent evenings and week-ends on software development. Gerry outlined how the payment method would work:

One of the first policies that we established was that for any product developed, the software team will get 25 percent of the income from sales—after front-end costs have been met. For instance, after the first $5,000 or so came in to cover development costs, the rest would be split 75 percent to Infometrix and 25 percent to the development team. This is done with the idea that it would be a pretty fair return to the individuals involved.

When asked how the 25 percent figure was obtained, Gerry responded that while working at Math Sciences Northwest, a similar 25 percent margin was used for personnel involved with developing pat-entable products. The firm retained first patent rights, captured initial start-up costs and split any residual earnings.

Reaching the Market

The size and shape of the market for Infometrix was something Gerry was working to define. Part of the problem, as he saw it, was to convince prospective customers that:

1. Infometrix existed.
2. The software Infometrix had available could be used to solve the client's specialized problems.
3. There was a value for statistical models in the natural sciences, a field which traditionally relied on controlled experiments for problem solving.

Whether the academic community or industry offered the best market for Infometrix was also a question Gerry had considered. He commented that academia offered a wider audience in the sense that he, Bruce and Clemens could make use of their established contacts and build a wider base from conferences and journals. Higher education and foundations were also more likely to be involved in basic research, which could readily use the software packages.

In Gerry's opinion, industry's emphasis on product development and improved production control offered opportunity for an equally viable market to develop with some initial "success stories." He saw two barriers that worked to block entry into this market:

1. An unwillingness to risk new attempts at improving production if the pay-offs had yet to be proven.
2. A tendency by business to keep information proprietary.

To reach a market for the software, Gerry said, a logical starting point would be three mailing lists of people and organizations who had inquired about ARTHUR or about articles published by Bruce Kowalski.

Obviously, those are people interested in statistical methods that can work in very messy problems. In our minds, they're a very good target market for the statistical programs we are selling. Most of these people are research chemists in universities or in industry.

To sound out possible markets for these software packages, a mailing that included a cover letter, listing of available programs, and reply form (see Exhibit 6) was made to about 150 scientists who had written regarding ARTHUR. About half were in academia and half in industry. A second mailing had just been finished in spring 1980 to those who had asked for reprints of articles previously published by Dr. Kowalski. These persons were largely in research disciplines concerned with chemistry. A third list of 50 names being reviewed for possible mailing, according to Gerry, came from one of Bruce Kowalski's recent graduates who had joined the faculty at another university.

The previous mailings had taken two to three days for Gerry to prepare and another two or three days to follow-up on replies. These tasks included typing a cover letter, addressing and stuffing envelopes and logging in replies by product interest and background of the respondent. Any professional typing required for the mailing was an added cost. The opportunity costs per mailing ranged from $240 to $360, using Gerry's estimate of $30,000 in potential salary he might otherwise have. He estimated that a phone follow up with those who replied would cost about $200 in long distance charges for calls made throughout North America.

Mapping a Strategy to Move Ahead

Major considerations in choosing marketing strategy were time and money, Gerry observed. He saw several areas that he could work on during the summer months. To begin with, Infometrix could seek more recognition for the software programs through talks each partner would be giving before the end of summer. Bruce had been traveling in Germany on sabbatical for some months and had already been speaking to professional groups and making contacts. Clemens was scheduled to travel to both Japan and Paris to speak about his research work at the University of Washington. The Infometrix software would be used as examples of how to solve problems in the natural sciences.

Expenses for the two were covered by the sponsoring institutions so no costs other than "lost time" would be born by Infometrix. Clemens had spent the first half of the year putting in about 20 hours per week on software development. During July, however, he had been forced to spend time preparing lectures for the upcoming trips.

Gerry was scheduled to appear in September at the annual meeting of the American Association of Cereal Chemists in Chicago to discuss applied pattern recognition. He reasoned that giving a speech and making contacts would be cheaper and more effective than going to the same gathering as an exhibitor. He planned to visit the Monsanto Company in St. Louis after Chicago and then visit Boulder, Colorado, to stay with friends. For each stop, he was working to arrange talks before industrial or academic professionals who would have an interest in the type of products and services Infometrix offered. By spending a little more on a plane ticket and staying at discount motels or in private homes, he would effectively reach three times the number of people as he would during the same length of time as an exhibitor in Chicago. Besides, Gerry explained, there were added costs such, as exhibitor's fees, display setup and time spent standing around the booth hoping people would stop to inquire about their firm and what it offered.

A second strategy Gerry saw was to seek consulting contracts to generate cash flow and build future leads. A risk in consulting, however, was underbidding, as had happened on a recent project. Gerry had doubled his estimate for the amount of time needed, but the actual time required had turned out to be four times the amount he had doubled.

A third option was to follow up the mail responses by phone. Fourth was the possibility of mixing consulting efforts with software development by joint venturing with some other company. Right now, this was a concept Gerry had talked about but had yet to explore or write down on paper ways to approach prospective participants. Finally, he mentioned the idea of contacting trade journals through news releases about new Infometrix products. He estimated that one day of his time to prepare such a release would represent opportunity costs and realized costs of $120 to $150.

Completing documentation of the computer programs and culling the list of names received from Bruce's former student were two immediate tasks according to Gerry. He doubted that documentation on the fourth program package would be finished before year end, due to time constraints on an hourly assistant working with Clemens. Gerry added that work on the other three packages had gone on since late 1979, with Clemens alone putting in about 600 hours of work on development.

Testing was done through the research group Clemens was associated with, and Gerry wasn't sure how much time this involved. The aim was to have a software program complete enough to enable a buyer to take the user manual and get the program running without further help from Infometrix. Gerry pointed out that any buyer of the software would receive three pieces of information from Infometrix:

1. A copy of the computer program;
2. User manuals (3 copies) with complete documentation;
3. A test run of the program with illustrative data.

The user would be responsible for setting the program up on his or her own computer system and making any changes for specific use. Gerry summed up the process: "Basically, we ship them all the information that should let them get it up and flying, follow up two weeks later with a bill and then keep our fingers crossed that a check will come in the mail 30 days after that." Refunds would be available if the user failed to set up the program. It was expected that an express courier service or mail would be used as the method of distributing the software.

Gerry had made no sales forecasts of the software yet. A purchase rate of ten percent of the respondees from the first mailing could conceivably bring in up to $10,000. While Gerry believed that the response rate had been favorable, he commented that added difficulties emerged when speculating on actual sales:

We're faced not only with finding the client who has the problem, but also with having to convince the client's management that this approach is the one to use. Often those are two different groups of people.

Educating the potential market was seen as a related problem according to both Gerry and Clemens. They said the social sciences were well acquainted with statistical models and techniques, while the natural sciences had relied on controlled experimentation. Consequently, many in the latter group had neither a sufficient grasp of statistical techniques nor understanding of their proper application in problem solving.

Another concern was in making the written material visually appealing through graphics. A friend of Bruce's had designed the stationery and logo for Infometrix and Gerry was considering contacting her to prepare a brochure, slide show, or both. Clemens had mentioned that graphics might also be useful to improve the marketability of the software programs through the way the output data was displayed. "Chemists," said Clemens, "really like to see pictures of the molecules and data they're working with."

Looking back at how his time had been spent in the last month, Gerry said that two weeks of this period consisted of preparing a paper and material for the upcoming Chicago conference. Another week was spent contacting firms in the area to survey possible employment possibilities. Evenings included work in putting an alumni association together comprised of former business school graduates of the University of Washington. And four days had been spent on re-roofing his house. His time was better spent, Gerry said, by doing the work himself—particularly after finding out what the roofing cost would be

if he hired it out.

Gerry said that the time he had spent to date on Infometrix was costly only in the sense of lost opportunities and income he would have otherwise been able to take advantage of:

> *My position is somewhat fortunate because my wife is a professional. She's, in effect, been covering our exposure somewhat grudgingly in the short term. In the long term, either Infometrix will go, or I'll be working at a full-time job somewhere and doing Infometrix on evenings and weekends.*

Gerry reflected on the venture to date and where it might be headed. He commented that two appealing goals stuck in his mind. The first was to have a sufficient cash flow to meet expenses (for both himself and Infometrix) and to establish a type of parity with his wife in terms of salary. Second was finding out whether sufficient promise existed of a "pay-off down the road" for Infometrix to be the success that he hoped. He wondered whether he should try to become a full-time employee of a consulting customer, for either the short- or the long-term future, should that seem possible. The immediate question he saw, however, was how best to spend his time and apply the available resources so that he could move ahead with Infometrix.

EXHIBIT 1 Company Profile, January 1, 1980

Infometrix was founded by Dr. B. R. Kowalski and Dr. G. A. Erickson in Seattle, Washington, on 13 January 1978. Dr. C. Jochum joined the company in December 1979, as director of software development. The purpose of the company is to assist groups and industries with complex problems through scientific insight and experience, computer software, mathematical modeling, and multi-variate statistical and pattern recognition techniques. The principals of the firm collectively have over two decades of experience in applying advanced mathematical techniques to multidimensional problems in industrial product quality control, source identification, environmental prediction, health effects, and analytical chemistry.

The founders of the firm are experts in the field of pattern recognition applications to chemical, industrial and environmental problems. Dr. Kowalski is the central architect of ARTHUR, a pattern recognition software system currently being used by more than 150 chemical laboratories worldwide. The ARTHUR system consists of utility, preprocessing and display routines, plus more than a dozen major non-parametric classification methods in cluster analysis, factor analysis, multivariate regression, discriminant analysis, similarity classification, and Bayesian classification.

In addition to their leading expertise in applied pattern recognition, the principals and associates of Infometrix have a wide range of experience in other mathematical analysis, computer modeling, and optimization methods. The experience of the Infometrix team includes studies in the following applications:

* Industrial product quality control
* Forensic science
* Air pollution warning models
* Source identification of oil spills
* Spectrum and waveform analysis
* Quantitative molecular structure/biological activity relations
* Computer-controlled synthesis design
* Control theory
* Automobile service market research
* Geochemical and geophysical exploration
* Semi-empirical quantum chemistry
* Air pollution dispersion modeling
* Downstream water quality effects of mining
* Stream origin identification of ocean-caught salmon

P.O.BOX 25888, SEATTLE, WASHINGTON 98125
(206)522-5139

EXHIBIT 2   License Agreement

INFOMETRIX, INCORPORATED

Software Program Sources License Agreement

Customer Name:

Address:

Infometrix, Incorporated (hereinafter referred to as IMI) hereby agrees to grant, and Customer hereby agrees to accept, a non-exclusive, non-transferable license to use and copy each of the software program sources and listings made available to Customer by IMI on the following terms and conditions:

1. Definitions

a)   Software Product as used in this agreement shall mean any software program in any form, including machine-compatible source code and listing, documentation and user information for each program as defined below.

b)   Source shall mean any machine-compatible program form including binary, machine-language, or ANSI FORTRAN coding stored on punched cards or magnetic tape.

c)   Listing shall mean any machine-compatible program form including any subroutines in any language format.

d)   Documentation and User Information shall mean any internal program explanation, user manuals, flow charts and directions for using and understanding the program.

2. Terms

Each Source shall be under a separate license effective from the date of execution of this Agreement by IMI, and shall remain in force until Customer discontinues use of such Source, or the License is otherwise terminated as provided herein.

3. Delivery

a)   Delivery will be made F.O.B. IMI's plant with shipping charges to be paid by Customer to carrier. Risk of loss shall pass to Customer upon delivery by IMI to carrier. In the absence of specific instruction, IMI will select the carrier, but shall not thereby assume any liability in connection with shipment, nor shall the carrier be construed to be the agent of IMI.

b)   IMI shall not be liable for any damages or penalty, delay in delivery or for failure to give notice of delay when such delay is due to the elements, acts of God, delays in transportation, delay in delivery by IMI's vendors or any other causes beyond the reasonable control of IMI. The delivery schedule shall be extended by a period of time equal to the time lost because of any such delay.

EXHIBIT 2 (continued)

4. Payment and Taxes

Customer shall pay in full in United States currency to IMI the license fee for each license covered by this Agreement within thirty (30) days of receipt of an invoice, therefore, from IMI. License fees are exclusive of all sales, use and like taxes. Any tax IMI may be required to collect or pay on the licensing or delivery of a source shall be paid by Customer and such sum shall be due and payable to IMI with the license fee as specified above.

5. Title

Title to and ownership of the Source shall remain with IMI.

6. Security

Customer shall not provide, disclose, transfer or otherwise make available any Source or any portion thereof, including but not limited to flow charts, diagrams, binary/object codes generated from Source and its listing and Documentation, in any form, to any person other than Customer or Customer's employees without the prior express written approval of IMI.

7. License and Right to Use

Customer shall have the right to use each Source or any portion thereof on a single computer system. Customer may copy the Source onto machine compatible form for secure storage to provide safety backup for the operating version on the single computer system. Customer may modify the Source provided, however, that any portion thereof included in a modified work shall remain subject to all terms and conditions of this License.

8. Assignment

This License Agreement, the license granted hereunder and the Source may not be assigned, sublicensed or otherwise transferred by Customer without prior written consent from IMI. No right to reprint or copy the Source, in whole or in part, is granted here by except as otherwise provided herein.

9. Termination

In the event Customer neglects or fails to perform or observe any of its obligations under this Agreement, or if any assignment shall be made of its business for the benefit of creditors, or if a receiver, trustee in bankruptcy or a similar officer shall be appointed to take charge of all or part of its property, or if it is adjudged bankrupt and such condition(s) is not remedied within ten (10) days after written notice thereof has been given to the Customer, this License Agreement and all licenses granted hereunder as to Customer shall immediately terminate. Within two (2) weeks after such termination, the Customer shall certify in writing to IMI that through its best efforts and to the best of its knowledge the original and all copies, in any form, including partial copies and modifications of the Source, received from IMI or made in connection with the License have been destroyed.

10. Warranty

IMI DISCLAIMS ALL WARRANTIES WITH REGARD TO ANY SOURCE LICENSED TO CUSTOMER HEREUNDER, INCLUDING ALL IMPLIED WARRANTIES OR MERCHANTABILITY AND FITNESS. IN NO EVENT SHALL IMI BE LIABLE FOR ANY SPECIAL, INDIRECT OR CONSEQUENTIAL DAMAGES OR ANY DAMAGES WHATSOEVER

EXHIBIT 2 (concluded)

RESULTING FROM LOSS OF USE, DATA OR PROFITS, WHETHER IN AN ACTION OF CONTRACT, NEGLIGENCE OR OTHER TORTIOUS ACTION, ARISING OUT OF OR IN CONNECTION WITH THE USE OR PERFORMANCE OF ANY SOURCE LICENSED HEREUNDER.

<u>11. Waiver</u>

Failure by either party to enforce any provision of this Agreement with respect to any Source Licensed hereunder shall not be deemed a waiver of that provision or any other provision of this Agreement with respect to such Source or any other Source Licensed to Customer hereunder.

<u>12. Acknowledgment</u>

Customer acknowledges that he has read this Agreement, understands it and agrees to be bound by its terms and further agrees that it is the complete and exclusive statement of the Agreement between the parties which supersedes all communications and understanding between the parties relating to the subject matter of this Agreement.

<u>13. Governing law</u>

This Agreement shall be governed by the laws of the State of Washington.

Executed this_____day of _____,19_____.

Infometrix, Incorporated   Customer

_____   _____
Authorized Signature   Authorized Signature

_____   _____
Title   Title

EXHIBIT 3 Income Statement

INFOMETRIX INCOME STATEMENT (FIRST QUARTER, 1980)

Income
  Professional Services

Hughes	*$4,250.00*	
Boeing	*2,000.00*	
Ferrous	*351.57*	
Sub Total	*$6,601.57*	
Total Income		*$6,601.57*

Expenses
Salary Expense

Compensation for Hughes and Boeing Projects	*$3,621.89*	
Sub Total	*$3,621.89*	

Operations Expense

Legal Expense	*$1,304.70*	
Taxes and Licenses	*15.31*	
Computer Time	*51.57*	
Typing Expense	*351.05*	
Misc. Expense	*359.55*	
Sub Total	*$2,082.18*	
Total Expense		*$5,704.07*
Net Income		*$897.50*

Income presented on cash basis.

Beginning balance, 1/1/80	*$48.50*	
Ending Balance, 3/31/80:	*$945.56*	
Net Income (Cash Basis) 1/1 to 3/31, 1980:		*$897.50*

EXHIBIT 4 Infometrix, Inc. Time & Material Billing Rates

(Effective 1 January 1980)

On T&M-based contracts, Infometrix uses the following billing rates, depending on the estimated (or bid) length of contracted effort (total man days):

Principal Investigators	Rate for Contracted Effort			
	1 Day	2-5 Days	6-20 Days	21-120 Days
Dr. B. R. Kowalski	$600	$500	$450	$425
Dr. G. A. Erickson	350	300	250	225
Dr. C. Jochum	300	275	225	200
Dr. R. Gerlach	250	225	200	175
Engineering Associates	175	175	175	150
Research Associates	125	125	110	100

Other Charges

Computer   at cost
Typing   at cost
Materials   at cost
Travel   cost plus lodging plus per diem
(per diem per individual) ($50/night of lodging)

Infometrix will perform all work on our premises and on a computer system of our choosing where the appropriate software is operational. Infometrix prefers progress payments, billed at the end of each calendar month during the contract, based on estimated study accomplishments and accumulated costs.

EXHIBIT 5 Infometrix Software Program Price List

Computer Program	Annual Lease Rate	One-Time Lease Rate	
		A	B
Path Modeling	$700	$2,500	$1,500
Underlying Variable Factor Analysis	$800	$2,750	$1,600
Generalized Standard Addition Method	$400	$1,500	$1,000
Protein Phylogeny	$300	$1,150	$800

Each computer program package includes the following:

1. Compatible program source code, available on magnetic tape or card
2. Three copies of the user manual, fully documented
3. Receipt via first class mail or common carrier

Each computer program is also subject to a one-time setup charge of $200.

Extra copies of the user manual are available @ $5 each ($10 for UVFA).

Programs obtained under the annual lease rate include automatic receipt of any subsequent updates at no extra charge.

Person desiring priority mail shipment shall add $10 to the above rates.

One Time Lease Rates under plan B are applicable to academic institutions.

Lease Rates Effective 1 July 1980.

EXHIBIT 6 Sales Letter

March 12, 1980

(To Medical Researcher)

Dear Doctor

Path Modeling may be the most important advance in data analysis since Multivariate Regression and Step-wise Regression analysis. Infometrix is pleased to announce the availability of the first Path Model computer program, PLS-1. This new method allows the analyst to specify directional relationships between macro-influence sectors, represented by latent variables, in any model of a complex system. And, the contribution of each measure to its latent variable is retained in the final result, avoiding the loss of variables experienced with Step-wise Regression in systems with highly co-linear (i.e. highly correlated) measures.

In addition to Path Modeling, three other computer programs are now available to aid statisticians and chemists: UFVA—Underlying Variable Factor Analysis; GSAM—Generalized Standard Addition Method; and PROTEPHYL—Protein Phylogeny. GSAM is potentially as revolutionary as PLS-1, to the field of Analytical Chemistry. GSAM allows the solution of complex, multi-component mixtures in the presence of interferences in the array of sensors. GSAM also allows an array of sensors to be redefined to enable measurement of other types of mixtures, as long as the sensors react somewhat differently to each of the suspected components of the new mixtures.

A brief information sheet on the new computer programs is enclosed. Fill out the reply form showing us which programs you're interested in, and mail it back in the enclosed envelope, or give us a call any time at (206) 522-5139.

Sincerely yours,

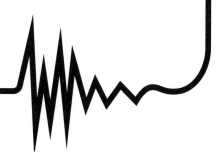

P.O.BOX 25888, SEATTLE, WASHINGTON 98125
(206)522-5139

EXHIBIT 6 (concluded)

Schematic Path Model Examples

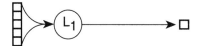

Muliple Regression Analysis of One Matrix onto a Single Feature

Two-Matrix Relationship Model and the Basis for Canonical Correlation Analysis

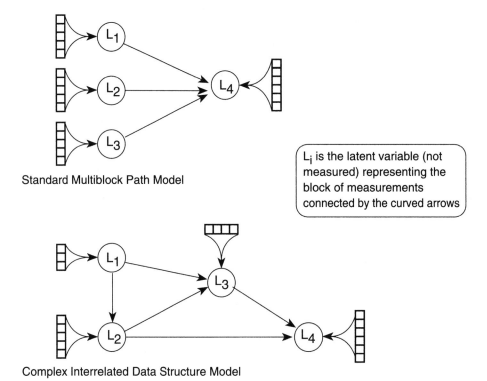

Standard Multiblock Path Model

L_i is the latent variable (not measured) representing the block of measurements connected by the curved arrows

Complex Interrelated Data Structure Model

Bill Foster

Bill Foster turned his desk calendar to February 25, 1980 and penciled in "Meeting with venture capital firms—Boston." In six weeks he would begin negotiations with two different venture capital groups in an attempt to raise up to $2,000,000 for starting a new computer firm, Alta Computing Systems. He expected it would take at least two years to prepare the first product for sale. Within the next six weeks, Bill explained, he needed to accomplish two specific tasks to be ready for the negotiations:

1. Complete the pro forma statements in the business plan; to date, financial issues had been discussed only in general terms and amounts.

2. Map a strategy with his three cofounders that would place them in the best possible bargaining position for striking a deal with the venture capital firms.

Bill's goal was to create a major computer company within five years, a company that specialized in producing an extremely reliable system for experienced data processing users, such as Fortune 1000 firms. He went on to add that without venture capital support the prospects that the business would ever get started were slim:

The venture capital market is a very close-knit group. Once a major venture capital firm turns you down, they might all turn you down.

He had spent the last six months inquiring about the venture capital market and recruiting a management team with a proven track record in developing computer hardware and software. Bill was currently living off $30,000 in savings which would be exhausted by summer. Consequently, he said, getting cash as soon as possible was essential for starting the business. Otherwise, he might be forced to put the idea aside and return to work to support his family. His three partners had either quit their jobs or announced their intention to do so. Bill said he hoped to have from 10 to 20 people working for Alta by June of 1980.

We're going to put together the pro formas, working off some basic assumptions and a general idea of how much money we'll need. Then we'll take the business plan to two groups. One will be made up of four venture capital firms in New York. The other will include a company in San Francisco, one in Connecticut and the lead firm here in Boston. The meeting on the twenty-fifth is with the second group, and I'm not sure what to expect. We've never been through this before.

There are a lot of issues to consider. For example, how much ownership should the venture capitalists versus the founders get? What should the price of the stock be? How do you work out different prices for different classes of stock? And how do we position ourselves for the possibility that we may later have to go back for more money? We're going to need several million dol-

lars of capital before we can call ourselves a profitable company, but we probably won't get it all up front. Finally, what criteria should we use for choosing the appropriate source and deal for capital?

Personal Background

Bill Foster grew up in California and graduated from San Jose State in 1966 with a bachelor's degree in math. Following graduation, he went to work for Lockheed in the San Francisco Bay Area. He completed a graduate degree in applied math at Santa Clara University while working for Lockheed and continued night school until 1973, when he also received his MBA from the same institution.

Bill reflected on his coursework in the business school:

> *The last course I took was on entrepreneurship, and the professor told us that the only way we would ever use his course or our MBA was if we went out and started our own business. Looking back at the last six months, he's probably right.*

In 1969, the Federal government canceled two major military projects, which sent the aerospace industry into a tailspin. The events prompted Bill to look for other work and resulted in his entry into the computer industry:

> *I used to drive right by this place called Hewlett-Packard on the way to work, and I really didn't know what it was. So I decided to stop in one day and apply for a job—and they hired me.*

Bill went to work for Hewlett-Packard (HP) in the company's then fledgling data products division. During the next seven years, he rose from programmer to engineering manager of a computing systems group. As manager, he was responsible for Hewlett-Packard's research and development for computer system hardware and software. About one-third of his time was spent talking with prospective customers to assure them that the product being considered was technically sound and able to perform the desired tasks.

In 1976, he was recruited by a rapidly growing New England-based minicomputer company to become the firm's vice president for software development. Bill recalled that the opportunity of working for the president of a smaller but faster-growing company appealed to him, as did the move to the East Coast:

> *I'd always lived in the Bay Area and thought that going to New England would be a very educational experience for both my family and me.*

Over the next three years, Bill established a reputation within the company as a good manager and became an officer of the firm. He said this work was rewarding, and the salary and stock option benefits allowed him to accumulate nearly $50,000 in savings.

The Decision to Start a Company

Bill recalled that he first began thinking of starting his own company in 1978. After returning from a business trip in England the following May, he told his wife that he wanted to quit his job and attempt to form a new business. This meant that he would give up the salary and prestige that went with being a vice-president of a Fortune 500 company. Since the firm had a restricted stock option plan, he would also lose the right to exercise the options which he had on about 800 shares.

The exercise price averaged $13 per share, compared with the current price of $70 on the open market. His annual salary was in the $50,000 range. Rumors within the company included speculation that he had been fired, since "they thought no one in their right mind would be crazy enough to walk away from the position and benefits I had." Within three weeks after returning from Europe, Bill submitted his resignation. He continued to work for another three weeks and left the firm near the end of July 1979.

Bill talked about why he decided to leave a job which he said he enjoyed very much:

I guess I'll never really know exactly why it happened the way it did. I had been thinking for over a year about starting a company. I tried to think about what I could do, but that didn't lead anywhere. I had no ideas that seemed worthwhile. Maybe I also didn't have the guts to do it. It didn't seem smart to leave the great job I had, making all that money and so forth.

But I knew a lot of other people who had gone off, started companies and become very successful. All of them were high technology-related. Most of the founders of Tandem Computer had worked for me when I was at HP. I knew many of the founders of Apple, too. I was somewhat envious of these people who had left other jobs and gotten involved with start-ups. It seemed to me that technically I was their equal. Yet my conclusion was that it just wasn't the right time for me to take the plunge; maybe never would be, and I had no ideas for what to do.

I almost feel foolish saying this, but when I went on another business trip to Europe in June of 1979, the first night I was there I woke up about three o'clock in the morning and had just decided to do it. When I got back home to Massachusetts, I was going to quit my job and try to start a company. It's almost as if I told myself I was really stupid not to have done it a year ago. I must have been thinking about it somewhere in the back of my mind, but I wasn't really

aware of it. I called my wife on the phone the next day and told her I was going to do it. She kind of said, "Oh, yeah, I've heard this before." When I got home, I talked some more about it, and then she knew I was going to do it.

I can't really explain why it was, but all of a sudden, I started thinking that the worst possible thing that could happen would be to wake up one day when I was 70 years old, look back over my life, and say to myself, "Gee, you never even tried to do it." I was 35, I was not being particularly challenged by my job, and I was envious of my friends who had gone off and done something similar. I finally realized that all of the constraints I had were basically artificial. I felt that I would be very disappointed with myself if I didn't at least attempt this...that all my options would be closed.

Once that happened, it was an easy decision. I had no qualms about it. Financially, it could have been a tough decision, but it wasn't. I had a lot of stock options that I had to leave behind. I didn't have a lot of money. It cost about $30,000 for our family of five to live on for a year. So my wife and I figured that if I treated this as an investment in myself, we could withdraw $600 a week and in a year's time, the business would either be on its way or would have flopped. I would reserve another $20,000 in savings to invest as my share of the equity. We would have to use the money we'd saved for our children's college, which was probably the biggest hang-up. But I had worked my way through school; if they had to work their way through, they could do it. That was not reason enough not to go ahead with the plan.

Starting to Look for Capital

The first step Bill took after leaving the

computer firm was to contact a friend whom he thought might be able to steer him to a venture capital firm. Bill explained that he knew nothing about that part of the financial community, but he "had a hunch" that there was a lot of money to finance a business such as the one he had in mind. The friend referred him to a Boston-based venture capital company. Bill described the experience:

> Three days after I quit my job, I went to talk to these people. I had no business plan, no partners. I didn't know if I should start the company on the East or the West Coast. I wasn't even sure what I was going to make, but I did know it would have something to do with general-purpose computer systems, since that's what I was familiar with. I was selling myself on my reputation as a technical manager.
>
> One of the venture capitalists and I spent two or three hours over lunch just basically talking about money being available, what they looked for, what they expected in terms of business planning and all the rest. I was impressed with the amount of time this partner was spending with me. He was very helpful.
>
> When I said I planned to do this in California, since that is where I was from originally, he gave me an introduction to two West Coast firms. They all owe each other favors. "You let me in this deal, and I may let you in another." They all talk to each other all the time. Besides, to do a large-scale start-up that might require as much as $10 million, they would have to collaborate with several other firms. They would not do that big a deal alone.
>
> I also found out that many venture funds normally do not do start-ups. They're not going to invest in three people and a briefcase where there's no track record. They ask, "Can this guy who's worked inside a big company do it

> on his own? Can he hire the people, can he meet his schedules? Can he do it without constant changes in direction?" Still, after I had visited three of the top venture capital firms in the business, I had the impression that if one of them would take the lead, the others might join in.

Developing the Business Concept

Bill decided to spend the next two months outlining the type of business he was going to start and developing a marketing strategy that would set his company apart from the competition. He spent the rest of July and August researching the computer market in search of a niche. In September he visited several friends in California from Hewlett-Packard. The conversation about computers came to Tandem, which focused on applications where failure could not be tolerated.

> These might be at banks for automatic tellers or funds transfers. Banks can lose literally tens of thousands of dollars in interest in the time it takes to get a failed computer back up. Other applications are in stock exchanges, airlines and medical systems. There are quite a few.
>
> Tandem has done very well, with sales of $24 million after only three years in business. They have a nice niche, but there's no competition for them, no similar product.

He began to look for ways to improve on Tandem's product (see list in Exhibit 1) and to write a business plan that would allow investors to see what he was trying to accomplish (see Exhibit 2). The type of product to be manufactured would be a commercial computer system in the "super mini" category for the end user market. Sales would be aimed at selected Fortune 1000 firms and independent system houses

(ISOs) Bill commented:

> *Today, the market for commercial computer systems in the $100,000 to $500,000 class is huge. It's expected to increase over the next five years from $3.5 billion to $20 billion. So, if we can get 1 percent of that market, we're a $200 million dollar company in five years.*
>
> *Our problem isn't going to be in getting orders. Our problem is focusing on who we want to sell to and where geographically. The key factor in this industry is not what you're going to be making but how you carry it out.*

Likely competition, according to Bill, would include Tandem Computer, Prime Computer, Digital Equipment, IBM and Hewlett Packard. A major advantage, he expected, was that he would be able to design fresh architecture while his established competitors would be held back from doing so by the investment they had in existing designs. This would put him in a better position to incorporate the latest technical advances.

Searching for Support

By October 1979 Bill Foster had developed a general business plan to use in "prospecting" for venture capital. He met with two San Francisco firms his Boston contact had suggested, and encountered much advice but no offers to invest.

> *I found myself working for the venture capitalists. They would say, "Do this; do that; go find a marketing person." That wasn't my objective. My objective was to work for myself. I found that I was wasting my time, doing the wrong things. I was constantly talking to the venture groups, looking for lawyers and CPAs.*
>
> *One group tried to get me to join*

> *with another entrepreneur who was also trying to start a company. He had a lot more experience and had already made a lot of money in the computer industry. They got us together and it was just like oil and water. There was no way I could see myself working <u>for</u> that guy and it would have been hard to work <u>with</u> him. Because of his experience, I was sure he expected to be my superior.*
>
> *This was really tough because I <u>knew</u> he was going to get his money. With his record, the venture capitalists were going to invest in whatever he wanted to do. I told my wife it would be really disappointing if two or three years out he would have built a really successful company while I never got off the ground. She said, "Look, what you want to do is run your own company. Don't start to lower your goals." So I called him up and said I wasn't interested. He said I was making a big mistake.*
>
> *Actually, my biggest mistake was to think that the venture capitalists were going to invest in me, Bill Foster. There's nobody who's going to put $2 million dollars on one individual; it's just too risky.*

He attempted to contact old acquaintances at HP to see if they might be interested in joining him in the venture. Bill recalled what he found:

> *I went to San Francisco with a list of 30 people whom I had been associated with and felt would be good to have involved in the company. I discovered there were only two still with HP. The others had gone on to start their own business or work for entrepreneurs. The start-up activity in California had been going strong from 1976 to 1979 while I was gone. It didn't take me too long to realize that getting a team together in California would be tough.*

By November, Bill was still in California trying to assemble a team and attract interest in the financial community. He explained his frustration at the lack of progress:

The venture firms all wanted to talk to everybody I tried to recruit. They were testing me, which I didn't realize. They wanted to see if Foster could attract those people. They'd say, "We may invest in Bill Foster. What do you think of his venture? Why would you join him? How would your job function?" They were really conducting job interviews! Remember, I knew nothing about raising money. It appeared that this was the way you do it. I didn't know any better.

Taking Another Tack

Bill finally decided to go back to New England and try starting his business there by lining up his management team <u>first</u> and then going to the venture capitalists. The traveling expenses to California had eaten into his weekly $600 withdrawals, and the real estate market had collapsed to the point where selling and buying a house was a difficult prospect at either end of the country. Added to that was the desire of his family to stay in New England where they had made new friends and enjoyed the change of seasons absent in San Francisco.

The major risk he saw in abandoning California as a start-up location was in breaking off discussions with the one venture firm with whom he had been meeting. Bill explained that this might destroy his credibility among such investors, since they didn't seem to like people shopping around for the best deal.

A number of calls came from friends who were curious about his progress to date. He contacted one of these friends who had started his own software firm af-

ter working with Bill at the computer company in New England. Their conversation led to an agreement where the friend would become the vice president of software development for Bill's prospective company, Alta. The friend had software developed that could be used for the venture and said he would provide it on a deferred payment basis—that is, if and when Alta became profitable, the friend would get paid for the software which was used.

Bill recalled his surprise at being able to bring the friend on as part of the management team:

My original plan when I approached him was to buy some of his software for my product. But when he learned what I was trying to do, he said, "Wow! this really sounds neat. I've always wanted to get into a manufacturing company instead of just a service company. I'll throw in my resources with you."

Bill was able to locate another individual who had some experience in hardware and a third, who was not in California, for marketing. Three days before Christmas, he got a telephone call from his partner who would be handling hardware engineering. The person had called to tell Bill he was backing out—his present employer had offered him a financial package that was too attractive to turn down. Bill's response reflected the setback:

That was a real blow. I had told one of the venture capital firms I was keeping in touch with that I was back to two people. I was convinced that the whole project was going to fall through. Things just weren't going well at all as we moved into 1980.

Bill contacted an individual who had an outstanding reputation in the hardware side of the industry. He admitted that there was little chance of convincing the person to come with Alta. Even so, he arranged a meeting with the man and the software vice-president. In Bill's words, "They hit it off. Both had respect for each other. What looked like disaster last month suddenly turned out to be good luck."

With a management team in place, Bill contacted a number of venture capital firms to line up meetings to discuss possible financing. Two groups expressed interest over the phone and agreed to meet with him in the near future. The Boston-led group could sit down with the founders in February and had technical expertise on board to understand the product aspects of the venture. The New York group wanted to bring in a California-based consultant to look at the business plan. Since the consultant was booked up with other commitments, the earliest that Bill could meet with this group of venture capitalists would likely be in March.

With this in mind, Bill set up a February appointment with the first group and thought about some of the advice he had received in the last six months:

> *Various people have told me that the most important thing in raising venture capital is to have a good relationship with your investors. They say that's more important than the terms worked out in the deal.*
>
> *Another bit of advice I'd heard frequently was that venture firms are somewhat like sheep. If you get one group to follow you, the others will be right behind, tlooking for a piece of the action. How you translate those observations into your negotiating strategy, I'm not sure.*

Projecting Financial Requirements for the Venture

Bill's experience from previous work in product development helped him imagine how long it would take to complete the first product and what would be required in staffing and money. He listed assumptions for creating pro forma financial statements for a business plan. (See Exhibit 3). He said the key factor during the first two years would be money spent on research and development (R & D). He planned to spend a fixed amount on it until sales were high enough that 6 to 10 percent of sales would cover it, and after that keep it at the high end of this range. He expected that most R & D costs would be tied up in salary, and that purchases of computer equipment wouldn't be significant until the second or third year.

His estimated current costs for software development professionals averaged $50,000 per year and for hardware development engineers averaged $80,000 including overhead expenses such as telephone, rent, and fringe benefits. Staffing would be primarily engineers until sales commenced. Then he would develop a sales force, adding administrative staff incrementally as needed. A bank would handle payroll paperwork and pay all employees from the first day the firm was in business.

Bill had received conflicting advice on how to show the year-end balance for cash on hand. An accountant suggested that he "pay by account" by getting more money in the first round than would actually be needed. He suggested that Bill might put $400,000 as the year-end figure to show the venture capital firms that he was being "frugal" in his spending. Venture capital professionals had mentioned that they didn't like giving out any more than was actually needed for funding during a given period.

He decided to construct pro forma statements for help in obtaining sufficient cash flow for operations and product development until sales could sustain needed working capital. He expected to break even about one year from the first shipment, although he wasn't sure when the exact timing of the first shipment would occur. Although he had yet to secure office space, he estimated that he would need approximately 10,000 square feet for the development phase.

As a general guide in forecasting, Bill decided to use the financial statements of similar computer firms. This would include Tandem, Prime Computer and Data General, among others. He expected that the margins and percentage ratios for the various accounts would likely be similar, even though the dollar volumes would be less than these firms. Percentages would likely differ in the first portion of the five-year projections, since there would be little sales, if any.

Because Alta was aiming for the end-user market as an OEM (original equipment maker), Bill figured marketing expenses would be a slightly higher percentage of total costs than at other computer firms. He said this would require a higher gross margin on the products sold by Alta. The company was expected to service the equipment once installed, and such revenues would be included in later years' projections.

The cash needed for purchase and lease of capital equipment was expected to range between $100,000 and $200,000 through the development phase of the business. Other assets would principally be current, with a set-aside for finished goods to be used as replacements in case a customer's computer failed for any extended period of time.

Bill outlined the accounts he needed to complete for pro formas. These included five-year projections for an income statement, balance sheet, and sources and uses statement (see Exhibits 4 and 5). He also developed further details regarding needed assumptions to project them (Exhibit 6). He then went to a local library to get copies of financial data from the annual reports of publicly-held companies that he thought would be similar to Alta in terms

of costs and margins (see Exhibits 7 and 8).

Looking at the information he had gathered and the base assumptions he had prepared, Bill outlined the work that lay ahead of him:

We've been talking in general terms about the money that will be needed to pull this off. Now I've got to figure out how that $1.5 or $2 million gets spent the first year, and what happens after that. My MBA background really helps out here . . . otherwise there's no way I would be able to put together the pro formas. I want to make sure that my numbers are precise for a couple of reasons. First, I've been told over the last six months that venture capitalists really focus on the financial side. They've got to. They might not understand the product side, but they do understand the financial and people aspects.

The other thing is that for about the first six months, you've got a honeymoon with the venture capital people. But then they are going to start looking over your shoulder to see if where you are is where your numbers said you would be. If you're way off, they can get pretty nervous.

He also saw other issues yet to be worked out: What type of employee stock option plan should be set up? When would a controller be needed for the company? Bill summed up the situation as he prepared for the first negotiation session:

I need to work on the pro formas and get them to a level of detail that will be useful in monitoring our performance. And I want to be informed enough so that we can be in the best position for getting the terms and percentages on the deal. But at the same time, I know that without any money by summer, the terms or the pro formas won't make a dime's worth of difference.

EXHIBIT 1   Thoughts about Competition

A survey of minicomputer users is conducted for *Datamation* magazine each fall. The 1979 survey (see *Datamation*, November 1979, pp. 95-8) noted the following preferences by minicomputer users about products currently available. The proposed product described would be at the top end of the price range for minicomputer systems, referred to as superminis. Three most important features cited by users in making a purchase of a minicomputer system are:

1. Vendor Reputation
2. Price
3. Operational Software

Other findings:

1. The top reason for switching suppliers was due to dissatisfaction with software support.
2. Customers tended to be loyal to their current main supplier.
3. Two or more suppliers were considered by 77 percent of all users when making an initial purchase of a minicomputer.
4. One in five users was either switching suppliers or considering a switch during 1979.
5. Delivery dates missed by suppliers was mentioned as a source of dissatisfaction by users.
6. Tandem Computer had the highest degree of customer loyalty: none of the 18 sites surveyed having a Tandem computer was considering a switch.

Competitive Features of the Proposed Alta Product

PRODUCT

— Reliability
— Price
— Modular Design of the CPU
— Use with non-English languages
— Large memory size for applications
— Stand alone system complete with peripheral equipment
— Growth of the 32-bit market
— Philosophy of not taking orders before product completion

MANAGEMENT TEAM
— Experience in hardware, software and marketing
— Risking savings and careers for the venture

DISTRIBUTION

— Targeted Market (Fortune 1000)
— Direct Sales Force
— Single product to boost installation base
— International Sales within five years

— Awareness of transitional needs from engineering to marketing

— Contacts within the computer industry
— Proprietary software available for use in development

EXHIBIT 2 Business Plan Draft

ALTA COMPUTING SYSTEMS, INC.

Proprietary Information

I - SUMMARY

The business of Alta Computing Systems is to design, manufacture and market small computer systems focused at commercial applications. Alta computer systems will sell in the $40,000 to $500,000 range. The product will consist of central processors and all necessary peripherals (discs, displays, tape, line printers), and system software (operating system, languages, utilities, communications). There are three design features that will provide significant differentiation from competitive products:

1. Highly reliable hardware architecture that can protect the user from almost any hardware failure.
2. Modular system architecture that permits the performance of any system to be expanded with additional central processing units.
3. A unique software offering including an operation system that is much easier to use than existing products.

A.   Reliability

Alta believes that one of the best possible uses of current and future technology is to substantially improve computer system reliability. While hardware costs continue to decrease, all other costs associated with computer system ownership are increasing: software, training and field service. Also, as the daily operations of businesses depend more on computers to do work that was previously done by people, the indirect costs of computer failure can become major. Unlike people, computers generally give little, if any, warning that they are about to fail. When they do fail, they are useless until repaired, and sometimes critical information is lost that is very difficult and expensive to recover. As the hardware costs drop and other costs of computer ownership rise, the percentage of the computer market that is willing to pay extra for high reliability will increase. Alta plans to take advantage of this technology trend.

B.   Expandability

One of the first questions potential computer purchasers ask is: What happens when I outgrow my system? Traditional computer manufacturers offer a family of computers based on several central processors of differing performance and cost. The user may upgrade the system with a more powerful processor, but this means that somebody is stuck with the old hardware, and the performance range form the smallest to largest model is limited.

The Alta approach is totally different. An Alta Computing System can consist of one to 10 or more identical central processing units. Thus, performance is increased by adding processors to the system. This architecture provides a very broad range of power, and gives Alta a family of computer models by replicating a single processor design, rather than designing several different processors.

EXHIBIT 2 (continued)

C.   Operating System

The operating systems of existing computer manufacturers are old and difficult to use. Most were designed about ten years ago when there was little understanding of the ways that small computers would be used in the '80s. Because of compatibility requirements, manufacturers have been forced to stick with their old systems and add new commands for new functionality. A significant advantage that Alta will have over all of its competitors is the ease-of-use of its operating system. The command language has the power required by application programmers but is also designed to be used by unskilled operators. It can be tailored for use by non-English speaking people so that commands and error messages have meanings in their language. The operating system also provides a transparent interface between the user and the multiprocessor architecture.

An important capability of the Alta operating system and central processor is the support of virtual memory. Alta will support applications as large as one million-plus bytes, even though physical memory will be much smaller. This means that all programmers, including Alta system software developers, are much more efficient than they would be in a limited address-space.

D.   Market

Alta will compete in the so-called "supermini" market, which had shipments of almost $1.5 billion in 1979 and is growing at approximately 30 percent per year (source: International Data Corporation). The large size of this market means that Alta can achieve its fifth-year revenue projections with 6 percent or less of the market. Alta will initially offer a highly reliable computer with excellent software development tools but no industry-specific applications. Hence, the Company will sell to computer-knowledgeable customers who will then add the required applications. Alta will sell primarily to *Fortune* 1000 companies, who will distribute computers within their company, and application system builders who will add application software and re-sell into specific vertical markets. The obvious customers will be those who already have specific requirements for reliability (financial, medical, manufacturing, communications), but Alta will also sell to customers with "conventional" reliability needs who recognize that the extra hardware cost may be more than offset by the "indirect" costs of down-time, particularly as hardware becomes cheaper.

Alta will sell to commercial users in the fast-growing 32-bit segment of the small computer market. According to Martin and Simpson Research Associates, Inc., this segment will grow at a compound annual rate of 56 percent through 1985 (*Electronic News*, Sept. 1979). Commercial applications are overtaking industrial, and will climb from 27 percent to 40 percent of the market by 1985.

E.   Competition

At this time the only general purpose computer manufacturer that has a product line focused at reliability is Tandem Computers. Tandem is a highly successful company that achieved approximately $109 million in revenues in its sixth year of operation. Alta's product will have several advantages over Tandem's, including: higher reliability, software-transparent architecture, lower price and a superior operating system.

Alta will also compete with the other established small computer manufacturers such as

EXHIBIT 2 (concluded)

Digital Equipment, Hewlett-Packard, Prime and IBM. All of these companies certainly recognize Tandem's success because they have all lost business to Tandem. However, it is difficult for any of them to make an adequate response because that would require developing a completely new product line from the ground up. This would not only be very expensive, but would create severe compatibility problems with their existing product line. Since most of their revenue comes from existing customers, compatibility is a key issue in all new product development programs. It appears that the strategy of these companies is to address the "Tandem" issue with an inferior technical solution consisting of a combination of existing products (thereby maintaining compatibility with minimum investment), and rely on their size and past reputations to win the business.

F.   Financing

Alta anticipates equity financing of between $1.5 and $2 million by the spring of 1980. It also expects to negotiate a bank line-of-credit of $100,000 or more for the purchase of capital equipment. Alta is currently completing a lease and rental agreement for computer equipment valued at $500,000 from one of its founders. This financing will carry the company for one year, by which time a prototype system will be ready. Alta projects a need for $3.5 million for second-year funding. It is the Company's objective to grow rapidly and achieve a 20-percent pre-tax margin on sales of at least $40 million by year five.

EXHIBIT 3   Assumptions for Financial Forecasts

1.   Revenues
     – All revenues based on a constant gross margin.
     – First customer shipments will occur no later than mid-1983.
     – Service revenues will grow at less than the industry average of 0.6 percent to 0.8 percent of installed base per month, and will account for less than 10 percent of sales through the period.
     – Reduced margins from OEM discounts will be offset by reduced marketing expense.
2.   Warranty
     – Because of high system reliability, warranty expense will not be a significant factor.
3.   Foreign Sales
     – Sales are expected to be made internationally by the end of the five-year period.
4.   Marketing Expense
     – A higher than average industry rate will be spent on marketing.
     – The sales force will be compensated through a very aggressive commission plan.
5.   Development Expense
     – The percentage of revenues spent on new product development will be at the high end of the industry average.
     – The development staff will remain at a constant level by the end of 1980, until the revenue base is supported with product shipments.
6.   Taxes
     – Loss carry-forwards for both state and federal taxes will be applied during the five year period.
     – A tax rate of 45 percent is assumed, which is reasonable in light of:
          • ITC
          • Jobs Tax Credit
          • Surtax Exemption
          • Tax Planning
7.   Accounts Receivable
     – Assumes initial turn cycle of 120 days, going to 90 days by the end of 1983. Representative companies, by comparison, range between 60 and 120 days.
8.   Notes Payable
     – Notes payable in 1980 and 1981 will be secured by the purchase of engineering and production test equipment.
     – Notes payable in later years will be secured by receivables (not to exceed 70 percent of receivables).
9.   Inventories
     – Assumes 2.7 inventory turns per year. Representative companies range between 2.5 and 2.8 turns.
10. Accounts Payable
     – Assumes $75,000 in 1980 and thereafter a 75-day turn cycle. Representative companies range between 60 and 110 days.
11. Property, Plant and Equipment
     – Early requirements will be financed through leasing. Assumes capital leases from an accounting point of view.
     – Currently anticipate the need for two computer systems—valued at approximately $400,000—for use in product development, corporate administration, and manufacturing control systems.
12. Interest
     – Interest income is 8.5 percent of cash balances, with a $20,000 reserve.
     – Interest expense is 16 percent of notes payable.

EXHIBIT 4 Spreadsheet for Five-Year Pro Forma Financial Statements ($000)

Income Statement	1980	1981	1982	1983	1984
Revenue					
Total Cost of Goods Sold					
Gross Margin					
Development					
Marketing					
G&A					
Total Operating Expenses					
Income (Loss) From OPS					
Interest Expense					
Interest Income					
Net Interest					
Income (Loss) Before Taxes					
Net Income (Loss)					

Balance Sheet	1980	1981	1982	1983	1984
Cash & Cash Investments					
Accounts Receivable					
System Spares					
Inventories					
Prepaid Expenses					
Total Current Assets					
Production & Test Equip.					
Electronice Test Equipment					
Computer Equipment					
Leasehold Improvements					
Subtotal					
Less-Accumulated Dep.					
Net Plant & Equipment					
Total Assets					
Notes Payable					
Accounts Payable					
Taxes Payable					
Accrued Expenses					
Total Current Liabilities					
Stock					
Rretained Earning (def.)					
Total Stockholder Equity					
Total Liabilities & Equity					

EXHIBIT 5 Spreadsheet for Five-Year Sources and Applications Forecast ($000)

<u>Cash Flow</u>

	1980	1981	1982	1983	1984
Cash Provided by (Used in) Operations:					
Net Income (Loss)					
Add: Charges Against Income Not Requiring Use of Cash: Depreciation					
Net Cash Provided By (Used in) Operations					
Other Sources of Cash					
Increase in Notes Payable					
Increase in Accounts Payable					
Increase in Taxes Payable					
Increase in Accrued Expenses					
Sales of Stock					
Total Sources (Uses)					
Uses of Cash					
Increase in Accounts Receivable					
Increase in System Spares					
Increase in Inventories					
Increase in Prepaid Expenses					
Additions to Property, Plant and Equipment					
Total Uses					
Increase (Decrease) in Cash					
Cash Balance Start of Period					
Cash Balance End of Period					

EXHIBIT 6   Additional Assumptions for Pro Forma Statements

I.   INCOME STATEMENT
Assumes average selling price per unit of $200,000.
Installation base by year is as follows:

	1980	1981	1982	1983	1984
Number Sold	0	13	91	183	365
Total Units Installed	0	13	104	287	652
Rate of Installation starting at	n.a.	one/wk 4 days	1 per 2 days	1 per 1 day	1 per mid year

Cost of Goods Sold at 45 percent of revenues.
Service revenues assumed to be negligible.
Development expense at $1.5 million or 10 percent of sales, whichever is greater.
Marketing expense at 20 percent of sales; 17.5 percent of sales in 1984.
G and A expense for 1980, a plug; thereafter, 5 percent of sales.
Interest expense and income based on assumptions in case materials.
Taxes assume loss carry-forward at 45 percent rate through 1982.

II.   BALANCE SHEET
Assets
Cash at $40,000 in 1980; 7 days sales in 1981; 8 days sales in 1982; 9 days sales in 1983; 10 days sales in 1984.
Accounts Receivable at 120 days in '81; 105 days in '82; 90 days thereafter.
System Spares equivalent to unit cost at 2 percent of installed base.
Inventories assumed to be $100,000 in 1980; thereafter, 2.7 times stock turn valued at cost of goods sold.
Prepaid expenses assumed to increase by $25,000 per year.
Computer equipment at $400,000 in 1980; 10 percent of sales in years 2–4; 15 percent of sales in 1984.
Production and Test Equipment and Electronic Test Equipment assumed to be 25 percent of amount for Computer Equipment, with relatively equal split between accounts.
Leasehold improvements of $50,000 assumed for 1980; thereafter one-fifth of annual sales through 1983 and one -sixth of annual sales for 1984.
Depreciation taken at 10 percent of total fixed assets in 1980; 14 percent thereafter.

Liabilities
Notes Payable assumed to be $150,000 in 1980; $500,000 in 1981; two-thirds of accounts receivable thereafter.
Accounts Payable assumed to be $75,000 in 1980; 75 day cycle thereafter.
Taxes payable at 45 percent after loss carry-forward applied.
Accrued expenses assumed to increase by $25,000 each year.

Equity
Venture Capital investment of $1.75 million in 1980; $3.5 million in 1981; and $1.8 million in 1982.
From partner/employees: $60,000 in '80; $40,000 in '81; $100,000 in '82; and $125,000 in both '83 and '84.

EXHIBIT 7   Data General Corporation Comparative Financial Statements ($000)

Consolidated Balance Sheets

	1974	**1973**	**1972**
Assets			
Current Assets	2,168	384	553
Short Term Investments	846	15,255	19,639
Accounts Receivable	22,842	11,90	6,124
Inventories	29,868	8,748	1,890
Prepaid Expenses	1,795	1,625	1,559
Total Current Assets	$57,519	$37,921	$29,765
Property, Plant & Equip.	17,673	11,516	5,557
Less Accrued. Depr.	3,968	1,708	642
Net Property, et al.	13,705	9,808	4,915
TOTAL ASSETS	$71,224	$47,729	$34,680
Liabilities and Stockholders' Equity			
Current Liabilities			
Notes Payable	2,049	—	—
Accounts Payable	10,813	5,380	3,864
Accrued Payroll	1,320	550	407
Taxes Payable	8,168	4,175	2,397
Other Accrued Expenses	2,088	2,171	932
Total Current Liabilities	$24,438	$12,276	$7,600
Stockholders' Equity			
Common Stock, $.01 Par Value			
Authorized 20,000,000 shares			
Shares issued and outstanding			
8,010,000 at 9/28/74			
7,903,000 at 9/29/73			
2,603,000 at 9/30/72	80	79	26
Capital in Excess of Par	$24,482	$23,096	$21,455
Retained Earnings	22,302	12,407	5,178
Less: Treasury Stock	1	1	1
Less: Deferred Compen-			
sation, ESOP	77	128	119
TOTAL LIABILITIES AND			
STOCKHOLDERS' EQUITY	$71,224	$47,729	$34,139

EXHIBIT 7 (concluded)

Data General Consolidated Statements of Income

	1974	1973	1972
Net Sales	83,196	53,306	$30,324
Costs and Expenses			
Cost of Goods Sold	38,268	24,521	——
Development Expense	8,514	5,970	——
G & A Expense	4,582	2,539	——
Marketing Expense	13,509	8,423	——
	64,873	41,453	——
Income from Operations	18,323	11,853	——
Other Income	722	1,108	——
Income Before Taxes	19,045	12,961	5,562
Provision for Taxes	1,265	6,220	1,665
Net Income	$9,895	$6,741	$3,897

Related Financial Information

	1972	1971	1970
Net Sales	$30,324	$15,341	$7,035
Net Income	4,297	1,561	633
Expenditures for Plant,			
Property and Equip.	3,897	770	456
Current Assets 30,232	23,020	5,225	
Current Liabilities	7,600	2,677	1,175
Working Capital	22,632	20,343	4,050
Stockholders' Equity	27,080	21,446	4,377
Per Share Income	$.49	$.2	$.11
Cumulative Computers Installed	4,170	1,710	690
Employees at Year End	840	480	240

Note: Dollars Expressed in Thousands.

EXHIBIT 8 Financial Statement Data from Prime and Tandem Computers ($000)

__Tandem Computer:__ Consolidated Statement of Changes in Financial Position

	1979	1978
Working Capital Provided From (Used For)		
Net Income before Extraordinary Credit	4,920	2,153
Add Back:		
Depreciation and Amortization	1,365	457
Deferred Income Taxes	737	—
Working Capital Provided From Operations	7,022	2,610
Extraordinary Credit	—	1,218
Acquisition of Property and Equipment	(5,770)	(2,387)
Net Book Value of Equipment Sold or Retired	337	84
Increase in Capital Lease Obligations	429	399
Increase in Deferred Income Taxes	304	—
Sale of Preferred Stock	—	1,000
Sale of Common Stock, Net	10,837	8,196
Tax Benefit of Stock Options	235	234
Net Increase in Working Capital	$ 13,394	$ 13,964

__Prime Computer:__ Consolidated Statement of Stockholders' Investment

	Common Stock				Treasury Stock	
	Number of Shares	$0 Par Value	Capital in Excess of Par Value	Retained Earnings (Deficit)	Number of Shares	Cost
Balance, 12/31/71	300,000	$8,000	$23,000	($1,000)	32,000	($1,000)
Sale of common stock	1,132,000	28,000	1,506,000	—	—	—
Treasury stock changes, net	(32,000)	(1,000)	26,000	—	(30,800)	(1,000)
Net loss for the year	—	—	—	(966,000)	—	—
Balance, 12/31/72	1,400,000	$35,000	$1,555,000	($967,000)	1,200	($2,000)
Sale of common stock	325,000	8,000	1,283,000	—	—	—
Treasury stock changes, net	—	—	32,000	—	4,000	1,000
Net loss for the year	—	—	—	(1,831,000)	—	—
Balance, 12/31/73	1,725,000	$43,000	$2,870,000	($2,798,000)	5,200	($1,000)
Public offering	400,000	10,000	2,451,000	—	—	—
Treasury stock changes, net	—	—	26,000	—	56,600	(9,000)
Net loss for the year	—	—	—	(532,000)	—	—
Balance, 12/31/74	2,125,000	$53,000	$5,347,000	($3,330,000)	61,800	($10,000)
Sale of common stock	—	—	15,000	—	312	(5,000)
Treasury stock changes, net	—	—	8,000	—	—	—
Net income for the year	—	—	—	692,000	—	—
Balance, 12/31/75	2,125,000	$53,000	$5,370,000	($2,638,000)	62,112	($15,000)
Sale of common stock	(52,886)	(1,000)	18,000	—	(62,112)	15,000
Treasury stock changes, net	—	—	20,000	—	—	—
Net income for the year	—	—	—	2,429,000	—	—
Balance, 12/31/76	2,072,114	$52,000	$5,408,000	($209,000)	—	—

Case 11

Bill Foster (B)

By the end of January 1980 Bill Foster was shifting his attention from working out the details of his venture plan to seeking a commitment for start-up capital. He knew that striking a deal with a venture capital group for financing would involve continued negotiations until both sides were willing to accept the terms presented. There were no assurances that the process would be completed within a week, a month or even later. Only one of his four partners had been associated with a start-up; none had been involved with venture capital financing.

Needs, he expected, would be for $6.2 million to cover a three-year development and market introduction effort. He would need about $2 million the first year to develop a working prototype and establish credibility of the team and concept. The founders themselves would personally be able to put in about $75,000 cash at most.

Possible Capital Sources

While recruiting his founding team and working out details of a business plan, Bill had also been gathering information about alternative potential financing sources.

My philosophy has always been "It doesn't hurt to talk to anybody. You might learn something." So I followed up every lead I got, whether it had to do with raising money, finding people or anything. You may run up a phone bill, but people are generally very helpful. I got leads from headhunters and investors, lawyers and friends. I talked to other people who had started companies.

They were probably the most helpful of all—those who had recently experienced what I was going through. They would reminisce about those exciting times. Of course, if they were successful and got their operations off the ground, they always liked to talk about it.

I got many of the new company leads by reading magazines. Some of them have articles about companies that have just started up. I'd just call some of the presidents of the companies that had been interviewed out of the blue, tell them what I was doing, and ask their advice. I met several of the people out in California through those articles.

Bill had found three major options: venture capital firms, private individuals, and other operating corporations. There appeared to be significant differences in the way each of these groups made investments and in the types of deals that might be struck.

Venture Capital Firms

The venture capital firms were the most obvious possibilities. There were a large number of venture firms actively seeking investments. In addition to the best known and perhaps most prestigious firms, there were a wide range of other, less well-known, firms he considered worth contacting. Most were smaller, more recently started, or simply chose to keep low profiles. Contacts with two of these latter firms who expressed interest in Alta had come through one of Bill's partners, Gardner Hendrie. When Gardner was considering joining the team, he had called an old friend, Charles Meyers, for advice. Charles had worked with Gardner 15 years earlier in an engineering company, then gone to California to become involved in venture capital, and through it became very successful. When Gardner explained why he was interested in learning the climate for venture capital, Charles said his company, Pacific Ventures, might be interested. Bill recalled:

Before I know it, Charles hops an airplane to come and talk with us. Right away he's very interested, partly on the strength of the business plan and partly because of his personal association with Gardner. But he felt we should have an East Coast firm in the lead. He'd be very happy with the New York firms we knew, but also suggested we contact Davidson-Mills, a lesser known Boston company they'd done some business with before. (It seemed that the best known Boston firms generally preferred second-round financings.) I had heard of Davidson-Mills, but had never bothered to call them. I didn't think they did start-ups, and I didn't think they were big enough. But Charles said they'd be good, and they'd feel good about our idea. One of the their partners had prior experience in the timesharing business and knew something about computers himself.

During his early discussions with the venture firms and in talking to the other recently started companies, Bill discovered some apparent ground rules in the venture capital community:

One rule is that you're not going to raise $7 million on day one. No one has put in that much money. The going first round for my kind of deal is around a million and a half. Maybe you can get close to $2 million, but probably not more than $2 million for a team of untried people. That much would get us just past a working prototype.

Number two is that they are going to have control—at least 51 percent. They're going to do it—there's no way you can get around it. At the same time, they won't commit to anything on round two. They'll talk about what they'll do if you do a good job, but if they don't like what you've done, you may not get that second-round money.

None of it is cast in concrete. You can talk and you can go through scenarios. They'd sit me down and tell me what other companies did. "In 1974 Tandem gave up 74 percent of their company for $1 million. The investor got 72 percent of Prime Computers for $600,000 in 1972." The new start-ups did a little better—the going rate seemed to be giving up about 60 percent.

I also found that many of the venture capital firms without technical backgrounds used outside consultants to help them evaluate high-technology ventures. The people they relied on were heavily booked and might take weeks to schedule.

Private Individuals

Another possible source of financing was from wealthy individuals. Certain tax provisions could make investments in firms such as Alta appealing; most of Alta's early expenses would be for research and development. If the funds for the R&D were provided by a limited partnership most of the expenditures could be deducted by the individuals against other sources of ordinary income. This would effectively lessen the actual after-tax amount at risk for those individuals. If the research proved successful, the investors would typically receive a royalty (normally 7 to 10 percent) on resulting sales. Such royalties would be taxed at long-term capital-gain rates.

Bill had been put in contact with a young individual who had taken an idea from an MBA thesis and built it into a very successful company, which he had recently sold for about $6 million. Now, to invest some of the proceeds he offered to lead a private placement with about 10 individuals each putting up $300,000 to $400,000. Because of potential tax benefits of such a placement and because some of the individuals in it did not get to see as many deals as venture capital firms did, Bill hoped his team would not have to give up so much ownership, maybe only 40-45 percent, if money could be raised this way. However, he expected this route would be more complicated and might require preparation of a private placement memorandum nearly as complex as a full-blown prospectus under SEC Rule 242. This might also require review by the state "Blue Sky" commission. "The SEC might not consider that even a wealthy lawyer is necessarily a 'sophisticated investor' when it comes to a computer start-up," he said.

Other Non-Venture Corporations

Once again, Bill found that people recommended to him as advisers for dealing with venture capital became capital sources themselves, as he began discussions with another company that soon expressed interest in financing the entire Alta start-up. Bill's contact, Gary Jameson, had formerly worked for a venture capital firm. Now he was vice president of administration in a company offering a product that depended on reliable computer systems. This company bought computers from major suppliers, then incorporated them in systems it sold to telecommunications firms. These systems required continuous absolutely reliable operation. Bill commented:

Gary's employer said they were very interested, and even though they were not in the venture capital business, they might fund us to the tune of $7 million. Again, this would be set up as partnership so that this company could get the more immediate tax benefits of expensing the R & D.

Gary said it might be impossible for me to raise money through venture capital sources—and I could be wasting my time talking to venture capital firms. Even though I had run R & D teams, I had never been the chief executive officer of a company, had never run the whole show. He said that venture capitalists were really conservative investors, and it was unlikely that any venture group would invest millions of dollars in a company in which the chief executive officer didn't have a proven track record.

This was the only non-venture capital company Bill had contacted for financing. After seeing the interest it expressed, however, he thought perhaps some other noncapital companies might have similar interests. He had heard that some major industrial corporations, such as General Electric, had in-house venture groups, but he wasn't sure how their investment strategies might differ from those of traditional venture capital companies.

Other Considerations

Striking a deal with any of the financing sources would, Bill expected, require detailed negotiations of unpredictable length with no assurance that a deal would ever be reached. The risks seemed heightened by the fact that the Alta team was untried in launching a company. One factor in their favor was that there had been a number of recent success stories of computer firms starting up and becoming industry leaders. Those deals also served as a growing data base to determine the increased values of the company for each round of financing.

Recent increases in the availability of venture capital also worked to Alta's advantage. Bill pointed out that more money now chased roughly the same number of high-quality investments, so his founding group should have good leverage in negotiating a deal. This could enhance terms for Alta on a whole range of issues, including relative percentages of ownership between investors and venture, relative privileges shareholders might seek through different types of common stock, preferred stock, or debt instruments with convertible provisions or warrants. The extent of voting privileges and membership on the board of directors would likely also be areas for negotiation.

Valuation of the company had to be considered somewhere in the process. With on-going companies, investors could look at the asset-bases and price/earnings ratios. With a start-up, the investor had to consider the concept, the projections, and the team, then decide on the venture's likely future value. Bill expected that more than one round of financing would probably be needed. How the first round of capital was priced and structured would, he supposed, influence the terms of later investment rounds.

Bill commented that an investor's main concern would be the likelihood of the venture's achieving a specified level of profitability in a given period of time. The track records with new products of his founding team could, he said, be a big plus. It had been in the start-up by Gene Amdahl whose record in the computer industry from his prior accomplishments at IBM had allowed him to marshall $17 million in start-up capital. Also in Alta's favor, Bill believed, was the fact that there had been a number of recent success stories of computer firms starting up and becoming industry leaders. Such venture precedents helped determine how stock prices and splits were negotiated between investors and founders at each round of funding.

Working Out Terms

All Bill's team members said they would agree to take smaller salaries than they had earned before. His own would, he expected, be less than half of this former salary and the others would be about 80 percent. The four founding members of the company would split whatever equity they could retain by dividing the number of shares by 4.2. Each of them would receive a 1/4.2 part except Bill. He would receive 1.2/4.2 or a "120 percent" share for putting the team together. Employee stock ownership and shares for other key employees also had to be considered.

Cash equity available among the team totaled between $50,000 and $75,000. Thus, to raise the necessary funds, a differential for stock paid by the venture capitalists and the founders would by required. No formula existed for setting a ratio differential. In some cases, the venture group might pay 10 times the rate of the founders; other times the ratio might go as high as 30 or 40. The figure was partly a function of initial funding required, available equity, willingness by the founders to give up a substantial or even controlling interest in the firm, and expectations on the time frame for future funding or start of shipments to generate revenues. Bill commented:

Let's say there are 3,000,000 shares in the company and that if the stock was being publicly traded, the current selling price was $10 a share. That would indicate that the value of the firm is $30,000,000. But what would it have to earn to produce that result? If current earnings are $1,000,000 for example, then the price/earnings ratio would have to be 30. Investors would have to be willing to pay 30 times present earnings for access to future earning streams in the company.

For a start-up like ours, you can look

at what our profits are projected to be in the future, adjust that by some perception of risk, and see what similar companies on the stock exchange are selling for in terms of their price-earnings ratios. Or, you could look at the historical pricing of other private placements in start-ups.

Another factor Bill thought important

to consider was that more than one round of financing would most likely be needed. If progress as measured against the plan went as scheduled, he expected a better stock price and /or differential could be negotiated in the second round. On the other hand, if delays occurred, he and the three partners would be in a weaker bargaining position and, at worst, might find themselves unable to raise any additional capital at all.

Debra Glassman

In late 1980, just over two years after completing her MBA at Northeastern University, Debra Glassman was concerned about how to improve the financial performance of her business venture, Everywoman's Sport Center. She reflected:

When I look back over my start-up activities during the past year, I don't see anything I would have done differently.

She was sitting on a wooden bench in the orange-carpeted "conditioning room" of the two-story warehouse which now housed her company. The room was filled with women in T-shirts, bending and stretching.

It's fulfilling for me to provide a place for women who want to be healthier and stronger, and to see them realize for themselves the potential of their own bodies. My only problem is that I need to increase the enrollment; I can barely cover my operating costs, let alone pay myself a salary. I don't know whether I'm not reaching the right people or whether the market isn't there. I figure I have six months. If the enrollment doesn't increase by then, I'll discontinue this venture and try something else.

Personal Background

"I have always loved sports," Debra began. In her high school in the late 1950s, girls had no opportunity to play team sports. On her own, she took up bicycling "when it wasn't cool for a girl to bike" and laughed at the surprised reaction of some of her classmates. She graduated from the University of Wisconsin in 1966 and earned a master's degree in Social Work from Columbia University in 1968. Her first job was at the YM\YWHA in Scarsdale, New York as director of youth services. From there, Debra went to Toronto. At the Addiction Research Foundation, she set up an extensive drug abuse program and directed a Crisis Intervention Center. Debra's resume appears in Exhibit 1. She continued:

As early as 1970, before women's issues became a big thing, I realized that the men I worked for seemed to resent me, and I didn't understand why. I was always very straightforward; I didn't bat my eyelashes or anything like that to call their attention to the fact that I was a woman. I had always been praised for saying what was on my mind. I found that I was using a lot of energy trying to deal with this problem and decided to go back to graduate school to get credentials to qualify me for a more responsible position, higher up, so there wouldn't be so many men above me to deal with. I tried law school for a term, because the intellectual challenge of problem-solving appealed to me, but it was not satisfying emotionally. The basis of the law seemed to be solution by compromise, and I like to aim for the ideal.

So I decided to get an MBA, with the idea of finding a responsible administrative position. Starting my own business crossed my mind, and I took a course in that area, which helped me a lot. The class was divided into groups and each group got to choose a new venture and prepare a report on how to start it. Our group—two men and two women—got along wonderfully; nobody felt threatened. In the academic setting, people accepted my frankness, and one professor included some of the women's issues I had raised in his new book. In it, he referred to me as "Debra Glassperson," which made us all laugh.

After graduating from Northeastern Business School in Boston in June of 1978, Debra became director and regional coordinator of mental retardation services at the Cambridge (Massachusetts) Family and Children's Service.

The job lasted eight months. The two men with whom I was working seemed to resent my having the control, which was part of the job description. This happened even though I made it clear from the outset that I would not take the job unless I had the authority to run the program myself. They would change plans we all had agreed upon earlier and "forget" to tell me. Again, I found myself spending energy on the woman issue that should have gone into my job.

At this point, in April of 1979, I decided that I could no longer hope to find a position within an existing organization that would be free of this conflict, and I began to think seriously about something I could do on my own. I liked working with women, loved sports, and was seriously committed to women's issues. Putting these together, I began to consider ventures involving women and sports. One area women have never taken seriously is making their bodies work for them, whether to achieve in competition or to maintain an adequate level of physical fitness.

First, I wanted to open a store selling women's equipment and clothing. I got excited about the possibility of conducting classes and clinics in the evening after store hours. Then, I realized that I was more interested in the classes than the clothes, and this led to the idea of a sports center for women.

I began to look around to see who was already doing what in this area and realized that no one was taking a common-sense physiological approach toward conditioning for women in sports. Some programs, like Gloria Stevens and Women's World, emphasized the cosmetic approach, the "you can be more attractive in six weeks" philosophy. (We don't care how your heart is as long as you look good.) It was still that same assumption about a woman's need to look good just on the outside.

Other institutions, the Ys and adult education centers, offered few good classes for women interested in a deeper understanding of how to use their bodies, and usually not in combination with sports. In short, there was nothing quite like my idea operating in the greater Boston area—no place designed for women, which used physiological understanding as a basis for improving physical performance, whether through conditioning alone or in combination with sports activity.

I wanted a low-key supportive atmosphere which would encourage women to learn about and take responsibility for their bodies. I wanted to sell the real thing, not an "image," and to have the women feel good and have fun. With this general idea in mind, I began some preliminary research, and it produced some very positive responses. I couldn't see any reason not to try a sport center for women, so I did.

Planning

Debra left her job April 20, 1979. By May 1 she had put together a business plan. Excerpts from her plan appear in Exhibit 2. She discussed it with a professor at Northeastern University, who was also a consultant specializing in new venture start-ups. She enrolled in a five-week Small Business Management course at a community college sponsored by the SBA (Small Business Administration) and an SBA-sponsored, all-day workshop on the same topic. She discussed the prospective venture with her family, who expressed willingness to provide the first year of financial backing. She contacted a friend who practiced law with a large Boston firm, for help with incorporation. "He also put me in touch with other people who had useful ideas," she recalled. Another friend recommended an accountant.

Debra decided on a name descriptive of her intentions—Everywoman's Sport Center. With the intention of opening in mid-September of 1979, she placed an ad during May 1979 in the *Boston Globe* offering employment for physical education graduates trained in conditioning and sports activities. She explained:

> *I thought of this as an informational step, as well as an opportunity to hire people. I was curious to see who was out there and what ideas they had. I got a number of responses from both men and women. Most of the women were enthusiastic, even though I didn't even have a building yet, but the men seemed uncomfortable—I don't know if it was the uncertainty of the new venture or the fact I was a woman.*
>
> *Anyway, I discussed with all of them the different sorts of conditioning and sports programs we might offer; and after a month or so, I had a pretty clear idea of what we would schedule initially. The aim would be to achieve overall fitness by improving muscular strength, cardiovascular endurance and flexibility. The means would be a program combining weight-lifting, inter-*

> *vals of jogging or aerobic dancing, and exercises to loosen and stretch the body. In addition to conditioning, we would offer instruction in specific sports and special recreational events like backpacking, canoeing and fishing.*
>
> *By the end of summer, I had selected six women whose attitudes and accomplishments I liked. They liked the fact that their ideas had helped to shape the program and that they would have flexibility in designing the specifics of their own classes. They all agreed to come to work at the end of September.*

Classes to be offered by the center in fall 1979 included Comprehensive Conditioning, Specialized Conditioning for Muscular Strength (Weights), Pregnancy, Post-Pregnancy, and Back Problems. Sports Instruction was offered in running, hiking, tennis, basketball, bicycling, swimming and self-defense. Several academic courses and a physical fitness laboratory completed the curriculum. Debra prepared mimeographed flyers describing the programs, which appear as Exhibit 3.

Physical Facilities

Along with her search for staff, Debra was looking for a building. She contacted several commercial real estate agents to help her find space, and described the type of building she was looking for: one with heat and plumbing, with not more than 2500 square feet, which could easily be converted into a small, high-ceilinged gymnasium and several conditioning rooms. She commented:

> *I don't like the word "exercise;" to me it implies "health spa," whereas "conditioning" implies something physiological, more comprehensive.*
>
> *Why Watertown? I wanted to start in a community without a special identity—not "the suburbs" like Newton,*

Belmont or Wellesley; or "affluent and single" like Cambridge; or "urban downtown" like Boston. I did want to be located in a central area, near public transportation. I used some demographics (Part B in the business plan of Exhibit 2). But mainly I drew on my own knowledge of Watertown and the surrounding areas and chose towns adjacent to areas I wanted to reach: Belmont, Arlington, Cambridge, Waltham, and Watertown. Watertown was my first choice, but I had also explored Brookline Village and several other focal points. I backed up my intuitive choices with demographic data, to check on their validity.

Looking at space was very discouraging at first. Few agents handle commercial properties which are so small. I saw a lot of warehouses but they were much too big and/or remote. After a month or so I put an ad in the Globe *under Space-Wanted. The owner of a small warehouse in Watertown, right near the Western Electric offices on Route 16, had a tenant who was consolidating his own operation in Waltham and asked if I wanted to see the property. He didn't advertise it because he was planning to use it for his own business. I saw it when it was still being used to store plumbing fixtures and thought it would work well. I signed a lease in late July 1979: 2200 square feet, $725 a month, 120 Elm Street, Watertown.*

Over the summer, Debra designed the layout of the center and most of the structural remodeling was done by her landlords. By September, the center consisted of a paneled and carpeted conditioning room, a small gym with 14-foot ceilings, concrete floors and stone walls, and an upstairs room which could be converted for conditioning as demand increased. Two bathrooms, each with a shower, had been added or remodeled, and sufficient light, heat and air-conditioning had been provided throughout. Off-street parking for a dozen cars was available, although the area was not well-lit. A small sign was painted near the door.

The property was zoned for 24-hour industrial use, so evening classes were no problem. The Watertown building code required no special regulations for indoor sport centers.

Equipment

"I am a very critical consumer; I pride myself on understanding my needs and only buying what I truly need," Debra remarked. Her search for weights illustrated her philosophy. Her first choice was "free weights" like barbells, dumbbells and weight benches, and weight-lifting systems like Nautilus and Universal, incorporating pulleys and counterweights. She explained.

I talked to a lot of people, salespeople included, until I had a clear idea of what equipment would be the most useful for the center. Nautilus equipment is good, but very expensive. Also, it is more of an individual thing, not adaptable for class use. On the other hand, free weights can be used simultaneously by an entire class. Free weights also allow you to isolate your muscles, one at a time, and to feel each one working—an excellent way to learn more about your body.

Once I decided on free weights, I decided to buy used equipment if I could. I looked in the want ads and saw what was available. Finally, I found a moonlighting ironworker who made barbells in his basement and specialized in custom orders.

Since it was early August when Debra began her search, she could not afford to wait the usual two months for delivery from conventional sources. Time pressure plus a price half of what she had seen elsewhere persuaded her to buy from the ironworker. For $850 she bought three sets of weights, three weight benches, half a dozen hand-dumbbells, assorted strap-on leg weights, and a stationary bicycle. She also bought a basketball stanchion on a movable base for $450. "It seemed to provide more flexibility than a stationary backboard in this small gym," she observed. In addition, Debra bought a volleyball net, and a selection of racquets, hockey sticks, and balls for soccer, basketball and volleyball.

Pricing

Debra's aim in pricing was to be moderate and affordable. She based her prices both on competitive programs at Ys and adult education centers (Exhibit 4) and on her operating costs, which she estimated at $27,000 for the first year. These, she said, included rent, utilities, staff salaries competitive with the going rate ($7-$10 per class/hour), and printing costs—both for promotional purposes and for the center's class schedules which were distributed before each session.

The first two sessions were each five weeks in length, to span the interval between the opening and the Christmas holidays. She thought two sessions, rather than one, were needed to accommodate expected growth after the first session. Having classes of no more than six customers and meeting twice a week was, she said, essential to maintain fitness and performance. This also required fewer participants to fill class spaces. A minimum of three participants was necessary to run a class. A "drop-in sports membership," entitling the holder to participate in scheduled recreational activities, cost $50/year. A "drop-in conditioning membership," giving unlimited access to conditioning

rooms, was priced at $100/year. This membership, although not required for participation, would provide a 10 percent discount on all classes and special programs.

Promotion

By September 1, Everywoman's Sport Center was one month away from opening. The core staff was hired, the building was leased and remodeling was under way. Types of programs had been decided upon, and the necessary equipment had been purchased. Now Debra turned to promotion.

She had already designed brochures and had them printed describing the philosophy and programs of the center. With the help of several friends she distributed them in highly visible spots throughout greater Boston: sports stores, grocery store, libraries, even on car windshields near a reservoir jogging track. She also mailed them to 100 people she knew might be interested, her core mailing list. She sent out a press release to two daily papers, the Boston Globe and the Boston Herald, as well as to local weeklies, the Phoenix and the Real Paper. Her aim was both to take advantage of free listings and to try to arrange for feature stories. To her delight, almost every paper showed an interest. Finally, she prepared an announcement and flier for the center's introductory open house on September 21, which she also distributed widely.

Operations

The first five-week session opened with 20 women enrolled in various classes and a running club, as tabulated in the enrollment history of Exhibit 5. The second fall session saw class enrollment rise to 47, and increasing interest in basketball, running and volleyball. The two winter sessions each included over 80 women in classes, and a floor-hockey group in addition to the other sports. To Debra's surprise, there was almost no interest in a fishing trip, a canoe trip, a rugby clinic, or a class for bad backs. Also, virtually no one had become a member. Debra could not account for the variations in demand for the center's programs, but she continued to test it out by offering new programs each session.

In the spring, enrollment began to level off, declining to a plateau of 55 for each of two sessions during the summer. The running and bicycling clinics continued to draw well, as did a massage program, and softball and soccer teams were formed. In addition, a Special Needs Sports Program was started—and enthusiastically received. Anticipating increased demand for the first session of fall 1980, Debra converted the upstairs space into a second conditioning room. She was surprised, however, when only 65 women enrolled in the first fall class. She commented:

I thought we would do better the second year. I want to figure out what we can do about it. We probably don't need "bring a friend" incentive membership programs, because people do that anyway, and I hate to commercialize something that happens naturally. During summer I began to give discounts for people who signed up for subsequent sessions to encourage continuity, though the return rate already seemed fairly good. An SBA consultant told me that a rate of 40 percent, 25 percent and 17 percent over three sessions was better than average, and mine was better than that.

The issue seems to be how to find ways, on a limited budget, to have more people learn about the center and stimulate a higher-than-average number to call for more information, then actually sign up. I've been told that a response of 1 to 2 percent on a mailing list is considered average. Mine was above that. So maybe the most important job is just

to reach more people.

Reflections after the First Year—October 1980

This has been a wonderful year for me. I have worked long and hard hours, but I enjoy it. I have found that it is exciting to live with uncertainty, and essentially to be able to make my own decisions. I may get discouraged but not frustrated. I always spend several hours at the center in the evenings, when there is the most activity, to be sure things are running smoothly and to be accessible to the women. I do the paperwork, telephoning and everything else during the day at my home/office.

The response from the women has been wonderful. Nearly all of them have discovered new sources of energy within themselves and are amazed at how much better they feel. One woman came to the center after a long illness, and another after an accident, and both have built up their strength again. I feel the center is making a real contribution.

I have been very careful about finances. I keep all my own books and do my own income statements. Then I give them to the accountant, who fills out the forms and sends them to the IRS. He is interested in the center, and we talk about my financial situation frequently. This tax year, 1980, I nearly broke even; the tuition revenues almost covered the operating expenses, excluding my salary. The cash flow has been adequate; I ask people to pay before the session, and if they cannot pay in full I ask for half now and half later. So far, I have only had two women who didn't pay—one owed me $35 and the other $40. I don't like to be taken advantage of, so I hired a collection agency just for the principle of the thing. Although I haven't yet been able to draw a salary, and have had to put small amounts of my own savings into the business every few months, I have always paid the bills promptly. I am compulsive about that. I'd call an aunt in Florida before I'd miss a payroll.

Assessing the promotion/publicity aspect is harder. I believe we've had good media coverage. The local dailies and weeklies have all carried our listings and done write-ups on us. I've been on radio and television half a dozen times, and I've lectured to schools and community groups. I wish I had time to do more of that. I am a very positive person. I talk with the expectation that people will be interested. I've also met with the SBA's ACE Counseling Service (Active Corps of Executives). They offered mainly encouragement, not much useful advice.

Looking Ahead

Clearly, there is a financing problem. Although I don't know what I would have done differently so far, I can see that something different has got to happen between now and June 1981. That will be two years of operation, and if I'm not more than breaking even by then, I'll want to know why.

Our need to increase enrollment and revenues can be approached from either end. The options for increasing revenues are, first, increasing tuition, second, encouraging individuals to take more classes per week, and, third, offering several special programs that are high enough in demand to pay their own way with a good profit. In the first instance, I have raised instructors' salaries, but I've kept class fees at $4/hour. I'm not anxious to increase tuition if I can avoid it. The second may be a possibility—we now offer a third "drop-in day" for free, and my sense is that three regular days may be too much. I am making progress on the third—but have a way to go. The Special Needs class, for instance, is well

received, and I have begun a post-part (following childbirth) class jointly with the Lamaze Institute. I wonder what else I should try.

One option for increasing enrollment might be to hire a development person to help me with expanding special programs and with looking for a corporate tie-in, a company that wants a fitness program available to its employees. In addition, such a person could study the present promotion efforts— the mailing list, media coverage—to make them more effective. If this person would pay for herself in time, I could put up money initially to pay the salary.

But a more basic question must be answered first. How much growth can I realistically expect at the center? My sense is that the health-and-fitness business may have peaked. I would like to know more about this market. If the number of competing programs that have arisen in just this past year is any indication, I would conclude that the market is mature. Tennis and racquetball centers are now offering classes in conditioning; so are certain companies and banks, for their employees. We do have something unique at the center, but we don't offer services that other programs provide like saunas and whirlpool baths. I don't think that demand is shrinking, but more programs are competing and the proportional market share for each is less.

I've even re-examined my original premise that the center should be only for women. I always thought that was such a positive thing. The center gives women an experience they can't get anywhere else. Some women may want a recreational opportunity that includes men; they want more of a social center. But I am determined that the center remain what I intended it to be and retain its unique woman/sports orientation in the increasingly crowded marketplace.

Even without knowing the long-range viability of the center, I have to plan for the next eight months—with regard both to programs and to additional financing. I have lots of ideas, and want to talk with as many people as pos- *sible in the near future. If the situation is one I can improve upon and make the business a success, I'll continue. If the circumstances are beyond my control, then I'll close the center and start some other business.*

EXHIBIT 1   Resume

DEBRA ALICE GLASSMAN

<u>EDUCATION</u>

<u>Master of Business Administration</u>, Northeastern University, June, 1978 Health Care Administration; G.P.A. 3.7; elected to Beta Gamma Sigma

<u>Master of Social Work</u>, Columbia University, June, 1969 Veteran's Administration Hospital Scholarship; major: Group Work

<u>Bachelor of Arts</u>, Cum laude, University of Wisconsin, June 1968

<u>PROFESSIONAL EXPERIENCE</u>

<u>MANAGEMENT-ORGANIZATION START-UPS</u>

Developed, directed and coordinated regional mental retardation services
<u>Director and Regional Coordinator</u>, Specialized Home Care
. Monitored and administered 1/4 million dollar budget
. Executed all contract negotiation and development
. Established all external service provision systems with regional staff
. Administered recruitment, public relations and training programs
. Developed and implemented all policies, procedures and operations
. Initiated an advisory board
. Formulated all agency policies as top management team member

Created and administered a counseling department and the overall planning and organization structure of a new family planning clinic
<u>Director of Counseling</u>
. Developed and implemented all counseling policies and procedures
. Recruited, trained and supervised staff of nurses and counselors
. Formulated company goals and policies as executive team member
. Served as management liaison with Union 1199

Established and implemented strategies, goals and policies of a new agency, including selection of the physical plant

EXHIBIT 1 Resume (concluded)

Created, coordinated and administered a new crisis intervention center
> Director of Crisis Intervention Center
> . Initiated and administered all planning and daily operations
> . Recruited and supervised all staff

Developed, coordinated and administered a new Department of Youth Services; planned and organized its expansion to a new and larger community center
> Director of Youth Services
> . Planned and developed all department goals, systems and operations
> . Supervised and coordinated all departmental programs and staff

Directed and coordinated all operations of a day camp
> Director of Day Camp
> . Evaluated and selected all campers
> . Hired and supervised all staff
> . Monitored all daily operations

EMPLOYMENT

> Cambridge Family & Children's Service, Cambridge, MA., 1978-1979
> Charles Circle Clinic, Boston, MA., 1973-1975
> Baycrest Geriatric Center, Toronto, Canada, 1971-1973
> Addiction Research Foundation, Toronto, Canada, 1969-1971
> Mid-Westchester YM-YWCA, Scarsdale, N.Y., 1968-1969

EXHIBIT 2 Excerpts from Debra's Business Plan

Debra's business plan was a collection of facts, figures and analyses in her own hand-writing, which she kept in a green folder. Background information included notes from her venture classes, xerox copies of articles documenting the growth of interest in recreational activities, and a brochure about small business and borrowing money. The following pages of the plan are reproduced (typed verbatim from Debra's notes):

A.   Description of Business

Sports education and training center for women of all abilities who have no structured sports programs or courses available to them. To teach and train the novice, the recreational person, and the professional athlete.

A need for this service exists due to:

1)   Increased cultural emphasis on physical fitness and exercise for well-being and longevity.

2)   Increasing number of women participating in professional sports

3)   Legislation guaranteeing women equal opportunity to participate in organized sports

4)   More leisure time

5)   More working women, accustomed to spending their earnings on themselves

6)   Changing lifestyles

7)   Inflation and recession—drop elegance and luxuries and opt for recreation

8)   Self-help emphasis coincides with women's movement

EXHIBIT 2 (continued)

B.   Market Area

	Income Over $9,000	Population by Age Group 25 - 65+	25 - 34	25 - 54
Arlington		18,123	3,356	9,924
	73%	13,230	2,450	7,244
Belmont		10,215	1,609	5,137
	75%	7,661	1,207	3,852
Boston (Central, Back Bay, Fenway, Allston, Brighton)	47%	91,650 43,076	21,080 23% 9,908	56,823 62% 26,706
Brookline		22,459	4,014	10,509
	75%	16,760	1,938	7,672
Cambridge		29,994	8,323	17,218
	56%	16,797	4,660	9,642
Lexington		9,362		6,400
	87%	8,145	1,480	5,568
Lincoln		1,937	508	2,505
	80%	1,550	406	1,204
Medford		20,449	3,476	11,283
	66%	13,496	2,294	7,446
Needham		9,012	1,592	5,699
	84%	7,570	1,337	4,787
Newton		29,164	5,061	16,756
	80	23,312	4,048	13,404
Somerville		27,314	5,608	15,425
	55%	15,022	3,084	8,484
Waltham		18,261	3,842	10,940
	68%	12,417	2,612	7,440

EXHIBIT 2   (continued)

Watertown				
		13,032	2,880	7,549
	67%	8,731	1,930	5,058
Wellesley				
		8,485	1,318	4,971
	87%	7,382	1,146	4,324
Weston				
		2,982	467	2,032
	89%	2,654	416	1,808
Winchester				
		6,767	1,263	4,240
	84%	5,684	1,060	3,562

Map of Communities Surrounding Watertown

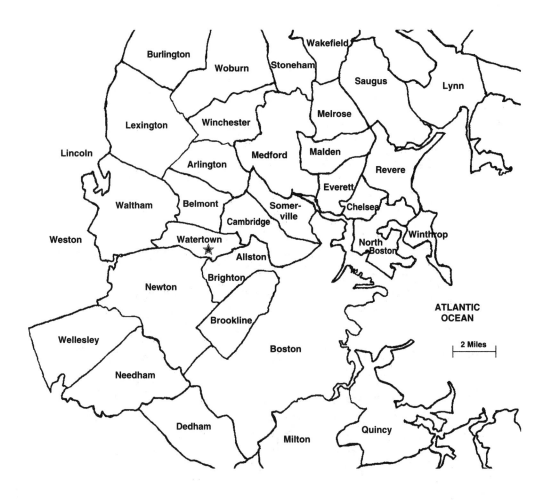

EXHIBIT 2 (continued)

C. Assessment of Competition

    Other adult education programs

    Affiliations with colleges (many scattered around the region)

    Boston Center for Adult Education (4.3 miles away)

    Cambridge Center for Adult Education (2 miles away)

    Boston YMCA (3.9 miles away)

    Cambridge YMCA (2.4 miles away)

    Joy of Movement Center - Boston (4.2 miles away)

    Joy of Movement Center - Cambridge (2.6 miles away)

    Increase in comprehensive sports programs for students enrolled in schools and colleges

    Little or no competition in the suburbs; mostly in Cambridge and Boston

D. Question of Profitability

    Problem: Income of women less than that of men, possibly they can't afford to take classes in a recession.

    Market Projections
    (Five weeks x $40)

1st	5 courses	50 people	$2000
2nd	5 courses	75 people	$3000
3rd	7 courses	100 people	$4000
4th	8 courses	125 people	$5000
			$14,000

<u>Expenses by Quarter</u>

<u>1st</u>	rent: $1800	brochures: $2000	salaries: $1000	total: $4800
<u>2nd</u>	rent: $1800	brochures: $2000	salaries: $1000	total: $4800
<u>3rd</u>	rent: $1800	brochures: $1000	salaries: $1400	total: $4200
<u>4th</u>	rent: $1800	brochures: $1000	salaries: $1600	total: $4400

EXHIBIT 2 (continued)

E. Financial Records
Cash Receipts

	1979 Aug.	Sept.	Oct.	Nov.	Dec.	1980 Jan.	Feb.	Mar.	Apr.	May	Jun.	Jul.	Aug.	Sept.	Oct.
Bank Deposits	5,200	0	6,256	12,335	1,780	3,242	4,167	1,369	5,060	2,309	3,058	1,004	3,733	4,534	1,943
Notes (Debra)	5,000														
Classes			575	10,000	1,654				800	1,400	800		1,000		
Drop-in Sports			20	1,945		3,141	3,894	1,089	3,995	909	2,258	1,004	2,733	3,634	1,943
Drop-in					20	16	20								
Conditioning			54			24	30	180							
Spl. Programs			50		12										
Fitness Lab			181	166	126	34	218	210	55						
T-Shirts						10	15	20	30						
Gift Certif.						25									
Capital Stock															
1/2 Paid-In		200		500											
Loan		5,000													
Conditioning Memberships					100		101	100							
Sports Memberships Teams													900		

EXHIBIT 2 (concluded)

Cash Disbursements

	1979 Aug	Sept	Oct	Nov	Dec	1980 Jan	Feb	Mar	Apr	May	Jun	Jul	Aug	Sept	Oct
Ads & PR	175	706	552	184	1,033	798	697	502	414	612	115	434	310	501	764
Instrs Fees			376	688	760	473	1,240	627	1,520	370	1,520	1,000	558	995	811
Ofc. Supplies		46	21	13	33	13	20						37	20	
Equipment		1,696	239	239	91	41								599	
Leasehold Imp.		850	37	105	80	21	10		15				48		150
Equipt, Sppl.			33	186		576	11	157					55	108	
Fitness Lab		115				26	164	30	41	44	102	61	55		38
Child Care						4									
Rent		725	725	725	725	725	725	725	725	725	725	725	725	725	725
Heat		104			135	96	266	271	122	103	150	13	93	22	106
Refund						72	84		165				59		
Rug Cleaning		152													
Tel		45	133	100	100	21	42	42	42	45	58	55	41	56	52
Ans. Serv.						15	43	49	69	58	39	41	67	43	56
Bank Charge		-6	-2	-2	-3	-5	-48	-5		-98	-5	-4		-8	-15
Loan Payback			2,400		5,000										
Insurance							73		24			73		15	
Membership					50										
Reimbursements					1,598										
Telephone					58										
Presents					81										
Reimbursement					1,714										
Incorporation		331				17		17							
Massage										72					
Loan Repayment									800						
Taxes								228							
Certificate						7			35	10					
Fitness Book															
Admin Pay								8		16	34	72		75	
Misc					5	37	25		25	5	40				
Accounting					85		400								
Teams														160	160
Prizes														75	
Total	175	4,764	4,514	2,238	11,545	2,933	3,756	2,621	4,027	1,962	2,778	2,470	2,048	3,386	2,847

EXHIBIT 3 Excerpts from Flyer

EVERYWOMAN'S SPORT CENTER, INC.
120 Elm Street
Watertown, MA 02172
926-3008

FALL SESSION II:
November 1 - December 19, 1980

SCHEDULED COURSES

Unless otherwise indicated, all classes meet for one hour, twice weekly, for six weeks.

Comprehensive Conditioning
Cardiovascular & muscle strength conditioning & flexibility for all fitness levels

	Day	**Eve**
Mon & Wed	7, 8, 9, 10	5, 5:30, 6, 6:30
	11, 12, 13	7, 7:30, 8
Tues & Thurs		4, 5, 5:30, 6,
		6:30, 7, 7:30
Fri (3rd day)		5:30, 6:30
Sat (3rd day)	9, 10, 11	

Classes are limited to 6 people
Fee: $48 (12 classes)

Aerobic Conditioning
Choreographed movements to music

	Day	**Eve**
Mon & Wed	7, 8, 9,	6, 7
	10, 11, 12,	5:30, 6:30*
		7:30

*A Fast-paced class
Fee: $48 (12 classes)

Weight Training
For highly motivated women pursuing their own fitness program who want to concentrate
on strength building
Mon & Wed 8 p.m.
Fee: $48 (12 classes)

EXHIBIT 3 (continued)

Start Anew After Childbirth

Registered Nurse-Childbirth Educators of Lamaze Childbirth Education & Physical Education Specialists of Everywoman's Sport Center will help you get back into shape-physically and emotionally-through exercise & discussion of post-partum issues.
Tues & Thurs 9:30-11:30; Fee: $60. Tues   9:30-11:30; Fee: $30. Children of all ages are welcome.

Conditioning for Back Problems
Tues & Thurs   7:30;   Fee: $48

DROP IN CONDITIONING

Use of the Conditioning Room:
        Tuesday   8-9:30 p.m.
        Thurs   8-9:30 p.m.
        Sat   9-11 a.m.
        Fee: $3/visit

PHYSICAL FITNESS LAB

Find out all about your level of physical fitness. Complete testing by appointment: Heart Rate, Blood Pressure, Pulmonary function, Strength, Flexibility, Body Composition, Hemoglobin. Fee: $35 for the complete test

SPECIAL NEEDS

Sports activities & conditioning for the developmentally disabled Sunday, 7-9 p.m. Can we offer one for your group?

DROP-IN SPORTS

Volleyball-Tuesday, 8:30-9:30 p.m., no advance sign-up needed; Fee: $2

SPORTS TEAMS

Our sports teams are going strong! Basketball-4 teams forming for scheduled competitive games. Soccer-Indoor & outdoor scheduled games for Fall and Winter. Are you interested in another team?

RUNNING CLUB

Join us! Progress charts, mapped routes, reading material, staff consultation, meetings-and more! Mon, Tues, Wed, Thurs 5-8 p.m. Fee: $50/year

SPECIAL EVENTS

EVERYWOMAN'S SPORT CENTER FIRST ANNIVERSARY PARTY Saturday, Nov. 8, 7:30 p.m. All welcome. Come celebrate our first year with us! Refreshments, Demonstrations and Slide Show

EXHIBIT 3 (concluded)

MASSAGE CLINIC

Through the giving & receiving of massage, try out the techniques & learn how it can release muscular tension, improve circulation, prevent injuries & strains, increase muscle tone & flexibility & restore the energy balance in your body. <u>Saturday, Dec. 6 & 13</u>, 9-12; Fee: $30 Fill out the Registration Form.

EVERYWOMAN'S SPORT CENTER REGISTRATION FORM

Name_____ Year of Birth_____

Address_____ City_____ Zip_____

Telephone(day)_____ (eve)_____

Courses-1st choice_____ Day & Time_____ Fee_____

  2nd choice_____ Day & Time_____ Fee_____

Membership/Clinics/Trips/Events_____ Fee_____

Were you looking for an activity/time that wasn't listed?_____

It is the responsibility of the participant to make certain that she is medically fit to enroll in any of the courses or activities offered by Everywoman's Sport Center, Inc. The participant hereby releases the Center, its agents, staff and independent contractors of all liability for any injury she may sustain while on the premises or using any of the facilities of the Center or in connection with any programs or activities of the Center at any other locations.

Date_____Signature_____

EXHIBIT 4   Competitor Information

In February 1981, the rates for exercise classes at certain competitive facilities were:

Joy of Movement Center (Cambridge)
    10 weeks - $59
    (Classes meet once a week for 1 hour; four free make-up classes are included.)

YMCA (Cambridge)
    10-week membership -$40
    (A membership includes unlimited attendance at exercise classes that meet three times a day, five days a week, and unlimited use of all other facilities, including swimming pool and handball court.)

 Women's World Health Spa (Several)
    6 weeks - $25. Introductory membership
    (Unlimited attendance at 30-minute classes, given every hour 9am-9pm on weekdays at 9am-2pm Saturdays. Also, sauna and whirlpool.)

Light n' Lively (Wellesley)
    6 weeks - $35. Introductory membership
    (Unlimited attendance at 45-minute classes, 9am-7pm five days a week and 9am-3pm Saturdays. sauna and whirlpool.)

EXHIBIT 5   Enrollment at the Center

Class	Number Enrolled
Fall I	20
Fall II	47
Winter I	85
Spring I	75
Spring II	65
Summer I	55
Summer II	55
Fall III	65

Case 13

Jude Goldman and Jan Whitted

A main concern of Jan Whitted and Jude Goldman in May 1977 was how to finance purchase of a $12,000 printing press and related equipment for turning their hobby of letterpress printing into a commercial business venture. Although the two had known each other for less than a year, they had set up shop near the Cambridge Common a few months earlier to print high-quality brochures, flyers and pamphlets for community groups, schools and business customers.

Now they wanted to expand from letterpress, a somewhat slow and artistic process, to the faster and more modern process of offset printing. Description of the process appears in Exhibit 1. Without the new press, they explained, their business would remain "pretty much a hobby" because letterpress was a much more time consuming production process than offset lithography, which had superseded letterpress for commercial printing in the early 1900s.

They had used up their savings to start the venture six months earlier and had also "tapped" their friends for loans to purchase chemicals and supplies. To finance a move into offset lithography, Jan said they were considering several financing options. Local banks were one possible source, though the first bank they had visited rejected their request for a loan. Another option was the Massachusetts Feminist Credit Union (MFCU), which supported feminist and political causes in the Boston area.

A third possibility was a woman they had recently met who appeared to be very interested in the business. Jude said the woman worked as a management consult-

ant and had told the two she was looking for a way to shelter some income from taxes. Working out a lease arrangement for the press might, she told them, be a way she could gain a tax deduction and help their venture at the same time.

Meanwhile, Jan and Jude said, they had to allocate their time to a number of other tasks. Securing credit, considering how to go about finding employees as the business grew, projecting financial statements, and serving their present customers all required immediate attention. Jude summed up the situation:

> We've already been to a trade show, and we know the type of press we want. It's $9,500 new, and from talking with others in business, we understand it's easier to finance a new press than an old one. We know the market is there for the type of printing we want to do. It's just a matter of getting the equipment and letting the people know we can take on the work.

The Partners

Jude Goldman graduated from Emerson College in 1975 with a B.A. in English literature. Because job prospects were "slim" at the time, she decided to enroll at Boston Technical High School to learn offset printing. Her motivation, she said, was to find a trade that would pay reasonably well, be in a field that was non-traditional for women, and bear some relationship to English. As she put it, "printing was closer than plumbing."

During school she also worked in a commercial printing plant and, on a volunteer basis, edited an "appropriate technology" magazine. She also developed an interest in the somewhat antique art of letterpress printing and considered setting up a workshop for others interested in letterpress. She recalled meeting Jan Whitted in August of 1976 while at the house of a local typesetter.

> *I was visiting this guy who did the typesetting for the magazine I edited. I asked him if he knew of anyone interested in developing a letterpress shop, and he said, "Yes, I just met somebody like that. She's downstairs."*

Jan picked up the story from there:

> *I was down in the basement picking through his trash for old bits of discarded type. I had developed a hobby of collecting type and letterpress cuts. Jude came downstairs, we started talking, and inside of a month we had set up a shop together.*

Jan Whitted had attended two Boston area schools, Wheaton College and Suffolk University, where she majored in English. During the late 1960s she was active in the anti-war movement, and in 1971, she co-founded a collective printing shop in Cambridge where she operated a press. She explained the development of her interest in letterpress over the ensuing five years.

> *When I first got into offset, I saw other people setting type by hand, figured I would never have patience for such slow work, even though it produced attractive prints, and I simply dismissed it. Later, after having a child, I spent some time in San Francisco with a friend who ran a letterpress shop, and it captured my interest. In 1975, I returned to the Boston area and worked at printing jobs with the idea that I would*

> *organize a workshop for letterpress. When Jude and I met, setting up shop seemed like the natural thing to do.*

Setting Up Shop

After some months of "knocking on doors" to locate suitable space and find prospective letterpress customers, Jan and Jude settled on 250 square feet available near the Cambridge, Massachusetts Common in January of 1977. They used part of $2,500 borrowed from friends to pay the first and last months' rent, at $125 per month, and to obtain the ink and other supplies needed to start printing. Jude sold her 1969 Ford Fairlane for $125 and Jan contributed an equal amount by keeping her son out of daycare for a month. The resulting $250 was enough for Jude to purchase some unused equipment from the printing plant where she had recently been employed as an offset press operator.

Both quit their jobs to pursue their new venture, "Tramp Printers," full time. Jan explained how they chose the name for their business:

> *We called ourselves Tramp Printers based on the old tradition of printers being itinerants and doing work whenever they could. We felt very much like that because we had gone around using other people's equipment for letterpress work before we found our location.*

People who came in for letterpress work to be done occasionally asked if either Jan or Jude knew of printers that did short runs in offset. The two would refer these customers to others in the business, but felt uncomfortable that potential sales were walking back out their door. The two also said there were few in the industry who performed offset work with the same high quality they strove for themselves in letterpress.

Jude explained that a "short run" in the printing industry was typically a job under 15,000 copies. Sometimes the total was as high as 100,000 copies. Since money was made on each copy printed, most printers sought out high-volume business to recoup costs of setup and maximize profits.

Sensing a potential gap in the market, the two began to discuss possibilities of specializing in high-quality offset work, emphasizing short runs other printers tried to avoid. The work would probably involve largely production of multi-color flyers, brochures and booklets. Emphasis on high quality might help avoid the extreme price competitiveness Jude said was common among printing shops in the Boston area. The Yellow Pages for the greater Boston area listed nearly 700 firms under the heading *Printers*. These included firms specializing in graphics as well as photocopying establishments. Quality, speed of service and price were the most frequent items mentioned in display ads for a company.

To learn more about offset presses, the two attended a printing trade show in Boston the same month they opened their shop in Cambridge. They went from booth to booth, talking with sales representatives about the equipment on display. Apparently, one of the sales representatives didn't take the two women discussing printing presses too seriously, Jude said.

We were looking at this press and told the guy standing there that we were going to buy such a machine. It had a price tag of $10,000 and we were asking him some questions about how it worked. The guy just laughed at us and walked away. So, we decided we were certainly not going to buy the press from him. Fortunately, we weren't interested in that particular brand anyway.

Even though the partners had decided on the type of press they wanted to purchase after attending the trade show, they expected it would be several months before they were ready to do so. They estimated that when the offset press was installed, break-even would be around $4,000 per month in revenues. This would include $2,250 in fixed costs. Rent would be at least $300 per month since more space would be needed to install the press and related equipment. Utilities, insurance, vehicle expense for making deliveries and calling on accounts, and a retainer for legal advice were also placed in their fixed costs estimate. Hiring a person to answer the phone and do bookkeeping for 30 hours a week was estimated at $550 per month.

Costs of goods sold included paper stock, which they estimated at 25 percent of projected monthly revenues, whether used for letterpress or offset work. Ink and production supplies, they estimated at 20 percent of paper costs; and sub-contracting for negatives and bindery work, they expected would cost about the same amount as ink and supplies. Other charges, such as advertising, postage, and servicing the machine, Jan and Jude estimated at 25 percent of paper costs. Another $100 they said should be set aside for interest expense on any loans or financial arrangements made to purchase equipment. Jan and Jude weren't sure whether this should be considered a fixed charge or be placed with the $250 per month payment expense for press equipment in cost of goods sold.

The two had approached suppliers about possibilities of obtaining trade credit on paper and other supplies. Jude commented on their experiences to date:

Suppliers regularly tell us the terms will have to be either prepayment or C.O.D. by certified check. When they say that, our response has been, "That's ridiculous! Look at the beautiful work we do." We walk right into their offices and tell them that what they are requiring is completely stupid. The funny thing is that sometimes their response has been to go ahead and give us credit after all.

Tramp Printers thus far had no employees, and could not afford salaries for the owners. Jan said that after a new offset press was installed they would like to find someone to help with office work. She and Jude also indicated they were considering use of apprentices, not only to help with the work, but to provide training for women in a traditionally male-dominated field. A concern they expressed when discussing personnel was that many of their customers regarded the business as a collective. Jude commented that because of her activist background and Jan's previous experience with a collective printing shop, people sometimes assumed their business was as much concerned with social causes as with making profit. Both said that this could work to their advantage in bringing in sympathetic customers. However, they added that this image might also pose problems when they attempted to hire people or bring them in for training.

Initial Sales

Initial clientele came from personal contacts or referrals by others in the printing business. To date, they had spent no money on advertising, and the two weren't sure what effect it would have on their business if they did. However, shortly after opening, Jan and Jude did attempt to promote their venture to local media. Jude recalled that they called a weekly newspaper, the *Boston Phoenix*, then a daily, the *Boston Globe*, and finally a local television station. To each she said that they were "missing a great story on the printing busi-

ness." As a result all three either did stories on the venture or said they planned to do so in the near future.

In the first four months of 1977, Jan and Jude worked on 31 jobs of varying sizes as listed in Exhibit 2. Each month, the dollar volume grew, with the total for the four months at $1,178.17. Jobs included preparation of brochures, business cards, programs, invitations, and advertising designs. The production was done on fixed assets valued at $1,586.83, as tabulated in Exhibit 3.

By requesting that customers pay cash upon delivery or within 30 days, they had been able to buy supplies and pay fixed overhead charges as they came due. Pricing was based on their stated belief that people would pay for high quality and not worry so much if the quote wasn't the "cheapest around." Jude explained that they attempted to price a job based on all the work that would be required. Another shop might initially leave off of the estimate some items that could be added to raise quality, such as adding a varnish. But Tramp Printers would include such items in the estimate from the beginning. Their target margin in bidding a job, Jan said, was "a typical figure for the industry, 20-percent profit before taxes."

Searching for Financing

Tramp Printers was initially capitalized at $2,750. Jan and Jude indicated that to be able to do offset work, an additional $12,000 would be required in equipment and supplies. Jan would then run the offset press while Jude handled letterpress work and sought additional accounts. To test their prospects for a bank loan, the two took a listing of their recent accounts and estimates for equipment needs to a loan officer at a nearby bank in Cambridge. Jude recalled their first dealings with a banker:

We went to see a loan officer at the

First State Bank of Cambridge.* We showed him the information we had and told him what great business prospects we were. Unfortunately for us, the numbers and the letters of intent weren't enough. He said we had no track record or assets to base a loan on, and that he would have to turn us down. But what really struck me was how apologetic he was about the whole thing. He said, "We make loans to all kinds of people: women, Chinese, you name it." He made a point of telling us the bank had turned down Dr. Land when he was starting Polaroid. He seemed almost proud of that fact.

Although they had been rejected by a bank, the two commented that there were plenty of other institutions in the area to approach for loans. One source they mentioned was the Massachusetts Feminist Credit Union (MFCU). Since Tramp Printers was a 100 percent female-owned partnership, Jude said the MFCU would probably be predisposed to support the company. She added that if the organization did show interest, she and Jan would work to complete a loan proposal. In the past, MFCU had lent small amounts, generally under $5,000, to women or community groups involved with social causes supportive of minority and feminist concerns. To Jude's knowledge, the credit union had never before granted a business loan, just support for non-profit activities.

A third potential source of funding was a recent acquaintance whom they discovered was employed as a management consultant by a prestigious Cambridge-based firm. The woman expressed enthusiasm about the venture, according to Jude, and said that she would be willing to help the two prepare a business plan for the loan request.

After the two told her about their busi-

ness and plans to purchase a press, the consultant had proposed a deal. She would purchase the press under her name for the full $9,500, taking out a personal loan for $7,500. Jan and Jude would contribute $2,000 for the down payment. The woman would then amortize the press over five years on a straight line basis, using the depreciation to reduce her tax obligations. She would also take a 10 percent investment tax credit which was allowable in the first year because the machinery would be devoted to a business enterprise which qualified under provisions of the current tax legislation.

Repayment of the $7,500 would be made over the five-year book life of the equipment. The woman would receive 5 percent of the printing company's gross margin, computed by subtracting cost of goods sold from revenues. Thus, payments would be subject to proceeds from operations, and not act as a predetermined dollar amount, as would be the case for principal and interest payments on a loan. Jan and Jude's lawyer saw nothing wrong with this approach. He said it was perfectly legal, and simply a form of a lease arrangement. Beyond the $2,000 down payment, Jan and Jude figured they would also need cash for some other equipment, as listed in Exhibit 4.

A fourth possible source of funding was the Small Business Administration (SBA). Jan pointed out that with the current emphasis placed by government on affirmative action and encouragement of minority and women owned businesses, they might stand a good chance of getting help. However, they also had been told by some suppliers and customers that obtaining such help required a great deal of paperwork plus total financial commitment in the form of personal guarantees, and could take many weeks for processing. Moreover, they were not sure how they

---

* Disguised name.

should balance ownership and income fairly if it turned out that through the guarantee one of them would be putting a greater amount of personal resources at risk than the other.

Moving Ahead with the Venture

Jude and Jan thought they should attempt financing for the offset equipment as soon as possible. While their current work in letterpress was paying immediate bills, it didn't allow sufficient volume to make the venture noticeably profitable or afford them salaries. They wanted the business to grow and provide them incomes. They said that, although they didn't regard the venture as a social experiment, part of their goal was to break down some of the traditional barriers women faced in learning skills and succeeding as entrepreneurs.

Jude remarked that friends in the printing industry had been very supportive over the past six months. The two were confident that a market was "out there" for the type of service they wanted to provide. Jan summed up their shared enthusiasm about the business:

Jude and I share a common personality trait. There is no doubt in our minds that the two of us can succeed in business. There are a lot of little things we must pay attention to in the coming months, but those we can probably work out on our own. What we need help on is getting money to buy a press.

Our friend has offered us a lease arrangement and maybe that's the way to go. But we want to make sure that we set things up the right way. This is a critical stage for us.

EXHIBIT 1   Printing: Letter Press vs. Offset Lithography, 1977

Letterpress is regarded as an artistic craft, preferred by persons desiring high-quality printing for artistic as well as commercial purposes. A desired type is chosen and hand set in a case frame for inking and printing. Ink is applied to the type and the paper is pressed against it to form the finished product.

Offset Lithography begins by making a photo of the page with a graphics camera, which is different from the regular camera. It doesn't see continuous tone, only black and white. The camera produces what is known as a line negative. The part of the negative which has the image area showing is clear acetate, and the remainder is black film. Shades are made with a second negative called a "half tone" which forms images with tiny dots to indicate shadings. The line negative and half tone must then be carefully overlaid to combine their effects.

If the object to be printed is written matter not "camera ready," a subcontract to lay out the copy as desired is given to a computerized phototypesetting firm. The print, its sizing and spacing, is then put on film by the typesetter, with the finished typeset film then ready for the offset process.

The film is then blocked out to desired size and positioned on a flat metal sheet that will fit on the press, with the emulsion side of the negative facing the emulsion side of the sheet. Stray pieces of dirt and dust which may have caused spots in the film to appear as clear acetate are opaqued with a paint solution.

The negative, and through it the sheet, are exposed to high-intensity light for approximately one and a half minutes, after which the negative is removed from the metal plate. Another chemical solution is then applied, this time to the metal plate which becomes a "positive" for printing. The desired image on the positive is reversed, much like an image viewed in a mirror, is reversed. Where the light has been able to pass through the clear acetate, a pink or green image appears on the metal plate, with the remainder still the original metal color.

The sheet is then put onto the cylinder of the press. The image that has remained on the plate will accept ink and the rest will accept water. Since the two liquids will not mix, ink sticks to the image and the rest remains clear. Paper is then fed through the press from one end to the other, pressing past the ink image to be printed as originally photographed. The process is called offset because the actual printing on paper is done indirectly from the metal plate. Lithography is a term for printing using an ink and water-based system.

EXHIBIT 2   Listing of Jobs in First Months of 1977

Month	No. of Jobs	Job Type	Revenue
January	2	Brochures	$72.72
	Total 2		$72.72
February	6	Ad & Proof Designs	31.20
	3	Menu	18.60
	1	Invitation	42.00
	Total 10		$91.80
March	1	Ad & Proof Designs	8.00
	1	Letterhead	26.45
	2	Cards	55.00
	1	Concert Program	114.30
	1	Invitation	47.00
	1	Brochure	19.70
	Total 7		$270.45
April	2	Brochures	73.16
	2	Envelopes	57.84
	1	Models "headsheet"	366.00
	2	Letterheads	81.66
	3	Cards	44.70
	1	Invitation	28.45
	Total 11		$651.81

EXHIBIT 3   Description of Physical Assets, May 1977

Assets Item	Amount Paid
Circa 1890 Chandler & Price 8 x 12 press	$250.00
Circa 1920 Chandler & Price 12 x 18 press	309.75
24 cases of type, representing over 200 fonts and 12 typefaces	545.50
60 antique printer ornaments & misc. borders	100.00
Imposing stone, galley rack and misc. printers supplies	376.63
TOTAL	$1,581.88

EXHIBIT 4   Intended Purchases of Equipment*

PURPOSE OF LOAN:

$2,000	Down payment on new ATF Chief 17
500	Plateburner
700	Cutter
500	Construction of light table and new wall for added press space
250	Miscellaneous chemicals and offset supplies
$3,950	

* Assumes remaining $7,500 for the offset press financed through other means.

Andrew Hammoude

We are four guys who are very competent technically. But none of us has any management experience. We have a prototype product and about $10,000 left from an original capitalization of $40,000. So where do we go from here?

Dr. Andrew Hammoude had prepared a draft business plan, which appears as Exhibit 1. As he had just said, and comments he had written in the draft of the plan itself indicated, there were still many important questions unanswered.

Background

He and his associates had developed a circuit board and accompanying software for IBM AT computers, which would enable them to perform "image processing." This product had sprung from a masters thesis project in electrical engineering by one of the founders, Alan Steiner. The project, suggested by Alan's supervising professor, was to design an imaging board. Alan finished the device and thought it could be marketed. Two colleagues, Tom Alexander and Jerry Stone, with whom he had worked in the University of Washington's Imaging Processing Lab, agreed. They believed the technology was the best available. Jerry Stone recalled:

We came into contact with a large number of different image processors with different capabilities, and so on. We had some applications to develop, such as things in pathology and radiology. So we looked at the available equipment, but it just wouldn't do the job.

Tom's board was a response to that. We set out to build a better workstation.

In January 1986 they began working in their spare time to develop "a state-of-the-art PC-based imaging system." Another colleague in electrical engineering, Andrew Hammoude, recalled becoming interested in the project and being invited to join.

I thought it over very carefully, because as the only full-time person in the company, I would be way out on a limb. When I listed the pros and cons on paper, a major factor for me was that I believed the technology was the best available.

Hammoude joined the venture in June 1988. Alan Steiner commented:

When we first started the company, there was a lot of work being done in radiology for PC-based imaging. Radiologists spend millions on imaging systems from GE and Phillips. Every time they need another console for their MRI machine, it's another $150,000. That console they're buying is just an archaic display with knobs and switches on it.

The Product

IMAGEsystems' product consisted basically of two parts, a circuit board for installation in I.B.M. personal computers and software to go with it, enabling a user to handle, display, and manipulate pictorial data, such as a chest X-ray or a Nuclear

Magnetic Resonance (NMR) image. Dr. Hammoude observed:

We haven't yet beta tested it. We haven't given it to a potential customer and said, "Here, use it." When they do, they will find it is really something new.

Many people are familiar with pictures generated on a computer screen, but these are referred to as "graphics" not "imaging," which our product makes possible. Graphics refers to synthesis, such as renderings artists make on televisions, like in the movie "Star Wars." With imaging the pictures originate in some other form external to the computer, in a camera perhaps. The computer may be fed image data from sensors, such as an X-ray machine, satellite signals, electron microscopic output, or astronomical telescope output. We do things like enhancing the display, transmitting it over phone lines, storing it, showing it on the screen in new ways, and performing processing functions to do such things as increasing the contrast. We might, for example, be able to improve poor quality in a photographic negative.

Normally with such things as a chest X-ray, for instance, you expose the film and then stick it up in a light box to analyze it with the human optical system, eyes. A couple of doctors might look at it, be concerned about some features of it, and so forth. The same is true with CAT scans and nuclear magnetic imaging. They can, I believe, do some computer analysis on such things, but it probably requires a mainframe at present.

What our system will let you do is apply computers to these images. Then they can be displayed on a TV screen without the actual physical records, which are often a great burden in terms of storage and retrieval. To compare the

X-rays of a given patient at two periods six months apart is a lot of trouble. Sometimes the records get lost.

Radiologists get their data either by a film sent to them by courier or by going down to the radiology lab directly. There is at present no way for them to pull an image up on a PC. Our system opens the possibility of storing the records in a remote archival setting and retrieving any of them over a phone line in a few seconds. The doctor need only dial up. That is a market we see.

We know one physician who has said it would be ideal. But we would have to do development work to perfect the system before he could start using it. We would like to develop a user system that is simple and menu-driven. We want to get it to the point where users don't have to develop code but can simply modify an ASCII file to the way they like to use the system. But that takes a great deal of work, not only developing the software, but also writing the manuals to go with it—not to mention debugging, producing, marketing and all the rest.

You may sometimes have a mix of both graphics and imaging combined. In an advertisement, for instance, there may be a photograph of a model, which is imaging, together with an artist-generated logo, which is graphics. When you have those two things together you may be able to use our product. But when the goal is graphics alone, the capabilities of our product are very limited.

Apollo and Sun, which are workstation manufacturers, can't use our product. Other third-party suppliers provide units for them. Sun and Apollo have more powerful computers than the PC AT, which is the only computer that our product runs on. If our company is successful, of course, we'll bring out a Sun line, a Macintosh line, and so forth.

The greatest advantage of our product is programmability. There are similar products available in the market, but only one is programmable. A second advantage of our system is the software. What we've written is, we think, much more advanced, sophisticated and broad-ranging than anything else available. For display capability and moving images around, it makes the system more user-friendly and appealing for people in graphic arts, publishing and printing, and medical diagnoses, for instance. Some other features of our system are a bit more arcane. We include a system for networking, to allow the software to interact in a computer network.

As regards price, I have some ideas. I know the minimum because I know what it costs to make the board. I know the maximum because I know what our competitors charge. But between those extremes I don't know where we ought to be. A major feature could be that we do things at low cost. Economies of scale could let us bring the cost of a system down to $5,000.

There are some markets where our advantages mean nothing. In machine vision, it isn't very interesting that we have a nice display capability. There are several areas, such as medical imaging, publishing and printing, graphic arts, and scientific research and development applications that constitute broad markets we might go after. But we have not defined a small segment of a market where the features of our product are dramatically important.

The total market for machine vision and remote sensing is very fragmented. Part of the reason for this is that images are so different. When you're formatting numerical data or words, numbers are numbers, text is text; even if you want to reformat the document in

French or Spanish, it's about the same. But the nature of images is different. The NMR image is quite different in nature from an ultrasound image and from a 35mm slide in both resolution and color. It's different in the very data content itself.

We seem to be faced with a market where there is no typical case. Every single end user seems to be involved with something a bit different. I was speaking to somebody in metallurgy, and what he was doing was so specific as to be completely unique. What the metallurgist needs is a value-added retailer (VAR) who can take our board and our basic display software tools and add specific software to solve his particular application.

That sort of market, if I see it right, is completely immature. It's true that boards to run on the PC have existed for some time, but there has not been the great array of problems wanting VAR solutions, requiring a programmable board like ours. There is no main player in that market.

Competition

We've got about five competitors out there who are producing PC-based imaging systems comparable to ours. Four of those we can pretty much write off in the sense that their capabilities don't overlap with ours. They run at higher speed but have a lot less versatility. Ours is programmable. It has a little minicomputer on the board that can be programmed. A person can put new instructions into the board by writing a program for the board and feeding it into that minicomputer.

The other four companies' boards are not programmable. They have only "hard wired" boards. There is no programmable processor on them. That limits the range of what they can do, although it lets them do it faster. They can, for instance, add a couple of functions or carry out convolutions, which is a very common image processing function. But they can't do anything else. Maybe someone says, "we just got a smoothing algorithm that was developed at Stanford University. Some guy has written a paper on it, and we'd like to try it out." With our board they could put that function in, whereas with our competitors' boards, they could not.

Only one competitor really has similar capabilities to ours. That's a company called Truevision, started by some former AT&T people. Reportedly they have about 35 employees, but we have no knowledge at all about what they are up to. They have a product they call a "vistaboard" that's very good. Our performance is better than theirs because in addition to the main processor on our board we have a second auxiliary processor which carries out very high-speed image number crunching functions. We have offset the slowness that normally accompanies programmability by adding this processor, which runs very fast. So we can run things faster than the Truevision board. But we think our system is unlikely to sell on the basis of hardware alone. The difference between us and True Vision doesn't seem great enough.

However, we have more programs than they do. Hardware alone is no good unless you've got programs to drive it. The scope, breadth and sophistication of our software greatly exceeds that of our competitors. With some modification, our software could run on the Truevision board, and with some modification theirs could run on ours. Of course, neither theirs nor ours has any applicability to the other four competitors, nor does theirs have applicability to us.

Truevision has a family of products, including systems for Sun as well as the PC and various others, as we would plan to have also. They have only a distributor here locally. I plan to look into the company further, find out where they are located, what they consist of, and so forth to be able to look over their specs and make a comparison. But what specific information should I most seek? And how much time should I be willing to spend trying to get it? I'm not sure.

Only one competitor, Data Translation, is public. It has 126 employees and sales of $25 million. Two of the other companies, Datacube and Matrox, are listed in Dun's Million Dollar Directory. But there is no information given about them.

We have very little idea about industry sales and distribution. Three months ago I knew nothing about marketing and sales. After working at it since then I feel I now know less than nothing. For instance, the approach to a retailer who caters to medical imaging end-users would be very different than the approach to scientific end-users in university research environments. But what should we do about it?

We've been told several times that it's vital for us to define our market precisely and not speak in general terms about the huge number of applications for handling pictorial data. Instead we should pick something very specific. We've been trying to do that but finding it hard. We've been energetic in looking up references, going through databases, calling competitors, talking to whomever we can, and trying to get information out of marketing companies. But we haven't had much success.

The best way to get market data, some have told us, might be to use a market research company. Should we hire a marketing consulting company?

If so, how would we choose one and how much should we be willing to pay for what? We just have no idea.

We could also get market information through buying a report by Frost and Sullivan entitled "The U.S. Commercial Image Processing Market." We could get information by subscribing to Dataquest's market research services. But the Frost and Sullivan report costs $2,000, and Dataquest's service costs $12,500. We don't have enough money. Should we get the money for that, or are there better alternatives?

Some industrially experienced people are critical of those market research studies. But bear in mind that we know nothing. Maybe their forecast is not very good, but their information about the present market might be helpful. If they say that 16.4 percent of the imaging market is in printing and publishing, isn't that helpful information? Wouldn't it be useful for us to know how many vision systems one of our competitors is selling?

It seems to be commonly agreed upon by analysts of the low-cost imaging field that it is about to grow explosively. The underlying reason is that the handling of image data is very pervasive in our society. People deal with visual information constantly. It is very clear that with numerical and text data, computers have taken over much of the human handling of those sorts of data.

The reason it has not happened with image data is the technical difficulty and expense of designing systems to handle it. But now the costs are coming down for things like the high-density memory needed to store images and the powerful processors needed to deal with it. For the first time, we are approaching a point where it will be possible to put together a non-trivial imaging system—one that can do something meaningful and useful with images—for less than $10,000.

Everybody knows this, and many expect the field will explode soon. The Frost and Sullivan estimate of the imaging processing market for 1990, we hear, is $1.58 billion. So, undoubtedly, there are other companies looking at it. Hearsay has it that there are several heavyweights out there, like IBM and Apple, looking at it and likely to enter.

Management Concerns

Right now there is really nobody out there who is the image processing company. We would like to be that company, dominating our market segments, known and respected for producing high-quality products, personnel, documentation, and support. We'd like to be a prestigious, thriving, profitable company at the cutting edge of innovation; the company that people try to beat. We are not yet thinking in terms of number of employees and sales. We are thinking only in terms of what we want the company image to be, and what we want to do. We want to be a presence in the image processing field.

If achieving our goals means we will be a hundred million dollar company in five years, then that's what we'd like to be. If it means we should have 80 employees, then that is what we would like to have. But we have been cautioned against the line of thinking that aims for sales and employment targets. We haven't begun to think in terms of pure profit making. But we're flexible.

Dr. Hammoude said his main concern at present was how to move ahead with management of the startup. The business plan draft that he had prepared included in its text some questions he and other founders thought needed answering. (See Exhibit 1.) Hammoude observed that none of the founders was experienced in management, commenting:

Of our specific business concerns, the first one of all is marketing. We realize that this is very important, and that the success or failure of the venture depends on how skillfully we market.

We have a bunch of ideas, but no discriminatory ability. For instance, we could place an ad. We could do a direct mailing. We could recruit sales reps. We could try to find distributors. We could try to generate some kind or royalty or licensing agreement with some big-time, heavy-duty marketing outfit. But we don't know what is the smartest or the best thing to do, and we don't know how to find out.

A second thing is the financial picture. Right now, we are doing everything on a shoestring. We are four guys working out of a spare bedroom in Renton. The other three are moonlighting, and working on the company evenings and weekends. I'm the only one who's full time. We're doing everything on the cheap. I run around xeroxing things and stand in line at the post office, sending information out.

That saves us money and lets us retain all the equity in the company. But in terms of efficiency, we're just a bunch of clowns. When we send out information, I hand write the envelopes, stuff them personally and stand in line at the post office. When I stand there, I think to myself, 'I just don't see the CEO of IBM doing this.'

Is this OK? We are spending three hours a day, three of us in cars, commuting to Renton to work together. The most massive inefficiency is that three guys are moonlighting. Instead of spending 16 hours a day, which they should, working on the company, they are spending three hours a day plus the weekend.

One thought is that we might place an ad, get a couple of orders, sell a couple of systems, take the money we make from that and build a couple more. If that is going to work, fine. The orders come in. We make some money, then gradually scale things up. Then we can rent office space somewhere and hire a secretary.

The other alternative, it seems, would be to "do it right." Get a quarter million, a half million or a million bucks, from where we're not sure, give up somewhere between 25 percent and 50 percent of the company, move to offices, hire a manager, bring in a marketing consulting company, pay them $30,000 for the consultation, pay an advertising agency another $30,000 to design an ad, place the ad, design brochures, manufacture brochures. Pay for a mailing list. Mail the stuff out.

The question is, what's the best way to do it?

It seems to us that one major milestone would be getting the business plan into a condition where, with a straight face we could show it to someone and they could read it with a straight face.

A second would be to get the venture capital we need. Until then we need some sort of interim financing. It's going to take a while for these things to happen; for us to get our act together. And in the meantime we have expenses. The more the act of getting the business together is costly, the more an immediate milestone is to get some cash.

If inevitably we're just not going to make it working out of a spare bedroom in Renton this way, I want to know now. If we should go big, how do we do it? What's the best way to get venture capital? How much should we get? Those are the kind of things we'd like to know.

Beyond that, what should we do about administration, taxation, legal aspects? I've done the rough of a business plan (attached as Exhibit 1) working from a guide on business plans from the

Small Business Administration. But I don't know what it means. It would be nice to have somebody tell us what is important. What else should be in the plan and how should I get it there?

We started with about $40,000 pooled from family and friends. About $22,000 was spent to work up the design and creation of the prototype, which was done by a company in California. We could manufacture more like it without much retooling cost. And we have about $10,000 of our original capital left. None of us is taking any salary.

We know that since we lack experience, we need help in finance, sales, marketing and overall management. But

which do we need the most? Or should we go out right now and hire a sales and marketing person and use that as a way to get financing? Or should we look for a financial expert first to get the money, and then hire two marketing people? Or should we be able to find one good management person who would take care of both needs?

Finally, as regards financing, we know we need money but we are a bit confused, still, about the various possible sources. We've heard there are alternatives like venture capital, or corporate partners and private investors. Somebody I spoke to on the phone recently asked, "Why don't you go public now?" Was that a joke?

EXHIBIT 1   Draft Business Plan (including some questions by Andrew Hammoude)

BUSINESS PLAN WORKING DRAFT
IMAGEsystems, Inc.
September 25, 1988

IMAGEsystems is a start-up company, and is involved in the development, manufacturing and sales of high-technology computer imaging hardware, together with appropriate support software. The following is a statement of our business plans for the next year of operation.

1. PERSONNEL

IMAGEsystems presently consists of four persons: Tom Alexander, Andrew Hammoude, Alan Steiner and Jerry Stone. The company was founded in January 1988. All four of us have advanced degrees in electrical engineering, and together represent an extraordinary concentration of skill and expertise in hardware design, software development and image processing technology.

Tom Alexander is currently working toward his Ph. D. degree in computer architecture at the University of Washington and has extensive experience in both hardware and software design.

Andrew Hammoude recently completed his Ph.D. degree at the University of Washington; his area of research was computer analysis of medical ultrasound images.

EXHIBIT 1 (continued)

Alan Steiner graduated from the University of Washington with a master's degree in electrical engineering. His research project was the design of a hardware imaging system, of which our first product is the direct descendant.

Jerry Stone also graduated from the University of Washington with a master's degree in electrical engineering. His thesis topic was the design of a machine vision system for automated inspection of printed circuit boards.

2. MANAGEMENT

None of the four principals has any management experience. We are well aware that this is a major problem, and are actively trying to deal with this lack of expertise.

To determine which management issues we should be most concerned with, and how we should deal with them, we have met with several institutions, such as the Small Business Administration, the Small Business Development Center, and the University of Washington Small Business Institute, which offer free consultations. This has led us to several other sources of management guidance. Two we think most likely to be useful to us are:

A. The M.I.T. Enterprise Forum
B. The Northwest Venture Group

Both of these offer management critique and guidance services at nominal cost; the M.I.T. Enterprise Forum through their Start-up Forums, and the Northwest Venture Group through their Venture Advisory Panels. We are planning to make use of both of these services, and hope that this will provide the sort of detailed and focused advice we need.

Some of the specific questions that we'd like to answer are: How should we deal with our lack of management know-how? Should we hire a manager? If so, how? Or would we be better off pulling in a management consulting company? How would we go about choosing a suitable consultant?

3. PRODUCT DESCRIPTION

Our first product is an image processing and display system. This consists of a single computer board, which plugs into an IBM PC/AT or any compatible, together with a complete software support system. Together, the hardware and software give the PC the ability to display, manipulate, and process images with a high degree of flexibility, thereby in effect converting the PC into a general-purpose imaging workstation. Some of the specific capabilities of the system are as follows:

Display: Display of multiply overlapping images; image zoom, pan and scroll; instant replay of stored image sequence; image annotation; superimposition of color graphics.

Visual improvement: Contrast enhancement; filtering (e.g., edge-enhancement); image averaging (e.g., for noise reduction); pseudo-coloring.

Storage and transmission: Electronic storage and transfer; image teleconferencing; image compression and decompression.

EXHIBIT 1 (continued)

Analysis: Histogram generation; statistical analysis; motion analysis; correlation, template matching, feature extraction; measurement.

Miscellaneous: Image addition, subtraction and convolution; image cropping and compositing; image warping.

A detailed description of the entire system can be found in the Product Overview, which accompanies this business plan. The following is a summary of the major distinctive features of our system.

1.   The processing hardware is <u>fully programmable</u>. It can be programmed to carry out virtually any image processing operation. This means that the user can write his own application-specific programs and is not restricted to the software library that we provide. Furthermore, our software system has been designed to allow the user to carry out this software expansion very easily.

2.   The processing hardware includes <u>two</u> programmable processors. In addition to the main system processor, there is a second, auxiliary processor, which carries out computationally intensive operations at very high speed. This second processor allows our system to operate at the substantially higher speed than comparable products from the competition.

3.   The hardware includes high-speed image transfer circuitry, which allows images to be displayed and manipulated with extreme versatility.

4.   The hardware is easily expandable; additional hardware devices (such as extra memory) can be incorporated into the system without difficulty.

5.   The hardware is constructed by means of **surface mount technology**. Surface mounted boards are easier to manufacture, allow higher operating speeds and are inherently more reliable than the more conventional through-hole assembly process.

6.   The software system allows **multiprocessing**—that is, the system can carry out several tasks simultaneously. For example, the user can initiate a lengthy series of processing operations on a particular image, and meanwhile continue to use the system for other things.

7.   Images are displayed in a fully **windowed** environment. That is, different images can be overlapped with each other on the display, allowing several different images to be viewed simultaneously. The windowing system allows extreme flexibility in the manipulation of images on the display.

8.   Extensive software support libraries are available with the system, including a complete repertoire of image display and manipulation functions.

9.   The software system allows easy expansion; it has been designed to allow the user to include additional programs without difficulty.

In summary, both hardware and software represent state-of-the-art technology. The hardware architecture incorporates several unique design features and is supported by a sophisticated software system. The result is a versatile, powerful, and interactive image processing system.

EXHIBIT 1 (continued)

Product Expansion

The above base system allows abundant opportunity for product expansion. We have already designed a digitizer board to work in conjunction with the base system and are planning several other expansion products, such as a memory expansion board, a high-speed processor board, and a second-generation, higher resolution imaging board.

4. COMPETITION

Various companies are currently producing image processing systems. Among these companies there are five with products similar to ours in terms of capability and price, which therefore represent our closest competition. These five companies, and the price of their most comparable systems, are:

Data Translation	$6690
Datacube	$9500
ITI	$6490
Matrox	$5995
Truevision	$5995

Comparisons among imaging systems can be made on the basis of many factors. However, the three most critical issues are:

- The versatility of the hardware
- The processing speed of the hardware
- The available software support

In terms of hardware versatility, IMAGEsystems and Truevision have a major advantage over the other four manufacturers. The systems from IMAGEsystems and Truevision are based on programmable processors, whereas the systems from Data Translation, Datacube, ITI and Matrox do not contain a programmable processor. The range of processing functions that these latter systems from IMAGEsystems and Truevision offer are fully programmable and can carry out virtually any image processing operation.

On the other hand, the four non-programmable systems have a clear advantage in terms of processing speed. Although their repertoire of processing operations is very limited, they can carry out these operations much faster than the two programmable systems; in fact, they can do operations in real time, which the programmable systems require several seconds to complete.

In a nutshell, IMAGEsystems and Truevision have designed for versatility, while the other manufacturers have designed for speed. Which of these two factors is the more important depends entirely on the application. The systems from IMAGEsystems and Truevision are not suitable for applications that require true real-time processing. On the other hand, the systems from Data Translation, Datacube, ITI and Matrox are almost completely useless for general-purpose image processing applications. This means that these latter systems address a market that is largely different to that addressed by IMAGEsystems and Truevision. For this reason, we consider Truevision to be our most serious rival.

EXHIBIT 1 (continued)

Since each system is fully programmable, there is little to differentiate IMAGEsystems from Truevision in terms of versatility. In terms of speed, however, IMAGEsystems has a distinct advantage; the dual processor design allows our system to operate at a substantially higher speed than the Truevision system.

In terms of software support, IMAGEsystems has a major advantage. The scope and sophistication of our software system greatly exceeds that of any of our competitors. None of the above companies has multiprocessing or windowing as part of their software system, and none allows the sort of flexibility and expandability that is possible with our system.

In summary, the versatility of our product greatly exceeds that of all our competitors, except Truevision. However, these competitors are able to carry out a limited range of processing operations at a considerably higher speed than IMAGEsystems. Our system is able to operate at significantly higher speed than Truevision, our nearest rival in terms of versatility. In terms of software, IMAGEsystems has a major lead over all competitors.

5. PRODUCTION

Manufacturing

Manufacture and assembly of the boards will be carried out by SCI Manufacturing in California; we will acquire the necessary parts and ship them to SCI for assembly. Availability of parts is, therefore, an extremely important issue for IMAGEsystems; inability to acquire parts would leave us unable to satisfy our orders. We will deal with this by maintaining adequate inventory of long-delivery items. At present, we have all the parts required for the first system already on hand. Long-delivery parts for the following 11 systems are on order, and we expect to take delivery of these well before our first production run. SCI manufacturing time is approximately three weeks per production run, so that, barring unavailability of parts, we can ship orders in a timely manner.

All software development will be carried out by IMAGEsystems. All documentation will be written in-house by IMAGEsystems.

Quality Assurance

The hardware will be tested at several stages during manufacture. Each board will first be subjected to a bare board test before any electrical components are mounted to make sure the board itself is correct. All components will then be mounted, and the complete assembled board subjected to a component test; this will ensure that each individual component is functioning correctly. These two tests will be carried out by SCI, and any errors corrected by them.

The completed boards will then be shipped to IMAGEsystems, and we will carry out a functional test by running hardware diagnostic programs to ensure that the system, as a whole, is functioning correctly. Any errors will be corrected either locally, or in-house by IMAGEsystems.

[How should the software by tested?]
[Should we carry out beta testing? How?]
[Should we offer a warranty? What will be the terms?]

EXHIBIT 1 (continued)

Distribution

The entire system (hardware, software, and documentation) is sufficiently small and light that packaging and shipping are not major considerations. Delivery will be by UPS or Federal Express.

6. PRICING

The direct costs to deliver a single system are as follows:

Parts	$1,200
Assembly	(1,300)
Testing	(100)
Other costs	
TOTAL	(2,650)

The price for a complete system will be $7,995. This is distinctly higher than the prices of similar systems from our competitors. However, we believe that this is easily justifiable given the significant advantages of our system, so that even at this price, we can successfully capture a portion of the imaging market. If this should prove not to be the case, this price allows room for price cutting while still maintaining profits.

7. MARKETING

The operations our system can carry out are useful in virtually any application that involves pictorial information, so that the potential market for this device is vast. Some of the applications that involve the handling of image data are:

Medical: X-ray radiology; ultrasound imaging; CAT scanning; magnetic resonance imaging; positron emission tomography; thermography; electron microscopy; optical microscopy; dentistry; 3-D reconstruction.

Scientific: Inspection and quality assurance; tolerance verification; missing parts detection; robotic; object location and manipulation.

Graphic Arts: Computer art; image overlay and compositing; animation.

Miscellaneous: Teleconferencing; security, access control; signature verification, fingerprint analysis; anti-counterfeiting.

Among these applications there are several broad markets for our system:

1. End-user. This refers to someone who wishes to buy the hardware board and support software alone. This implies that the person already owns a PC system, and now wants to add advanced image handling capability. Typically this would be someone in an R & D environment, either industrial or academic.

EXHIBIT 1 (continued)

2.   Turn-key system user. This refers to someone who has a specific and immediate need for image handling capability, but who does not have the time, inclination, or know-how to assemble and configure the required system piecemeal. This user wants to have a complete working system shipped, one that can be operated without requiring any particular knowledge of its inner workings.

3.   The OEM market. This refers to a company that is manufacturing a system, for example a turn-key system as described above, of which our hardware is an integral part.

In addition to these major markets, two other potential markets are worth mentioning:

4.   Standard software only. Our standard software is general and portable to other systems, so it does not necessarily require our hardware to be useful.

5.   Contract programming. In the case of any of the above markets, the user may require high-level, application-specific software in addition to the more general standard-system software.

Our initial marketing effort will be directed towards the end-user and OEM markets. The last two markets mentioned above, though potentially important in the future, are very small in comparison to the gigantic size of the first three markets. Furthermore, any attempt to address these markets would divert effort away from the continued development of our existing product, and at this stage we cannot afford this distraction.

The turn-key market would require that we be able to provide service and maintenance for the installed system. This is practical only in the Seattle area, and even there, the drain on our manpower is very undesirable at this stage in our operation. Furthermore, supplying the turn-key market would greatly complicate our inventory, packaging, freight and insurance requirements.

In the case of the end-user and OEM markets, however, we can ship the system simply and rapidly and can guarantee quality by means of a warranty. Furthermore, both of these markets can be reached by means of the same marketing strategy, which is not true of the turn-key market. Our initial marketing effort, therefore, is simplest when directed at end-user and OEM.

Marketing Plan

At present we do not have a coherent marketing plan, and this is one of the issues that we hope to get assistance with from the two previously mentioned advisory services.

However, we do have several ideas that we intend to put forward for criticism:

1.   We are planning to place an advertisement in *ESD* (*Electronic System Design*) magazine. This magazine is most closely concerned with the sorts of imaging applications for which our system has been designed. All of our competitors advertise regularly in this magazine.

2.   We are planning to attend "Electronic Imaging West '89" in San Jose, California in March. This trade show is an ideal forum for presentation of our system. All of our competitors will certainly be in attendance.

EXHIBIT 1 (continued)

3. Should we do direct mailing? It is possible to buy mailing lists from *ESD* magazine and other sources, consisting (supposedly) of persons who are likely to be interested in our system.

4. Should we recruit sales representatives? If so, how?

5. We have decided that selling via distributors is not practical because of the large price mark-up they will require. Is this a reasonable conclusion?

6. If possible, we will publish an article on our system, in *ESD* magazine or elsewhere. We published an article in *ESD* in March 1988, and this generated quite a lot of interest in our system.

7. We plan to make a demonstration of our system on request to any seriously interested persons in the Puget Sound area. Since the entire system is easily portable, this is quite practical.

8. Should we pursue some sort of licensing or royalty arrangement with some organization that already has a powerful marketing infrastructure? What are we talking about? How do these arrangements get set up and how do they work?

We would like to get answers to all of these questions.

Some minor marketing activity has taken place already. As previously mentioned, we published an article in *ESD* in March, and this generated approximately 95 inquiries requesting information about our system. In April we attended "Electronic Imaging West '88" in Anaheim California, and this also generated numerous requests for information. Finally, Texas Instruments wrote our system up in the summer issue of their Pixel Perspectives newsletter, and this too resulted in several inquiries. We have responded to all of these inquiries by sending out a package of information about our system.

8. SCHEDULE

10/1/88	Manufacturing prototype completely functional
12/1/88	Software version 2.0 ready for release
12/1/88	New brochure ready for mailing
12/1/88	First ad runs in *ESD* magazine
1/1/89	Documentation completed

9. FINANCIAL PLAN

To date, July 1, 1988, the following costs have already been incurred:

Parts	1,814.63
Prototype	17,114.25
Legal fees	1,249.70
Office supplies	672.42
Telephone	660.25
Trade shows	792.00
Travel	1,795.28
Advertising	978.34
Freight	355.09
Miscellaneous	123.17
TOTAL	25,555.13

EXHIBIT 1 (concluded)

Costs over next six months (7/1/88 - 12/31/88):

Prototype		4,000.00
Parts (first 5 systems)		6,000.00
Assembly (first 5 systems)		(6,500.00)
Testing (first 5 systems)		(500.00)
Long-delivery inventory		2,832.50
Advertising	Ad design	(1,000.00)
	Ad placement (ESD)	2,450.00
	Brochure design	(1,250.00)
	Brochure production	(2,000.00)
	Brochure mailing	(100.00)
Documentation		(1,000.00)
Packaging		
Telephone		650.00
Office Supplies		(500.00)
Miscellaneous		1,000.00
Total		(30,000.00)

Costs over following six months (1/1/89 - 6/30/89):

1989 Trade Show	Booth rental	1,188.00
	Booth design	1,000.00
	Travel	396.00
	Hotel, per diem	480.00
Capital equipment	Logic analyzer	4,000.00
	Oscilloscope	2,000.00
	Laser printer	1,200.00
	SMD rework station	5,000.00
	DSP Assembler	500.00
	GSP C compiler	1,000.00
	Office equipment	1,000.00
Salaries		4,800.00
Telephone		1,300.00
Office supplies		500.00
Miscellaneous		1,000.00
Total		25,284.00

Are these figures realistic? This is a "shoe-string" budget, with three of the four principals moonlighting, the fourth working for nothing, and everything being done on the cheap. Is this a realistic way of going about things, or are we heading for disaster? What is the current dollar value of the AT-based image processing market? How much of this market can we expect to capture?

Case 15

Dan Handel

In the fall of 1984 Dan Handel was seeking capital to manufacture stained glass. He had worked with his two partners since the previous summer, contacting potential financing sources that would be able to supply the $800,000 they believed necessary for start-up. So far, they had elicited only one outside offer. It came from two investors who wanted to put up $300,000 in return for 40 percent of the equity and other terms, which Dan said would effectively give them control of the firm.

The enterprise would produce decorative glass in sheet form with a rolling mill. Current industry practice used a hand-operated batch process, which Dan and his partners said was more costly, less efficient and limited in capacity. Dan commented:

> We've got a couple of wealthy investors who are willing to kick in with a loan and stock arrangement that would give them 40 percent equity. There's another engineer we know who has $40,000 he'll contribute if we try to make it with other funds and our present cash flow. And I suppose we can keep looking for other people who would be interested in us.
>
> In any event, we need to take another look at our plan and see if there's a way to improve it. I think we need to ask ourselves if we can do it cheaper and what do we have to have to get started in the glass business.

Origins of the Enterprise

Dan Handel, Dave Smith and Jack Rogers all had become acquainted from having worked for Rayshield, a Seattle company that manufactured glass with radiation shielding properties. The glass was useful in shielding windows for X-ray and nuclear reactor applications. They started West Coast Specialties as a "moonlight activity" in Dave's garage in 1978. Dan described how it began:

> While I was working for Rayshield, one of my partners who had been hired by Boeing as a consulting engineer discovered a need for a product that didn't exist. He did some design work, and we contacted a company that was an approved distributor for Boeing's 747 program. That got us started making control switches for the plane and we went from there.

By 1984, this business, although it was begun with virtually no capital and still operating only part-time, had grown to a net worth of nearly $74,414, as can be seen from the balance sheet in Exhibit 1, relying on what Dan termed a strategy of internal growth.

> Initially we stayed away from any work that didn't have a high enough profit margin. This gave us time to work on other products that would have even higher margins. If you're going to get bigger without outside financing, this type of strategy is essential. Otherwise you'll just be making wages, and never get rich.

Manufacturing of the switch consisted

mainly of assembling parts purchased from outside suppliers, using small hand tools. It was performed on benches occupying about 300 square feet of an industrial building leased by West Coast Specialties. The current business was profitable, but Dan characterized its immediate future in supplying aircraft parts as "not that promising." All three had experience in ceramics and glass technology, so discovering that a shortage of stained glass existed caught their interest. Dan recalled:

Sometime in late 1983, one of my partners heard through the grapevine that there was a booming demand for stained glass. In fact, the company we worked for gave some thought to the possibility of manufacturing it. But they chose not to, so we decided to give it a try on our own.

Using their knowledge of glass production, the three partners came up with a concept they believed would give them a competitive edge in the domestic market, estimated at up to $40,000,000 or more in sales per year. Dan described it:

Each of the existing producers uses a labor intensive batch method of production and typically produced up to five tons of colored flat glass a day. Our plan is to adapt continuous production on a small scale that would be cheaper but turn out between 80 and 120 tons a day.

Dan stated that competitors were located mainly in the Midwest and eastern U.S., used hand methods of production and had shown no intention of expanding capacity.

Prototype Testing

The partners assembled a jury-rig production machine to test their process idea.

This occupied about 500 square feet of floorspace in the plant, which was otherwise empty except for the switch-making operation. Total floor space in the plant included 18,000 square feet of paved open ground-floor work area plus 2,000 square feet of office space. It was situated in an industrial zone and adjacent to a rail spur.

The jury rig consisted of a heating and pouring unit for the glass, which then passed through rollers as a sheet and fell onto the floor where it shattered. Dan observed wryly that demand from buyers of decorative glass was sufficient that there had been offers to buy this scrap in its present form.

Each of the planned two full production machines, they expected, would have both a larger pouring capacity and, most importantly, a long output conveyor on which the glass would be properly cooled to make it less brittle and be cut into regular sheets for packing and shipping rather than falling on the floor and breaking as it now did. An overall machine in final form would be approximately 140 feet long by 30 feet wide, including an 80 foot Lehr conveyor. Each furnace would be able to make one color at a time. Changing colors was expected to take up to a day, and colors would probably be changed once a month. Orders for various colors would be met either through inventory or lead times that could be months ahead.

The partners expected to store inventory along sides of the building where a conveyor (known as a Lehr) would run the length of the facility. Storage bins for each color of glass produced would also be needed, since cutting and packaging left up to half the finished product as waste (known as cullet). Dan noted that there could be unanticipated problems in going from the prototype facility to one designed for continuous production.

We've never rolled glass before. So,

we're not sure what will happen if we scale up to a full-sized mill.

Seeking Capital

The three spent 1984 contacting possible capital sources based in Washington State. They had drafted a venture plan, which is attached as Exhibit 2, to inform potential investors about the proposed business and advantages its production process should give it over competitors. Dan recalled his experience in meeting with various investors:

The fact that we're already in business helps a lot in dealing with the bank. But getting venture capital, that's a different story. Most of the money is flowing to high technology. And glass production is not high technology. Venture capitalists are looking for ventures that are open-ended and have huge potential. We project a good return, but there's a limit to the market, and that seems to turn them off.

They want a phenomenal upside because they know that only a certain number of ventures they invest in are going to succeed and some will totally fail. If they don't make up for the losers with big winners, they're not going to get the return on investment they want.

Dan believed that since solid demand seemed to exist for decorative flat glass, the risk of failure would be low. But that argument had not yet prevailed with investors.

Sales

One man who had taken an interest in the business and was offering to invest $40,000 to become a fourth partner was Jeffrey Holden, whose biographical sketch also appears in the business plan of Exhibit 2. He had undertaken to investigate the market for stained and decorative glass

sheet, and had concluded that demand currently exceeded supply. Orders from existing suppliers were requiring two months and longer to fill.

One company in Hempstead, New York, which currently imported such glass from abroad, apparently with some difficulty, responded to Mr. Holden's inquiry with a letter stating the following:

It was a pleasure speaking with you over the phone today, and I am quite interested in all aspects of what we discussed.

As you know, my firm is mainly in the glass selling business. We are importers from several countries and we service all different kinds of domestic accounts. A large portion of our business is what we call "bending" accounts. These bending accounts require a large amount of opalescent glass in the various colors.

If you can produce this glass as well as the quality and specifications of Wissmach, then I would be very much interested in purchasing about 600,000 square feet per month—12 months per year. This purchasing can be done on a Letter of Credit basis but I would have to be given the exclusive rights to sell east of the Rockies.

I am anxiously awaiting to hear from you.

Don was encouraged by the letter, but at the same time had reservations, commenting:

Here we've got the opportunity to sell to just one buyer and they would sell everything we make. I'm reluctant about doing this because of our past experience with government contracts. Essentially, you end up with monopsony power and that one buyer has really got you by the throat.

Instead, I'd like to aim for a distri-

bution system that includes both whole-sale and retail channels and work out the product line and pricing to fit with some sort of system like that.

Moving Ahead with the Venture

Other options available, as Don saw it, were one or a combination of the following:

1. Go with Jeff Holden's $40,000 and existing orders for aircraft parts; and pursue orders from glass retailers and wholesalers.

2. Continue seeking venture capital from other sources.

3. Scale down the present venture plan.

He could also consider other sources of capital. Don said that his banker would probably be willing to lend up to $40,000—probably as a line of credit with compen-sating balances. Another possible source was the Small Business Administration (SBA), although he didn't know how much money it could provide. He knew it would sometimes guarantee bank loans up to 90 percent, but only after approval of a fairly substantial amount of paperwork, which could take weeks to prepare and process.

The timing was an important factor, according to Don. The building space for expansion was already under lease near downtown Seattle. The prototype of the production process had been tested and the method appeared to be feasible. Most important, Don stated, was that taking immediate advantage of current market conditions would allow West Coast Specialties to become a major producer of stained glass before other competitors moved in to "fill the gap."

"I'm convinced we should act quickly and decisively," he said. "The question is what that action should be."

EXHIBIT 1 Balance Sheet - As of Sept 30, 1984

WEST COAST SPECIALTIES, INC.

ASSETS			LIABILITIES	
Cash		$3,738	Accounts Payable	$6,952
Accounts Receivable		22,502	Taxes Payable	550
Other Receivables		262	Due Stockholders	2,270
Prepaid Rent		3,000	Unearned Investment Credit	370
Prepaid Income Tax		200		
Inventory		41,106	Sales Commission Payable	1,826
Mach'y & Equipt	9,570		Total Liabilities	11,418
Less Acc Depn	5,766			
		3,804	Capital Stock	42,000
			Retained Earnings	32,086
Goodwill & Organization Expense		11,220	Net Income (3/31/84 to 9/30/84)	328
Total Assets		$85,832	Total Liabilities	$85,832

Note: Investment Credit not figured; depreciation is estimated; taxes are estimated.

EXHIBIT 2 West Coast Specialties Business Plan Draft

Briefly

West Coast Specialties, Inc., designers and manufacturers of specialized electrical systems, propose establishment of a company to manufacture rolled flat glass. The principals of West Coast Specialties, Inc., have had long individual experience in engineering and production of glass products. Using this background a prototype glass melting furnace was constructed and energized. It proved to be successful in producing opalescent flat glass of such quality as to insure volume sales to a market in need of an additional source.

West Coast Specialties, Inc. has the skills and the factory facility to engineer and manufacture a production unit to produce 20 tons per day (9,000,000 square feet per year). It has the management capability and the factory space to insure efficient productivity as well as strong industry ties. Experience biographies of the principals are attached to this report. Banking relations are with National Bank of Commerce, First South-Stacy Branch; accountants are Kelly & Payne, 200 First Avenue West; attorneys are Culp, Dwyer, Guterson, & Grader, Hoge Building. All are in Seattle.

The Product

The product is a soda-lime type of glass, melted from standard raw materials, rolled into sheet form, cut to size and used as decorative panels, windows, and in leaded glass forms (windows, lampshades, etc.). The sheets of glass are cut to standard sizes and are colored in the melting process to a minimum number of combinations specified by several customers.

It is assumed from industry data (augmented by our knowledge of the industry and the capabilities of the three domestic producers) that the current domestic consumption of rolled, flat, colored, decorative glass is approximately 35,000,000 square feet per year. It is established that deliveries from domestic producers are quoted from 12 to 18 months from receipt of order. Production is being allocated and new customers, even if in need of continued substantial volume, are forced to purchase through jobber-retailers. The most important producer (Kokomo Glass Company) has stated that this market condition will continue for five to six years, and this statement has been confirmed at the user level (McGowan Stained Glass Studio, Seattle). In this market, 9,000,000 square feet of glass is definitely salable.

The three domestic producers of this type of glass use methods of manufacture that predate the industrial revolution but are time-honored in this craft. Since it is a highly labor intensive craft, in which the production worker is subjected to extremely hot working conditions, the application of proven automatic methods provides a substantial competitive edge. The use of such methods as (1) controlled furnace drain system, (2) continuous melting furnaces, (3) automatic stirring mechanisms, and (4) variable energy sources, allows lower direct labor cost, automatic assurance of quality and flexibility of manufacture previously unknown in this segment of the industry.

We anticipate no patent issuance since there is no specific proprietary technology involved. Rather, the applied technology is that of standard, proven methods and equipment long accepted in other segments of the glass industry (i.e., container manufacture, but hitherto not used in the production of opalescent flat glass). Two of our engineers are critical to the application of such technology, each having had strong practical background in glass melting technology and production methodology.

EXHIBIT 2 (continued)

At the outset, and for the first two years' production, we will produce only opalescent sheet. At full capacity, a pretax profit target is 40 percent to 45 percent of sales, and expected return on invested capital should be in the range of 50 percent. Our forecasts indicate a higher percentage of each measurement. The selling price, FOB Seattle, is planned at $0.80 per square foot and the costs to produce this square foot are as follows:

The Variable Costs: Raw materials, direct labor factory overhead	$0.2666/sq.ft.
The Fixed Costs: Overhead and G&A	0.1686/sq.ft.
Total Costs: Based from 6 mega sq.ft.	$2,611,600
Sales Income from 6 mega sq. ft.	$4,800,000

The raw materials cost $0.1030 per square foot represented by sand, soda ash, aluminum hydrate, calcium carbonate, sodium, silicon flouride and coloring agents. Possible shortages of one or more of these ingredients may be dealt with by adjustments in composition of the glass. Since the glass industry is large nationally, there are many alternate sources of raw materials. A prime example of substitution ability is use of scrap recyclable glass. Suppliers of the above are such firms as Lane Mountain Sand, Spokane and Seattle, and Van Waters & Rogers, Seattle. Judicious buying and reasonable scheduling will allow for continuity of raw material receipts without extraordinary in-house inventories.

The Plant & Facilities

Our present plant facility consists of 18,000 square feet of factory space and 2,000 square feet of offices, situated in an Industrial Zone inside the Seattle city limits. The site is served by a rail spur and is adjacent to Port of Seattle pier facilities. The factory building is a Butler-type, built in the late 1940s. It is long and narrow and ideally suited for glass production. We have a two-year lease at $3,000 per month, rising to $4,000 per month in May 1985. Additional space is available in the same complex of buildings as needed. The factory space is leased by West Coast Specialties, Inc. in anticipation of glass production, and would be, together with appropriate office space, sublet to the glass company.

With one furnace in this facility our production from an eight-hour shift would be 3,000,000 square feet per year. Addition of second and third shifts (since the pre-determined furnace output controls the hourly volume) will add a total of 6,000,000 square feet annually.

To produce this 9,000,000 square feet, we anticipate building one all-electric melting unit consisting of a basic opal melter and two colorant melters. These melters, constructed of steel frameworks with refractory and insulating brick, are fed by an automatic batch charging system. They deliver molten glass into a conditioning and mixing forehearth. Specially engineered water-cooled rolls flatten the molten glass delivered by the forehearth and feed the sheet into an 80 foot long annealing Lehr. From the Lehr, the sheet is delivered to the cutting and packing area. (See attached graphic of the furnace.) By the addition of fossil fuel energy, the annual output can be increased by 14,500,000 square feet. To produce be-

EXHIBIT 2 (continued)

yond that amount, a duplication of the production unit will be required. There is sufficient space already under lease for it.

Personnel

A constant concern in the glass industry is the seven-day work week. This necessitates rotating shifts, holiday and weekend premium pay and a generally awkward personnel problem for direct workers. The design of our productive equipment allows for a three-shift, five-day week, since the melting equipment can be made dormant without loss of quality.

A survey of local rates (Northwestern Glass Company) shows the average hourly rate to be $10.32 per hour for production and maintenance workers, including fringe benefits. Foremanship average salaries are $2,884 per month, including fringes. We anticipated starting rates to be at the low side of the local rate ranges. At optimum production, we anticipate 20 production and maintenance workers, three foremen and a superintendent to handle the manufacture of the product.

The four management persons will be supported in the office by an accountant, a purchasing agent and a receptionist/stenographer. This support will represent salaries of $6,000 per month. The general management, development, engineering, production management, financial management and selling will be personally done by the management personnel at combined salaries of $30,000 per month. (We are fortunate to have close connection with the Department of Ceramic Engineering at the University of Washington and can partially staff our evening and night shifts with competent graduate students.) The area provides a good semi-skilled labor market.

Fringe benefits include medical and life insurance, paid holidays, paid lunch and coffee break periods, shift premiums (24 cents and 32 cents per hour) and vacation pay.

Research & Development

No innovative research and development is planned during the first 18 months of operation. Thereafter, upon scheduled production stoppage for color changes, experimentation will start to create color patterns heretofore impossible to produce due to equipment limitations. The cost of such experiments is minimal. Direction will be set by capabilities and market testing. At the end of the sixth quarter of profitable operation, an R&D budget will be set, providing about $100,000 per year to maintain technical leadership and to modernize colored glass styling to open new uses by architects and decorators.

We anticipate no diversification in production for the first five years of operation but will prepare to enter the market in clear (as opposed to opaque) colored flat glass for such uses as tub and shower enclosures, decorative windows, etc. We are competent to do our own research and development without recourse to outside consultant groups.

Sales and Marketing

Initially all sales will be made to distributors of such glassware. We have been contacted by the leaders in this field and have been assured of their intention to buy at least 7,000,000 square feet of glass per year. As soon as we are assured of financing, we will enter into contracts with two or more national distributors.

Meanwhile, we have a letter of intent from an interested established distributor. The

EXHIBIT 2 (continued)

acute and continued shortage of this type of decorative glass has forced the distributor to disappoint his long-term customers. He is keen to maintain his good customer relationships and to accept new ones in this growing market. This distributor sells to glass retailers, such as Washington Glass Company in Seattle. By the 18th month of operation, we will have contacted original equipment users of opalescent glass (such as Pendleton Lamp Co., Oklahoma City) to sell to them on a direct basis.

At this writing, glass manufacturers are demanding payment in advance of shipment of goods. National distributors such as Bienenfeld Industries and Amworth Industries have indicated willingness to cooperate with us at the outset in pre-payment of orders.

We anticipate no need to advertise at the beginning of operations, but a modest budget should be set up at a later date for advertising in such publications as *Stained Glass, Glass Industry* and membership in such organizations as The Stained Glass Association of America, Glass Grafts of America and the Flat Glass Marketing Association.

The current (since 1980) boom in the sales of colored flat glass is directly traceable to the hobbyist's strong interest in Tiffany-type lamp and window crafting. Also, the restoration of turn-of-the-century buildings—together with use by architects and decorators of nostalgic decor, such as stained and colored glass structural members and objects d'art— has caused a shortage of opalescent glass estimated to be about 14,000,000 square feet. This estimate is ours, based upon our knowledge of the productive capacity of the several producers and the reports of users and distributors as to the backlog of unfilled orders on hand. There are no available figures through the government or trade associations that give other than general data pertinent to "flat glass." No professional surveys have, to our knowledge, been made. We estimate that the current market will hold for the next five years and that our price structure will allow for a continually expanding segment of that market. With the input of more product into the market, it is anticipated that hobbyists, heretofore frustrated in efforts to get glass to work with, will renew their enthusiasm and that the volume will increase.

Location of the plant in the Seattle area has the advantage of low electric power rates, which allows for waste-free melting of glass, plus the option of switching to fossil fuels should electricity shortages occur. Geographic shipping limitations are not significant at this writing. The product is sold F.O.B. Seattle. Our pricing can be reduced below that of competitors and still provide comfortable profit margins. Should geography pose eventual problems, it would be relatively inexpensive to set up a companion plant in a more favorable market location.

Use of up-to-date technology in fabricating opalescent glass sets us apart from the competition. Other manufacturers use hand methods which have not changed markedly since the industrial revolution and consume an inordinate amount of direct labor hours. The domestic producers are Kokomo Opalescent Glass Company, Kokomo, Indiana; The Paul Wissmach Glass Co., Inc., Paden City, West Virginia, and Advance Glass Co., Newark Ohio. Each company is a closely-held, old-line firm, and we are advised by their customers that they have no plans for plant or production expansion to fill the market needs.

Glaverbel, S.A., of Belgium is exporting opalescent glass to this country, yet the quality of the product is not up to that of the domestic producers. Glaverbel's sales are the result of the shortage of opalescent sheet of any kind. This latter holds true also for the small

EXHIBIT 2 (continued)

amount of the product imported from Saigon to our west coast. No estimates of the total square footage of imported goods are available. Our methods of manufacture allow us to meet the highest quality standards now being met by the domestic manufacturers and to diversify into other flat rolled glass products (i.e., cathedral, antique, and transparent colored glass). The sample glass from our prototype furnace has met with approval from users and distributors. Although plastic polymers have made inroads into other segments of the glass industry, there is no attempt for their producers to enter this market, nor is the product suitable.

Key Personnel

DANIEL HANDEL
Experience History
1979 to Present: West Coast Specialties, Inc.
Together with J. Rogers and R. Smith, he formed this company to design, manufacture and sell electronic and electro-mechanical components to the aircraft industry. Currently supplying Boeing and McDonnell-Douglas with components especially designed for them, the company has grown from a garage operation to a profitable, debt-free, small business. In addition to the business management phase of this enterprise, he has contributed to production planning and operation.
1973 to 1979: Rayshield Company
Upon leaving Stanford University, where he spent a post-graduate year after receiving a degree in engineering form the Department of Metallurgy at Washington State University, he joined this engineering and research company as a project engineer and sales engineer. The scope of his responsibility was wide...personally supervising the production of glass frit (colorants) for industry; engineering the development of processes and products for the glass industry in general; installing equipment (primarily all-electric glass melting furnaces) in the United States, Japan and India. In addition he acted as sales engineer, domestically and abroad. His last assignment was in systems design and cost evaluation for raw systems proposal in response to customer inquiries. This activity resulted in final preparation of equipment quotations and patent licensing agreements. He left this post in 1979 to attend the Graduate School of Business at the University of Washington. He received his MBA degree in 1981.

DAVID E. SMITH
Experience History
1979 to Present: West Coast Specialties, Inc.
Together with D. Handel and J. Rogers he formed this company to manufacture and sell electronic and electro-mechanical components to the aircraft industry. He has had direct responsibility for the electrical engineering applied to the development of the product line. Moreover, he has handled field sales as well as field service problems.
1976 to 1979: Engineered Industrial Systems
Employed as an electrical and mechanical engineer by this firm of engineering consultants, he designed and supervised the installation of various production facilities for the

EXHIBIT 2 (continued)

Boeing Company.

1973 to 1976: Rayshield Co., Inc.

At this company, consultants and manufacturers for the glass industry, he was chief electrical engineer, designing systems for the melting and control of glass fabrication. In addition he had responsibility for the electrical portion of field construction.

1970 to 1973: Aluminum Company of America, Wenatchee Works

At this aluminum smelter he engaged in the design, construction and installation of electrical equipment, both power and control. He automated various areas of the aluminum producing areas.

He holds degrees from Washington State University in both Mechanical Engineering and Electrical Engineering.

JACK D. ROGERS

Experience History

1983 to Present: West Coast Specialties, Inc.

Although an original participant in this organization, he did not dedicate his total time until late 1983. Since that time, he has engineered the furnace and ancillary equipment for a proposed rolled sheet glass production facility, formulated compositions for this product and organized suppliers and subcontractors for cooperative action. In addition, he has built and operated a prototype melting furnace for this glass venture.

1973 to 1983: Rayshield Co., Inc.

On joining this firm of consulting engineers and manufacturers to the glass industry as a ceramist, his first assignment was the completion of a development project to create a tin oxide electrode that would endure in contact with molten glass. In addition, he was totally responsible for the development and experimental casting of a man-carrying glass sphere for undersea search and rescue work, involving one of the most massive glass castings ever attempted.

1967 to 1973: A variety

From his entrance into college in 1967 to his completion at the University of Washington as a Ceramic Engineer he held a number of industrially oriented jobs. To afford his education and to support his family he was variously an electronics technician at the Boeing Company, a quality control technician at Stoneway Sand & Gravel Company, a laboratory technician and inspector at Herman Adalist & Associates, and once again an electronics technician at the Boeing Company.

JEFFREY M. HOLDEN

Experience History

1977 to 1984: The Rayshield Group Companies - Vice President & Director

He was employed in 1977 as vice president of the parent company and of the international sales company of this specialized engineering, consulting and manufacturing organization. He was named as director of both companies, as well as their Western Hemisphere Trading Company, in 1978. In 1979 he became a director of the subsidiary company operating in England.

He was responsible for all operations, except research and development engineering,

EXHIBIT 2 (continued)

although charged with the administration thereof. He voluntarily resigned in early 1984 to negotiate for the purchase of Irish Crystal Glass (Galway), Ltd. on a personal basis.

1963 to 1977: Reeves Rubber, Inc. - Executive Vice President

He was employed in 1963 by this manufacturer of molded and extruded rubber products as sales manager. In 1964 was made vice president and corporate officer. In 1972 was named executive vice president, with responsibility for all company departments and operations—in addition to sales.

He served as acting president form August 1972 until the president returned to semi-active participation in the business in August 1974. During this period he handled all management duties as well as policy planning, development, finance and sales.

Between 1963 and 1972, sales volume tripled, with profits substantially in excess of those standard in this industry. In 1972 a complete re-organization of the company was undertaken. Management controls were developed and applied, and profit planning was established, resulting in a doubling of 1975's volume by the end of 1977.

1961 to 1963: Cannon Electric Company

He was employed as director of procurement at the outset of the Korean War by this dominant manufacturer of electrical connectors. Circumstances demanded a heavy subcontracting program and accelerated purchasing activity. He assembled a staff and contracts were let in the manufacturing disciplines of die-casting, screw machine work, lathe work,

Financial Forecasts (see attached tables)

EXHIBIT 2 (continued)

Pro Forma Operating Statement (Unaudited)

	4Q-84	1Q-85	2Q-85	3Q-85	4Q-85	1Q-86	2Q-86
A. Net Sales (Billed)	84,910	103,768	149,816	279,710	1,027,710	1,338,270	1,380,000
B. Cost of Goods Sold	61,920	72,860	130,400	255,620	342,152	444,600	484,000
1. Raw Materials	16,324	22,000	122,200	96,000	152,000	86,000	114,000
2. Direct Labor	13,920	18,000	40,000	92,000	*134,000	140,000	140,000
3. Mfg. Overhead	24,600	28,860	48,400	119,420	*196,152	205,600	230,000
a. Indirect Labor	4,000	4,000	8,000	16,000	42,000	42,000	42,000
b. Energy & Rent	9,200	11,300	17,600	46,800	46,800	46,800	47,800
c. Insurance & Taxes	2,000	4,960	8,200	10,020	17,692	24,200	24,600
d. Depreciation	600	600	600	20,600	30,600	30,600	30,600
g. Miscellaneous	8,800	8,000	14,000	20,000	*30,000	32,000	55,000
f. Crafting for Glass				6,000	30,000	30,000	30,000
4. Inventory Change	7,076	4,000	80,200	-51,800	-141,000	13,000	
C. Gross Margin (A-B)	22,990	30,908	19,416	24,090	685,558	893,670	887,000
D. Selling, Administrative							
& Misc. Expenses	16,000	59,000	97,000	80,000	181,600	250,000	262,000
5. Misc. Expenses	7,000	42,000	77,000	50,000	*10,000	10,000	10,000
6. Salaries	4,000	12,000	12,000	12,000	39,600	60,000	60,000
7. Commissions & Sales							
Expenses	5,000	5,000	8,000	18,000	132,000	180,000	192,000
E. Net Operating Profit (C-D)	6,990	28,092	77,584	55,910	503,958	643,670	625,000
F. Interest Expense		9,000	9,000	9,000	9,000	9,000	9,000
G. Net Profit Before Federal							
Income Tax (E-F)		37,092	86,584	64,910	494,958	634,670	616,000
H. Estimated Tax					137,572	306,640	287,000
I. Net Profit After Taxes (H-G)		29,774	86,584	64,910	357,386	330,030	338,000

* Glass Production treated as a regular operating expense, not as Misc.

EXHIBIT 2 (continued)

Cash Flow Forecast

	4Q-84	1Q-85	2Q-85	3Q-85	4Q-85	1Q-86	2Q-86
Cash at Start	3,738	16,306	678,414	536,888	382,560	334,878	943,148
Uses of Cash							
Cost of Goods							
Sold and Inventory	54,844	68,860	210,600	307,420	483,152	431,600	484,000
G&A, Selling & Misc.	16,000	59,000	97,000	80,000	181,600	250,000	262,000
Equipt & Prepaid							
Expenses		80,000	284,800	1,000	0	0	0
Loan Payments		9,000	9,000	9,000	39,000	39,000	39,000
Income Tax							442,212
Sources of Cash							
Loan & Stock Sales		800,000					
Trade Credit	83,412	77,768	159,816	249,700	897,710	1,298,270	1,350,000
Depreciation		600	600	20,598	30,600	30,600	30,600
Net Cash Flow	12,568	661,508	-440,984	-127,122	224,558	608,270	153,388
Cash at End	16,306	677,814	237,430	409,766	607,118	943,148	1,096,536

EXHIBIT 2 (concluded)

Pro Forma Balance Sheet (Unaudited)

	9/30/84	3/31/85	6/30/85	9/30/85	12/31/85	3/31/86	6/30/86
Assets							
Cash	3,738	678,414	237,430	110,320	334,878	943,148	1,096,536
Receivables	22,764	5,000	40,000	70,000	200,000	240,000	270,000
Inventory	41,076	30,000	110,200	162,000	303,000	290,000	290,000
Prepaid Expenses	3,200	3,200	3,200	4,200	4,200	4,200	4,200
Current Assets	70,778	761,614	390,830	346,520	84,206	1,477,348	1,660,736
Fixed Assets (cost)	13,954	93,954	378,754	378,754	378,754	378,754	378,754
Accum. Depreciation	9,570	10,770	10,770	31,970	62,570	93,170	123,770
Fixed Assets (net)	4,384	83,184	367,384	346,784	316,184	285,584	254,984
Other Assets	11,220	11,220	11,220	11,220	11,220	11,220	11,220
Total Assets	86,382	856,018	769,434	704,524	1,169,482	1,774,152	1,926,940
Liabilities							
Current Part of Loan		100,000	100,000	100,000	100,000	100,000	100,000
Trade Payables	6,952	6,436	6,436	6,436	6,436	6,436	6,436
Income Tax Payable		0	0	0	137,572	442,212	287,000
Accruals	2,746	3,000	3,000	3,000	3,000	3,000	3,000
Current Liabilities	9,698	109,436	109,436	109,436	247,008	551,648	396,436
Balance of Loan		400,000	400,000	400,000	370,000	340,000	310,000
Due to Stockholders	2,270	2,270	2,270	2,270	2,270	2,270	2,270
Total Liabilities	11,968	511,706	511,706	511,706	619,278	893,918	708,706
Capital Stock	42,000	342,000	342,000	342,000	342,000	342,000	342,000
Retained Earnings	32,414	2,312	84,272	149,182	208,204	534,234	876,234
Total Liabilities & Net Worth	86,382	856,018	769,434	704,524	1,169,482	1,774,152	1,926,940
Working Capital	61,080	652,178	281,394	237,084	595,070	925,700	1,264,300

Michael Hoppe

The following is the report of an MBA student at Arizona State University, who in 1989 set out to find a company to buy as a way of entering self employment. Names have been disguised.

Entrepreneurship Paper

This paper will trace the methods and activities that were a part of my search for a business to purchase. The acquisition of a going business concern seemed like the most promising alternative for me to begin my career as a self-employed businessman. I do not have any great ideas for new products or inventing revolutionary new technology. Also, because my capital is very limited, the financing of an existing firm with a track record of established profits is considerably easier.

Before I began my search, I formulated some thoughts about the "ideal" company to purchase. The current owner would be 55-70 years of age and ready to retire. The business should be mature and not have experienced significant growth over the past two years, because the current owner should be content with his current workload and income level. These ingredients usually indicate that a more aggressive owner and management could increase sales and profit levels in a reasonably short period of time. This could permit me to increase the value of the company and sell it at a substantial profit after two or three years.

The business would also need to be "asset heavy," allowing use of the company's own assets for collateral. I felt it was essential that the owner consent to a non-compete contract for a minimum of four years. Since I do not have any highly technical expertise in any one area, I would insist upon a management consulting contract for myself for one year, or for one business cycle. Ideally, the owner would undertake a considerable portion of the financing to reduce the amount of outside financing required and thus eliminate the need to dilute my ownership. I would also want current customer lists, prospective customer lists, as much inside information as possible about selling techniques the owner had used over the years, and a subjective or quantitative evaluation of them, if available.

While my "ideal" owner and company may appear to be cast in a fairly rigid mold, I think there is ample room for flexibility. Not all the above characteristics are essential. The only area that would seem to be missing from this ideal is the *product*.

Because of my limited experience, I deliberately left this area more flexible. I did not want to limit myself to a few product lines. I would prefer a product (or service) that was on the verge of taking off, and would shortly be an item desired in everyone's home. The important factor for my business is that it must make a profit the first year, and that sales can be increased 30 percent or more by the second year. This would give me an income and asset base to expand into areas where a new product or market might be developed, and very large returns could be obtained.

With this ideal owner and company implanted in my mind and my notebook, I began to search for a company. I knew full well that such a search process might take many months or even years.

Initial Search

I began seeking conversations with numerous people to learn how a person can discover which businesses are for sale. I felt there was a "good old boy" network, but was not at all certain about how to get into it. Being a student, I started by talking to professors from both previous and current classes whom I thought might be involved in some consulting work in the business community. I hoped they might direct me to useful contacts and also might provide some inexpensive advice on pitfalls and "cons" to beware of.

This initial search led me to the Business Advisory Services Group at Phoenix Commercial Bank. After several telephones calls and transfers around the department, I obtained an appointment with Dave Brown. He said he could "tell me things I'd never read and might take years to learn."

He also said to be careful of companies whose assets were severely understated and whose owners did not want to increase their book value so as to be liable for increased taxes. After a company has been purchased, the federal tax collectors at the Internal Revenue Service will typically audit that firm in the next tax year, and if the assets were not transferred at a realistic value, I could be held responsible for a large tax liability. He said that since a company of interest to me would probably be some form of corporation, and if I purchased such a firm, only the stock would change hands. It would be entirely too costly to dismantle the existing corporation and form a new one with myself as the stockholder.

He also stressed to me the importance of obtaining good legal and tax advice before signing any documents. He gave me the names of two attorneys and some tax people who were very good and had handled many acquisitions over the years. Finally, since the department he worked in performed a considerable number of valuation studies, he offered the bank's services to me. His advice was well taken, and he stated that although very few firms that are for sale flow through his department, he would inform me if he found one that fit my criteria. He also gave me the names of two business brokers in Denver: Robert Haller and Dean Valley.

I visited one of the brokers immediately, since his office was near the bank. He asked what my net worth was and told me he did not deal with clients whose net worth was below a million dollars. I left with very little new information except his advice to construct a personal financial statement.

Next, I called Dean Valley and chatted on the phone. I told him what I was looking for and went to visit him. He was more a real estate salesman, selling Mom-and-Pop type operations than a business analyst. For some reason, which I cannot specify, I did not like or trust him and did not analyze any of the businesses he represented. None of them came close to my criteria for the "ideal" acquisition anyway.

A Tavern

By now I was getting anxious to analyze a business, so I started reading the business opportunities section of the local newspapers and the *Wall Street Journal*. Finally, with some apprehension, I began making calls. I inquired about a tavern in the west end and decided that, even though it did not meet my criteria, I would go and take a look. It was for sale by a broker whose name I do not recall. He gave me the address and told me to meet him there.

I was not expecting a plush club, but I also did not expect such a rat hole. The owner wanted $20,000 cash. For this I would receive ownership of the fixtures, furnishings and company name. He offered to sign a non-compete clause for a 15 mile radius, and said he would help me learn the business for three months at the rate of $100 per day. I would also receive $1,000 of inventory which consisted of 10 barrels of beer, some unspecified gallons of wine, and beer and wine glasses.

The rent was $560 per month, with three years left on the lease. Utilities and insurance had averaged $160 per month and were not anticipated to change. The current owner said he was withdrawing $40,000 per year, which was the entire profit. He had owned the tavern for five years and was now retiring.

The furnishings and assorted contents of the tavern appeared to be in rather poor condition. I felt the entire tavern would need complete remodeling and, definitely, new fixtures. I also got the feeling that the owner might decrease the purchase price or extend more favorable terms. But the remodeling might cost something like $5,000 to $20,000, and I was not sure how I could finance that. Also, I was not sure I would want the current customers patronizing the tavern if it were mine. They seemed like a pretty rough bunch.

So that opportunity has left me with some real problems to ponder. But at least by looking at it, I began to get into the water and become motivated to continue my search.

A Store

After a few more days of reading advertisements and making telephone calls, I decided to look at an import shop in the south end of town. I made an appointment and met the broker at his office. There we went over, in moderate detail, the aspects of the business and the terms of sale.

The owners were two gentlemen from India. They imported goods from India to the United States and sold wholesale as well as retail. They said the wholesale business had been keeping them busier

than they had anticipated, and they had not been able to devote adequate time to the retail business.

The retail store has no real track record of sales. The owners kept it open only five hours per day, and said they didn't really know what the volume of business was. The store has two-and-one-half years left on its lease in a small shopping center. The center is relatively modern, and even on a Wednesday afternoon appeared to have an adequate volume of traffic. The rent is $882 per month for 1,260 sq. ft., of which 200 sq. ft. is office and bathroom. There is no storage space except in the office.

The owners want $24,000 cash for which I would receive the inventory which they said this is worth $20,000 wholesale or $50,000 retail (wholesale is 40 percent of the retail price). I would also receive the minimal amount of fixtures, which they valued at $2,400, and a machine for imprinting T-shirts. This machine transfers designs, pictures and slogans to T-shirts, which they sell for $9.95 at a cost of $4.00 each. They claimed the machine cost $1,600 six months ago. They said that as wholesalers they would also give me a discount on merchandise I purchase from them for two years. The amount of the discount was unspecified, and so far, I do not have a firm commitment from them on it.

Some of their inventory appeared to be of minimal marketable value. Most of it was made up of carved wooded boxes, tables, plus brass ashtrays and water pipes. There were also 150 Indian print dresses that to me looked hideous. I suspect that, perhaps, it would cost me around $20,000 cash to rent a store and buy inventory with comparable or higher marketable value. Anyway, I don't know if they transferred the goods to the store at an inflated price.

The fixtures were mounted to some cheap carpeting, which was stained. Shelving had been homemade out of 1-by-12-foot boards. I don't think it would cost a great deal to replace something like that if

I tried to set up a new store myself. Finally, the fact that there weren't any profit and loss statements or documentation on the cost of the inventory has left me suspicious. The store is not set up as a separate business entity from the wholesale operation, so I suppose I would have to incur additional expense to form a corporation.

I expect I could lose a maximum of around $20,000 if the inventory proved to be of no value. I felt I could liquidate the inventory for around $10,000 if I had to shut down, but I have no idea of a maximum profit. The profit potential seems entirely dependent upon the volume of business attainable.

The break-even volume per month would seem to be:

Rent	$882
Utilities & Insurance	140
Return on Investment at 20%	4,000
Fixed Costs	$5,022

Break-even Sales = 5,022/(1-0.4) = $8,370/mo

When $2,000/mo. is added for my salary, the break-even sales volume increases to $11,666/mo. or $140,000/year. This equates to $112/sq. ft., or an inventory turnover of almost three times. This appears to be a "double" turnover rate, but much above five times would appear to be high. If the turnover was five times per year (I have assumed that $20,000 is an adequate inventory), the sales volume would increase to $250,000 per year.

Sales	$250,000
COGS (40%)	100,000
Gross Margin	150,000
Fixed Costs	84,264
Profit Before Tax	$65,736

Feeling uneasy about this company too, I began reading the business opportunities sections of newspapers again. One positive result was that I started to feel more adept at screening businesses for sale against my established criteria.

Hospital Equipment

The next company I chose to investigate further was advertised as a hospital equipment firm. From a preliminary screening over the telephone, it seemed to meet most of my criteria, so I made an appointment to meet with the broker.

This business has been in operation for two years. Its owner has three other firms, which he says are more profitable, and since he felt he could not devote an adequate amount of time to this business, he wanted to divest himself of it. It is a wholly owned subsidiary of another firm in which the owner is sole stockholder. Its line of work is supplying hospitals with total nurse-patient communication systems. This firm has an exclusive franchise with Bunting Corporation to sell all of its products in the Rocky Mountain region. Because Bunting manufactures the product and delivers only when ordered, I see no need for warehouse facilities.

The profit margin is claimed to be an incredible 50 percent of sales, something I have not yet verified. All the sales have been to hospitals. The owner feels he has been successful with relatively minimal effort because he provides the installation. This he contracts out to electrical contractors in the area of the job, thereby eliminating the need for any permanent employees.

A balance sheet as of July 31, 1988 is attached as Exhibit 1. The accounts receivable are due from hospitals where work is nearing completion. The owner claims that none of these are in arrears. Construction is said to be in progress at several unspecified jobs that the owner said are continuing on schedule and have no unforeseen cost overruns in them. The inventory consists primarily of several demonstration units for sales presentations. The accounts payable are owed entirely to Bunting Corporation for goods received.

A profit and loss statement for the year ended July 31, 1988 is attached as Exhibit 2. As can be seen, the profit is very high for such a low sales level. The ending inventory figure is very high when compared with the number on the balance sheet. The administrative expenses are only direct expenses. There are no salary payments to the owner.

The company has two salesmen who will leave with the owner. I suppose this business is not large enough at present to warrant more than myself and a secretary. The owner will agree to a consulting contract at $300/day plus expenses. He will also sign a non-compete clause and will turn over all customer and contractor information sheets.

The owner stated that the overriding theme of the sales presentation and of the entire product line is that of efficient patient care. The competitors do not install their equipment unless pressured to do so. This appears to be the firm's competitive advantage.

Now for the deal. The owner wants $100,000 for the company. I buy the assets and the liabilities. He wants $50,000 down and the remaining $50,000 to be paid quarterly over five years at 6-percent interest. He has hinted to me that the terms are flexible.

What do I receive for this? I don't exactly know. The owner is not willing to give me an overabundance of information without some commitment on my part. He mentioned to me that with a binder, he would allow me to go through his accounting books, and we would itemize everything included and not included in the purchase. The broker has said he signed a statement that everything exists as he has presented it in the financial statements.

At this point, I considered letting this business pass. I did not have access to $50,000—even though the owner might lower the down payment to $30,000. In talking with the owner, I discovered that he felt a minimum of $20,000–$30,000 would be needed for working capital with a business volume of $2 million. I did not know where I could raise $60,000–$90,000 that would be necessary for the down payment and working capital requirement. Also, since the business did not meet the criteria of a large hard-asset base, I did not feel I could borrow the money because of the lack of collateral.

Then, out of nowhere, the broker asked me if I would consider taking on partners. He said he and his own partner would be interested in a 50-percent position if it was agreeable to me. Since this took me slightly by surprise, I informed him at the end of our meeting that I would get back to him after I studied the business a bit further. This is where the deal now stands, December 1989.

Future Analysis

To conclude this report, I will detail action and information I think I need to gather before a final discussion can be made on this deal.

An analysis of the specific assets and liabilities that are included in the company must be made. This will not be possible until some earnest money is presented. Also, an analysis of the profit and loss statement items should be made to learn the actual profitability of the company and determine if there are unallocated costs that should have been charged against the business.

Also I want to know exactly the specific products I have a franchise for in the four states and whether there are any restrictions, requirements, etc. included in the franchise agreement. I need to satisfy myself that it is indeed an exclusive franchise, and I need to learn what terms of payment Bunting Corporation requires.

The owner thought I could take over the office next door to him. I need to determine the cost and terms of the lease. He is also in the process of negotiating a contract for a $2 million installation, and I must determine whether I would receive the contract and the profit.

I expect to contact my lawyer before I get to the earnest money stage. He should help me cover all the bases by giving me advice about things to look for and questions to ask of the owner and his partners.

I expect I should visit several of the installations the company has made locally and one or more projects that are still under construction. This should let me get more feel for the dynamics of the business, and obtain an appreciation for problems encountered during construction. I also want to learn how much supervision is re-

quired of the contractors. This, I suppose, will entail analysis of past practice and of the type and cost of people who do such work.

Since the owner has been using the salesmen from his other company, I need to learn how much they are compensated and how much time they have devoted in the past year to this company. Finally, I guess I should look for contacts in the hospital business to check on the reputation of this company.

But this is all new to me. How can I tell how well I've been doing and whether I'm on the right track about where to go from here? What else, specifically, should I look for or investigate? If I do decide to try making a deal, how should I begin?

EXHIBIT 1 Balance Sheet

CURRENT ASSETS:

CASH	$8,142
ACCOUNTS RECEIVABLE	109,964
CONSTRUCTION IN PROGRESS	52,970
INVENTORY	4,420
OTHER ASSETS	
EQUIPMENT	14,962
TOTAL ASSETS	$190,278
LIABILITIES	
ACCOUNTS PAYABLE	82,942
OWNERSHIP	
RETAINED EARNINGS	107,336
	$190,278

EXHIBIT 2   Profit and Loss Statement   **June 30, 1987–July 31, 1988**

SALES		
Columbus Hospital		$496,370
Columbus Hospital other		54,390
Madigan Hospital		53,508
Madigan Hospital other		14,232
Other		83,740
Gross Sales		$702,240
Beginning inventory	$18,350	
Purchases	291,930	
Ending Inventory	71,314	
Cost of Goods Sold		$238,966
Gross Profit		$463,274
Installation Expenses		
Intermountain Business Systems	$32,842	
Madigan Installation	9,580	
Administration Expense	55,290	
Installation material		
(Columbus Hospital)	62,932	
Total Expense		$160,644
Net Profit		$302,630

Case 17

ImageSystems

The M.I.T. Forum

Dr. Andrew Hammoude and his partners had applied to the Seattle chapter of the M.I.T. Forum to have their business plan reviewed and to receive expert advice for their venture. (Please see the Andrew Hammoude case for further background.) The M.I.T. Forum was an activity organized by the Alumni Office of the Massachusetts Institute of Technology. Entrepreneurs could submit their plans to a local chapter of the Forum, which would then select one for review by a volunteer expert panel. The panelists would be chosen based on relevance of their expertise to the particular venture. They would review the plan, meet with the entrepreneur, examine the product or service and develop appropriate advice.

This advice would be presented at a public, two-hour meeting in the evening. The meeting would begin with dinner. By the time dessert was being served, the presentation would begin. The entrepreneur and his or her colleagues would stand before the assembly and describe their enterprise. Then each member of the expert panel would present his or her observations and advice. After that, members of the audience would be invited to ask questions and make comments, which would conclude the evening.

IMAGEsystems was the subject of an M.I.T. Forum meeting in Seattle on November 14, 1988. The panelists included two founders of profitable and rapidly growing small firms in microcomputer applications, a sales executive from a major microcomputer manufacturer, and an analyst from a venture capital firm. The following is a digest of their comments and those of others in the audience after the entrepreneurs' presentation.

Panelists' Comments
Entrepreneur #1

I came out of a very technical background myself and went through much the same thing as you. When we first started our company and were talking to the banks, looking for cash flow commitments to fund our operations and our receivables. The banks were not ready to put more at risk than we were. So you should quit your jobs when you are ready to become a company. Until that, you have not made a commitment that you are a company.

Divide responsibility now. Write it down. Have succinct job descriptions of what each of you is going to do. There is an instinct for all of you to want to be involved in all aspects of the company. The result is that you will all be juggling parallel work, which will lower your efficiency tremendously. Communication is an n-factorial process. When there are four of you, that's not much of an overhead. But when you grow to eight, 16 or 32 people n factorial becomes a very large number. You need to establish clearly defined channels of communication and responsibility. With the latter must go ownership. You must own responsibility. If you have that early on, then you won't be in each other's way, and you will be effective. Decide what it is now and get it done.

You have spent 30 years obtaining technical skills that will give you an unfair advantage in the marketplace. It is important that you obtain similar levels of business skills. You must draw on those to be successful. You must find assistance for those: financial, legal, sales and marketing.

The model we followed was a good one. You don't need a CPA, but you do need a part-time bookkeeper. You need to get off on the right foot. Get in touch with one of the significant accounting firms, have somebody help you set up the books correctly and get you going. Have them recommend someone who can help you on a part-time basis. But get your books set up correctly first. The accounting firm also will know the banking community and can help by making introductions for you there, which can go a long way in helping you get your line of credit.

You don't need a lawyer in house, but you need one to get set up correctly. There are certain issues that we struggled with early on that paid dividends later. Think about your current team. You're all best of friends now. So were the five of us when we started our company. But as our organization matured, our personal goals changed and some of us parted ways. You need to think now, while you're all still good friends, what will you do, how will you divide the stock, what are the rights of people that leave the company with their stock? Should there be buy-back options? Will the company self-destruct if one of you decides to change lifestyle?

The company will live or die based on its ability to sell products in the marketplace. This is not the time to give somebody in the company on-the-job training in sales. You need to find somebody who has been there before and who has taken a company through the stages

you are struggling with. You should consider a staged approach. Somebody who has taken a company to thirty or forty million in sales is not what you need at first. Such a person would be very expensive. But you do need somebody who has taken a company out a few years to around three to five million in revenues. You want that person to have ownership in the company, to own stock, to lust after making it succeed and seeing that stock mature into something of value.

Can you bootstrap the company and grow internally, or do you need outside capital to grow and fund the company? We cannot answer that for you. It is a question you have to answer yourself. But here are some questions to consider.

You are looking at what is claimed to be a fast-growing market with a limited window of opportunity for introducing this product and achieving market penetration. So there are certain boundary conditions that will control whether you can grow from inside or need outside capital.

What is a significant window of opportunity? If you are going after less than 30 percent of the market, you ought to get out right now. How long can you afford not to be a significant player and still be able to capture 30 percent of the market? What do you expect the life of your sales cycle to be? Does it take two weeks or six months from first contact to closing a sale? Each has different implications for recovering return on investment.

How long a production run can you afford? How long will it take to do a run? What are the cash requirements to initiate that production run? When must you pay for all the costs? Basically, the question is what volume of inventory can you support today to support the sales and cash flow? Answers to these questions will reveal whether you can bootstrap your company or will need outside capital to enter the market through the window of opportunity you have.

Be extremely conservative with your costs and sales estimates. A company that fails in this area will not be a candidate for additional venture financing. It's far better to start with more cash than to run out and find you need more and are at the mercy of the venture capitalists.

Judging from your plan, you are positioning your product as basically the "high-priced spread," versus something cheap and ubiquitous. That may be appropriate, but I'm concerned that the company may be driven by academic rather than market goals. What is the real market opportunity for entry? Almost every other word you speak should be "customer." You must be customer driven, market driven. Maybe the high-priced spread is the right approach, but you really need to understand who the clients are and how you can meet their needs.

So in summary, you have a tremendous challenge and exciting time ahead of you. I wouldn't exchange running a company for anything. Yours is an exciting business, and it is admirable that you are asking the questions you are. I wish we had done that at your stage of growth.

Entrepreneur #2

From my experience since starting our company just two years ago, I'd say you have to hock everything you have, take out a personal loan, open a garage someplace and get started. You need that level of commitment before anyone will be willing to buy your products. They won't buy if they think you are hedging.

If you want to become known as the lead company in the industry, with 30 percent of the market or more, you will have to buy market share out of profits. You must set a goal of reminding yourself every morning to become a customer-driven company. To do that you must get early sales revenues from somewhere. For a venture capitalist to be interested, you must ask who is the end-user and why will he buy? Are the unfair advantages I have worthy of the price?

I would go out in brute force; buy a list of all the system integrators in the United States. Get on the phone and start calling, working down from the top. You need to wrap something more around the technology that you have for a specific purpose and niche. Look for a niche in which somebody is selling hundred-thousand-dollar-plus workstations, because there you can sell for a higher price. That will let you show some profit, which is the only way you will motivate investors.

The big players are coming into this industry. There are no entry barriers. You have an opportunity to enter with low investment, seed capital and guerrilla tactics, personal loans, licensing of the technology, selling one-offs here and there to individual R&D groups. This can give you a toehold. But in about two years these opportunities will not exist. The market you're addressing seems to be a large number of vertical segments—people building products for specific end-user, vertical applications in fairly narrow markets number from 25 to maybe several hundred, if you are lucky.

In a couple of years it's not going to be much of a hardware game anymore. The big computer makers will be bringing in products and pulling the distribution channels together for more effective distribution. That will bring down margins and raise barriers to entry.

Microcomputer Company Sales Executive

You have to be the best in some area and get some wins soon. We are looking hard at the possibilities of this market. We use market consulting firms quite often. Second and third opinions can really help. You have to consider what segments you want to work, how big they are and how fast they are growing.

There are three major areas of distribution we consider: (1) direct sales with your own sales force—loyal but costly, and it has to be large for mass market, (2) distributors—they are order-takers; you must advertise and generate sales for them. (Plusses are that they will hold inventory), (3) value added resellers—people providing solutions to a problem, who take pieces of hardware and software and provide a total solution to their customers; they really know their market. They are people you could really get on the bandwagon with, but only after you decide on what market you are really going after.

Venture Capital Analyst

What are your goals? To develop a nice little company and maybe sell it off or continue running it? Or to go public? Some entrepreneurs prefer the former, but we are only interested in the latter.

You must understand and properly project your cash requirements. Venture capitalists don't like to be surprised by urgent calls for more cash. How much you aim to raise should be tied to a set of milestones or goals closely aligned with product development and with some sort of customer satisfaction or adoption rate.

If you write a plan and decide you will need $5 million to become self-sustaining, don't try to raise it all at once—that would sell you short. If you can take a smaller amount first and use it to reach a greater valuation for your company, then you can charge a higher price for ownership.

Banks are an unlikely source for you. I am on the board of two companies with sales of around $30 million. Neither of them got bank money until they had three quarters of profitability. Venture capital is next least likely, because it wants hotter deals than yours is at this point. Our deal structure depends on the business, its plan, prospects, etc. But the typical deal is 60 percent going to the investors and 40 to management, with half of that set aside to cut in other key people the company will need to recruit in the future. There are pros and cons to that, and some other venture capital firms do it differently, but that's the way we typically work.

Individual investors would be a better bet for you. Accountants, consultants and lawyers can lead you to them. Your most likely source, though, is suppliers and customers. See if you can't figure a way to get a customer sold to the point of putting up $200,000 to get you started.

You should go out and hire a big-six accountant. A lot of companies have developed accounting software packages. Each accounting firm has its favorite. Get the right package the first time, because correcting it later can be a disaster. One company I knew had its MRP supplier go into Chapter 11. The company was shipping about $8 million in hardware revenues. The hardware price was over $55,000, there were a lot of parts in it, and we had no idea where they were. We couldn't get the source code, because the company was in Chapter 11.

Part-time bookkeepers can be very helpful in accounting and even beyond that. Having the proper controls set up within the company, so one partner can't take money without the other one knowing it, is very important.

A company we were involved in down in Dallas had two very good people running it. The president was 65. The other was a very bright 35-year-old marketing woman with an MBA from Northwestern, who was one of the sharpest marketing people I ever met. I got a call from her on a Thursday asking me to please come down.

She had done some snooping and found out that the president's wife had terminal cancer. His company had been in trouble since it started, so we had been putting money in every three weeks. That president had been embezzling to pay medical bills, because he wasn't taking any salary, and he had no insurance coverage on his wife. He never told anyone in the company or any of the directors. So you have to set up controls in the company to make sure money doesn't disappear.

Comments from Members of the Audience

(Each paragraph denotes the start of a different person's comment.)

An engineer is always in the final stages of development. Don't make that mistake.

Could you sell your product to GE or Phillips rather than the user? Their expertise is not image processing but rather in manipulation of the signals coming back. Your opportunity is to sell the OEM a better tool set.

Those big companies are looking for strategic partners because they know they cannot do things fast internally.

To enter the radiologist market you might try selling to medical schools.

There is a company called Strider Technology that does imaging for radiological applications.

(Dr. Hammoude) *We will have to look into that.*

You and your partners should use a Saturday to develop matching lists of goals.

(Response from Dr. Hammoude) *We do have different temperaments. I am glad my partners heard you say this. I think we should have more bull sessions, but have encountered resistance from some of my partners. It's hard to justify a bull session when we have got to get software out.*

How many people in this room have seen a market research projection from Dataquest, or from Frost and Sullivan or anyone else that was right for three years ahead? You will learn far more from just meeting with several of your clients.

(Computer Sales Executive) *The first thing you need to do is identify what market you are really after. We use focus groups of a dozen or so behind a videotaping mirror. It is frustrating the way our message does not get across.*

You should visit computer hardware companies in Seattle and Portland to describe your product and get ideas.

If you can get a strategic partner you may be able to use market research they have done.

Four sources of market information are (1) customers, (2) competitors, (3) potential competitors, and (4) market research firms. To get information from that fourth one free, call another company that has bought it and borrow the report from them.

Be careful not to waste your time on people who don't know the market. Identify several thought leaders around the country and go see them.

You could pick one industry, like real estate, and lash together a demonstration of your product, something zippy, then rent a small booth in a show and take orders.

That suggestion is dangerous. If you can't deliver, it can ruin your company.

(Entrepreneur #1) *We find that general market data are not very helpful. But specific questions such as "What are the advantages of this competitor" can be very powerful. You can task somebody to go learn that.*

(Venture Capital Analyst) *Investors may find the "top down" market information of interest because it gives clues about total potential for growth.*

It is very hard to get market data from a company like Dataquest about a market that has not developed yet.

(Venture Capital Analyst) *You will need some of those reported market numbers to use as references in developing your business plan. You can't pull them out of thin air for that purpose. But since you have not identified a need for what you are developing, I don't see how you could possibly generate any numbers and I can't imagine any source you could go to for numbers. Don't quit your jobs until you know what the need is for your product. Who needs it?*

You should get the market reports simply to verify the numbers you have come up with and possibly to identify surprises that you have not thought about.

I used to be a venture analyst, and I remember looking at marvelous numbers in business plans. They never came true.

Don't keep working for perfection. Pick a niche and get started. You can move to other niches later.

I'm not sure you need a niche. Can you make it cheap enough to go after larger markets?

You have no market, no user, no sales experience, no manufacturing experience. You have a product that is difficult to sell because you have to educate. You have no money, consensus or plan. Why don't you sell your technology as soon as possible for whatever you can get for it and do something else.

(Entrepreneur #1) *I think there is a lot of merit to that comment. But I think our country would lose a lot of its special value if all the founders of small companies understood the odds that they are up against. They would not do startups. I think it is important that sometimes there is a little naiveté, there is bravery and things are born. I think you are asking the right questions. I think you're going in the right direction. The odds are overwhelmingly against you. But a lot of people have made it.*

(Moderator) *I think from the M.I.T. Forum's standpoint, we'll close on that comment rather than the previous one. Thank you.*

Fred Ingersoll

In December of 1989, Fred Ingersoll said he was one step away from turning his idea for a business venture into reality—to print baseball logos on high-quality T-shirts to sell in retail stores around the country. He had spent the past three months imprinting shirts slowly by hand, soliciting orders for them and trying to find a bank that would lend him $350,000, which he figured was necessary to capitalize the business properly. He had been told, to his disappointment, that to secure such a loan he would have to invest $100,000 in equity, an amount he didn't have. His list of estimated first-year costs appears in Exhibit 1.

Without the money, he said, approximately $200,000 in orders he had lined up could not be filled in time to meet spring and summer shipping dates. According to Fred, that would mean losing his present customer orders, and sure demise for his Atlanta-based venture. If funding was not forthcoming by the end of the month, he expected he would have to choose between continuing limited production by hand, closing the business, or looking for another alternative to keep his enterprise going.

Getting a Business Idea

Fred Ingersoll graduated from the University of Georgia in 1979 with a B.S. in Economics. His first job after college was as a bank examiner for the Comptroller of Currency in the Southeast Region. Fred recalled that the work helped him understand "what business financing was all about." His job involved reviewing business loans made by commercial banks in the six-state region. He said that although

this work was a valuable learning experience, he longed to become more closely involved with actual business operations.

In 1983, he went to work for a company selling novelty T-shirts. He switched employers three years later, although the type of work he was doing was the same. Fred described the product as poor quality T-shirts imprinted to be sold in places where people would not expect the shirts they bought to last with continued use. The sales approach relied heavily on impulse buying. He went on to explain how the T-shirts were processed for selling to retail customers:

The fabric was purchased from a factory in the Far East. The nylon and cotton blend was out of proportion to what a high quality T-shirt would contain, and the weave was poor and thin.

We'd get the T-shirts, apply lettering or pictures on the front, and sell them to vendors or small stores as novelty items. When you wash a shirt like that, it's possible that after three or four times through the machine, you'll have to throw it away. The dye will fade or run, the shirt will shrink, and any flaws in the weave will get worse—the T-shirt can literally fall apart in your hands.

As a result, Fred said, he had little faith in the products he was selling. He started considering the possibility of selling T-shirts of high-quality cotton weave that would be imprinted with a more permanent dye and would last as long as sports shirts purchased in clothing stores. He talked to his boss about the idea but was told that there was no incentive to make a costlier product that might lose out in the intense price competition prevailing in that business. His boss explained that his company operated on a very thin margin. A difference of just pennies on an order of a thousand shirts, he said, would not only hurt the company's profitability, but would force him to raise his price slightly, and this would prompt his customers go to a different manufacturer for the $20 or $30 total savings on a typical purchase order.

Fred commented on his experience in the novelty T-shirt market:

> I'd call these independent vendors you'd see in Atlantic City or other tourist places in the summer. Some of them would set up for a week or two and peddle as many novelty items as they could. Then they would literally 'pack up shop' and move somewhere else.
>
> The business is really seasonal and for the guy out on the beach who decides to buy a T-shirt with something funny on it, the $2 or $3 doesn't seem like much. He knows there's no chance for him to return the shirt if it's defective. He goes to the beach maybe once or twice during the summer and it's just not worth his time to complain about such a small amount of money. The retailer knows that and consequently buys low quality to get a low price.

Deciding to Venture

By 1989, Fred decided he couldn't continue to sell a product he didn't believe in, even though sales for cheap novelty T-shirts were growing despite their generally poor-quality reputation. He thought about other options he might have if he quit his present job. The idea of imprinting high-quality T-shirts that would last longer still appealed to him. The prospect of being his own boss was also pleasing, and he thought his experience in the field gave him a good idea of how to succeed.

First, he said, there would have to be some customer orders from major retailers to lend the product credibility and assure sufficient volume. Second, the design on the T-shirt would have to be popular with a large segment of the population, and be inoffensive for display in stores. Fred recalled seeing many people in New York wearing hats and shirts with a New York Yankees baseball logo imprinted. He reasoned that sports-related designs and logos would sell throughout the country, and could be regionalized depending on local team and fan loyalties.

Since the logos were registered trademarks, Fred called the Commissioner of Baseball's office to see what would be needed to buy rights for using the designs on T-shirts. He was referred to a department that specialized in handling royalties and promotions for the major leagues, and discovered they were interested. Their philosophy, Fred recalled, was that high-quality products with team logos helped to promote major league baseball. A percentage would typically be negotiated as a minimum royalty that would increase as the person's sales of a product increased. In Fred's opinion, the figures quoted him were an insignificant cost. He should be able to make the venture work if he could get sufficient orders and capital to purchase equipment. Encouraged by these findings, he quit his job with the T-shirt company and set out to see which stores would be willing to order his shirts for the upcoming 1990 baseball season.

He purchased a few dozen high quality T-shirts from a department store and used a homemade setup to print logos on them. With the completed samples, he called on buyers for department stores and sporting goods shops in southern and mid-Atlantic states. Several said they would be willing to take delivery on such shirts for spring and summer. By the end of 1989, he had obtained orders for approximately $200,000, including one from a nationwide department store chain, and several from regional department stores who would display the shirts either with other sporting goods equipment and clothing, or as an added line in their sportswear sections.

Planning for Operations

Fred's present production method used screen printing, which could be done either by hand or machine. The simple procedure used a fine mesh screen over a wooden frame large enough to be placed on a T-shirt. The letters or design would be blocked out on the shirt with masking tape. Ink would then be forced through the screen onto the shirt by spreading it with a squeegee. The masking tape was then peeled off and the shirt left to dry.

This, he said, was hard and tedious work that could produce blisters from using the squeegee all day. He estimated that the mesh was about eight times as fine as would be found on a screen door, so pressure had to be applied to push the ink through it. He explained that the ink needed for imprinting was a very thick solution and tended to be cohesive.

In a more sophisticated process, which he planned eventually to use, a stenciled screen would be prepared. This would eliminate the need for masking tape and would print a more accurate image. To make this screen, a logo or design would first be cut from a sheet of red acetate. This formed a "positive" image of the emblem, identical to the way the logo would look when printed on a T-shirt. Next, the positive image was placed atop a light-table, and the screen, stretched over an oblong wooden frame and saturated with a light-sensitive emulsion, was positioned on top of it, as illustrated in Exhibit 2. The light source would then be turned on for up to 10 minutes, hardening the emulsion wherever the light was not blocked by the ac-

etate stencil between it and the light. Finally, the non-hardened part was washed away with water, leaving porous a part of the screen in the exact shape of the image.

Supplies such as the acetate, screen, and emulsion could be purchased from any graphic arts supplier. A light-table, Fred said, could be built for about $600:

> *Essentially, you build a wooden table which has a piece of glass resting on top. Beneath the glass, you cram as many light bulbs as you possibly can to provide a high-intensity light source.*

In use, a screen which had been prepared by this process was placed over a T-shirt resting on a hard back palette shaped like the shirt. The shirt could then be printed, with ink passing through the screen to the shirt only where the light had been blocked out by the acetate, which thereby kept the emulsion soft and let it be washed away.

Fred wanted to automate as much of the printing as possible, particularly by doing away with hand application of the ink and squeegee. After chasing down leads to see if such equipment could be purchased anywhere, he learned of a man who had been in the specialty T-shirt printing business, left, and then returned to concentrate now on developing designs to be used on shirts. This man owned the type of equipment Fred sought and, although he wanted to keep it, agreed to sell plans and specifications for a modest price. Fred said the next step would be to take those "specs" to a machine shop to obtain bids for building a printer and dryer. He observed:

> *The printer and dryer have to be compatible units. The printer applies pressure to force ink through the screen and the dryer allows the ink to be baked quickly onto the shirt. The dryer is essentially a long conveyor belt passing*

through a heat source. When that's fin-
ished, you can fold and pack the shirt for
shipment.

Advantages of automating the printing process were to allow more production per worker, and to assure consistently high quality in affixing ink to the shirt. Fred estimated that to have the main machine made by a machine shop would cost about $60,000. Other equipment would then be purchased or made to complete the set-up for production.

Fred estimated he would need 2,000 square feet of space to house the equipment and inventory. He knew of loft space in old warehouses near downtown Atlanta that could be leased for as little as $2 per square foot per year. His main concern was that the location be properly wired for the electrical equipment. He stated that the machinery would use "quite a bit" of electricity, since the dryer had to operate at a high enough temperature to bake the ink onto the T-shirt for a permanent fix. He estimated that leasehold improvements could run as much as $10,000, and annual electricity bills around $4,000. He guessed that 60-65 percent of his cost of goods sold would be for blank T-shirts. Other major expenses would be for salary and printing supplies. Costs of office furnishings and related items would, he expected, be insignificant.

According to Fred, finding workers with both experience in screen printing and artistic skills to help prepare the designs would probably not be hard:

I've got a friend who does screen
printing, and he's carrying more trained
workers than he actually needs. I've
talked briefly with a couple of them and
they would be willing to come and work
for me, assuming I get the money I need.
Jobs in the printing business are pretty
hard to find right now and it seems to

me we'd all come out ahead with this
type of arrangement. It's not as if I'd be
raiding his shop.

From his past experience in the business, Fred said that much of the work would still be manual. All the folding, packing, and storage of shirts would be done by hand, and he estimated that at least half of the production labor time would be spent performing such tasks.

Orders would be taken by the dozen, the minimum being one dozen for any single baseball team. He had called department stores to ask if there were any standards for the number of shirts by size that should be packed with an order. One person explained that most orders came with two shirts small, four each medium and large, and two shirts extra large. Fred explained that if the major stores were comfortable with this combination, he would arrange his production accordingly.

If he imprinted only baseball logos, he expected his business would be highly seasonal. People who sold similar products told him it was common for 80 percent of annual sales to be delivered in about 40 percent (or nearly five months) of the year. Thus, he could either (1) produce for a portion of the year and then shut down, (2) search out offsetting lines that peaked at different times of the year, or (3) seek custom work for slack times.

Another option, he said, might be to seek rights for major league football as well as baseball logos; however, he hadn't pursued this possibility. Instead, he had contacted wholesalers and retailers of specialty items to seek custom work for slow periods. They would provide shirts, and Fred would print the desired wording or artwork at a specified rate. This work would reduce the shirt inventory he needed. He said he might be able to build the custom part of the business to as much as 25 percent of total sales during slack months.

Developing a Marketing Strategy

Fred estimated that a selling price 60 percent above the $3 or $4 paid for a lesser quality T-shirt would be competitive and affordable to a wide segment of the population. Display in retail clothing and sporting goods stores might associate them with quality that could command a premium price. To his knowledge, no one else was currently providing stores with similar quality shirts carrying baseball logos. Possible competitors such as Wilson or Rawlings had stayed with sports uniforms and focused on football instead of baseball. Many buyers Fred talked with said they liked the appearance of his samples and would order " . . . as many as you can get us, if the shirts take off."

Payment terms for customers, Fred figured, would be net 30 days. He expected that once he was able to establish credit, his payables would be on a similar basis. A few stores had indicated willingness to order shirts with baseball logos and colored borders around the neck and sleeves. For these, Fred said he would buy the fabric and ship it to a mill for sewing to customers' specifications. Current orders for such shirts accounted for nearly 25 percent of total orders received to date (shown in Exhibit 3).

According to estimates Fred had heard, total sales of the entire sports clothing products market ranged between $100 million and $300 million per year. This size market meant that there would be numerous trade shows and significant amounts of money invested in advertising each year, Fred said. However, he preferred to put all of his available capital into inventory during early years of the venture. He explained that it made more sense to him to build on current accounts than to spread himself too thin by promoting a larger customer base.

He knew there were about a dozen cities with teams in each of the two main baseball leagues, American and National. He had been told that attendance was around 20 million people per year in each of them, with some teams, such as Los Angeles, drawing over two million per year while others, such as Atlanta, drew about half that. In football, he estimated that there was a roughly comparable attendance; while in hockey, the total number was about half as large.

Fred had heard estimates for football products sales ranging between four and 10 times those of baseball products. Coincidence of the football schedule with "back to school" and Christmas seasons was cited for part of its larger appeal, he added. He speculated that a related benefit that would come with rights to produce football as well as baseball logos was that the same concessionaires and stadium owners were often involved.

Seeking Capital

Fred discovered during the final months of 1989 that bankers he talked to did not share his optimism about the venture. When he pointed to over $200,000 in orders lined up for the upcoming 1990 summer season, a banker countered by stating the business existed only on paper; there were no established lines of credit, no equipment, inventory or accounts receivable to secure a loan, hence no basis for lending. Despite the orders and $5,600 Fred had invested from his total personal savings of $7,600, the responses he reported from lending officers had a common theme. He recalled:

Since the company was a start-up, they said that there was no track record to show I'd likely be able to repay the loan. They also said there were too many steps between an order and creation of a receivable. The stores could cancel, I might not be able to produce the product in the quantity or quality desired, and I might not be able to meet shipping deadlines. In essence, I was being told that my orders were worthless—there was no evidence that the orders would clearly become deliverable products or any other form of collateral.

During conversation with one large Atlanta bank, Fred was told that he should consider going to the Small Business Administration (SBA) for help with financing. The SBA, he was told, only considered persons who had been rejected by a commercial lending institution, a requirement Fred would have no trouble meeting. He made an appointment and met with an SBA loan officer in November 1989. Fred described how the SBA might be able to help finance his start-up:

They guarantee a bank loan. The bank is responsible for helping the business along and taking the active role. The SBA is a back-up for the bank in case the loan defaults. The limit on this program is $500,000 and the SBA will guarantee up to 90 percent of the total. The catch is, they won't touch anything that has a debt-to-equity ratio higher than three-and-one-half or four to one. For me, that means finding $100,000 in equity to get the $350,000 I need to get started.

Fred mentioned that he had an uncle who might be willing to lend the $100,000; but if the money came as a loan, it would show up on the balance sheet as debt. Stock issued to the uncle was another possibility, although Fred didn't want to lose control of the business. Also, he would have to take time out for the added administrative tasks of incorporating, preparing and issuing stock certificates, holding directors' meetings, keeping minutes and preparing corporate tax reports. Fred commented that his uncle's present portfolio "is not one you should clutter up with a

bunch of risky paper from a start-up company." He understood, moreover, that the SBA would require all shareholders of the company to accept full personal responsibility for repayment of such a guaranteed loan.

A third idea he had would be for his uncle to invest in a certificate of deposit at the bank where Fred had been discussing possible loan arrangements for SBA participation. With a $100,000 certificate at the bank pledged against his loan, the bank would have recourse. If the business failed and could not repay, the bank could take over the $100,000 certificate for coverage.

Fred said he was unaware of other leveraging possibilities. As it now stood, he thought the SBA might provide the guarantee if a bank would finance the loan. One bank said it would grant the loan if he could provide the $100,000 in the form of equity. His uncle said he would provide such equity if there were some sure method arranged for him to receive repayment over a period of time, and if Fred could assure him that he was being treated fairly.

Current interest rates were in the range of 9 percent annually. Part of the funding would consist of a seasonal line of credit, requiring a zero balance for at least 30 consecutive days sometime during the year. Compensating balances, wherein the bank required that a minimum balance be maintained by the borrower, would not be required if Fred maintained an account with the bank and honored terms of the credit line.

Fred remarked that a typical SBA guarantee commitment stretched over five years at most. Beyond that, a commercial bank should be willing to lend the amount needed for the business, with equipment and current assets secured if necessary. Since the guarantee limit was $500,000, Fred added that he would have to move from reliance on the SBA anyway, or the business would never be able to grow as large as he wished. He explained that his strategy would be to use increased sales and retained earnings to obtain a larger commitment from the bank each year. He estimated, based on a collection period of 30 days and stock turn of 4, that to obtain a loan of $500,000 secured against 80 percent of accounts receivable and 50 percent of inventory, sales would have to be in excess of $6,000,000 per year.

Fred summarized options he currently saw as follows:

1. Raise the $100,000 in equity, either through his uncle or other sources he had not yet found, to leverage the $350,000 needed to set up production for the venture.

2. Operate the business using a manual screening process, and cut back on the volume of orders received, either by eliminating certain customers or filling only a portion of each order to the retailer.

3. Arrange for trade credit through suppliers and other sources of cash, and reduce start-up needs, lessening the amount of money needed to begin operations, and secure a smaller SBA loan.

4. Search out some other yet-to-be-discovered option. One he was not at this point ready to accept was to abandon the business entirely without attempting to satisfy his obligations, and glean the most possible from what he had accomplished so far.

Deciding upon Action

The longer his venture continued without the necessary financing, the dimmer Fred said prospects became. He pointed out that peak production to meet present orders should have begun by the first of December and continued through May. He was attempting to meet orders by doing the printing by hand, but this was a much slower process. While two dozen shirts with the same logo could be printed in an hour by hand, 20 dozen could be printed with proper machinery. Time for folding and packing would remain the same either way.

To date, he had been able to obtain lines of credit from two of the five suppliers he was using, one for $10,000 and the other for $20,000. The other three required him to pay by certified check or C.O.D. He had considered approaching customers for funding, but said this would be highly unlikely. The retail stores had placed orders on the assumption that Fred would be able to meet shipping deadlines and that the shirts would sell. While Fred could start the business at a lower volume and with less funding, he thought he would lose growth potential if he started too small. Starting small and remaining small was a prospect he said he did not want, commenting:

It's kind of a vicious circle. The bank won't touch me unless the SBA comes in. The SBA won't go in unless I have the capital to keep the debt to equity ratio at four-to-one, or less. But I've got the concept, orders, and competitive edge in designs, fabric, and printing that I would use. That's why the stores, not to mention the baseball commissioner's office, have gone along with me in the first place. It seems to me there has been a real value created there that I should be able to capitalize on somehow.

EXHIBIT 1   Financial Forecast

ESTIMATE OF START-UP COSTS
FOR FIRST YEAR OF OPERATIONS

Expense Category		Amount
Machinery (Printer and Dryer)		$60,000
T-shirts		
Standard (1455 dozen @ $4.00/shirt)	$70,000	
Special (480 dozen @ $5.00/shirt)	$29,000	
Total, Current Orders	$99,000	
Standard (725 dozen @ $4.00/shirt)	$35,000	
Special (240 dozen @ $5.00/shirt)	$14,400	
Total, Re-orders and inventory for	$49,400	
1991 (Expect to fund one-half of re-orders and inventory from funds provided by operations)		
Total, All Orders		$148,400
Salaries ($6/hour, times factor of 1.3 to include benefits, insurance and other compensation; estimated for 2 persons @ 40 hours/week for six months)		$16,000
Rent, Utilities, and Leasehold Improvements		$24,000
Ink and Production Supplies		$24,000
Selling and Administrative Expense (Includes salary for principal @ $1,000 per month for one year)		$54,000
Other Expenses and Working Capital		$23,600
TOTAL FUNDING REQUIREMENTS		$350,000

EXHIBIT 2   Diagram of the Inking and Printing Process (manual process)

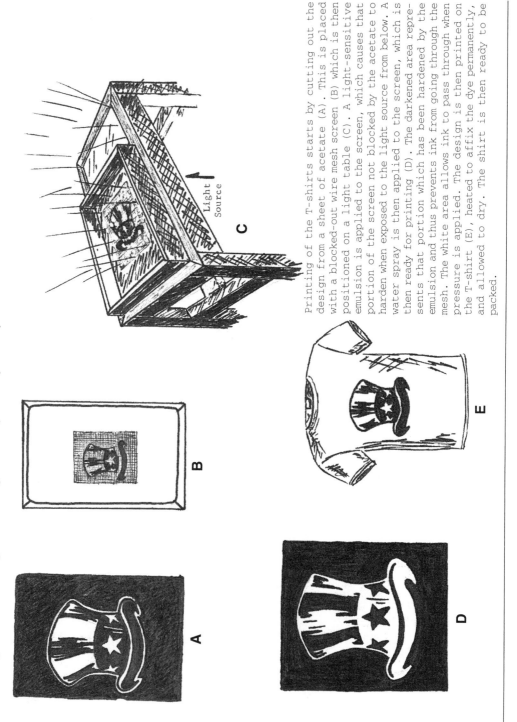

Printing of the T-shirts starts by cutting out the design from a sheet of acetate (A). This is placed with a blocked-out wire mesh screen (B) which is then positioned on a light table (C). A light-sensitive emulsion is applied to the screen, which causes that portion of the screen not blocked by the acetate to harden when exposed to the light source from below. A water spray is then applied to the screen, which is then ready for printing (D). The darkened area represents that portion which has been hardened by the emulsion and thus prevents ink from going through the mesh. The white area allows ink to pass through when pressure is applied. The design is then printed on the T-shirt (E), heated to affix the dye permanently, and allowed to dry. The shirt is then ready to be packed.

EXHIBIT 3 Orders Received as of December 31, 1989

Type of Customer	Quantity (in dozens)	Type of Shirt (std. or spl.)	Revenue (per shirt)	Total Revenue
Department Stores				
380		standard	$7.00	$ 31,920
185		special	$9.00	$ 19,980
Sub Total	565			$ 51,900
Sporting Goods Stores Nationwide Chain				
600		standard	$7.00	$50,400
200		special	$9.00	$ 21,600
Sub Total	800		—	$ 72,000
Other Sporting Goods Stores	475	standard	$7.00	$ 39,900
95		special	$9.00	$ 10,260
Sub Total	570			$ 50,160
Total, T-shirt Orders	1935			$174,060
Custom Work	960		$2.50	$ 28,800
TOTAL, ALL ORDERS	2895			$325,020

Price estimates based on cost of $4.00 per standard shirt, $5.00 per special order shirt, and $2.00 per shirt on custom work. Fred assumed that these "splits" would continue in roughly the same proportions for future volumes of business. Delivery dates range from late February through June, with some indicating a willingness to reorder if sales meet expectations.

Case 19

Intelligent Devices, Inc.

You say I'm going to fail and I say I'm going to be a success. One of us is wrong.

Ben Bailey leaned back in his chair and talked about how he convinced the management of Onyx Systems, Inc. to let him sell their products in New England. He recalled that he had confronted the company's marketing vice president in front of the firm's president to convince the CEO that, indeed, Ben could sell the Onyx computer line. The tactic worked, Ben added. The Onyx president agreed to a contract giving Ben's 18-month-old business venture (Intelligent Devices Corporation) the exclusive right to sell Onyx computer hardware and software in the four-state region of Connecticut, Massachusetts, New Hampshire and Rhode Island.

Now, in February of 1981, the contract had been in force for nearly five months. Ben said that he needed to sell at least 22 systems in the next six weeks, or Onyx would be able to terminate the agreement. To date, he had sold three systems, one of which he was using as a back-up to demonstrate to potential buyers and to replace the other two systems should one of them need servicing.

Ben talked about this dilemma and the opportunities he saw for selling the Onyx line to a recent acquaintance who was also involved in selling computers. They discussed Ben's situation and what steps he might take to meet the terms of the contract and beyond that build his company into a diverse electronics supplier for both manufacturers and users. Said Ben:

I'll tell you right off; I've got a problem. I have an incredible machine in Onyx, a geographical area that is locked up, and no one in my company to market the product the way it deserves. My time is committed to designing circuit boards for a chip manufacturer that originally got the company going. I've got three guys working on commission to sell these computers, and I'm convinced that it's the best product on the market for the price. The catch is that it takes time to cultivate a sale, and that's what I always seem to be running short of—time.

Origins of the Business Venture

For the past five years Ben had attended Babson College, dabbling in several on-campus enterprises, and starting his own company in August of 1979. The business evolved from "tinkering" with a single board computer kit that was marketed to colleges and universities. Ben worked with a Babson professor to improve on the kit by designing a printed circuit board that would eliminate the tedium of manually wrapping tiny wires to the proper terminals that routed instructions for the computer to function. The kit manufacturer agreed to have Ben and the professor produce the circuit boards, and their venture, Intelligent Devices Corporation, was born.

Over the past year, Ben had worked on related projects for the manufacturer, effectively positioning Intelligent Devices Corporation (IDC) as a custom supplier of circuit boards and software to the larger firm, which was based in Texas. IDC's offices had been set up in rented space one mile from Babson College, in the town center of Wellesley, Massachusetts. Ben lived on campus with his wife, who was working toward her business degree and helping with the company on a part-time basis.

Ben described his computer knowledge as being largely self taught. He recalled that he first became interested in computers in 1977 and eventually switched majors to graduate with a B.S. in quantitative methods from Babson in June 1979. After a summer of interviewing with corporations, Ben recalled that he made the decision to start IDC on the strength of the circuit board order and the desire to see if he could make it as an entrepreneur.

Financing for the company came from loans contributed by the Babson professor who was working with Ben on the venture. To date, the loans totaled $12,000 and were the only sources of capital, in addition to operating revenues. Ben admitted that his personal budget was "bare bones," yet the business income had been sufficient to cover operating costs and pay a small salary to himself and two others working part time for IDC.

Searching for a Versatile Computer

The events leading to involvement with Onyx, Ben recalled, stemmed from his personal interest in keeping up with products on the market. His father had commented on the need for a computer to help automate tasks involved with his legal business. Ben looked at the range of products being offered and found that a gap existed between the low-end microcomputers (e.g., Apple, Radio Shack's TRS-80) and minicomputers manufactured by industry giants such as Prime, Digital Equipment Corporation (DEC), and Data General.

On a chance visit to New York City, Ben noticed an Onyx C8001, which retailed for $14,000. He remarked that the specifications were very close to the type of ma-

chine needed by his father, yet the salesperson knew little about the computer. Ben said he was told by the salesperson that Onyx had just had a management shakeup and perhaps Ben might want to speak with the company directly about their products. Ben outlined what happened next:

I figured that if I could wrangle an exclusive distributorship out of them for a box as incredibly good as this one appeared to be, I could make money on it. I didn't think that there was anything less than $100,000 that could compete with it. After making a number of calls to Onyx, I finally talked with someone who said they'd love to discuss the possibility of my selling their products. That was all I needed.

Ben flew to California to meet with the top management of Onyx. He proposed that Onyx make his company, IDC, the exclusive distributor for Onyx's products in most of New England. Ben pointed out that he had an existing business that could market the machines, in contrast to the fact that there was virtually no sales nor service support for the Onyx products in that area at present. In addition, he brought a contract for the company to consider and ultimately sign. Ben recalled how he put the legal document together:

I worked off a boilerplate contract. The main changes were to include performance requirements and to add two features that would work to my benefit. One was to name IDC as the sole distributor of Onyx products in New England. The other was that if Onyx failed to ship their product within 90 days after receipt of a purchase invoice, I would have legal recourse to acquire all of their patents, trademarks, and property rights. It's a pretty tight contract, and I had a lawyer glance at it for me. I suppose they ended up signing because they didn't have anything going in New England and were anxious to build an installation base. My timing was critical to getting the contract.

Negotiations with Onyx started in August 1980, and the contract was signed by early October. Late that month, the first computer was shipped to IDC, giving Ben's company a second product line, the Onyx C8000 series of computers.

Features of the Onyx C8000 Series

The Onyx computer, according to Ben, competed with machines in the $60,000 to $100,000 price range. Its memory put the machine in a class above microcomputer systems currently becoming popular among hobbyists and small business users. Ben said the machine was extremely reliable and that he could probably make additional revenue by servicing the equipment, in case one of its four sub-assemblies failed.

Compatibility with standard software was another feature which made the Onyx computer attractive, according to Ben. Traditionally, computer manufacturers, including IBM, had designed their hardware to use only their own software. Their objective was to lock in customers, since to change hardware suppliers they would have to buy new software.

An alternative strategy for a hardware manufacturer was to design its machines to work with software already used by many prospective customers, as was happening in the microcomputer or low end of the market. Onyx was designed to fit "UNIX" software, which many expected would become a standard for machines at the high end of the market. Ben stated that UNIX had a wide following among persons knowledgeable in the industry and that this should be a strong selling point for the Onyx. He commented:

UNIX was developed 15 years ago at Bell Labs. Since it came out of a laboratory, versus commercial, environment, it was essentially given away to universities for students and faculty to work with. As a result, many computer professionals in the industry today grew up beating on the UNIX system. They like it because they are familiar with it and because it's versatile, friendly to the user, well-tested and well-documented. That's the same strategy DEC used to get their minicomputers moving. They keyed on universities and the result is that they are right behind IBM in the industry. DEC also has machines that run on UNIX, but their comparable model to the Onyx system costs about five times as much.

Ben had heard that applications software to go with UNIX was being developed by a number of companies.

Ben's Onyx Marketing Strategy

Terms of his selling agreement with Onyx, Ben said, allowed him to purchase computers at 40 percent off list price. He described how re-selling to a dealer or systems house would provide a profit for IDC:

Let's say a machine sells for $20,000. We get 40 percent off, so we pay $12,000. We might sell it to a dealer and give a discount of 10 to 35 percent, depending the number of computers ordered. That should net us between 5 and 15 percent, after we pay commissions and expenses, or around $1,000 to $3,000 per machine.

The contract provided that any inquiries from potential buyers in New England were to be forwarded to Ben, as the sole distributor in that area. Any orders of 50 computers or more were to be forwarded to Onyx for direct purchase from the factory, with IDC receiving a commission on them.

To advertise the fact that IDC was distributing Onyx products, Ben was writing press releases to send to periodicals such as *Computer Retailing, Computer Business News, Computer Dealer,* and *ComputerWorld.* He said there were seven categories within those publications that could promote companies and products, and he intended to use every one. He wondered if there were a best method for gaining maximum benefit from this promotion approach.

Trade shows were another promotional avenue. Ben lamented that since IDC's working capital consisted mainly of funds from operations, he doubted that he could afford the $1,000 to $2,000 needed to rent booth space at a trade show, prepare promotional literature, and pay expenses for his transportation and lodging. Although Boston hosted some regional computer trade shows, Ben said that the main expositions were usually held in New York, Chicago or Los Angeles.

Overhead costs for operating the sales effort were minimal. Ben had already secured office space for the other work that IDC was involved in, and no computer inventory carried beyond the one system spare. Ben estimated that one in the office would be sufficient to support 10 machines in the field. His sales force of three would be paid strictly from commissions and equity shares in the company. Ben commented:

We're not a distributor—we don't stock a thing. Plus, I don't want to tie up capital in inventory. I'd rather seek out compatible products that we could sell. We're also not an independent systems house (ISOs), because we don't have the talent or experience to work with end users in providing installation or support. When we sell the product, we're like a distributor. In every other respect, we're representing the factory.

I think this is a strategy we can make money with, and I'd like to build on the base we have with the circuit board, software design and Onyx series. Our natural buyers for Onyx would be ISOs and OEMs (Original Equipment Manufacturers).

Ben said that any software purchased from IDC would be added to the cost of the Onyx hardware and UNIX operating system. He estimated that this would add from $200 up to $7,000 to the customer's cost. He expected his cost for software would be 40 to 50 percent off list price. For warranty and support services, he planned to offer 24-hour turn-around on hardware failures. Defective machines would be shipped back to the factory while the customer used Ben's spare as a temporary replacement. Eventually, Ben thought he might stock sub-assembly components and have a technician available for immediate repairs under a service contract IDC would offer its customers.

The time needed to realize a sale Ben found difficult to estimate. Sometimes, he commented, only one 15-minute phone call was required. However, he was also still working with people who had expressed interest in the computer months earlier. He currently had six leads he hoped would become eventual sales. This would still leave him far short of the 25 systems he was obligated under the Onyx contract to sell by the end of March.

Meeting Provisions of the Contract

The contract with Onyx imposed performance requirements on quarterly and cumulative sales. Ben explained:

There are two tests of performance in the contract. Have I failed to sell 25 systems a quarter for two consecutive quar-

ters as spelled out in the contract? Only if both conditions exist can Onyx cancel the contract. So, I could sell 25 systems this quarter, fail the test the next three months, and still keep the contract by selling enough the subsequent quarter to meet the 25-unit test and the cumulative total.

The president of Onyx, Ben said, had given verbal assurance that Ben would not be held to the 15 units specified for the first quarter, which ended December 31, 1980. Delays in signing the contract and failure to furnish certain software were cited by both sides as reasons to waive the volume test for the first quarter. Ben wondered if a verbal agreement was enough. "I don't have a written commitment on that yet," he said, "and frankly, I'll believe one when I see it."

He hadn't talked with Onyx about their reaction should he fail to sell the 25 units by the end of March. He suspected that the marketing vice president would just as soon see him fail, so that Onyx wouldn't have to be encumbered with the exclusivity feature for the New England states. Ben said he was confident that a sufficient market existed for the computer. He mentioned one corporation in the automotive industry that had signed with Onyx to take delivery on 100 systems per month, and Onyx apparently had other customers, chiefly OEMs, who were buying 50 or more systems each month.

He characterized the competition selling Onyx products in the rest of the country as "high-powered." Ben had discovered that one distributor had been making sales calls in New England and advised Onyx's president of the possible contract violation. In another case, a customer told Ben it could go through an Onyx distributor based in Kansas City and receive 25 percent off list price, compared to the 10 percent Ben was offering.

Ben confirmed the exclusivity arrangement with Onyx, then phoned the Kansas City firm to inquire about their discount schedule. He learned that the firm was offering its customers higher discounts than he could for volume purchases. The comparative discount schedules are summarized in Exhibit 1. This, he said, suggested that Onyx might be giving other distributors a better discount than he received. Excerpts from the Onyx agreement with IDC appear in Exhibit 2.

Ben said his most important task for now was to generate enough sales over the next six weeks to prove to Onyx that he was making progress and would, in fact, succeed.

He also felt pressure to spend time on the chip kit part of his business, commenting:

For what I know how to do, maybe my time should be invested in other places: namely design. The circuit boards and proprietary software offer the highest margins and also have the potential for larger volume.

At the same time, I don't want to lose the contract with Onyx. Everyone I've talked to is amazed that I was able to get the exclusive feature in setting up a selling territory. Besides, the machine is incredible, and there's no reason we can't make a lot of money selling their products.

I wish that I could come up with a strategy that would allow us to meet the volume requirements. In lieu of that, perhaps there's an opportunity to re-negotiate the contract and still keep the attractive features I originally put into it. Either way, I'm convinced that IDC can succeed in being a growing and profitable company. That's the ultimate test for me.

EXHIBIT 1   Comparative Customer Discount Schedules

IDC			Kansas City	
No. of Units Ordered	Discount Off List Price		No. of Units Ordered	Discount off List Price
1-3	10%		1-25	25%
4-9	20%		26-50	30%
10-25	30%		51-100	35%
26-50	35%		Over 100	40%
Over 50	House Accounts			

EXHIBIT 2 Excerpts from Onyx Contract (Some sections have been abbreviated to shorten the document)

Onyx manufactures a product line of general purpose computer systems, hereinafter referred to as "the C8000 System," which Onyx wishes to be distributed through IDC.

1.   DEFINITIONS

(a) "The C8000 System" refers to a general purpose computer system with an integrated fixed disk and cartridge tape drive that is a self-contained unit manufactured by Onyx and more particularly described in Exhibit I attached hereto and incorporated herein by this reference.

(b) Replacement Parts" refers to . . .

2.   APPOINTMENT

(a) Subject to the terms stated herein, Onyx appoints IDC and IDC hereby accepts such appointment, as Onyx's sole and authorized distributor of the C8000 System within the states of Massachusetts, New Hampshire, Connecticut and Rhode Island.

The relationship of Onyx and IDC established by this Agreement is that of independent contractors, and nothing contained in this Agreement shall be construed to (i) give either party the power to direct and control the day-to-day activities of the other or (ii) constitute the parties as partners, joint venturers, co-owners or otherwise as participants in a joint or common undertaking.

(d) Nothing herein shall prevent Onyx from selling direct to End Users or OEMs within IDC's area of exclusive distribution, provided that said End Users or OEMs enter into written agreements with Onyx requiring said End Users or OEMs purchase annually a number of C8000 Stems exceeding fifty (50) per annum.

(f) Nothing herein shall prevent Onyx from dealing directly with customers which have purchased systems from IDC who wish to purchase quantities as specified in 2(d) so long as Onyx pays to IDC within 30 days of delivery of any C8000 system to such customer a sum

EXHIBIT 2 (continued)

equal to the schedule in Exhibit VI.

(g) Nothing herein shall prevent Onyx from dealing directly with the purchasing department of any National Retail Computer Store chain nor prevent such a National Computer Store chain from selling or servicing Onyx C8000 Systems at any one of its franchised or owned outlets regardless of that outlet's location.

3.   OBLIGATIONS OF IDC

IDC hereby agrees that it shall:

(c) Purchase annually at least one hundred (100) C8000 Systems in quarterly shipments of at least twenty-five (25) C8000 Systems, except that the first quarter of this Agreement shall cover the period from the date of execution of this Agreement until December 31, 1980 and for said first quarter IDC need purchase not more than fifteen (15) C8000 systems.

(f) Stock and Maintain an inventory of subassemblies as dictated by accepted statistical methods of predicting expected failure rates given the failure and quality assurance information supplied by Onyx to IDC on the entire population of C8000 Systems except those regarded as being in hostile environments.

4.   OBLIGATIONS OF ONYX

(a) To exert good faith efforts to manufacture and deliver C800 Systems to IDC in accordance with IDC's purchase orders.

(j) Refer to IDC all customers located within the area specified in 2(a) who annually require fifty (50) or fewer systems from Onyx. Onyx will make every effort to ensure that neither Onyx, its employees, or its customers sell into the exclusive distribution area as specified in 2(a) and Onyx will refuse to sell C8000 Systems to those who continue to violate this agreement except as provided in sections 2(d), 2(f) and 2(g).

(k) Deliver to IDC within 90 days of order C8000 Systems ordered by IDC. Should Onyx fail to deliver within 90 days goods ordered by IDC, Onyx, if IDC so requests, will make available to IDC all Industrial Property Rights related to the C8000 System without regard to IDC's intended use of said Industrial Property Rights and IDC will have an option to acquire said Industrial Property Rights for a period of 30 days after each such failure of delivery by Onyx. IDC's refusal to exercise this option for any particular delivery failure will not alter this Agreement or preclude IDC from exercising this option on subsequent delivery failures.

(m) Onyx will represent to the public that IDC is a distributor of Onyx computers wherever distributors, dealers, OEMs, ISOs or any seller of Onyx computers appears in advertising by Onyx at Onyx's expense.

(n) Onyx will represent IDC as a factory authorized service center.

5.   ORDERS AND DELIVERY

EXHIBIT 2 (continued)

6.   PAYMENT

IDC shall pay to Onyx the net purchase price of all goods ordered herein 5 days prior to Onyx's scheduled shipping date for those goods. Onyx may at its option extend credit terms to IDC, but these credit terms are subject to revocation by Onyx.

7.   FORCE MAJEURE

Each party to this contract shall be excused from the nonperformance or late performance of any obligation hereunder that is caused by acts of God, wars, riots, strikes....

8.   LIMITED WARRANTY

9.   LIMITATIONS ON WARRANTIES, LIABILITY AND BRINGING ACTION

10.   PRODUCT CHANGES

11.   INDUSTRIAL PROPERTY RIGHTS

(a) IDC agrees that the Industrial Property Rights to the Goods are and shall remain the sole property of Onyx except as provided in section 4K. The use by IDC of any Industrial Property Rights (including, but not limited to, any trademark, trade name or copyrighted material) is authorized only for the purposes set forth herein; and upon termination of this Agreement for any reason such authorization shall cease.

12.   TERM AND TERMINATION

(a) The initial term of this Agreement shall commence on the date hereof and shall continue for 64 months thereafter.

(b) This agreement or any contract made pursuant to this Agreement may be terminated:

(i) By either party for substantial breach of any material provision of this Agreement by the other, provided that written notice has been given to the other of the alleged breach and such breach has not been removed within 30 days after the giving of such notice.

(ii) By Onyx if there is a transfer of the majority interest of IDC, if any assignment is made of IDC's business for the benefit of creditors, if a receiver, trustee in bankruptcy or similar officer is appointed to take charge of a substantial part of Buyer's assets, if IDC fails to

EXHIBIT 2 (continued)

respond within 10 days to a demand by Onyx for adequate assurance of IDC's ability to perform under this Agreement of any contract made pursuant to this Agreement, or

(iii) By Onyx if IDC shall fail to purchase 25 C8000 Systems per quarter for two consecutive quarters and IDC has not, as of the date of the above mentioned failure, purchased at least the cumulative total required as of that date according to Exhibit V.

(iiii) As provided by section 13 hereunder.

13.   ASSIGNMENT

This Agreement is personal to the parties hereto and any delegation by either party of its duties of performance under this Agreement or any assignment by IDC or Onyx of its rights hereunder without prior approval of the other party is prohibited and shall, at the option of the other party, void this Agreement provided that Onyx shall be able to assign its rights to receive payments hereunder.

14.   PATENT INFRINGEMENT - INDEMNIFICATION

(a) Onyx agrees, at its own expense, to defend IDC and any customer thereof ("indemnitee") from and against any claim, suit or proceeding, and to pay all judgment costs finally awarded against IDC or said customer by reason of such claim, suit or proceeding, insofar as it is based upon an allegation that the Goods or any part thereof furnished by Onyx infringes any United States letter patent....

15.   EXPORT

(a) IDC shall comply with all applicable provisions of the Unites States Export Administration regulations....

16.   GENERAL

(a) This Agreement together with Exhibits attached hereto constitutes the entire agreement between the parties relating to the subject matter hereunder and no modification of this Agreement shall be binding on either party unless it is in writing and signed by both parties

EXHIBIT I - PRODUCT SPECIFICATIONS

EXHIBIT II - REPLACEMENT PARTS PRICE LIST

EXHIBIT III - SYSTEMS PRICE LIST

EXHIBIT IV - CONFIDENTIAL STATEMENT AND NOTICE

EXHIBIT 2 (concluded)

EXHIBIT V - IDC MINIMUM PURCHASE SCHEDULE

EXHIBIT VI - COMMISSION SCHEDULE

Cumulative Systems Sold To Each Customer By Onyx	Commission To Be Paid In Accordance with 2(f)
1-10	5%
11-25	4%
26-40	3%
41-60	2%
Over 60	1%

Case 20

Knight Brothers

In November 1980 Richard Knight and his brother, James, were reviewing the business plan they had prepared for setting up a retail store to sell microcomputer time by the half-hour. They had chosen a location in Harvard Square, a very busy intersection in the Boston area, and had lined up computers they would lease and set up for operation in the store. What remained, as they saw it, was to obtain venture capital, set up the store and open for business. To do this, they felt their plan needed to be in good order, and they needed an idea of just how much capital they should seek from what sort of people, and on what terms. A copy of the plan, such as they had prepared it to date, appears in Exhibit 1.

Born in Providence, R.I. in 1944, Richard Knight had attended boarding school and earned a B.A. degree from Colorado College. After a tour of duty in the U.S. Army, he took a job with the First National Bank of Boston. In 1970 he decided to leave the world of corporate finance, remarking, "I hate suits and I hate, absolutely despise, organizational politics." Subsequently, he and his wife traveled to many parts of the world, until she injured her leg, and they decided to return for extended medical care in Boston. He recalled:

> At that time I had nothing to do. I was interested in finance, the stock market, data manipulation, forecasting, and so on—just things I had picked up since leaving college. But I wanted to learn more about business and to try fooling around with forecasting and computers, so it seemed like business school would be a good thing to get involved in.

He enrolled in the MBA program at Boston University and found a professor who would allow him to store data on his computer account. As a part-time student, his course of study took several years, during which he made extensive use of his computer access to develop forecasting programs.

> The tuition at B.U. was fairly high, but I figured I was getting around $30,000 worth of computer time that more than made up for it.

When his access to the terminal ceased upon graduation in 1979, he turned to microcomputers to carry on his work, operating in conjunction with a Boston stock brokerage firm.

James Knight, Richard's brother, who was 10 years younger, had earned an undergraduate degree in banking at Boston University and more recently had applied for admission to the MBA program at Dartmouth. Soon after graduation, with his wife expecting their first child, he looked around Providence for a company to buy and develop. Failing to find one, he moved to New York, where he became involved in Dynamotion, a company which manufactured a jingle-bell box for point-of-purchase sales. James commented:

> It was such an odd concept that I thought we should get orders first and then manufacture the product only after we were sure there was a market. But the financial backers disagreed, made me president and told me to go ahead anyway. A month later I left to join an in-

vestment firm. Three months later Dynamotion went broke.

At the investment firm James worked first in institutional sales for five years and then in mergers and acquisitions.

The Knight brothers had also tried a venture together as crude oil brokers in the late 1970s. Their father had suggested the opportunity as one that might yield commissions as high as $250,000 or more per day if they could close a big deal. Over a six-month period the brothers ran up a phone bill of over $4,500 attempting to set up oil purchases between suppliers and sellers, with themselves as middlemen, but they could not close a deal. Richard remarked:

Everyone was too greedy. Sales kept falling through because different people involved all wanted bigger and bigger cuts, first $1 million, then $2 million and so forth. There was so much money involved. It was hard for us to believe that a multimillion dollar deal would be entirely aborted because it wasn't more "multi."

During that time, Richard negotiated to take over a bankrupt oil refinery in Puerto Rico, but that deal also fell through, just before papers were signed. "Too much graft, corruption and payoffs involved," Jim observed. Nonetheless, both men looked back on the oil endeavor as "an incredible adventure." By contrast, Jim said his work in mergers and acquisitions at the New York investment bank made him "bored to tears." Richard said he felt the most important lesson from the oil venture was understanding the reason they failed.

The scheme was entirely feasible, but we had no credibility and no credit. We had not proven to anybody that we could conceive and capitalize a venture,

so they refused to believe in us or back us.

Some other venture attempts by Richard that never progressed beyond the pencil and paper stage included selling thermostats, a Mazda dealership and a pasta pushcart to provide homemade pasta with several alternative sauces from a small wagon in Harvard Square to people rushing out of the subway stations headed home without groceries.

The decision to pursue the idea of a computer time rental store was made in the fall of 1980 when James came from New York to Boston on personal business. He and Richard met for lunch at the Parker House and discussed the concept. Richard had suggested the idea 18 months earlier, but James had flatly said it would not work.

Richard wanted to set up a store full of APPLES with $15,000, but I figured it would cost 10 or more times that much.

Since that time, however, James had noticed the spreading popularity of microcomputers. The idea of renting them on a hourly basis in a retail store to hobbyists, small business managers and larger firms with temporary word-processing overloads seemed like it might succeed. Rental cost in Harvard Square, he and Richard knew, would be high, in the range of $2,000 per month for a suitably sized storefront on ground level. But the traffic in the area was high, consisting largely of college students, but also shoppers and business people going between the local subway station and downtown Boston. It also included many who were fairly affluent. The two men knew of no other computer time rental store in the country. The only related firms they knew of in the area were an arcade with pinball machines and computer games approximately one-third mile east of Harvard Square, and a small microcomputer retail sales store approximately one-third mile north of the Square.

Harvard, which was right on the Square, was among the most expensive universities in the nation to attend, and included many bright students who were both "well-heeled" and fascinated with computers. Recently it had made computer programming literacy one of the requirements for liberal arts graduation. In addition, many of its graduate students had use for the machines in their studies and research. The two brothers started preparing a prospectus and soon produced the document appearing in Exhibit 1, replete with computer generated alternative financial forecasts.

Beyond the initial store, they contemplated additional enterprises. They figured they would expand from the first store to 20 others at different locations within a year-and-a-half. After that, they surmised that their concept might become obsolete as larger companies moved into retailing on a larger scale and more people installed microcomputers at home. Second, however, they wanted to explore the concept of a laser printing service. Xerox was just introducing a machine which would allow quick and very high-quality printing with any defined typeface, and the two could see that it would permit them to provide a high-quality and very flexible printing service to any customer in the country by telephone. The machine would cost on the order of $150,000 to install, however.

Third, they wanted to market a new point-of-purchase marketing aid consisting of a "light box" about a foot long with 50 spaces for L.E.D. letters and numbers, which could be individually programmed by a retailer to flash advertisements on a running loop basis like a stock exchange ticker tape display or the Times Square News. This too would take substantial capital.

Their immediate objective, however, was to raise capital for the first store. Once they were able to do that, they felt they would have established credibility in the financial community, which would let them move on to additional and larger enterprises in the future.

EXHIBIT 1   Think Tanks Business Plan

TABLE OF CONTENTS
- I. INTRODUCTION
- II. CONCEPTUAL PLAN
- III. DEFINITION OF MARKET
- IV. PRODUCT SCOPE
- V. LOCATION
- VI. COST ANALYSIS
- VII. STAFFING AND INVENTORY
- VIII. PROJECTIONS
- IX. CONCLUSION

EXHIBIT 1 (continued)

I.   INTRODUCTION

It is our intention to form a partnership to purchase microcomputers (hardware) and the peripheral equipment necessary to adapt the microcomputers to many different uses along with the programming (software) that will facilitate adaptation of the microcomputers to the greatest number of prospective clients.

In connection with this we intend, once established, to offer our clients the opportunity to lease or purchase the computers, peripheral equipment and the programming from us, should their need for access to a computer make it more sensible for them to have it at their place of business or residence instead of coming to us.

We intend to lease store space in the Harvard Square area of Cambridge. Renovations will be made to the store to make it modern and suitable to our needs. We will advertise primarily on the radio in the Boston/Cambridge area to make people aware of the services we are offering.

The general partners will keep the limited partners apprised on a timely basis of the completion of the various stages of development.

II.   CONCEPTUAL PLAN

Over the next 10 years, usage of microcomputers by the average American household will undergo a major expansion. It has been established that the demand will exist in the next decade for the home computer to handle such matters as the family bank account, grocery shopping, and budgeting of family energy consumption among many other uses. Given this need, the American public will have to become far more familiar than currently with the computer and its uses. As this is primarily an educational process, the benefits to the organization that can establish a foothold in the confidence of the American household will be sizable. Establishing our store, which we plan to call Think Tanks, at this time will allow us to take full advantage of the opportunities outlined above.

A perceived roadblock to the widespread use of the computer in the home or small business is the cost of acquiring a computer. From marketing studies we know that the consumption of high-ticket home usage items can be readily achieved. As evidence of this, the BETAMAX system and the VHS system have become extremely popular. A BETAMAX, or comparable machine, costs slightly under $1,000.00 per unit. The cost of the microcomputers currently available appears to present a certain argument for elasticity of the demand for high-ticket items for the home.

Even though we cannot control the cost of the hardware to the consumer, we can offer a far less expensive way for the typical consumer to explore the product and have use of it. An individual will be able to walk into our store and will be met by one of our employees. The employee will be familiar with the operation of microcomputers and will attempt to ascertain the exact interests of customers while helping them learn and experiment with the various systems. We feel that the ability to offer many different microcomputer products and allow customers to investigate the advantages and disadvantages of each system will bring us people who are not only curious but also interested in purchasing.

In addition to the regular computer services the client might wish to perform, a separate area of the store will be devoted entirely to computer assisted games. For example the person interested in playing backgammon with one of the acknowledged experts could sit down in front

EXHIBIT 1 **(continued)**

of a television type screen and attempt his skill. The customer interested in this type of service will have access to the games on the computers in return for the payment for the time the computer is used. The inherent market for this type of service in the proximity to a college should be large.

The success of the game SPACE INVADERS is well-documented. We will be able to offer many games of this type on a comparable cost basis.

The use of the CRT, or Cathode Ray Tube, is an important part of the concept. The idea of sitting in front of a simple keyboard and typing is not appealing, but the ability to look at what you are typing or look at the game you are playing is quite intriguing.

Computers now being tested as a learning tool with children in school systems have been quite successful and the reception to them has been quite good.

III.   DEFINITION OF MARKET

We project that the average age of our initial customers will be on the low side. Somewhere in the mid-twenties to start is the best estimation that we are able to make. We would hope that the age will rise, as people in the area become more familiar with our store.

The application to so many areas is exciting. We believe that the possibilities for the near future from the neighborhood concept are of a most exciting nature. Once the store becomes a member of the community, the sales potential for servicing local business accounts in, for example, accounts receivable or inventory control is tremendous. A local doctor might send a secretary down to our store at the end of every week to input data on patients the doctor has seen during the week, what types of problems they sought help on, what the diagnoses were, how much time the doctor spent with each patient, and billing information. This would computerize the doctor's records, giving cross-reference ability on ailments and telling where the doctor stands from a personal financial point of view so he or she can plan accordingly.

If initial demand meets our expectations, we want to be prepared to expand into other sectors of the greater Boston-area market. This area is one of the largest population centers in the United States, and it has an extraordinarily high percentage of students because it contains many colleges and universities. In the Harvard Square area there are five: Harvard University, Massachusetts Institute of Technology, Boston University, Northeastern University, and Boston College. Their combined student population exceeds 100,000.

Cambridge is regarded by industry as a high-technology center and was the forerunner of what is currently described as the Route 128 technology belt.

We foresee the prime customers for our concept to include: small businesses, professionals, students, leisure-time users, elementary schools, high schools, learning systems users and database users. Let us consider each of these perceived potential markets.

Small Business

There exist well in excess of 2000 small businesses in the immediate area of the proposed store location. The potential for this market is substantial. Traditionally, small business has not been able to take advantage of many factors which for the larger businesses bring about economies of scale. One area in which the small business has been at a severe disadvantage has been information systems.

EXHIBIT 1 (continued)

Typically, the small business has not had any form of sophisticated inventory control. The application potential of the microcomputer to this area is extensive, from information aspects to reporting and keeping accounting control. How many small businesses can monitor their cost of goods sold in an efficient manner? The time required in taking inventory could be eliminated with a computer providing all this information. The business owner could tell at any time what type of a mark-down should be used while still remaining profitable.

Keeping track of accounts receivable is a problem, and their aging can cost the small business a lot of money. Using a microcomputer the small business could analyze the profitability of various products in inventory. In planning, this would be most useful information. Many accounting costs which the small business now sustains could be reduced by adding a microcomputer. Many other applications are possible with the use of a microcomputer, but the above gives a feel for the potential of this segment of the market.

Even though the microcomputers address themselves to the small-business market, there is still a gap. We believe that the problem is twofold, the first being the educational or confidence gap. No one likes to be regarded as unsophisticated or unintelligent. The owner of a small business who lacks expertise to operate a small computer may consequently hold back from buying one. If to this inhibition we than add the factor of cost, we would expect to find that a large sector of the potential market has not purchased. We propose to solve these two roadblocks by offering computer time on a low cost basis so users can learn without any type of capital contribution.

Then, should a customer decide that the benefits of the microcomputer are as extensive as we think, and that acquisition of a computer is desirable, we will offer to sell or lease one. This makes sense because of the reluctance of the small business to commit to a capital expense. We would offer attractive terms to induce business owners to enter into the lease and get the hardware installed.

To summarize, for the small business the microcomputer's advantages are extensive, incorporating such positives as inventory control and the ability to compete effectively from an informational decision-making point of view with large businesses of the same industry. Our approach to this segment of our market is to show customers the obvious advantages of adding the expertise of the microcomputer to their business. This can then be accomplished in three ways; leasing time on our microcomputers, leasing the customers their own microcomputers, or selling them microcomputers.

Professionals

Programs at our store will offer multiple uses for the professional sector of the economy including some of the same advantages provided to the small business sector. The professional is typically in a service-oriented business involving significant personal interaction with each client. One factor that places a ceiling on effectiveness of practitioners is their ability to handle the flow of information and statistics on each new client. The strain placed on a professional's time is significant, and there is an optimization point after which the value of additional clientele can become negative. Although this optimization point can be raised by adding more staff, there is a cost trade-off which makes this impractical beyond a certain level. More importantly, the time of the professional becomes occupied with managing the increased staff, rather than

EXHIBIT 1 (continued)

drawing an enlarged clientele and thereby increasing the revenue base. Insofar as we help increase the time that professionals can spend on increasing their income, we provide a valuable service.

There are the additional benefits allowing the professional with a small office to compete effectively with larger offices. This becomes especially important as we examine the move to more advertising and competition on the part of professionals, from doctors to accountants to lawyers. The professional who does not have all the cost effectiveness of the large firm will be forced to innovate in order to survive. We offer innovativeness to the professional with a smaller office.

The uses take several forms. Word processing and accounting are only two of many useful capabilities for professionals. For lawyers, time records could be stored on the microcomputer which, in turn, would easily handle the billing of the clients. The information which the lawyer keeps on his clients could be stored and cross referenced.

For doctors the uses include standard office accounting work, as well as keeping track of lab reports. An MD could cross reference all of his or her cases, which would provide the ability to analyze types of services being provided to the community on an on-going basis. The ability to call up a patient's prior records in legible hard copy just before the patient arrives for an appointment should be a definite plus.

Other professionals have many needs for services we are discussing. There are many one-person accounting offices that do both individual and business work. Addition of a microcomputer would allow the accountant to prepare the quarterly statements for an organization in a fraction of the time currently needed. It would also allow opportunity to compare the results of the client company over comparable periods of time. This would be a most useful tool as it could reveal discrepancies quickly and help the accountant home in on important changes in financial position.

To other professionals the aid of a microcomputer will be invaluable. Stockbrokers in smaller firms now lack access to the type of computer capability which larger firms afford their employees. To be competitive with counterparts in larger firms, stockbrokers in smaller firms need computerized help in such areas as cross-referencing of clients' holdings by position. Most larger firms already have such a service in place. In addition, it would be of significant benefit to have the computer maintain a call sheet that the broker could use to track conversations with present and prospective clients regarding their holdings and suggestions they were given.

It is readily apparent that the uses for professionals are manifold in nature and exciting in scope. The capability of a professional to provide more and better services on a more timely basis will be greatly enhanced by use of a microcomputer. Further, the option of not having to increase overhead by making a substantial purchase should make time-renting or leasing alternatives attractive to professionals.

Students

One of the most fascinating of all the markets for the services we are proposing is the student population. Advantages of the Harvard Square area in this connection are readily apparent. The student population of the area, which exceeds 100,000, makes the location ideal for marketing the services of the store to students.

EXHIBIT 1 (continued)

As you will recall, in conceptually analyzing the project we came to the conclusion that one of the major roadblocks for some market sectors was an educational gap. That is not true of the student market. There, that educational factor should work very much to our benefit. The younger the customer on average, the greater the prior exposure to computers. Students in college today are products of the computer age, where it is natural to rely on the machine for part of the work. The more quantitative the field of study in which the student is engaged, the greater the interaction with data processing equipment.

We do not envision students as likely candidates for purchase of computers. However, the interest they should have in using our facilities we feel will be significant. Uses to which students can put our microcomputers appear to be never ending. Let us analyze a few of them.

Presently, students have access to computers only through their schools, and the schools set very definite restrictions upon who can use computers and for how long. The emphasis in time-sharing at those institutions goes to the statistically oriented courses. In addition, it is quite unlikely that there is a computer for the eye to see. Many students are simply allowed access to terminals which operate remotely via telephone connections with large computers from which the university leases time. The advantages of students actually seeing computers in front of them we feel are significant. This will encourage them to be more participants than just programmers of homework into keyboards.

For students taking courses in quantitative areas, the benefits of working with numbers and formulas is apparent. Moreover, the word processing-related functions are helpful with writing and on-line editing of manuscripts. The writing and reorganization of term papers becomes far more facile. Development of quality resumes is one of the prime concerns of students in their last year. We could assist in development of resumes.

Access of students to data bases in conjunction with empirical research can aid some required schoolwork. A student will be able to tie from our computer directly into many large data bases, such as Dow Jones, with a telephone hook-up, which we will provide. Cross-referencing ability will be beneficial to students outside of the normal work which would be called for by their colleges.

Our store will provide many other services which we believe will interest students. The largest of these falls into the leisure time sector of our services. We will offer many games with various degrees of sophistication on the microcomputers. Among sophisticated games a student can choose to play backgammon against some of the best players in the world to improve skill. This holds true for many other games, including gin rummy, poker, blackjack, chess, checkers, cribbage and others too numerous to mention. The microcomputers will be programmed to play at different skill levels, which will accommodate anyone from beginner to the most advanced of players.

Less sophisticated games we envision installing include some now available through such manufactures as Atari. These will be available in the store in an area slightly separated from the computers in a physical sense. In this way those who are playing the games will not disturb the more serious students who might be working on formulas. The range of games will be more than enough to satisfy even the most enthusiastic devotee. We envision a different pricing structure for games which are less complicated. These pricing policies will be discussed later when we will take up the entire pricing structure of the store.

EXHIBIT 1 (continued)

We believe that student demand will be a function of intelligence and curiosity level. Students are today far more accustomed to computers in their day-to-day life than older people. Most students have been using computers on a regular basis since high school and have been made aware over a period of time that there are many other functions which computers can perform in addition to homework assignments. The interest of students in the sophisticated games the microcomputers will offer has been documented in our research in the university systems. There is today a definite demand in this area made up of the students who wish to spend time playing chess on the computer, for example. In summary, we feel that the student sector offers us a large untapped market for the store's services.

Graduate Students With Degrees

The application for the services in this store should run somewhat congruently with those of the student population, but with an important difference. Undergraduate students have access to computers of the university to aid them with their studies. But many graduate students must do research on their own under limited budgets. We will be able to offer this sector the most cost-effective manner in which to use computers.

Word processing capabilities of the microcomputers can be important to the graduate student who is attempting to get published. The store will offer a full complement of computer on-line word processing type functions which would be helpful with a doctoral dissertation. The more quantitative the work that the individual is engaged in, the better we will be able to service him or her.

Leisure Time

The leisure-time sector of our perceived market is large indeed. Even though not all sectors of our market may be as versed in computers as the student population, we expect that the surrounding community in general is sophisticated. This statement is backed by voluminous amounts of empirical data on the socioeconomic composition of the Harvard Square area. We believe that leisure-time activities in this community are such that it would be perfectly normal for individuals to stop in to our store after hearing about us and experiment with various products we offer.

We anticipate demand from this sector of our market for the following services: sophisticated games which can be played on the microcomputer; less sophisticated games, that a parent might bring children in to play on a Saturday afternoon; the learning about microcomputers to ascertain practical fit with a household; and the pursuit of other outside hobbies or interests. Cooking could be an example. A person would be able to access a vast number of recipes. A dieter could select recipes screened to exclude cholesterol.

This market segment is exciting in offering so many different possibilities. There are, of course, many more than have been discussed here, and new combinations of services are being developed every day.

Elementary and High Schools

Many schools already use computers in one way or another as a learning aid. However, the budgetary crisis that confronts most school systems aids us in that we offer a less costly service

EXHIBIT 1 (continued)

through our leasing option, and as a result of the low cost of the microcomputer. We could provide programming to schools that would enable students to learn how to use computers all by themselves. The additional advantage of the microcomputer that comes into play here is that it is in front of the student who is working on it. It is not some abstract "thing" that the student never truly understands. We will explore the feasibility of offering part or all of these services on a limited basis as a good-will gesture to build up our community identity and bring us additional business from other market sectors, such as, for example, the parent who hears from a child or the person who reads about the concept in a newspaper.

The amount of programming available in this area and the instructive games which can be demonstrated are exciting.

Instructional Systems

Instructional systems will become more microcomputer-oriented in the future. The market here is large and the ability of our store to exploit it is great. A tremendous amount of learning takes place outside the formal classroom structure that can be economically accomplished on the microcomputer. This can be seen by looking at self-teaching aspects of microcomputer programming. Certainly if the microcomputer can teach the individual who is operating it how to do so without any outside help, then it will be able to teach accounting, cooking, English grammar or applied statistics. What could be more exciting than being able to expand into new areas of learning on your own time and in accordance with your schedule? Courses for the microcomputer to provide will be developed by leading authorities in their fields.

For businesses interested in teaching salespeople a new marketing approach, we could develop a system to their specifications. For a brokerage firm wanting to provide institutional clients with explanation of a new product in the financial futures area, our store could prepare computerized teaching materials and other services. The possibilities are expansive for servicing this market sector.

Data Base Access

The final perceived market is in data base access. Throughout the country there are large data bases on everything from the number of golden retrievers who had litters last year to the movements of multi-national corporations into new markets overseas. These data bases are being added to every day by all of us. All we must do is write a check and the bank upon which we wrote the check is increasing its data base. The possibilities for data base access are far too numerous to mention so we shall only discuss a few here.

The electronic mail concept widely discussed for the last few years in connection with the office of the future is currently available to larger corporations. They can send mail on an overnight, or if they wish immediate, basis through expensive equipment. But if an individual or small- to medium-sized business should wish to accomplish this, the cost is prohibitive.

The application of microcomputers we will offer in this area is exciting. An individual will be able to walk into our store and access a data base or send a letter to Texas for delivery the next day. We will be able to offer these services to the person who has no other access to them. A local business interested in expanding sales but handicapped by limited capital and lacking an extensive sales organization will be able through our store to reach buyers based upon extensive information about each of them.

EXHIBIT 1 (continued)

Among more whimsical uses of the data bases, we could generate the record of every major league football team against another team and screen for factors such as the defensive nature of the team in the past to form conclusions as to advisable coaching directions and the amount of passing they should utilize. In connection with this, we could provide information on how all the various people who predict these outcomes are thinking.

This mentions just three of the endless possibilities.

Summary of Market Sectors

We must conclude that the uses of the microcomputers that we will install to meet the demands of the markets are limitless and bounded only by the imagination and the software available. However, our store will not enter all of the above-mentioned markets on the first day of operation. We believe that a gradual rollout of services is better in keeping with sound financial practices and the common good of the partnership. It is our intention to provide those services through the store that are in greatest demand. That will maximize cost effectiveness for the partnership and contribute to optimization of return to the limited partners.

Experience of the General Partners

Richard D. Knight is 36 years old and has lived in the Harvard Square area for the past nine years. He holds a Bachelor of Arts degree from the Colorado College in Colorado Springs, Colorado, and a Master's in Business Administration from Boston University with a major in the application of microcomputers. For the past five years he has been an independent computer consultant specializing in the microcomputer area. Most recently his work has included the development of volume momentum models for stock, commodity and option trading for Burgess and Leith, an investment banking and brokerage firm in Boston, Massachusetts.

James A. Knight is 26 years old and a resident of New York City. He holds a degree in finance from Boston University. He lived in the greater Boston area for four years while associated with the investment banking firm of Shearson, Loeb, Rhoades, most recently as a vice-president. He has extensive experience in all facets of the financial markets and the capital raising process.

IV.   PRODUCT SCOPE

Products offered by our store will vary from the low end of Atari games to the high end of a Hewlett-Packard computer with disc drives and a color plotter. Equipment will cost from $600 per game to the Hewlett-Packard at $25,000. In between will be small microcomputers from Apple and Radio Shack with the add-on equipment necessary to expand functional performance of the units. In addition, because we believe that a significant portion of our revenues will initially come from our word processing capability, we have projected the purchase of two Digital Equipment (DEC) word processors that are, in our judgment, among the very finest available in cost-effectiveness. In the high-quality area, we intend to purchase a color graphics printer, which will give us the finest possible hard copy output for the demanding segments of our perceived market.

We will also have a large selection of software to meet user requirements. The cost of the software is low in relation to the time utilization.

EXHIBIT 1 (continued)

The scope of the product must also include certain cards, chassis, monitors, plugs, connectors, modems, etc. One of the more interesting peripheral components will be two Apple graphic tablets, which will work in conjunction with the Apple computers and enable users to perform a far broader range of functions.

In summary, we intend to cover the microcomputer market thoroughly. Installation of the various units must be timed from a cost effective roll-out point of view. The microcomputer field is expanding so rapidly that new product substitutions might occur within the next few months if they offer better scope or less cost.

V.   LOCATION

Why Harvard Square? Well, it has long been one of the leading high technology areas of the country. The Greater Boston Area presents excellent demographics for this type of product introduction. Especially important to us, as we analyze the location, is the combination of high percentage student population with high-income level in the rest of the population. A study done for the Cambridge Seven group was filed with the city of Cambridge and the Commonwealth of Massachusetts, in connection with the proposed building of residential housing in place of the old subway yards in Harvard Square. Extensive demographic analysis done in connection with that study identified as target groups for the housing project families with $45,000 in annual income and young (under 35) professionals. It concluded that there were more than enough in these groups to justify the building of a major multi-million dollar housing project.

These results indicate first, that the area is conducive to new investment on a large scale; second, that the income level of the local community is such that it can justify an expensive housing unit expansion; third, that type of clientele we would like to attract exists in the area and; fourth, that the overall outlook for the Cambridge/Harvard Square area is excellent.

We conclude that Harvard Square offers us the best overall mix on high income level, proximity to the universities, large professional population, technological interest and cost effectiveness.

VI.   COST ANALYSIS

In estimating costs for setting up the store and beginning operations we have made some assumptions, which follow:

1. The cost of equipment will range in the $150,000 area.
2. The space in Harvard Square area will be available immediately.
3. The renovations can be completed within 30 days.
4. The cost of the microcomputer hardware, software and add-on equipment will not materially vary before the end of the year 1980.
5. We will be able to hire adequate staffing.
6. The store will be in operation in 1980.
7. The amount allocated to rent includes heat and electricity.

EXHIBIT 1 (continued)

In line with this, we intend to purchase the following equipment:

Hardware

Six APPLE 48K	$6600.00
Twelve disc drives (APPLES) four with monitor	5640.00
Four APPLE soft cards	50.00
Three Zenith 19" color monitors	2250.00
Three PAPER TIGER with graphics	3000.00
Three APPLE graphics tablets	2100.00
Two Centronics 636 Printers	1700.00
Four SANYO black and white monitors	600.00
Two Centronics printer interface cards	380.00
Five APPLE serial intersect cards	1000.00
One APPLE clock/calendar card	250.00
Two Silenttype printers	1000.00
Two APPLE expansion chassis	1100.00
Two Corvus 10 megabyte Hard Disc	8800.00
One Diablo Daisywheel letter quality printer	3000.00
One Hewlett-Packard HP-85 with disc drive	5000.00
Five DC HAMET micromodem II	2000.00
One PRINACOLOR IS 8001 (color graphics printer)	6000.00
Two Digital Equipment word processors	40,000.00
One Hewlett-Packard 32K with disc drives and color plotter	25,000.00
Four Radio Shack 264002,64K with one drive	14,000.00

TOTAL HARDWARE $130,170.00

All hardware is subject to replacement by comparable equipment.

Games

Five Texas Instruments	$3000.00
Five Atari	3000.00

TOTAL GAMES $6000.00

Software, Etc.

Software, Cables, plugs, connectors, parts, library inventory, disc inventory, data base subscription, paper inventory $16,600.00

Working Capital Costs

Rent	$90,000.00
Telephone	5,000.00

EXHIBIT 1 (continued)

```
Salaries ............................................................................................... 43,200.00
Advertising ......................................................................................... 20,000.00
Renovations ....................................................................................... 20,000.00
Office misc .......................................................................................... 2,500.00

                        TOTAL ............................ $180,700.00
```

Sales Analysis and Pricing

The pricing formula we have determined to be best is based on the sophistication of the machine. The more sophisticated and costly the machine, the higher price it will rent for. At the low end of the spectrum is the game segment, which will be priced at $1.25 per quarter hour. The APPLE segment will be priced at $12.00 per hour. The Digital Equipment word processors will be priced at $19.00 per hour. The top end of the equipment represented by the Hewlett-Packard equipment with the graphic plotter will go for $21.50 per hour. We expect to do the bulk of business in the lower sectors of our pricing structure.

VII.   STAFFING AND INVENTORY

Under the projections we have run for the store, there is essentially no cost to carry the inventory because there is virtually no inventory, except for discs and programs, which are not material.

Staffing of the store will be accomplished primarily with graduate students of the area in need of extra money. Richard Knight has agreed that during the start-up phase, he will devote his efforts on a daily basis to operation of the store. He, plus one full-time staffer, should be adequate for administration and handling customer inquiries. We do not anticipate any dramatic increase in staff, even if the utilization rates should hit the higher end of our prediction.

VIII.   PROJECTIONS

In the equations we ran to estimate revenues at various levels of equipment utilization, we assumed that the store would be open six days a week for 52 weeks per year. We assumed alternative machine utilization rates in the computations shown below for different activities to examine their impacts. For example, Assumption One shows everything at a 30 percent rate of use and in Assumption Two we increase the use on the games up to a 50 percent rate. In Assumption Three we project that the games are used 70 percent of the time. Costs remain constant throughout, because we have budgeted our fixed expenses to meet the different levels of demand. It is interesting to note that the optimization of revenues and therefore of profits comes from the APPLE system.

In the projection below all equipment will be assumed to have a utilization rate of 30 percent except for the games which will have the following utilization rates: Assumption One, 30 percent; Assumption Two, 50 percent; Assumption Three, 70 percent.

EXHIBIT 1 (continued)

NAME(GAMEW) = GAMEW

UNDER THE 30-PERCENT ASSUMPTION 11/16/80

PROJECTIONS FOR MICROCOMPUTER UTILIZATION
UNDER 3 ASSUMPTIONS

	Assumption One	Assumption Two	Assumption Three
Revenue	272,160.00	324,000.00	375,840.00
Expenditures	160,700.00	160,700.00	160,700.00
Profits	111,460.00	163,300.00	215,140.00

The effect of other assumptions on profits can be seen in the table following.

IX.   CONCLUSION

It is our belief that the demand for the product we intend to market will be significant in nature and require us to expand our operations in the near future. The potential of expanding the number of stores in the greater Boston Area and then expanding into other markets in other cities is high.

We believe this concept is the tip of the future and will enable our investors to participate in what we consider to be the coming boom in the microcomputer market. The evidence of this exists partially in the offering of Apple on Wall Street and the enthusiastic reception that company is receiving.

As a final note, this offering memo and the projections which it contains were prepared by a microcomputer of the type we intend to utilize.

EXHIBIT 1 (concluded)

OTHER UTILIZATION RATES ASSUMED (%)				PROFIT CALCULATIONS ($)		
GAMES	APPLES	DIGITAL	HEWLETT	REVENUES	EXPENSES	PROFITS
30	30	30	30	272,160	160,700	111,460
50	30	30	30	324,000	160,700	163,300
70	30	30	30	375,840	160,700	215,140
30	50	30	30	361,029	160,700	200,329
30	70	30	30	449,897	160,700	289,197
30	30	50	30	286,231	160,700	125,531
30	30	70	30	300,302	160,700	139,602
30	30	30	50	298,821	160,700	138,121
30	30	30	70	325,481	160,700	164,781
30	50	50	50	401,760	160,700	241,060
50	50	50	50	453,600	160,700	292,900
70	50	50	50	505,440	160,700	344,740
50	30	50	50	364,731	160,700	204,031
50	70	50	50	542,469	160,700	381,769
50	50	30	50	439,529	160,700	278,829
50	50	70	50	467,671	160,700	306,971
50	50	50	30	426,939	160,700	266,239
50	50	50	70	480,261	160,700	319,560
30	70	70	70	531,360	160,700	370,660
50	70	70	70	583,200	160,700	422,500
70	70	70	70	635,040	160,700	474,340
70	30	70	70	457,303	160,700	296,602
70	50	70	70	546,171	160,700	385,471
70	70	30	70	606,898	160,700	446,198
70	70	50	70	620,969	160,700	460,269
70	70	70	30	581,719	160,700	421,019
70	70	70	50	608,379	160,700	447,679

Case 21

Jack Logan

The central issue in my mind is this: What is the quickest payback I can get for this company and how much can I make? I'm getting two years to find out the answers and I'll be able to draw a salary during that time.

In December 1988 Jack Logan was negotiating possible purchase of Northern Bus Sales from the present owners who were operating the suburban Boston company from their offices in Albany, New York. Northern was a franchised distributorship which sold school buses manufactured by Cardwell Bus Bodies. The territory included Massachusetts, New Hampshire, Rhode Island, and Maine and was, according to Jack, considered to be one of the most competitive areas in the country for selling school buses.

He currently worked for the two Albany partners under a commission arrangement that would expire in early 1990. Over the next year, Jack said one of three things would happen:

1. He and the present owners of Northern Bus Sales would have agreed on a price for Jack to purchase the company.

2. Jack would continue to work under the present commission arrangement while establishing an equity position for himself as a partner.

3. The two sides would break off negotiations and Jack would seek other business opportunities on his own.

The Albany partners were asking $300,000 for the company: $120,000 down and the remaining $180,000 in five equal payments spread over five years. Jack had proposed a purchase price of $150,000 arranged over a five-year period with no more than $30,000 down. Jack summed up what he believed the reasons were for the disparity in valuing the school bus franchise:

These guys picked up the franchise in 1987 for a song. Their whole purpose was to work a quick turn-around and sell the company for a profit. The $300,000 is based on a multiple of the gross margin, but that's completely unrealistic. They have no interest in leaving Albany and coming to the Boston area to run the business. That's why they hired me.

From my point of view, the franchise has been dying for years. The previous owner had the company 15 years and virtually ran the business into the ground. The financial statements give you a pretty good idea of what shape the company is in.

Copies of the company's 1987 financial statements appear in Exhibit 1.

Personal Background

Jack Logan's father and uncle had owned and operated a school bus leasing company in Boston's western suburbs while Jack was growing up. Jack helped out with the family business occasionally and, after graduating in production management from Boston College in 1980, worked for his father and uncle full time. By 1986, Jack had decided to pursue an MBA and seek other business challenges. He enrolled as a full-time finance major at Babson College in the fall of 1987. One course that he mentioned as being particularly exciting was a new ventures class where he and three other students simulated buying a company:

> *Four of us, two buyers and two sellers, stayed up all night bargaining. It was the best experience I had at Babson.*

His involvement with the family business meanwhile helped him keep abreast of what other bus companies in the area were doing. He commented that the quality and turnover of sales representatives was a good indication of how strong a company was. It was common practice, he said, for a salesperson to work for a school bus distributor for a year or two, and then go to work for a competitor.

About the time he started graduate school, Jack recalled, he became aware of the condition that Cardwell Bus Body's distributor, Northern Bus Sales, was in. The owner, he said, had established a poor reputation for himself and the company, constantly losing credible sales people. Jack commented:

> *His wife had divorced him, his son had run away from home, and the Internal Revenue Service was after him on seven counts of tax evasion. Add to that he was $100,000 in debt and the general opinion that he was a liar and a bad business man, and you can see why I figured he was on the way out.*

At this point, the Albany partners purchased the franchise and began looking for someone to operate the business. Jack had been in contact with Northern by purchasing a few buses from it for the family's

leasing company. When he learned of the ownership change, Jack called the partners in Albany, and inquired about their plans for managing the franchise. He was told they were planning to turn the franchise around over the next three years and would be willing to let Jack run Northern on a day-to-day basis.

He negotiated an annual salary of $50,000, plus a 10 percent commission on all sales. In return, he would pay $3,200 monthly to the Albany partners as their return on equity and be responsible for his own selling and administrative expenses. In addition, it was agreed that the two sides would begin negotiations either to add Jack as a partner or to have him completely buy out the business.

Jack said this arrangement would let him accomplish a number of career objectives. The salary would allow him to support his wife and four children. He could continue at Babson during the evening and complete his MBA. Working for the company would allow him to assess it as a prospective acquisition. One year, he said, should be long enough for determining the franchise's sales potential. Moreover, he felt that experience gained through his father's and uncle's leasing company was a valuable learning aid:

> *Since my family was in the same business when I was growing up, I know what the other people are doing and thinking. I can walk into a bus yard and know what's going on in five minutes. In that respect, the experience is helpful. However, specialization can lead you to over emphasize the importance of one part of the business, and that can work against you.*

The School Bus Industry

School buses comprised a billion dollar market in the United States each year, according to Jack, with sales dominated by six bus body manufacturers. Jack guessed that Bluebird and Wayne were the industry leaders, with Cardwell a smaller volume competitor. All were based in the Midwest and were similar in terms of production and distribution. The chassis, engine, drive train and frame assemblies, were customarily manufactured by Ford, General Motors, and Navistar. Sales representatives would order chassis through these three producers and specify which of the six bus body companies would receive the chassis assembly. The body would then be fitted by the bus manufacturer to the chassis and the finished bus would be delivered to the distributor who had ordered the vehicle. Delivery took about four months after placement of the order with a chassis manufacturer.

Jack ordered nearly all chassis through Navistar. He thought they made good products and he wanted to preserve a good relationship he had developed with the Navistar dealer in Massachusetts. He used sales estimates to determine order sizes for chassis and tried to time orders so as to head off anticipated price increases, possible contract disputes or other events that might adversely affect the cost and delivery of chassis to bus body manufacturers. To take advantage of volume discounts, chassis were typically ordered once a year and carried as inventory until bodies were attached, busses were shipped to the distributors, and buyers were lined up.

Bodies were ordered as sales were made to customers, since body construction was generally customized. Differences in state and local regulations, combined with buyer desires for special options, prevented body manufacturers from taking advantage of mass production techniques that chassis manufacturers employed.

Demand for school buses was influenced by a number of economic and political factors. Weather conditions in New England required that sand and salt be applied to highways during the winter months. The salt corroded bus bodies so they needed replacement within five to 10 years. Jack noted that among local school districts, Waltham replaced its buses every six years, Wellesley every five years, and for communities along Cape Cod, every 12 years. In Massachusetts alone, he estimated that one eighth of the 10,000 school buses on the road were replaced each year due to rusted bodies and engine wear. Jack guessed that another 250 buses each were sold in Maine and New Hampshire annually.

Although there were exceptions, nearly all school buses were used by local school districts to transport students from their homes to school and back. The need for buses depended on the type and size of school district (e.g. urban or rural), extent of special activities that required transporting students, or the presence of integration efforts. A school district might own and operate its own fleet of buses or contract with an independent company such as the one Jack's father and uncle owned.

Jack saw market trends pointing in different directions. A switch to diesel fuel, court ordered busing, requirements that vehicles be accessible to the handicapped, and consolidation of schools and school districts all helped boost demand for school buses.

Countering such demand was increased pressure on officials to control costs. As a line item, transportation was the largest non-educational expense for a school district. It also seemed to Jack that resistance to busing was growing, influenced by opposition in northern cities such as Boston. Moreover, passage of property tax rollbacks, such as California's Proposition 13 and Massachusetts' "Prop 2 1/2" in recent elections, had caused local officials to wonder aloud whether further attempts to curb property and other taxes might continue to occur. School districts derived operating funds mainly from local property taxes, plus state aid and federal assistance to meet special educational needs. School districts in Massachusetts were more dependent than those elsewhere in the country on property taxes. Up to two-thirds of a school district's budget might be financed through this revenue source.

Jack said current law provided that the Federal government would reimburse local school districts for up to 80 percent of their transportation costs. Thus, a district that spent $1,000,000 in 1987 for transportation would be reimbursed $800,000 in 1988 for the incurred expense. Jack mentioned that this system was prone to confusion among school officials:

> They'll look at the cost of using school buses, and decide that they should patch up and repair their fleet instead of getting replacements.
>
> What they keep forgetting is that of the $36,000 they pay for a new bus, they are only paying $7,200 of that. So when they defer purchases, they're not cutting very much out of their budget . . . but a lot of them don't seem to grasp that. I guess that it's politically expedient to put off the decisions if you can.

Competition in School Bus Sales

Northern Bus Sales was one of seven principal distributors operating in New England. Jack outlined the competition as it presently existed, pointing to one dealer as the reason for recent price competition and reduced margins:

> His actions have screwed up the market terribly by trying to force everyone else out. Customers now have the attitude that when they call for a bus, they can find one in stock ready for driving off the lot. So what's happened is that we're being forced to carry a larger inventory than we would like and some people are even cutting the normal

> 10 percent profit margin to as low as 3 percent.

The largest nearby bus distributor was based in New Hampshire. Jack described the Wayne Bus Body affiliate as a huge operation which could pre-purchase and inventory buses. It offered financing and leasing services which other competitors, including Jack, lacked financing to do. He estimated that the firm held between 20 and 33 percent of the market for New England.

Jack guessed that Tico Bodies, based in Weymouth, Massachusetts, sold 350 buses each year, as did a distributor near Scituate, Massachusetts. The latter owned a fleet of 400 school buses for inventorying and leasing. They also provided financing to customers. Jack described the other three competitors as smaller and less aggressive. One was based in Rhode Island, another had recently been purchased by a private partnership, and a third was rumored to be going out of business.

Sales were made either through bidding on major fleet purchases by school districts and leasing companies or by selling individual units as they were needed. Jack said the former approach favored larger distributors with financial strength to order in greater volume and offer attractive payment terms in bidding. He estimated that as many as half of the orders put up for bid probably had the sale already "locked up" through a particular distributor. Jack remarked that he had bid 10 contracts for each eventual sale he had made in the last year, adding, "At least I'm getting known."

Jack described his selling approach as one of knowing who was buying what and getting friendly with them. His week consisted of sales calls to school officials and fleet owners throughout his four-state territory, concentrating on suburban and rural areas of Massachusetts. He estimated that he spent 30 of his 50 working hours per week making personal sales calls, but no more than four per day.

He had developed a list of what he saw as every potential customer in eastern Massachusetts. It included information on past purchases made by that district or company and whether they had purchased from Cardwell or one of its competitors. Jack said he drew upon school officials, fleet operators, bus dispatchers and drivers, and school secretaries to gather the information and get an idea of what was liked or disliked about such things as different makes of buses, service received from distributors, and future purchase plans. Jack followed up on sales calls through letters and order forms he had developed as promotion tools (see Exhibits 2 and 3).

He said about 60 percent of his sales were filled from his inventory, the remainder involving direct orders that he placed with the Cardwell factory in Indiana. During 1988, he had sold 45 new buses at an average price of $35,000 each. All but five were full sized models. He elaborated on the strategy of selling half-sized buses, which were considered specialty vehicles in the industry:

> The half-size buses are only about $4,000 cheaper than the full-sized version. From a selling point, that's not much of a savings. However, I've found that there is a spot market for bus chassis, and in particular, the half-size ones. So if I have the chassis in the factory and can't use them here, I can probably find someone else in the country who would be willing to pick them up at a premium. I stocked five of the half-size models this year and made money on them, even after carrying costs.

Other selling opportunities included used buses and vehicles modified to serve the handicapped or counter rising fuel costs. Jack explained that he spent nearly as much time selling a used bus as a new one. Consequently, he limited his dealings in this area to buses he could take as "trade ins."

Buses with wheelchair lifts were becoming popular and Jack added that increasing interest was being shown in buses powered by diesel or propane gas. In some cases, the profit margins tended to be higher than in selling the standard full size versions.

Jack described his sales terms "cash on the driveway." He said that while he didn't extend financing assistance as did his larger competitors, he did make an effort to see that the vehicles were properly serviced and his customers kept satisfied with the vehicles' performance:

> I've had a guy on salary who takes care of servicing buses. I'm finding out though, that it's cheaper to have my customers service their own vehicles and then reimburse them for the cost— granted that the bus is under warranty and the problem wasn't their fault. Maybe this is a change I should make permanent.

Jack said the past year had convinced him a person could still make money in the school bus industry. However, he regarded the current economic situation as the most volatile he had ever witnessed:

> School officials who used to look at transportation costs only when they replaced their fleet are paying much closer attention to busing expenditures. They look at me and say, "Why, only three or four years ago, I could buy a new bus for just $20,000. What happened?" My response is that, sure, prices have gone up. But it's still a lot cheaper to buy some buses and consolidate the physical plant rather than keep a lot of half-empty schools open and eat the overhead that goes along with a building. The

selling job is getting tougher instead of easier.

Financial Aspects of an Equity Position

Jack said he had a "silent" partner whom he could rely upon for financing the acquisition of Northern Bus Sales from the Albany partners. He added that unless he was certain that he could clear a minimum of $60,000 to $80,000 in salary each year, he wouldn't go ahead with his plans to buy the company:

> *I can't see risking my own money if someone else will pay me just as much to work for them. I figure I can get a job paying $60,000 a year without the hassle of tying up personal equity.*

Cash was important for financing inventory. Payment for the chassis required access to a substantial line of credit, which Jack was not receiving through the New York partners. Finance charges on a full-size chassis, which wholesaled for $24,000, totaled $7 per day. The carrying charge commenced when the order was placed with the manufacturer and continued until the unit was sold.

Selling and administrative costs consisted of the travel expenses Jack incurred in making sales calls and the rental for the top half of a house in suburban Boston which had been converted to office use. Jack guessed the financial condition of the company had improved since the last fiscal year, although he wasn't sure by how much until the 1988 financial statements were completed. "If anything," he said, "the figures should support my argument for a lower purchase price than the partners in Albany proposed."

Jack acknowledged that his relationship with the current owners was not very amicable. He questioned the value of financial statements as a basis for negotiating a pur-

chase price or equity position for himself:

> *There's a lot in the statements which shows up and a lot that doesn't. They show that a badly run franchise can do nearly a million dollars in gross sales and still lose money. You can also see that the previous owner took a lot out for himself.*
>
> *I reviewed all the techniques for financial projections I learned at business school and none of them seemed to apply. For instance, in a region as big as mine, there will always be more potential sales than I can make. What I sell depends on how well I develop my territory, because I have a lot of bad will to overcome. I'm estimating 25 percent more chassis per year to project sales of new buses, with an eventual peak of 250 buses per year. My assumption is that demand for new buses will stay about the same. If that changes, my outlook on taking over this company could change as well.*

Considering Alternatives

Jack said his present position at Northern offered him a range of possibilities to consider over the next 12 months. First, there was the chance that he and the partners in Albany could come to an agreement on a purchase price for Jack to take over the company. Should Jack maintain the present situation, he mentioned that there might be an option for him to buy into the company as a partner—with either a one-third or one-half interest in the firm:

> *I know that they're looking to get their investment back out of this company as soon as they can. So, if I were to come in with a lower proposal as a partner, then I could have some say in how the business should develop and also show my sincerity in taking over Northern Bus Sales. At the same time,*

I don't want to pay more than a minority interest is worth. I'm not sure how to start in setting a value on the business as a partnership.

Other options Jack mentioned included diversifying the business to insulate sales from any possible budget cutbacks by school districts. Leasing of school buses was becoming more common, as was use of passenger vans for school and general business use. Jack pointed out that the Albany partners owned a van franchise in addition to Northern Bus Sales and that there might be an opportunity to build that segment of the transportation market into the business. Splitting commissions on sales he lined up with motels, corporations or special transit services might, he said, be one way to get into that market.

Sticking to school bus sales was another option. Although Jack had been unable to get factory concessions in the past, he said that if he could it would improve his profit picture and help him remain price competitive with other distributors. The concessions were similar to those offered to automobile dealers. A customer might be sold a vehicle at or near the wholesale "sticker" price. However, the dealer would receive a concession of up to $1,400 from the bus body manufacturer which effectively lowered the wholesale cost of the bus. Jack said that he was still talking with Cardwell representatives to try and set up a concession arrangement for a portion or all of his sales.

Developing the sales territory was another priority of Jack's. He had thus far concentrated on Massachusetts and, to a lesser extent, New Hampshire. To bid contracts in Maine he had been relying on a sub-dealer, but he was disappointed with the results:

You need to be a special sort of a person to sell in Maine. The towns are spread out and those old-timers are hard to convince when it comes to selling. Bidding contracts really hasn't accomplished much. I need to personally develop the contracts on my own, but to do that, I'd have to hire someone to manage what I've developed in Massachusetts.

Jack reflected on prospects for the bus distributorship going into 1989:

I'm convinced that you can make money in this business if you are willing to commit the time and dedication. If you can't take the high highs or low lows, forget this business—or any sales business for that matter.

I think I know my own needs, and the extent to which I can take risks. Plus, I know the bus business. What I don't know is where the industry is headed in the next few years or how long this intense competition can keep up without some of the distributors falling by the wayside. If I could get a clearer picture on that, I'd be in a better position to know what this company is worth and whether it's worth my time to invest in it. Right now, I honestly don't know how to assess the situation.

EXHIBIT 1 Financial Statements

NORTHERN BUS SALES, INC.
BALANCE SHEET
December 31, 1987

ASSETS

CURRENT ASSETS:
 Cash $172,647.38
 Accounts receivable   282,452.18
 Inventory   140,116.20
 Deposits   1000.00

  TOTAL CURRENT ASSETS $596,215.76

ORGANIZATION EXPENSE, net of amortization 1,490.74

                $597,706.50

LIABILITIES AND STOCKHOLDERS' DEFICIENCY

CURRENT LIABILITIES:
 Demand notes payable due a bank $142,876.44
 Advances from Cottrell Capital Corporation 143,978.68
 Accounts payable   349,888.20
 Accrued payroll and excise taxes 33,037.02
 Accrued taxes on income   456.00

  TOTAL CURRENT LIABILITIES $670,236.34

STOCKHOLDERS' DEFICIENCY:
 Common stock, without par value
  Authorized 200 shares
  Outstanding 100 shares   20,000.00

 Deficit $(92,529.84)

                $597,706.50

EXHIBIT 1 (continued)

NORTHERN BUS SALES, INC.
STATEMENT OF EARNINGS AND DEFICIENCY
Year ended December 31, 1987

SALES		$1,984,506.78
COSTS AND EXPENSES:		
Cost of sales	$1,875,652.08	
Depreciation	1,516.72	
Selling and administrative	198,325.36	
Interest	24,218.90	
		2,099,713.06
LOSS BEFORE TAXES ON INCOME		$(115,206.28)
TAXES ON INCOME:		
Federal (Note B)	$(23,132.44)	
State	456.00	
		(22,676.44)
NET LOSS		(92,529.84)
DEFICIENCY END OF YEAR		$ (92,529.84)
Loss per share of capital stock outstanding		$ (925.30)

See notes to financial statements

EXHIBIT 1   **(continued)**

NORTHERN BUS SALES, INC.
STATEMENT OF CHANGES IN FINANCIAL POSITION
Year ended December 31, 1987

SOURCE OF FUNDS:

From operations:			
Net loss			$ (92,529.84)
Non-cash items:			
Depreciation and amortization			<u>1,859.98</u>
TOTAL FUNDS FROM OPERATIONS			$(90,669.86)
Monies borrowed			142,876.44
Monies advanced from Cottrell Capital Corporation			143,978.68
Sale of common stock			20,000.00
Increase in liabilities:			
Accounts payable			349,888.20
Accrued expenses			33,493.02
Proceeds from sale of equipment			<u>2,000.00</u>
			692,236.34
DISPOSITION OF FUNDS:			
Equipment additions		$3,516.72	
Organization expense		1,864.00	
Increase in assets:			
Accounts receivable		282,532.18	
Inventory		140,036.20	
Deposits		<u>1,000.00</u>	
			<u>428,949.10</u>
INCREASE IN CASH			<u>$ 172,617.38</u>
CASH, END OF YEAR			<u>$ 172,617.38</u>

See notes to financial statements.

EXHIBIT 1 (continued)

NORTHERN BUS SALES, INC.
NOTES TO FINANCIAL STATEMENTS
Year ended December 31, 1987

NOTE A Summary of significant accounting policies:

(1) Inventory: Inventory is valued at the lower of cost (first-in, first-out method) or market.
(2) Depreciation and amortization: Cost of equipment is depreciated using the straight-line method over the estimated useful lives. Organization expense is being amortized using the straight-line method over a five-year period.
(3) Taxes on income: Investment tax credits are used to reduce the income tax provision in the year such credits are claimed.

NOTE B Federal Taxes: The Company was credited with the tax savings or benefits by Cottrell Capital Corporation and its subsidiaries by utilization of Northern Bus Sales, Inc. loss on operations through filing of a consolidated tax return.

NOTE C Operations: The Company sold in 1987 thirty-two (32) new buses and nine (9) used buses. In December 1987 three (3) of the new buses sold were repossessed, the gain or loss on resale of these vehicles is not ascertainable at present. Two of the used buses sold in 1987 necessitated the engagement of an attorney to seek payment or repossession. Seven new bus orders were in house December 31, 1987 to be delivered and sold in 1988.

EXHIBIT 1 (concluded)

Krasner and Company
Certified Public Accountants

798 Center Street
Albany, New York
(716) 675 5636

May 3, 1988

Northern Bus Sales, Inc.
P.O. Box 275
Wellesley, Massachusetts 02181

Gentlemen:

In Connection with our examination of the financial statements of Northern Bus Sales, Inc. for the year ended December 31, 1987, we made the following clarification to Note C - Operations.

Lee R. Myles during 1987 sold thirty-two (32) new buses and nine (9) used buses. In December 1987 three (3) of the new buses were repossessed, the gain or loss on resale of these vehicles is not ascertainable at present. Two of the used buses sold in 1987 necessitated the engagement of an attorney to seek payment or repossession. L.R Myles had written orders for seven (7) new buses as of December 31, 1987 to be delivered and sold in 1988.

Other executives of the Company sold thirty-one (31) new buses in 1987.

Sincerely,

Oliver J. Krasner

EXHIBIT 2 Letter to Potential Buyers

NORTHERN BUS SALES, INC.
DISTRIBUTOR OF CARDWELL BUS BODIES

An Open Letter to School Bus Purchasers:

Cardwell Body Works endeavors to continually upgrade its product not to meet minimum specifications, but to augment your purchasing dollar.

In order for you to realize maximum advantage of your purchases not only must your outlay be considered, but the workmanship, service, cooperation, sales counseling and most importantly follow up you receive will be weighed.

Northern Bus Sales has serviced the school transportation industry since 1973. I myself have been a principle in it only since 1987. What I lack in longevity I make up in honesty. Prior to entering the school bus business I believed honesty and integrity would be my mainstay in the field and were the qualities sought after most by school bus users.

These past few short years have proven my theories correct. I will continue to adhere to my disciplined code of ethics knowing that in doing so I will win your trust. Once I win your trust I will gain your business.

Sincerely,

NORTHERN BUS SALES, INC.

Jack C. Logan
(President and General Manager)
JCL:dd

"Truth is truth
To the end of reckoning"
        William Shakespeare

288 WILMINGTON AVENUE   WELLESLEY, MASSACHUSETTS 02181

EXHIBIT 3   Price Sheet

NORTHERN BUS SALES, INC.
DISTRIBUTOR OF CARDWELL BUS BODIES

*"For what is worth in anything
but so much money as 'twill bring?"*
Samuel Butler

Dear School Bus Purchaser:

Thank you for the opportunity to quote you on your future bus purchase. As you are aware the quality of a product such as a bus body determines its value in the marketplace.

I believe Cardwell is the best school bus body made both in dependable service and durability. To enhance the quality of this product I have included the following options to my quotation:

SPECIFICATION	APPROXIMATE VALUE
Three rub rails	70.00
Ventilation rain visor	120.00
12" wrap around rear bumper	60.00
74" headroom	250.00
Cove mouldings	40.00
Aluminum aisle strips	30.00
65,000 BTU double fan rear heater	70.00
Fuel tank door	20.00
Fully welted seats	60.00
42 oz. seat material	120.00
Locking driver's window	20.00
Tiltback driver's seat	80.00
Windshield external defrost fan	50.00
Body solenoid switch	40.00
Electric windshield washer	50.00
Chrome door handle	50.00
External defroster fan	50.00
Total	$1,180.00

To compare my price with other body figures add $1,180.00. Cardwell gives you the most for your money.

Sincerely,

Jack C. Logan, President

288 WILMINGTON AVENUE   WELLESLEY, MASSACHUSETTS 02181

Case 22

Janet Luhrs and Renee Williams

In October 1988 Janet Luhrs and Renee Williams were moving forward with a product idea Renee had developed called "Babypak," a fabric sling for a parent to use in carrying a baby. Traditionally, American mothers had carried babies in front and Japanese mothers in back by means of such slings. After trying both methods, Renee had preferred the Japanese arrangement and had consequently developed a Japanese-style sling with what she regarded as improvements in configuration and strength over the Japanese product.

After considerable work on improvement of the product, unsuccessful attempts to sell through mail order, design and development of a box-type package and exploration for suitable manufacturers in the Orient, the two had visited the headquarters of Toys 'R Us and received an order for 15,000 units, to begin with a first shipment of 5,000. This put them, Janet observed, "in the process of trying to figure out the best way to set up our business so it will be a successful one."

Renee Williams

Renee Williams had attended art school and beautician school following graduation from high school, and then gone to work as a beautician. She commented:

> One of my classmates who had dropped out before graduating from high school had also become a beautician, and by the time I was ready to go to work she already had her own beauty salon. So I went to work for her.

After working a while in other shops, Renee decided in 1977 to open her own. She recalled her reasoning at the time.

> I figured, that if my friend could set up her own business without even graduating from high school, then I ought to be able to do it, too. Besides, the shop I was working for at the time didn't seem to me to be treating people very well. I wanted to leave, and it turned out some of the other beauticians did too. So when I opened my own salon several of them came to work for me.

A problem, she said, was that running a salon and managing other people was very demanding work, which provided meager returns. Beauticians who worked for her, she found, often made more money than she did after she paid for wages, rent, health insurance and other costs of doing business. The salon was always profitable, but revenues in the best year were only $150,000, leaving income after expenses for her and her husband, who worked as receptionist, of around $30,000. When the difficulty of operating it was compounded by arrival of her first baby in 1982, she sold the salon and opened a small solo salon in her home, to which some of her clients followed her.

Occasionally she came up with other product ideas.

> I've always been inventive. Even back in school I used to think I would like to invent something and patent it. The trouble was that at the time I

couldn't think of any products worth patenting.

While operating the salon she had tried commercializing some ideas with a friend she had met in art school, Janet Luhrs, about whom she said:

Janet is also inventive, and we had fun working together even though our ideas didn't pan out.

They had tried making some products they called "Terrific Toilets," which were toilet covers, and packaged "Schmores" for microwaves. A combination of peanut butter, cookies, chocolate and sugar in plastic bags, the schmores were supposed to be a product that could be quickly heated to a sweet, gooey consistency in microwave ovens. Renee recalled the result:

The trouble was that the sugar crystallized into a hard substance that made the schmores hard to eat.

Renee and Janet had also tried working up a video program for high school students. After paying a small fee the students would progress through a series of videotaped lessons presented by well-known personalities. After watching these, the students would prepare and present their own fashion show. Renee recalled:

We showed it to schools and they liked it. The problem was they didn't have any money to pay for it, so they just took the lesson plans we had developed and used them on their own without the tapes and without paying us anything.

Baby Pak

Then had come the Baby Pak idea. When Renee's first baby arrived in 1982, a Japanese lady had given her a sling from Japan, which Renee had used with pleasure and then passed along to another mother when her baby outgrew it. Arrival of Renee's second baby in late 1986 had prompted Renee to wish for another such sling and consequently to design a copy for herself which a friend who was skilled as a seamstress helped her make. Working through a series of a half dozen prototypes, Renee added improvements to the design which fitted it better to the baby and made it stronger. A flyer depicting applications of the Baby Pak appears in Exhibit 1.

Having created what she considered to be a superior product, she decided to try selling it. She had noticed advertisements for baby products offered by other individuals in a diaper service newspaper and decided to telephone some of them to learn how selling through the paper worked. Running the advertisements cost, she found, around $60 per month. After enlisting her mother-in-law's help as a seamstress to make the products, she ran advertisements in that paper and in *Mothering* magazine, but found that the volume of sales did not cover the costs of advertising.

She concluded that she needed to find a source of greater sales volume and it occurred to her that a store like K-Mart or Toys R Us might afford such an opportunity. For help in writing letters to them, she decided to ask her friend, Janet Luhrs. "If there's one thing I can't do it's write anything," Renee observed, "and Janet is a good writer."

Janet Luhrs

Janet picked up the conversation from there.

Writing and art are two strong points with me, so when Renee asked me in April to help her out with these letters, I was glad to.

Following high school Janet had gone to art school, where she met Renee. Janet recalled her own career.

In high school I had been the best in art. But in art school everyone else had been the best, too. It was really competitive, and I just didn't feel like buckling down on it at that point. So I needed to move on to something else and went on to the University of Washington where I got a bachelor's degree in journalism.

After journalism school I worked for a while in the newspaper business and then did my own freelance writing. Then I went to law school. I had met my husband, and he had gone to law school. A woman I had worked with in the writing business had also gone to law school. So why hadn't I gone to law school? One morning I woke up and said 'I think I'll go to law school.' I had been getting tired of the writing anyway, and thought maybe going to law school would lend another dimension to my writing and my research.

Law really wasn't for me, although I enjoyed parts of it, like working for the public defender up in Alaska and conducting trials. A lot of it is just too dry. I'm good at writing and artistic work. But in law you just gobble up what some judge said and spit it back out in a nice way.

Then when I had a baby I found I couldn't flip my brain on and off to do law. That work is intense and I found I could not do it all day and then go home and say goo goo. And besides I just didn't want to work full-time any more. It was just too much.

Also, I had continued to do freelance writing all through law school, and in fact, I have one account, a newsletter, that I still do work for. Then I got pregnant again, and when I'm that way, I'm just a wreck and can't do anything.

But about three months after I had

the second baby, I started to get "antsy" again and think about what else to do. I thought maybe I'd start writing again, and then Renee approached me with this baby pack design and asked if I wanted to go into business with her. It was perfect, so I said sure.

First Steps

The two women asked advice of anyone whom they thought could help. Renee told her hairdressing clients what she and her partner were trying to do and through one of them met a successful inventor in Bellingham, Washington who gave them suggestions and leads on packaging the product. Janet asked her husband, a maritime lawyer, for leads and through them located a man who specialized in making arrangements for manufacturing in the Far East. Through inquiries with manufacturers' representatives they learned about sales markups and "hidden" costs. For instance, there might be a requirement that 98 percent of the products be perfect or else the buyer could cancel the deal. And to obtain a UPC bar code for the box they found they would have to pay $300 to a company which monopolized the standard code.

A manufacturer's representative told them that the best way to follow up on the encouraging mail response they had received from Toys R Us would be to make a personal appointment and both fly to New Jersey to meet with the buyer. Renee recalled:

It was hard for me to accept the idea of such a big expense. But we did it, and everything worked out perfectly.

Janet added:

Others told us either we wouldn't get in to see the buyer at all, or if we did, he'd only give us five minutes. But he was very friendly, we had no trouble getting in, and he spent two hours looking over the product and giving us helpful advice.

One of the things a sales representative told us was that we had to ask for an order to get one. If he had not told us that, I would have just waited for the buyer to tell us he would place an order. And he probably never would have. But in the interview we did ask for the order, and we got one for 15,000 units, the first delivery to be for 5,000. He didn't even try to beat us down on price, but took what we offered, $15 a unit.

Renee concluded:

I couldn't believe we would be able to get an order without a successful test marketing program first. But we did.

The partners had also explored possible manufacturing arrangements. Currently, it appeared that a local firm would be able to have them made in the Orient and deliver them to the partners for $7 per unit, including customs. It also appeared that there would be no problem with import restrictions that applied to clothing.

The supplier wanted guarantee of payment on delivery, however. This would require more cash than either partner could provide and consequently they had started to prepare a business plan, excerpts of which are attached in Exhibits 2 and 3, and

approached banks for possible loans. Rainier bank had said it could probably provide a letter of credit guaranteeing payment if the two women could produce enough cash to back up the letter. Renee figured she could raise part of the money from her house but not enough.

Next Concerns

A question on the mind of both women was how to turn these beginnings into a longer term business with high profitability. A schedule of activities Janet saw as necessary to start the company appears as Exhibit 2. She had also prepared a financial forecast which appears as Exhibit 3. Both had young children and wanted to be able to stay home with them. Neither had much capital. Janet observed that she hated borrowing money and did not want to be in debt personally. Renee said she had thought of selling stock, but did not want more partners and was not anxious to have the profits diluted by other owners.

I read in a magazine about two women who were making a lot of money selling designer bottles, and we heard about a couple of women back east with another product. The first pair seem to be making a lot of money and the other two are just squeaking by. We want to know what will determine which we will be like and figure out a way to be like the ones who are really successful.

EXHIBIT 1   Baby Pak Advertising Flyer

1 - Although Baby Pak is best used as a back pak:

Baby Pak
The Best Baby Carrier!

P.O. Box 25332
Seattle, Wa.
98125
(206)633-4514

2 - You can also use Baby Pak as a front pak for smaller babies.

3 - Or as an emergency high chair. (Directions: Sit baby in contoured seat of Pak. Insert legs through leg holes. Criss-cross shoulder straps across baby's chest, and around chair back, criss-cross and thru D-rings and tie straps.)

4 - Or a safety seat for shopping carts. (Use directions from #3 above.)

5 - Or a safety seat for high chairs. (Use directions from #3 above.)

If baby falls asleep while on your back, use receiving blanket folded into a triangle to hold baby's head close to your body. Tuck corners of blanket under shoulder straps, or simply use a shawl around baby and yourself.

EXHIBIT 2   List of Activities   (copied from handwritten notes)

Sept '88
    Letter of credit - #1 for $53,000
    Manufacturing Order - # 1 Thaw, 5,300paks
    Miscellaneous - Incorporate
Oct. '88
    Loan on A/R, Bank Pays - #1 Box co. $3,500 for 5,000, R. Mann $1,000
    Box Orders - #1, 5,300 boxes
    Miscellaneous - Work with R. Mann on box design
Nov. '88
    Make Sales - 2,400 pks to Kids R Us, Target
    Miscellaneous - Source RSVP better price on pak mfg.
Dec. '88
    Box Orders - Receive Box #1
    Payments to others - Box co $1,590 #1
Jan. '89
    Letter of credit - LOC for run #2
    Loan on A/R, Bank Pays - Loan on A/R - Pays Thaw $53,000
    Manufacturing Order - Order Thaw 5,000 pks #2
    Deliver to Stores - 5,000 pks to Toys R Us #1, 100 pks to REI, run #1
Feb. '89
    Receive payment from stores - REI $1,500, apply to box co #2
    Box Orders - Order box #2
    Payments to others - Box co, $1,500 #2
Apr. '89
    Letter of credit - LOC for run #3
    Payment to Bank - $60,000 #1
    Receive payment from stores - Toys R Us $75,000 less 3,000 hold back
    Manufacturing Order - 5,000 paks #3 Thaw
    Box Orders - Receive boxes #2
    Payments to others - Box co $1,500 #2
May '89
    Loan on A/R, Bank Pays - Loan on A/R #2
    Box Orders - Order boxes #3
    Deliver to Stores - 2,600 pks Toys R Us, 560 Kids R Us, 100 REI, 1,755 Target, run #2
    Payments to others - Box co $1,500 #3
Jun '89
    Make Sales - Large sales push for run #5 K Mart
Jul '89
    Letter of credit - LOC's for run #4
    Manufacturing Order - Thaw for 5,000 pks #4
    Box Orders - Receive box #3
    Make Sales - Dallas trade show
    Payments to others - Box co $15,00 #3
    Miscellaneous -
Aug. '89
    Loan on A/R, Bank - Loan on A/R #3
    Payment to Bank - Pay $50,150 on loan #2
    Receive payment from stores - $75,000
    Deliver to Stores - 2,600 pks to Toys R Us, 560 Kids R Us, 100 REI, 1,755 Target, run #3

EXHIBIT 2 (continued)

Payments to others - Box co $1500   #4
Oct. '89
Letter of credit - For run #5
Manufacturing Order - Thaw run #5, 13265 pks
Box Orders - Receive boxes #4
Payments to others - Box co $1,500 $4
Nov. '89
Loan on A/R, Bank - Loan on A/R #4
Payment to Bank - $50,150 From Thaw #3
Box Orders - Order box #5, 0.47/box, 13,265 pks
Deliver to Stores - 2,600 toys R Us, 560 Kids R Us, 100 REI, 1,755 Target, run #4
Jan. '90
Letter of credit - LOC #6
Manufacturing Order - 13,265 pks, Thaw, #6
Box Orders - Receive box #5 for 13265 pks, $3,117, 0.47/box
Payments to others - Box co $3,117
Feb. '90
Loan on A/R, Bank - $132,650 on #5
Payment to Bank - pay on #4
Receive payment from stores - Receive #4, $75,000
Box Orders - #6 for 13,265 pks, $3,117
Deliver to Stores - #6, 5,015 Service PX, 8,250 K-Mart
Payments to others - Box c $3,117
Apr. '90
Letter of credit - #7
Manufacturing Order - 13,265 pks, Thaw #7
Box Orders - Receive #6 for 13,265 pks, $3,117
Payments to others - Box co, $3,117
May '90
Loan on A/R, Bank pays Thaw- $132,650 onA/R #6
Payment to Bank - #5
Receive payment from stores - Receive #5 for $198,975
Box Orders - Order box #7 for 13,265 pks, $3,117
Deliver to Stores - #6 to first yr accts 5,015 and to K-Mart 8,250
Payments to others - Box co, $3,117
Jul. '90
Letter of credit - #8
Manufacturing Order - Thaw #8 for 13,265 pks
Box Orders - #7 for 13,265 pks, $3,117
Make Sales - Dallas show
Payments to others - Box co. $3,117
Aug. '90
Loan on A/R, Bank Pays Thaw - $132,650 on #7
Payment to Bank - Pay #6
Receive payment from stores - #6 for $195,975
Box Orders - #8 for 13,265 pks $3,117
Deliver to Stores - ## to first yr accts 5,015, to K-Mart 8,250

EXHIBIT 2 (concluded)

        Payments to others - Box co, $3,117

Oct. '90

        Letter of credit - #9

        Manufacturing Order - Thaw #9

        Box Orders - Receive #8 for 13,265 pks $3,117

        Deliver to Stores - #8 to first yr accts 5,015, to K-Mart 8,250

        Payments to others - Box co $3,117

Nov. '90

        Loan on A/R, Bank Pays Thaw - $132,650 on A/R #8

        Payment to Bank - Pay #7

        Receive payment from stores - #7 for $198,975

Feb. '91

        Payment to Bank - #8

        Receive payment from stores - #8 for $198,975

        Deliver to Stores - #9

Exhibit 3a Financial Forecast Sept. '88 - Aug. '89 (copied from handwritten notes)

	Sep'88	Oct'88	Nov'88	Dec'88	Jan'89	Feb'89	Mar'89	Apr'89	May'89	Jun'89	Jul'89	Aug'89	Totals
Revenue													
Toys R Us								72,000			37,440		109,440
4% Hold Back						1,500					1,500		3,000
REI											3,000		3,000
40 Sm. Specialty											3,375		3,375
Kids R Us											1,125		1,125
Toys R Us Canada											900		900
Toys R Us Intnl											26,325		26,325
Target													
K-Mart													
Total Revenue						1,500		72,000			73,665		147,165
Cost of Sales													
Thaw					53,000				50,150			50,150	153,300
Eagle Box		5,300		1,590				1,500	1,500	1,500	1,500		12,890
Richard Marin		1,000											1,000
Total Cost of Sales		6,300	—	1,590	53,000	—	—	1,500	51,650	1,500	1,500	50,150	167,190
Gross Profit		(6,300)	—	(1,590)	(53,000)	1,500	—	70,500	(51,650)	(1,500)	72,165	(50,150)	(20,025)
Expenses													
Salaries $1K Each								2,000	2,000	2,000	2,000	2,000	10,000
Payroll													
Outside Services													
Supplies													
Repairs and Maint													
Advertising													
Deliv and Travel			1,500							1,500	1,500		4,500
Acctg and Legal		50	50	50	50	50	50	50	50	50	50	50	550
Rent													
Telephone		20	24	24	24	24	24	24	24	24	24	24	260
Utilities													
Insurance			200	98	98	98	98	98	98	98	98	98	1,082
Other Expenses													
Total Expenses		70	1,774	172	172	172	172	2,172	2,172	3,672	3,672	2,172	16,392
Net													(36,417)

Exhibit 3b Financial Forecast, Sept. '89-Aug. '90 (copied from handwritten notes)

	Sep'89	Oct'89	Nov'89	Dec'89	Jan'90	Feb'90	Mar'90	Apr'90	May'90	Jun'90	Jul'90	Aug'90	Totals
Revenue													
Toys R Us			37,440			37,440			37,440			37,440	149,760
4% Hold Back		3,000				1,560			1,560			1,560	7,680
REI			1,500			1,500			1,500			1,500	6,000
40 Sm. Specialty			3,000			3,000			3,000			3,000	12,000
Kids R Us			3,375			3,375			3,375			3,375	13,500
Toys R Us Canada			1,125			1,125			1,125			1,125	4,500
Toys R Us Intnl			900			900			900			900	3,600
Target			26,325			26,325			26,325			26,325	105,300
K-Mart									123,750			123,750	247,500
Total Revenue		3,000	73,665			75,225			198,975			198,975	549,840
Cost of Sales													
Thaw			50,150			132,650			132,650			132,650	448,100
Eagle Box		1,500	3,117		3,117			3,117			3,117	3,117	23,319
Total		1,500	53,267		3,117	135,767		3,117	135,767		3,117	135,767	471,419
Gross Profit													
Expenses													
Payroll													
Salaries $1K ea.	2,000	2,000	2,000	2,000	2,000	2,000	2,000	2,000	2,000	2,000	2,000	2,000	24,000
Outside Services													
Supplies													
Repairs and Maint													
Advertising											1,500		1,500
eliv and Travel													
Acctg and Legal	50	50	50	50	50	50	50	50	50	50	50	50	600
Rent													
Telephone	24	24	24	24	24	24	24	24	24	24	24	24	288
Utilities													
Insurance	98	200	98	98	98	98	98	98	98	98	98	98	1,278
Other Expenses													
Total Expenses	2,172	2,274	2,172	2,172	2,172	2,172	2,172	2,172	2,172	2,172	3,672	2,172	27,666
Net													325,134

Exhibit 3c   Financial Forecast, Sept. '90- Aug. '91   (copied from handwritten notes)

	Sep'90	Oct'90	Nov'90	Dec'90	Jan'91	Feb'91	Mar'91	Apr'91	May'91	Jun'91	Jul'91	Aug'91	Totals
Revenue													
Toys R Us			37,440			37,440		1,560		1,560		1,560	
4% Hold Back			1,560			1,560							
REI			1,500			1,500							
40 Sm. Specialty			3,000			3,000							
Kids R Us			3,375			3,375							
Toys R Us Canada			1,125			1,125							
Toys R Us Intnl			900			900							
Target			26,325			26,325							
K-Mart			123,750			123,750							
Total Revenue			198,975			198,975		0		0		0	266,863
Cost of Sales													
Thaw			132,650										
Eagle Box		3,117											
Total		3,117	132,650			198,975		1,560		1,560		1,560	
Gross Profit		(3,117)	17,425			198,975							
Expenses													
Salaries $1K ea	2,000	2,000	2,000	2,000									
Payroll													
Outside Services													
Supplies													
Repairs and Maint													
Advertising													
Deliv. and Travel													
Acctg and Legal	50	50	50	50									
Rent													
Telephone	24	24	24	24									
Utilities													
Insurance	200	98	98	98									
Other Expenses													
Total Expenses	2,274	2,172	2,172	2,172									
Net													

Case 23

Bob Mighell

It was the end of spring quarter 1991 and second year MBA student Bob Mighell was working to make what he considered to be a major decision. Should he purchase the Biopsy product line from his former employer, Branton Instrument Company, and start his own company or should he move ahead with a job search and work for someone else?

The Biopsy Product Line

A biopsy procedure consists of a doctor removing a small piece of tissue from a patient and observing the sample under a microscope. The biopsy equipment sold by Branton Instrument Company* was specifically used to obtain samples from the stomach, the intestine and the small bowel. These instruments were used by gastroenterologists who specialized in digestive diseases.

The original instruments were developed in 1957 by James Branton, founder of Branton Instrument Company, and Russell Robins, a gastroenterologist at the University of Washington's Medical School. The products were never patented, which Russell Robins attributed to a "folly of youth." The product line expanded through the early 1960s to include three different instruments. Those three instruments had, according to Branton, changed little since they were developed. A typical example of these instruments is depicted in Exhibit 1.

Bob Mighell's Background

Bob was born and raised in the Seattle area but decided to move away and attend

* disguised name

Dartmouth College right after graduation from high school. At Dartmouth Bob's interest in both medical products and entrepreneurship was kindled. He spent five years at Dartmouth working as a research assistant while earning degrees in both Liberal Arts and Mechanical Engineering. The research dealt with artificial joints. Bob's job required him to work in a machine shop where he learned to operate end-mills, lathes and other general machine shop equipment. His engineering degree thesis was written on Bob's design of a surgical instrument he developed for installing artificial joints.

During his last year at Dartmouth, Bob took an entrepreneurship course at the Tuck School of Business, which was located right next door to Dartmouth's Engineering School. In the course, Bob prepared a business plan to manufacture and sell snowboards, which at the time were an emerging sport. After graduation he took the business plan back to Seattle, incorporated as Edge Snowboards, and tried to raise the money to get the venture off the ground. Bob could only get $500,000 committed out of the $1,000,000 needed and the project folded.

After the snowboard project, he went to work for Branton Instrument Company as a manufacturing engineer. After two years with Branton, Bob decided he really wasn't interested in being an engineer all his life and would rather run his own small company. His experience with his snowboard venture had left him feeling he needed to know more about business management. With that in mind, he entered the University of Washington's MBA program in the Fall of 1989.

Possibility of a Buyout

The idea for the buyout originated in 1987 when Bob was having lunch with his usual group of manufacturing engineers, and his boss at Branton. They were talking about the different products Branton made and Bob's boss made the comment, "You know, someone could probably buy that biopsy line, set it up in their garage, and make a pretty decent living with it." Although Bob didn't follow up with the idea at the time, he remembered it and had always thought there might be a possibility that he could buy the biopsy line. Even though he worked as a manufacturing engineering and the biopsy line was officially under his control, he never once in the two years he was at Branton had to do anything with that particular product line. Bob thought that this was a good sign since the only things he ever heard about were the problems and if he hadn't heard anything about biopsy department in two years, the process must be well in control.

After Bob had left Branton to pursue his MBA, he had remained close friends with several of his co-workers. Bob called Brad, who had worked with him as a manufacturing engineer and asked what Brad knew about the biopsy line. Brad had been with Branton for several more years than Bob and knew much more about the biopsy line. Brad told Bob that there were only two people who worked in production on the biopsy line and neither of them worked more than half time. The other half of their time was taken up working on other products. The main pieces of equipment Brad knew that were required to produce the biopsy instruments were a couple of small jewelry lathes and an old end mill. Brad didn't know whether the end-mill and the lathes were used for producing other products or not. He also didn't know much about the sales figures but thought that they might be going down. He told Bob that he thought that Branton was planning to phase out the biopsy department over a period of five years. Brad said he thought the chances were pretty good that Branton would want to sell the biopsy line but the person Bob really needed to ask was Mark Rathman, the vice president of operations.

Bob's call, the next day, to Mark was very brief and went like this:

> *Bob: Hello Mark, this is Bob Mighell. I don't know if you remember me, but I worked there two years ago as a manufacturing engineer.*
>
> *Mark: Sure, I remember. How's the MBA program?*
>
> *Bob: It's great! A lot of hard work but I am learning quite a bit.*
>
> *Mark: So, what can I do for you?*
>
> *Bob: I was interested to know if you would be willing to sell your biopsy line?*
>
> *Mark: You bet! Do you have a buyer in mind?*
>
> *Bob: Well, actually I was thinking of buying it myself. Can we get together and talk about it?*
>
> *Mark: Sure. This week is pretty bad since we are just finishing up the quarter, but how about next Friday at 7:00 AM?*
>
> *Bob: Sounds great, I'll see you then.*

Mark had not hesitated a moment in saying that he would be willing to sell the biopsy line and Bob felt encouraged that he should pursue this opportunity. Before meeting with Mark Rathman, Bob wanted to learn a little more about biopsy equipment in general and Branton's instruments in particular.

Information Gathering

Bob invited another former coworker, Bill, over for dinner and explained that he was interested in buying the biopsy line. Bill had never worked very closely with the biopsy line and said he couldn't offer Bob much help, but he had an extra product catalog and price list that he would be willing to drop by the next day.

The catalog offered Bob his first complete picture of what he would be buying. There were basically three products that were being offered: The Multipurpose Suction biopsy, the Hydraulic biopsy and the Crosby-Krugler biopsy. They were all fairly similar in construction and appearance to the product shown in Exhibit 1.

Bob next spent some time at the University of Washington's Medical School Library researching the topic and found several references to Branton's instruments. The earliest reference, dated July 1959, was an article in *Gastroenterology* which was the official publication of the American Gastroenterological Association. In the article, Russell Robins and James Branton described their Multipurpose Suction biopsy instrument, which was almost identical to the one Branton was offering for sale in 1991. This product had basically not changed for over 30 years and was still selling.

In prepation for the meeting with Mark Rathman, Bob made a list of questions, which he sent in a letter to Mark (see Exhibit 2). He had two aims for the letter. The first was to remind Mark of the meeting and the second was to let Mark know that Bob was serious.

Bob recalled that his meeting with Mark was very informative. Mark explained that Branton wanted to get rid of the biopsy line for several reasons. He said he felt that the sales had been rather flat for a few years at what he estimated to be around $100,000–$120,000 per year. The total company sales were around $70 million

and this little department was a "pain in the neck." Other products were expanding and this product line was taking up valuable space in a increasingly cramped building. He said they found it a problem that none of the FDA required procedures had been written on how to assemble the product. When Mark was pressed by Bob on the actual sales figures for the last few years, Mark looked up the last two years and said that 1989 sales were $115,000 and 1990 sales were $97,000. The 1990 sales were split among the biopsy products as follows:

	Total	Foreign
Multipurpose	$27,653	$ 6,000
Crosby-Krugler	$ 7,175	$ 3,000
Hydraulic	$ 5,610	$ 3,000
Repair Work	$56,257	$ 5,700
	$96,695	$17,700

Bob asked Mark if he could have a copy of a tabulation which Mark had been reading. Mark said that would be no problem and called in his secretary to make some copies (see Exhibit 3). The reports also showed a gross margin for the product line of around 40 percent which seemed terrible to Mark and was another reason he was interested in selling. Bob remembered from his time at Branton that other product lines he had worked on had gross margins in the 60 to 70 percent range.

Mark also mentioned in this meeting that the marketing department had just recently sent a letter to their biopsy customers saying that they were planning on discontinuing the product line. He said that they had gotten some response back from doctors who were very disappointed with the news. He seemed to remember that the doctors who were the most disappointed were the pediatric doctors. Mark said that if Bob were to buy the company, he would not have any problem in having Branton's salespeople refer all sales leads to Bob's company.

Bob left the meeting with Mark with the agreement that Mark would talk with Tony Perri, Branton Instrument's president, and see if he would approve the sale of the biopsy line.

At this point Bob recalled thinking that if he bought the biopsy line, he would run the company as a one-man shop. With his manufacturing and machining background, he thought he could easily handle the production. Combining this with his MBA, he felt he could take care of marketing and financing requirements of the company as well. With $100,000 in yearly sales and a 40 percent gross margin, it seemed to him there would be enough money for him to support his wife and two young children.

Before calling Mark back, Bob returned to the Medical School library to do a little more market research. In a reference book entitled the *Medical Device Registry* he found a list of five other manufacturers who made products listed under the subheading "Suction Biopsy Instruments." He called all five but could only get information from two of the companies. One had gone out of business and two would not give out product information to non-doctors. From the information he did receive from the two companies, it did not appear that their products performed the same function as Branton's equipment.

Other information that Bob gathered from the library included information on medical product and supply companies from *Standard & Poors 1990 Handbook* (see Exhibit 4) as well as information on medical manufacturers from *Robert Morris Associates 1990 Annual Statement Studies* (see Exhibit 4).

After several days of trying to get through to Mark, Bob finally reached him on the phone and found out that Tony had given approval to sell the biopsy line.

Mark said that they would be willing to sell the line for what they had in inventory, which he said was $73,000 as of 12/31/90. He also said that for that price he would throw in some of the equipment as well. Bob asked Mark if he had any sales figures prior to 1989 easily available. Mark said he had some for 1987 and 1988. 1987 sales were $153,000 and 1988 sales were $138,000. Mark sounded a little surprised as he read the numbers to Bob and he said, "It looks like sales aren't level after all, it looks like there is a downward trend."

Bob still wanted to speak with two other people in the company. The first was Sarah Morgan who was the marketing manager for medical products and the other was Dennis Olson, who actually produced the product. Mark said that he would speak to Sarah and Dennis and let them know Bob would be calling.

Bob's first call was to Sarah Morgan. She sounded a bit confused at first and thought he was someone else. She said that she had heard that someone was interested in buying the company a couple of months ago, but she didn't know that it was Bob. Bob thought that it couldn't be him that she was thinking of since he had only been talking with Mark for less than three weeks.

Bob was particularly interested in finding out if Sarah could explain the downward trend in sales. She said that she had never really paid much attention to the biopsy line and, in fact, never advertised the product, never went to any medical shows to promote the product nor ever raised the prices in the five years she had been on the job. She felt that the product was mainly sustained by word-of-mouth advertising between doctors. She assumed that the drop in sales was due to the expanding use of endoscopes by gastroenterologists. Endoscopes have fiber optics and allow the doctor to view where he is going in the body.

Bob asked Sarah about the letter she

sent telling the customers that she was going to drop the product line. She said that she had sent the letter in January to about 1500 doctors. The doctor's names had come from a list of doctors who had bought the product over the past several years. She mentioned that she had gotten some letters back from a few doctors saying that they were disappointed with Branton's decision to drop the product line. She talked about the pediatric doctors that Mark had mentioned and felt that there might be a special market niche. She said that she would send Bob some product literature and a list of some of the doctors who wrote back in response to her letter.

Sarah also told Bob that she had just received the first quarter's sales results and that for the first quarter of 1991, biopsy sales had been $50,000. She felt that the high sales for that quarter were due to the letter she had sent out.

The next person Bob spoke with was Dennis Olson who was in charge of making the product. Dennis was a goldmine of information according to Bob. Dennis had been making the product for the last 20 years and knew everything about how to manufacture the whole product line. Bob found out that, although there were current drawings for all products, there were indeed no written procedures on how to make any of it. Dennis proudly showed Bob a part that was about the size of a pinhead that had six holes drilled through it, a slot down the middle and was threaded on the outside. Although Bob had worked in a machine shop for several years, he wasn't sure that he had the skills required to make a part that complicated.

Dennis also showed Bob the equipment that was used in making the biopsy instruments. The main pieces were an end-mill, like Bob thought, and the jewelry lathes but there was also an industrial size lathe that was required as well. Both the end-mill and the large lathe were used exten-

sively to make products other than biopsy equipment. Dennis also mentioned another piece of large equipment that he used for honing certain parts that was located in the basement. Honing is the process of smoothing out a hole made previously with a drill.

Dennis told Bob that he had entertained the thought of buying out the biopsy line and running it himself but was too concerned about the liability issue. Bob told Dennis that he too had worried about the liability issue and had called an insurance firm that had been recommended to him by an owner of a small medical device firm. The insurance agent said he would need to know a bit more about the product's history but estimated that the insurance would probably cost around $12,000 per year.

Bob and Dennis were talking about the letter that Sarah had sent out when Dennis said, "Wait a minute, I think I have a copy of that somewhere." After rummaging through several files he pulled a copy of the letter out and showed it to Bob. The letter was dated January 14th and the letter said that Branton would stop selling the biopsy line on February 1st.

As Bob and Dennis were talking more about how the instruments are assembled, Bob asked Dennis about how much time he spent working on the product. Dennis said that if he were to devote the required time to keep up with the orders, he would work on it about 20 hours a week. He said that he hadn't really been working on the product due to priorities in other areas and he figured that there was at least $20,000 in backorders. Bob was interested in the backorders because Mark had mentioned that Bob could take all the backorders with him if he bought the biopsy line.

After his meeting with Dennis, Bob called Sarah again to verify what he had read in the letter. She confirmed that the letter had said that they would stop taking orders for new products on February 1 but they had actually taken orders until March 1. She also said that they had been telling any customers that called that they had committed themselves to providing repair work for the next five years. The next day Bob received a packet from Sarah that contained product information as well as a short list of doctors who used Branton's biopsy equipment and their phone numbers.

Bob decided that he would call a few of the doctors on the list to get their views of the product and hopefully learn more about the biopsy market. The general consensus he found among the doctors was that Branton produced very good products that "last forever" but they were all beginning to use endoscopes instead of the Branton instruments. One doctor Bob spoke with was Russell Robins who had developed the instruments with James Branton. Dr. Robins himself admitted that he was no longer really using the instruments. Some doctors said that they hadn't used the instruments in three or four years while some of the pediatric physicians said that they used them as much as twice a week. For a certain procedure on infants though, there was no other comparable product on the market.

Bob was interested in this pediatric market but wanted to find out how many pediatric gastroenterologists there were in the United States. Through the American Gastroenterological Association he found out that The American Board of Pediatrics is the association that would board certify this specialty. Bob called the Board and they told him that they had just given their first board for a pediatric gastroenterologist in 1990 and 267 doctors had passed. Bob called one of these pediatric specialists on his list from Sarah and the doctor estimated that there were no more than 500 practicing pediatric gastroenterologists in the United States.

One doctor told Bob that if he really wanted to talk with more gastroenterologists he should attend the big yearly Digestive Disease Week convention being put on by the American Gastroenterological Association at the end of May in New Orleans. This was the year's biggest convention of gastroenterologists and over 7000 were expected to attend.

Decision Time

Bob felt he had gathered quite a bit of information over the past two months but now he had to put it all together and make a decision. Should he continue pursuing this opportunity or should he focus his attention on getting a job with another company. Graduation was less than three weeks away and he wanted to get on with whatever his career was going to be.

EXHIBIT 1   Biopsy Instrument Example

Peroral Hydraulic Suction Biopsy Instrument

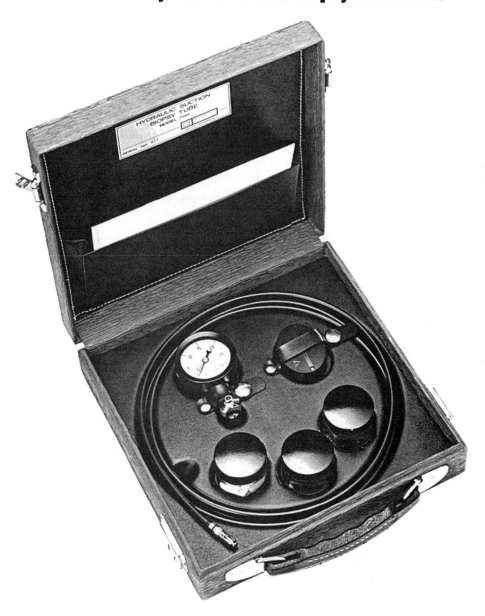

EXHIBIT 1   (concluded)

The most advanced biopsy instrument available for obtaining multiple biopsies from any level of the gastrointestinal tract

The Branton Peroral Hydraulic Instrument is an excellent diagnostic aid for obtaining biopsies from the more distal, previously inaccessible areas of the small bowel.

The instrument has the significant advantage of being able to deliver biopsies rapidly to the exterior while the tube itself remains in place. This makes it possible to follow physiological processes as they occur by both morphologic and chemical techniques.

With the Branton Hydraulic Instrument, both normal and pathological physiology can be studied in patients under normal circumstances, without anesthesia, fasting, or other procedures normally required.

Improved technique.

The Branton Hydraulic Instrument was first used for experimental production of the lesions in idiopathic sprue, and has been used for histochemical, electron microscopic and biochemical studies of fat absorption in man. It has been used in many other experimental applications and has also been used in routine diagnostic applications. As an example, biopsies of lesions in the ileum or distal jejunum have shown tuberculous lymphoma and regional enteritis. Prior to the availability of this instrument, such diagnosis would have required laparotomy.

Precision design.

Capsule design and controlled suction limit the size of the biopsy. However, careful patient management should be observed during biopsy procedures to reduce to a minimum the possibility of bleeding.

The fluid delivery system insures consistent and rapid delivery of the biopsy. Improved methods of attaching the tube to the capsule have resulted in better performance with less maintenance than in earlier models.

Each unit complete.

Each hydraulic instrument (Catalog #9127-002) comes as a complete kit including the capsule, radio-opaque double lumen plastic tube, vacuum gauge, sample jars, instructions, carrying case, actuating pump, and CO_2 cylinder.

The capsule and knife with spring.

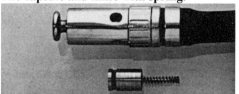

Capsule cross section

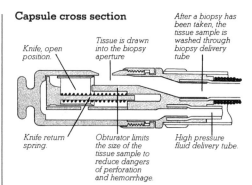

Knife, open position.

Tissue is drawn into the biopsy aperture

After a biopsy has been taken, the tissue sample is washed through biopsy delivery tube

Knife return spring.

Obturator limits the size of the tissue sample to reduce dangers of perforation and hemorrhage.

High pressure fluid delivery tube.

Actuating Pump

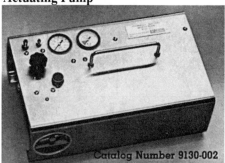

Catalog Number 9130-002

The Branton actuating pump (Catalog #9130-002) is an improved design featuring quiet operation and push-button control. Tyrode's solution can be used safely in the pump and capsule. Carbon dioxide gas is utilized to actuate the pump mechanism which, in turn, delivers solution to the tube at controlled pressure. Carbon dioxide does not enter the patient tube.

Each pump unit consists of a 5 lb CO_2 cylinder, pressure multiplier with stainless steel chamber for use with Tyrode's or saline solution, pressure regulating valve and electric control.

Ordering Information.

Description	Catalog Number
Complete unit 115V (including instrument and pump)	9127-002
Complete unit 230V (including instrument and pump)	9127-003
Hydraulic suction instrument (only)	9129-001
Hydraulic actuating pump only 115 V	9130-002
Hydraulic actuating pump only 230 V	9130-003
CO_2 cylinder	4026-001
Monofilament plastic mesh for handling specimens.	
Sufficient for approximately 500 biopsies.	1905-001
Silicone lubricant for knife and capsule (5.3 oz. tube)	1906-002

Note: Since the capsule, knife and tube of the 7mm hydraulic instrument are carefully matched and fitted at the factory, it is essential that all three parts be returned together when service is required.

EXHIBIT 2   Bob's Follow-up Letter

March 30, 1991

Mark Rathman
Vice President, Operations
Branton Instrument Co.

Dear Mark,

I am writing in response to our phone conversation last week about the possible sale of Branton's biopsy department. I look forward to meeting with you at 7:00 on Friday, April 5th, to discuss this possibility further. In preparing for our meeting, I have come up with a list of questions. Not all of them need to be answered right away but I hope they will help in guiding our meeting.

1)   What exactly is involved in the business? What percentage is new product manufacturing and what percentage is service? What are trends in the industry?

2)   What were the sales and earnings for at least the last five years and what are your projections for the next few years?

3)   Where and how are the products sold? Do your current salespeople promote and sell the product?

4)   Do you have any separate financial records for the biopsy department?

5)   What assets would be included in the purchase? Such as: product name, patents, trademarks, customer and mailing lists, credit records, supplier arrangements, know-how for performing the work, documentation, tooling and equipment.

6)   Inventory and receivables: How much do you normally carry? How will it be valued and by whom? How much would be transferred in the sale?

7)   What liabilities would be included in the purchase? What do the accounts payable consist of and who will be responsible for them? Any impending lawsuits, customer claims or other outstanding obligations of the biopsy department?

8)   May I speak with James Branton about biopsy equipment and Sarah Morgan about the market for this product?

Thank you for your time and I look forward to meeting with you on Friday.

Sincerely,

Bob Mighell

Exhibit 3   P&L by Product, 1990

	Multipurpose Biopsy	Crosby Kugler	Hydraulic Suction	Ulcer Maker	Parts & Labor
Sales	27,653	7,175	5,610	1,025	57,661
Discounts	0	0	0	0	711
Returns	0	0	0	0	693
Net Sales	27,653	7,175	5,610	1,025	56,257
Material	4,323	1,068	1,178	363	8,956
Labor	3,842	1,279	665	127	9,991
Overhead	6,635	2,010	1,608	303	16,725
Total Costs	14,800	4,357	3,451	793	35,672
Gross Profit	12,853	2,818	2,159	232	20,585

Exhibit 4   Selected Stock Data - Medical Products and Supplies (from Standard and Poors)

Year	Profit Margin %	Dividends % of Earnings	Price Earnings High	Price Earnings Low
1965	6.94	29.73	35.70	22.54
1966	7.53	25.53	37.28	27.62
1967	9.24	25.86	53.12	29.83
1968	10.58	26.87	55.78	40.75
1969	11.73	26.92	58.28	41.41
1970	12.98	27.50	58.71	34.66
1971	14.62	26.14	45.83	39.10
1972	16.54	24.27	52.94	38.73
1973	20.07	22.31	46.45	34.49
1974	24.01	20.14	31.12	16.91
1975	27.19	18.02	26.03	19.00
1976	31.15	18.27	21.18	16.82
1977	35.32	20.25	15.15	11.39
1978	40.98	21.83	14.91	11.18
1979	36.21	29.97	13.17	10.62
1980	41.12	30.42	15.46	9.96
1981	45.69	30.79	11.59	8.12
1982	48.79	31.63	17.37	11.69
1983	52.52	34.81	18.23	15.19
1984	55.36	40.63	16.37	11.98
1985	53.10	36.80	17.15	10.93
1986	71.96	45.38	26.73	17.70
1987	112.46	28.65	20.72	14.75
1988	124.71	27.73	15.91	12.08
1989	125.07	28.04	17.10	12.86

Exhibit 5   Selected Robert Morris Ratios

Annual Sales	0-1MM	1-3MM	3-5MM	5-10MM	10-25MM	25MM & Up
ASSETS	5.4	10.6	4.7	14.8	7.7	9.6
Cash & Equiv.	34.6	27.2	28.2	26.9	34.4	28.4
Net Receivables	26.7	28.4	36.5	27.5	24.8	28.9
Inventory	4.0	4.2	2.0	2.9	0.8	2.3
Other Current	69.7	70.3	71.4	72.2	87.5	67.2
Fixed Assets	20.5	24.0	25.5	18.6	26.2	23.5
Intangibles	4.4	0.4	0.3	3.3	1.7	4.0
Other	5.3	5.3	2.7	5.8	4.8	5.4
Total	100.0	100.0	100.0	100.0	100.0	100.0 LIABILI-
TIES						
Short Term Notes	11.9	6.2	12.8	7.4	9.3	7.2
Curr. L T Debt	6.0	4.9	2.6	1.9	1.6	1.3
Trade Payables	14.6	11.3	14.3	10.7	12.7	8.3
Taxes Payable	0.5	0.9	0.2	0.7	0.8	1.5
Other Current	17.3	9.0	9.9	9.2	11.5	8.5
Total Current	50.3	32.3	40.3	29.8	38.0	28.8
L T Debt	19.4	13.8	16.0	9.7	8.8	13.4
Deferred Taxes	0.0	1.2	0.2	0.8	0.4	1.8
Other L T	10.3	5.2	1.5	5.0	7.6	3.1
Net Worth	20.0	47.4	42.0	54.5	47.2	54.8
Total	100.0	100.0	100.0	100.0	100.0	100.0
INCOME						
Sales	100.0	100.0	100.0	100.0	100.0	100.0
Gross Profit	49.4	53.5	42.9	47.3	41.8	44.6
Expenses	47.4	45.9	38.9	39.7	35.7	30.8
Operating Profit	2.0	7.6	4.0	7.6	6.0	13.9
Other Exp.	1.0	1.5	1.0	1.0	1.6	2.0
Profit Before Tax	0.9	6.1	3.0	6.6	4.5	11.9
RATIOS						
Current	1.4	2.3	1.9	2.4	1.9	2.3
Quick	0.8	1.5	0.9	1.8	1.1	1.5
Sales/Receivables	7.6	7.0	6.9	6.3	5.8	5.8
COS/Inventory	4.0	2.6	3.2	3.1	3.9	2.9
COS/Payables	15.7	9.5	8.0	8.5	11.8	10.7
Sales/WC	13.8	5.9	6.6	4.6	5.7	3.8
EBIT/Interest	2.2	3.9	1.9	8.7	6.3	4.3
Fixed/Worth	0.8	0.4	0.5	0.3	0.4	0.4
Debt/Worth	5.8	1.2	1.2	0.9	1.2	0.7
Sales/Fixed Assets	12.6	8.3	9.1	9.4	7.4	8.2
Sales/Total Assets	2.3	1.8	2.1	1.6	1.9	1.5

Case 24

Jeff Mills and Marv Wilson

In late February 1990 Jeff Mills and Marv Wilson were seeking advice about how to respond to an offer from their employer for them to buy him out. The company, Vashon Yachts Incorporated, manufactured wood and fiberglass boats ranging in size from small rowboats to large custom cruisers and sailboats as long as 60 feet. Sales in the preceding year had been nearly $1,440,000. Profits, Jeff and Marv guessed, could have been as much as $160,000 before taxes, depending on how the accounting was handled, after a draw of around $25,000 for the owner. The offer from Ed Jenkins, owner of the company, was to sell out for a price of $550,000, with $160,000 down and the balance over 12 years at 8-percent interest. One question on the minds of Jeff and Marv was whether to accept the offer as it stood. If not, then another was whether to make some kind of counter offer or to do something else, and if so, what.

Large Custom Boats

Vashon Yachts produced two general categories of boats, custom and production types. The custom boats, some sailboats and some power cruisers, typically were larger, over 40 feet in length, selling for $250,000 to $450,000—depending on size, features and extent of completion before delivery to the customer. To buy such a boat, a customer would hire a marine architect to prepare plans, then hire a company like Vashon to perform construction following the plans. The company charged for this work on the basis of its own costs for labor plus materials and a markup of 25 percent on that sum. The total price was never fully set in advance. Mr. Jenkins might make a general estimate of the overall costs based on the plans, but this estimate was never written nor firm. The customer would be billed on a monthly basis as work progressed and could at any time halt the job.

Construction of a custom yacht began with ordering supplies, including hull materials as well as components such as engine, propeller and other mechanical, electrical and plumbing parts. At the same time, hull construction began by "lofting" or laying out sections of the hull cross-section to make a wooden pattern which was externally shaped like the hull. Around this pattern would be formed a fiberglass external mold. Once this external mold was solidified, the internal wooden pattern was broken apart and extracted. Then fiberglass to form the hull was laid up inside the mold where the wooden pattern had been. The hull was laminated in several layers, with fiberglass on the outside. The inner layer was a combination sandwich whose middle was in some areas plastic foam and in other areas balsa wood, depending upon the types of forces and temperatures that would be acting at different points in the hull.

Laying up the hull materials was something of an art, to produce both a smooth shape and finish and to assure adequate strength, especially at joints and other points of stress, such as where engine mounts and sail fittings were attached. Many of these fittings were fabricated as one-of-a-kind items in the company shop out of durable and attractive, but expensive and hard-to-work, stainless steel. Jeff Mills observed that the man who cut, bent, welded and polished these parts to a chrome-like luster took considerable pleasure and pride in these creations. Jeff commented:

> *From conversations with customers, my impression is that very few other companies building boats like these make their own rigging attachment hardware as well. Most have it custom made by outside shops. Being able to show it in process to prospective customers when they visit our shop always seems to draw out their admiration and probably helps us sell boats.*
>
> *Our man who does this work just loves it. He used to build motorcycles in California, but when he moved up here where he liked the country better, he had to work on a line with 50 other welders all doing the same thing, which he didn't like. Here he gets to start from scratch and make everything his own way, which is much more fun. He doesn't make as much money as he did on the production line, but he enjoys living and working here on Vashon Island and has said he plans to stay here forever.*

Hulls were formed in two shells, a top including the deck and a bottom. These were permanently mated after major internal parts such as engines, bulkheads and floors were installed. Interior walls and floors were typically made of sheet plywood and, like the deck, bonded to the lower hull with plastic. Much of this construction involved adjusting arrangements and shapes as work proceeded. At times the company would tell a customer that certain parts should be made stronger or shaped differently than the original plans called for. Negotiations would follow in which the customer would have the final say. Customers often imposed their own

ideas regarding cabin shapes, layouts and trim, while they typically deferred to the marine architect on hull shape and to Vashon regarding internal structure.

The rate of dollar expenditure in building a hull might range upwards of $30,000 per month plus the cost of major items such as engines. The company normally billed customers on these big jobs monthly and expected payment within 30 days. If payments from a customer lagged, the company would slow its pace of work by pulling men off the project until further payments came. No boat went out the door until all customer payments on it had been received.

One large cabin cruiser had sat for nearly a year awaiting progress payments. It had been ordered by an underworld figure who was a very promptly-paying customer and, according to Vashon employees, one of the most amiable and pleasant to deal with. Work had progressed to a point where his boat was about 40-percent complete and the customer had invested approximately $320,000 when he was arrested, tried and sent to jail for racketeering. He kept his payments current throughout the trial, but stopped them when he went off to prison. At that point the company filed a lien on the vessel and stopped work while the racketeer sought from prison to find a buyer. After a year the boat was sold to another man who owned a chain of 100 movie theaters, and work as of early 1990 was again underway.

Most of the large custom vessels were taken away by customers in semi-finished form with additional work such as interior decoration, painting, rigging and other finishing to be done elsewhere. Some customers would set dollar limits on what Vashon was to do, for instance saying that work should stop when $200,000 worth had been performed, because that was all they could afford to spend on it.

Production Boats

A second and quite different category of boats included what the company referred to as "production boats." These were standard hull shapes made in permanent molds. These vessels typically went out the door for around $30,000 each, much less than the custom boats for three main reasons. First, they were smaller, around 25 to 35 feet as opposed to 40 to 60 feet for the custom boats. Second, they were made from permanent molds, which meant that the cost of making a mold could be amortized over many craft. Third, people who bought them tended to take them away in an even less finished form than did custom boat buyers, to complete the work themselves. Sometimes, however, the company custom-finished these hulls to order.

Production sailboats also sold somewhat differently than did custom vessels. Whereas in custom boats quality of workmanship and the amount of work that could be expected per dollar of cost were the major selling factors, in production boats the more important thing tended to be reputation of the hull design. When one of the production boats was successful in winning races a large number of orders for that design would regularly follow. If later another manufacturer's boat took the prize instead, orders for the former winner's boats would drop off.

People

Employees of the company could be grouped into two categories, one for those who stayed permanently and a second for those who came and went from the workforce on a short-term basis, sometimes because of surges in workload, other times for personal reasons. There were roughly eight permanent people, while short-timers ranged in number from around eight to as many as 24. Top pay among the permanent employees, except

for the owner, was $14 per hour. Short-timers' pay ranged from minimum wage, which might be for high school students working part time, up to top scale for more skilled workers.

The owner, Ed Jenkins, had been in the business of constructing "spec" houses during the '60s. "Spec" referred to a practice of building a house speculatively before a customer had been lined up, the builder investing his own money coupled with a bank loan to put up the building, which would later be sold during or after construction, rather than before as was done with non-spec homes. This speculation practice could be highly profitable when sales came easily, or it could be ruinous for the builder if the houses sold slowly, since profits were then rapidly consumed by interest carrying charges of bank loans on the unsold property. During the aerospace downturn and local "Boeing crunch" of the late '60s Mr. Jenkins' construction company had been wiped out by consequently depressed conditions of the Seattle housing market.

He had then worked for a couple of years, until 1982, in a company owned by his wife's family, building low-cost production boats before borrowing a stake from the family to set up his own custom boat business. With this stake he had bought five acres of Vashon Island real estate for $300,000, and with Al Downey, one of the craftsmen from his former house construction business, poured a concrete slab and put up a 40 by 80 foot building in which to make boats. Revenues from the first boats were used to finance others, to develop molds for production boats and to put up additional building space. Jeff Mills commented that Ed Jenkins seemed to have a knack for locating bargains on building materials, such as used steel beams suitable for his buildings, and for putting up buildings cheaply using plant labor.

Initially, Mr. Jenkins had been involved in all company functions, lining up customers, buying supplies, supervising the workforce and laboring on the boats himself. As time progressed and the workforce grew, however, he had largely withdrawn from production activities. By 1990 he still performed the selling and purchasing, and typically came into the plant for an hour or two each morning, "to chew everybody out about how the work is going," according to one of the shop men, but after that he would leave for the day and not return.

Al Downey, the craftsman whom Mr. Jenkins had brought with him from housebuilding, was an experienced boatbuilder, who had constructed his first vessel 19 years earlier at age 18 and continued to build others ever since on an off-hours basis. In contrast to Mr. Jenkins, who did not do much sailing personally and built boats on what one employee described as a "cut and try" basis, Mr. Downey was an experienced sailor, who had grown up near the water on a nearby island and served several years in the Coast Guard in addition to building and sailing his own boats. He and his wife currently lived on a boat. His approach to boatbuilding was careful and systematic. He performed all the company's lofting work on custom boats and was presently supervising the company's largest job, the racketeer's custom cruiser.

Jeff Mills was an MBA graduate from the University of Washington and an experienced sailor who had grown up sailing boats as a youngster in Southern California. He graduated from college in California with a degree in economics and worked for a couple of years as assistant branch manager in a California bank. Much of his work there had been to substitute for other branch managers in the chain when they were temporarily away from work on vacation or due to illness. He had moved to the Pacific Northwest in 1985, taken a job at Vashon Yachts and en-

rolled in the MBA program both to get away from a situation he was not enjoying in California and to pursue his love of sailing.

Through an uncle, he had met Ed Jenkins, who hired Jeff for his extensive racing experience and his skills as a rigger. Jeff started at the bottom in the company, as a glass laminator, despite his college training, but rose as he learned the business. By early 1990 he was supervising construction of a $400,000 custom sailboat being built for a wealthy California housing contractor. Jeff estimated that his time was spent approximately 20 percent on supervising the work of others and 80 percent performing work on the job himself.

Marv Wilson, 25, had been a bicycle racer before shifting his interests to sailing. At Vashon, he too was responsible for supervising one of the major custom boat projects currently in process. Self-taught, he had been with Vashon Yachts for four and one-half years and had worked on all aspects of boatbuilding. His specialty, however, had become design of metal parts and structural features on the boats.

Outside work, Marv had been pursuing real estate interests of his own. With savings from his job he had bought a small house during the mid-70s. It had shortly doubled in value, both as a result of his own remodeling work and as a result of generally rising real estate prices. Selling the house, he had found five acres of land which had been attached by the Internal Revenue Service because of the owner's default on taxes, and after considerable legal work he obtained title to it at a very low price. In his spare time he then built a house, which he sold off with two of the five acres for $200,000, retaining the other three acres himself. With the proceeds, he bought some waterfront land on which he was currently constructing another house in his spare time.

Don Evans had been with the company for seven years, since graduating in urban planning from a university in Southern California. He was regarded by other employees as a great sailboat racer and was especially skilled at fiberglass laminating and finishing. Earlier he had quit Vashon to create his own business. He rented one of the large buildings and some molds from the Vashon to build, on subcontract for Vashon, a "star" racing boat which won some races and sold well. Because of the substantial markup taken by Vashon in selling his boats, however, it was difficult for Don to make enough profit to buy Vashon's molds as he intended. After about two years the star design lost favor with racers due to success of another company's boat in races, and sales declined sharply. Ed Jenkins offered Don his job back at Vashon, and Don rejoined the company, where he too supervised some of the boatbuilding.

Facility

The company was located on five acres of land in the woods on Vashon Island, a short ferry ride from Seattle. Boats were built in three large buildings plus a breezeway. The breezeway consisted of a cement slab plus roof covering a 40-by-60 foot space between two of the company's 40-by-80 foot buildings. The third building was nearby and was 40 by 160 feet. All the buildings were constructed with high roofs and overhead cranes to facilitate working on large boats. In the yard surrounding the buildings were parked production boat molds not being used plus some partially completed boats which had been moved out of the buildings where all of the hull fabrication was done.

Equipment in the plant consisted largely of scaffolding set up to hold the hulls and allow workers to climb around on them, plus assorted tools. Most substantial of the tools were those in the metal-working area. These included a large electric welder, a large band saw for cut-

ting plate, a drill press, grinders and sanders for shaping and finishing metal parts. There were no machine tools such as lathes, milling machines or other precision equipment. No permanent or elaborate mounting arrangements were required for any of the tools, and the scaffolds were all temporary.

On neighboring lots were a couple of other small manufacturing plants. Elsewhere on the island were a large ski manufacturer plus other small marinas and boat yards, none with facilities to handle the large jobs, however. Other than that there was little industrially zoned land on the island, although there was one parcel of five acres for sale directly across the street. It was believed that rezoning for light industrial use could be obtained for this land, on which the asking price was $250,000.

The Deal

Ed Jenkins first approached his four employees, Jeff Mills, Marv Wilson, Al Downey and Don Evans about the possibility of one or more of them buying him out in early December 1989. Jeff recalled:

We asked him how much, and he said around two or three hundred thousand. But he didn't say for what, and each time we would ask it seemed more things were to be left out of the deal. We started running around adding up the value of the assets. The major power tools were worth maybe $70,000, but there seemed to be some question about whether those would be included. The small tools could be replaced for around $35,000. The molds currently used for production boats we guessed might cost around $200,000 to replace.

The real estate would add a lot more, but that was not to be sold. Instead, Ed offered us a five-year lease at 24 cents per square foot per month on the buildings and 15 cents on the breezeway. He let us look at his income tax statements for the past five years, and those showed sales rising each year from $540,000 in 1984 to $560,000, $780,000, $995,000 and $1,440,000 for the other years up to 1989.

No profits were shown because he had been able to expense things out. Shop labor was used to put up the plant buildings, make the molds, and so forth. We can see that Ed has been doing well financially. He has built a fancy custom boat of his own, bought lots of tools, bought a small island and a company airplane.

We tried to estimate how much profit was in the boat sales. There was no breakdown of sales or expenses by different line of boats, but we know the custom work was marked up 25 percent on labor and materials, and we think the margin on production boats must be around twice that. In 1989 we made about 10 production boats and the rest of the sales came from custom work.

Ed finally came up with a firm offer of $560,000 to include all the molds and shop equipment. He asked for $160,000 down and the balance over 10 years at 8-percent interest.

We put our heads together and decided that each of the four of us could come up with $40,000 for a down payment. That would fully commit all of my assets and all of Al Downey's except for the boat he and his wife live on. Marv could generate his share by selling some of his land and still have other land left. Don Evans has money in his family that he could tap for his share.

We got all enthused about owning our own business, but still felt the price was too high. So we went back to Ed with a counter offer of $400,000 for the molds, tools and company name. But he turned that down cold. He did say he would relax the terms, let us take 12 years instead of 10 for the payout and lower the interest rate from 8 percent down to 7 percent. But that was as far as he would go.

Then we started considering other options. Marv thinks we should try to own our own building. But that would take much more capital than we have. There aren't any other large plants on the island we could get, and all of us would have problems with moving. I might be willing to do it if the opportunity looked good enough, but Al Downey isn't even willing to consider it. Marv and Don might be willing, but right now they don't think so.

Meanwhile, we have been noticing that the general economic downturn of the country may be affecting our boat sales. We have three large custom jobs under construction but no more on order at the moment. We probably have a couple of 35 footers on order, but only Ed knows about that, since he handles all the sales. He is talking with prospective buyers fairly frequently and may have other things coming along as well that we have not yet heard about. But right now the backlog seems to be shrinking a lot in custom boats, and we are not facing any orders on production boats.

On the other hand, we get lots of inquiries, often as many as 10 a day. Ed often seems to us to be pretty abrasive to these people. So quite a bit of sales potential may be getting deflected away. We get the impression from customers that we are unique in this area in being able to make several large boats at a time. Most yards around the country can build at most only one or two large custom boats at a time.

For my own part, I feel there are several options. I am sailing in races every other weekend. At the end of June, I will sail in one from Victoria to Maui and then either sail a boat back or else fly back and sail in some other races here.

Another option for me would be to become a permanent skipper on someone else's boat, which would let me sail all the time. And of course I still have that MBA.

I'm clearly not in this for the money at $14 an hour, which is what all four of us are paid. I love sailing and I enjoy working on boats. But we can all see that if we had our own company we might be able to still sail a lot and have more personal freedom and money at the same time. I'm convinced Ed would like to get his money out of this company so he could move on to other things himself. The trouble is that his price seems too high and we don't have enough money to finance it. So where can we go from here?

Bruce Milne

As 1979 ended, Bruce Milne, the sales manager of a minicomputer sales company office in Seattle, was considering how to structure ownership in a new company he planned to start with two of his co-employees. The company they worked for sold DEC minicomputers to accountants for the combined functions of accounting and word processing. Bruce had watched with increasing interest as microcomputers had expanded in capabilities and he expected that it was only a matter of time before they too would find application in both accounting and word processing. Because they were much cheaper than minicomputers he expected that once they entered the market for those functions they would spread rapidly. His idea for the new company was to capitalize on that opportunity. To get started he wanted Brian Guthie and Lauri Chandler to join him as partners.

Antecedents of the Idea

Bruce Milne had been engaged in ventures of one kind or another since childhood. He recalled:

When I was 8, I was already trudging around selling Christmas cards. I liked to buy the stock, go around presenting it to people, make the sales and collect the money. To me it was fun.

Later, as a business major at the University of Washington, he "always had two or three businesses going at once," he recalled. "It was to prevent starvation, because nobody was paying my way."

For instance while working as a lifeguard, he met parents who wanted swimming lessons for their children. Consequently, he rented time at a local pool and set up a swimming school which employed up to four instructors. He continued:

I'd been a swim instructor and a coach. Then I became a lifeguard for the city. Parents were always asking if there were someplace they could send their kids for lessons. I saw that there were a lot of private pools, and a lot of people in one housing complex wanted lessons. I went to a private pool there, and they let me use the pool until two o'clock on my own. For instructors I hired some fraternity members at the University. I had all the paper boys in the north end put flyers out, and I had a little pyramid scheme where for every customer you bring in, you get a dollar off on your own child. We had a babysitting service where if you bring them for a half-hour they could have a babysitter for two or three hours, so you could go shopping at the Northgate shopping center. We were deluged because we had the cheapest babysitting service in town, plus swim lessons.

He also bought, repaired and sold used Volkswagens, ran a barber service, sold cookware, imported and sold Swiss watches and renovated houses.

After graduation in 1970, Bruce spent the remainder of his savings on a trip to Europe, after which he returned to Seattle and looked for a job. He made application to the University of Washington Business School. He was accepted, but decided not to go. He worked for a company called Canadian American Security Holders (CASH), which was a collection agency. "I thought you'd make money quick at that," he said. "But it was a fly-by -night operation." He soon looked for another job.

In the newspaper classified section, he noticed two jobs of possible interest, one selling office copiers and the other selling computers. "My dad always told me to go to work for a big company," he recalled. After interviewing both he chose the latter and in 1971 went to work for Burroughs Corporation, "It was lucky I made that choice," he said, "because the other job would have been a dead end."

He went through Burroughs' training program and became a sales representative. "The job started at only about $600 to $700 a month," he said. "It took me about five years working full time to get up to the level of income I'd had working part time for myself." He once again went to the University, where he took a couple of night courses toward an MBA, but then dropped out.

In 1973 he encountered a new opportunity in the company.

I had gone to school in Mexico during my sophomore year and always thought it would be interesting to get into international business in some way. There was a guy from Burroughs who was flying through on his way to Japan. My boss said, "I'll see if he can interview you between planes." So I went and said I wanted a job internationally. I was cocky at 24. I said, "I can outsell anybody you have." He said "OK." So I went sight unseen to Puerto Rico. I took a pay cut. I guess a lot of people didn't like that job. It was funny. My three worst subjects in school were Spanish, accounting and computer programming. And so now I was selling

computers for accounting applications in Puerto Rico.

By age 24 he became the youngest sales zone manager in the company. He also got married to a co-worker from Burroughs in Seattle with whom he had stayed in touch.

She had been in real estate sales, and got her job as a Burroughs sales representative after she sold the local sales manager his house—a big 12,000 square foot place in West Seattle that had been a girls' school.

Beginnings of a Business Idea

Software for computer accounting systems at the time was almost entirely a custom activity in the mid-1970s, he recalled.

At one point my wife and I set up another business on the side called Systems Analyst Programmers, because Burroughs would not let us hire any programmers, and we needed them to sell and service the systems for Puerto Rican customers. At Burroughs you had to do your own programming, so we did this other business on the side to try to save some of the installations we had. At one point we had guys from about 10 different companies working for us.

I also picked up software on trips to the United States. Wherever I went around the country, to Chicago or Los Angeles, I'd head straight for the software backroom, rip off a copy of everything they had and take it on the plane with me back to Puerto Rico. So I built a library, even though I wasn't a technical guy, because the software they had in South America was garbage.

Then in 1974, Bruce again decided to apply to business school.

Everything seemed to go in two-year

cycles. After about 18 months in one spot I'd start to get the feeling it was time to move on. I applied to Harvard, IMEDE and Wharton. Then to my pleasant surprise on three successive Saturdays I got acceptances from each one. I felt great. My grades had been passable, but not so good as to give me confidence I'd be accepted.

He started at the Harvard Business School in 1975, majored in finance and spent the following summer working as an intern at nearby Digital Equipment Corporation (DEC).

The question I worked on was basically how do we train the original equipment makers (OEM's) who resold and installed DEC's computers, something DEC itself didn't do. That gave me a great exposure to their OEM channels who developed and sold systems and helped develop the custom software that always had to be part of the package.

During my second year I developed a thesis on "The role of the distributor in a computer environment." It was one of these two-credit courses you could devote your life to. My wife and I sold the report to a number of big companies, including IBM, and made several thousand dollars on it that helped pay tuition. It was the most comprehensive report on that topic available at the time.

It looked at the time like software was going to be a marketing bottleneck. Prices of computers were coming down. People were projecting that computer prices were going to come down by 75 percent, while costs of marketing would triple. Companies like IBM, Burroughs and NCR only sold direct. DEC did almost all its selling through the OEM systems houses. The question was how would you extend the channels around

them? How would you manage those channels? How would you recruit? What should be the credit policies, and so forth? Stores selling software were unheard of.

Following graduation in 1977, Bruce and his wife sought a way to return to the West Coast. Bruce took a job with a Portland, Oregon DEC distributor, Alpine Corporation, to help develop a sales office in Seattle. There his belief that better ways of standardizing and distributing minicomputer software were bound to come continued to grow. He recalled:

I said to Alpine management, "you guys already have a lot of software. Why don't you get a guy in Boston, a guy in Philadelphia, and one in Baltimore and make them dealers to resell your stuff so people won't always be reinventing the wheel. You can get leverage and build a big company." There were no big companies selling minicomputers at that time. The biggest we had at DEC was about $3 million a year, and every year the biggest would go out of business, because they would grow, and they would have all this custom software, they'd overextend themselves . . . and we'd be eating their receivables. They were always trying to supply the stuff with lots of custom applications. DEC would help put them out of business because it would take four months to make shipment, and meanwhile the distributors would run out of cash.

His interest in microcomputers also continued to grow as their capabilities increased. In his travels Bruce became acquainted with John Torode, who studied computer science at the University of Washington, then went to Berkeley to teach, while on the side developing a company to make microcomputers. He was the first, according to Bruce, to develop a machine with two floppy disk drives. It seemed to Bruce that it was only a matter of time before machines like that began to benefit from development of standardized software and find application in offices such as those of the accountants to whom he was selling minicomputers.

Teaming

One of the people he began discussing these ideas with was a co-worker, Brian Duthie. Brian had studied industrial engineering and business at Berkeley, then joined Western Electric in 1969, where he worked in product testing. After hours he studied computers at a nearby technical school. Jobs with other companies followed, selling minicomputers for a sales firm, developing software for an insurance company, then working for a computer consulting firm, mainly installing a purchase order system for Boeing. Seeing insufficient growth in that job, he joined Alpine, where he found himself working for Bruce. Together, the two were responsible for over 40 percent of sales in the 40-person company.

When Bruce, frustrated by Alpine's rejection of his business development ideas, first began talking with Brian about creating a new company, the idea was that they might begin developing microcomputer systems on the side. Bruce developed a connection with Altos Computer in California and suggested that Brian might develop software to go with Altos hardware to make a complete system they could sell to accountants.

But attendance at a night course gave Bruce a different perspective. One of the speakers who had developed several successful companies stressed the idea that he had never been able to do it part time. It was necessary, he said, to take the full plunge if the company were going to be ambitiously growth-oriented. Brian, however, was cautious. Neither he nor Bruce had much savings, and Brian's wife was expecting their first child.

Hoping to persuade Brian, Bruce suggested they visit John Torode in California to see his dual floppy microcomputer. On the trip they could also visit the only company Bruce knew of that offered a standard general ledger software package for minicomputers. Bruce commented:

> Brian, like a true techie, was glad for the chance to get inside a computer "factory" and meet the machine's designer. Then we went over to the software company, told them we might be interested in distributing their product, and asked for a demonstration. We had a yellow pad with us that we took notes on. The demonstration was supposed to last 45 minutes. But after 20 minutes we said we had seen enough. The notes we took on the yellow pad were deficiencies and we already had four pages of them. Like any good programmer, Brian always knew he could make something better. And if this was the leader of the industry, they were in for real trouble.

Now Brian was ready to go with the new venture. The idea would be to sell DEC minicomputer systems with existing software for the short term to derive income, which would support development of better software by Brian for the longer term. The software would be for microcomputers, and when it was ready, the new company would sell systems combining it with Altos computers to accountants.

Bruce had also persuaded his secretary, Lauri Chandler, to join the team. Lauri had become skilled at word processing on the minicomputer systems Alpine sold.

Designing the Ownership Structure

As Bruce saw it, each of the three would bring different ingredients to the new venture. Brian would be crucial as the "resident genius" software developer. He would also be important in helping sell and install minicomputer systems for income while the company was getting started.

Lauri would help with two functions. One would be to run the office of the new venture itself. The other would be to serve as a consultant on the word processing aspects of the minicomputer installations sold during the company's first phase of existence.

Bruce would take primary responsibility for selling minicomputer systems during the first stage. He expected one major problem would be to obtain the computers to sell, since the company, because of its smallness, would not initially qualify as an OEM for DEC. "It's ironic," he observed. "One of the very systems I helped set up at DEC would now prevent us from becoming an OEM for them."

However, Bruce had become well-acquainted with DEC's channels and believed he would be able to buy through contacts he had in a consortium headquartered in North Dakota. This would reduce the discount they would receive on equipment from 30 percent down to perhaps 25 percent, but he expected it would enhance speed of delivery, since the buying consortium always had more units on order than a typical systems house handling DEC products, and therefore could provide faster and more dependable delivery.

Bruce would also be responsible for raising capital. Each of the three, it appeared, would be able to muster $10,000. To do so, the three would have to commit all their personal savings and, in some cases, borrow from relatives. Bruce would be able to go without salary in the near term, thanks to his wife's income, but the other two would need to be paid. So it seemed clear to all three that more capital would have to be raised. Bruce knew of three individuals he might be able to raise another $10,000 each from within a couple of months if they could get the company set up and operating. One was an entrepreneur with a cheesecake manufacturing company to whom Bruce had sold a minicomputer. The second was a lawyer whom Bruce had tried to sell without success, but had nevertheless become a good friend. The third was a former competitor who had recently made large profits from shares he held when his employer went public.

> *If the new firm were able to raise another $30,000 from these individuals, Bruce expected that it might last only a few months, after which, if Brian were successful in developing the microcomputer software, they would need another infusion two or three times that large to move ahead with its distribution. How he would accomplish that, he was not sure. He supposed it would necessitate recruiting more shareholders from somewhere.*

Bruce also knew some sales prospects to whom he thought the new company would be able to sell minicomputer systems in the near term. But as in the case of the potential sources of capital, that possibility remained to be tested.

His immediate problem was how to structure ownership between himself and his two initial colleagues, both to get the company started and to establish a base for further development in the future.

Case 26

John Morse

Midway through a two-year MBA program at the University of Washington, John Morse had begun a venture search with the objective of achieving self-employment upon graduation. Now graduation was just two weeks away and, although he had generated many possible venture ideas, John had not yet found one he was sure he wanted to pursue. He felt it was time to review the steps taken in his search to date and decide whether to continue it or to adopt a different approach.

Background

As the ninth of 12 children, John spent the first 18 years of his life (1952-1970) growing up in a suburb north of Chicago, going right from high school to college. He spent one year at Boston College, his sophomore year abroad in Rome, and finished up the last two years at Northwestern University in 1974 with a B.S. in Sociology. During the next four years, until starting his MBA program in 1978, he held the following jobs: waiter, bartender, phlebotomist, law clerk, factory worker in a sausage plant, hospital purchasing agent, and purchasing agent for a printing plant. John said his experiences working with other individuals as his supervisors and "carrot danglers" were not very rewarding or fulfilling.

I seem to be intimidated and uninspired in that environment. I suspect it would be a frustrating life for me as an employee, and it would probably be riddled with continual disappointment. My nature is especially attracted to the

independence associated with being one's own boss. I am far more secure with the uncertainties this entails. Three or four years ago, in 1976, I realized what I wanted out of a career in business was to run one, ideally my own. My plan was to get a master's degree in Business Administration, spend three to five years as an employee gaining experience and capital, and then launch a business.

For part of his MBA program, John spent a year as an exchange student in England. While there, he took a course in entrepreneurship which triggered the thought that it might be possible for him to start a business of his own following graduation, if he could line up a suitable venture idea. Upon returning to Seattle in June 1979, he approached one of his professors at the University of Washington about doing a feasibility study of a new venture idea as an MBA research project. Since John did not have a specific venture idea in mind, the professor suggested that he come back before fall quarter (three months hence) with a study proposal.

During the next three months, once or twice a week John would go into a vacant classroom for a couple of hours at a time with a notebook. He would try to force himself to think of business innovations. He relied largely on his imagination and inspiration. He would try to picture in his mind where business trends were headed. Some ideas that came out of those sessions were:

1. Develop a product for a fast grow-

ing market segment—senior citizens.

2. Start a service to capitalize on the increase in foreigners visiting Seattle (for example, day care or tour bus guide service).

3. Develop a marketing device (for example, a nondefaceable billboard to put up on stall walls) to take advantage of the captive market in public toilets.

4. Set up camps for adults.

5. Begin a service to alleviate some of the difficulties facing the growing number of women executives traveling alone to Seattle on business.

6. Organize an information network with subscribers hooked up via computer terminals.

About three weeks before he was scheduled to get back to his professor with his proposal for a topic, John came across an article in *Newsweek* on "Snob Ice Creams" that he said "came the closest to eureka" since he began searching for a business idea. He now wanted to investigate the feasibility of manufacturing locally a top-quality ice cream to compete with brands currently imported from the Midwest. During the next week-and-a-half he tried to get a feel for what he was considering. He went to the library and pulled some books on ice cream manufacturing. He called all the local ice cream manufacturers to find out what they manufactured in the way of high-quality ice cream. He contacted, either by phone or in person, a number of retail ice cream stores to find out whose ice cream they were distributing and what sort of demand it was generating.

This informal research left John less than convinced that his ice cream manufacturing idea was bound to be a sure-fire success. His professor also expressed

doubts, noting that the gourmet brand uppermost in John's mind was imported not only to Seattle but also to Los Angeles from the Midwest. If the Los Angeles area with its many millions of people did not represent a large enough market to justify setting up a local manufacturing plant, the professor asked, how could the Seattle area, which was only a fraction that size and even closer to the Midwest, justify doing so? Instead of plunging ahead with the "hot flash" idea of manufacturing gourmet ice cream, he suggested that John might undertake, under his sponsorship, a methodical search for a business venture as a research project. The professor pointed to three donated boxes of IEA (International Entrepreneur Association) manuals as a possible source of ideas but left the door open to any other sources John might want to mine.

John took a sample of an IEA manual home and discovered it to be a report on a business venture that might appeal to an aspiring entrepreneur. It outlined, step-by-step, what an individual might do to pursue the profiled venture. Some of the items covered were market research, a suggested list of readings, sources for equipment and supplies, and typical cost figures. At the end of each manual was a section devoted to business, legal and governmental considerations in establishing a new venture. A list of manuals available to him in the school library appears in Exhibit 1.

Unsure how he was going to approach the search, but with the desire to do it, John arranged with his professor to begin the MBA research project in fall quarter, two weeks away.

Anticipating a Market

Weeks 1 and 2

In discussion with his professor, John decided to attempt a systematic search for a business venture by reviewing the various manuals in the light of his desires and

Seattle's business makeup. But he began the search far from convinced that this method would lead to anything tangible or practical. He chose to combine his search through manuals with a review of the Puget Sound area. It seemed to him that it should be possible to view the marketplace as a "case study," and analyze the Puget Sound area for its demographics, economic factors, market profile and any apparent trends. From some such combination of information, he figured, it would be only a matter of deduction to recognize where opportunities existed for a successful start-up.

Week 3

John began his search with a visit to the Seattle office of the Washington State Department of Commerce. He asked for any information that they had on local and state demographics, market studies, consumer profiles, trade figures, growth projections, economic forecasts and anything else they thought relevant.

> *What stumped both them and me was the question: relevant to what? Since I wasn't really sure what information I was seeking, I couldn't be specific. They gave me all the publications they had that might have any connection, even remotely, to the somewhat broad boundaries of my request.*

They included a 1978 *Pocket Data Book of the State of Washington* (a reference volume of population, economic, government, education, and human resource statistics and trends), a "Community Level Target Industry Identification Program" report, the "Washington State Economy Review of 1978, Outlook for 1979," "Washington State Exporter's Guide," and the "International Trade Directory." He also spent an hour speaking with the Small Business counselor in that office about general trends in the state, as he perceived them,

and what he felt were the areas for opportunity. Energy and transportation were cited as the industries providing the greatest opportunities.

Later that same day John visited the Seattle Chamber of Commerce with the same request for information. They too indicated that his request was very broad and gave him a number of publications, including a 1978 Economic Review of the Seattle-Everett area, a booklet entitled "Corporate Headquarters: Central Puget Sound Region," a sample of "Business Profiles," a "Business Migration Study: An Analysis of Out-Migration Patterns in Seattle Firms," and a listing of other publications available through the Chamber of Commerce. Both the state and city Commerce Departments recommended a visit to the Seattle City Library's business department.

Week 4

Skeptical about where his search was going, John next visited the city library with the same request used at the Commerce Departments. The librarian in the business section presented him with a large volume of statistics profiling metropolitan Seattle consumers. "It could conceivably have been a great marketing aid, but since I didn't know yet what I was trying to market, I had a hard time extracting any value out of that book," he recalled.

The librarian also pointed out a file cabinet of resource documents which contained a drawer devoted to the Small Business Administration. John perused that file and while finding it of general interest, came away with no concrete information.

> *At this point I had accumulated a small library of information and the more I looked through it, the more confused I became as to what I was trying to learn. From all this data I discovered that trying to absorb all the information available on the Puget Sound area and then translate it into some business*

opportunity(s) was far too broad, difficult and abstract for my purposes and abilities. I also discovered that the approach I was taking could offer no more direction than that which I was already bringing to it. The flip side of that, however, was the realization that there is a wealth of information and assistance available to the individual who knows exactly what information he is seeking.

Four weeks into the project John was still devoting most of his mental energy searching for a business idea that would anticipate a market, either a new product or service that would capitalize on a currently unmet need or else a business that would take advantage of a growing market demand. He began to think that perhaps the best way to enter a market would be to let an innovative or quality product or service lead him into the market rather than entering a market first and then searching for an idea.

Week 5

I remember once reading an article which stated that even when you are not looking for a job, it is prudent to keep an eye on the "Help Wanted" classified ads so that you can get a feel for which employers are having a hard time finding and/or keeping employees, which professions are (not) in great demand, pay scales for various positions, and so forth. Using that same line of thinking I started to read the 'Business Opportunities' section in the classifieds to learn what I could about the business climate as evidenced by what types of businesses were up for sale, where, and at what price.

So far, John was still avoiding analysis of the IEA manuals, feeling they were "somebody else's song," which he did not want to imitate. He was trying to be highly

methodical, keeping and analyzing a log of his time and the degree of output different approaches were producing for him. The log was something he had agreed with his professor to do as part of the research paper he was supposed to produce for course credit. However, he found the chronicling difficult and was acutely aware that the sixth week of the search was at hand and, so far, no satisfactory venture idea had turned up. He intensified his efforts at becoming more systematic.

Establishing a List of Possible Ventures

Week 6
John observed:

My single most difficult step in undertaking a methodical and rational search for a business (and it really didn't begin until this point) was overcoming the gut feeling that it is inspiration and innovation that lead the entrepreneur to the marketplace, not scientific inquiry. The prospect of starting or buying a business before having an outstanding idea or product seemed like the proverbial cart before the horse. At the same time, there was fear that by forcing entry into one market, I could be preempting the discovery or recognition of a successful enterprise in another field. Fortunately, I came to see that line of thought as counterproductive. The way I was able to bridge the gap between my desire to be creative and methodically arriving at a list of possible ventures was the belief that the latter does not have to preclude the former.

Next he began to write down what it was he was looking for versus what he was trying to avoid in various types of businesses, as shown in Exhibit 2. As he did this, he also noticed that the venture search project was becoming the main focus of his school interest, notwithstanding three other courses he was taking.

Weeks 7 through 12

A help, John found, was Kenneth Albert's *How to Pick the Right Small Business Opportunity.* One of its features was a capability assessment guide, which he used to take an inventory of his strengths and weaknesses. He continued:

> The Alberts book revealed to me that it was easy when looking at existing entrepreneurs and executives to be impressed with what I don't know without counterbalancing it with how much I do know, which is also important.
>
> A hard part of trying to be systematic was figuring out what step to take next. As with any exercise, if you know where you're going to end up, the direction of your steps is fairly obvious. But otherwise, it's confusing.
>
> One thing I discovered, though, in thinking of potential business ideas, was that step-by-step progression had to take place in their development, and that I should avoid sitting back and viewing the 'go-no-go' decision as a quantum leap.

Other outside reading John did at this stage was Sandman and Goldenson's, *How to Succeed in Business Before Graduating,** plus the record of another student's venture search and an article in the *Harvard Business Review* on the origin of venture ideas.** The Sandman book seemed to him limited to ventures of only short-term viability. The other student's study did not

seem to have found much pay dirt. The article suggested that most venture ideas come from jobs and hobbies rather than from any systematic study such as John was pursuing.

Also in the seventh week of the project, John xeroxed a 13-page index of major groups in the Standard Industrial Classification. His intent was to go through this index and circle any industry or product that he could conceivably get involved with in some capacity. In weeks eight and nine, he went through this list two more times on different days to check and recheck his choices. He applied the same procedure to a Seattle Yellow Pages index. By the end of the fourteenth week, he had consolidated the products and services list as shown in Exhibit 3. A couple of hours scanning the *Thomas Register* and the *National Directory of Associations* revealed to him no additional ideas or categories that weren't already covered in the consolidated list.

Week 13

During spring break John began reading through some of the IEA manuals in an attempt to identify positive and negative features of each of the profiled ventures (Exhibit 4). He commented:

> Some of the available manuals (e.g., Christmas tree lot) I didn't even glance at, either because they were too small-time or they didn't even have a minimal attraction. The ideas most worth serious consideration in the manuals I read seemed to be a cookie shop, a secretarial service and a mobile restaurant. The mobile restaurant (vending truck) seemed potentially viable as a business to take downtown during the lunch hour rush. After thinking about it, however, I decided that I didn't want to get involved with retail food service. That clouded the cookie shop idea as well.
>
> The secretarial service had the appeal

---

* Sandman, Peter, and Dan Goldenson, *How to Succeed in Business Before Graduating*, New York, Collier Books, 1968.

** Vesper, Karl H., "Finding New Venture Ideas, Don't Overlook the Experience Factor," *Harvard Business Review.*

of low capital required and seemed like maybe it could be a good interim step and experience-builder in case I didn't get something else going. But those advantages still left me feeling unmotivated, so I decided not to follow through with it.

It began to seem to John that the more effort he spent defining what he was looking for, the less time he would have to spend searching for it, but with the trade-off for defining versus searching not being one-for-one. This impression persisted. John sketched what he meant on a time-line as follows:

how I would assign 30 points or allocate $30 among the criteria to indicate its importance to me," he recalled. Then, although his knowledge of what these businesses entailed in terms of financial, technical and personal resources was sketchy, he computed two scores for each line of business: one by counting the number of plusses and the other by multiplying the number of plusses by their respective criteria priority weightings and adding up those totals.

With these numerical values computed for each of the business categories, he selected eight products and five services that were both high-rated numerically and

```
/Defining————————————————————————————>/Search——————————>time

                              versus

/Defining——————————>/Search————————————————————————————>time
```

The first of these two patterns, he believed, was more difficult but more efficient. It also occurred to John at this time that his search process might be helpful in clarifying what he was seeking in a job, even if it did not yield a business.

Week 14

By the fourteenth week of the project, John felt ready to narrow his search further. He began by listing 11 criteria he considered important in the evaluation of a business. Then he took a list of product and service areas he had consolidated earlier and went through each business category, rating it against his criteria (see Exhibit 5). He assigned plusses and minuses subjectively based on how he felt about it. He also assigned priorities to the criteria (indicated by the number next to each criterion in Exhibit 5). "I asked myself

comfortable to his "gut feeling." They were:

PRODUCTS	SERVICES
Frozen Desserts	Circulation Library
Ice Cream	Day Care
Sporting Goods, Wholesale	Freight Forwarding
Cookies and Crackers	Lodging, hotel, motel, hostel
Cider, Fruit and Vegetable Juices	Delivery Service
Woolen Goods	
Salad Dressings	

Next, he began pruning this list, beginning with day care. He commented:

A friend who is a good friend of a woman who runs a day care business told me about all the headaches she encounters trying to run a business that deals with people's most precious concern, their children. That conversation and subsequent reflection made day care an easy deletion. Owning a lodge struck me as beyond my immediate skills, experience, finances and interests so I dropped it form the list. The circulating library is really a take-off on the information services that I was trying to structure in my thoughts before I began this project. I realized that unless I had something concrete, this business idea would have to wait. Since six of the remaining eight products were food-related, I decided to concentrate my interviews with the food industry and the remaining two services on my pared-down list, freight forwarding and a delivery service.

Interviews

Weeks 15 and 16

Now began what John regarded as the most enjoyable and rewarding phase of the project, interviews with business owners and executives. The interview process, visiting firms, talking with people about getting into businesses like theirs, and getting around to see and hear what was happening, gave John what he described as the most tangible feelings of accomplishment and progress.

Throughout this project I felt my status as a student was a real asset and could probably make information and individuals far more accessible than they may be otherwise. It seemed a natural and logical move then to contact business owners and executives and see if I could draw on their experiences and knowledge to aid in my search.

He prepared a questionnaire (Exhibit 6) to guide his interviews, then visited nine people, all of whom were in the food business, either manufacturing or wholesaling. Which questions on his list were appropriate varied among interviews. Sometimes items would come up in the interview that led to new questions.

To find interviewees John used two references, the *King County Manufacturer's Directory* and *Contacts Influential.* He chose these sources for three main reasons: (1) they listed companies by their S.I.C. (Standard Industrial Classification) numbers, which made it easy to locate prospects; (2) they gave valuable information about these companies such as when they were established, their sales volume, number of employees and whether the office is a branch or headquarters, and (3) they listed names of company presidents or owners.

He was hesitant to let interviewees know that his reason for pursuing this project was to consider entering their lines of work as a potential competitor. He suspected they would be reluctant to answer the questions. John's professor argued to the contrary and, as it turned out, John's fears were unjustified. In fact, he found all whom he interviewed were helpful and encouraging. Two of them spoke with him over lunch, and one invited him to sit in on his annual marketing meeting.

In reviewing the notes taken during the interviews, John said the following points appeared to represent a consensus of the interviewees' remarks:

An individual must have money and related experience to get started in the food business. Also mentioned on more than one occasion as necessary were traits of courage, desire, ambitiousness, and determination.

The most instrumental factors in determining a company's success seemed to be good business management (awareness of costs and cost efficiencies, working capital management, and common sense), good product, and integrity in that order of frequency among the interviewees.

Respondents were about evenly divided on the relative advantages and disadvantages of a small business in the food industry. On the plus side for small firms were quick response time, simplicity and close supervision, while heavy investments, distribution channels, and governmental requirements favored large companies.

The trend in the food industry is toward more convenience foods and prepared high quality frozen foods.

Good business sense, obviously, is important. Also frequently mentioned were the ability to get along with and motivate people and the ability to be a jack-of-all-trades.

In order, the three biggest problems facing the businesses seemed to be (1) government (local and federal) interference; (2) finding and keeping good employees; and (3) financial management, maintaining good cash flow and finding money to expand the business.

To date, John had not looked for possible acquisitions, and none had presented themselves. But he recognized that buying a business was another possibility worth considering.

A product-oriented business, especially manufacturing, seemed to call for buy-out rather than starting from scratch. Product development could take too much time; equipment and setting up would cost too much capital. In contrast, an established business, if its owner were willing to sell it for a small down payment borrowed at the bank, and take payments over time, could be a way around those problems.

Services seemed less difficult capital-wise, but they presented other problems. Among delivery service firms, for instance, John called five individuals before one agreed to speak with him. The owner described a heavy role of government licensing and regulating in his business, as well as in freight forwarding. John decided that line of work was not for him.

Week 17

By the seventeenth week of the project and halfway through his planned interviewing, John said he was disappointed with his progress and frustrated by the shortage of time left before he would be done with school and have to move on.

Up to this point, I hadn't really considered what I would do if the right opportunity didn't turn up. But a glance at the calendar and a pinch of foresight was telling me that, ready or not, school was almost over. Thinking it would help me clarify my thoughts, I took out a piece of paper, titled it "Going For It" as immediate entrepreneurship, and then listed the pros and cons of pursuing a venture tenaciously right away (Exhibit 7). Even though I didn't really make a conscious decision, judging from the subsequent six weeks, I chose to continue trying to arrange something.

Having already established a set of business criteria and attached relative weightings to them (Exhibit 5), John slowly began to conclude during the interviewing process that a good share of the criteria would be met only if the business he attempted were successful.

Selecting a Business

Week 18

In the eighteenth week of the project, and with graduation only a few weeks away, John saw two major concerns in deciding on a business venture. First, he was approaching this decision as though he had a gun with only one bullet, so the aim had to be excellent. Second, it seemed to him that undertaking risk was directly related to conviction. Starting and/or running a business seemed likely to require heavy investments in time, energy and probably money, at least relative to his meager resources. Without a solid commitment and the necessary determination, that investment could be wasted.

As he reflected on his situation, several options were on his mind. One was to continue searching. In that line, he felt he should consider not only the degree of effectiveness his procedure had demonstrated so far, but also how it could be done better. He had collected a log of activities and time spent, as shown in Exhibit 8, which he thought might be useful in refining his process. There was also the question of whether one or more of the ideas generated so far should be carried further.

Overall, there seemed to be four broad choices: (1) continue searching for more ideas, (2) investigate several present ideas further, (3) select one idea and put all efforts into going ahead, and (4) look for employment in someone else's organization.

EXHIBIT 1 International Entrepreneur Association (IEA) Manuals

1.	Dive-For-A-Pearl-Shop	28.	Tool & Equipment Rental Service
2.	Plant Shop	29.	Ghost Dog Making
3.	Balloon Vending	30.	Contest Promotions
4.	Tennis & Racquetball Club	31.	Parking Lot Striping
5.	Athletic Shoe Store	32.	Maintenance Service
6.	Pizzeria	33.	Antique Store
7.	Pet Shop	34.	Pet Hotel & Grooming Service
8.	Handwriting Analysis by Computer	35.	Janitorial Service
9.	Tune-Up Shop	36.	Do-It-Yourself Auto Repair Shop
10.	Flower Vending	37.	Old-Fashioned Ice Cream Bar Stand
11.	Furniture Store	38.	Dry-Cleaning Shop
12.	Window-Washing Service	39.	Copy Shop
13.	Instant Print Shop	40.	Stuffed Toy Animal Vending
14.	Adult Bookstore	41.	Adults-Only Motel
15.	Mail Order	42.	Robot Lawn Mower
16.	Hamburger Stand	43.	Mini-Warehouse
17.	Quit-Smoking Clinic	44.	T-Shirt Shop
18.	Consignment Used Car Lot	45.	Muffler Shop
19.	Cheese & Gourmet Food Shop	46.	Worm-Farming (expose)
20.	Swap Meet Promoting	47.	Psychic-Training Seminars
21.	Art Show Promoting	48.	Trade School
22.	Bicycle Shop	49.	Auto-Parking Service
23.	Rental List Publishing	50.	Rent-A-Plant
24.	Liquor Store	51.	Auto-Painting Shop
25.	Popcorn Vending	52.	Employment Agency
26.	"Who's Who" Publishing	53.	Furniture-Stripping Service
27.	Antique Photo Shop	54.	Carpet-Cleaning Service
		55.	Ten-Minute Oil Change Shop
		56.	Fried Chicken Takeout-Restaurant

EXHIBIT 1 (continued)

57. Mobile Restaurant
58. Bonsai Collecting
59. Day-Care Center
60. Coffee Shop
61. Earring Shop
62. Stained Glass Window Manufacturing
63. Low-Cal Bakery
64. Lie Detection by Voice Analysis
65. Bust-Developing Product
66. Sunglass Shop
67. Custom Rug Making
68. Newsletter Publishing
69. Self-Service Gas Station
70. Flea Market-Finding Products
71. Homemade Candy Stand
72. Seminar Promoting
73. Mattress Shop
74. Hot Dog Stand
75. Hot Tub Manufacturing
76. Car Wash
77. Vinyl-Repairing Service
78. Yogurt Bar
79. Weight Control Clinic
80. Skateboard Park
81. Cookie Shop
82. Computer Store
83. SBA Financing-New Businesses
84. SBA Financing-Existing Businesses
85. Hidden Franchise Laws
86. Roller Skate Rental Shop
87. Free University
88. Roller Skating Rink
89. Burglar Alarm Manufacturing
90. Import & Export
91. Burlwood Tables Manufacturing and Retail Store
92. Homemade Cake Shop
93. Digital Watch Repairing Service
94. Sculptures by Computer
95. Video Cassette Recorder
96. Liquidated Goods Broker
97. Selling Your Business
98. Pinball Arcade
99. Kitchen-Remodeling Service

100. Gift Shop
101. Women's Apparel Shop
102. Used Car Rental Agency
103. Windsurfing School
104. Free Classified Newspaper Publishing
105. Promotional Gimmicks
106. Candid Key Chain Photos
107. Used Bookstore
108. Handicrafts Co-Op
109. Salad Bar Restaurant
110. Sculptured Candle Making
111. Coin-Op TV
112. Plastics-Recycling Center
113. No-Alcohol Bar
114. Health Food Store
115. Donut Shop
116. Shrimp Peddling
117. Soup Kitchen
118. Pipe Shop
119. Roommate-Finding Service
120. Backpacking Shop
121. Hobby Shop
122. Discount Fabric Shop
123. Paint & Wall Covering Store
124. Do-It-Yourself Cosmetic Shop
125. Secretarial Service
126. Furniture Rental Store
127. Pet Cemetery
128. Seasonal Christmas Tree And Ornament Business
129. Tropical Fish Store
130. Gourmet Cookware Shop
131. Flower Shop
132. Do-It-Yourself Framing Shop
133. Insulation Contracting
134. Automobile Detailing
135. Private Post Office
136. Telephone Answering Service
137. Sailboat Leasing
138. Exterior Surface Cleaning
139. Consulting Service
140. Intimate Apparel Shop
141. Flat-Fee Real Estate Agency
142. Travel Agency

EXHIBIT 1 (concluded)

143.	Chimney Sweep Service
144.	Sandwich Shop
145.	Cross-Country Trucking
146.	Specialty Bread Shop
147.	Security Patrol Service
148.	Maid Service
149.	Children's Apparel Shop
150.	Coin Laundry
151.	Shell Shop
152.	Churro Snack Shop
153.	Jojoba Plantation
154.	Video Store
155.	Financial Broker
156.	Vitamin Store
157.	Raising Money
158.	Hottest New Businesses and Future Trends
159.	How to Get Free Publicity & Promote Your Business
160.	Manufacturing & Distributing Products
161.	Legal Ins & Outs of Small Business
162.	How to Intelligently Buy a Business
163.	Getting Into Import & Export

164.	Women Getting Into Business
165.	Businesses You Can Start for Under $1,000
166.	Mail-Order Business
167.	How To Franchise Your Business
168.	Franchise Pros & Cons
169.	Selling Ideas
170.	How to Develop a Successful Plan
171.	Businesses You Can Run and Keep Your Present Job
172.	How to Make Quick Profits in Real Estate
173.	Tax-Saving Angles for Small Businesses
174.	Advertising Techniques for Small Businesses
175.	Recession-Proof Businesses
176.	Preventing Bad Checks, Pilfering & Embezzlement
177.	Four Millionaires Tell How They Did It
178.	Negotiating Techniques
179.	How to Protect Your Ideas
180.	How to Test Market Your Products & Ideas
181.	Millionaire's Secrets to Success

EXHIBIT 2   Thoughts about Preferences

LOOKING FOR
Something that I can be proud of; a product or service that is a contribution; allows for quality input/differential.

A business that I can sell.

Stability - a business that I can sink my feet into without concern that its market/usefulness will quickly vanish.
A business that I am interested in, will make it easy to spend the extra hours to make it fly.

A business that will utilize my talents, staple, no gimmicks.

Challenge - competitive.

Ideally a product rather than a service.

A business that can be flexible in its location, allow for the best of two worlds.

Opportunity for eventual absentee ownership.

Very profitable business, both financially and spiritually. One that will give me and the company the power (freedom) to enact some positive contributions.

Flexible work hours; both in days and hours.

Slow, healthy growth in a growth industry.

Independence.

A business of ideas, innovation in substance, not style.

A business centered around communications, communication skills important.

Success criteria that match my abilities.

A market that I can relate to, get excited about and enjoy dealing with. Not necessarily high labor intensive; will allow for small, sole beginning.

AVOIDING
Franchise; a business that appears to be a commodity.

Faddish business, more a fashion.

High technology/capital requirements.

Being a middleman, a conduit.

Fast buck business.

Fabricated need, product oriented.

Business/industry in tail-end of product life cycle.

High capital requirement.

Art, cultural, design business.

EXHIBIT 3   Products and Services from S.I.C. List and Yellow Pages

Products

Bakery
Cocoa and Chocolate Products
Coffee
Dairy Products
Fruits and Vegetables, Wholesale
Frozen Desserts
Frozen Fruits
Games
General Merchandise Store
Wholesale Groceries
Retail groceries
Hardware; Wholesale and Retail
Ice Cream
Knit Mills
Wood Products Dealer
Musical Instruments
Records and Tapes
Slippers
Sporting Goods; Wholesale & Retail
Book Store
Hobby, Toy and Game Store; Whole-
    sale and Retail
Wooden Goods
Vaults and Safes
Children's Vehicles
Wines; Wholesale and Retail
Cookies and Crackers
Salad Dressings
Stereo, Video Cassette Equipment, Retail
Pies
Bicycle Rentals
Camping Equipment
Carpet and Rug Dealer
Cider
Vending Machines
School Supplies
Dehydrated Foods
Fruits and Vegetables
Nuts
Soda Fountain
Swings
Vending Trucks

Services

Amusement Park
Bridge Teacher
Camps
Chauffeur Service
Circulating Library
Cold Storage Lockers
Day Care
Messenger Service
Food Lockers
Freight Forwarding
Gymnasium
Motel, Hotel, Hostel
Laundry
Linen Supply Delivery Service
Picnic Grounds
Resort
Trucking, Local Cartage
Air Port Terminal Services
Accounting & Bookkeeping Services
News Dealers
Floor Laying
Library and Information Center
Rental Business
Taxicabs
Local - Suburban Transit
    Transportation, Chartered, on Land,
    Rivers, Air, Etc.
Transportation Broker
Food Broker

EXHIBIT 4   Survey of IEA Businesses

FREE CLASSIFIED NEWSPAPER PUBLISHING

+ high return
+ could lead to many more opportunities
      in related fields
+ little know-how necessary
- mechanical
- not very exciting, largely a money
      machine

GIFT SHOP

- retail
- high risk
- out of my league

DONUT SHOP

+ food
- restaurant business, retail headaches

BACKPACKING SHOP

+ product line
+ growth industry in good area of
      country
+ personality of market
- high investment, risk
- barriers to entry
- retail

PIPE SHOP

+ clientele
+ specialty
+ stable
- boring
- retail

GOURMET COOKWARE SHOP

+ specialty shop
- cannot relate to the market
- retail
- risk

TROPICAL FISH STORE

+ product
- small time
- risk

HEALTH FOOD BAR

+ could be an idea whose time has come
- a tavern, or a restaurant; either one
      is unacceptable

SCULPTURED CANDLE MAKING

+ product
+ has low investment, easy startup
- small time
- art and art shows, flea markets

PAINT AND WALL COVERING STORE

+ stable
+ reasonable profit
- not a comfortable industry
- heavy investment

SECRETARIAL SERVICE

+ good employee relations
+ reasonable investment
+ tap marketing skills
+ reasonably stable
+ easy growth/management
- lack of familiarity
- competition, mature market

EXHIBIT 4 (continued)

HOMEMADE CANDY SHOP

+ easy start up
+ quality output
+ business atmosphere (customers)
+ growth and expansion potential
+ stable
- product
- roadside scenario

SEMINAR PROMOTING

+ an idea that has its financial merits
+ down the road it certainly offers a
   source of revenue
- not exactly what I am looking for

STAINED GLASS WINDOWS

although it is a product, it does
not offer anything other than a
short term attraction

CAR WASH

- doesn't grab me
- high risks
- high investment
- out of my ball park

FURNITURE RENTAL STORE

+ stable, over established
+ profitable, easy absenteeism
- doesn't excite me
- high investment
- little outlet for quality, creativity

INSULATION CONTRACTING BUSINESS

+ timing
+ seasonal
- not my style
- this is where the pack is
- heavy investment in money & time to
   get going

FURNITURE STRIPPING

+ appears to involve minimum startup
+ craft
- reasonably stable
- tough to break away from "Mom & Pop"
- small ROI

SCULPTURE BY COMPUTER

- not me

MOBILE RESTAURANT

+ dealing with food
+ relatively low start up
+ opportunity for creative application
+ reasonably simple
- difficult quality input
- questionable future in terms of growth
   and potential

EXHIBIT 4   (concluded)

SUN GLASS SHOP

+ stable market
+ low investment
+ easy absentee
- too narrow
- not exciting enough

DIGITAL WATCH REPAIRING

+ low start up
+ work and location flexibility
+ good growth potential
- an area I do not feel comfortable with
- seems high risk

NEWSLETTER PUBLISHING

- lack of interest/expertise

YOGURT BAR

+ product, different
- market seems saturated
- somewhat faddish

DAY CARE CENTER

+ good future
+ good product-opportunity for contribution
+ good customer base
+ room for quality differential
+ could be fun
+ survives on its own momentum
- dependent on high volume
     high start up costs
- governmental influence
- competition can be fierce, money

KITCHEN REMODELING

- do not have the skills to do the job
- high investment in time and money

EXHIBIT 5 Comparisons

BUSINESS PRODUCTS	Favorable Content	Business Flexibility	Product	People Contact	Independence	Quality Differential	Artistic Contribution	Fun	Stability	Status	Income	Total "+"s	Total Points
Weights	2	3	3	2	3	3	1	2	5	3	3		
Cookies and Crackers	+	+	+	-	+	+	-	+	+	+	+	9	27
Bicycle Rentals	+	-	-	+	-	-	+	+	-	-	-	4	7
Camping Equipment	+	+	+	-	+	+	-	+	+	+	+	9	27
Carpet and Rug Dealer	+	-	-	+	-	+	-	-	+	-	+	5	15
Cider	+	+	+	-	+	+	-	+	+	+	+	9	27
Vending Machines	+	-	-	-	-	-	+	-	+	-	+	4	11
School Supplies	+	-	-	+	-	-	-	+	+	-	-	4	11
Foods (Dehydrated)	+	+	+	-	+	+	+	+	-	+	+	9	23
Fruit and Vegetable Juice	+	+	+	-	+	+	-	+	+	+	+	9	27
Nuts	+	+	-	-	+	-	-	+	+	+	+	7	21
Soda Fountain	+	-	+	+	-	-	-	+	+	+	-	5	14
Swings	+	+	+	-	+	+	+	+	+	+	+	9	27
Vending Trucks	+	-	-	+	-	-	+	+	-	-	-	4	7
Woolen goods	+	+	+	-	+	+	-	+	+	+	+	9	27
SERVICES													
Amusement Park	+	-	-	+	+	+	+	+	-	+	+	8	19
Bridge Instructor	+	-	-	+	+	-	-	+	-	+	-	5	12
Camps	+	+	-	+	+	+	+	+	-	+	+	9	22
Chauffeur Service	-	-	-	+	+	+	-	-	+	-	-	3	10
Circulating Library	+	-	-	+	+	+	+	+	+	+	+	9	24
Cold & Food Storage Lockers	+	-	-	-	+	-	-	-	+	-	+	4	13
Day Care	+	-	+	+	+	+	+	+	+	+	-	8	21
Messenger Service	+	-	+	+	-	+	+	+	+	-	-	6	15
Freight Forwarding	+	-	+	+	-	+	-	+	+	+	+	7	20
Gymnasium	+	-	+	+	-	+	+	+	-	+	-	6	13

EXHIBIT 6   Interview Questions

COMPANY_____INTERVIEWEE_____

1. What does an individual need to get started in your business?
2. What factors are most instrumental in a company's success in your business? (e.g., service, location, contacts, product).
3. How much is product and how much of it is service?
4. Do you feel that a small company is at a distinct disadvantage in your business?
5. How important are economies of scale?
6. What trends do you see developing in your industry? Why?
7. Do you see a market that is currently not being satisfactorily served?
8. Do you see any opportunities in the _____ industry? Why do you think this is?
9. Would you characterize your industry as extremely competitive?
10. What are the competitive pressures?
11. What skills or attributes do you consider most essential in successfully running a _____?
12. How are they different from running, say, a cardboard box plant?
13. How much people-contact do you have? What type?
14. What do you consider to be the biggest problems you are faced with in running your business?
15. How large a market is there for top-of-the-line _____?
16. Are you currently trying to serve it? Why? Why not?
17. What sort of work week does your _____ have (# of days, shifts)?
18. What sort of work week do you have?
19. Could you, if you wanted, have a non-conventional work week?
20. Could you locate anywhere in the greater Seattle metropolitan area without serious consequences?
21. Can you think of anything particular to your industry that would influence a decision to buy a going concern vs. starting from scratch?
22. What background did you bring to your business?
23. What experience do you consider most helpful in running your business?
24. What attracted you to the _____ business?
25. Were your expectations and hopes realistic?
26. If you knew then what you know now, what would you do differently?
27. Would you start up your business today? Why(not)?
28. If you were to start your business from scratch today, what do you think would be the biggest difficulty?
29. If you were to start your business today, how much technical and product know-how would you need?
30. Dealing with such a stable and established product, do you sometimes find this too staid, too conventional?
31. Are there opportunities for creativity?
32. What do you feel are the greatest rewards from your position?
33. What do you find exciting about your work?
34. What do you consider to be the biggest challenges in running a _____?

EXHIBIT 7   Going For It

PROS	CONS
Little to lose, in a position to take a risk, short-term needs are mounting.	Precarious financial situation; short.
The earlier I dedicate the time, the easier it should be.	Lack of experience/exposure.
Personal financial needs are slight.	Am I prepared to handle the setbacks?
It's what I want to do.	Will I choose a business only for the sake of choosing?
It would be exciting.	Want vs. need (is the timing right)?
I owe it to myself/personal tranquillity.	Is the opportunity really there? Am I forcing it?
Pass?	
If not now, when?	Do I need the pressure this search is causing?
Overcome a fear.	
Start up something and sell it in a few years if it's not what I'm looking for.	
I'll be disappointed.	
Quit delaying; sink or swim. •	

EXHIBIT 8   Time Log

CALENDAR	ACTIVITY	TIME EXPENDED
Weeks 1&2	Trying to figure out what I was going to do and how I was going to do it.	?????
Week 3	Visited State Dept. of Commerce (and spoke with Maurice Alexander)	two hours
Week 4	Went to downtown branch of the city library (business section)	four hours
	Read booklets and pamphlets gathered thus far.	six hours
Week 5	Started reading "Business Opportunities" section in Times and P-I classifieds	one hour
Week 6	Started log; started writing down what I'm looking for and avoiding in a business.	three & 1/2 hours
Week 7	Xeroxed S.I.C. index; started circling interesting categories	two hours
	Read "Business Opportunities"	one hour
Week 8	Read Sandman's book " Albert's book " Business Opportunities"	two hours one & 1/2 hours one hour
	Screened S.I.C. index twice	three hours
Week 9	Skimmed *Thomas Register,* *National Directory of Assoc.*	one hour one hour
	Read "Business Opportunities"	one hour
Week 10	Drew up "Capability Assessment Guide" Began screening index to Yellow Pages	two hours five hours
	Read "Business Opportunities"	one hour
Week 11	Continued screening Yellow Pages index	four hours

EXHIBIT 8   (continued)

CALENDAR	ACTIVITY	TIME EXPENDED
	Read "Business Opportunities"	one hour
	Read Alberts book	one hour
Week 12	Read "Business Opportunities"	one hour
Week 13	Read or skimmed twenty IEA manuals	eight hours
	Read Albert's book	one hour
	Read "Business Opportunities"	one hour
Week 14	Read or skimmed twenty IEA manuals	eight hours
	Consolidated the Yellow Page and S.I.C. indices and narrowed the list via the criteria checklist.	six hours
	Read "Business Opportunities"	one hour
Week 15	Devised a questionnaire for interviews	two hours
	Used Manufacturers' Directory and Contacts Influential to locate prospects for interviews	three hours
	Read "Business Opportunities"	one hour
Week 16	Called to arrange interviews	1/2 hour
	Interviews with: Bill Mynar	one & 1/2 hours
	Howard Stanford	one hour
	Eugene Holland	one & 1/4 hours
	Bob Lindsay	two hours
	Used *Contacts Influential* to locate prospects in freight forwarding and delivery service	one hour
	Read "Business Opportunities"	one hour
Week 17	Called to arrange interviews	1/2 hour

EXHIBIT 8 (concluded)

Wrote down pros and cons of "Going For It"	one hour
Interviews with:	
Jim Reynolds	one hour
Henry Gai	one & 1/2 hours
Paul Baertch	one & 1/2 hours
Cecil Neilsen	one & 1/2 hours
Dave McDonald (including sitting in on marketing meeting)	six and 1/2 hours
Read "Business Opportunities"	one hour

Note: The time expenditures listed above are rough estimates. They represent time spent only on listed activity and do not include travel time, waiting time, time spent locating information, etc.

Case 27

Vic O'Brien

In December 1971 Vic O'Brien, an electrical engineer at Colossal Technology Corporation in Seattle, faced a decision of whether to give up on his attempt to set up a hi-fi speaker manufacturing and retail business, or to press on with it, and if so, how. He had opened the store as a part-time activity run by other employees during his working hours. Since opening the store in July, his sales totaled $2,850, contrasted with rent of $1,450 and employee salaries of $4,360.

Vic had not paid himself any salary to date and the savings he had used for start-up were eroding faster than he could replenish them from his job as an engineer. He commented that he wanted the new business to succeed, but if there was no way to do so, he didn't want to "throw good money after bad."

Personal History

Born in Tacoma, Washington, the son of a newspaper circulation manager, Vic O'Brien graduated from high school in 1960 and attended Gonzaga University for two years, majoring in liberal arts. He then married, moved to Seattle and took a job with the phone company to support his family, which soon included a new baby. By working full time for the phone company he was able to qualify for tuition support from the company to attend the University of Washington, where he shifted his major to physics but took as many electives in electrical engineering as possible. By carrying a full course load, he was able to qualify for university housing at low rent.

His interest in electronics developed in high school, where he built an ultrasound modulator as a hobby project. In college he put together a hi-fi system. Components such as tuners and amplifiers he found were cheapest if made from kits. For a speaker he decided to follow do-it-yourself instructions he found in *Popular Electronics* magazine. He bought the basic speaker, which then needed mounting in some sort of box, through the mail from Lafayette Radio. Then he built a cabinet for it in the dirt-floored garage behind his house. Instructions for building the box called for arranging holes and baffles with measurements to be made using other electronic instruments. To buy these and the other electronics parts he needed at wholesale, Vic obtained a state resale tax number and city business license and called himself a business, O'Brien Research Associates. When the speakers were finished, their sound pleased him. He recalled:

The guy who wrote the article really didn't know what he was talking about technically, but the speaker sounded great anyway. What impressed me even more, though, was how much less the unit cost than buying something with comparable performance at a retail store.

As another hobby project, Vic decided to install an intercom in his house. To maximize discounts he could get on parts and also to earn money to pay for them, he decided to set himself up as a business installing intercoms for other people as well. He placed a classified advertisement in the local paper, which brought him his first customer. He met his next customer in the parking lot of an electronics supply store. Vic described what followed.

He turned out to be a builder. So I asked him if he would like some intercoms installed in the house he was building, and he said he would. Out of that I was able to pay for wiring my own house.

Vic's interest in business continued to grow as he started reading books about it. One told about James Ling, an entrepreneur who was becoming spectacularly successful in the '60s after starting as an electrical contractor, particularly impressed Vic. He began thinking how he might be able to emulate Ling.

Following his graduation in physics from the University of Washington in 1964, Vic quit the phone company and went to work as an electronics engineer for the standards laboratory of a large Seattle company, Colossal Manufacturing. His interest in entrepreneurship, however, continued. He found many at Colossal, he said, who felt confined and restricted by their jobs, and consequently formed outside businesses, both as creative outlets and as potential career-escape vehicles.

One of these entrepreneurs was another engineer in the standards laboratory with whom Vic became friends. Vic recalled:

Management drove him into his own business with the kind of stupid policies big companies are so good at coming up with. The standards lab was set up just to serve Colossal divisions, but they all had this beautiful expensive equipment for measurement work. So some outside companies started buying service from the lab, and it started making money on that too, which was fine.

But then a new manager came into the lab. He was the bullslinger type who gets along great with management but is not strong technically. Good technical types often deprecate their work when you ask about it, but if you let them show it to you they get all enthused. Bullslingers, on the other hand, will tell you how great it is but won't have anything to show you. When a bullslinger moves around in the organization, he tends to attract others like him. They all keep looking up at higher management to see how they are doing, instead of down where the action is. It's like a basketball team with its players all watching the clock, and pretty soon they lose the game.

In the standards lab they decided to make more money off outside customers by raising prices. And at the same time they decided to make the other Colossal division managers happy by giving them higher priority in the lab. This meant the other divisions didn't have to plan and schedule their work as carefully. It also meant that the outside customers got poorer service for the higher prices.

My friend saw this as handwriting on the wall and set up his own lab outside to catch customers as they dropped away from Colossal. Then as the workload in Colossal's lab began to decline, management started surplusing some of its test equipment. This meant they were selling off very expensive equipment for as little as 10 cents on the dollar. My friend would buy it, which strengthened his own lab and gave him the capability to take more work away from Colossal, causing it to surplus still more equipment, which he would buy, and so forth. Before long our management was laying people off right and left. I got my termination notice but was picked up by another department.

A Speaker Manufacturing Venture

Vic continued his outside interest in hi-fi speakers, spurred on by concerns about his job at Colossal. He and his brother pooled $500 of savings, bought a table saw, other tools, plywood, speaker cones, wire and other materials and began fabricating speakers in his basement. As with the intercoms, he ran classified advertisements in the local papers, this time offering "engineering prototype speakers for sale, half price." To their disappointment, very few sales resulted.

They did receive a phone call from another man who was selling stereo hi-fi systems door-to-door. He asked the two what they would charge to make speakers for him. They responded with a price of 25 percent above raw materials cost. He immediately placed an order and, because the brothers were short of working capital, also provided them with an inventory of speaker cones he had already bought for another local man to use in building speakers for him. Production began in batches of 12. To carry plywood, Vic bought an old Volkswagon van. Finding the rear doors too narrow to accept 4-by-8-foot sheets, he cut slots at the door edges to widen the entry. Vic commented:

> We were working hard, building speakers, spending money, and buying materials and tools, but for some reason we weren't getting anywhere. We began selling some of the speakers direct ourselves, but when the man we had been building for found out we were doing that, he became very unhappy, especially since we were selling inventory of speaker cones he was providing for us free. It also turned out that when he visited our shop, he had been taking note of just what tools we had and exactly how we were building things. He was setting up his own shop to copy our designs. So to some extent we were both cheating on

each other. I decided that if I was going to be successful in business, I needed to learn more about how it was supposed to work by going back to school.

Business Education

Vic and his brother liquidated their business in 1967 by transforming the remaining raw materials into speakers and selling them. With tuition provided by his continuing Colossal job, Pat enrolled in the University of Washington Graduate School. Vic said:

> They wouldn't admit me to the Business School. I don't know why. So I got in as an unmatriculated graduate student and every quarter with a lot of effort persuaded professors in the business school individually to admit me to their courses on an overload basis. After I had taken a bunch of courses successfully in that way, I went back to the admissions office and showed them I was earning good grades and was headed toward graduation anyway, so they might as well admit me. They did.

At the suggestion of the friend who started his own standards laboratory, Vic also took a night course at the University on small business management. Sponsored by the Small Business Administration, but taught by a series of professors, the course especially influenced Vic's thinking about how a company might be managed more effectively than he believed Colossal was. He recalled how the instructor had divided the class into two competing teams.

> My friend who had the laboratory was made leader of one, and I was leader of the other. We were given some Tinkertoys, and each team was supposed to build as high a tower as it could in a given period of time. One team was hierarchically organized with a leader at

the top directing it, and the other was egalitarian and non-directive, with each person adding to the effort as he saw fit.

My team was the non-directive one, and we built a tower that was vastly higher than the directive team did. Most of us also rated the project as more enjoyable than most of the people on the directive team did, although there were a few people who dissented with the majority in both groups. The instructor told us that it always turns out that way. The non-directive team always builds a higher tower and likes the job but there are a few people on it who don't like the non-directive way of working. I decided that the next time I had a business it would be egalitarian and give maximum freedom to the individuals working in it so we could outperform our competitors the way my team had in building the Tinkertoy tower.

Vic's Work at Colossal

In 1969, Colossal's industry underwent a substantial downturn and Vic's discomfort with his job at Colossal increased. Vic continued:

People were getting laid off all around me. One day in 1969 my boss called me into his office, where his desk was all covered with pink layoff notices for different people. My wife had just had a new baby. I looked at those notices and asked what he wanted to see me about. He told me we should go to his boss's office, which we did. His boss said we should go down to the cafeteria where we could talk. The look on his face didn't make me feel easier. I figured this was it for me. Then they handed me my five-year pin, congratulated me on receiving it, and had a big laugh about how they had scared me. To them it was all a big joke. But it really made me mad.

Vic also felt he and others were often not recognized for their contributions to the company. He described an episode in which another employee had been responsible for developing a piece of electronic equipment. After working several months, the man had been unable to make it work. With a contract deadline near, Vic had taken over the job, and by dint of great effort and many overtime hours had "pulled off a miracle and got the thing working." No congratulations had followed, he said, simply other tough cases of a similar nature as recognition of his exceptional troubleshooting performance. Later he noted that one of his superiors presented a paper on Vic's technical accomplishments. "He did the paper better than I could have," Vic said. "So that may have been best for the corporation. But after all, it was my work. How could I get ahead in this kind of a system?"

Vic enjoyed some parts of his work at Colossal, notably the electronics, but other aspects he did not.

The huge parking lots, commuter traffic, numbered badges and hierarchical atmosphere turn me off. The individual often doesn't matter at all in that kind of a system. One day, just as an experiment, I made a conscious effort to do absolutely no work all day. Normally I really put out a lot, but when I cut it down to zero it produced no effect at all. Nobody even noticed, which I guess is why so many people at Colossal devote their efforts to politics, social activities, and other games instead of getting work done. In a small company, things could never be that way for long.

Opening a Store

By early 1971 Vic had completed his MBA studies and, now freed from coursework but still employed by Colossal, he decided to start another business, this time a hi-fi retail store. This, he thought, should be a more effective way to sell his own speakers than the classified advertisements had been, and by selling at retail he expected he could realize a higher profit margin than he had earlier, when manufacturing for the man who sold door to door. He still had the table saw and other tools from his earlier manufacturing adventure. His wife, who had recently inherited property worth approximately $10,000, agreed to invest half that amount if Vic would sell the dune buggy he had built and invest the proceeds from that as evidence of his "moral commitment."

From one of his university courses in taxation he had concluded that a "Subchapter S" corporation combined the desirable feature of permission to write off for tax purposes any company losses against personal income, as in a proprietorship, with the limited liability advantages of a corporation. To form one, he looked up the state statute, which he found gave good instructions, and phoned the office of the Washington Secretary of State to clarify issues as he ran into them. Since he understood three directors were required, he recruited a friend, not associated with the business in any other way, to join himself and his wife on the board. He made application to the U.S. Patent Office to register the company's name, Sound Array, for trademark protection.

An additional reason for forming a corporation, Vic said, was so he could issue stock in lieu of pay until the company built up cash for that purpose.

Only the government can issue dollars. But stock is another form of currency, and anyone can issue as many shares of that as he wants by simply forming a corporation. In a sense, it's a legal way of printing your own money.

Vic authorized his new corporation to issue up to 50,000 shares at a par value of $1 a share. To himself he issued 2,439 shares for investing that number of dollars in terms of equipment, purchased supplies and cash. An opening balance sheet for the store appears as Exhibit 1. He later had the corporation issue debentures, convertible into 5,000 shares of common stock at her option, to his wife for $5,000 she invested.

To find a location, Vic decided to concentrate on the area near his house, since he wanted it to be convenient in his off-work hours. He looked up census data on personal income and learned that the north end where he lived, although it contained many modest homes such as his own, which had been built as part of a military tract in World War II, on the average had fairly high personal income. There were several small business districts near his home, each having one or two blocks of small stores. He drove through all of them, looking for any empty storefronts. One he noticed had recently been vacated by some sort of photographic enterprise. Inside it had been partitioned into many small rooms for sales, picture taking and developing. The room bordering the sidewalk was 12 by 16 feet with a large display window along the walk.

One thing Vic particularly liked about that location was the rent: $225 per month on a two-year lease. In addition to the price, Vic commented on two other reasons favoring this location:

It's about two miles from a major shopping district serving the University of Washington. I figured that by locating near the University, we could sell to the University market and tap a good labor supply at the same time. Hi-fi is still pretty much a hobby-oriented business and the heavy buyers are young men in the 18-35 year age bracket. If you figure that half the 30,000 students at the University are male, that's a pretty good base to draw from.

Vic signed the lease. Then, after work and on weekends, he and his wife went to work on the empty building, cleaning up, constructing shelves and decorating. They moved shop equipment for making speakers from Vic's basement and set it up in one of the back rooms. To ration his modest capital carefully, Vic ordered a small inventory of medium-priced hi-fi equipment, tuners, amplifiers, turntables and other accessories. These he obtained through the former door-to-door salesman, who was now in the manufacturing business himself, having copied Vic's speaker cabinet designs and shop facilities. The man was doing quite well selling his speakers to dealers in Seattle and also western Canada.

Vic spread the products out on the shelves but found the inventory was insufficient to keep the store from looking bare. He decided to fill the shelves by displaying some stuffed toys his wife had designed and been selling on her own. In addition, he visited thrift shops and stores such as the Goodwill and Salvation Army to obtain antique looking electronic goods to cover blank space and to sell if anyone took an interest in them.

Initial Operations

The store opened for business on July 1, 1971. Prices were set substantially below the competition on all items, the lowest being speakers made by the company, depicted in Exhibit 2, which were sold at approximately half the price of competing lines in other stores. Vic did this to compensate for the limited range and selection available in his store, which was less than half that of competitors, the nearest of which was in the University business district, about two miles away.

Other disadvantages he began to notice were that the only parking available at his store was along the curb in front and at the side of the corner on which the store stood. There was no lot. However, he also noted

that the severity of this problem was not terribly great, since there was relatively little traffic in the area. Many cars passed in the morning and evening when people were traveling to and from work, but during the day there was very little street traffic, and almost none on the sidewalk. There was no large grocery or other store in the area. On the street running north from Vic's store were half a dozen businesses, such as a beauty salon, an antique store, a dry cleaner and small restaurants on each side of the street. Running south were houses on his side and a graveyard across the street. To the east and northwest were simply houses.

To operate the store and make speakers during the day while he was at Colossal, Vic hired his next door neighbor, an engineer recently laid off by Colossal. This man agreed to work for $4 per hour, half in cash and half in stock. This, Vic figured, would not only save money but also enhance employee dedication to company success. Teaching the new salesman to make speaker cabinets and install the speakers in them was easy, Vic said, not so much because the man was an engineer, but simply because the job was very elementary and uncomplicated. He recalled:

We decided to start with one model called the Sound Array 3. It's similar to some name brands we sell, but much cheaper. Our speaker is a three-way system with a $1\,1/2$-cubic-foot box housing a 12-inch woofer and a tweeter which we hook together with appropriate cross-over circuits. What we're essentially doing is making the box and then putting the speakers and wires in. I guess you could call us a wood-processing operation.

An illustration of the company's initial speaker product appears in Exhibit 2.

Vic's View of the Speaker Industry

Vic regarded speakers as part of a growing market that was changing from being hobby oriented to reaching the general consumer. The industry had seen great changes in the past 10 years as transistors and solid-state circuitry made their way into stereo components. He mentioned five speaker manufacturers that were doing well in the Seattle area: KLH, JBL, EPI, DR and Austin. He commented on how speakers were priced and marketed:

> In any given market there are more brands than strong dealers. If a strong dealer pushes your product, then you'll do well. Manufacturers and distributors are willing to haggle over margins and differentials in wholesale and retail price, because there is a lot of margin to work with. They know that if they can get a dealer to push their line, he'll sacrifice margin for extra volume. That's where we have an advantage. We can sell our own products directly to the customer and avoid the mark-ups in between—our price is half that of our competitors, and we still get the same dollar margin from the sale. The only thing we need now is enough volume to put us over break-even.

Another concern Vic expressed about the speaker industry was what he termed "marketing hype." He explained that manufacturers would put out response graphs which indicated how much distortion existed from hearing the music through the speaker as compared with sitting in front of a live band or orchestra. Supposedly, good speakers would show a frequency response graph that was flat for different volumes that a listener might desire. Retailers would then use the graphs that were flattest to push a particular brand, even though a customer might be listening to two similarly priced speakers and prefer the sound of the one which appeared to have worse response.

Vic explained that there were many ways the charts could be rigged and that their apparent flatness was not necessarily a valid measure at all. Much more useful, he said, would be to have a spectrum analyzer, which could be employed both for designing better speakers and for demonstrating their qualities relative to other brands. He noted, however, that the cost of such an instrument was far beyond what he could afford at present.

Speaker parts, on the other hand, were comparatively cheap. Vic said the rule of thumb that speaker manufacturers typically used in designing and pricing their products was that the speakers in a system should be worth one-fifth the price of the system. Thus, a $100 dollar system would have $20 worth of speaker parts in it. The remainder would be spent on the cabinet, advertising, overhead, dealer margin and profit. By selling Sound Array 3 speakers at approximately $120 each, Vic explained, he could install components at two to three times normal costs and still earn a tolerable margin. A bigger cost, he said, was that of the speaker cabinets.

Selling

Store sales were $300 in July, largely thanks to friends of Vic's who came to see the shop. Sales dropped to $150 in August when Vic's neighbor quit to accept another engineering job and recommended a friend to take over the store's operation during the day. Vic hired the individual and soon hired still another man the neighbor recommended. Both were described by Vic as "hippie types," with long hair and old clothes.

The men would work in one of the back rooms building speaker cabinets, then come forward to the showroom when a customer came in. Vic described the scene as less than conventional:

> *When one of these guys sees a customer coming he tends to get excited and run to the door. Then, while he's standing there blocking the doorway before the customer can get in, he does a number about how great the speakers are. Meanwhile, the other employee, who is very shy, usually gets so uncomfortable from this that he goes into the back room to hide.*
>
> *I'll admit our place doesn't look much like a retail store and there's probably some skepticism on the part of customers when they come in. But, we're offering them a pretty good deal in terms of a high-quality speaker at a really low price.*

Vic's own approach was to invite customers to hear how name brand speakers sounded and then let them listen to the Sound Array speaker for comparison. Vic said his strategy was to let people realize that they could get the same quality sound for half the money they would normally spend.

By September, with two men in the shop, sales rose again to $300, and in October, after a third man had walked in the door, asked for a job and been hired, they rose to $1,000. Vic began to take heart that things were picking up and that the unstructured form of management he found so effective on the Tinkertoy class project was going to work for him in business too. Employees were allowed to work on a flexible hour basis as long as someone was around to run the store. The business, he said, was small enough that a worker could determine when a shelf needed to be adjusted, the floors swept or other work around the store required attention.

Vic admitted they hardly looked like conventional salesmen, with long, sawdust-filled hair and tattered clothing, but

he believed them to be intellectually bright, particularly the one he had most recently hired, and his impression was that about one customer out of four who came in the shop bought something, a figure he understood to be comparable to the experience of other hi-fi stores. One customer who came in asked if he could look at what was going on in the shop, and then asked if he could simply buy parts to make a speaker himself. One of Vic's salesman readily obliged. Later, when Vic asked what price the parts had been sold for, he learned that the salesman, not knowing what to charge, had given a figure equal to three times what Sound Array had paid for them. Apparently, the customer happily paid the price and left with the parts.

He noticed, as other customers occasionally came in and bought parts, that not only were they willing to wait, while employees scurried around the shop gathering them up, but also the customers seemed to be reasonably confident that they would be able to put them together. The thought occurred to him that if customers could make buying and assembly decisions well on their own, perhaps he could sell through mail order. He also surmised that there might be problems in selling beyond the Pacific Northwest region if mail order were attempted:

> *People think that you can operate all over the country with mail order and that since Washington is 3 percent of the population, you can sell 97 percent of your product outside the state. But I have my doubts when it comes to speakers. People like to come into the store and listen to the equipment before they decide to buy it.*

In order to go to a mail-order distribution strategy, Vic expected money would have to be spent on advertising and in development of catalogs and instructions.

The most that Vic calculated he could afford in ad space at present would be a single one-inch column in the leading metropolitan newspaper, or presumably a somewhat larger space in a more localized paper, since ad rates scaled up and down with circulation volume. He said he had no idea what preparing a catalog would cost or what other means of advertising might be available to him to help boost sales.

Pressure for Decisions

In November sales turned down again to only $450, and in December, when Vic had hoped they would be buoyed by Christmas buying, the total came only to $550. At this rate there was not enough to pay for the parts, rent and utilities, let alone three men in the shop plus something for Vic, who like them paid himself on the basis of hours worked at $4 an hour, but all in stock, no cash. Vic's savings were low, and he could see that if he were to shut down there would be some time required to accomplish that and to find someone else to take over the remainder of his two-year lease.

It seemed there were many directions the company could take if there were only more time and capital. It might be possible to open other sales channels for the speaker manufacturing operation, as the former door-to-door salesman had done. Or the company might perhaps be able to sell through mail order, if it could work up a suitable catalogue and mailing list. The company had as yet done practically no advertising, as other hi-fi stores were able to do with apparently good results, so there seemed to be potential for improvement there. Undoubtedly there were also other options he had not yet thought of. But he wondered what he could do about any alternatives with only about $2,000 of savings left.

Those savings were taking on a new meaning for him as the large company for which he worked, Colossal, was also sinking into trouble. More and more layoff notices were coming around, and Vic feared that although his technical work at the company was progressing well there might be one of those unwelcome pink slips coming his way any day.

EXHIBIT 1   Opening Balance Sheet of Sound Array, Incorporated

```
Start of Business, July 1, 1971

Cash                            216.83
Accounts Receivable                  0
Inventory                     1,457.00
Prepaid Expenses                324.57
                             _____
        Current Assets                              1,998.40

Leasehold Improvements           76.25
        Less: Depreciation           0
                             _____
        Net                                76.25

Equipment and Fixtures          961.64
        Less Depreciation            0
                             _____
        Net                               961.64

Lease Deposits                  475.00
Organization Expense             64.50
                             _____
                                          539.50

        Fixed Assets                                1,577.39
        Total Assets                                3,575.79

Accounts Payable              1,136.79
Taxes Payable                        0
Accrued Expenses                     0
Unearned Revenue                     0
Notes Payable
        Within One Year              0
                             _____
        Current Liabilities                         1,136.79

        Long Term Notes                                    0

Capital Stock Issued
  and Paid For                                      2,439.00

        Total Liabilities
            and Capital                             3,575.79
```

EXHIBIT 2 Speaker Construction

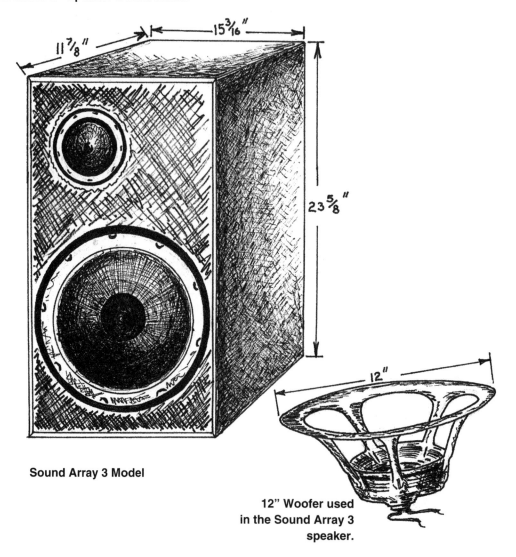

Sound Array 3 Model

12" Woofer used in the Sound Array 3 speaker.

A typical speaker designed by Vic O'Brien and made by Sound Array is shown at left. Wood was cut and assembled to the dimensions shown. Then the speaker components were mounted and wired together within the enclosure.

The tweeter (high pitch sound) is the circle at the top left of the speaker. The woofer (low pitch sound) is at the bottom and also shown below dismounted.

A fabric cover would be mounted in front of the speakers and the wood would be finished, depending on customer preference.

Vic estimated that it took about eight hours of employee time to complete one speaker.

Laurence Osborne

Laurence Osborne was frustrated in February 1981 by his lack of success in attempts to refinance his new enterprise, First Watersign Corporation of Cambridge, Massachusetts. Its product was a small appliance that could, among other things, enhance the potency of a drug which, although illegal, was beginning to show some promise as a medicine and, he believed, might some day be legalized. He noted that the drug, marijuana, was widely used socially, and he thought this fact, coupled with the high cost of law enforcement, which was having only limited success anyway, might eventually lead to legalization under government control, as had happened with alcohol and the elimination of prohibition.

Mr. Osborne's product, called the "Maximizer"™, was a redesigned electric hotpot converted into a double boiler. As the water boiled, steam surrounded an inner container, bringing the contents to exactly 100 degrees centigrade. The water itself served as a timer. The moment that the unit boiled dry a thermostat turned it off to complete a calculated heating cycle. Data from U.S. government research on marijuana showed relationships between the heating cycle and potency in activating the drug, THC (tetrahydrocannabinol). Depending on the sample, narcotic potency could be increased by as much as 50 percent through regulation of this heating process.

Osborne said that although marijuana remained illegal, its acceptance for treatment of cancer chemotherapy patients seemed to be growing in the medical community. He had filed for a patent covering his cooking process, which could be used to regulate potency for either medical or commercial purposes. He commented:

The upshot is that when we get that patent, we'll have virtual control over any form of legal marijuana processing for 17 years. Between now and then, I'm betting that we'll have legal medical marijuana, and we'll be the only ones with the technology. Somebody is going to pay well for this mini-autoclave we made out of kitchen appliance parts. And besides, it's a dandy rice cooker as well.

At present, however, Mr. Osborne was out of cash. Developing the product, including injection molds, jigs, and four-color mail-order advertisements in *High Times* had used up his initial investment capital, which had come mainly from old friends and by borrowing on his life insurance. His first manufacturing run was also partly financed by pre-selling much of it to retailers highlighted in the first advertisements. The first 5,000 Maximizers, whose assembly and shipment he directed and participated in himself, sold as fast as they could be put together.

Following this first run, Osborne located a manufacturer to whom he could subcontract the entire assembly and packing operation. After work had begun on the second run, however, the U.S. Drug Enforcement Administration unveiled a new set of statutes designed to criminalize makers, distributors, and users of "drug paraphernalia." Included in this newly illegal category were small pipes, rolling papers, and virtually anything else that was sold to be used with marijuana. Despite a letter to Osborne from the National Institute on Drug Abuse which affirmed, in response to a query from him, that a double boiler was not such paraphernalia, he saw the marketplace for his product falling apart. Stores known as "head shops" because they sold the newly condemned paraphernalia went out of business throughout the country, eliminating Maximizer sales through that channel. With sales of *High Times* magazine, in which his advertisements ran, also under adverse pressure, the mail order component of his sales dropped by 75 percent in three months. His firm barely survived the summer of 1980. He could foresee that without Christmas advertisements, sales would continue to drop, leaving him with an apartment full of unsalable cookers.

In order to pay his creditors, refinance the company, and move his operation forward, Mr. Osborne prepared a written business plan as a prospectus for recruiting more capital. Excerpts from this document appear in Exhibit 1 of this case. As he began using it in search of backing, he encountered repeated rejections and soon became concerned that his creditors might seize the inventory on hand, or even attach his company's bank account.

Laurence Osborne

Starting businesses was something Larry Osborne had done from an early age. As a young boy, tired of his lemonade stand, he located a clam bed during summer camp and "cornered the market." He traded clams as fish bait for comic books and traded comics for candy bars. Later, as a Harvard freshman in 1962, he led a rock band and promoted it vigorously. Taking it to Los Angeles the summer of 1963, he returned with a surfboard and started a chain of surf shops called "Surf City" on Cape Cod, as well as in New Hampshire and Maine. He plowed all his

earnings back into this seasonal business, which he finally sold in 1968.

Following graduation from Harvard in 1966, Larry taught writing at the University of North Carolina. His attempt to join the Army ended when he told recruiters that his skills would be useful in the Saigon black market. Classified 4-F, he entered the Harvard Business School instead in 1967, graduating in 1969. During the summer between his first and second years of MBA study, he was funded by a Kansas City industrialist to design a media workshop for young African Americans. Then in the second year of MBA studies, he completed two final projects: a truck rental plan for Ryder systems and a study of marijuana as a free-trade phenomenon within a regulated economy.

After he received his MBA, *Time* magazine asked Osborne to contribute to one of the first school-oriented drug abuse efforts. Deciding he could do it better himself, he gathered a group of experts who specialized in the field, and soon, he recalled, became a minor celebrity when William F. Buckley. Jr. publicly praised his small educational publishing firm, The Creative Learning Group. It was during this time that Osborne developed the professional friendships with those in the field of drug research that led ultimately to the marijuana process on which he later applied for a patent.

His publishing firm began growing. Within two years it was selling drug education curricula to schools nationwide, as well as to the U.S. Army, the U.S. Navy and the Smithsonian Institution. In 1973, however, President Nixon eliminated federal funding for school drug education, forcing The Creative Learning Group into receivership.

From what he had learned about marijuana from reports of U.S. federal experimentation with it, he undertook in 1973 to obtain a patent on the process for creating from it the narcotic, tetrahydrocanabinol.

He recruited a chemist to help him, with the understanding that the two would share ownership in the patent. They were also going to share in the costs of applying for the patent but, to Osborne's disappointment, the chemist neglected to do so.

When The Creative Learning Group terminated, Osborne undertook to continue in the publishing business by dropping drug education and instead following a new direction. He used his limited remaining resources to develop the first Russian language computer typesetting system. His aim was to reproduce current Russian articles for use in Russian language classes. These were needed, he explained, because the only other Russian language writings widely available in the U.S. were very old classical works of less current interest. The lack of current works was apparently due to the high cost of setting Cyrillic type, over $100 per page, which pushed up printing costs to levels schools could not afford. He found that with a computer he could do it much cheaper, recalling: "Even *Pravda* could not do it as cheaply as we could."

Just as he began to enter the market with this innovation, however, the U.S. Congress passed the "Jackson Amendment" that denied favorable trade status to the U.S.S.R. because of its emigration policies. BORIS (Binary Operated Russian Interface System) was liquidated after only six months. With the office space and publishing facilities he had available, he struck up an alliance in 1974 with two men who had just left their jobs with a magazine to form one of their own, *New Age*. Eventually, their magazine grew beyond the space Osborne had available, and they moved out.

Meanwhile, after learning through personal friends that Harvard University had a trove of antique glassware that it wanted to sell, Osborne formed a company called University Antiquaries to purchase, clean, catalog and pack nearly 20,000 of natural-

ist Louis Agassiz's original hand-blown specimen jars. These he sold at a gallery in Boston and through mail order advertisements.

In 1976, Osborne received news from the U.S. Patent Office that the patent he had applied for had been granted. Having earlier been disappointed that his chemist partner had not paid the share of filing expenses that Osborne thought he should, Osborne now contacted the man and again asked him to pay up. Osborne recalled:

> *I told him that if he wasn't going to pay up, I was not going to pay the required $100 issuing fee and our application would lapse. He said, "fine, let it lapse." So I didn't pay the fee, and a month or so later, it lapsed.*
>
> *My hope was that he would not apply for the issuance himself. He could have, but didn't. I also didn't, because I wanted to wait until marijuana was closer to legalization before I started the expiration clock that would begin ticking when the patent was issued with its 17-year life span.*

By 1977, the jar venture inventory was exhausted. Osborne, also exhausted, took a break by attending Harvard Divinity School. In the spring, financial pressures led him to perform freelance air courier deliveries. Tiring of that, he dropped by the Harvard Business School and read on the bulletin board about a harpsichord company that wanted consulting help. He recalled:

> *The founder had died and his widow was concerned that the company was losing money. It turned out they were trying to operate with only a 15-percent markup. I fixed that, developed a mailing list and started a newsletter for them to help promote their products. That turned it around and I found myself with some success in the manage-*

ment consulting business. That fall I joined another consulting firm, Management Directions, where I worked on jobs like developing product sales manuals and multimedia for sales meetings in companies like BMW, Volkswagen and American Optical.

The Cooker Design

One day the attorney who had helped Osborne with his marijuana process patent called to say that *Playboy* had talked to him about an article they were developing on the question of who would get rich if marijuana were legalized. He suggested Osborne give the reporter a call, which he did. During the conversation, the reporter asked Osborne why he did not make a machine to carry out the optimal cooking cycle Osborne had developed. When Osborne replied that it would take expertise, the reporter said, "Well, you're a consultant. Why don't you hire one?"

Taking up the challenge, Osborne began calling cooking appliance companies and asking them where he could find a good consultant on how to design one. Following up the names he was given, he called one consultant in Connecticut, who said he would give the job some thought. Osborne described what happened next.

One week later, the consultant called and said, "I think we have your problem solved. The fee will be $1,200. Do we have an agreement?" I asked if the cooker could be designed to sell for around $29.95. When he said he thought so, I said then we had a deal, and asked what the secret was.

Then he proceeded to tell me that he would control the temperature with a fluid that vaporized at exactly 100 degrees centigrade. The time would be controlled by having a circuit close when just the right amount of this fluid boiled away.

I asked what sort of fancy fluid we would have to get for that mechanism. He said, "Now just think a minute. What readily available fluid vaporizes at exactly one hundred degrees centigrade?"

I said, "My gosh! You just charged me $1,200 for telling me about a double boiler!"

In the spring of 1979, the cooker project moved ahead. Using a quickly-written prospectus offering 20-percent interest-bearing bonds, Osborne was able to raise enough money to pay for the designer, the model makers, the injection molds, and advertising layouts to roll out the product in November.

He also decided to try reactivating the process patent he had applied for earlier, since now he would be using that process in his new cooking appliance.

Initial Operations

Since he expected the Maximizer would be used by those wishing to improve marijuana potency, Osborne decided to place his first advertisements for it in the *New England Journal of Medicine*, directed to the attention of medical researchers. Other small advertisements, which he placed in *New Age* magazine, described the Maximizer as a small steam cooker without reference to any other use. If his product were going to end up in *High Times*, Osborne reasoned, let it first be marketed as a "medical instrument or a simple appliance." A researcher at the Mayo Clinic ordered one, as did a number of *New Age* readers who said they used it as a versatile steam cooker and praised its efficiency.

By August 1979 Osborne had raised only $30,000. Although he regarded this as "a drastic under-capitalization," he went forward with a production run of 5,000 units to coincide with a November double-page advertisement he had scheduled with *High Times*. The ad offered to mention the names of any shops buying more than two dozen Maximizers. This brought in enough orders to yield what Larry characterized as his "last increment of investment" from his own customers, the shops. By the day the first order was shipped the venture's bank account had been reduced to less than $250. But the product sold readily, and within six weeks the entire run had been shipped.

With the cash that was coming in from these first sales, Osborne started his second production run. He also worked on a prospectus for raising more capital, which he believed was desperately needed. He calculated that he had enough either to keep advertising or to finish the second run, but not both.

A Process Patent

Osborne regarded his Maximizer product as the financial engine that was keeping First Watersign Corporation afloat. He expected, however, that the process patent embodied in the Maximizer, rather than the product itself, would be by far the most valuable asset of his corporation. So far, he had learned that no patent identical to the one he was applying for had been issued in the interval since the earlier application had lapsed. So he thought the chances of getting it again were good.

With the help of his patent attorney, he had identified three areas that he believed could be protected:

1. The method of treating the plant material to maximize and/or stabilize the THC content.

2. The device which provided the environment to effect the process.

3. The means of storing the processed plant material.

If the first two claims were granted, Osborne expected that his company would control not only the device, but the process itself, in the same manner that DuPont had

benefited by its patent on the process for making nylon. A process patent, he said, could be more lucrative than a product patent because it generally reserved to the owner the sole rights to both the process and the product as well.

The Search for More Capital

The result of his quest for capital Osborne summarized as follows:

My search for funding for the MAXIMIZER was a long story that I can make short. Nobody wanted to touch it.

Possible investors Osborne had approached during his initial fundraising included several venture capital firms that specialized in startups. He recalled:

They loved the prospectus. Some said it was the best written business plan they'd ever seen. But they felt the area was taboo. The fact was that the burgeoning paraphernalia industry was generating considerable profits, but few people had any solid numbers and the major players were, to say the least, considered marginal operators and novelty distributors.

It seemed to Osborne that the first production run had demonstrated that manufacturing costs could be contained and that the market was nearly unlimited. Hence, he reasoned, it should be easier to attract investors for the second run. In fact, however, it seemed harder to raise money for the second run than it had for the first one nearly a year earlier. He observed:

Here I am with a 400 percent R.O.I. after the first run and still nobody is putting in the money we need. I stopped pursuing institutional investors a long time ago, and now it's just rich eccen-

trics. Recently, I almost got $15,000 from a family friend, but then, just as he was about to sign the check, his son was committed to a drug abuse clinic.

So here I am, in debt, with 750 Maximizers from the second run ready to sell and not even $45 to pay for a mailing, which would sell at least $1,500 worth. I need to pay my parts suppliers or they'll never go along with a third run. I have to pay for the Christmas ads, and I'd love to send something to my investors as well. I'm pretty cer-

tain we'll get that patent, and I'm not sure that those paraphernalia laws are constitutional in the long run.

The bottom line is that I would be making more money doing just about anything if I dropped this venture. But if I hold on, I might end up with the entire technology for medical, or even legal, marijuana.

Sometimes I think this is pioneering; sometimes I think that someone must have put some pot in my corn flakes to get me to even try the idea. You tell me. What would you do? Hang in there, or just let it go?

EXHIBIT 1   First Watersign Corporation Prospectus

(This document has been abridged to reduce case length)

EXHIBIT 1 (continued)

IN BRIEF

Purpose

The First Watersign Corporation, a small privately held research and manufacturing firm in Cambridge, Massachusetts, is raising $200,000 for expansion of their business operations. A first year test-marketing through limited channels sold nearly 9,000 of the company's unique and proprietary product. The enthusiastic response of customers, wholesalers, and retailers has demonstrated both feasibility and profitability of the product, and indicates a likelihood of rapid growth once the total market is aware that the product simply exists. For the purpose of raising expansion capital, 25 percent of the common stock of the company is being offered. The offering price is $53.35 per share, and purchasers will receive with each share a warrant good for purchase of one further share at the same price during a two-year period.

Product

The company's product, the MAXIMIZER^{tm}, is a unique time-cycle multi-purpose appliance. Although it is marketed chiefly as an all around cooker, it incorporates proprietary techniques which allow it to increase the potency of marijuana by as much as 200 percent through the non-destructive decarboxylation of precursor plant cannabinoids. Units have been supplied to every research project in the country where legal marijuana is used by medical volunteers participating in the national testing of THC and smoked marijuana as a therapeutic medicine. The sale of the appliance through food channels has already prompted a special letter from the National Institute on Drug Abuse affirming the legality of the MAXIMIZER^{tm} for production and sale to all markets.

Return

The entire offering will be returned in profits the first year if 0.1 percent of the estimated market responds. Should marijuana become legal for medical or recreational use, the company will probably control the processing patents and all machinery for the potency control/increase used in the entire industry.

Taking into account all production and marketing costs, the total potential profitability, before taxes, is nearly $34,000,000. At a ratio of one unit sold at wholesale ($4.00 net at $16.00) to one unit sold through mail order ($16.00 net at $29.95) the figures add up as follows:

$$1,700,000 \text{ units wholesale } \times \$4.00 = \$6,800,000$$
$$1,700,000 \text{ units retail } \times \$16.00 = \underline{27,200,000}$$
$$\$34,000,000$$

The $29.95 price came from a standard marketing formulation which suggests a price of "five times cost of goods" as a retail price which will permit enough flexibility for wholesaling and marketing. Since the manufacturing cost at normal levels reduces at $6.00 from the current $8.00, the $29.95 price was not only still within "impulse purchase" range, but conformed to standard pricing formulas.

EXHIBIT 1   (continued)

It was also noted that the original "Isomerizer," which sold at $129.00, did not lose sales volume when the "KIK" appeared at $69.00. In fact, both items were able to sell at the same volumes (approximately 8,000 units per year) simultaneously. It appeared that as the price dropped, this market grew proportionately. It was felt that the $29.95 price would absolutely insure a market test of nearly 10,000 units in that particular market. Despite the unexpected effects of the paraphernalia ordinances, which drove the two other manufacturers out of business, the company was able to enter this market, and sell nearly 8,000 units during the first year.

The MAXIMIZER^{tm} was designed to be manufactured from parts which are readily available and which are, for the most part, either stocked or easily manufactured by a number of domestic suppliers.

A primary consideration was that the manufacturing process not be defined by the test market, and that the early seed capital not be expended for permanent dies or molds. Accordingly, the major part of the product is assembled from an already available appliance which is taken from its manufacturing process at an intermediate stage and sold to the company in lots of 5,000. The only part of the product which is produced in company molds is the polypropylene top.

Since entering the market at the 1979 Christmas season was considered important, design and early manufacturing were done almost simultaneously. When the company contracted for final assembly suddenly was unable to handle the job, untrained workers were used to produce the first 4,200 units. Although unit cost was high, due to multiple revisions of design, parts, and manufacturing operations, it was indicative of the simplicity of the product that the job was completed in less than six weeks.

Enthusiastic acceptance of the product in the marketplace resulted in stock-out by the first week in February. Due to long lead times on some components, assembly of the second run was not started until the last week in April 1980. At this time, the company had located an appliance firm with private-label manufacturing as a specialty. Current manufacturing procedure is to ship all parts to this company, which then prepares the sub-assemblies, assembles and tests the product, and packs it in 12-pack cases.

Since there is no part of the appliance which cannot be made or obtained in large volume, and the assembly firm is geared towards much larger runs for other customers, production could be increased to well over 200,000 units per year without the necessity of seeking any other suppliers or assemblers. The new assembly procedure has provided an almost defect-free run while cutting the labor cost in half.(Exhibit 19).

Personnel

Since the founding of the company, it has been solely managed by Laurence O. Osborne. Osborne, who previously managed a small-business consulting firm, has a long history of managing start-up situations. Familiarity with the drug field came through his management of a major drug-abuse publishing company in the early seventies, a position which also provided extensive training in the area of printing, publishing and communications. Management of a direct-mail marketing firm (1974-77) provided experience in that area. His biographical information sheets are included as Exhibit 20.

Throughout the first year, Osborne has been aided by a number of professionals func-

EXHIBIT 1 (continued)

tioning either as consultants, part-time employees, or suppliers. Judith Preston, who holds an MBA form Boston University, is active as the corporate treasurer and comptroller. Office management and shipping functions have been assumed by several individuals as the office became more systematic, and manufacturing is handled entirely by the Appliance Development Company of Boston.

One of the major reasons for the placement is to obtain the funds necessary to provide trained management to help manage the expansion of the corporation into its new and growing markets.

Financing

At this time, 30 percent of the stock in the company is held by Laurence Osborne, 10 percent by Donald A. Jenkins, Esquire, the patent attorney, and approximately 5 percent by outside stockholders and holders of convertible debentures. The remainder is authorized, but unissued, treasury stock.

The original bondholders invested in the project at the ratio of $100,000/15 percent of the corporation. The value of the corporation was arrived at by a formula of five times estimated profits at 20,000 units-per-year sales. So as not to dilute initial investors, the original ratio has been maintained for the purposes of the offering. To further facilitate the placement, investors are offered warrants which may be exercised at any time during the next two years and which allow purchase of an equal number of shares at the same price.

The offering represents an enlargement of the original offering, which was for convertible debentures, rather than for common stock. As $35,000 was raised during that offering, the current offering will raise approximately $165,000, returning $125,000 to the corporation after payment of commissions. Since the corporation currently has 12,500 shares of common stock authorized, the price per share is $53.35. The objective is to sell 25 percent of the common stock. When this is accomplished, Osborne will still own 30 percent, Jenkins 10 percent, outside shareholders will own 30 percent and will be able through the use of their warrants to increase their holdings to 60 percent of the corporation during the next two years, if company performance indicates a highly profitable investment.

Investors should regard the company as a speculative investment which provides its payouts either in the form of regular dividends or in the appreciation of the value of the stock in the case of a possible buy-out by a larger firm in the appliance or biomedical field. At sales levels of more than 30,000 units annually, the one product alone would return in its profits more than the total amount of this offering. Should growth proceed as expected, the company could be sold for several million dollars within its first three years of operations.

EXHIBIT 1   (continued)

MAXIMIZER MANUFACTURING COST BREAKDOWN

PART	COST
Drawn aluminum body	1.30
Tubular heater	.55
Phenolic base	.48
Top, with valve	.50
Inner container (screen bottom)	.58
Inner container (solid bottom)	.38
Screen	.04
Cord set with strain relief	.28
Thermostat	.65
Pilot light	.13
Label for bottom	.05
Box	.24
Boxwrap	.04
Label for box	.05
Two instruction booklets	.08
Guarantee-Registration card	.05
Plastic lens	.05
Order entry form	.05
Shipping, all parts	.20
PARTS TOTAL	$5.70
Slot base	.10
Finish on body	.25
Coating on body	.10
Logo on body	.05
All assembly and packing	1.75
TOTAL MANUFACTURING COST	$7.95

EXHIBIT 1 (continued)

Figure 16 FIRST WATERSIGN CORPORATION CASH FLOW PROJECTION FOR THE 12 MONTHS ENDING JULY 31, 1981

	AUG	SEP	OCT	NOV	DEC	JAN	FEB	MAR	APR	MAY	JUN	JUL	TOTAL
Cash Balance	2,500	2,167	7,317	3,692	16,527	26,452	23,422	16,924	3,439	2,864	15,674	16,883	3,200
Cash Receipts													
Wholesale	4,960	6,160	8,400	11,600	10,800	6,800	6,000	7,600	8,800	9,200	10,000	10,800	101,120
Mail Order	3,744	9,360	15,600	18,720	20,280	6,240	7,800	6,240	6,240	7,800	8,580	9,360	119,964
College Reps	—	5,000	7,000	12,000	9,000	4,000	2,000	4,000	7,000	10,000	4,000	2,000	66,000
Magazine Features	—	—	—	9,360	15,600	6,240	3,120	1,560	780	780	312	—	37,752
Direct Mail	—	—	3,120	7,800	6,240	2,340	1,560	1,560	780	780	312	312	24,804
TOTAL SALES	8,704	20,520	34,120	59,480	61,920	25,620	20,480	20,960	23,600	28,560	23,204	22,472	349,640
Cash Available	11,204	22,687	41,437	63,172	78,447	52,072	43,844	37,884	27,039	31,424	38,878	39,355	352,840
Cash Disbursements													
Manufacturing	1,747	10,020	23,845	20,695	23,845	10,675	10,020	21,045	10,675	—	—	—	132,567
Shipping	440	1,000	1,550	2,600	2,300	1,025	1,050	1,050	1,150	1,400	1,145	1,110	15,820
Marketing	1,500	6,000	7,000	15,000	10,000	4,000	7,500	4,000	4,000	4,000	7,500	7,500	78,000
Salaries	3,350	3,350	3,350	3,350	3,350	3,350	3,350	3,350	3,350	3,350	3,350	3,350	40,200
Office	2,000	2,000	2,000	2,000	2,000	2,000	2,000	2,000	2,000	2,000	2,000	2,000	24,000
TOTAL DISBURSEMENT	9,037	22,370	37,745	43,645	41,495	21,050	23,920	31,445	21,175	10,750	13,995	13,960	290,587
Minimum Cash Desired	3,000	3,000	3,000	3,000	3,000	3,000	3,000	3,000	3,000	3,000	3,000	3,000	3,000
Total Cash Needed	12,037	25,370	40,745	46,645	44,495	24,050	26,920	34,445	24,175	13,750	16,995	16,960	293,587
Excess (or deficiency)	(833)	(2,683)	692	16,527	33,952	28,022	16,924	3,349	2,864	20,674	21,883	25,395	59,253
Financing													
Borrowing	—	10,000	—	—	—	—	—	—	—	—	—	—	+10,000
Repayment	—	—	—	—	2,500	—	—	—	—	5,000	—	2,500	15,000
Interest (@ 20%)	—	—	—	—	—	4,600	—	—	—	—	—	4,600	9,200
Total Effects of Financing	—	—	—	—	—	—	—	—	—	—	—	—	—
Cash Balance, ending	2,167	7,317	3,692	16,527	26,452	23,422	16,924	3,439	2,864	15,674	16,883	18,295	45,053

EXHIBIT 1 (continued)

Figure 16 (continued) CASH FLOW PROJECTION (60% OF ORIGINAL ESTIMATES) FOR THE 12 MONTHS ENDING JULY 31, 1981

	AUG	SEP	OCT	NOV	DEC	JAN	FEB	MAR	APR	MAY	JUN	JUL	TOTAL
Cash Balance, Beginning	2,500	2,167	5,133	7,897	16,200	35,942	31,629	23,747	8,088	533	6,719	9,344	1,700
Cash Receipts													
Wholesale	4,960	4,321	5,760	8,160	4,800	3,360	3,840	5,280	5,280	5,760	6,240	6,720	64,480
Mail Order	3,744	5,616	9,360	11,232	12,168	3,744	4,680	3,744	3,744	4,680	5,148	5,616	73,476
College Reps	—	3,000	4,200	7,200	5,400	2,400	1,200	2,400	4,200	6,000	2,400	1,200	39,600
Magazine Features	—	—	—	5,616	9,360	3,744	1,872	936	468	468	187	—	22,651
Direct Mail	—	—	1,872	4,680	3,744	1,404	936	936	468	468	187	187	14,882
Total Sales	8,704	12,937	21,192	36,888	35,472	14,652	12,528	13,296	14,160	17,376	14,162	15,423	215,099
Cash Disbursements													
Manufacturing	1,747	10,020	23,845	10,675	—	—	10,020	18,475	10,675	—	—	—	85,457
Shipping	440	600	233	1,560	1,380	615	540	630	690	840	687	666	8,881
Marketing	1,500	4,000	6,000	8,000	6,000	3,000	1,500	1,500	2,000	2,000	2,500	2,500	40,500
Salaries	3,350	3,350	3,350	3,350	3,350	3,350	3,350	3,350	3,350	3,350	3,350	3,350	40,200
Office	2,000	2,000	2,000	2,000	2,000	2,000	2,000	2,000	2,000	2,000	2,000	2,000	24,000
Total Disbursements	9,037	19,970	35,428	25,585	12,730	8,965	17,410	25,955	18,715	8,190	8,537	8,516	199,038
Minimum Cash Desired	3,000	3,000	3,000	3,000	3,000	3,000	3,000	3,000	3,000	3,000	3,000	3,000	3,000
Total Cash Needed	12,037	22,970	38,428	28,585	15,730	11,965	20,410	28,955	21,715	11,190	11,537	11,516	202,038
Excess (or deficiency)	(833)	(4,867)	(12,103)	16,200	35,942	38,629	34,747	8,088	533	6,719	9,344	13,251	14,751
Financing													
Borrowing	—	10,000	20,000	—	—	—	—	—	—	—	—	—	+30,000
Repayment	—	—	—	—	—	—	—	—	—	—	—	—	—
Interest (20%/annum)	—	—	—	—	—	7,000	—	—	—	—	—	7,000	14,000
Total Effects of Financing	—	—	—	—	—	—	—	—	—	—	—	—	—
Cash Balance, Ending	2,167	5,133	7,897	16,200	35,942	31,629	23,747	8,088	533	6,719	9,344	13,251	14,751

EXHIBIT 1 (continued)

Figure 17 FIRST WATERSIGN CORPORATION UNIT SALES AND INCOME PROJECTION FOR THE 12 MONTHS ENDING JULY 31, 1981

	AUG	SEP	OCT	NOV	DEC	JAN	FEB	MAR	APR	MAY	JUN	JUL	TOTAL
Retail Outlets	125	140	160	180	200	205	210	230	240	250	270	280	280
Inventory of Units	2,203	1,763	763	213	113	313	1,788	2,388	1,338	188	1,288	2,143	2,203
Units Produced	—	—	1,000	2,500	2,500	2,500	1,500	—	—	2,500	2,000	500	15,000
Unit Sales													
Wholesale	320	450	600	850	500	350	400	550	550	600	650	700	6,520
Mail Order	120	300	500	600	650	200	250	200	200	250	275	300	3,845
College Reps	—	250	350	600	450	200	100	200	350	500	200	100	3,300
Magazine Features	—	—	—	300	500	200	100	50	25	25	10	—	1,210
Direct Mail	—	—	100	250	200	75	50	50	25	25	10	10	795
TOTAL UNITS SOLD	440	1,000	1,550	2,600	2,300	1,025	900	1,050	1,150	1,400	1,145	1,110	15,670
End Inventory/Units	1,763	763	213	113	313	1,788	2,388	1,338	188	1,288	2,143	1,533	1,533
Gross Income/Sales	8,864	21,560	35,320	61,480	59,120	24,420	20,880	22,160	23,600	28,960	23,604	22,872	352,840
Less Manufacturing	3,520	8,000	12,400	20,800	18,400	8,200	7,200	8,400	9,200	11,200	9,160	8,880	125,360
Shipping	440	1,000	1,550	2,600	2,300	1,025	1,050	1,050	1,150	1,400	1,145	1,110	15,820
GROSS PROFIT	4,904	12,560	21,370	38,080	38,420	15,195	12,630	12,710	13,250	16,360	13,299	12,882	211,660
Less Marketing	1,500	6,000	7,000	15,000	10,000	4,000	7,400	4,000	4,000	4,000	7,500	7,500	78,000
Salaries	3,350	3,350	3,350	3,350	3,350	3,350	3,350	3,350	3,350	3,350	3,350	3,350	40,200
Office	2,000	2,000	2,000	2,000	2,000	2,000	2,000	2,000	2,000	2,000	2,000	2,000	24,000
Interest	1,850	1,850	2,050	2,050	2,050	2,050	2,050	2,050	2,050	2,050	2,050	2,050	24,200
Depreciation	180	180	180	180	180	180	180	180	180	180	180	180	180
Net Profit	(3,976)	(820)	6,790	15,500	20,840	3,615	(2,450)	1,130	1,670	4,780	(1,781)	(2,198)	45,080

EXHIBIT 1 (continued)

Figure 17 (continued)

UNIT SALES AND INCOME PROJECTION (60% OF ORIGINAL ESTIMATES) FOR THE 12 MONTHS ENDING JULY 31,1981

	AUG	SEP	OCT	NOV	DEC	JAN	FEB	MAR	APR	MAY	JUN	JUL	TOTAL
Retail Units	125	135	140	145	150	150	150	150	150	150	150	150	150
Beginning Inventory/Units	2,203	1,763	1,163	233	173	1,293	1,678	1,138	508	1,318	2,978	3,291	2,203
Units Produced	—	—	—	1,500	2,500	1,000	—	—	1,500	2,500	1,000	—	10,000
Unit Sales													
Wholesale	320	270	360	510	300	210	240	330	330	360	390	420	3,912
Mail Order	120	180	300	360	390	120	150	120	120	150	165	180	2,307
College Reps	—	150	210	360	270	120	60	120	210	300	120	60	1,980
Magazine Features	—	—	—	180	300	120	60	30	15	15	6	—	726
Total Units Sold	440	600	930	1,560	1,380	615	540	630	690	840	687	666	9,402
Ending Inventory of Units	1,763	1,163	233	173	1,293	1,678	1,138	508	1,318	2,978	3,291	2,625	2,801
Gross Income/Sales	8,864	12,936	21,192	36,888	35,472	14,652	12,528	13,296	14,160	17,376	14,162	15,423	216,789
Less Manufacturing	3,520	4,800	7,440	12,480	11,040	4,920	4,320	5,040	5,520	6,720	5,496	5,328	75,216
Shipping	440	600	233	1,560	1,380	615	540	630	690	840	687	666	8,881
Gross Profit	4,904	7,536	13,519	22,848	23,052	9,117	7,668	7,626	7,950	9,816	7,979	9,429	132,692
Less Marketing	1,500	4,000	6,000	8,000	6,000	3,000	1,500	1,500	2,000	2,000	2,500	2,500	40,500
Salaries	3,350	3,350	3,350	3,350	3,350	3,350	3,350	3,350	3,350	3,350	3,350	3,350	40,200
Office	2,000	2,000	2,000	2,000	2,000	2,000	2,000	2,000	2,000	2,000	2,000	2,000	24,000
Interest	600	800	1,100	1,100	1,100	1,100	1,100	1,100	1,100	1,100	1,100	1,100	12,400
Depreciation	180	180	180	180	180	180	180	180	180	180	180	180	2,160
Net Profit (loss)	(2,726)	(2,794)	889	8,218	10,422	(513)	(462)	(504)	(680)	1,186	(1,151)	299	13,432

EXHIBIT 1   (continued)

Figure 18a   BALANCE SHEET AS OF JULY 31, 1980 (Financial statements prepared by CPA without audit)

<u>ASSETS</u>

<u>Current Assets</u>

Cash	2,502.00	
Accounts Receivable 5,538.00		
Prepaid Advertising 1,188.00		
Inventory <u>24,244.00</u>		
Total Current Assets		$33,472.00

<u>Fixed Assets</u>

Proprietary Molds	$5,200.00
Mold Inserts and Mandrils	1,155.00
Factory Tools and Machinery	1,162.00
Office Equipment	<u>4,850.00</u>
Total Fixed Assets	$12,367.00
Less: Accumulated Depreciation	<u>1,582.00</u>
Net Fixed Assets	<u>10,785.00</u>

TOTAL ASSETS   <u>$44,257.00</u>

<u>LIABILITIES AND STOCKHOLDER'S EQUITY</u>

<u>Current Liabilities</u>

Accounts payable	$5,748.00
Accrued expenses	478.00
Accrued Interest (Note 2)	<u>5,175.00</u>
Total Current Liabilities	$11,401.00

<u>Long-Term Liabilities</u>

Bonds Payable (Note 2)$36,000.00		
Loan Payable - L. Osborne (Note 3)	3,337.00	
Loan Payable - B. Osborne	<u>5,000.00</u>	
Total Long-Term Liabilities		<u>44,337.00</u>
Total Liabilities		$55,738.00

<u>Stockholder's Equity</u>

Common Stock	0.00	
Retained Earnings (Deficit)	<u>$11,481.00</u>	
Total Stockholder's Equity		<u>(11,481.00)</u>

TOTAL LIABILITIES & STOCKHOLDER'S EQUITY   <u>$44,257.00</u>

"See Accountant's Compilation Report"

EXHIBIT 1 (continued)

Figure 18b STATEMENT OF INCOME & RETAINED EARNINGS FOR THE YEAR ENDING JULY 31, 1980

Sales		$120,217.00
Cost of Goods Sold:		
Parts	$73,339.00	
Labor	12,026.00	
Total	$85,365.00	
Less: Ending Inventory	24,244.00	
Total Cost of Goods Sold		61,121.00
Gross Profit		$59,096.00
Operating Expenses:		
Advertising	$18,403.00	
Professional Fees	8,408.00	
Telephone	7,185.00	
Commissions	7,087.00	
Office Expenses	6,990.00	
Refunds and Bad Checks	6,200.00	
Shipping and Mailing Expense	5,690.00	
Interest Expense	5,175.00	
Rent	2,250.00	
Depreciation	1,583.00	
Marketing	444.00	
Bank Charges	383.00	
Accounting	250.00	
Mass. Corp. Excise Tax	228.00	
Travel	228.00	
Insurance	46.00	
Total Operating Expenses		70,550.00
Net Loss		$(11,481.00)
Retained Earnings - July 31, 1979		
Retained Earnings (Deficit) July 31, 1980		$(11,481.00)

"See Accountant's Compilation Report"

EXHIBIT 1   (continued)

Figure 18c   STATEMENT OF CHANGES IN FINANCIAL POSITION   FOR THE YEAR
ENDING JULY 31, 1980

<u>SOURCE OF WORKING CAPITAL</u>

Operations:		
Charges not requiring use of working capital		$1,583.00
Issuance of 5-year bonds		36,000.00
Receipt of loans payable		<u>12,000.00</u>
Total Sources of Working Capital		$49,583.00

USE OF WORKING CAPITAL

Operations:		
Net loss for the year	$11,481.00	
Purchase of Fixed Assets	12,367.00	
Decrease in loans payable	<u>3,664.00</u>	
Total Uses of Working Capital		<u>27,512.00</u>

TOTAL INCREASE IN WORKING CAPITAL   <u>$22,071.00</u>

<u>COMPOSITION OF WORKING CAPITAL</u>

	End of initial year	Beginning of initial year	Increase or (decrease) in working capital
Current Assets			
Cash	$2,502.00	— 0 —	$2,502.00
Accounts Receivable	5,538.00	— 0 —	5,538.00
Prepaid Advertising	1,188.00	— 0 —	1,188.00
Inventory	<u>24,244.00</u>	<u>— 0 —</u>	24,244.00
Total Current Assets	<u>$33,472.00</u>	— 0 —	
Current Liabilities			
Accounts Payable	$5,748.00	— 0 —	5,748.00
Accrued Expenses	478.00	— 0 —	478.00
Accrued Interest	<u>5,175.00</u>	<u>— 0 —</u>	5,175.00
Total Current Liabilities	<u>$11,401.00</u>	— 0 —	
Working Capital	<u>$22,071.00</u>	— 0 —	

TOTAL INCREASE IN WORKING CAPITAL   <u>$22,071.00</u>

EXHIBIT 1 (continued)

Figure 18d NOTES TO THE FINANCIAL STATEMENTS FOR THE YEAR ENDED JULY 31, 1980

Note 1   SUMMARY OF SIGNIFICANT ACCOUNTING POLICIES:
Inventory is stated at standard cost, which approximate actual cost on a first-in, first-out basis and does not exceed market.

Depreciation of equipment is computed using the straight line method over the estimated useful lives of the assets.

The tax year ends on December 31 and as of this date the initial State and Federal Tax Returns for December 31, 1979 have not been prepared.

The Corporation was incorporated on July 31, 1979. This financial statement of July 31, 1980 presents the activity during the 12 months since incorporating. Some start-up costs were paid for in June and July of 1979 and all have been expensed during this fiscal year ending July 31, 1980.

Note 2   BONDS PAYABLE:

The 5-year bonds consist of the following:

20% Notes due August 1984	$11,000.00
20% Notes due October 1984	11,500.00
20% Notes due November 1984	2,500.00
20% Notes due January 1985	11,000.00
	$36,000.00

These Notes are secured by all assets. Interest of 20 percent per year is payable semi-annually on the date of purchase. As of July 31, 1980, $3,600 of interest has become due but unpaid. The bonds are convertible into a percent of common stock, calculated at 15 percent ownership for every $100,00 of bonds.

Note 3   LOAN PAYABLE L. OSBORNE:
The original amount of the loan to Laurence Osborne was $7,000. The balance has been reduced by taking repayments against the loan in lieu of salary.

Note 4   ERRORS
There are two errors in this statement. The amount for "bad checks and returns" is high by $3,400. The accountant noted this debit memo in the bank return, and it was not reconciled with a later deposit of the same amount. A large check had been mis-endorsed, and had to be redeposited. The gross sales would likewise be over-stated by the same amount.

EXHIBIT 1   (concluded)

Figure 18d   (concluded)

The accounts payable are closer to $15,000. Two pages of the older payables were somehow not included. They do exist, although there has been about $3,000 of payments made on them since the end of July.

Finally - the first run was a production debacle. A firm hired to do the assembly went suddenly bankrupt, and we had to become an appliance manufacturing firm on the spot. Only a small portion of the workers were trained, and the entire assembly line was makeshift. We managed to get 4,400 out in about a month of continuous effort, but the labor cost per item was close to $4.00 when the smoke finally cleared. Added to this much higher cost, 1,100 of the first run were sold at an average of $9.50 to distributors to obtain the cash to complete the run.

This combination of high cost and a low average sale price on the first run is combined with the much more efficient second run, the costs of which are accurately represented in the $7.95 cost of goods sold total in the exhibit. One banker insisted that our unit cost was close to $10.00. If we hadn't learned how to make them after the first run, that could well have been true - but since May, the second run, we've got that cost contained.

Dick Redman

In the fall of 1990 Dick Redman and two associates working with him at Pacific Mogul Tours in Portland, Oregon, were considering which of several alternative career directions to take. One would be simply to stay with Pacific Mogul in their present jobs. A second would be to attempt a buy-out of their employer. A third would be to undertake a start-up of their own, by one of several possible routes. They had been trying to explore each of these options discreetly without compromising their jobs, but this was becoming increasingly difficult. Consequently, all were feeling pressure to make clear decisions promptly and take decisive actions one way or the other.

The Tour Business

Travel tours produced by Pacific Mogul could be bought from any travel agent. Someone wanting to take a trip through the Canadian Rockies, for example, could arrange the trip without buying such a tour, either by arranging tickets with airlines and accommodations directly or by doing so through a travel agent who would make them directly. There might be a flight to Vancouver, followed by a train ride to Banff, then a hotel stay in Banff, where the person might arrange to take a sightseeing bus, and so forth. The individual, with or without an agent, would plan these details directly and personally cope with any problems they produced on the trip.

Alternatively, the person might purchase from a company like Pacific Mogul a pre-packaged tour in which all of these tickets and accommodations were already set up for pre-established itinerary. Then the traveler would write out one check for the whole package. The tour might again begin with a plane ride to Vancouver, and perhaps there the traveler would be met by a tour guide who would lead all those who had bought that particular itinerary through the travels it entailed. Advantages for the traveler of this arrangement would be that the same trip, when bought as a package would be cheaper than buying the individual components of the trip separately. Additionally, it would be more convenient to have all the arrangements worked out in advance rather than having to take chances and piecing them together. Having a tour guide to solve any problems that arose enroute could further enhance convenience.

The function of Pacific Mogul in this process was to design and arrange the different components of the tour, airline reservations, hotel reservations, tour guide and so forth. The company would set it up for some anticipated number of travelers, perhaps 30. Travel agents then would make commissions on sales they made to travelers. The advantage to the travel agent or retailer who sold the tours to consumers was the ability to offer individual customers the rate and convenience advantages of group travel without having to organize a group. For its part, Pacific Mogul would, in effect, collect groups of travelers by selling through all interested travel agents, and would make its profit through buying the tickets and accommodations at quantity discounts.

To make this work, Mogul had to be

able to do several things. One was to design attractive trips. The itinerary, accommodations, sightseeing excursions, and timing of events had to be such that people would like to experience them. It would be a mistake, for instance, to combine too many days of traveling without an appropriate number of days of layover and relaxation. But too many of the latter in series might let travelers get bored. Accommodations had to be suitably matched in quality to tour price, and the total price had to fit pocketbooks of people likely to want to do the things the tour involved. Any misalignments might not sell, or worse, would produce unhappy customers, who in turn would spoil the tour company's reputation with travel agents.

Selection and training of tour guides was also important to the process. Mogul normally hired college students in summer. They did not receive much in the way of cash, but had all their expenses paid to accompany tours. At the conclusion of a tour each customer was asked to rate the quality of all elements of the tour, including the guide. Those guides who received lowest ratings were promptly dropped from Mogul's roster.

To maintain tour components, Mogul's president, Walter Langdon, and his son, who was vice-president of the company, continually traveled to various hotels, arranging for blocks of rooms at needed dates, and negotiating prices and terms. Hotels customarily allowed cancellation of reservations only up to a certain date before use, after which Mogul would have to pay.

To market tour packages, the two also visited key agents in selected parts of the country, according to the particular tours and markets for which they were aimed. The company spent approximately $40,000 per year on elaborate colored brochures with photographs and written information describing the tours. These were given away at trade shows and mailed to agents around the country. Typically, trade shows were sponsored by major airlines. At those shows wholesalers who made substantial use of the particular lines in their tours were given free booths for displaying tours and distributing literature. Travel agents were given free travel to attend these shows, where they would circulate among the booths, picking up information on tours they felt their clientele might find of interest. In its Portland office Pacific Mogul maintained several WATS lines, so travel agents could make collect telephone calls to obtain information about its tours.

The Three Associates

Dick Redman began his MBA studies at Portland State in 1986 and graduated in 1988. For three summers during school, he worked as a tour escort for Pacific Mogul. He recalled:

> I would welcome 40 people from all over the USA, when they arrived in Portland to begin the tour. Then for the next 14 days I would accompany them around, making sure everything worked as advertised on the itinerary they had bought and doing my best to solve any problems that arose in such a way as to keep every customer as happy as possible.

Upon graduation, Dick was invited by Walter Langdon, Mogul's president, to join the company full time as vice-president for operations. This, in effect, meant he was in charge of all the tour escorts and responsible for seeing that things went smoothly during the tours. In negotiating to accept this job, Dick told Mr. Langdon that the salary was less than he could earn elsewhere with his MBA. Mr. Langdon, he said, replied that if Dick did his job well and got along in the company, there would be opportunity in the near future to obtain a share of ownership in the company as well as profit sharing as additional incentive.

Jack Miller, like Dick Redman, was in his late 20s when he, too, joined Mogul Tours in 1988. Prior to that, he had graduated from college in liberal arts, spent two years in the military and then joined the sales office of a major hotel chain, where he rapidly rose to national sales manager. He then briefly worked for another Pacific Northwest tour wholesaling company before joining Pacific Mogul as vice president for marketing. He was now responsible for opening facilities negotiations, which were then followed through by Dick Redman, and for carrying out sales campaigns directed by the president. Jack said he chafed somewhat at this direction and wanted to make more of the marketing decisions himself.

Ellen Wilson was in her late 30s. She had worked as a stenographer before getting married and then had quit her job to raise a family. When her children were grown, she began to look for another job and happened, in 1981, to meet the son of Walter Langdon, who at that time was just beginning to set up Pacific Mogul. She recalled:

> I came in on the ground floor when the company was just starting and worked on a lot of different aspects of getting it going. Essentially, I handled all of the internal operations of the office except bookkeeping, while Walter designed the tours, set them up and sold them to the agents.

As of late 1990, Ellen was in charge of office operations, responsible for seeing that paperwork, including correspondence, ticket processing, reservation confirmation and other records—as well as phone communications—were handled effectively. She said, however, that she would prefer to have more influence on policy decisions of the internal operations, not just responsibility for seeing that they were implemented.

Like both Dick and Jack, Ellen said she was dissatisfied with her pay. The three of them, although they had never seen financial statements of the company, believed that Walter Langdon and his son were taking home substantial bonuses. The company was prospering, as judged by the number of tour sales it was closing compared to competitors. Both Langdons were exhibiting signs of prosperity and both had withdrawn substantially from operations, leaving it to employees to carry on the work all day while the two owners put in only brief appearances at the office each morning. Essentially, the trio felt that they were doing most of the management work for low pay while the Langdons were reaping the rewards of leisure and high pay.

Buy-Out Negotiations

The ownership sharing opportunities, which Dick Redman had discussed earlier with Walter Langdon, had to Dick's disappointment, never materialized. Whenever he attempted to bring the subject up, Mr. Langdon indicated that the right time had not yet arrived, and Dick had begun to wonder if it ever would. Then, to his surprise, he learned that the Langdons had been discussing with outside parties the possibility of selling the company. Jack Miller was surprised at this news also. He and Dick approached Walter Langdon and suggested that rather than selling the company to outsiders it might make sense to sell to employees instead. Mr. Langdon, Jack recalled, said, "All right, why don't you see what you can do about making me an offer?" Jack continued.

> That was all I needed. Through some people I had met who knew about the financial community, I got in touch with a local stock brokerage house. I didn't

know exactly how much we needed, but the business appeared to be very profitable, and it didn't need a lot of capital for fixed assets. The brokerage house said that some of their clients liked to get involved in private placement deals, so they should have no trouble raising as much as a million dollars.

But when we went back to Walter with that, he really blew up. He said he would want at least a million and a half, and that we had no business going around talking about the company being for sale. Through his attorney, he sent a letter to the broker saying something to the effect that any representation by us was without the knowledge or authority of the owners of the company, and any actions the broker would take based upon these representations would be at the broker's own risk. The broker called us to apologize and gave us his sympathy.

Neither Dick, Jack nor Ellen had any substantial savings with which to buy the company, or alternatively, to start one. Consequently, Dick and Jack began searching for contacts who might be able to help, and found two additional alternatives. Details of the terms could not be worked out because the exact amount needed had not been established. However, the first source, a venture capital group with enormous financial resources, indicated willingness to consider providing all the capital needed in return for 60 percent of the stock. Terms would include continuing the three associates at pay approximately 30 percent above their current rates and giving them a free hand in running the business; nobody in the venture capital group had any experience in the travel business, nor did they want to acquire any.

A second potential source was a travel agency, which said it might be willing to share ownership on an equal basis, 50 percent for it and 50 percent for the three as-sociates. Salary conditions would be similar to those suggested by the venture capital group. The agency had, to a limited extent, developed some tours of its own, which it would turn over to the three as part of the deal. Financial resources of the agency were somewhat limited, however, and its main customer was one airline which had been considering some schedule changes. If it eliminated certain flights in which the agency specialized, the agency would have serious problems and could possibly fail. Financing from the agency would be provided on an installment basis to ease the drain.

Strategic Options

It seemed to the three that there were several directions they might choose to pursue. One would be to continue trying to buy out the Langdons, either wholly or partially. Perhaps they could satisfy the Langdons and achieve their own desires through a buy-out that worked in stages or based upon some sort of contingencies. However, they did not know what the Langdons might find acceptable in that regard, or how to find out, since prior attempts to explore the subject had failed.

A second option would be to set up a new tour wholesaling company. This would require substantial expenditures. Dick expected the biggest expense would be salaries for setting up an office, working up tour packages, preparing advertising materials, arranging reservations and selling to travel agents. This could take several months, during which income would start and rise slowly as tours were sold. Preparation of advertising brochures would probably cost about $60,000, he said. Printing he expected would cost another $20,000, and other advertising from $40,000 to $60,000. All these estimates had to be rough, Dick said, because the only people privy to financial information at Mogul had been the two owners.

Other major items he estimated were mailing expenses for the brochures, as much as $30,000, attending trade shows, possibly $20,000 to $30,000, and other company travel, at least $2,000 per month. Taking incoming phone calls collect and making outgoing sales calls might cost around $2,000 per month. Office space should be available for $1,000 to $1,500 per month. Office supplies, utilities and other expense items might add another several thousand, but he was not sure. There would be expenses for minor supplies in connection with tours for things such as bag tags, but these should not be much, perhaps $6 per customer. Dick's feeling was that if the company managed to sign up between 1,500 and 1,800 customers during the year, mostly in the summer, it would be doing fairly well.

Once they decided what to include in the tour, they could estimate selling prices and variable costs for tours in a relatively straightforward matter. Typical markups of the industry could be computed by working back from their prices and a knowledge of variable costs. The three associates worked up a half dozen tour designs based upon what they knew to be selling well for other firms, and Dick computed likely sale prices and variable costs for those tours, as shown in Exhibit 1. How sales might vary from one tour to another, he was not sure. He noted, however, that gross margin did not vary too greatly among them anyway. On the average, he expected each tour might run 10 times with around 30 travelers.

A third option would be to keep their jobs with Mogul and continue as before. The company was growing, and the three were advancing, both in responsibility as the number of people subordinate to them expanded, and financially through salary raises and bonuses. Since they were largely running the company while the Langdons were not around, it seemed to them their bargaining positions might be good for attempting to obtain more substantial raises and perhaps a share of company profits. Should this fail, they all believed they would have no trouble obtaining other similar jobs, since they felt they had built good reputations based upon the work they had performed for Mogul.

Issues of Concern

How to work things out with the owner was something all three associates had been considering. Dick commented:

> One matter that concerns us is loyalty. How much do we owe our employer? How far should we go in any of these strategic directions based on that loyalty? All three of us have learned a lot working here, and we are grateful for that. But we are somewhat dissatisfied, and we have been frustrated in trying to work things out with the company so far. Our employer is probably pulling somewhere on the order of $200,000 to $400,000 of profit out of this company, based upon mostly our work, as we see it. For that we don't seem to be getting paid very much, and we would like to see that change.
>
> The company is healthy and growing, but the owner's price seems awfully high, since people in the financial community have told us a P/E ratio of around two or three is more typical for a company like this.

An additional concern was division of ownership and responsibilities. Discussions among the three associates had tentatively concluded that Jack Miller would most likely become president, since he had the most experience as a travel business executive. But Jack's feeling was that the office or president should carry with it a substantially higher salary than those of vice presidents, which the other two would then hold. The other two disagreed with this and felt that since they were basically partners and peers, they should share equally in ownership and salaries.

Starting a new company would raise some of the same concerns. The three believed it would be crucial to obtain accommodation commitments from certain popular hotels that could pick and choose among tours because they tended to fill in advance. Also crucial would be to recruit enough of the 30,000 travel agents around the country to sell the tours actively in competition with the other 400-odd tour

wholesalers currently in operation. For this reason, the three expected that raising capital for selling expenditures would be needed. Whether these kinds of commitments could be obtained, the three did not know. But they agreed it would be unethical to contact prospective accommodation operators and travel agents for a company of their own as long as they were employed by Pacific Mogul. They believed word of such attempts would get around and would both end their jobs and make it difficult for them to obtain similar jobs elsewhere.

EXHIBIT 1 Estimated Tour Pricing

Tour	Per Traveler* Selling Price	Per Traveler Variable Costs**
A	$1,110	$852
B	$1,190	$844
C	$1,250	$914
D	$1,490	$1,186
E	$1,750	$1,396
F	$1,090	$824

---

*   Assumes an average of 30 travelers per tour.

**   Includes expenses and salary of tour guide or escort.

Riverfront Press

We've been given just enough money to hang ourselves. If we can't get a loan for $65,000 to buy a larger press and put our accounts in order, we won't be able to survive. Going into 1980, things were looking up; we had received a $35,000 loan last October, which allowed us to move into our present location. Because we expected to get additional funding from the SBA, we started taking work that we had to job out so we could build a larger client base and make sure the market for our work would be there.

But the financing hasn't come through, so now we're losing money hand over fist. We might be forced to close the shop next month, in July, when vacations are scheduled and work eases up. But the last thing we want to do is quit. We've spent four years developing this business and are just on the verge of making it profitable. Our reputation for quality work is outstanding, and it seems inconceivable to us that we can go this far only to have the business fail.

The key is to find someone who will look at our business plan and say, "Yes, this is a worthwhile investment." We desperately need a second printing press. Right now, we're incredibly discouraged.

Jude Goldman pointed to a list, reproduced in Exhibit 1, that showed operating losses incurred from jobbing out work (having other shops perform it on subcontract) from February to May of 1980. She said the business was well on its way to bankruptcy if present trends continued.

The partners said they weren't sure if lending institutions had rejected their requests due to the business plan, a copy of which appears in Exhibit 2, or other factors. Jude summed up the position which she and Jan had taken in dealing with banks and the Small Business Administration during the past month:

The theory goes that by giving women the tools to produce, they can become a more viable part of the economic mainstream. We've been trying to say, "Look! You're not giving us the tools. How can we be expected to accomplish anything given that kind of situation?"

History of Riverfront Press

Jude Goldman and Jan Whitted cofounded Riverfront Press originally as "Tramp Printers" in August of 1976, after a chance meeting during which they both discovered they shared an interest in printing. The two set up a letterpress shop near the Cambridge Common in 250 square feet of space rented for $125 per month. Loans from friends, proceeds from selling Jude's 1969 Ford Fairlane, and cutting back on their personal budgets gave them $2,750 to capitalize the business and start production.

By early 1977, the two decided that there was a commercial potential related to their hobby interest, particularly for high-quality, short runs of offset printing. Jan recalled that customers would come in to have letterpress done and ask if the two knew of other printers who did similar work in offset. Jan explained:

We didn't really like referring potential customers to other printers. And the people who came to us for letterpress work clearly let us know that there was a need for high quality offset printing. So, six months after moving into this shop, we bought our first offset press.

Financing of the first press was done through a combination of a loan and financing agreement with a private individual. The two had been turned down by a local bank in their first attempt to secure funding. The loan officer had told them that there was simply no track record to look at or fixed assets that could be secured.

By chance, they met a woman who was a management consultant in the Boston area. Her income, she said, had put her in need of a tax shelter. When she learned what Jan and Jude were trying to do, she proposed that she finance the press by taking out a loan under her name. Jan and Jude would have to find $4,000 to pay for the down payment for a $9,500 press and purchase the auxiliary equipment that would be needed.

In return, the woman was to receive 5 percent of the gross margin from the business for the book life of the press—five years. In addition, she would get an investment tax credit and benefits of depreciation. For Jan and Jude, borrowing needs were thereby reduced and they had a press with which to exploit the market niche they saw in offset printing. Jude reflected on the loan and lease arrangements:

Today, I can't believe our lawyer let us go ahead with a deal like that. But at the time, the woman was invaluable to us. She helped us write our first business plan. After the bank had turned us down, we went to the Massachusetts Feminist Credit Union. Their credit committee listened to our presentation and approved a $5,000 loan, which is

the highest they can go.

We spent $2,000 on the press and the rest on equipment and supplies. We weren't sure what the significance of the 5 percent off gross was until we had signed the contract with the woman. At the time, it was the only way we could get enough money to buy the press.

Operations

With the new press installed, Jan and Jude divided the work as follows until the end of 1979. Jan ran the offset press while Jude took care of letterpress work and building up more accounts. Both handled administrative functions. In 1978 another person was hired part time to answer the phone and keep books. Apprentices were used as a way to provide training for women interested in printing and to allow the partners time for administrative responsibilities without the presses "being down."

Past problems in hiring decisions had led them to pay the "going wage" for personnel. Currently, they employed one person for bookkeeping and managing accounts and another to handle pre-production work for the offset press. Jude talked about past situations in hiring people that had become a source of frustration:

We were confused about our identity, which led us to try to hire women, instead of looking for the best person for the job. We advertised in the women's papers and sure enough, people who responded were politically motivated, technically incompetent, and expected us to carry them with high salaries.

Establishing credit with suppliers was another issue the two had dealt with from the beginning. Since they had virtually no capital, they would counter requests for prepayment with a certified check or

C.O.D. by showing the suppliers the quality of their work and using the argument that they should be treated the same as established customers. The result, Jan said, was that they were able to get credit on purchases of paper and other supplies.

Pricing was estimated on each job that came in. An estimating form and estimate sheet were completed for the order, listing the type of work that was to be done. Jude explained that there were two reasons why price quotes might vary from one printer to another. The first was due to the estimating process. Many printers simply quoted a price on what the customer originally asked for. If later changes and modifications were desired, the customer was charged extra for each "add-on." Jan and Jude, on the other hand, would spend time with the customer to make sure all aspects and special features that customer might desire were discussed when the order was first taken. This way, a complete price could be quoted and there would be less misunderstanding about what the final product would look like when completed. A second reason for price variations had to do with Riverfront's current scope of operations, Jude explained.

We can't buy paper as cheaply as some people can. We don't do bindery operations in house on some things such as folding and stapling. So our prices are higher for those kinds of work.

Jude said their price estimates were based as much on quality as on matching existing competition. Since the business emphasized quality, they had decided from the beginning to price on the high side for brochures, pamphlets, flyers and business cards—which comprised most of their business.

Costs for paper stock were about 25 percent of total receipts, typical for the printing industry. Other fixed and variable costs included rent, labor, loan commitments and supplies for the office and production facilities. Pro forma cash flows can be seen in the company's business plan and loan proposal, which is reproduced as Exhibit 2 .

Jude estimated that their share of the local printing market was under 1 percent. The printing industry was very fragmented, she said, each firm tending to specialize toward a particular client base. Riverfront Press had relied on academic institutions and non-profit groups at the start, although they were now mainly serving corporations in the hotel and entertainment industry. She added that roughly 25 percent of their business currently came from federal purchasing set-aside programs for women or minority owned firms. Referrals and repeat business made up over half their sales. The other half consisted of new clients who learned about the company from publicity or other sources.

The partners had relied on media coverage for advertising during the early stages of their venture, and they had concluded that the press "is always looking for a story." They remarked that this avenue of promotion had been more successful than paid advertising and they anticipated no major expenditures for advertising in the near future.

For the past two years, Jan and Jude had been attempting to position the business to make a steady profit. Their progress had been slowed due to an accident Jan suffered when a bus she was riding on was sideswiped by another bus. From the time of the accident in June of 1978, up through early 1979, neither had drawn a salary. Friends would come in at night to help keep up with orders while Jan was recovering. The incident also resulted in their decision to hire a press operator, which set them on a course of expanding the business to reach profitability.

Pursuit of Financing

By 1979 the two had concluded that if the business were ever going to get beyond break-even, a larger printing press and a new location was essential. Financing the move, however, they saw as a problem. They had dealt with the same loan officer at First New England Trust (disguised name), since opening an account there in mid-1977, attempting to keep their financing in order and refine their business plan. The partners had visited several banks during their first attempts to get a loan prior to 1980. A friend had suggested that they approach another Boston bank that had a division set up to assist small businesses in the central city. But so far they had decided to stay with their current bank where they felt the loan officer had become familiar with their business. Jude explained that he had been very helpful in suggesting ways to learn more about finance and monitor their cash flow. When it came to getting a loan from the bank however, the officer always told them that they needed to do "a couple more things" to put their business in order. Jan recalled:

Every time we go in there he tells us, "You're such nice girls; you've been working so hard. I wish I could help you. If you would only do x, I could help you." Our response has been to do that and then return. By that time, he's thought of something else we should do, like read a book on financial management.

It's become really frustrating. He won't give us the money, and he won't turn us down for the loan so we can go back to the SBA. Meanwhile, when we go to the SBA to talk about a second loan, they tell us that we need to be refused by a commercial lending institution before they can consider our request. At first, the praise, gratitude and encouragement were enough. Now,

they aren't enough. We need the money.

Jan and Jude explained that their success in getting $35,000 from the SBA in late 1979 was due to persistence. They had used the rejection from the first bank they had approached in 1977 as their "entre" to get funding for a second press and additional equipment for expansion. At first, the only thing the SBA would offer was advice. Jude recalled the sequence during 1978 and 1979 when they kept attempting to borrow $70,000 for the venture:

The SBA turned us down . . . and they turned us down . . . and they turned us down. And we kept coming back . . . and coming back . . . and coming BACK.

Jan continued:

We approached them with a package that would buy us a larger press, take care of some of our payables, consolidate our loans and move us into a bigger space. After a year of fighting and going back, they would say, "Change this, change that." They finally approved a loan for half of what we had asked for. Not only that, what they took out of the loan was the equipment, which was the only collateral possible in the loan. So we had an uncollateralized loan without the means of production.

Jude completed the story:

So the loan would take care of our cash flow and payables and move us into a bigger space that we didn't need without the press. They made the vague promise that if we were in a better position in four months, they would put in the money for the larger press. We later found out that this is a syndrome they use to give you enough money to kill your business. That's exactly what they did to us, and we should have never accepted that loan. But we were desperate; we took it.

The loan was approved for $35,000 and funds were received in February of 1980, one month after moving into a new location in East Cambridge. To prepare for getting a larger press, Jan and Jude decided to adopt a strategy of jobbing out. This meant that they would go after business and subcontract the work to other printers until they had assembled the financing to purchase the press, at which time they would be able to do those jobs internally. They admitted that the mark-up for themselves would be smaller than in-house work during this interim phase. However, they stated that this strategy should allow them to test the size of the market and to build an established base of clients. This, they hoped, might help persuade a lender that investment in a press was justified.

The purchase price of the needed press was $20,000. It and the existing press were capable of running 10,000 impressions per hour, although Jude pointed out that 7,000 would be better, to reduce equipment breakdowns and problems in production. She said the new press would accept larger sheets of paper so that more pages of a book or a larger poster could be printed simultaneously. Jude added that the press had an improved inking system which would provide a higher quality product for half tone effects. They estimated that business volume could be doubled in the first year if the new press were added to their production capacity.

Facing the Current Dilemma

As of June of 1980, the two partners found themselves losing money and no closer to securing a second loan package than they had been six months earlier. Current projections showed the business ending 1980 near break even, with

$135,000 in sales. For 1981, break even was estimated to be $200,000, contingent upon obtaining the second press. By jobbing work out, their margin had been reduced to 5 percent on work that would otherwise bring 20 percent. Payables were running between 60 and 90 days while their receivables were at 60 to 120 days. Jude blamed the situation of slow payment principally on a few government customers, whose billing procedures and payment schedules meant that a check might take as long as three or four months to finally reach the printing company.

Jan and Jude summarized where they stood with their current options for financing the $65,000 loan package:

The last time we talked with First New England Trust, the banker told us that we should bring in another partner who would contribute some equity to the business, and most importantly, have an MBA. He doesn't believe that we can manage the money.

The Small Business Administration has changed loan officers, and the one we dealt with last year is gone. His replacement told us he knew nothing about any kind of promise that we could get more money four or six months down the road. By now, everyone at the SBA should know who we are. When we go walking down the hall it seems as though everyone says, "Hi Jan; hi Jude." It's ridiculous how much time we've spent over there.

We've been trying to re-negotiate the financing deal we set up with the management consultant in 1977. The arrangement still has three years to run and we can't afford the lost revenue. We're telling her she should consider the 5 percent as a re-investment and put the money back in to purchase the second press. Then we would set up payment terms to repay the entire amount as a loan. Her feeling is that she took a very big risk on the deal originally and she's entitled to the 5 percent as it currently stands.

Jan and Jude said that getting customers was not a problem. They simply needed to establish a volume that would support their overhead costs and allow an improved cash flow for profit and re-investment. If they were to move back to the previous location, they felt they would simply be back to where they had started three years ago, with no progress to show for all their efforts and sacrifices. They said closing the business was an option, but one they felt was out of the question. Jan summed up their outlook for the venture:

We want to be the major two- and three-color printer of newsletters, booklets and pamphlets in the New England area. That would mean revenues of well over a million dollars per year. To abandon that goal is to ignore the market we know exists for this type of service. We can't see calling it quits when we are so close to becoming a successful enterprise.

I guess the lessons we've learned in our financial dealings are to be very direct, forceful, and get a deal right away. Otherwise, they can keep you on the string forever. But I'm not sure how we should apply those lessons right now to get ourselves turned around.

EXHIBIT 1   Riverfront Press 2/80-5/80 Loss Attributed to Subcontracting

In 1979, its third year of operation, Riverfront Press showed a profit. Despite this, a substantial loss was incurred during the first five months of 1980. This loss is directly attributable to the volume of work subcontracted by the company. Under present circumstances, a loan of $65,000 would reverse this trend within six months after the necessary equipment is installed. Table 2 demonstrates the money lost on two typical jobs. The following chart shows how the company lost money while subcontracting in order to buy into its target market. This situation would never have occurred had the company's initial loan request for equipment been approved.

DOLLAR VOLUME SALES INVOICED	COST OF SUBCONTRACTING
$525	$345
3659	750
775	542
350	345
1,760	1,422
165	123
400	375
1,150	902
1,715	752
525	323
525	345
271	189
714	650
1,150	494
275	142
945	672
525	345
405	360
TOTAL: $15,834	$9,076

NOTE: The above does not reflect the cost of paper and labor supplied by Riverfront Press. Paper, figured at 25 percent of sales accounts for $4000, labor at 5 percent of sales was $800; therefore, gross profit on the work totaled $702.

ADDITIONAL SUBCONTRACTING FOR THE PERIOD:

NEGATIVES: $700. Majority of work performed before our camera was operational. Outside negatives now average $50 per month.

BINDERY COSTS: $800. All this work could have been done on proposed equipment.

TYPESETTING: $2300. Approximately 80 percent of the work performed for Riverfront clients will not be billed to us. Instead, it will be billed to customers by our associate, Minerva Graphics, eliminating most of our cost in this category.

EXHIBIT 1 (continued)

TABLE II
RIVERFRONT PRESS
COST ANALYSIS FOR SUBCONTRACTED WORK

JOB		SUBCONTRACTED	IN HOUSE
A	Paper	$120	$120
	Printing/Binding	345	200
	Misc. Labor	69	30
	Total Cost	534	350
	Billed At:	555	555
	Net Profit	21	205
B	Paper	348	348
	Printing/Binding	451	290
	Misc. Labor	23	25
	Total Cost	822	663
	Billed At:	1150	1150
	Net Profit	328	487

EXHIBIT 2 Business Plan

RIVERFRONT PRESS
20 Thorndike Street
Cambridge, Mass. 02141

I. SUMMARY

Riverfront Press is a four-year-old commercial printing company which has experienced rapid growth. It became apparent in 1979 that capital was needed to physically expand the business and to add equipment, thereby increasing the capacity and profitability of the business. A loan package of $70,000 was submitted to the Small Business Administration. The central point of the financing was a 25" offset press which would enable the company to:

a) stop jobbing out work to other printers, a highly unprofitable practice which increases accounts payable and cost of sales to a dangerous point; and

b) fully pursue its established market and to grow in a stable and profitable way.

The request was approved for $30,000. As allocated, funds were dispersed for accounts payable, loan consolidation, moving expenses, construction, a graphics camera and a paper cutter. The company has been able to work more efficiently and decrease some outside costs. However, the SBA loan did not include funds for the 25" press. The $30,000 served only to stabilize the company toward a break-even point; the profit and growth picture have not been improved. Considering the company's potential in terms of market, staff and management, this is a serious situation.

Riverfront Press is a classic example of a contemporary women's business in its potential and in its problems. Initially undercapitalized in a capital-intensive field, the company has yet to become credible to the banking establishment. The company must obtain financing and equipment now to improve its profit and position as it reaches for its true market share.

Most women's businesses are concentrated in service and retail areas which cannot contribute to the basic needs of government and industry. As a manufacturing concern, Riverfront Press is in an excellent position to provide a necessary product for both the public and private sectors while improving its own status and that of women in the mainstream of the economy. The company is both competent and reliable. Relationships with Massport, the University of Massachusetts and others with affirmative action purchasing programs (as well as with those who have no such program) have resulted in quality work, delivered on time, at a competitive price.

EXHIBIT 2   (continued)

With the proper working tools, Riverfront Press will quickly become a healthy, profit-making business.

AMOUNT REQUESTED: $65,000

PURPOSE: Equipment, Leasehold Improvements, Cash Flow

19" x 25" Offset Press	$20,000
Plate Burner, folder, stitcher	5,000
Leasehold Improvements	4,700
Trade Debt	6,000
Working Capital	29,300
NET LOAN REQUEST	$65,000

II. BACKGROUND

Riverfront Press is a commercial printing company located in Cambridge, Massachusetts. It began as Tramp Printers, a custom letterpress shop, in January of 1977. It has grown into a commercial offset printing plant specializing in short-run, high-quality work. This service is used by the public and private sectors alike. It is an alternative to quick copy centers which handle short runs but cannot provide a quality product.

III. INTRODUCTION TO THE COMPANY

In olden times itinerant printers traveled from town to town in search of daily work and new experiences. They were called "tramp printers" and provided a colorful tradition for the graphic arts as well as a name for this company.

Tramp Printers was begun as a custom letterpress shop offering finely crafted, custom designed books, invitations, broadsides and cards. In January of 1980, the company moved to larger quarters in the Lechemere area of Cambridge. This area is being developed as the "riverfront." The name Tramp Printers was changed to upgrade the company image and to closely identify the business with the new location.

EXHIBIT 2 (continued)

Six months after opening, it became clear that letterpress buyers and others frequently needed high quality, short run offset work. Financing was obtained through the Massachusetts Federal Feminist Credit Union. In June of 1977, Tramp Printers expanded into commercial offset printing by purchasing a small, duplicating press.

In the first year of offset production the company grew rapidly. Customers required books, brochures and magazines as well as letterheads, business cards and flyers. Then, as now, the business offered quality work to the short run printing buyer. Service is personal and attentive. Management is competent and organized in both business and production.

For six months, the company experimented with a sales representative. It was decided that sales could be more efficiently handled (and more profitably) by one of the partners. Jude Goldman has established substantial accounts in the target markets. The projection includes 70 percent of sales to be generated through her efforts.

Riverfront Press continues to grow into its fourth year. Projections for 1980 include: 1) increasing gross sales by increasing visibility in target markets through direct sales; 2) improved service and productivity through addition of larger press and bindery equipment; and 3) increased profitability through decreased outside expenditures.

IV. ORGANIZATION AND MANAGEMENT

The principals of Riverfront Press are Jan Whitted and Jude Goldman. They are equal partners and are together responsible for all management decisions.

Whitted is a self-taught printer who has been in the trade for nine years. Previous to forming Riverfront Press, she managed her own shop, served as a printing consultant to school and community groups and gained extensive experience in all phases of letterpress and offset production. At Riverfront, her skills are utilized in production management. She has charge of routing, scheduling and personnel. Whitted is responsible for a substantial part of physical production.

Sales at Riverfront are managed by Goldman, whose education in trade school and college and work background in market research and printing have prepared her for technical work and management. She is also responsible for purchasing, estimating and quality control.

EXHIBIT 2   (continued)

Whitted and Goldman complement each other well in their skills. They work together on all decisions in management, combining their efforts to meet the challenge of a young business.

V. PRODUCT

Riverfront Press produces commercial offset printing and, through a sub-contractor, provides computer typesetting.

The company produces short run (under 100,000 copies) of books, pamphlets, magazines, brochures and posters as well as business stationery.

Offset lithography is a photo-mechanical process which utilizes the resistance between ink and water to transfer an image from one flat surface to another.

Bindery operations are currently obtained through sub-contractors. The majority of this work (folding and stapling) could be easily and more profitably handled in-house.

VI. THE MARKET

The printing industry in the United States is large, diversified and growing. Despite the severe recession of 1974-75 and the current economic outlook, it continues to grow at a steady annual average gain of 7.9 percent (see Table 1).

In 1977 the commercial printing industry grossed approximately $15 billion. One-third of this figure was generated by general job printing, with 60 percent done in lithography.

According to the U.S. Department of Commerce 1972 Census of Manufactures, $.75 of each dollar of receipts in commercial printing (lithographic) was spent in cost of materials and payroll. The percentage of receipts spent on payroll and materials by Riverfront Press has consistently fallen on or near this industry standard.

Riverfront Press is a new and aggressive company rapidly expanding its market share. Its growth rate is higher than the stated average; its sales reflect the efforts of a young company to provide a higher quality product and better service in order to increase in market share.

Clients fall into four categories. The first includes universities, publishers, consulting and design firms. Retail establishments with exclusive or discriminating clientele are the second group.

EXHIBIT 2 (continued)

Members of the public and private sector who have a commitment to affirmative action are the third type of customer. In 1980 the company has pursued more work from the fourth category, corporate customers. Our client base has been enlarged to include firms such as Thermo Electron and the Cabot Corporation.

VII. SALES STRATEGY

Short-run, high-quality printing buyers such as locally based corporations, universities, design firms, and local and state agencies, have been targeted as the market for Riverfront Press.

Sales are solicited by direct client calls. Goldman acquaints the prospect with the company's work and evaluates their potential as a client for quality, volume, and budget.

Riverfront Press also obtains business by bidding on government contracts at the city, state, and federal levels. These bids are furnished whether they are part of an affirmative action program or not.

Very little advertising has been done by Riverfront. Money budgeted for advertising is primarily used to produce and mail promotional pieces which demonstrate our abilities to full advantage.

Word-of-mouth advertising is one of the company's best allies in the sales promotion. Many long-standing accounts were originally generated in this way.

Extensive media coverage has been received because the business is a small, quality shop and because it is woman-owned. Articles in the *Boston Globe*, the *Phoenix*, *Equal Times*, and *Inc.* magazine, and appearances on Channel 4's "Woman '77," Channel 38's "Tom Larson Show," Channel 5's "Sunday Open House," and a National Public Radio Broadcast have increased visibility and volume.

VIII. THE COMPETITION

Riverfront Press is in attractive position competitively. This is due to its service and its status as a woman-owned company.

Riverfront's customers need short-run printing and demand close attention and high quality, often difficult to obtain for a small job. Business which goes elsewhere lands at copy centers or much larger companies.

EXHIBIT 2 **(continued)**

The short-run printing industry is dominated by copy shops which are too numerous to count. They produce fast, cheap work of inconsistent quality, and their ability to handle complicated work (multi-colored or photographs) is limited.

Service at Riverfront is complete and attentive. The quality of the work is guaranteed. This places the company in competition with larger printers who are rarely interested in short run work. Riverfront Press is necessary to the printing buyer with a small job and exacting standards. Aggressive sales, service quality and competitive pricing enable Riverfront to expand and hold its market share.

As a 100 percent woman-owned company, Riverfront Press is eligible for many set-aside programs. The competition here is minimal.

IX. PURPOSE OF THE LOAN

Long-term financial projections for Riverfront Press include a larger product, increased sales, and higher profitability. In the short term, this means some plant renovations and the purchase of equipment.

The major purchase is a 19" x 25" offset press ($20,000), which will increase production capacity and product size while decreasing cost of sales. A larger plate burner, folder, and saddle stitcher ($5,000) will also accomplish the same goals.

Following installation of this machinery, working capital ($29,300) is required for increased costs.

Leasehold improvements totaling $4,700 will be necessary and we request $6,000 to cover existing trade debt.

X. EQUIPMENT LIST

1966 Miehle 20 x 26, #2341	$18,500
Baumfolder 22 x 28	4,500
Boston Wire Stitcher $4-110	400
Nuarc Flip Top Plate Maker	1,000
Total Equipment Purchase	$24,400

EXHIBIT 2   (continued)

XI.   PARTIAL LISTING: RIVERFRONT PRESS ACCOUNTS

American Type Founders, Boston
Apt Corporation, Cambridge
Boston Public Schools
The Cabot Corporation, Boston
Computer Corporation of America, Cambridge
General Electric Co., Lynn
Harvard University, Cambridge
Houghton Mifflin, Boston
Massport, Boston
MBTA, Boston
Planned Parenthood, Cambridge
Radcliffe College, Cambridge
Studio Associates, Boston
Senator Paul Tsongas, Boston
Thermo Electron, Waltham
Tufts University, Medford
University of Massachusetts, Boston

TABLE 1
Printing, Publishing and Allied Industries: Projections 1975-1985
(value of shipments in millions of dollars)

SIC	Industry	1975	1976	1985
27	Printing, publishing & allied industries total	38,950	42,654	82,940
2711	Newspapers	9,684	10,850	20,000
2721	Periodicals	4,179	4,338	6,200
2731	Book Publishing	3,760	4,120	8,430
2732	Book Printing	1,180	1,290	2,360
275-2-4	Commercial Printing	11,450	12,650	27,100
2761	Manifold Business Forms	2,307	2,526	6,000
27-	Other Printing & Publishing	6,350	6,880	12,850

(1)   Estimated by Bureau of Domestic Commerce.
(2)   Compound annual rate of growth.

Exhibit 2 (continued)

Riverfront Press Cash Flow Projection (copied from handwritten spreadsheet)

	MAY	JAN - JUNE	JULY	AUG	SEPT	OCT	NOV	DEC
			Gross Sales - 1980: $137,614					
SALES	38,114	12,000	2,000	12,000	15,000	18,500	20,000	20,000
Accounts Rec. 30		3,435	3,600	600	3,600	4,500	5,500	6,000
Accounts Rec. 60			6,182	6,000	1,000	6,000	7,500	9,250
Accounts Rec. 90		3,000		4,800	2,900	400	2,400	3,000
Misc Income		4,500						
Loans		65,000						
Total income		10,935	74,782	11,408	7,000	10,900	15,400	18,250
FIXED								
Rent		718	718	718	718	718	718	718
BRK Trust/MFFCU		280	280	280	280	280	280	280
/GMAC/Loan		282	282	282	282	282	282	282
Life & Dis. Ins.			200			200		
Property & Auto				282			282	
Medical				280	280	280	280	280
Vehicle Exp. Gas		172	70	172	172	172	172	172
Repairs		60			60			60
Telephone		200	150	200	200	200	200	200
Prof. Dues		24	135	35	35	35	35	35
Partners Salaries		1,548	1,548	1,548	1,720	2,150	2,150	2,150
Payroll - Office		688	320	688	1,989	1,989	2,075	2,075
Payroll - Production		1,032	480	2,408	2,408	2,408	2,408	2,408
Payroll - Taxes		172	80	464	482	655	655	663
SBA Loan A		198	198	198	445	445	445	445
Loan B					1,200	1,200	1,200	1,200
Paper		3,000	500	3,000	3,750	4,625	5,000	5,000
Ink		30		75	100	100	100	100
Supplies (Pres)		420	70	420	526	648	700	700
Subcontracting NEGS		50	50	50	50	50	50	50
Advertising		200	0	275	0	275	0	275
Legal		150	150	150	150	150	150	150
Accting/BKKPNG		540	350	540	623	623	623	623
Office Supplies		150	0	100	100	100	100	100
Postage & Freight		15	75	15	30	30	30	30
Bus Development		80	80	80	80	80	80	80
Purchases:Equipment			25,000	4,700				
Other Expenses			6,000					
Total Disbursements		10,009	36,726	12,260	15,670	19,849	18,015	18,076
Total Cash Flow		926	38,056	-852	-8,679	-8,949	-2,615	174
Beginning Balance		-16,296	-15,370	22,636	21,784	13,105	4,156	1,541
Ending Balance		-15,370	22,636	21,784	13,105	4,156	1,541	1,367

Gross Sales - 1981: $287,620

	JAN	FEB	MAR	APRIL	MAY	JUNE	JULY	AUG	SEPT	OCT	NOV	DEC	TOTALS 1981
	18,760	14,260	18,260	22,260	25,260	30,260	18,260	20,260	25,260	30,260	32,260	32,260	287,620
	6,000	5,628	4,278	5,478	6,678	7,578	9,078	5,478	6,078	7,578	9,078	9,678	
	10,000	10,000	9,380	7,130	9,130	11,130	12,630	15,130	9,130	10,130	12,630	15,130	
	3,700	4,000	4,000	5,628	4,278	5,479	4,452	5,052	6,052	5,479	4,052	5,053	
	19,700	19,628	21,936	18,236	20,086	24,170	26,160	25,660	21,260	23,187	25,760	29,860	275,643
	893	893	893	893	893	893	893	893	893	893	893	893	10,716
	280	280	280	280	280	280	280	280	280	280	280	280	3,360
	282	282	282	282	282	282	282	282	282	282	282	282	3,384
	200			200			200						
		282			282			282			282		1,128
	280	315	315	350	350	350	350	350	350	350	350	350	4,060
	172	172	172	172	172	172	172	172	172	172	172	172	2,064
			60			60			60			60	240
	200	200	200	200	200	200	200	200	200	200	200	200	2,400
	35	35	35	35	35	35	35	35	35	35	35	35	420
	2,580	2,580	2,580	2,580	2,580	2,580	2,580	3,010	3,010	3,010	3,010	3,010	33,110
	2,075	2,075	2,075	2,075	2,548	2,548	2,548	2,548	2,548	2,548	2,591	2,591	28,770
	2,408	2,537	2,537	2,537	2,537	2,537	2,537	2,623	2,623	2,623	2,623	2,623	30,745
	706	719	719	719	766	766	766	818	818	818	822	822	9,259
	445	445	445	445	445	445	445	445	445	445	445	445	5,340
	1,200	1,200	1,200	1,200	1,200	1,200	1,200	1,200	1,200	1,200	1,200	1,200	14,400
	4,690	3,565	4,565	5,565	6,315	7,565	4,565	5,065	6,315	7,565	8,065	8,065	71,905
	187	142	182	222	252	302	182	202	252	302	322	322	2,869
	656	490	639	779	884	1,059	639	709	884	1,059	1,129	1,129	10,056
	50	50	50	50	50	50	50	50	50	50	50	50	600
	0	275	0	275	0	275	0	275	0	275	0	275	1,650
	150	150	150	150	150	150	150	150	150	150	150	150	1,800
	623	623	623	623	623	623	623	623	623	623	623	623	7,476
	100	100	100	100	100	100	100	100	100	100	100	100	1,200
	30	30	30	30	30	30	30	30	30	30	30	30	360
	80	80	80	80	80	80	80	80	80	80	80	80	960
	18,922	17,539	18,212	19,812	21,054	22,582	18,907	20,422	21,370	23,290	22,744	23,787	248,272
	1,278	2,089	3,724	-1,576	-968	1,588	7,253	5,238	-110	-103	3,016	6,073	27,371
	1,367	2,645	4,734	8,458	6,882	5,914	7,502	14,755	19,993	19,883	19,780	22,798	
	2,645	4,734	8,458	6,882	5,914	7,502	14,755	19,993	19,883	19,780	22,798	28,781	

Exhibit 2 (concluded)

NOTES TO CASH FLOW PROJECTION

SALES: 1980   Gross - $137,614
This is based on current sales efforts of J. Goldman/existing house accounts.
    1981   Gross - $287,620
Based on a 5 percent increase in current commercial accounts, pursuit of
    government contracts, and the addition of new sales generated by a sales
    intern taken on in October, 1980. (Goal, increase in new accounts of
    $150,000.)

ACCOUNTS RECEIVABLE:
    20 percent in 30 days
    60 percent in 60 days
    20 percent in 90 days

DISBURSEMENTS:
Rent: 3550 sq. ft./ 5 year lease with option $718/mo. through December, 1980,
    then $893/mo. (At present we sublet space which we may need in 1981.)
    Heat and electricity are included in the rent.

Notes Payable: All current notes/see schedule
    Brookline Trust - press lease
    MFFCU - 5 year note
    Shawmut/GMAC - Auto Loans

Insurance: Life and Disability coverage for two partners, limits $50,000 each.
    Medical Insurance - to cover all employees

Partners Drawings:
    1980 - $12,814
    1981 - $33,110

Payroll:
    Office - 1 @ $4 (to $4.50)/40 hr. wk.
    Feb. 1981 add 1 @ $3.50/ 20 hr. wk.
    Oct. 1980 add 1 FT Sales @ $12,000.
    Pressroom - 1 @ $6 (to $ 6.50)/40 hr. wk.
    Aug. 1980 - add 1 @ $8 (to $8.50)/ 40 hr. wk.

Payroll Taxes: 10 percent of drawings and payroll
Paper: Computed at 25 percent of sales.
Ink/Suppliers: 4 percent of sales
Legal: Retainer of $1800
Accounting/Bookkeeping: Retainer of $2400 Bookkeeper @$5.5/ 15 - 20 hr. wk.

Michael Shane

The first time you try to start a business is the easiest. Everyone expects you to fail. It's the second or third time around that can shake your confidence. People expect you to do better than the time before; and if you don't, they think that something is wrong. Not only that—you're going into another unknown area, just when you've gotten comfortable with what you've been working on so hard before.

Michael Shane, was reflecting on his "third time around" for starting a business. His latest idea for a venture was to get involved with the growing computer industry—perhaps as a distributor for retail computer stores. Two months earlier, in December of 1979, he had assembled a core of five people to find out if a "super distributor" was needed. In addition to himself, Michael's brother, Tom Shane, and sister, Sandy Fromm, were helping in planning and learning about the industry through calls to computer stores and going through trade magazines. His administrative assistant, Elaine Cresto, had worked for Michael in his previous business for the past five years and agreed to help with this possible venture. To survey stores, Michael had just hired Dick Sanders, the only one of the five who would admit to knowing "a little bit about computers."

Now, in February of 1980, the five were working out of Michael's recently purchased condominium in suburban Boston. Each had a telephone line for making calls to stores and manufacturers throughout the United States to learn about trends and needs in the industry. Michael explained

that if there was need for a "super distributor," their next step would be to develop a strategy for the venture. If not, perhaps they might be able to discover through market inquiry another niche relating to computers that would afford them a business opportunity. The trick, Michael emphasized, would be to interpret the information they got correctly. Otherwise, the past months of preparation and nearly $20,000 already invested in the unnamed venture could turn out to be a complete loss.

Wig Flair

Michael Shane was 17 years old in 1967 when he started his first business. Using $235 in savings he began selling wigs, which he bought from New York wholesalers for $35 and sold for $35 out of the trunk of his car. His mother had owned several beauty salons and most of the wigs she carried cost from $38 up. He reasoned that by starting at a low price and building volume he would be able to buy in larger quantities at lower costs to net a profit. Emphasis on service and fast delivery paid off. Soon his cost dropped to $30 per wig, then dropped further as his sales rose to $100,000 per month by the end of the first year.

He rented 2,500 square feet of warehouse space in Canton, Massachusetts, and quit Babson College as a sophomore to become a wig distributor. He chose the name "Wig Flair" for the business and began selling to retail stores. With profits he began to buy larger volumes and varieties of wigs and go to more exclusive boutiques and retail chains. Timing decisions, he said, came from an intuitive sense, based on casual observation of fashion trends, that the market was ripe for wider distribution of wigs. Enlisting his younger brother, Tom, to help in the stock room after school, Michael developed contacts for buying wigs directly from a Hong Kong-based manufacturer instead of going through New York suppliers.

To support further growth he took in as 50-percent partner a customer who ran a wig salon at night and worked as a meat salesman during the day. By 1969, their joint company had developed a nationwide network of sales representatives who called on beauty supply houses. It also employed a telephone sales force, which sold to wig wholesalers. All Wig Flair sales were C.O.D. Volume continued growing, and in 1970 Wig Flair bought its own Hong Kong manufacturing plant.

Later that year, with sales at $12 million, the two sold out for 150,000 shares of U.S. Industries, then traded on the NYSE at $12 per share. They also received employment contracts of $60,000 per year each, plus dividends of $100,000 per year each. In addition, they received incentive options, which could earn them up to another $5.5 million over the next five years, if performance met projections. The projections were, in fact not met, as the market for wigs declined in profitability. But Michael was able to sell his U.S. Industries shares at $27.

His partner stayed on, but Michael left Wig Flair a year after selling out. He explained.

> It wasn't like we were building toward anything, and I hated it. I realized that my partner was only interested in the money. I was interested in money, but also in creating something. Just sitting there and drawing money on my five-year employment contract and not making waves was of no interest to me.

> When I left the company, I didn't know what I was going to do. I was 21 years old and I had good instincts and some money. I wanted to be independent. I figured I'd dabble in some things for a while.

Michael started investing, mostly in real estate. One deal his accountant introduced him to was a retail blue jeans business needing capital. He invested $25,000 in what became a five-store operation. He also arranged with the Wig Flair plant in Hong Kong to make jeans with its spare sewing capacity. The first $300,000 order, however, was patterned on Hong Kong styles unacceptable to Americans. Michael wrote off his investment and gave his interest to a store manager.

Faded Glory

Subsequently, however, the manager had a dispute with his partner that threatened to break up the jeans business. The Hong Kong plant manager called Michael in a panic to say that he was going to lose the jeans business. Michael had been thinking that there was still opportunity in jeans. His brother, Tom, commented on Michael's vision:

> He told me in 1973 that he thought the next thing in fashion would be blue jeans that went beyond the traditional concept of dungarees. He turned out to be right.

Michael purchased $10,000 in denim, and set up the factory to begin production of private label fashion jeans. His own vision of the situation was as follows:

> In those days, there was no fashion denim like we know fashion denim today. Hard blue denim, like Levi's, that's all there was. They weren't even washing them out. But you had to be stupid

not to see everybody bleeding their blue jeans out in the bathtub. So we took them, washed them out, and put studs on them or dragons or pansies, or whatever, and that was fashion. We were fashion, and the first year we had $12 million in sales.

This new business, Faded Glory, was a family affair. Michael allowed some of his brothers and sisters to obtain ownership on favorable terms, but retained voting control himself. His brother, Jim, managed internal administration, while Michael took care of marketing and other "outside" functions. Tom continued to work in the back room, filling orders and taking inventory in his spare time from undergraduate work at Boston University. Sandy joined the two in early 1974 to set up a sales force and telephone system to keep in touch with retail customers. She recalled:

My job was to build a sales group that would rely on telephones as the main way to get orders and service accounts. I started by myself, sitting with one phone in a big empty room. Five years later, there were over 40 people working the phones and a field sales force of 100, calling on thousands of stores we had as customers.

Although Faded Glory had a head start in fashion jeans, competitors quickly appeared, not only with other designs but also aggressive prices and service. Telephone salespeople called individual stores periodically to inform retailers of lines and promotions available. The calls also obtained information about retailer problems, such as late delivery, with suppliers' services.

In addition, a field sales force called on stores to get orders. Eventually, phone salespeople collaborated to coordinate for better service. For very large accounts, a VIP "hot line" was set up to provide still better service. Mass mailings were also used to provide stores with posters, product announcements and promotional literature.

Tom Shane continued his description of how Faded Glory developed and grew:

Initially, we were selling to specialty retail stores—boutiques—which were relatively small. I was responsible for seeing that the orders were filled, and Jim made sure that the volume of the jeans we needed came from overseas at the right times. In the early days, you would get the requisition from the salesperson, grab a basket, and walk around the back room filling the order. We added data processing capabilities as our sales increased, and we finally had to move out of our original warehouse to larger facilities.

Faded Glory's distribution system provided retail stores with much better service than they had previously received. We had a competitive edge because we could make large volume purchases, promise shipments to be ready at the start of the five or six fashion seasons each year, and maintain service credibility with individual stores.

Refining Distribution Capabilities

While Wig Flair relied on relatively few accounts, keying on large retail department stores for sales, Tom recalled that Faded Glory had developed a more extensive distribution system:

In the case of Faded Glory, we were selling to specialty retail stores, which were relatively small. I was responsible for seeing that the orders were filled and the volumes of the jeans we needed came at the right times. At first, it was pretty simple. You would get the requisition from the salesperson, grab a basket, and walk around the back room filling the order. As our sales increased, we added data processing capabilities and finally had to move from the Canton warehouse to larger facilities.

In the company phone bank, Sandy had directed employees who called stores periodically to inform retailers of the different lines of jeans currently carried and any special promotions being conducted, and to learn of any problems stores might have in terms of delivery or other parts of the relationship. A field sales force also called on stores to obtain initial orders and solicit reorders. Sandy recalled that over time they merged the two functions so that the person on the phone handled both sales and service of a particular account:

We divided the workload by geographic region so a person might be handling all the stores in North and South Carolina, for instance. The field sales force still recruited new accounts and helped with promotion and displays. As for any national chains, they typically bought from one central area, such as New York, so the person who had New York would handle that particular chain.

Sandy added that much of a typical phone salesperson's time was spent on responding to incoming calls and taking orders for a particular design of jean. A "VIP hot line" was set up to provide quick service to the company's largest customers. Mass mailings provided stores with posters, product announcements on accessory outerwear, and other promotional literature. These efforts, according to Tom, provided retail stores much better distributor service than they had previously received. Making large-volume purchases, having shipments ready at the start of each of the five or six fashion seasons per year, and maintaining service contact with indi-

vidual stores was a competitive edge he cited as central to the firm's success. He commented:

A lot of things we did were strictly by seat of the pants. But it didn't take long to find out which jeans were the dogs and which ones were the stars. You simply tried to order less dogs and more stars and make sure that the retail outlet got the kind of attention that you knew you would like to have if you were in their shoes.

Faded Glory's sales grew to $40 million in its second year, as it focused on the high-end fashion business. Pretax profit was about $6 million. Gross margin reached 45 percent and Michael guessed it might reach 60 percent. Instead, however, it started dropping, down to 32 percent as sales reached $50 million. The company booked $175 million in orders its third year, but delivered only $55 million because the Hong Kong supplier refused to expand capacity.

Michael went looking for suppliers elsewhere and soon took over a Nicaraguan plant that had been foreclosed by its bank. Progress there, however, was shortly terminated by a revolution. One of the plant managers was shot. The factory was closed and a $700,000 write-off was taken by Faded Glory.

The search for yet another supplier in Guatemala was interrupted by a disagreement between Michael and Jim over how Jim managed. The company now had 600 employees, including eight of Michael's relatives. In 1978, Michael asked to be bought out. He recalled:

I wasn't interested in keeping the company at the $50 million level. Also, I was getting up every morning and saying, "There's got to be more to life than the garment business and making money." I wanted to do other things. I *was a little interested in politics among other things, so in early 1979, I sold out to my partner and my brother.*

His brother, Jim, and sister remained with Faded Glory, as did his administrative assistant, Elaine. Tom had graduated from Boston University in 1977 and was now entering his second year of law school at Suffolk University.

Considering a Computer Venture

Michael spent the end of 1978 and first half of 1979 working with one of the major political parties in its Washington, D.C. office. He developed a friendship with the director of an East Coast educational institute and recalled that whenever he visited or traveled with this friend, the man would be carrying around a portable computer. He showed Michael how the machine worked and the capabilities microcomputers have for problem solving. Michael said his friend's fascination with computers further piqued his own interest in the machines. A subsequent trade show he attended inspired him to serious discussions with his brother about the prospect of entering the computer industry. He observed:

I was attending a blue jeans trade show at the Coliseum in New York. Half of the floor was being used for jeans while the other half had a trade show for personal computers going on. I wandered over and started talking with some of the sales manufacturers representatives and manufacturers and found out that they regarded themselves as the kingpins of the future. I realized that computers could be a good bet if I started another business.

I met with several guys who owned retail stores. I was willing to match the capital they had in the business for a 50 percent interest, but I was perfectly

happy to let them run it. I'd have been delighted to have been a passive investor, just talking to them once a week or so, and offering them my expertise where it was needed. What I was looking for was someone I saw eye-to-eye with in business philosophy and who had the ability to run a big company. But I never found the situation I was looking for.

Elaine Cresto had joined Faded Glory in 1974 as a result of seeking part-time work through an employment agency, which in turn, referred her as a two-week replacement for a secretary on vacation. She recalled fearing that if she insisted upon a permanent part-time referral, the employment agency might never call her back. But now, six years later, she was still working for Michael. Her duties gradually increased, as she kept telling Michael, "I don't have enough work to do." One aspect of her work, she remembered, was occasionally clipping an article on computers from a magazine at Michael's request, and filing it for future reference. She said the articles ranged from impacts computers were expected to have on society to information about major manufacturers and their product lines. When Michael asked her to help think about a new venture that would be involved with the computer industry, Elaine said it came as no surprise to her.

By autumn of 1979, Michael, Tom and Sandy were contemplating ways to begin dealing in small computers and peripheral equipment. Their consensus was to explore whatever gaps might exist in distribution channels between manufacturers and retailers. Michael stated that start-up capital would be provided from his personal savings and that the apartment complex where he lived could serve as an office initially. It had recently been converted to condominiums and he decided to make a down payment on both his unit and the one immediately above it.

Michael requested another three phone lines for the condo, in addition to the two already present, and ordered subscriptions to magazines carrying computer advertisements and information. Sandy and Elaine scanned the magazines to find names of computer stores and products that they most often sold, as well as information about their typical customers. Tom spent much of his time talking with the stores by telephone, calling manufacturers to inquire about their products, and discussing overall strategy with Michael.

The common advice to get a good lawyer and accountant to start a business was true, Michael said. "But first and foremost," he emphasized, "you need a good market researcher." He placed an advertisement in the *Boston Globe* in late November for someone to conduct studies for the prospective venture. Elaine screened the respondents by phone, commenting that she was looking for persons who had experience in the computer industry and who seemed to come across well over the phone. One person whom she advised Michael to interview was Dick Sanders, who recalled his reaction when he first read the ad and later met Michael:

I told myself this must be a waste of time; it was a real small ad. On the other hand, I was out of work because the company I was with had just gone bankrupt. My job prospects were pretty dim except for a major local mainframe manufacturer, and I had the feeling that I would just get lost in their type of environment. So I went in to interview and was immediately impressed to find out that Michael had an entrepreneurial spirit. I quit interviewing elsewhere and was hired in three days. Most managers look for the big, glossy position announcements and tend to value a job by the size of ad in the classified section. I'm glad that this time I didn't.

Dick had spent most of his professional career with a Boston-based market research firm which specialized in the computer industry. In his words: "I've been doing market surveys all my life." He said his task now was to design a survey to send computer stores that would determine:

1. Whether need for a distributor existed.

2. How such a venture should be set up.

3. What type of services should be provided to both manufacturers and retailers.

4. How to position the business to take advantage of growth trends and set it apart from other competitors.

He explained that the "hunch" they were all basing the venture on presumed that computer retailers were not getting good service, nor low enough prices to encourage wider sales of microcomputers and related peripheral equipment. At the other end, he said, manufacturers were burdened with selling small lot quantities to individual stores. This required maintaining nationwide sales forces and inventory systems, which drained manufacturer's resources away from their primary strengths in product development.

By December, the five had each "mapped out" their own work responsibilities to learn more about the computer industry and plan the venture. Dick was focused on putting together his mail survey. Michael was calling on manufacturers to learn about products and discuss terms that could be established for a distributor relationship. Elaine was still compiling information on manufacturers and distributors by going through magazines and reading about them. She also reviewed advertisements sent in by a hired clipping service. The service had been instructed to send any ads by computer stores that appeared in major newspapers around the country. Dick said they soon found that the information was of little value to them:

> *You get charged 50 cents an article and they started pulling every Radio Shack ad in the country. Needless to say, we didn't rely on them too much after that. We've ended up doing most of the clipping ourselves.*

Sandy and Tom were responsible for planning operations of the potential venture. Tom said he expected inventory control and shipping to require methods similar to those used in the jeans business. Sandy added that they would likely use a phone bank as a sales and service link with retail stores:

> *I've found out that when you set up a telephone system like we used with Faded Glory, you don't need a telephone for every person. If you have nine outgoing lines for every 12 or 15 people, that should be enough. Part of their time is spent recording information on each store in a loose leaf notebook, which all of the sales people use. They also might be reviewing literature on a particular product that we're trying to sell. The question of whether you can get by with nine lines or 12 is based to a large degree on how many incoming phone calls you expect to receive.*

She explained that the Faded Glory sales force had attempted to call each retail store at least once every two weeks. This allowed each retailer to keep abreast of any promotional activities and also stay in touch with the distributor. It was, she said, a means of showing that service was being stressed.

Besides dealing with likely operational issues, both Tom and Sandy were also contacting computer stores by phone and through personal visits to outlets in the New England area. Tom estimated that everyone was averaging at least 50 hours per week on the potential venture, and Sandy guessed she was putting in up to 80 hours a week if her week-end visits to computer stores were included. Having a telephone for each person was a logical step in Tom's view:

> *I probably spend 40 percent of my time on the phone. Michael's probably on the phone 70 percent of the time. Sandy's on the phone about 30 percent and Elaine 20 percent—the phones are not going unused.*

Often, Dick said, the owners appeared to be people who were simply opportunistic and/or interested in computers but had little, if any, business knowledge or financing capacity. The flow of newcomers into this industry was pointed up, he noted, by a recent *Datamation* article, which predicted that, by 1983, there would be over 2,000 computer stores in the United States.

Working on a Market Survey

Dick said he usually followed a number of rules when putting together a market survey. First, the mailing list should include precisely those people or firms whom the survey was trying to reach. Second, the questions should be written out. Then they should be reviewed by several people to make sure that they wouldn't be misinterpreted by respondents. "Finally, and probably most important," Dick added, "is to ask yourself, just what is it that you want to find out."

He said that reviewing the questions for clarity wasn't much of a problem, since he had been doing surveys for so long. He recalled that a questionnaire typically took him about two hours to write and proof. Dick related his methods in composing a survey:

You want to stay away from essay-type answers; have questions they can check answers to. You want to keep the appearance light. Otherwise, they'll look at it and say, "I'm not going to take the time to finish this." Make sure that they receive a copy of the results and assure them that the survey won't be published without their permission. And finally, offer a little reward up front—it doubles the response rate. On our last survey we estimated that by offering a drawing for a camera we roughly doubled our response rate.

The four prepared their own lists of retail computer stores from names out of magazines. The only other alternative, Dick said, was to purchase a list from one of the subscription houses or magazine publishers.

Current Distribution Patterns of the Microcomputer Industry

While considered an "infant" when compared to established industries such as autos, steel and chemicals, data processing equipment was widely hailed in media articles as "the greatest growth and glamour industry since World War II." Technological advances had made it possible for computing power to be packaged in ever smaller equipment that was easier to use in a variety of applications and by people with little, if any, technical background in electronics or computer science.

Current terminology divided computer products into three major classifications: mainframes, minicomputers, and microcomputers. Each was designed to address a particular customer application and evolved as advances were made in data storage.

Mainframes came from the industry giants such as IBM, Control Data, Honeywell, and Cray Research. The machines were designed for very complex and exacting scientific and analytical needs and could cost well over a million dollars, including software and peripheral equipment. Distribution in this segment was by one of two routes: the manufacturer sold directly to the end user, thus using a strategy called OEM (original equipment manufacturer), or sold to an intermediary systems house. The systems house would then add peripheral equipment made by other manufacturers and custom design software for more specific applications. The final product was then sold as a "turnkey" package, where the buyer would simply have to turn on switches and the system would be operational.

Minicomputers were generally less expensive units with substantial computing power, memory and speed, although less than that of mainframes. Recent products called "super minis" had somewhat blurred the distinction between minis and mainframes. Distribution channels for minis were similar to mainframes, with salespersons typically making four or five calls to a prospect before a purchase was made. Principal manufacturers included Hewlett-Packard, Digital Equipment, Data General, Prime computer and Tandem. Customers were considered to be medium and large businesses or government agencies, with lengthy lease or purchase periods and service agreements with the manufacturer or the systems house.

Microcomputers represented a radical departure from other computer products in several respects. Microprocessor chips as a form of central processing unit or "brain" for the computer instead of massive cabinets full of electronic circuits and magnetic tape drives had been in existence only since the mid-1970s. These chips made microcomputers unique in size. For the first time, computers could be small enough to be placed on top of a desk. Previously, computers had to be housed in special rooms with temperature and humidity controls. Now, not only did they not need such rooms, but they also cost tens of thousands of dollars less, under $10,000 for the first time. Programming also became vastly simpler and for the first time software was becoming standardized, as well as much cheaper, easier to use and widely available.

Users for the first time included small businesses, home hobbyists who would use the machines for recreation or developing applications for personal use, schools, and larger businesses. An increasing number of companies had started manufacturing peripheral equipment specifically for microcomputers, including printers, memory storage units, special-purpose plug-in circuit boards and plotters. The largest manufacturers were Apple Computer, Tandy's Radio Shack division and Commodore. An assortment of companies followed, from IBM to small ventures, some of which had already failed, including two of the earliest, MITS and IMSAI. It was widely expected that there would be many more entries and many more failures among the makers of microcomputers before the industry stabilized.

Since the value added per unit with microcomputers was much less than that for minis and mainframes, the use of direct sales people calling on individual accounts didn't make economic sense. Apple, for example, had used mail order as a strategy to build sales and gain a leadership position in the industry but was currently selling mainly through regional distributors to retail computer stores. Distributors were mostly regional, serving at most two or three states.

Radio Shack added its TRS-80 microcomputer to its existing line of stereo equipment and sold the machine in the retail outlets it had developed throughout the United States and overseas. Other manufacturers used a combination of mail order and retail sales through locations

such as the estimated 700-1,000 computer stores in the U.S. For mini and mainframe builders, as well as peripheral equipment manufacturers, the addition of a microcomputer to their product line could be touted to existing customer accounts as an added product from their sales forces.

The fact was, Michael pointed out, that no clear distribution pattern yet existed for microcomputers. He said the trend toward selling microcomputers in retail computer stores appeared to be the most likely avenue to persist. Whether the stores would remain largely independent, be comprised of chains such as Radio Shack or Computerland, or be a retail outlet of a computer manufacturer, such as Digital Equipment's computer stores, he hoped he could devine from the market survey.

Sandy commented that the inquiries they had made to date had already provided some clues as to what they could expect from Dick's more formal survey:

> *We've found that the retail outlets are used to waiting five or six weeks for delivery on an order and when it comes, the manufacturer often requires them to pay C.O.D. In part, the payment terms are due to the fact that most of the retail stores are fairly new. Another factor is that these store owners come from a technical background, and they have no concept of what retailing is all about. So they often fail. If you look at a list more than six months old, many of the store numbers have been disconnected, and people have gone out of business. About one out of every six stores we tried to contact had gone out of business in the last six months. But for every one that closed, two more are opening up. At that rate, we figure there will be about 1,500 independents by the end of 1982.*

She added that the people running the retail stores were much more willing than the jeans store operators to talk on the phone about their products. They gave their thoughts on where the industry was headed, even though she gave them only her name and simply said she was interested in learning more about computers. In many ways she thought retail personal computer stores were similar to stereo outlets in the 1960s, when hobbyists were the major "promoters." The general public was just becoming aware of the products offered and what the terminology meant in terms of performance or application.

Michael continued his commentary concerning difficulties that computer retail stores seemed to be up against:

Retailers aren't getting the newest products as fast as they want, nor can they reorder quickly. The underlying issue here is that entrepreneurs in any new business always have limited capital. To compete in the long run with the big manufacturer's stores like Radio Shack and Xerox, the independent computer retailer needs fast delivery of the best products available. This way he ties up and risks less capital. There is need for someone who will do the market research and take the risk of stocking new products, so stores can concentrate on what they do best, which is making sales. What is needed is, in a sense, a buying service.

A Printer Possibility

Michael had sent requests for product information to every manufacturer in the microcomputer business he could locate. The response of one company, LRC, was to send a salesman to call on him. Michael recalled:

The LRC salesman said his company is coming out with this new 40-column printer and they want us to carry it. He had no sales figures because there are no

40-column printers on the market, as yet. Everyone is selling 80-column printers, but the salesman said it is logical that hobbyists using a small computer will want a small printer. His argument makes sense to me.

When we asked about terms, he said if we take 55 printers COD, LRC would give us a $5,000 credit limit. We figure the gross margin would be about 14 percent. We don't like the terms, but I know we're not in a good negotiating position. Here he is calling on us in our condominium where we have nothing at all to show him.

Other Start-up Issues

As Dick faced the task of designing a survey, the other four were concerned about other issues. Education about the products and the industry was a must, according to Michael, since none of them had a technical background in computers or electronics. Dick was acquainted with computers from the perspective of following the industry and market trends, although he admitted that he still had trouble trying to figure out how to simply turn on a machine:

We'll have manufacturers come in to talk about their product and they'll start in on some heavy technical presentation. They don't realize that Michael and I are thinking about goats when they're talking about ROMS and RAMS. So, we've got some catching up to do in learning about the jargon and products.

If the venture were attempted, Michael thought they should try to develop a sales force dedicated to maintaining close contact with the stores and keeping up with product developments. Sandy pointed out that this might be hard, since experienced technical sales people were in short supply and were prone to switching companies for higher salaries or improved benefits. "Company loyalty doesn't seem to extend very far down the ladder in the computer industry," she lamented.

Dick remarked that people they had talked to with computer experience "want the moon for a salary." The five were hoping to start people at $12,000 per year and increase the amount as they developed experience. With Faded Glory, the sales staff had worked on a straight salary basis. Whether any commission incentive should be included in this venture idea wasn't yet known. Dick added that they would probably settle for people who simply had general sales experience, figuring that someone who had sold Tupperware was better than someone with no sales experience at all.

Another concern was finding a more suitable office and warehouse facility to work from. The Canton Massachusetts warehouse, which had been used in previous businesses, was currently under lease. The tenant indicated he might vacate it when the lease expired in April, but Tom and Sandy continued to spend part of their time searching for other space in the Boston area.

Another question was what their initial product line should include. Michael suggested distributing first some relatively non-technical product with potential for high volume to offset the low margins he expected they would be able to command. He wanted 20- or 30-percent-margin product lines but believed that realistically, they would have to settle for 10 to 15 percent to attract manufacturers to an unknown business like theirs.

One possible initial product to distribute would be floppy disks and diskettes. A manufacturer they had investigated seemed to have a good reputation for such products, yet held a mere 3 percent market share in sales. Michael and Dick reasoned that if they told the manufacturer they could boost market share to over 10 percent, they might be able to get advantageous distribution rights. Their strategy would then be to build on that success by adding microcomputer peripherals to their line. Another emphasis, they stated, would be to concentrate on products compatible with the leading computers such as those of Apple, Radio Shack, and Commodore—which together currently comprised 60 percent of the total installed base of personal computers.

Industry standards for negotiating margins followed the assumptions that retail stores required 30 percent off list price for every item sold. Michael and Dick estimated they would need between 20 and 30 percent to act as a full service distributor, even though some distributors in the industry were taking as little as 6 percent on products. Dick pointed out that these companies simply purchased products from manufacturers and resold them to retailers with no attempt to provide service or assistance beyond product delivery.

The two figured they could attempt to purchase from manufacturers at 50 percent off the suggested retail price. They would keep 40 percent of the discount and pass the remaining 60 percent along to the retailers. To be successful, manufacturers would have to agree to forego 10 to 20 percent of the list price which they were now keeping for themselves.

Another element of strategy Michael believed would be extremely important was advertising. He commented that since the venture would be starting from scratch, a disproportionate amount would be needed for promotion. He said that they would probably spend 10 percent of annual sales on advertising for the first year or two until the venture became recognized as a leading distributor of computer products.

Dick said conversations with retailers and manufacturers indicated that a gap did exist in terms of distribution. Most of the retail emphasis was being put on carrying only the leading printer, CRT, or other peripherals for each particular product line. One result was that periodic price cutting, rather than product variety, was the major competitive tactic being used, and lesser known manufacturers were having difficulty selling their products. Another result was that retailers became dependent on a small number of suppliers. At the mercy of those suppliers, the retailers found that fast delivery was the exception. Maintenance and repairs often required shipping machines back to a manufacturers and could take weeks to accomplish. Shortages of user-oriented software impeded selling new microcomputer systems to the general public.

Possible Implications of a Formal Market Survey

As March 1980 approached, Dick considered it important to find out what a formal survey could tell him about market potential for the prospective venture. He, Michael and Tom believed that, if they decided to move ahead, conclusions from the survey should form the basis for structuring the venture. If the type of service, markets, pricing and related issues were handled appropriately, the business could succeed. If not, Michael's third attempt in starting a business might result in failure.

Dick reviewed a number of questions that he hoped the survey results would help answer:

We want to find out what the stores

think of the manufacturers and their products. Which ones are the best? Worst? Where are the retailers getting their sales people? How are they hiring them? Who are the stores selling products to? What needs could a distributor fulfill?

We want to know what kind of money it takes to start a store. Who are the store's competitors? What about problems with software and maintenance? How much do they spend on advertising? Should they put out a catalog featuring the store's product line? Does the store use mail order?

What does the future hold for retail computer stores? Where would they invest capital if they had more of it to spend: inventory or another store? What are their sales revenues? What about in three years?

The answers to these questions will tell us if there is a place for us as a distributor. And it will tell us how to structure our business, in terms of what products to go after and what services to offer. Also, we'll be able to develop some expectations about growth and competition down the road.

At the same time, we can't forget the importance of getting our name out to people in the business. That's very important. Right now, we have manufacturers come to the condominium with their product, they look at the five of us, look around the room in disbelief, and say, "Hey! What's going on here? You call yourself a business?"

Michael Shane (B)

Market Research Responses

As described in the case on Michael Shane, he decided to conduct a market survey to help him decide whether to establish a new wholesaling company in the microcomputer industry and, if so, what form it should take. Dick Sanders, who had professional experience in market research, was hired to design and conduct the survey. He prepared a questionnaire and mailing list with the help of Michael and his associates.

One day was spent getting the mailing out. Within a week, results began coming in the mail, and a week after that Dick started tallying answers on large sheets of paper. By the end of January, 45 stores had responded. A number of other replies were received but discarded. Some were discarded because their answers indicated that those respondents had not understood the questions. Also discarded were answers that came not from retail stores but rather from systems houses. These were vendors which packaged software and hardware for end users and sold microcomputer products as custom-designed turnkey systems.

Another 80 questionnaires were returned as undeliverable. Dick commented that these returns did not bother him. He said it simply indicated that one of every six stores had gone out of business in the last six months, reflecting the recent emergence of the computer store as a retail growth phenomenon. To offset the loss, Dick speculated that two stores were popping up for every one that closed. His assessment was supported, he said, by a recent *Datamation* article which predicted that by 1983 there would be over 2,000 computer stores in the United States.

Exhibit 1 is a summary of the survey results Dick prepared. The task now, he said, was to figure out just what the implications of these results were for design of Mike Shane's business.

Exhibit 1   Dick Sanders' Summary of Survey Results

I.   Store Demographics

A.   The following table analyzes the demographics of the responding stores.

Table 1
Demographics

Average number of stores per business	1.3*
Range of number of stores per business	1 to 6*
Average length of time in business	24.2 months
Ranges of length of time in business	3 to 48 months

Types of locations (% of responding stores)

Small Mall	42%
On a Main Street Location	19
Downtown Business Area	13
Industrial Park	10
Office Building	8
Shopping Center	6
At a University	2
Total	100%

* One return was not used in the averages in that they answered for the whole Computerland chain (107 stores), and this would have distorted the independent stores' figures.

Exhibit 1 (continued)

II.   Sales Ratings of Personal Computer Manufacturers

Table 2

Percent of the Responding Stores Mentioning

Manufacturer	Carry the Mfr.	Mfrs. Being in their top 4 in Sales	Mfrs. Being their Top Seller	Mfrs. Being in their Top 4 in Sales	Mfrs. Being their Top Seller
Apple	67%	67%	38%	67%	23%
North Star	31	27	8	13	4
Commodore	29	25	8	18	11
Cromemco	25	21	8	11	9
T.I.	23	17	0	29	11
Ohio Scientific	21	19	8	18	4
Alpha Micro	17	17	4	16	4
Atari	17	13	0	24	0
Vector Graphics	15	13	10	11	11
Exidy	15	13	0	2	0
Dynabyte	10	8	0	2	0
Pertec	8	8	4	11	2
Compucolor	8	6	0	4	0
NEC	8	8	0	11	4
Altos	8	4	0	2	0
SWTPC	6	4	2	4	0
DEC	4	2	0	2	0
IMSAI	4	2	0	0	0
Tandy	4	0	0	0	0
Heath	4	0	0	2	0
Many (20 companies)*	2	0	0	-	-
Data General	-	-	-	4	2
H-P	-	-	-	7	0
Many (13 companies)**	-	-	-	2	-

* Others Receiving One Mention: MSI, Western Digital, Polymorphic, Digital Micro, Micromation, Computex, SD Systems, Zilog, Industrial Microsystems, Micro V, Percom, Hazeltine, Interec, Ithaca, Thinker, Elf, RCA, Interact, and Rexou.

** Others Receiving One Mention: MSI, FUSI, AMD, ISC, Micromation, Zilog, Ind. Micro., Prime, Polymorphic, Digital Micro, TEI, Rexou, and Micro V.

Exhibit 1 (continued)

III.   Salespeople

The following tables describe what a store looks for in potential salespeople and also whether they have a formal or informal training program once hired.

Table 3
Desired Characteristics of
Potential Salespeople

Desired Characteristics	% of Responding Stores Mentioning
Sales Experience	52%
General Sales Experience	43%
Computer Sales Experience	6
Retail Sales Experience	3
Technical/Computer Knowledge or background	46
Motivated/Hungry People	14
Good Personality	11
Ability to Analyze Customer Needs	9
College Degree	9
Programming Experience	9
Business Knowledge	9
Ability to Communicate	6
Honesty	6
Others*	3

*   Others were: Appearance, Female, Non-Computer Experience, Young, Intelligent, and Anything Noteworthy.

Exhibit 1 (continued)

Table 3A
Type of Training Programs

	% of Responding Stores
Formal	32%
Informal Floor Training	68%
Total	100%

IV. Sales by Product Category

Table 4
Percent Each Category Represents

The following table analyzes the percent of total sales each product category represents for the responding stores.

Product Categories	Average % for All Responding Stores	Percent of Stores Offering	Percent Breakdown Encountered the Most
CPU	37%	80%*	60%*
Peripherals	20	88 *	20
Software	11	88	10
Books	5	71	10
Turnkey Systems	27	58	0
Total	100%		100%

* The stores not offering CPUs and peripherals were stores offering only turnkey systems.

Exhibit 1 (continued)

V.   Sales By Market Sector

The following table describes stores' sales according to the market sector they are being made in, both now and projected for 1983.

Table 5
Sales By Market Sectors
Now vs. 1983

| Market Sectors | Now | | | 1983 | | |
	Average % For All Responding Stores	Ranges For All Responding Stores	Breakdown Most Encountered	Average % For All Responding Stores	Ranges For All Responding Stores	Breakdown Most Encountered
Small Businesses	53%	0-100%	60%	58%	0-100%	80%
Home/Hobbyist	23	0-75%	20	18	0-85%	20
Educational	14	0-60%	10	14	0-32%	0
Scientific	6	0-50%	10	6	0-30%	0
Others	4	0-70%	0	4	0-60%	0
Totals	100%		100%			100%

VI.   Need for Distributorship Offering Better Terms, Immediacy, Low Quarterly Buys

The following table expresses how stores viewed the need for distributorships which could offer better financial terms, immediate availability, and the opportunity to purchase smaller quantities than some distributors or manufacturers might offer—at prices not much higher than they were currently paying.

Table 6
Need for These Specialized Distributorships
by % of Responding Stores

% Seeing a Need	80%
% Not Seeing a Need	20%
Total	100%

Exhibit 1 (continued)

Table 6A
Reasoning Behind Responses
of Either Needing or Not Needing
These Specialized Distributorships

Reasons for Needing	% of Positively Responding Stores Mentioning	Reasons for Not Needing	% of Negatively Responding Stores Mentioning
Immediate Deliveries	86%	Can Margins be Maintained?	33%
Ability to Buy in Small Quantities	60	Not Needed	11
Better Credit Terms	40	Are an OEM	11
Ability to Get Better Systems	9	Are a Franchise	11
No Long Commitment for Blanket Orders	6	Are a Distributor Themselves	11
Better Prices (Higher Margins)	3	Question on Support Capabilities	11
Help with Floor Planning	3	Would Just Create More Problems	11
Provide Product Knowledge	3		

Exhibit 1 (continued)

Current and Future Sources of Distribution which Stores Use

The following table analyzes the sources of distribution which stores are currently using to buy both their systems (CPUs) and peripherals—now and anticipated for 1983.

Table 6B
Methods of Distribution Stores Are (Will Be) Using
Now and in 1983
Average % Of All Responding Stores

	Systems		Peripherals	
Methods of Distribution	Now	1983	Now	1983
Manufacturers (Direct)	63%	58%	45%	46%
Distributors	32	39	50	51
Parent Companies or Franchise	3	1	3	1
Other	2	2	2	2
Total	100%	100%	100%	100%

VII.   Store Startup Factors

The following tables examine two factors of store startup: Characteristics which stores perceive manufactures look for when granting the rights to sell their products; and also the stores' opinions as to the amount of capital necessary to comfortably open a store.

Table 7A
Characteristics Manufacturers Look for in Stores
When Granting Rights to Carry Their Products

Characteristics	% of Responding Stores Mentioning
Financial Stability	40%
Good Personnel	29
Nothing Needed (NONE)	27
Ability to Provide Service for the Equipment	20
Good Location	9
Commitment From the Store (Blanket Orders)	7
Ability to Provide Sales Support	7
Sales Potential	5
Good Store Image	5
Been in Business for a While	5
Formal Business Plan Done	5

Exhibit 1 (continued)

Table 7B
Amount of Capital Necessary to
Open a Computer Retail Store Comfortably

Categories of Necessary Capital	% of Responding Stores Mentioning
$50-75K	2%
76-100K	31
101-150K	40
151-175K	12
>175K	15
Total	100%

VIII.   Competition as Viewed by the Stores

The following table analyzes just whom stores view as their major competitors—both now and anticipated for 1983.

Table 8
Competition as Viewed by the Stores

Types of Competition	% of First Place Ranking Received		Weighted Average Ranking	
	Now	1983	Now	1983
Large Computer Chains (5 or more stores)	31%	51%	.85	1.00
Small Independent Stores (1 to 5 stores)	40	13	1.00	.81
Direct Sales by Mfr's Salesfo (IBM, DEC, DG, etc)	21	10	.75	.68
Manufacturer Owned Stores (DEC)	7	23	.42	.76
Sales thru Office Supplies Salesforces (Moore Bus. Forms sells for TI)	0	2	.12	.33
Other*	Negligible	Negligible	Negligible	Negligible

* Others were: Radio Shack, Mail Order, Sears, and Audio/Retail stores.

Exhibit 1   (continued)

IX.   Sources For Software

The following tables analyze computer stores' sources and methods of software acquisition.

Table 9A
Sources of Software, Current and in 1983
(Avg. % Each Source Represents for All Stores)

Sources	Average % for All Responding Stores Now	Average % for All Responding Stores 1983
Manufacturers	30%	29%
Independent S/W Houses	45	47
User Developed	12	14
Other Sources*	13	10

* Other sources were: Self-developed by the store.

Table 9B
Independent Software Houses Most Mentioned

Independent Software Houses	No. of Mentions	Independent Software Houses	No. of Mentions
Personal	8	Creative	3
Hayden	6	Microsoft	3
Serendipity	6	Micro Source	3
Peachtree	5	Independent Consultants	3
Muse	5	Retail Sciences	2
Instant	4	Programma	2
Structured Systems	4	Others* (20 companies)	1

* Others were: Quality, Softside, Daykin 5, Dr. Daileys, Basic, Bus Enhancements, Abacus, Astra, Digital Research, Program Design, Mad Hatter, Rainbow, Q Type, Indecom, AMS, International Micro, Microware, Softape, Laselle and National.

Exhibit 1 (continued)

Table 9C
Methods Software Distributors Use
to Contact Stores

Methods	% of Stores Mentioning
In person sales call	11%
Telephone sales call followed by in-person sales call	18
Telephone sales call only	25
Saw ad and called them*	74
Other**	20

* Publications where ads were seen: Byte (12 Mentions), Interface News (4), Creative Computing (4), Kilobaud (4), Computer Retailing (2), Computer Dealer (2), Computer Business News (1), and Computerworld (1).

** Other methods were: Direct Mail, Word of Mouth, Customer Requests Upon Seeing Ads, and Manufacturers Send Salespeople to the Stores.

Table 9D
Methods Stores Would Use to
Find Additional Software

Methods Ranked by No. of Mentions	% of Total Mentions
Through reading industry magazines	44%
Would develop software themselves	13
Go to manufacturers	9
Check out other dealers' products	9
Ask manufacturers where to go	7
Directly to industry software houses	4
Shows	4
Inquiries after seeing ads	2
Others	9
Total	100%

Exhibit 1   (continued)

X.   Maintenance/Repair Performance and Manufacturers Mentioned as Having Maintenance Problems

Table 10A analyzes how maintenance, repairs are being handled by the stores. Table 10B analyzes manufacturers mentioned as having the greatest degree of breakdowns.

Table 10A
Handling of Maintenance/Repairs

Methods	Average % of All Responding Stores	Ranges Encountered for All Stores	Breakdown Most Encountered
In House	85%	0 - 100%	90%
Sent Back to Mfrs	14%	0 - 100%	10%
3rd Party Maintenance*	1%	0 - 75%	—
Total	100%		100%

* Only one store was using.

△ Stores were able to repair 85% of their customers' equipment problems in-house, with only 14 percent of the cases being sent back to the manufacturers. This high degree of in-house repairability is of utmost importance in any area of the computer industry, as downtime is the industry's major problem. This high in-house capability is mostly due to the business of microprocessors, and the ability to replace chips and boards independently.

Exhibit 1 (continued)

Table 10B
Manufacturers Mentioned as Having
Equipment which Experiences
the Most Downtime

Manufacturers	% of Stores Mentioning a Mfr. as Having Downtime Problems—Based on the Number of Stores Carrying Each Manufacturer	% of Stores Mentioning a Mfr. as Having Serious Recurring Downtime Problems—Based on the Number of Stores Carrying Each Mfr.
Imsai	100%	100%
Ohio Scientific	80	30
Pertec	75	—
Compucolor	75	50
Commodore	57	7
SWTFC	50	—
Cromenco	42	—
Apple	38	12
Exidy	29	14
Vector Graphics	29	—
Dynabyte	20	20
North Star	14	—
TI	8	—
Peripherals		
Centronics	40	—
Other Peripheral		
Manufacturers	44	22
No Problems	20	—
No Serious Problems	—	65

Exhibit 1 (continued)

XI.   Advertising Expenditures

The following table analyzes the average amount stores are spending per month on advertising.

Table 11
Advertising Expenditures
Responding Stores

Average Per Month- All Responding Stores	Average Per Month- Stores Which Were Advertising	Range Per Month- All Responding Stores
$810	$920	$80 to $5,000

XII.   Mail Order Business

The following table expresses the degree to which stores are involved in mail order business, now and anticipated for 1983.

Table 12
Stores Selling Through Mail Order
% of Responding Stores

	% Involved in Mail Order		Average % of Sales Represented All Stores	
	Now	1983	Now	1983
% Selling Systems - Mail Order	25%	25%	6%	6%
% Selling Peripherals - Mail Order	25	21	6	6
% Selling Software - Mail Order	19	15	4	5
% of Stores Selling Anything Through Mail Order	2	25		
% of Stores With No Mail Order Business	75	75		
Total	100%	100%		

Exhibit 1 (continued)

XIII.   Buying Motives of Computer Retail Store Customers

The following table lists the major buying motives (related by the stores) as to why customers buy personal computers and why the customers chose their store in particular.

Table 13
Buying Motives
% of Mentions by Responding Stores

Buying Motives of Customers For Personal Computers	% of Total Mentions	Buying Motives of Customers in Selecting Particular Stores	% of Total Mentions
Business needs	29%	Application/system solution	20%
Curiosity	21	Good equipment/demo	
Low price	12	Systems	16
Child education	6	People related	
Service offered by stores	6	Knowledgeable salespeople	16
Home/hobbyist interest	6	Honesty/soft sell	3
Prestige	3	Store reputation	10
Desire to learn about		Good service	10
Computers	6	Location of store	8
Interest created by		Store atmosphere	5
advertising	4	Support	5
Gadget appeal	2	Direct mail/advertising	3
Atmosphere of the stores	2	Dollar savings	2
Total	100%	Total	100%

△ 50% of the total mentions as to why stores felt customers were interested in personal computers were a combination of business needs and curiosity. These two factors explain the interest of the major sectors in the marketplace, business and the home/hobbyist contingents.

△ Store owners said the major reasons customers chose their stores in particular were their stores' ability to provide application/system solutions to problems (20%), and the good equipment/demo systems (18%) they displayed on their store floors, which attracted customers. Knowledgeable salespeople were also mentioned as being important. This factor and the system solution factor are closely related to the primary aim of stores' being able to interpret and then supply application solutions to problems and needs of customers.

Exhibit 1 (continued)

XIV. Problems Faced by Computer Retail Stores

The following table lists the major problems which computer retail stores feel they are faced with.

Table 14
Major Problems of Computer Retail Stores

Major Problems	Ranking According to Weighted Average of Mentions	% of Mentions as Being Primary Problem
Margins too low on equipment	1.00	22%
Cash flow, lack of strong financial backing	.87	32
Getting good employees	.81	22
Keeping abreast of technology	.64	4
Training required with each new product or new salesperson	.62	6
Servicing the equipment	.47	2
Keeping good employees	.42	6
Inventory control (balance between cost and immediate delivery needs	.40	4
Unhappy with store location	.22	2

△ The major problems computer retailers said were greatest were: Margins too low on the equipment, cash flow (lack of strong financial backing) and getting good employees. Almost one of every three stores (32%) mentioned cash flow as their major problem, while collectively the three just-mentioned problems represented the primary one for three out of every four stores (76%).

Exhibit 1 (continued)

XV.   Application Usage

The following tables analyze the major applications for which end users—both small businesses and home hobbyists—buy personal computers.

Table 15A
Major Applications for which Small
Businesses Buy Personal Computers

Applications	Weighted Average Ranking Of Mentions	Number of Primary Mentions Received
General accounting	1.00	32%
Word processing	.90	21
Inventory control	.76	16
Accounts receivable	.87	16
Billing	.62	5
Mailing lists	.58	5
Accounts payable	.51	5
Total		100%

△ Other Applications mentioned were: Payroll, Process Control, Data Base-Management, and Property Management.

Table 15B
Major Applications for which Home
Hobbyists Buy Personal Computers

Applications	Weighted Average Ranking of Mentions	Number of Primary Mentions Received
Games	1.00	57%
Child Education	.81	20
Personal Accounting	.76	23
Total		100%

△ Other applications in order of number of mentions were: Adult Education, Software Development, Energy Conservation, Custom Business, Word Processing, and Mail Lists.

Exhibit 1 (continued)

XVI.   Stores

Table 16A
Year When Stores Will Reach Their Peak
or Saturation Point

Years	% of Responses
1981/2	12%
1983/4	22
1985/6	35
1987/8	5
1989/90	13
Beyond 1990/Never	13
Total	100%

Table 16B
What Factors Will Allow Smaller Stores (1-5 units)
to Survive versus Large Chains

Factors	% of Total Mention
Sevice	26%
Turnkey systems	18
Market niches/application solutions/market positioning	11
Support	8
Product selection	7
Product expertise	7
Price cutting	7
Personal service	5
Location	3
Good sales people	2
Word of mouth advertising	2
Higher margins	2
Acting as a service bureau	2
Total	100%

Exhibit 1 (continued)

Table 16C
What Stores Would Invest in
if They Had Additional Capital

Investments <u>% Of Total Responses</u>

Increase inventory	32%
New store(s)	19
Software company	17
Turnkey system Hhuse	9
Expand current store	7
Additional software	4
More/better salespeople	4
Advertising/seminars	4
Distributorship	<u>4</u>
Total	100%

Table 16D
Will Particular Stores be Seeking Additional
Capital in the Near Future?

% Yes	67%
% No	<u>33</u>
Total	100%

Exhibit 1 (continued)

Table 16E
Fastest Growing Manufacturers
in the Personal Computer Marketplace

Manufacturers	% of Total Fastest Growing Responses Received	% of Total New Participants Responses Received
Apple	29%	—
Alpha Micro	10	—
Commodore	8	—
Vector Graphics	8	—
North Star	7	—
TI	6	25%
Ohio Scientific	6	—
Japanese manufacturers	4	12
Cromemco	4	—
Atari	4	13
Heath	3	—
Altos	3	—
DEC	1	11
IBM	1	13
Dynabyte	1	—
Industrial Microsystems	1	—
Others	4	—
Mattel	—	7
NEC	—	7
HP	—	4
Data General	—	2
Tano	—	2
Edo	—	2
Pexou	—	2
Total	100%	100%

Exhibit 1 (continued)

Table 16F
Important Technological Developments
Stores Foresee in the
Personal Computer Industry

Technological Developments	% Of Total Mentions	
Memory (Disk) Related	(49%)	
Bubble memories		16%
Increased memory capacity		12
Increased memory per dollar		9
Hard disks		5
New disk technology		3
Video disk association		2
Eliminate disks for other storage medium		2
Product Improvements	(34%)	
16/32 bit processing (faster)		12
Better graphics		5
Decrease size of system		3
Laser technology		3
Voice recognition		3
Home terminals		2
Flat CRT's		2
Increased overall capabilities		2
Plasma CRT's		2
Software	(9%)	
User oriented software		3
Better software		2
Standard languages		2
Data base capability		2
Pricing	(8%)	
Decrease printer prices		5
Decrease in whole system prices		3
Total		100%

Exhibit 1 (concluded)

XVII.   Revenue Size of Stores

The following table analyzes the current and anticipated 1983 revenue sizes of responding stores.

Table 17
Revenue Size of Stores

	% Of Responding Stores	
Revenue Classifications	Now	1983 (est.)
Under $100K	9%	0%
$101 - 250K	36	4
$251 - 500K	22	9
$501 - 750K	7	24
$751 - 1,000K (Million)	13	18
Over $1 Million	13	45
Total	100%	100%

△ 45% of the stores expect to have grown to over $1 million in sales by year end 1983.

△ The average sales for current stores were approximately $430,000, based on the midpoints of the ranges they fell in. By 1983, these reporting stores expect to have average sales of $905,000. This represents an average growth of 110% over these 4 years, or 21% a year compounded growth.

Case 33

Think Tanks

In conjunction with their business plan, which appears as the Knight Brothers case, the two brothers had also drafted an investment proposition, as follows below:

November 16, 1980

The following is a business proposal for the formation and operation of a limited partnership. This memorandum is to provide a limited number of investors information pertaining to the private placement of Units of Limited Partnership Interest in THINK TANKS, a New York limited partnership organized to purchase microcomputers and operate them in a retail store.

SUMMARY

INVESTMENT OFFERED Limited partnership interests are offered in the aggregate amount of $300,000.

MINIMUM PURCHASE The minimum purchase is $25,000.

PAYMENT SCHEDULE The first payment of $12,500 upon subscription. The final payment of $12,500 on March 15, 1980.

OFFERING PERIOD The offering will terminate at 5 p.m. on December 15, 1980 (unless extended by the partnership to not later than December 30, 1980 or the commencement date, if earlier).

CONDITIONS TO CLOSING THE OFFERING All subscriptions will be returned to investors unless received prior to December 15, 1980 (or December 30, 1980 in the event that the partnership has extended the offering), the partnership has accepted subscriptions for interests totaling $300,000.

BUSINESS OF THE PARTNERSHIP The partnership will purchase microcomputers and will sell time on them through a retail store in the Harvard Square area of the Cambridge, Massachusetts. In addition, the partnership intends to purchase microcomputers for lease or sale to individuals and/or businesses.

MICROCOMPUTERS The partnership intends to spend approximately $150,000 in the acquisition of microcomputers and related high-technology equipment.

MANAGEMENT The managing partner will be responsible for the managing of the partnership's business. Mr. Richard D. Knight and Mr. James A. Knight, individual general partners, have an aggregate in excess of 10 years' experience in the computer and financing businesses.

FINANCING The general partners do not anticipate the need for debt financing of any kind in connection with the purchase of the microcomputers or the operation of the business.

PAYMENTS TO THE GENERAL PARTNERS The partnership will pay the general partners a management fee of $30,000 per annum plus an amount equal to 3 1/2 percent of the net profit (payable monthly).

ALLOCATION OF THE PROFITS AND LOSSES Profits and losses of the partnership will be allocated 95 percent to the limited partners and 5 percent to the general partners until the sum of the cash distributions to the limited partners equals the amount contributed to the partnership by the limited partners. Thereafter profits and losses will be allocated 80 percent to the limited partners and 20 percent to the general partners until the sum of the cash distributions is equal to TWICE the amount contributed to the partnership by the limited partners. Thereafter profits and losses will be allocated 60 percent to the limited partners and 40 percent to the general partners.

PARTNERSHIP DISTRIBUTIONS The general partners will distribute quarterly, in their discretion, the amount of cash in excess of that required to conduct the business.

SUMMARY OF PROJECTED
RETURN PER $25,000 INTEREST

YEAR	Cash Investment	Tax Loss	Investment Tax Credit	Cash Flow
1980	$12,500	$2000	-$0-	-$0-
1981	12,500	10,250	412.50	2,000
1982		2775	-0-	18,000
1983		1450	-0-	22,000
1984		-0-	-0-	30,000
1985				30,000
1986				30,000
1987				30,000
1988				30,000

The assumptions which are made in the summary table with regard to the projected tax losses and the investment tax credit are in line with the business plan of the partnership and generally accepted accounting principles.

The projections as to the cash flow are based upon the business judgment of the general partners in connection with the utilization studies which have been performed projecting the store's sales.

Greg Thompson

In late September 1975, three years after receiving his MBA degree from the University of Washington, Greg Thompson was thinking about preparing two proposals. One would be for presentation to a bank executive to solicit a contract for flying canceled checks from bank branches in southern Washington to a central office in Seattle. The second would be to a bank loan officer for financing the purchase of an airplane with which to carry the checks. Questions facing him included what information to include in the proposals, how to obtain it, and how to present it.

Personal History

Flying had been a favorite hobby of Greg's for over 10 years. He was a licensed pilot and had served on the board of directors of a local flying club, "where I learned the many difficulties of doing things by committee," he recalled. In 1972 he had led a team of students in preparing a prospectus for a commuter airline as part of an MBA entrepreneurship course. That project was not carried further than the class, however. Greg recalled:

We abandoned the commuter airline idea because it simply required too much financing. So after graduating we took different jobs. Two members of the team started a small restaurant after hours to serve Mexican food, and the third one set up a manufacturer's rep operation in Denver.

I vacationed around for a while after getting my degree and then innocently sat back waiting for the phone to ring with job offers. By the time summer ended, it was clear that would not happen, so I began to hustle. Through the placement office, I interviewed with a small contracting firm that really looked interesting, but they didn't offer me a job. I sent some applications to Boeing and had two or three interviews with them. At the time I really didn't know what I wanted to do, but it began to become clearer to me what I didn't want to do. These were big government contracts where I would be some sort of coordinator or administrator. I had never been comfortable with the prospect of being a tiny cog in a huge machine, and that was what this was. The jobs were ambiguous, with no clear idea what was expected of you. Somehow you were responsible for something, but with no clear authority over anyone or anything—just shuffling papers.

The life insurance routine also left me cold. At first I thought, "Why not sell life insurance?" My major had been in marketing. But when I went for an interview to one of the companies, they kept me waiting for half an hour. During that time I wandered around the office and came across a chart on the wall that showed what volumes of business the different salesmen were doing. A very few were doing big volumes, but more were far below that. Then when they got around to interviewing me, they told me about commissions and volumes and what I could expect. They made claims about what other salesmen typically did, which were way out of line with what I had seen on the wall.

That convinced me I didn't want to work for them.

But by now my savings and student loan money was running out, and I needed to get a job somehow. So I got hold of a Boeing company telephone book and started looking through the different sections that made up the company. The hydrofoil program caught my eye. I had been in the navy for three years before returning to graduate school, and I liked the sea. So I called up the marketing manager of the hydrofoil program from his number in the book, and told him I had majored in marketing and transportation, and that I wanted to go to work for him. That got me an interview, and the interview got me a job as a market analyst.

Greg was still in this position when the idea for air-freighting bank checks came up, and although he now worked for a very large company, he liked his job.

The part of Boeing I work in is actually a small one. In it I can see the whole picture of what I'm doing and how it fits in. In our small group a salesman and a market analyst work together on each project. We learn about the prospective customer, work up a demand analysis and cash flow, and build the basis for a sales and financing proposal. I like being able to see the whole thing and follow it all the way through to a sale.

Check Flying Service Idea

In July of 1975 Greg read in the newspaper about the crash of a helicopter near Seattle. He was surprised to notice in the article that the craft had been used just to fly canceled checks between bank offices. This, he thought, was certainly an expensive way to move checks around, since air transport in general is fairly high-priced;

helicopters are especially costly to operate, generating expenses per mile and per payload pound that are two or three times as much as those of airplanes. He figured it must be worth a lot to banks to get fast delivery service on canceled checks. It occurred to him that with a plan he might be able to out-perform other modes of transport for some routes. But he did nothing further with the thought at the time.

Then in early September 1975, he attended a cocktail party where, by chance, he met a man who happened to be on the planning staff of a major Seattle bank, one of the three banks that had been experimenting with the helicopter service for transporting checks from nearby cities around the Puget Sound. The air transport subject came up, and Greg let it be known that he might like to try ferrying checks by airplane—perhaps from more distant areas where advantages over the helicopter would be greater. The planning officer said he knew the bank's float control manager, who was responsible for arranging transport of the checks. Greg recalled:

He gave me his card, told me to call the man, and said he would contact the man himself to announce that I would be calling. I probably would not have called the man, but this setup really didn't leave me much choice. I felt literally pushed into it.

The phone call lasted nearly two hours. The float control manager and I just seemed to hit it off right from the start. It turned out the bank was dissatisfied with the combination of air and ground service they were using for various routes and was open to new possibilities. They can save a great deal of money by getting checks in just a few hours or even minutes earlier to beat deadlines on interest at the Federal Reserve Bank. So it doesn't help when their contract delivery service sends the bank an announcement that its schedule is going to be changed. The delivery service does this because it is a big outfit with many customers, and it finds a way to reduce its costs by striking a new compromise in delivery timing among them, rather than accommodating each individual customer on an individual basis. At the bank such changes can disrupt handling and processing schedules, making things harder and possibly delays that cost the bank more money.

It also doesn't help when check shipments get mixed up or lost, which had happened to the bank at times on commercial airlines where their freight may be stacked with everyone else's. The checks are not negotiable, but it is enormously inconvenient and expensive for the bank.

At the close of their meeting, the float control manager suggested that Greg come back in a few days with a proposal for ferrying checks from Vancouver in southern Washington to Seattle, roughly 140 miles north. He gave no indication of present costs on the route or of the expected price for Greg's service, but did describe the present method of transport, which was by truck and typically took two hours and 25 minutes per trip.

Another option Greg quickly noted was to bring the checks by commercial airline, perhaps with a special attendant to make sure nothing happened to them. From flight schedules at the airport he laid out three sequences for using commercial service out of Portland airport. A copy of his tabulation can be seen in Exhibit 1. From the bank's description of its needs he estimated that roughly 25 percent of the checks would be ready for departure by 3:15 p.m., another 50 percent by 4:14 p.m., and the remaining 25 percent by 5:15 p.m.

If he had a plane Greg expected he could fly the routes himself. He could use the international airports in Portland and

Seattle, for instance. Or he could use smaller local airports, since his plane would be small. To reach Portland, Oregon, he could fly in and out of a local airport just across the state line in Vancouver, Washington. That would cut the driving time from airport to Portland down to around five to 10 minutes, or roughly half the time it would take from Portland International, where the commercial flights went. Landing and taxiing the aircraft would take perhaps another 10 to 15 minutes, and flying to Seattle between 70 and 90 minutes. Then taxiing and unloading at Seattle might require roughly 10 to 15 minutes. To reach Seattle, he could use Boeing field, which was about 10 minutes from downtown, rather than Seattle-Tacoma airport which was approximately twice that time away from the city. The purchase price of a small plane suitable for these routes and capable of carrying the load he expected would be around $15,000 to $18,000. From personal savings he expected he could raise around $5,000 as a down payment to buy it, if the bank would lend him the rest.

At present he enjoyed his market analyst job at the Boeing company, and he was not particularly anxious to leave. His work involved several international trips per year, often to exotic places like the South Pacific, where there was interest in hydrofoils for tourist excursions. His salary was not particularly high, around $13,000 a year, but it was enough to live on and do some recreational flying on weekends. He observed:

Making more money or being my own boss are not things that particularly motive me. But I certainly would like the idea of being able to own an airplane and do more flying. I wonder how feasible it would be to try combining a check transporting service with personal flying. Would I have to quit my job at Boeing? How big a dip would it put in my income, and for how long? What kind of help should I be able to get from the bank? What should I present to them to persuade them to grant that help, and what steps should I take to prepare that presentation?

Should I be concerned about whether they might just take all the work I might put into a plan and use it to give the job to someone else instead of me? Should I propose a trial period with them? If so, how long, and what would be the best way to keep going with them beyond that? I imagine there might be quite a few people out there who now

pay to fly, like I do, and would gladly offer low-cost service to get a subsidy for their flight time by taking over the work. Should the pricing I put into my proposal be based on this or on how much it's now costing the bank to fly checks by helicopter? How should the pricing basis, whatever it is, change with time? Or should it? What are all the most important issues, like this, that should be considered in my proposal to the bank. What should be the most effective way to organize and to present them?

EXHIBIT 1   Airline Delivery Time Using Flight Schedules

Check Pick-up Time	3:15 p.m.	4:15 p.m.	5:15 p.m.
Arrival Portland International	3:50	4:50	5:50
Ready for Departure (90 min. check on time-min.)	5:20	6:20	7:20
Next Available Flight	5:45 (UA flt 792)	7:55 (NW flt L09)	7:55 (NW flt 10)
Arrival Sea-Tac	6:30	8:30	8:30
Ready for Pick-Up (1 hr. unloading time)	7:30	9:30	9:30
Arrival Computer Center (35 min. driving time)	8:05	10:05	10:05

Case 35

Paul Van Hague

Need for a Venture Plan

In April 1980, Paul Van Hague, a mechanical engineer, was looking for help to create a business around a new type of saw to be used in sawmills for cutting lumber. It differed dramatically from the standard type of circular saw presently in use. The new saw gripped the circular blade on opposing circumferential edges with chain links (like holding a phonograph record by the edges) rather than having it mounted on a shaft through the disk's center as existing saws did. A photograph of the saw appears in Exhibit 1.

In performance, it differed from conventional rotary saws by making a thinner cut (kerf), thereby producing less sawdust and hence less waste from the lumber. Several years of development effort had been applied to the saw, and considerable progress had been made. However, still more work was needed to complete final development and introduce production machines. To do this, Paul expected a substantial amount of capital and creation of a company would be needed. He was looking for help in developing a plan to bring this about.

He had already gathered information, made performance analysis calculations for the saw, and formulated parts of a business plan to introduce it commercially. He commented:

What we have at this point is still in the development stage. We've made a prototype and we think it demonstrates that the principle works. But the prototype is not a production machine, and we are a distance away from a commercial model. There are still some unknowns.

In a letter requesting assistance from a professor at a nearby university he wrote as follows:

Enclosed find the Preliminary Organizational Setup for incorporation of my company. It is an attempt to "design" an organization which:

1) Allows me to keep control by owning 51 percent of the voting stock.
2) Gives four or five people who help me set up this business an opportunity to earn up to five percent of voting stock each.
3) Gives investors maximum assurance of a good return on their investment (and avoids double taxation at the same time) by having most investment in the form of subordinated debentures with a reasonable interest rate.

I would very much appreciate your comments on this preliminary setup. Thank you in advance for your help.

Excerpts from Paul's preliminary planning notes are attached as Exhibit 2.

Present Status

Four people had participated in development of the new saw: Paul, his two brothers living in Holland, and his father, who had originated the concept in Holland but was no longer living. A prototype of the saw had been designed, built and tested in Holland, where it was presently housed in a fabrication shop but not used.

Patents on the saw had been obtained in the United States as well as several other countries. An abstract of the U.S. patent description read as follows:

Abstract

A circular sawing machine having one or multiple circular sawing blades driven at their outside periphery by one or more single or multiple strand chains of the type having inside and outside links connected by pins, the saw blades having for this purpose teeth, the teeth which go in between the inside links of the chain doing this with little clearance, and the teeth going in between the outside links of the chain carrying cutting elements wider than the saw blade, but still capable of passing with ample clearance between the outside links.

The saw blade or blades are not supported by a shaft, but shaped annular or flat. The annular saw blades can be supported by circumferentially grooved rollers located at the inside periphery of the saw blades with the blades fitting in the grooves and in addition indirectly by rollers on extensions of the chain pins rolling on a hollow cylindrical member attached to the frame of the machine just outside of the periphery of the saw blades.

The latter rollers can roll in grooves in these hollow cylindrical members, thus not only supporting the saw blades radially, but also axially.

If the chain and cylindrical hollow member enclose sufficiently more than 180 degrees of the circumference of the saw blades, or if there are two or more chains on sufficiently opposed sides of the saw blades, the rollers on the internal periphery of the annular saw blades can be omitted and the saw blades can be flat circular plates instead of annular plates.

Initially, the Van Hagues intended to introduce the saw in the European sawmill industry. Work had been done with one European company that had expressed strong interest. However, after the Van Hagues had developed a prototype and were about to proceed with a production model, the company changed its mind and canceled the order. Paul recalled that this was quite discouraging to his brothers and him. Other European mills had been watching to see how things went with the first customer. When that one canceled, he said, the feeling was that other European mills, which he characterized as very conservative, would consequently be unlikely to try the saw. Therefore, his brothers had backed away from working on the machine and suggested that Paul, since he had emigrated to the American Pacific Northwest, might pursue the development there instead. Paul commented:

It's kind of slow going. The lumber industry isn't doing well right now, and that makes it hard to find people who are interested. My feeling is that the industry will come back, though. When it does I'd like to have a company and machine in place ready to take advantage of the rebound, which will likely include expansion and modernization of existing sawmills, as well as construction of new ones.

Personal Background

Paul Van Hague had been trained through a five-year course of study in Holland as a mechanical engineer, followed by an additional year of training in research and development. After graduating in 1965 he worked for 15 years for both European and U.S. companies mainly in machine design. After emigrating to the United States, he passed the professional engineers' examination and became qualified as a registered mechanical engineer. This field was, he said, "not all that easy." He continued:

> There are a lot of companies that have lost money on new mechanical equipment because they did not design and test with sufficient care to avoid the many things that can go wrong with new machinery.
>
> Quite a bit of my work was in heavy machines. But there were other types as well. Machine design is basically similar in different fields, although the emphasis varies. I worked for Ingersoll-Rand for several years on underground mining machinery, for instance, and there the emphasis is on compact design.
>
> I also worked in the lumber industry. I designed a chipper that worked very well, and some other things. In lumber it's important to maintain very small deflections, as opposed to compactness. Once you catch on to that, the machine design is very similar to that in mining.
>
> More recently I started doing consulting work for a company that makes fiberglass parts, gratings mostly. They needed a machine to sand their product. They tried one that was built for sanding plywood. Prices on it start at $25,000 and go to $700,000. It is very expensive and way too costly for such an application. It doesn't impose such high loads or need such high accuracy in plywood processing. So worrying about keeping deflections small is not so important as in wood machinery.
>
> At first it was hard for me to catch on to these different requirements. But now I am succeeding quite well. This customer needs lighter weight and lower costs. You can get that if you realize how little the loads are and the fact that deflections are not very important.

Origin of the CPC Saw

Inception of the novel saw idea had occurred about 12 years earlier to Paul Van Hague's father, who had been engaged as an engineer by a company in the stone cutting business. It was having problems with a large reciprocating saw used to slice boulders into slabs. Paul recalled:

> My dad fixed that saw for them. There were some basic design errors in it. While he was doing that, he decided that the basic concept was not very good. So he started thinking about a better one and came up with this circular saw idea.
>
> He approached the owner of the stone company, which was relatively small, about possibly developing the idea. But the owner said, "we really don't need it. You fixed the old machine so well." Then that little company was bought out by a big company. My dad tried to interest them in the project too, but they had other contracts, and were just not doing any machine development, period. Meantime my dad had talked to some of the people who sintered small pieces of diamond into copper alloy for cutting the stone, and they offered to provide him with a blade free of charge for the new type of saw. So he kept pushing ahead with the idea.
>
> But it was hard to find a machine builder. Stone cutting saws are big, and there isn't that much market for them, especially in Holland which has to import the stones. There is more stone industry in Italy, and dad went there and talked to some people. But it would still require a big machine. That's where the stone saw project stopped. Building a prototype stone saw would just be too much. So he decided to see what the potential would be in the lumber industry. That seemed like a bigger market with different requirements, such as more

emphasis on speed, which began to interest my younger brother.

The younger Van Hague, who held a Ph.D. in physics and worked as a specialist in optics for a Dutch university, offered to finance development of a wood-cutting prototype. His job afforded him access to shops where some of the parts could be made experimentally. Some help came also from Paul's older brother, who was head of a research institute space system group. Together, the three carried on the work as something of a hobby after their father died.

Performance Aspects

The principal advantage of the saw, the three believed, was that it wasted less lumber. Because it was held at top and bottom, as depicted in Exhibit 1, the blade was more firmly supported and, therefore, could be thinner. Consequently, it made a thinner cut in the wood and transformed less wood into sawdust. Paul estimated that as much as 5 to 8 percent more usable lumber could result from a log.

At the same time, he said, the saw took less energy to push through the wood. Partly this was because it did not chew as much wood into sawdust. And partly it was because the log passed through the center section of the blade rather than just past the bottom of the blade which in conventional machines pushed against the log's advance. Instead, the log encountered the blade where the blade was moving more vertically and less against the advance of the log. The amount of this energy saving, however, he said was not very important.

He had discussions with people in the wood products industry and the sawmill machinery industry as well as business contacts, bankers and prospective investors whom he sought out for help in moving the venture forward. Using this information he had prepared planning

notes, excerpts from which appear in Exhibit 2. Views he encountered sometimes agreed and sometimes conflicted with each other. For instance, three different employees in one very large wood products company, estimated the value of sawdust and scrap variously as $2, $15, and $30-$40 per thousand board feet. Distinction between sawdust and chips was not always clear when people talked about scrap, he noted, although chips were considered much more valuable for use in paper making. Sometimes, however, the scrap was simply burned for fuel, regardless of its composition. "I don't think the wood lost to sawdust is worth more than about $10 to $15 a thousand board feet," Paul said, "but first I was told it was $2, so some of my estimates used that."

Machinery life was another area of question. Without extensive and expensive testing it was difficult to determine just how long a new machine would last. Not only was construction of a prototype expensive, but then it had to be proven by processing a lot of logs. "Even the big machinery makers usually can't afford that," Paul observed. "They often have to collaborate with a lumber manufacturer."

He had followed the customary engineering practice of making estimates during design of machine life based on theoretical computations. However, these were never certain until actual application over years had verified them. Paul judged that technological obsolescence made 20 years a logical life target. He noted that one northwest plant recently torn down had been running its original equipment since 1912. He had also been told that the majority of equipment currently used in the sawmill industry was 40 years old or more. One experienced member of the industry commented:

In spite of old age, that machinery is still running great. The industry is ridiculously conservative. We just don't

*make major changes in equipment. Saw-
mills have been being built the way they
are now for 40 years and more.*

One aspect of the new "CPC" (Circumferential Power Chain) saw design that
Paul Van Hague thought fit well with
present trends was the movement of mills
into processing smaller logs. The original
old growth timber was being used up, and
younger trees that had been planted to replace them were harvested when smaller
in diameter. The new machine allowed use
of a smaller blade for any log, since without a shaft in the middle more of the blade
could pass through the wood. Paul explained:

*The market in saws can be rather ex-
tensively segmented. Not only are there
different sizes of logs, but there are
hardwoods, softwoods, seasonal differences in cutting, and different types of
sawing for different stages in cutting up
a log. We are now thinking through design of a resaw for use at the tail end of
a mill, in addition to one for the front
end. There are a lot of possible choices.
It isn't just the lumber industry. There
are a lot of other applications too. I think
my calculations show that the potential
is there.*

*I looked at application in the do-it-
yourself market and in equipment for
small cabinet shops, furniture shops,
and so forth. I talked to Omark Corporation in Portland, Oregon. They're the
world's leading maker of chain saw
blades, but they recently bought a factory that makes small circular saw
blades for table saws and the like. They
were very interested in making saw
blades for an application of this to any
market that company could serve. But
they only want to make the blades, because otherwise they start competing
with their own customers.*

*I also know a company in California
that can help with the blades, but not
the machine. Their man in charge of
long-range research said he would talk
to some of their customers about it. We
have some features that might particularly fit that application. For instance,
we have small feed forces because the
circular cuts perpendicular to the feed
action, whereas in a conventional circular saw the saw either pulls the material
in or tries to push it out. That gives our
design some advantages, in terms of
both accuracy and safety.*

Contacts

Paul had discussed use of the new machine with some large forest products companies. They seemed, he said, to be
interested but moving very slowly. Moreover, different ones seemed to be interested in different applications calling for
different saw designs, none of which
would work for a whole sawmill. Paul
commented:

*The sawmills seem to be coming un-
der a cost squeeze with the foreign countries leaning more toward buying raw
logs. Also, the mills are having to adapt
more to smaller logs. All this may make
them more interested in new types of
machinery.*

*There are a few mills willing to in-
vest in new machinery, but only after it
is on the market. Once you have a production machine, there are people willing to put it into a plant and try it out.
The big mills have manufacturing laboratories for trying new ideas. A large
part of what they are doing is trying out
the different machines that are on the
market. So once you have something
that is marketable, it's easier to find
people who are willing to buy through
the regular route of capital investment.
Then it's just a matter of the financial*

people feeling it's worthwhile to risk buying that piece of equipment. The gap between having a prototype and having a production machine for a mill to try, though, seems tough to get across.

I've talked to a number of people I thought might be interested in helping refine and produce our machine. There are two other machine designers I met who have very strong backgrounds in this field and might be interested in joining me, but they don't have money to invest.

Looking for potential manufacturers, I got in touch with a small machine building company in Vancouver, Canada, through a venture capital firm up there. To them our machine looks very big, maybe too big for them. If I spent more time with them maybe they would pick up on it. But they don't seem to have much money. It often seems that the people who understand technical subjects either don't have any money, or if they do, they also have so many good technical ideas of their own that there isn't any left over.

Two other people I approached in Oregon are an electrical engineer and another man who considers himself more of a management expert...I must say he is a very good talker. I did find two smaller mills down there who seem interested in working with us if we can bring them a machine to try.

Seeking Capital

In search of capital, Paul Van Hague had talked to other people in business, including bankers and venture capitalists. None, he said, had been very helpful as yet.

Bankers I have talked to all seemed very friendly, and expressed a lot of interest in the company and me. But when it comes to the money, they turn me down. I couldn't even get a second

mortgage on my house.

It's much the same with venture capital firms, only worse. People had told me they were greedy. There seem to be quite a few examples around town where venture capitalists—not just their firms, but the individuals—have taken advantage of entrepreneurs. I think one of their problems is that they want very large profits very fast. They don't understand products that don't become obsolete fast and that take a long time to wear out. They may also shoot you down because of a bad investment they made in some other company they see as similar, even if it isn't. This was one of my painful experiences.

I called the head of a well-known venture capital firm down south and made an appointment to meet with him. When I arrived at the agreed-upon time, he wasn't even there. His assistant had never heard of me but was very nice and offered to hear my story. My impression of the head of the firm may be wrong, but I can't help thinking that he sees himself as sitting in the driver's seat with all the money, so he doesn't have to care. Why else wouldn't he show up, or at least send a apology later if he had to miss the meeting without giving notification?

Anyway, I talked to his assistant for two hours or so. He was very pleasant. He was even interested and wanted some references, which I gave him and he checked. And then after that it suddenly stopped. He sort of gave me a preliminary turn down, and I had a feeling that there was something I didn't know.

When I checked further, I found out they had invested in a California company that makes scanners and computer programs for the lumber industry. This investment didn't grow as fast as they had expected. I think that may have biased them against me.

I followed up the California company further by getting some brochures. They were fairly ordinary. Someone who had bought from them said they were one of the first pioneers with a new technology, but they had lost their lead and were now in the middle of the pack of about 10 other companies. It seems they definitely had a good application, and as soon as that was recognized a lot of other companies jumped in and gave them competition. The opportunity that company was capitalizing on was reduction of labor costs in the lumber industry, which is definitely a promising direction. It occurred to me that we could combine technology like that with our new saw and make it more attractive. But, of course, that would require still more capital.

I'm still willing to talk to venture capitalists, although from what I've seen and heard they don't seem to be too venturesome. I just don't know if the right amount of capital for us to attempt to employ is large enough to interest them, or if the payback will be fast enough and high enough. I have heard from others that too often they want to move too fast. Going into the sell stage too fast has produced some very unnecessary failures.

Looking Ahead

You can't tackle the whole job of getting a machine like this on the market all at one time. I feel there is a lot of potential. I have discussed it with so many knowledgeable people. I feel I have a pretty good idea. I don't think I have overlooked any major technical things. But there is still work to do. I can feel

very confident about it, but development takes time. It doesn't take all that much money if investors are willing to be patient.

I think the first step now would be more development. Maybe it would not require much money. But it is development, and there are not many people willing to invest in just development. Of course, many don't understand it.

As I mentioned, it's very difficult to work up good data on machine life. We have some from the prototype, but probably not enough. One finding from the testing we did was that we must make changes, particularly in the drive, which will be different on the next machine. The chain has a bad reputation at high speed. With a double belt drive it looks like we will be able to go faster and with little or no wear.

I would really like to meet someone who understands this financial stuff and knows how to put a financing proposal together. Instead, I am doing it more or less by myself. It is a struggle because I'm not a financial person. I know something about it from taking accounting courses and so on, which leaves me not completely ignorant. But it's not my field.

My most immediate job is to keep day-to-day things going and feed my family. My brothers and I still do a little work on the machine, but we are also doing other things. A little while ago I hired a young engineer to work with me. But a customer hired him away. It seemed to make both of them happy, so that's okay, I guess. But it didn't help me move toward what I'd really like, which would be to build a business around a proprietary product like this saw.

EXHIBIT 1 The CPC Saw Prototype

CPC saw with removed protective covers.

Patents granted :
USA 3,799,021

Canada 148,037

Great Britain 1393563

Germany 2121200

Austria 316848

France 72.14553

Italy 960882

Belgium 782.295

For further information contact :
Ir. G. Hammerschlag
Gezichtslaan 82
Bilthoven - the Netherlands
Tel. (030)-782889

EXHIBIT 2 Excerpts from Paul Van Hague's Planning Notes

PAUL VAN HAGUE, P.E.
Machine Design - Research and Development - Metric Conversion

THE CPC SAWING PROCESS AND ITS ADVANTAGES

The Sawing Process Generally

Sawing can be defined as cutting a piece of material by moving a thin blade with teeth across it, causing each tooth to remove a small chip of material.

This method of cutting has the following advantages:

1) Compared with shearing and punching it does not significantly deform the material next to the cut, nor does it induce stresses or hair cracks into the adjacent material.

2) Compared with flame cutting, due to the absence of a significant heat input, it does not affect the quality of the material next to the cut and does not cause distortion of the material.

3) Compared with milling, turning and other machining operations, to which it is of course related, it wastes less material due to the narrow cut (or "kerf" as the saw cut width is often called).

4) Compared with more exotic cutting methods, like electric discharge, electro-chemical, ultrasonic, water jet, abrasive jet, laser beam and electron beam cutting, its major advantage is its low cost.

Thus we see that sawing is the major method of cutting material in lumber manufacturing, woodworking and natural stone processing, while it is used extensively in cutting of metal and plastic raw materials produced in bar and extrusion form.

However, sawing has a problem of its own, as everybody who ever used a hacksaw or other hand saw knows. The thin blade gets easily deflected from its nominal position, causing the saw cut to deviate from its intended path and causing inaccuracy in the pieces made.

Every saw has this problem, whether it be one of the many kinds of reciprocating hand saws, the powered reciprocating frame saws, bandsaws or circular saws. Circular saws and bandsaws are often used with so called "saw-guides," pads of babbitt, Teflon or other material having low coefficient of friction. These pads are held against the saw blade and give additional support beyond what shaft (circular saw) or wheels (band saw) can give. Circular saws can be made thicker. However, this solution causes, besides of course a more expensive blade,

EXHIBIT 2 (continued)

more waste of material, since the saw cut will be wider. In fact, it will be a gradual change from saw blade to milling cutter if the blade is made thicker and thicker.

The CPC Principle

The CPC (Central Passage Circular) saw is a circular saw driven not by a central shaft, but by peripheral special chains, guided radially by rollers on the chain pins and axially by saw guides, eliminating the need for a central shaft.

The major advantage of this system is that it allows support of the saw blade for a given saw blade thickness and height-of-cut superior to conventional circular saws, both single arbor and double arbor types, while keeping the advantages of conventional circular saws over band and reciprocating saws.

Our mathematical calculations show that the CPC saw blade support is also much stiffer than that of double arbor circular saws, allowing a kerf for the CPC saw of only one-half to four-tenths that of a double arbor saw.(Of course again, not all of this increase in stiffness has to be used to reduce kerf; some of it could be used to increase accuracy.) In addition the CPC saw has the advantage that even if the saw blade is deflected, it will make a continuous cut, whereas the double arbor saw, if its two saws are deflected differently, will make an ugly ridge in the center of the sawn product.

It must also be mentioned that the CPC sawing principle has another advantage over both single and double arbor circular saws in that it cuts over the full height of the cut more or less perpendicular to the grain (like a band saw). This means that feed forces are very small, the resulting deflections of the machine and the material to be cut will be small, and the accuracy of the cut will be high. Also, when cutting wood, the cuttings will be short and crumbly (not like planer shavings), will easily fill up the gullet spaces in the blade and be easily sucked out of the gullets by a vacuum sawdust removal system, allowing very clean cutting.

Description of the Saw

A CPC sawing machine (Central Passage Circular saw) lets logs and beams pass across the central part of the circular saw. This is not possible with any other circular sawing machine due to the center shaft and its bearings, which block the passage of the central part. A conventional circular saw has a penetration limited to one third of its diameter. A CPC saw has a capacity of more than half of its diameter.

EXHIBIT 2 (continued)

Direct drive and guidance at the outside periphery, sawing teeth of hard metal (carbide) and large gullets for the sawdust between the sawing teeth guarantee a quiet and precise operation of the CPC saw and consequently straight pieces of timber.

Conventional circular sawing machines have a strongly varying direction of the motion of the sawing teeth with respect to the fiber direction of the wood. The cutting direction of the teeth of a CPC saw is always perpendicular to the fiber direction of the wood. Consequently, the sawdust is of a granular nature and can be easily removed.

A CPC sawing machine can be moved easily by truck to a working site, if it appears to be more economical to saw the trees on the spot and to transport the sawn timber afterwards.

Comparison with Band Saws

Band saws do not have a stiff support of the saw blade, mainly because the blade must be thin to bend over the wheels. As a result, band saws are the least accurate of the major saw types. They are popular in the lumber saw mills, because they can saw thick logs, cants, or lumber with narrower kerf than shaft-driven single or double arbor circular saws. Of course some of the advantage of the thin kerf is lost again due to their inaccuracy, requiring substantial removal of material in finishing. The CPC principle also allows thin kerf, but without the inaccuracy inherent in the band saw process and without the need for the large machine frame with the big wheels, the pit in the floor, the expensive and difficult-to-handle blades, and the larger filing room.

Comparison with Frame Saws

With a CPC saw, trees can be sawn into beams or boards and thus it can do work that used to be done with reciprocating saws. Reciprocating saws are big, expensive machines, and reciprocation of their heavy saw frame causes large acceleration and deceleration forces, resulting in wear of the bearings and guides. CPC sawing machines have no dynamic forces and are small compared to reciprocating sawing machines of comparable capacity. The attainable cutting speed of the CPC saws is twice that of reciprocating saws. Moreover, the sawing process is a continuous one, whereas the backward motion of reciprocation saws is idle.

Reciprocating frame saws, like band saws, can saw thick material with relatively thin kerf. However, the reciprocating motion means that in their extreme positions the saw blades do not move, while the feed of the material continues, causing momentarily very large bites per tooth, resulting in rough and inaccurate cutting and requiring large finish allowances. Also, the reciprocating movement does not allow high saw speeds, not even close to those of circular and band saws.

EXHIBIT 2 (continued)

Finally, the continuous acceleration and deceleration of the saw frame requires a large fly-wheel (if at least a somewhat reasonable saw speed is required) and a machine frame that can take the substantial acceleration and deceleration forces, leading to a rather large and heavy machine.

Estimated Savings with CPC Rotary Gang Saw

The savings from using a CPC Rotary Gang instead of a conventional rotary gang result from the thinner kerf and higher accuracy inherent in this new design. Feed speeds will be comparable to those of conventional rotary gangs. See the following table of saw characteristics.

Saw Characteristics	CPC Rotary Gang	Conventional Rotary Gang
Kerf	0.120"	0.160"
To be removed by planing per cut	0.030"	0.050"
Feed speed - max. practical	100 ft/min	100 ft/min

To determine yearly savings, the volume of wood that is converted into lumber instead of sawdust and planer shavings will be calculated for the following "typical" sawmill operation.

- Depth of cut: 4"–12", 7" average
- Feed speeds: 50–100 ft/min, 70 ft/min average
- Average number of cuts per pass: 5
- 2-shift operation, 250 days/year/4 hours of actual sawing per shift (2000 hrs. of sawing/year)

Length of cut sawed in one year:
2000 (hrs/yr.) x 60 (min/hr) x 70 (ft/min) x 3 (cuts/pass) = 42,000,000 ft/year

Volume in cubic feet of timber turned into sawdust and planer shavings with conventional rotary gang saw:
42,000,000 x 7/12 (height of cut, in ft) x (0.160 + 0.050)/12 (thickness of wood removed, in feet) = 428,750 cubic feet/yr. (= 5,145,000 bd. ft./yr.)

Same for CPC rotary gang saw:
42,000,000 x 7/12 x (.120 + .03)/12 = 306,250 cubic feet/yr. (= 3,675,000 bd.ft./yr.)

EXHIBIT 2 (continued)

Savings with CPC rotary gang per year:
428,750 - 306,250 = 122,500 cubic feet/yr. = 1,470,000 bd.ft./yr.

Assume value of lumber = $200 per 1,000 bd. ft.
Assume value of sawdust and planer shavings = $2 per 1,000 bd.ft
Value of savings is then:
(1,470,000/1,000) x ($200. - $2.) = $291,060

Savings with CPC Rotary Gang Saw

Estimated cost of conventional rotary gang: $200,000.
Estimated cost of CPC rotary gang: $300,000.
Assume interest on invested capital is 10%.
Higher interest cost CPC gang: 10% of $100,000. = $10,000/yr.
Higher depreciation cost CPC gang (assuming depreciation in 10 years): 1/10 x $100,000. = $10,000./yr.
Total increase of operation costs: $20,000./yr.
Net savings with CPC rotary gang:
$291,060 - $20,000 = $271,060/yr.

Assuming that the average thickness of the lumber produced with this rotary gang operation is 1.25 inches, the yearly production will be approximately: 42,000,000 (length of cut, ft/yr.) x 7/12 (depth of cut, ft) x 1.25 (thickness of lumber, inch) = 30,625,000 bd.ft./yr.

Note: Power consumption, number and skill of operators required, and maintenance cost for a CPC rotary gang are expected to be about the same as for a well-designed conventional rotary gang.

Summary

The CPC saw has superior stiffness of support of the saw blade over conventional shaft-driven single and double arbor circular saws, allowing approximately one-half the kerf of double arbor saws and one-third to one-quarter the kerf of single arbor saws for the same depth of cut. Also it does not have the problem of a possible mismatch of the two saw cuts, as double arbor circular saws have.

Further, its cutting more or less perpendicular to the grain leads to small feed forces contributing to accurate cut and crumbly cuttings that can be easily removed with a suction system.

Main advantages of the CPC saw over band saws are its more accurate cut, the less massive machine and the smaller, easier-to-handle-and-sharpen saw blades.

Main advantages of the CPC saw over frame saws are its higher speed, neater and more accurate cut and generally less massive machine.

EXHIBIT 2 (continued)

Estimated North American Market for CPC Rotary Gang Saw for Lumber Manufacture

I.   Softwoods
Production of one CPC rotary gang saw in two-shift operation will be approximately 30,000,000 bd.ft./yr.

Assume that lumber production from side boards will be approximately the same in magnitude. This means that there is a need for one rotary gang for approximately every 60,000,000 bd.ft. of lumber produced.

Yearly softwood production in North America (U.S.A. and Canada) is approximately 40,000,000,000 bd.ft.

Potential market for rotary gangs in softwood production: 40 billion/60 million = 666 machines

Assume life of a machine approximately 20 years. Thus market would be: 666/20 = 33.3 machines/year   At $30,000 per machine this would be $10,000,000 per year.

Accessory, spare parts and saw blade business would boost this to approximately $20,000,000 per year.

II.   Hardwoods

Harder wood and thinner boards would reduce production of rotary gang to approximately 15,000,000 bd.ft./yr. Assume again approximately the same amount of lumber from sideboards, thus one rotary gang per 30,000,000 bd.ft./yr.

Yearly hardwood production in North America is approximately 7,500,000,000 bd.ft./yr.

Potential market for rotary gangs is: 7.5 billion/30 million = 250 machines

Assume life of a machine approximately 20 years. Market would be then: 250/20 = 12 machines/year   At $300,000 per machine this would be $3,600,000 per year.

Accessory, spare parts and saw blade business would boost this to approximately $7,000,000 per year.

III. Total Rotary Gang Business in North American Wood Sawing Industry

$20,000,000 + $7,000,000 = $27,000,000 per year.

EXHIBIT 2 (continued)

Estimate of Capital Needs for Business Development

Four phases can be distinguished in this business development:

1) Preparation
2) First Production Machine
3) Growth
4) Stabilization when limit of market potential is reached

As no capital is needed in the final stabilization stage, this phase is not considered here.

Growth is considered only up to a yearly sales volume of $30,000,000 even though market investigation showed that total business potential, including spare parts, repair work and accessory equipment is in the $50,000,000 to $100,000,000 a year range for North America alone. The first three phases will not be discussed in more detail.

Phase 1 - Preparation

This period prior to design and manufacturing of the first production machine, estimated at approximately six months, is needed for the following activities:

1) Preparation of organization, including incorporation.
2) Negotiations with potential customers.
3) Completion of tests on prototype and demonstration of prototype to potential customers.

Expenses for this period will be:

Labor: 1 man 6 months, at $3,333 per month	$20,000
Materials for tests	10,000
Travel, office expenses and other overhead	20,000
Initial cash payment for license agreement	50,000
	Total $100,000

Income: none
Investment Requirement: $100,000.

EXHIBIT 2 (continued)

Phase 2 - First Production Machine

Assume that the first order consists of a rather large $300,000 machine (a conservative approach for calculating capital needs), that the customer wants delivery 18 months after placement of order, and is willing to pay 25 percent of price at placement of order, 25 percent of price six months and 12 months after placement of the order, and the final 25 percent at delivery of machine.

Expenses and income are calculated for this period on a monthly basis (See Table 1 below.) Personnel expenses are based on the assumption that during this period manpower will be on a constant level, a highly desirable situation in a high-technology business. Personnel listed in Table 1 are needed with approximately the salaries and overhead shown.

Table 1: Personnel Requirements of Phase 2

Skill	No.	Avg. Monthly Salary	Total Monthly Expense
Genl Mgr/Engr/Salesman	1	$3500	$3500
Design Engineer	2	2100	4200
Draftsman	1	1500	1500
Assembly Man	2	1500	3000
Secretary	1	800	800
Total direct salary expense			$13,000
Overhead (80%)			$10,400
Total monthly personnel expense			$23,400

Cost estimating, buying, production control and quality control functions will be performed mostly by engineering personnel (who always do this to a certain extent, even in large organizations). Quality control and production control functions will be performed by assembly people, also.

Parts manufacturing will be subcontracted and is estimated at 45 percent of the $135,000 sales price. Payments for parts are assumed to be distributed as follows: $3,000 per month the first six months after receipt of order, $15,000 per month the next six months and $4,500 per month the last six months.

Table 2 shows the personnel and parts expenses on a month-by-month basis. It also shows a 5 percent license fee payable at delivery of the machine, the progress payments for the machine by the customer and the investment capital required on a month-by-month basis. It is assumed that accounts receivable are equal to accounts payable, which eliminates the need to consider them in these calculations. The total amount to be invested will be $303,500. Note, if the first machine turns out to be less expensive, the capital required will be proportionately less.

If sufficient preparatory work with the customer can be done during the six-month, Phase 1

EXHIBIT 2 (continued)

period, final design and manufacturing of this machine will be possible in nine to 12 months, leaving six to 10 months of the 18-month, Phase 2 period for endurance testing of this machine and a strong sales effort helped by being able to show the machine to potential customers.

This would not have significant influence on the amount of capital required.

Table 2: Cash Flow and Capital Required in Phase 2
on a Month-by-Month Basis (Expenses in $)

Month	Payroll+ Overhead	Parts	Licenses	Total	Income	Invest. Req'd
1	23,400	3,000		26,400	75,000	—
2	23,400	3,000		26,400		—
3	23,400	3,000		26,400		4,200
4	23,400	3,000		26,400		26,400
5	23,400	3,000		26,400		26,400
6	23,400	3,000		26,400		26,400
7	23,400	15,000		38,400	75,000	—
8	23,400	15,000		38,400		1,800
9	23,400	15,000		38,400		38,400
10	23,400	15,000		38,400		38,400
11	23,400	15,000		38,400		38,400
12	23,400	15,000		38,400		38,400
13	23,400	4,500		27,900	75,000	—
14	23,400	4,500		27,900		—
15	23,400	4,500		27,900		8,700
16	23,400	4,500		27,900		27,900
17	23,400	4,500		27,900		27,900
18	23,400	4,500	15,000	42,900	75,000	—
Total	$421,200	$135,000	$15,000	$571,200	$300,000	$303,300

Note: Cash on hand at end of period: $32,100.

EXHIBIT 2 (continued)

Phase 3 - Growth

Assumptions for the ensuing four years would include the following:

The first year (third year from startup of venture), one rather large $300,000 machine per quarter is sold; the second year three such machines per quarter; the third year 10 machines; and the fourth year 25 machines per quarter. Not all machines will cost $300,000. Quantities will be different and jumps in sales will not occur exactly at the first of each year. However, these assumptions should allow estimation of the order of magnitude of capital requirements.

It is assumed that all machines will be delivered nine months after receipt of order, and that customers will make progress payments of 25 percent at placement of order, 25 percent three months and six months after placement of order, and the final 25 percent after delivery of machine. Personnel increases are assumed to take place at the same time sales jump, thus the first of each year. Personnel costs assume an average direct salary of $1,700 per month plus 80 percent ($1,360 per month) overhead.

Parts manufacturing will be subcontracted at cost 45 percent of sales price of $135,000 per machine. Parts will cost $6000 per month during the first three months and $9000 per month during the last three months of the period between placement of order and delivery of the machine.

Table 3 summarizes expenses (including a 5 percent license fee payable at delivery of the machines), income and capital needed. It assumes again accounts payable equal accounts receivable, and therefore do not need consideration. Note that the third year still requires a significant investment, but the following years show an increasing profit.

EXHIBIT 2 (continued)

Table 3: Cash Flow and Capital Required in Phase 3 on a Quarterly Basis

Year	Quarter	Expenses in $				Income in $	Investment Capital Required in $	Profit/Loss
		Payroll + Overhead	Parts	Licenses	Total			
3	1	128,520	18,000	—	146,520	75,000	*39,420	—
	2	128,520	108,000	—	236,520	150,000	86,520	—
	3	128,520	135,000	—	263,520	225,000	38,520	—
	4	128,520	135,000	15,000	278,520	300,000	—	21,480
	Total	514,080	396,000	15,000	925,080	750,000	164,460	21,480
4	1	275,400	171,000	15,000	461,400	450,000	—	11,400
	2	275,400	351,000	15,000	641,400	600,000	8,520	**32,880
	3	275,400	405,000	15,000	695,400	750,000	—	54,600
	4	275,400	405,000	45,000	725,400	900,000	—	174,600
	Total	1,101,600	1,332,000	90,000	2,523,600	2,700,000	8,520	229,200
5	1	697,680	531,000	45,000	1,273,680	1,425,000	—	151,320
	2	697,680	1,161,000	45,000	1,903,680	1,950,000	—	46,320
	3	697,680	1,350,000	45,000	2,092,680	2,475,000	—	382,320
	4	697,680	1,350,000	150,000	2,197,680	3,000,000	—	802,320
	Total	2,790,720	4,392,000	285,000	7,467,720	8,850,000	—	1,382,280
6	1	1,606,500	1,620,000	150,000	3,376,500	4,125,000	—	748,500
	2	1,606,500	2,970,000	150,000	4,726,500	5,250,000	—	523,500
	3	1,606,500	3,375,000	150,000	5,131,500	6,375,000	—	1,243,500
	4	1,606,500	3,375,000	375,000	5,356,500	7,500,000	—	2,143,500
	Total	6,426,000	11,340,000	825,000	18,591,000	23,250,000	—	4,659,000

*$32,100 was left from Phase 2

** Accumulated profits of previous two quarters

Preliminary Organizational Setup of Efficient Machinery Company

At present, Efficient Machinery Company is a sole proprietorship owned by Principal Founder. As soon as a significant business volume has been developed and/or other circumstances make this desirable, the company will be incorporated and 20,000 shares of common stock at a value of $1 each will be authorized for issue. The following types of stockholders will be distinguished:

EXHIBIT 2 (continued)

1) Principal Founder
2) Working Co-Founders (can work for company in their spare time or as employees)
3) Investors
4) Vendor Investors
5) Customer Investors

Founders

Upon incorporation, the principal founder will receive 10,200 shares in return for contributing his sole proprietorship to the incorporated business. Working co-founders will receive, for every "unit" of work performed for the company, either $50 in cash and a common stock share of $1 or a subordinated debenture of $50 and a common stock share of $1. A unit of work will consist of three and one-half hours of work, regardless of the kind of activities the co-founders perform.

After March 31, 1981, a unit of work will consist of three hours of work. The subordinated debentures will be payable within 10 years from date of issue with 12-percent interest, compounded daily, payable periodically or when debenture is paid back at the option of the company. Each working co-founder can earn his way up to 1000 shares of the company. After the company has been incorporated, key-employees, not co-founders, may get co-founder status, allowing them to earn shares as outlined above, upon invitation by the company.

Investors

Investors will receive for every $51 invested in the company a subordinated debenture of $50 and a common stock share of $1. Vendor investors are vendors who accept payment for articles, services, etc. supplied by them in the form of subordinated debentures. For each $50 in such subordinated debentures, they can buy a share of stock for $1.

A customer willing to buy a first machine, a model that has been upgraded but not yet proven, or a machine that is in any other way a risk to him, may be offered opportunity to buy a certain number of shares at par value ($1), but not more than one share for every $100 of equipment purchased. Such a customer will be considered a customer-investor.

Investor subordinated debentures will yield 12 percent interest and be payable within 10 years of issue, like co-founder subordinated debentures. Interest again can be paid either periodically or when the debenture is paid back, at the option of the company.

Further Methods of Investment

When 5000 of the 20,000 shares authorized have been issued to investors, the stockholders can decide by majority vote to authorize issue of more shares of common stock in batches of 20,000 shares with a par value of $1 each. Principal founder and co-founders, if employees of the company when stock issue is allowed, as well as key employees of the company having

EXHIBIT 2 (concluded)

co-founder status, will receive a percentage of new stock equal to the percentage of existing stock they own, at par value ($1 for each share).

Existing investors will have the option to buy a percentage of new stock equal to the percentage of existing stock they own at par value ($1 for each share) provided they invest at the same time in a certain amount of subordinated debentures. This amount, as well as the interest rate and pay-back conditions, will be set by the company. If existing investors do not exercise this option within one month from date of authorization of stock issue, the company may sell the stock to other investors on the same conditions offered to investors holding old stock. When new stock is issued, existing investors will receive for every share of par value $1 they own, X non-voting shares of par value $1 per the following formula:

  X = (total no. of new shares) / (total no. of old shares)

Non-voting stocks, if corporation is liquidated or sold, will participate in dividends and in distribution of available funds as if they are common stocks.

Management

The company will be managed by a president assisted by a management committee consisting of himself and up to six vice-presidents. Major decisions, to be defined in more detail at incorporation, will have to be approved by the board of directors.

Changes

Changes in this preliminary organizational setup will not be made until all prospective founders and investors have been notified of the intended changes and had a chance to give the management of the company their opinion about them. Until the company is incorporated, contributions made by prospective co-founders and investors will be loans to principal founder under conditions negotiated individually with him. He will inform prospective co-founders and investors of all such arrangements made.

Effectiveness

This preliminary organizational setup will go into effect when signed by principal founder and one or more co-founders and/or investors.

Case 36

Joe Walkuski

Now that he had filed for the patent, what next? Joe Walkuski pointed to a sketch of a hood and jacket, shown in Exhibit 1, that he had designed to keep a person warm and dry in cold, wet weather. At the suggestion of his brother-in-law, Joe had filed for a patent that he hoped would protect the unique design of the hood, which he said had the advantage of fitting close to the head and not restricting vision as other hoods did. Now, in April 1981, Joe was trying to decide how he could proceed with his ambition to commercialize his hood and become a successful entrepreneur.

A year had passed since he sewed the first prototype. Joe was now completing his first year of school at the Fashion Institute of Technology in New York City, where he was studying to become a Fabric Development Specialist. Although he wanted to finish developing the jacket and hood, he had another year of school remaining and no money of his own to invest in the venture. He was looking for summer work in the fabric industry, although uncertain about whether that was best, rather than pursuing his product idea full time. He observed:

Right now, I'm not sure what I should be doing. I'd like to gain experience by working in the industry, but I'd also like to finish school, and I'd like to keep moving with the hood and jacket and see if I could develop a market for it. I want to reach a point of designing my own outerwear, from selecting the fabric up through the finished product. That's what being a fabric development specialist, which is what I'd like to become, is all about.

Competitive products on the market range from $65 to $185. I think mine's better, but I don't know how to price it or what the best method to distribute it would be. If I don't find a job this summer, I'll probably go home to upstate New York, do some hiking and design some more jackets to go with the hood. I have a lot of questions right now about what else I might need to compete successfully and how to go about getting it.

Personal Background

Joe Walkuski was an avid hiker and climber who started college as an atmospheric sciences major. He said his treks into the Adirondacks often meant encountering cold weather or storms, and the foul weather gear he wore tended to restrict his vision and movement. Frustration in trying to stay dry and move about easily prompted him to wonder whether a hood could be designed that would fit around his head better. He began experimenting with various patterns until he came up with one he thought might work. In January 1980 he bought enough material to make a jacket and hood. With his mother's sewing machine, he completed the first prototype in February. Since the hood's drawstring was positioned to follow the top (or crown) of the head, side vision wasn't blocked by the edge of the hood when turning to look right or left. A vent in the front (along the neck) was to aid body ventilation, so the wearer wouldn't become hot and sweaty. Joe said this was important because body temperature was controlled to a great degree by the temperature of the head.

The jacket was a pullover with large pockets and loose-fitting sleeves. Both jacket and hood were made from Gore-Tex^{tm}, a synthetic fabric that combined features of breathability with being waterproof.

Investigating the Hood's Market Potential

Joe tried out the complete hood and jacket and was pleased with it. He thought others might like to have a jacket like it and sewed a couple more to show to friends and mountaineering shops near his home. One such store in Latham, New York, offered to sell the garment on consignment. This encouraged Joe to contact various suppliers and ask what the cost of raw materials would be in limited quantities.

One weekend in spring, Joe took his jacket to show to his sister and brother-in-law in New Jersey. As they talked about the possibility of Joe visiting different stores in the New York area during the summer to sell the coat, his brother-in-law suggested patenting the concept and design of the hood. Joe decided to seek advice from a patent attorney. He described how this led to filing for a patent.

I started looking through the phone book until I came to patent attorneys and ended up talking with three different firms. They convinced me I should abandon the idea of trying to sell the jacket during the summer, and instead, seek patent protection so no one else could use the same concept in making hoods. I chose an attorney who said he would hand-deliver the jacket to Washington, D.C., and do all of the paperwork. I figure that I've spent about 50 hours of my time on the application,

mostly in drawings of the hood.

The patent application consisted of drawings and a precisely worded description of the hood which Joe termed "hat theory." After spending a couple of sessions with his attorney to learn what patents could and could not accomplish, Joe submitted his drawings and written description of the hood to the lawyer. By autumn 1980 the application had been filed with the U.S. Patent Office. Joe said he had spent $1,300 on the patent application thus far, and the process would take one to four years to complete. Meanwhile, he could put "patent pending" on the product to dissuade competitors from copying his hood. He explained that the filing date was important since, should the patent be approved, he would be able to challenge any use of his hood concept by manufacturers who started making identical products after the filing date.

He added that the design was otherwise relatively easy to copy. The drawstring made the hood unique by the way it traveled from the forehead in the front to the top of the neck in the back. Conventional hoods had drawstrings along the outline of the face, as illustrated in Exhibit 2. Consequently, Joe said, his design let the hood fit the head snugly and follow its movement more naturally than traditional hood designs. His list of competitively advantageous features for outdoor enthusiasts appears in Exhibit 3.

Through summer and fall Joe looked in retail stores and magazines to see which companies were producing similar garments using the Gore-Tex fabric. He pointed out that the principal manufacturers were located in the Western United States. North Face was in Berkeley, California, while REI Cooperative, Early Winters, and the Yak Works were in Seattle, Washington. Smaller companies included Log House Designs in Vermont, Pack Form in

Rhode Island (although they didn't appear to be using Gore-Tex), Sea Bee Sports in Vermont, Chuck Roast in New Hampshire and Eastern Mountain Sports, Inc., a retail chain based in New Hampshire that specialized in hiking, camping, and skiing equipment. A grid comparing competitors, prepared by the casewriter in discussion with Joe, appears in Exhibit 4.

Other companies, such as Sierra West, Sierra Designs, Class Five, Eddie Bauer, and Frostline Kits, offered outerwear garments, but they either did not use or did not stress using Gore-Tex fabric in their product line. Joe emphasized that most of the companies appeared to be doing well in sales of coats, jackets and parkas. Financial information and other data on size of the market was difficult to find, he added. Most of the companies were privately owned and did not publish annual reports for the general public. Moreover, this segment of the apparel industry seemed relatively new, made possible by the growing popularity of outdoor recreation and improvements in synthetic fibers. Census data were specific only to the extent of calling the market segment "waterproof outer garments," in which traditional raincoats purchased in the spring and early summer formed the market peak.

In contrast, the peak season for jackets such as his, Joe said, was autumn and early winter. Its typical buyers were cross country skiers, hikers, campers, kayakers and mountain climbers. Garments made with Gore-Tex seemed to be aimed at the higher priced end of the recreation market, since fabric with that feature costs more.

Magazines such as *Sport Style, Ski, Sail,* and *Outdoor Life* contained advertisements of some garment manufacturers, Joe remarked. Further sources of information were catalogs and brochures of the manufacturers themselves, typically printed in color on slick paper. Joe summed up his perceptions of the market potential for garments such as his.

All the manufacturers seem to be doing really well. I had a couple of stores in the New York metro area lined up to sell my garment on consignment last summer, even before I decided to file for the patent. I wish that there were better information on the size of the market or buying habits. I do know that W. L. Gore and Company puts out the top-of-the-line fabric, and that most of the companies making and selling jackets started out small. As for huge conglomerates moving in on this part of the apparel industry, I can't think of any.

Moving Into Startup

Joe had sewn six jackets at home by the end of the summer 1980 and had enrolled in a two-year program at the Fashion Institute to study textiles and fabric. In his spare time, he worked on patterns, and tested finished coats by walking around Manhattan or going on weekend hikes in upstate New York. He mentioned that testing and quality control were important considerations for him, and that the school's laboratory facilities allowed him to do some strength testing of the jackets and fabric. One benefit the school offered was what Joe called the "gripping machine," which he described as follows:

Essentially it's a machine with two mechanical hands on each side. You put a piece of fabric in the machine and it pulls at the garment until either the seam or the fabric tears apart. Most people believe that the seams should be stronger than the fabric. I think that the reverse should be the case, because if you tear the garment at the seam, the integrity of the fabric is still there. If the fabric rips, you have to start patching up the coat in areas where it originally wasn't intended to be sewn together.

He added that most producers, such as North Face and Early Winters, relied on users trying the garments out in actual field conditions to assess performance. These companies would then state in promotion literature that the jacket had been "subjected to extensive field testing." Guarantees for the products were either implied or stated. Joe thought that if he used Gore-Tex fabric, consumers would expect high quality and that this would help build a reputation for high quality in his products.

Three types of firms produced apparel. First were proprietary manufacturers who controlled all steps of production, from initial design to selling the finished goods to retailers. Second were contracting firms that owned designs and bought fabric for a third type of firm to sew into garments. This third type consisted of jobbing companies that did not hold title to fabric or designs, but simply cut and sewed to specification, then returned the finished garments to the contracting companies, who then sold them to retailers.

Joe had talked with Maryland-based W.L. Gore, Inc. about obtaining raw materials. They gave him cost figures and mentioned that they did not perform assembly work for garments. Joe said he was reluctant to have another company sew the garment together, for fear of losing control over quality of his product. Moreover, if he were to continue designing and producing jackets, he wanted to work in a separate location from his home or apartment. He had a distaste for working and living in the same place, and problems with zoning restrictions might arise by working out of the home. He estimated that approximately 3,000 square feet of space would be needed for sewing machines, cutting table, related equipment, and inventory storage. He hadn't yet explored the availability or price of space for setting up an office and production facility.

By relying on Gore's fabric standards, conducting field tests of the garments, and using the school's test facilities, Joe explained that his test equipment needs should be kept to a minimum. He did, however, want to obtain a seam-sealing machine so the seams could be waterproofed at the factory for a ready-to-wear garment. Otherwise, consumers had to buy small tubes of liquid sealer to apply to seams after buying the jacket. Joe pointed out that at least one manufacturer had added a sealing machine to its production process, figuring that the convenience aspect was a major selling point for the garment. He admitted that the machine wasn't a necessity for start-up. Rather, it would provide a competitive advantage to help promote his garments.

Joe estimated some of his start-up expenses, as shown in Exhibit 5. Purchasing minimal amounts of raw materials to begin making the jackets and hoods, he estimated materials costs at close to $32 for a pull-over jacket. Based on the garments he had sewn the previous summer, Joe estimated that from 10 to 12 hours of labor at $3 an hour, would be required to complete one jacket and hood. His overall estimate for a large Anorak-type outergarment was around $62 in variable costs, as tabulated in Exhibit 6.

Also, there would be machinery purchases, inventory requirements, and costs for leasing space and having an office. Joe figured that inventory would require an initial $7,000 investment, supplementing his existing inventory valued at $792, as shown in his estimated balance sheet in Exhibit 7. The minimum Joe figured he would need to get started was $18,000: $10,000 in fixed assets, $7,000 for raw materials, and $1,000 for office and miscellaneous expenses. He mentioned that family and friends might be able to supply $10,000 in start-up capital, although he was not sure.

Developing Sales

Distribution of outerwear, according to Joe, generally involved the manufacturer selling directly to retail outlets. Sometimes, a factory outlet store might be set up to sell directly to consumers at the point of production. Other strategies included sales by mail order (e.g., L.L. Bean), and selling kits through mail order or retail stores for the consumer to complete product assembly in the home (e.g., Frostline Kits).

One friend in Joe's home town who ran a mail order catalog business offered advice on how to sell his product. Some of this advice, coupled with Joe's reluctance to offer large discounts to retail stores, had led him to prefer mail order or factory outlets for distribution. Joe explained:

> The discount structure is such that retail price is about twice as much as wholesale. When I first started talking with stores and heard what they wanted, I told them they were crazy—they weren't putting any effort into the product. So I'm trying to stay away from the retailer and reach the consumer directly.

Looking Ahead

As Summer 1981 approached, Joe saw two main options for applying his time and advancing his career interest in fabrics. One was to seek employment with a manufacturer such as W.L. Gore where he might learn more about production processes for making fabric or clothing and develop more industry contacts. However, he feared that if he chose that option he might, by not moving fast enough, lose the opportunity to start a venture. He had seen that styles constantly changed, companies were always coming up with new design ideas such as his, and consumer interests could shift away from the kinds of garments his invention best fitted.

Another option he saw would be to concentrate full-time on his hood design as the basis for a business venture. Joe said he thought his strengths lay in being self-motivated, being good in dealing with people and public relations aspects of business and possessing organizational skills. He was nearly finished with the first year of his two-year program at the Fashion Institute and added that he would like to finish school during the coming year. One course he was currently taking involved business management. He believed there was much he still needed to learn, commenting:

> Sometimes I wish I had majored in apparel production management instead of fabric development. My goal is to be involved in all aspects of the production process, from designing the fabric to managing the way the garment is put together and made ready for sale. The part of the industry that is exciting to me is what I call applied outerwear—jackets like the ones I've made. If nothing else, I could spend the summer at home, designing more jackets with the hood I came up with. I turned down a summer job with White Stag, but Gore is still a possibility.
>
> Pricing has been a problem for me, and I want to make sure that any garment I offer for sale has been fully tested and meets the highest expectations as to quality and performance. The potential is there for a business. I just wish I knew how to proceed with all the pieces to the puzzle to make it work.

EXHIBIT 1   Hood and Jacket Design

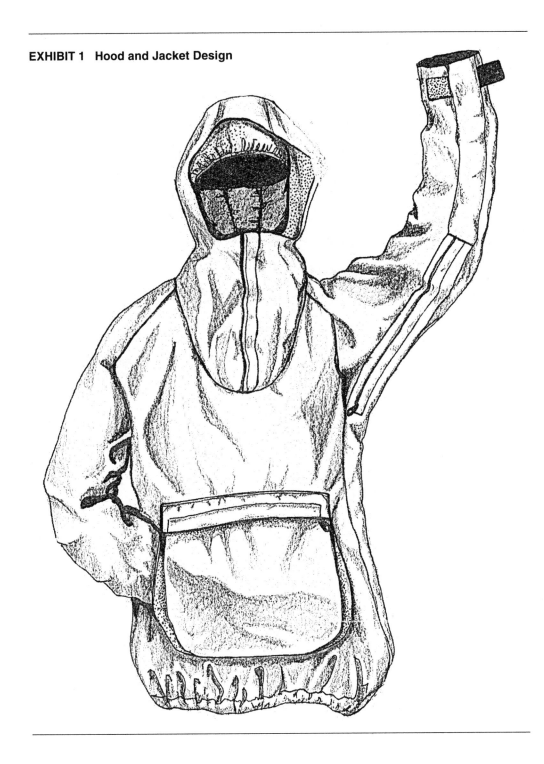

EXHIBIT 2 Example of a Competitive Hood

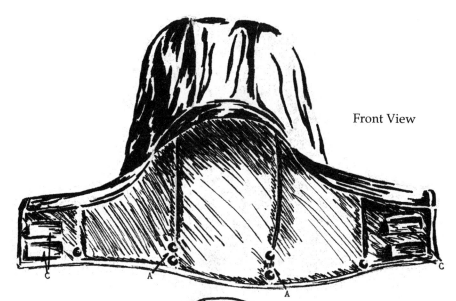

Front View

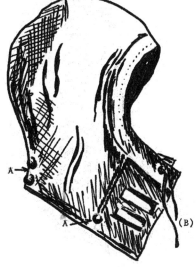

SIDE VIEW OF HOOD

Drawings not to scale; portray design of a commercial hood now sold by an outerwear manufacturer.

This version of a hood is attached to the coat by fastening the metal snaps (A) to their counterpart along the coat's collar. The hood is contoured to the head and made snug by pulling on the drawstrings (B), which reduces the front opening. A final "seal" is made by fastening the rectangular snaps, which are made from a plastic-like fiber and can be attached and pulled apart many times (C).

EXHIBIT 3   Competitive Features of the Hood and Jacket

(The Anorak Pullover)

HOOD FEATURES

* Circum - Crown Drawstring
* Three Piece Construction
* Front Vent Formed by Full Cut Sides (to vent excess heat)
* 12" Velcro Closure
* Beak to Cover Vent
* Nylsilk Nylon Lining
* Velcroed Fold for Collar Formation
* Baggy Cut for Ease of Movement

SLEEVE FEATURES

* Raglan Design
* Radical Arm Hole Cut
* Velcro-Closed and Adjustable Cuff

SIDE PANEL FEATURES

* Runs from Cuff to Bottom Hem
* Has Double Protected Inset Zipper, Underarm
* Enhances Upward Stretching Freedom

FRONT PANEL FEATURES

* Large Expansion Pocket, Zippered at Top
* Kangaroo Style
* Pack Belt Goes Behind
* Jacket Stuffs into Pack Belt to Form Carrying Pouch

EXHIBIT 4 Competitive Products Grid

FOR SALE OF FUNCTIONAL OUTERWEAR GARMENTS

Company	Use of Gore-Tex	Price Range of Product	Hood Design	Test-ing	Primary Area of Sales	Esti-mated Company Size#	Use of Fac-tory Sealed Seams	Primary Method of Distribution	Primary Method of Production##
Walkuski (Functional Outdoor Garments)	Yes	Medium	New	?	New England Northeast	Small	Yes	Mail Order Factory Outlet	Manufacturer
Yak Works	Yes	High	Trad.	Y	Western U.S.	Small	No Retail	Mail Order	Manufacturer
R.E.I. COOP	Yes	Low	Trad.	Y	Western U.S.	Medium	Yes	Retail (Own Store) Mail Order	Manufacturer Manufacturer
North Face	Yes	Medium	Trad.	Y	Western U.S.	Medium	No	Retail Mail Order	Manufacturer
Early Winters	Yes	Medium	Trad.	Y	Western U.S.	Medium	Yes	Retail Mail Order	Manufacturer
E.M.S., Inc.	Yes	Medium	Trad.	Y	Eastern U.S.	Medium	No	Retail (Own Store)	Mail Order Contractor
Other Traditional Producers*	Yes & No	Medium to High	Trad.	Y	Nationwide	Small to Medium	No	Retail Mail Order	Manufacturer Contractor
Eddie Bauer	Yes	High	Trad.	Y	Nationwide	Medium	No	Retail (Own Store) Mail Order	Contractor
Frostline Kits	Yes	Low	Trad.	Y	Western U.S.	Medium	No	Mail Order	Manufacturer
Major Retail Chains**	Yes & No	Low to Medium	Trad.	Y	Nationwide	Medium to Large	No	Retail (Own Store) Retail (Own Store) Mail Order	Contractor

#Estimated Size of Company: Small, Medium or Large; guessing at sales volume. ##Primary Method of Production (in order listed): Manufacturer (controlling process all the way through) or Contractor (jobbing out for cutting and sewing to complete the garments). **Sears, J.C. Penney's, and regional retail chains.
*Includes Sierra West, Class Five, Log House Design and others.

EXHIBIT 5 Cost Estimates

FUNCTIONAL OUTDOOR GARMENTS

LIST OF START-UP COSTS   (If I'm starting again from scratch)
Costs based on minimum order requirements per supplier.

Raw Materials
        Gore-Tex (500 yds, laminate and lamination fee)
            500 yds. ripstop nylon @ $1/yd. $500
            Lamination fee (twice) @ $5.35/yd.x 500 yd.
        Sub Total $5,850 $ 5,850

        Velcro @ $.27/yd; minimum order of 100 yds.
        Quantity of 1,000 yds., enough for 250 jackets $270

        YKK Zipper @ $.75/meter; order qty of 200 meter $150

        YKK Zipper Tabs @ $.10 each; order qty of 750 $75

        Thread @ $4/cone (use one cone per ten jackets)
            Quantity of 25 cones $100

        D - Ring, drawstring, and cordlocks (estimated) $ 90

        Total, Raw Materials $6,535

Fixed Assets
        Building   ?

        Seam sealing machine $6,000

        Four sewing machines (new) $4,000

        Cutting table/machine $2,000

Administrative Overhead (Excluding direct labor)   ?

Total Start-up Costs (Excluding undetermined
    costs for building lease or purchase and
    administrative overhead, ofc. equipt, mktg, etc.) $18,535

Note: No allowance has been made for wastage of material, subsequent cash flow
needs or costs for labor and selling expense.

EXHIBIT 6 Pricing

FUNCTIONAL OUTDOOR GARMENTS VENTURE

Detailed Pricing Estimate

Item	Unit Cost	Quantity Used	Total Cost
Gore-Tex	$6.58/yd.	4 yds.	$26.32
Nylsilk hood lining	1.25/yd.	0.4 yd.	.50
Velcro	1.175/yd/side =	0.33 yd. @ 1 1/2"	.40
Velcro	.788/yd/side	2.5 ft.	.65
Zipper	.45/yd.	4 ft.	.60
Zipper tabs	.10 each	3	.30
D-Rings	.05 each	1	.05
Drawstring	.06/yd.	2 yds.	.12
Cordlocks	.20 each	2	.40
Thread	n.a.	insignificant	-0-
"Cushion" for wastage	n.a.	n.a.	2.00
TOTAL COST, MATERIAL			$31.34

Estimate is based on the material used for one large size pull-over jacket.

Direct labor is estimated at $30.00 per jacket; thus material and labor costs, as above, total $61.34 per jacket.

Material costs based upon invoice price as stated for 5/1/80.

EXHIBIT 6 (concluded)

PRICING

> $ 31.34 = Cost of materials for a Large Anorak
> $ 30.00 = Cost of Labor
> $ 61.34 = Total Cost of One Large Anorak

Labor is conservatively estimated, actual cost of labor would hopefully be decreased due to mass production.

> * Calculated retail price of 1 Large Pull-over (Spring 1980) = $80.00

> * Calculated retail price of 1 Large Pull-over (Winter 1981) = $125.00

The increase in cost is due to the cost of the patent application and a more logical appraisal of overhead estimates and other costs. The increase is not due to any increased cost of materials.

Factory seam-sealing process would further add to the cost of the jacket, from both the retail price and start-up costs involved.

Actual market prices for comparable quality jackets range from $65 to $185.

Pricing has been the most difficult task to date, receiving only limited priority.

EXHIBIT 7   Balance Sheet

FUNCTIONAL OUTDOOR GARMENTS

For the Period Ending 4-10-81

Current Assets

Cash		$ 0
Accounts Receivable*		230
Inventory**		
Gore-Te	520	
Velcro	60	
Nylsilk Nylon	12	
Fibre fill	150	
Other materials	50	
Total		792
Total Current Assets		1,022

Total Assets $1,022

Current Liabilities

Accounts Payable	0
Pending Orders***	150
Total Current Liabilities	$150

Total Liabilities $150

Owner's Equity $872

Total Liabilities and Owner's Equity $1,022

    *   Pending Orders
   **   Stated at cost (5/1/80)
  ***   Stated at cost of materials plus labor

Case 37

Windsurfer (A)

The Start-up

Hoyle Schweitzer's inspiration to start a company to manufacture sailboards came from a 1965 conversation with an acquaintance, Jim Drake. The two were comparing two sports they enjoyed, surfboarding and sailing when it occurred to them that it might be possible to combine the two by mounting a sail on a surfboard to propel it.[1]

They began constructing prototypes in quest of a design that could be steered without a rudder, as a surfboard was, but with power coming from the sail rather than a wave. When they achieved a design that worked they applied for a patent for a "wind-propelled apparatus in which a mast is universally mounted on a craft and supports a boom or sail." Twenty two months later, in January 1970, the patent was issued as number 3,487,800. An excerpt from the *Patent Gazette* containing the announcement of this patent appears as Exhibit 1.

Schweitzer, his wife and Drake formed a company, Windsurfing International, to make and sell their invention. The novelty of it attracted attention and even practical jokes: When they displayed it at a boat show, someone modified the sailboard by adding a large helm and portable toilet. But it began to catch on. The Schweitzers bought out Drake in 1973.

Success of the product, however, inspired imitators, and to protect it Schweitzer filed suit for infringement of his patent. In the legal combat that followed, it was discovered that another man, S. Newman Darby, had created a similar device which looked like a door with an upside-down kite stuck into the socket in the center. The rider stood in front of the kite and leaned back against it as the wind blew it forward and propelled the flat door-like board across the water. Darby made no attempt to patent his invention, but a description and photograph showing it in operation appeared in a 1965 issue of *Popular Science*. Thus Schweitzer's patent became threatened.

Schweitzer claimed that his design represented a significant innovation beyond Darby's "prior art," as required to keep his patent valid, because of differences in design of his windsurfer's triangular sail and boom in contrast to Darby's kite-like arrangement. This novelty, Schweitzer asserted, gave much more control to the operator.

Would-be competitors disputed Schweitzer's claim of advance beyond prior art and sold imitations as the sport caught on and the market for sailboards rapidly grew. Schweitzer sued one imitator after another, resulting in a series of court decisions. By 1981 he had spent over a half million dollars on lawsuits and won 40 of them. But there were by then over 100 imitators still doing business. The U.S. Patent Board of Appeals decreed in favor of Schweitzer that his "hand-held wishbone rigging combined with the vehicle swivel mast attachment produces, in our opinion, a unique sailing apparatus which functions with the user in a manner that is completely unrecognized in any art before us." But subsequently the Patent Office rejected

---

[1]Mamis, Robert A., "Hoyle Schweitzer's Decade of Discontent", Inc, February, 1982, p. 54.

that decision, which in turn led to another appeal.

The litigation continued, leading to still further decisions. One from the U.S. Court of Appeals which was rendered in early 1986 appears in Exhibit 2.

EXHIBIT 1   Excerpt from Patent Gazette, January 6, 1970

106   OFFICIAL GAZETTE   JANUARY 6, 1970

3,487,798
SEWING MACHINE FOR PRODUCING BELT LOOPS AND THE LIKE
Nerino Marforio, Milan, Italy, assignor to S.p.A. Virginio Rimoldi & C., Milan, Italy
Filed Aug. 28, 1968, Ser. No. 755,932
Claims priority, application Italy, Sept. 7, 1967, 20,221/67
Int. Cl. D05b 23/00, 37/04
U.S. Cl. 112—121.27   11 Claims

A sewing machine for producing belt loops and the like from off-cuts of random length which are sewn end-to-end to form a continuous lengthwise strip, including means for preventing the cutting knife from cutting said strip along any portion thereof which is of a thickness other than the uniform thickness required for the loops, and also including means for automatically sorting reject loops from satisfactory ones, as well as a counter means adapted to count only the satisfactory loops.

3,487,799
ROOF SEAMING MACHINE
Sven Olof Grönlund, Marumsgatan 16, Skara, Sweden
Filed Apr. 12, 1968, Ser. No. 721,024
Int. Cl. B21d 39/02, 19/04
U.S. Cl. 113—55   2 Claims

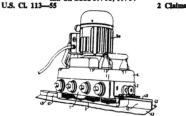

The present invention relates to roof seaming machines for forming standing seams to interconnect adjacent roofing sheets and is of the kind comprising a carriage with pair-wise arranged rolls which successively perform the seaming operation when the carriage is moved along the upstanding sheet flanges. One of the rolls of each pair, hereinbelow termed the folding roll, is adapted to be displaced outward relative to the other roll, herein termed the counter roll, and is acted upon by a compression spring such as to be biased toward the counter roll and to assist in folding the upstanding sheet flange or sheet flanges for producing a single or double seam. Accordingly, one of the rolls must be movable towards and away from the other roll in order to enable the spring to act

on the folding roll and to enable the folding roll and the counter rock to adjust themselves to various thicknesses of the seam.

3,487,800
WIND-PROPELLED APPARATUS
Hoyle Schweitzer, 317 Beirut, Pacific Palisades, Calif. 90272, and James Drake, 385 Mesa, Santa Monica, Calif. 90402
Filed Mar. 27, 1968, Ser. No. 716,547
Int. Cl. B63b 15/02; B63h 9/10
U.S. Cl. 114—39   14 Claims

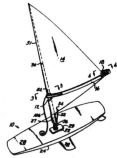

Wind-propelled apparatus in which a mast is universally mounted on a craft and supports a boom and sail. Specifically a pair of curved booms are arcuately connected athwart the mast and secure the sail therebetween, the position of the mast and sail being controllable by the user but being substantially free from pivotal restraint in the absence of such control.

ERRATUM

For Class 114—77 see:
Patent No. 3,487,807

3,487,801
METHOD AND APPARATUS FOR STABILIZATION OF VESSELS
Mario C. Calvi, Santa Susana, Calif., assignor to The Ralph M. Parsons Company, Los Angeles, Calif., corporation of Nevada
Filed Oct. 31, 1966, Ser. No. 590,723
Int. Cl. B63b 43/06
U.S. Cl. 114—125   16 Claims

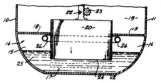

A ship stabilization system having passive tanks opposite sides of the ship with an interconnecting passage for the flow of liquid between the tanks. The effective cross-sectional area of the interconnecting passage varied to maintain the natural period of flow of the liquid in excess of the period of roll of the vessel. The cross sectional area is varied in one embodiment by shifting transversely one of the walls defining the passage, and

EXHIBIT 2   U.S. Court of Appeals Decision, January 28, 1986[2]

Background

(1) Proceedings in District Court

Windsurfing International (WSI) sued AMF, BIC and Downwind, alleging infringement of its '167 patent. AMF then sought a declaratory judgment that the patent is invalid for obviousness, unenforceable because of patent misuse, and not infringed. Also, AMF sought the cancellation of WSI's registrations of "WINDSURFER" and related trademarks[3] on grounds that the marks had become generic. BIC sued WSI, seeking a declaration that the '167 patent is invalid for obviousness, unenforceable, and not infringed.

Consolidating the three actions, the district court held a non-jury trial on 13 dates between November 19 and December 11, 1984, filed an opinion July 15, 1985 and entered judgments on September 11, 1985. AMF, BIC, and Downwind appeal from the judgments holding the '167 patent valid and infringed. AMF and BIC appeal from the grant of injunctions.[4] WSI cross-appeals from the judgments holding it misused its patent and refusing to enjoin Downwind.

(2) The '167 Patent

The patent in suit relates to the sport of "sailboarding,"[5] in which participants ride boards propelled by wind striking sails attached to the boards.

A preferred embodiment of the claimed invention is shown in Figure 1 of the '167 patent:

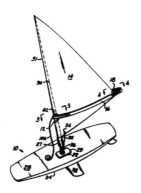

---

[2]282 F. 2nd 995 (Fed. Cir. 1986)

[3]U.S. Trademark Registration No. 962.616. 997.974 1.180.024. and 1.195.641. The district court held that WSI's trademarks have become generic. The district court has not yet entered judgement to that effect and the trademark issue of genericness is not part of this appeal.

[4]The district court permanently enjoined AMF, but "preliminarily" enjoined BIC pending termination of a related action by Intervener James R. Drake claiming an ownership interest in the '167 patent.

[5]We refer to the patented structure as a "sailboard" and not as a "windsurfer" because whether the latter term has become generic is not yet final.

EXHIBIT 2 (continued)

A participant stands on the top surface of surfboard 10 behind universal joint 36, grasps boom 16 or boom 18 (depending on wind direction), and controls the speed and direction of the board by maneuvering the boom to which sail 14 is attached. If a participant begins to lose control in a sudden wind surge, he or she merely releases the boom and the universal joint allows the sail to fall freely into the water.

Claim 15 from the patent is representative:

Wind-propelled apparatus comprising body means adapted to support a user and wind-propulsion means pivotally associated with said body means and adapted to receive wind for motive power for said apparatus, said propulsion means comprising a mast, a joint for mounting said mast on said body means, a sail and means for extending said sail laterally from said mast *comprising two opposed booms secured to said mast for guiding said sail therebetween and adapted to provide a hand-hold for said user on either side of said sail while sailing,* the position of said propulsion means being controllable by said user, said propulsion means being substantially free from pivotal restraint in the absence of said user, said joint having a plurality of axes of rotation whereby said sail free falls along any of a plurality of vertical planes upon release by said user.

The understood limitation sets forth the boom and was added when WSI's U.S. Patent No. 3,487,800 was reissued as the '167 patent.

Issues

Did the district court err in: (1) holding the claimed invention nonobvious[6] (2) finding infringement; (3) holding patent misuse; (4) enjoining AMF and BIC; and (5) refusing to enjoin Downwind.

Opinion

(1) Non-obviousness

On appeal, AMF[7] argues that the district court erred in upholding the '167 patent because it: (a) improperly deferred to decisions by the U.S. Patent and Trademark Office Board of Appeals (Board); (b) compared preferred and commercial embodiments with the prior art; and (c) considered commercial success having no nexus with the claimed invention.

---

[6]35 U.S.C. § 103 provides:
A patent may not be obtained…if the differences between the subject matter sought to be patented and the prior art are such that the subject matter as a whole would have been obvious at the time the invention was made to a person having ordinary skills in the art to which said subject matter pertains.
[7]Because BIC raises many of the same arguments, and Downwind relies principally on the arguments raised by BIC and AMF, this opinion hereinafter refers to the three parties collectively as AMF, unless otherwise indicated.

EXHIBIT 2 (continued)

(a) Deference

[1] In deferring to the Board's decisions concerning the allowance of the claims in the reissued patent, the district court was recognizing the statutory mandate that all patents are presumed valid. The district court carefully considered whether the evidence not presented in the "fiercely contested adversarial proceeding" before the Board would ease AMF's burden of proving facts compelling a conclusion of invalidity.[8] Concluding that the evidence at trial was merely cumulative of that before the Board, the court correctly held that evidence did not enable AMF to carry the burden.

AMF contends that, because the Board did not mention the obviousness of replacing the rig, shown in a publication referred to as the "Darby reference," with the boom disclosed in the '167 patent, no deference is due the Board decisions. The district court carefully reviewed the administrative record and stated that such argument "oversimplifies the depth of the Board's review and assumes the Board ignored other issues raised in the parties' extensive briefs." We agree. Merely because a decision does not mention a particular point "forms no basis for an assumption that it did not consider those elements." Moreover, the district court correctly noted that "the Board . . . reaffirmed its original holding that combination of the hand-held wishbone rigging [boom] with the vehicle swivel mast attachment produces . . . a unique sailing apparatus....'" We are satisfied that the district court did not err in this case in giving "deference that is due to a qualified government agency presumed to have properly done its job."

(b) Comparison

[2] The district court conducted a thorough *Graham*[9] analysis before concluding that the claimed invention at the time it was made would not have been obvious to one of ordinary skill in the art. AMF attacks the district court's findings as clearly erroneous, asserting it compared to the prior art not the claimed invention but commercial and preferred embodiments as representative of the claimed invention (claims, not embodiments, are focus of obviousness inquiry). Those embodiments include a "scoop" on a slimmer hull-shaped board, a skeg (or fin on the bottom at the back), and footstraps. Thus, they argue that the advantages found by the court are attributable to a combination of those design improvements and not to the claimed invention.

The district court did determine that it would have been obvious to replace a kite sail

---

[8]The "proceeding" referred to comprised the initial application for reissue, a protest, an appeal to the Board, a remand to the examiner, a second appeal to the Board, and an appeal to the Court of Customs and Patent Appeals. The district court described these events in its opinion. 613 F. Supp. at 942-44, 227 USPQ at 934-35.
[9]Graham v. John Deere, 383 U.S. 1, 17-18, 86 S.Ct. 684, 693-94, 15 L.Ed. 2d 545, 148 USPQ 459, 467 (1966).
[10]Contrary to BIC and Downwind's contentions, a conclusion that it would have been obvious to replace the sails and add a boom does not require a conclusion that the claimed invention considered as a whole would have been obvious. The claims include more, e.g., a universal joint and its relationship to board, mast, boom and sail.

EXHIBIT 2 (continued)

with a force and aft sail, and to add a second opposed boom.[10] Properly looking to the claimed invention at the time it was made as a whole, the district court correctly concluded that "the combination of the hand-held wishbone rigging with the universal joint produced a vehicle that performs in a manner previously undisclosed by any of the prior art references before us and, indeed, a vehicle with a performance potential that is even now not yet fully realized."

WSI's expert, Dr. Bradfield, conceded that certain advantages were due to particular added improvements, but he consistently maintained that the overall performance capabilities of the claimed invention were mainly due to the combination of the universal joint and the wishbone rigging. The district court found that testimony credible and AMF has shown no basis on which this court could engage in the normally inappropriate process of substituting a contrary credibility determination for that of the district court.

(c) Nexus

Before concluding that the combination of the universal joint with the wishbone rigging would not have been obvious, the district court reviewed the objective evidence, and correctly sought a nexus between WSI's commercial success and the merits of the claimed invention.

In essence, AMF says that the commercial success found by the district court was due in large part to "other economic and commercial factors unrelated to the technical quality of the patented subject matter." Particularly, AMF argues that the great commercial success found by the district court was due to (1) sales of accessories amounting to 10-15 percent of the gross receipts; (2) an extensive advertising campaign and European promotional effort; and (3) more efficient manufacturing and design changes. They argue that WSI's commercial success is of little probative value because it occurred so many years after the date of invention and was not the result of providing any solution to some existing problem or long-felt want.

[3] Having carefully reviewed the record before use, we conclude that the district court did not impermissibly credit the evidence of commercial success. It specifically found that SWI's commercial success should not be "significantly diminished" by testimony that 10-15 percent of gross receipts are from paraphernalia. The court accorded some weight to motivational factors leading to German licenses, but concluded that "widespread recognition and use of the invention" indicated that it would not have been obvious. The commercial success of the invention was found to have been "well beyond the effect" of WSI's promotional efforts.

Absent some intervening event to which success must be attributed, the delay in achieving the great commercial success of the claimed invention in this case does not detract from the probative value of the evidence of that success. Similarly, AMF's suggestion that objective evidence of non-obviousness can be considered only when the invention solves a long-existing problem is unwarranted. Providing a solution to a long existing problem is but one type of objective evidence useful in making obviousness/non-obviousness determinations. Further, the district court correctly noted that copying the claimed invention, rather than one within the public domain, is indicative of non-obviousness.

[4] Having carefully considered AMF's arguments and the evidence relied upon by the district court, we conclude that AMF has not discharged its burden on appeal, i.e., of per-

EXHIBIT 2 (continued)

suading us that the district court committed reversible legal error in its determination that the invention would not have been obvious, or that the court's probative findings underlying that determination were clearly erroneous. Accordingly, the presumptive validity of the '167 patent remains unscathed and the judgment upholding claims 15-21 of the '167 patent is affirmed.

(2) Infringement

Downwind alone appeals from the judgment of infringement, urging that its structure does not have a "joint having a plurality of axes of rotation." Downwind employs a flexible rubber tube or rod connecting the mast and the board.

[5] Claim interpretation is a question of law, but we have been shown no basis for upsetting the district court's interpretation of the claims as covering a structure that permits the mast to pivot with respect to and about a number of axes. Downwind's contention that a flexible rubber tube is not "mechanical," and does not rotate, and thus is not a "joint" within the meaning of the claims, is without merit. The word "mechanical" does not appear in the claims, the twisting of the flexible tube is about an axis of rotation, and the tube forms a joint between the mast and board.

[6, 7] Whether Downwind's accused device infringes the claims as interpreted is a fact question, and a finding on that question will not be upset unless clearly erroneous. None of the accused infringers has attempted to rebut the testimony on which the district court relied in finding infringement. Downwind has not shown that the claims must be given its own unduly narrow interpretation or that the district court's finding of infringement was clearly erroneous. Accordingly, the judgment of infringement is affirmed.

(3) Patent Misuse

AMF's allegation of patent misuse is based on this paragraph included in license agreements between WSI and 11 licensees:

Trademarks

LICENSEE hereby acknowledges that the terms "WINDSURFER," "WINDSURFING," and "WINDSURF" and the company logo are all valid trademarks. LICENSEE hereby agrees not to use any of the trademarks identified in this paragraph 10 in any form or fashion in its company name or any of its literature or advertising or promotional material or on any products whatsoever.

The district court said that whether that provision gives rise to a patent misuse defense depends on whether the registered trademarks are generic. Having found the marks generic, the court concluded "that Paragraph 10 has an intrinsically inhibiting effect on competition beyond the scope of the patent...."

The court went on to determine that the "level of misuse" did not warrant rendering the patent entirely unenforceable because the court found the "record insufficient to determine

EXHIBIT 2   (continued)

fairly the extent to which WSI sought to enforce the provision and the extent of any monetary gain to it" and also found the record insufficient to support a finding that "WSI necessarily would or should have known that its mark had become a common descriptive name for the product."

The court set the damages issue for determination at a later time, deferred until that time "the resolution as to what relief, if any, WSI's misuse of its patent privilege warrants," and decided to enforce the '167 patent.

In its cross-appeals, WSI contends that a mere inclusion in a patent license agreement of a promise not to infringe a licensor's trademark does not constitute patent misuse. Acts constituting misuse, says WSI, must be "coercive" toward an improper advantage. WSI argues that it was merely asserting rights it possessed under the trademark laws and, thus, the patent misuse defense should fall.

[8] The doctrine of patent misuse is an affirmative defense to a suit for patent infringement, and requires that the alleged infringer show that the patentee has impermissibly broadened the "physical or temporal scope" of the patent grant with anticompetitive effect. We have seen cited to no authority, and are aware of none, for the proposition that patent misuse may be found on the basis of a patent license agreement provision recognizing and forbidding use of the licensor's validly registered trademarks.

[9, 10] To sustain a misuse defense involving a licensing arrangement not held to have been per se anticompetitive by the Supreme Court,[11] a factual determination must reveal that the overall effect of the license tends to restrain competition unlawfully in an appropriately defined relevant market. A provision in a patent license agreement requiring the licensee to acknowledge the validity of registered trademarks, and to avoid their use, cannot possibly restrain competition unlawfully in an appropriately defined relevant market. The license agreement provision merely asserted and recognized WSI's rights derived from the trademark laws. The assertion of trademark rights can have procompetitive effects, and thus under only the most rare of circumstances could such assertion, separately or as a provision in a patent license agreement, form in itself the basis for a holding of inequitable conduct such as that labeled "patent misuse." It is not an uncommon precaution when licensing a product sold by the licensor under a trademark to prohibit the licensee from using the licensor's trademark on the licensee's product. That is but a matter of business prudence and in no manner misuses the patent right.

That the marks were found generic after trial and long after execution of the license cannot of itself prevent a full enforcement of the '167 patent. Trademark registrations enjoy a statutory presumption of validity. As the district court found, AMF failed to show that WSI granted the licenses or enforced its rights in the marks with knowledge that they were or had become a common descriptive name, and AMF failed to show that WSI should have had that knowledge. On the present record, the district court was improperly persuaded to rest its holding of misuse entirely on an after-the-fact determination that the marks are generic. Be-

---

[11]Recent economic analysis questions the rationale behind holding any licensing practice per se anticompetitive.

[12]We need not, in view of our determination, discuss the parties' contentions respecting the purging of misuse.

EXHIBIT 2 (continued)

cause that was error, the holding that the facts of record established a misuse of the patent right must be reversed.[12]

(4) Injunctions

[11] The law empowers district courts to "grant injunctions in accordance with the principles of equity to prevent the violation of any right secured by patent, on such terms as the court deems reasonable." The statute makes clear that the district court's grant or denial of an injunction is within its discretion depending on the facts of each case. Hence, the district court's grant or denial of an injunction is reviewed under an abuse of discretion standard.

The holding of misuse having been reversed, we need not address AMF's contention that the district court should not have enjoined further infringement of the '167 patent in light of that holding.

AMF argues that the district court improperly ignored its intervening rights, a defense it contends was raised in the pleadings and at the injunction hearing, citing *Seattle Box Co. v. Industrial Carting & Packing, Inc.*, made no mention of its intervening rights defense at the trial.

[12] Nothing in *Seattle Box* addresses the point at which the intervening rights defense must be raised to preserve it. Intervening rights, however, is "an affirmative defense . . . that must be raised at trial." That it failed to make any attempt to prove the defense at trial is in this case fatal. AMF cannot be held to have resuscitated the defense by the mere submission of affidavits at a post-trial hearing. To so hold would run counter to the finality attaching to trials. District courts are under no obligation to consider a defense abandoned at trial. Accordingly, no abuse of discretion having been shown, we affirm the district court's grant of injunctive relief against AMF and BIC.

On its cross-appeal, WSI urges that the district court abused its discretion in refusing to enjoin Downwind. In denying injunction relief against Downwind, the district court stated from the bench:

I am prepared to say at the present time that I do not believe that an injunction against Downwind is appropriate. As bad as Windsurfing's problems I am prepared to believe may be, I do not believe that enjoining Downwind, which is such a small operation, would solve their problems, not that I think an injunction's purpose is simply to solve its problems; and so I mention that because I don't think you need to argue further on that.

The relative size of multiple infringers should not alone serve as a basis for enjoining

---

[13]Downwind said its infringing sales were between 1,000 and 2,000 sailboards a year since it began operations in 1981. AMF was selling about 1, 800 sailboards a year during the same four-year period. That sailboards are Downwind's primary product, and that an injunction might therefore put Downwind out of business, cannot justify denial of that injunction. One who elects to build a business on a product found to infringe cannot be heard to complain if an injunction against continuing infringement destroys the business so elected. The district court, recognizing the absence of bad faith on the part of all parties, weighed the effect of its orders on each. In so doing it indicated that WSI's entire business was built on sailboards and accessories, and thus that Downwind and WSI were in the same boat. Under those circumstances, no warrant appears on this record for denying the requested injunction against continued infringement by Downwind.

EXHIBIT 2 (concluded)

continued infringement by some and not by others.[13] The district court articulated no other basis for denying injunction relief against Downwind. On the present record, therefore, we must conclude that the district court abused its discretion in refusing to enjoin Downwind. Accordingly, we remand the case to the district court to reconsider WSI's request for an appropriate injunction against Downwind.

CONCLUSION

The judgment of the district court upholding the validity of claims 15-21 of the '167 patent and finding them infringed, and the grant of injunctions against AMF and BIC are affirmed. The judgment that WSI is guilty of patent misuse is reversed. The case is remanded with instructions to vacate the order denying an injunction against Downwind and to reconsider WSI's request for that injunction.

The appeal is affirmed in part, reversed in part, vacated in part, and remanded.

Windsurfer (B)

Trademarking

In addition to patenting physical features of utility in his sailboard design, Hoyle Schweitzer also applied for trademarks on the name "Windsurfer" and on logos with that name used by his company, Windsurfing International. As the market for his product grew, his trademark as well as his patent came under attack from imitators, and Schweitzer sued in response. Excerpts from the *Trademark Gazette* depicting logos which he registered appear in Exhibits 1 through 3. A description of litigation which ensued appears in Exhibit 4.

EXHIBIT 1   Initial Trademark Registration, 1973

TM 182   OFFICIAL GAZETTE   APRIL 17, 1973

SN 432.256. Mattel, Inc., Hawthorne, Calif. Filed Aug. 9. 1972.

SAND WITCH

Owner of Reg. No. 887.081.
For Toy Model Automobile (Int. Cl. 28).
First use July 24. 1972.

SN 432.257. Mattel, Inc., Hawthorne, Calif. Filed Aug. 9. 1972.

THUNDER BOLT

For Toy Model Automobile (Int. Cl. 28).
First use July 24. 1972.

SN 432.258. Mattel, Inc., Hawthorne, Calif. Filed Aug. 9. 1972.

TOAST-A-TUNE

Owner of Reg. No. 691.606.
For Musical Toy (Int. Cl. 28).
First use July 24. 1972.

SN 432.260. Mattel, Inc., Hawthorne, Calif. Filed Aug. 9. 1972.

ALIVE '55

For Toy Model Automobile (Int. Cl. 28).
First use July 24. 1972.

SN 432.415. Eldora A. Hurley, d.b.a. Earl H. Hurley Associates. Corry. Pa. Filed Aug. 10. 1972.

EXERGLIDE

For Play Swings and Exercise Apparatus for Children and Adults (Int. Cl. 28).
First use June 7. 1949.

SN 432.423. Gayla Industries, Inc., Houston. Tex. Filed Aug. 10, 1972.

SKY-SPY

For Toys—Namely, Kites (Int. Cl. 28).
First use Aug. 11. 1970.

SN 432.424. Gayla Industries, Inc., Houston. Tex. Filed Aug. 10, 1972.

DYNASOAR

For Toys—Namely, Kites (Int. Cl. 28).
First use July 29. 1968.

SN 432.646. Western Publishing Company, Inc., Racine. Wis. Filed Aug. 14. 1972.

Owner of Reg. Nos. 885,922. 931.702. and others.
For Playing Cards (Int. Cl. 16).
First use Aug. 1, 1972.

SN 432.649. Western Publishing Company, Inc., Racine. Wis. Filed Aug. 14, 1972.

Owner of Reg. Nos. 900,803 and 909,516.
For Children's Educational Playing Cards (Int. Cl. 16).
First use Apr. 3. 1970.

SN 433.078. S. S. Kresge Company, Troy, Mich. Filed Aug. 17. 1972.

LI'L MISS KAY SMART

For Children's Toy Jewelry and Children's Toy Cosmetics (Int. Cl. 28).
First use on or before June 18, 1972.

SN 433.097. X-Potential Enterprises, Fountain Valley, Calif. Filed Aug. 18. 1972.

SUPER STIX

For Construction Toy (Int. Cl. 28).
First use June 12. 1972.

SN 433.188. Western Publishing Company, Inc., Racine, Wis. Filed Aug. 18. 1972.

GOLDEN

Owner of Reg. Nos. 896,937, 899,690, and 931,795.
For Jigsaw Puzzles (Int. Cl. 28).
First use July 5, 1972.

SN 433.306. Windsurfing International, Inc., Santa Monica. Calif. Filed Aug. 21. 1972.

WINDSURFER

For Surfboards (Int. Cl. 28).
First use Aug. 15, 1969.

SN 433.342. Montgomery Ward & Co., Chicago. Ill. Filed Aug. 21. 1972.

MY TOWN

For Children's Toys (Int. Cl. 28).
First use June 8. 1972.

SN 433.517. Raider Tackle Manufacturing Co., Chicago. Ill. Filed Aug. 23. 1972.

GATORCRAWLER

For Fishing Lures (Int. Cl. 28).
First use January 1969.

EXHIBIT 2 Trademark Registration from 1974

TM 166   OFFICIAL GAZETTE   AUGUST 20, 1974

SN 7,271. Fantasy Boats, Costa Mesa, Calif. Filed Nov. 26, 1973.

FANTASY

For Boats and Structural Parts Therefor (U.S. Cl. 19).
First use on or before May 15, 1959.

SN 8,013. Windsurfing International, Inc., Santa Monica, Calif. Filed Dec. 3, 1973.

Owner of Reg. Nos. 909,519 and 962,616.
For Sailboats Comprising a Surf Board Type Hull and a Sail (U.S. Cl. 19).
First use on or about Aug. 15, 1969.

Class 14 — Jewelry

SN 3,092. Urschel Tool Co., Cranston, R.I. Filed Oct. 9, 1973.

kenwood

For Jewelry for Personal Wear and Adornment (U.S. Cl. 28).
First use Mar. 19, 1973.

SN 4,511. Bulova Watch Company, Inc., Flushing, N.Y. Filed Oct. 25, 1973.

LONGCHAMP

For Clocks, Watches and Parts Thereof (U.S. Cl. 27).
First use Oct. 15, 1973.

SN 4,595. Empress Pearls, Inc., Los Angeles, Calif. Filed Nov. 21, 1973.

DRIFTWOOD

For Pearl Jewelry Sold Only Through At-Home Parties (U.S. Cl. 28).
First use July 2, 1973.

SN 4,596. Empress Pearls, Inc., Los Angeles, Calif. Filed Nov. 21, 1973.

IMAGINATION

For Pearl Jewelry Sold Only Through At-Home Parties (U.S. Cl. 28).
First use July 2, 1973.

Class 16 — Paper Goods and Printed Matter

SN 877. KCL Corporation, Shelbyville, Ind. Filed Sept. 13, 1973.

AMBER-ZIP

For Reclosable Bags for Hospital Use (U.S. Cl. 2).
First use at least as early as May 19, 1972.

SN 2,751. Farm Journal, Inc., Philadelphia, Pa. Filed Oct. 4, 1973.

COUNTRYSIDE LIVING

Owner of Reg. Nos. 775,394 and 920,415.
For Magazine Published From Time to Time (U.S. Cl. 38).
First use at least as early as Sept. 20, 1973.

SN 7,943. Dayco Corporation, Dayton, Ohio. Filed Dec. 3, 1973.

401

For Printing Blankets (U.S. Cl. 50).
First use on or about July 28, 1972.

SN 7,944. Dayco Corporation, Dayton, Ohio. Filed Dec. 3, 1973.

501

For Printing Blankets (U.S. Cl. 50).
First use on or about July 28, 1972.

SN 7,945. Dayco Corporation, Dayton, Ohio. Filed Dec. 3, 1973.

600

For Printing Blankets (U.S. Cl. 50).
First use on or about July 28, 1972.

SN 7,948. Dayco Corporation, Dayton, Ohio. Filed Dec. 3, 1973.

427

For Printing Blankets (U.S. Cl. 50).
First use on or about July 28, 1972.

SN 7,949. Dayco Corporation, Dayton, Ohio. Filed Dec. 3, 1973.

606

For Printing Blankets (U.S. Cl. 50).
First use on or about July 28, 1972.

SN 8,370. The Saml Dodsworth Company, d.b.a. Dodsworth Co., Kansas City, Kans. Filed Dec. 10, 1973.

UNI-SUN

For Bank Checks (U.S. Cl. 37).
First use on or about Nov. 1, 1973.

SN 8,409. Texace Corporation, San Antonio, Tex. Filed Dec. 10, 1973.

CAPALOG

For Periodicals—Namely, Product Catalogues (U.S. Cl. 38).
First use as early as 1946.

SN 12,869. E. R. Squibb & Sons, Inc., Princeton, N.J. Filed Feb. 7, 1974.

RYTHRO-LOG

For Diagnostic Worksheets for Laboratory Use (U.S. Cl. 37).
First use Sept. 6, 1973.

EXHIBIT 3   Trademark Registration from 1978

JUNE 27, 1978   U. S. PATENT AND TRADEMARK OFFICE   TM 289

SN 133,616. Bunny Osbrink, Inc., Doraville, Ga. Filed July 11, 1977.

For Tennis Skirts, Golf Shirts, Hats, Visors, and Halters (U.S. Cl. 39).
First use October 1976.

SN 134,078. The United States Shoe Corporation, Cincinnati, Ohio. Filed July 15, 1977.

For Shoes (U.S. Cl. 39).
First use at least as early as May 17, 1977.

SN 134,079. The United States Shoe Corporation, Cincinnati, Ohio. Filed July 15, 1977.

For Shoes (U.S. Cl. 39).
First use at least as early as May 4, 1977.

SN 134,080. The United States Shoe Corporation, Cincinnati, Ohio. Filed July 15, 1977.

FREEMOC

For Footwear (U.S. Cl. 39).
First use at least as early as Aug. 1, 1921.

SN 134,343. Uniform Guild, Inc., New York, N.Y. Filed July 18, 1977.

Guild
Professionals

Owner of Reg. No. 788,771.
For Uniforms for Nurses, Nurses Aides, Medical Receptionists, Waitresses and Beauticians, and Coats or Aprons Worn by Bakery Sales Personnel, Laboratory Technicians and Factory Personnel (U.S. Cl. 39).
First use at least as early as June 1, 1977; July 1936, in a different form.

TM 971 O.G.—20

SN 138,095. William W. Artzt, Palm Beach, Fla. Filed Aug. 19, 1977.

BEND 'N STRETCH

Applicant disclaims the word "Stretch" apart from the mark as shown, without waiving any common law rights thereto. Owner of Reg. No. 948,595.
For Children's and Infants' Wearing Apparel—Namely, Pajamas, Sleeping Garments, Overalls, Shirts, Undershirts and Underwear (U.S. Cl. 39).
First use on or before June 28, 1969.

SN 138,550. Windsurfing International, Inc., Marina Del Rey, Calif. Filed Aug. 22, 1977.

WINDSURFING

For T-Shirts, Jackets and Wet Suits for Waterskiing (U.S. Cl. 39).
First use at least as early as February 1970.

SN 139,674. Chief Apparel, Inc., New York, N.Y. Filed Sept. 1, 1977.

LE DISQUE

The mark "Le Disque" translated into English means "the record" (i.e., disc).
For Men's and Boys' Tailored and Pre-Cut Clothing—Namely, Coats, Jeans, Slacks and Tops (U.S. Cl. 39).
First use June 30, 1977.

SN 139,974. L & K Co., Inc., Shelby, N.C. Filed Sept. 6, 1977.

SHELBY STATION

Applicant disclaims the word "Shelby" apart from the mark as shown, but without waiving any of its common law rights to the mark shown in the drawing or any feature thereof
For Ladies' Jackets, Tops and Dresses (U.S. Cl. 39).
First use as early as March 1977.

SN 141,910. The Enro Shirt Company, Inc., Louisville, Ky. Filed Sept. 20, 1977.

CLUBHOUSE

For Men's Dress Shirts and Sport Shirts (U.S. Cl. 39).
First use Aug. 15, 1977.

SN 142,293. Karman, Inc., Denver, Colo. Filed Sept. 23, 1977.

CHUTE #1

For Western Clothing—Namely, Shirts (U.S. Cl. 39).
First use Sept. 5, 1977.

EXHIBIT 4

WINDSURFING INTERNATIONAL[1]
INC., Plaintiff-Appellant.
v.
AMF INCORPORATED.
Defendant-Appellee.
United States Court of Appeals.
Federal Circuit.
Sept. 9, 1987.

Three actions relating to validity, infringement and enforceability of reissue patent for sailing surfboard were consolidated. Appeal was taken. The Court of Appeals held that the district court lacked jurisdiction over action.

MARKEY, Chief Judge.

Appeal from a judgment of the United States District Court for the Southern District of New York holding that Windsurfing International's (WSI's) "WINDSURFER" trademark has become generic and ordering (1) cancellation of its U.S. Trademark Registration Nos. 962, 616 and 1,195,-641 on that mark, and (2) rectification of U.S. Trademark Registration Nos. 997,974 and 1,180,024 by addition of a disclaimer. 613 F. Supp. 933, 227 USPQ 927 (S.D.N.Y. 1985). Because the district court lacked jurisdiction to entertain AMF's claim for cancellation, the judgment appealed from must be vacated.

BACKGROUND

United States Patent No. 3,487,800 for a "Wind-Propelled Apparatus" issued in January 1970. WSI, the assignee, has manufactured and sold the patented "sailboard" since 1969. WSI filed an application for reissue in 1978, and U.S. Patent Re. 31,167 ('167 patent) issued on March 8, 1983.

In 1981, after other manufacturers had entered the "sailboard" market, WSI sued AMF Incorporated (AMF) and others for patent infringement. The district court stayed the action pending the outcome of reissue proceedings. When the '167 patent issued in March 1983, AMF filed a complaint in the same court seeking a declaratory judgment, *inter alia*, that the '167 patent was unenforceable because WSI had misused it.

WSI had since 1977 been sending letters demanding the cessation of all use of "WINDSURFER" except in reference to WSI's products. On August 16, 1983, after an AMF dealer ran a newspaper advertisement using "Windsurfer" to refer to one of AMF's products, attorneys for WSI wrote to the dealer demanding that it cease using "WINDSURFER" and requested a prompt reply "to preclude the necessity of instituting more formal proceedings to protect [WSI's] trademark rights." AMF advised the dealer to stop running the advertisement, and the dealer did so.

In November 1983, AMF filed its answer to WSI's a infringement complaint, amended its complaint for a declaratory judgment, and filed a counterclaim, seeking in both latter instances

---

[1] 828 F.2d 755 (Fed. Cir. 1987).

EXHIBIT 4 (continued)

cancellation of WSI's registrations. AMF did not designate its counterclaim as one for declaratory judgment, though, like its amended complaint, it was clearly such. In its amendment and counterclaim, AMF alleged that "windsurfer" did not function as a trademark because it had become generic. The district court consolidated the actions.

In November 1984, shortly before trial, WSI moved to dismiss AMF's trademark claims for lack of subject matter jurisdiction, arguing that AMF had alleged insufficient facts to create a "case or controversy" under Article III of the Constitution. The district court denied the motion.

The district court held a nonjury trial in November and December 1984 and issued an opinion on July 15, 1985. About WSI's no-case-or controversy argument, that opinion said:

On the eve of trial WSI moved to dismiss the trademark issues on the grounds of lack of case or controversy. The motion was denied. WSI again raises the issue in its post-trial brief. The fact that WSI has sent correspondence threatening to sue at least one of AMF's dealers, along with the fact that the trademark issue is intimately connected with AMF's misuse defense (which AMF clearly has a right to assert), is sufficient in this action to create a "case or controversy" and we decline to overturn our earlier ruling.

The foregoing quote is the entirety of the district court's opinion relating to whether a "case or controversy" exists on the trademark issue. On the merits, the opinion said "windsurfer" had become generic. No judgment was entered at the time the July 15, 1985 opinion was issued.

On September 11, 1985, the district court entered judgment on the patent issues and an injunction. AMF appealed. This court affirmed the judgment that the '167 patent was valid and infringed, reversed the holding that the '167 patent was unenforceable because of patent misuse, and remanded for the district court to reconsider the scope of its injunction.

On January 6, 1987, the district court entered judgment on AMF's complaint and counterclaim, having determined that "'windsurfer' has become and is generic," and ordered the cancellation of two of WSI's trademark registrations and the addition of a disclaimer to two others. No reference to the presence or absence of a case or controversy was made in connection with that judgment. WSI appealed.

ISSUE

Whether the district court had subject matter jurisdiction to entertain AMF's challenge to WSI's trademark registrations.

OPINION

As in any federal case, an action under the Declaratory Judgment Act must present a "case or controversy" within the meaning of Article III of the Constitution. Because this court has jurisdiction to decide the question only because the district court's jurisdiction was based in part on 28 U.S.C. § 1330(a), we look to the discernible law of the regional circuit where the district court sits, here the Second Circuit, in deciding whether AMF's trademark claims presented a "case or controversy" to the district court. We may also look when necessary to guidance from other circuits. Because declaratory judgment actions involving trademarks are analogous to those involving patents, we may also, when necessary, find guidance in the precedents of this court.

EXHIBIT 4 (continued)

[1] The test of determining whether an actual case or controversy exists in a declaratory judgment action involving trademarks is two-pronged. First, the declaratory plaintiff must have a real and reasonable apprehension of litigation. Second, the declaratory plaintiff must have engaged in a course of conduct which brought it into adversarial conflict with the declaratory defendant. Both prongs of the test must be satisfied.

[2] Assuming without deciding that, as the district court's opinion suggests, AMF reasonably feared litigation *if* it began using "windsurfer" in connection with its products, the record contains no evidence that AMF has engaged in any course of conduct, or indeed, any conduct at all, that has brought it into adversarial conflict with WSI respecting WSI's trademarks. AMF acknowledges that it has avoided using "windsurfer" and has so instructed its dealers. Thus AMF fails to satisfy the second prong of the test.

In its complaint and counterclaim, AMF alleged merely that "AMF is interested in using the mark descriptively in connection with its products." AMF cites testimony that AMF has a "desire" to use "windsurfer" in its advertising and promotion, and that other members of the trade have the same "desire." Rather than use the mark, get sued, and fight it out in court, AMF was saying, "We would like to use the mark, but before we do, we want a court to say we may do so safely." Thus AMF's complaint and counterclaim sought an advisory opinion, something a federal court may not give.

A justiciable controversy is one that touches the legal relations of parties having adverse *legal* interests. AMF's "desire" to use "windsurfer" and "windsurfing" descriptively may render its commercial interests adverse to those of WSI, but absent a combination of AMF's use of the mark and threats or suits by WSI, the legal interests of AMF and WSI are not adverse. ("A vague and unspecific 'desire' to practice an invention if a patent should turn out to be invalid smacks too much of the hypothetical and contingent.")

AMF argues that, under section 14(c) of the Lanham Act, its status as a competitor of WSI gives it standing to seek cancellation of WSI's trademark registrations. AMF cites a number of cases from the Court of Customs and Patent Appeals, but those cases involved appeals from the Trademark Trial and Appeal Board, not from district courts. Section 14(c) of the Lanham Act does authorize persons interested in using marks that have become the common descriptive names of articles to petition the Patent and Trademark Office to cancel registration of those marks. It does not, however, authorize suits for cancellation in district courts.

Under the Lanham Act, district courts have the power to cancel registrations, but only in an "action involving a registered mark." "Involving" cannot mean the mere presence of a registered trademark, but must be read as involving the right to use the mark and thus the right to maintain the registration. (In a dispute over a franchise agreement licensing a trade name, "the mere existence of the protected trade name and attendant symbol herein does not provide a basis for federal jurisdiction."); (antitrust defendant's defense of trademark registration made the case one "involving a registered mark" giving the court jurisdiction to order cancellation of that registration). There must, therefore, be something beyond the mere competitor status of the parties to serve as a basis for the court's jurisdiction. Such a basis may, for example, be a suit for trademark infringement (counterclaim of trademark genericness entertained in suit for trademark infringement), or a "case of actual controversy" referred to in the Declaratory Judgment Act, 28 U.S.C. § 2201. As discussed above, AMF's status as a competi-

EXHIBIT 4 (concluded)

tor of WSI does not create such an "actual controversy" effective to create jurisdiction in the district court.

[3] AMF argues that the district court had "pendent jurisdiction" because AMF's allegations of patent misuse concerned trademark provisions in WSI's patent license agreements. Pendent jurisdiction allows federal courts to consider state claims with federal claims when they "derive from a common nucleus of operative fact." It is inapplicable here. Moreover, if AMF's patent misuse theory created a "case or controversy" respecting WSI's patent rights, it did not do so respecting WSI's registered trademarks. The parties here have incorrectly assumed a nonexistent identity of the trademark and the patented invention. WSI, for example, argues that AMF had no standing to challenge the trademarks because it was enjoined from infringing the patent, and AMF argues that it could have used the mark on products made under its pre-reissue "intervening rights." Neither party recognizes that the mark is registered for various classes of goods and services, and that nothing limits its use to the patented structure.

CONCLUSION

AMF's mere desire to use "windsurfer" and "windsurfing" in connection with its products does not constitute a course of conduct placing AMF in legally adversarial conflict with WSI respecting WSI's trademark registrations. AMF, in its complaint and counterclaim, did not present a justiciable controversy. On the contrary, it impermissibly asked the district court for an advisory opinion. The district court therefore lacked subject matter jurisdiction to entertain AMF's claim for cancellation of WSI's registrations, on the ground that "windsurfer" had become a generic term or otherwise. The district court must therefore vacate the judgment appealed from. The case is remanded for that purpose.

Venture Plan Excerpts

Appendix 1 contains excerpts of important elements ranging from tables of contents to footnotes of financial projections from a variety of unrelated venture plans. A listing of the excerpts appears in the detailed table of contents at the front of the book. The appendix is intended to illustrate alternative ways to convey information effectively in plans and to serve as a starting point for exploring ways to make plans better. Selected to stimulate ideas more than to serve as models, any of the excerpts can be criticized and improved upon. Questions the reader may wish to consider in examining them include:

- What information does this excerpt convey? What seems to be its purpose in a venture plan? Where in the plan should it appear? For what types of plans would it be most suitable and for what types least suitable?

- What alternative forms of presentation could be used to convey the same information as this excerpt? Which ones would be most appropriate for what circumstances?

- How much can be discerned about the particular venture from just the excerpt itself? Would there be any way to modify the excerpt so that it would be able better to stand on its own without making it longer?

- How does this excerpt compare to other excerpts in its effectiveness? What makes the difference?

- What are three ways of changing this excerpt to make it better? Which would improve it most? How hard would it be to accomplish that improvement? Would it probably be worth the required effort and cost?

- Which of the excerpts could most usefully be added to venture plans in one or more of the cases in this book?

1 TABLE OF CONTENTS EXAMPLES

Venture A

Venture B

Venture C

2 EXECUTIVE SUMMARY EXAMPLES

A. Passenger Airline

The company plans to offer scheduled jet passenger service in the Seattle-San Francisco, Seattle-Denver and San Francisco-Denver markets. The company expects that its principal competitors will include the following commercial airlines: United, Western, Alaska, Northwest, PSA, Wien and Frontier. All of these competitors are larger, have a history of successful airline operations and have greater financial resources than does Air Washington.

The company intends to compete on the basis of price, flight frequency and passenger service. For example, Air Washington's proposed fare in the Seattle-San Francisco market is $77. This fare represents a savings of 45 percent to 62 percent over current Tourist Class fares in that market. The proposed fare in both the Seattle-Denver market and San Francisco-Denver markets is $109. This fare represents a savings of approximately 57 percent over the current Tourist Class Fares in these markets.

Air Washington plans to provide a total of 11 round trips per day in its system, consisting of 6 round trips per day between Seattle and San Francisco, 2 round trips per day between Seattle and Denver, and 3 round trips per day between San Francisco and Denver.

The company plans to offer a high level of in-flight passenger service, including full meal service appropriate to the time of day, competitively priced liquor, full baggage service, and advance reservations and seat assignments. Few of the carriers currently service the company's proposed markets offer this combination of passenger service.

Most of the company's competitors incur greater costs, primarily due to higher equipment and labor costs. The company plans to operate modern, efficient airplanes with highly motivated and productive employees, thereby achieving cost savings that will allow it to charge lower fares and still generate a profit. For further details and elaboration see Exhibit B.

B. Word Processor

This document describes the following investment opportunity:

1) An OEM venture primarily involved in product development, marketing and assembly of component elements produced by other companies under contract. This venture will produce "new printer" devices that are capable—in the initially considered manifestation—of producing hard copy equivalent in quality to that produced by a carbon-ribbon Selectric typewriter—in multiple fonts/graphics—at a rate of 10 pages/minute—with an OEM price of $2,500.

2) A 3-phase initial investment is contemplated, probably utilizing an R&D limited partnership structure. The proposed funding level is $650,000. Phase I requires $150,000 for technology "maturation"/risk assessment and market research. Of this amount, the first $50,000 will be devoted to "proving" the highest-risk technological element. Phase II requires an additional $250,000 investment to create a pre-production prototype. Phase III will require an additional $250,000 to enter initial (demonstration quantity) production and to perform initial OEM marketing. Phase II and III investment will be triggered by achievement of predefined objectives.

3) The venture will receive assignment of several basic patents and will probably generate a significant number of additional patents.

4) A development team has been assembled, centered around the inventor of the technology, Gilbert Springer, and assisted by a venture development consultant, Stuart Lichtman. Additionally, a very strong OEM printer salesman has been located and is available to the team. The venture does not yet have the strong, marketing-oriented chief executive entrepreneur required for long-term success—nor will such a person be required prior to the 12th to 15th months.

5) Timing of the venture involves about six months for technology maturation, 9 to 12 months additional for completion of a pre-production prototype, and an additional six months to initial deliveries (the 21st to 24th month). Active marketing is projected to start around the time of completion of the pre-production prototype (15th to 18th month); background marketing will commence about three months prior.

C. Tunneling Machine

The goal of this business plan is to secure venture capital for financing of the Ramex Corporation. The capital would be applied to the design, development, production and marketing costs of a proprietary tunneling machine. Based on an optimistic forecast, it is estimated that approximately $1.5 million would be required; however a commitment of approximately $2.6 million is requested, which would cover such contingencies as strikes, excessive lead time on critical components, interim financing for production machines, or unanticipated development problems. The design concept of the Ramex machine is based on the use of a massive reciprocating cutter head, which is driven by a 2-stroke, free-piston diesel engine. Energy developed by the reciprocating cutter head is used to fracture the rock at the tunnel face. The cuttings produced are then picked up and conveyed to the rear of the machine for removal from the tunnel. This concept offers several advantages over rotary machines, which are currently the accepted standard in the industry. These advantages include sharply higher penetration rates, greater reliability and reduced manufacturing cost of both cutters and machine. Because of these advantages it is believed that this machine will be capable of dominating the entire industry within a few years.

The development and testing of a full-scale prototype is expected to take two years. During the design and development phase the company would be primarily engineering oriented. As the development progresses, administrative functions would be phased in to produce and market the equipment. The first year of operation would be spent producing design drawings and in supervising the fabrication of the prototype by subcontractors. The second year would be spent in assembling the prototype and testing it in the shop. The last phase of development would be the on-site use of the machine by a prospective buyer. This last phase would provide the first expected source of revenue for the company. At the conclusion of this test period Ramex will begin full-scale marketing and production based on customer orders.

The basic design concept is a significant technological advance, and it is expected that the patents pending will insure that Ramex will retain exclusive rights for its production. The Ramex Corporation also expects that the tunneling machine will have excellent profitability potential both because of its proprietary nature and improved performance characteristics. Preliminary figures estimate that the production costs for a typical machine will be $380,000 and the selling price to be $1.2 million. Based on these estimates for a 10-foot diameter machine, the company can operate profitably with the sale of one machine per year. It is expected that sales volume will exceed $20 million per year within five years. The total potential market exceeds $60 million per year.

3 DESCRIPTIONS OF PRODUCTS AND SERVICES

A. Yacht Exchange

We propose to establish a mechanism by which yacht owners in Hawaii and the Puget Sound region can exchange sailing time on their vessels. We believe a significant market for this service exists, as it will provide the yacht owner with an opportunity to explore new waters at a cost of little more than that of sailing out of his own marina.

CONCEPTUAL PLAN

Pacific Yacht Exchange proposes to act as an intermediary between individuals who wish to trade sailing time on their boats. Traditional impediments to doing this have been problems associated with the mechanics of the exchange and with security. We intend to capitalize on the economies of scale available in both these areas.

Potential customers will be first contacted by advertisements placed in sailing periodicals based in the Northwest and Hawaii. Those who respond will be sent a brochure describing our service and the sailing opportunities in the matched area. An application form will also be sent which will be used as the primary screening device. This form will require both a resume' of sailing experience and a set of personal references. In addition, general facts about both the applicant and his yacht will be requested for matching purposes.

Having carefully examined and checked an applicant's qualifications and background, we will make arrangements to inspect the client's boat. This step is felt to be necessary in order to exclude poorly maintained vessels (and their owners) from consideration and to confirm some of the facts on the application form. A further benefit will be to enhance our credibility and rapport with the client. We also plan to take color photos of each yacht to provide to the client who will be matched with it.

Physical matching of clients will be accomplished with the aid of a microcomputer. Specific matching criteria to be used will be (in order of importance): boat size and equipment, age and family status, and personal factors (i.e., smoker vs. non-smoker). For the initial exchange we anticipate providing a model contract specifying the dates of the exchange and recourse should problems occur. Liability considerations will be clearly spelled out in the contract. The penalty for failure to provide sailing time received will be equal to the cost of a barebones charter rental. Whether P.Y.E. or the client should be responsible for collection is undetermined at this time. Legal advice will be sought in drafting the model contract. Future exchanges between the two parties will be accomplished without our participation.

While P.Y.E. will make every effort to insure that the exchanges go smoothly and will offer personal assistance should problems arise, we expect that the parties involved will take primary responsibility for the successful completion of the exchange.

B. Disk Drive Venture

PRIAM, a California corporation, was founded to develop, manufacture, and market mass storage devices for small business computers, distributed processors, and word processors. The initial product is a low-cost disk drive based on state-of-the-art Winchester technology.

Winchester disk technology was first introduced by IBM for its large systems due to the significantly lower cost, higher reliability, and higher capacity offered by this new technology. IBM shipped the first Winchester disk (IBM 3350) for the large S/370 systems in early 1976. PRIAM intends to rapidly bring this new 3350 technology to the small business computer market, thereby leap-frogging competitors who are using non-Winchester technology or early versions of Winchester (i.e., IBM 3340).

The uniqueness of PRIAM is that this product will be the lowest possible cost 30-40 megabyte Winchester disk drive using a fast-access mechanism.

The market for low-cost Winchester disk drives under 50 megabytes is expected to explode over the next five years. Unit shipments will reach levels experienced by today's floppy disks. This explosion will be driven by small business computing, distributed processing, and word processing demands for reliable, low-cost mass storage. The fastest growth segment within these markets will be multiple-terminal systems, which demand fast disk access capability to satisfy multiple users running multiple programs that share on-line data bases.

Competition also senses this market opportunity, and a variety of entrants are making plans or introducing products. Most entrants will find Winchester technology surprisingly difficult to design and manufacture efficiently. Shugart and CDC will be the toughest competitors. Shugart can be beaten on performance in multiple-terminal applications and matched in cost at the 30-megabyte capacity level. CDC can be beaten on cost. However, both companies have strong, established market positions and product introduction leads that will need to be overcome by PRIAM's superior price-performance product.

The PRIAM strategy is to capitalize on the window that has opened as a result of the expected shift to Winchester disk technology. The high twin barriers to entry of the difficult technology and heavy capital requirements will be overcome with a Winchester-experienced team and institutional-level financial backing. Product development will focus on achieving the low-cost design in a small, reliable package. Later product enhancements and additions will be aimed at building a disk product family. Financial leverage will be used during the launch, since most successful OEM businesses generate cash after momentum has been achieved. Manufacturing rights may be sold in Europe or Japan in order to minimize dilution. PRIAM will sell its product direct to OEM's in the U.S., but will initially use distribution offshore. Selling expense will be minimized by focusing on OEM's rather than end users. Other overheads will also be minimized to allow more effective price competition. PRIAM will target on the multiple-terminal small business computer (SBC), clustered word processing, and distributed processing markets. Initially, one or two large OEM's will be targeted to get the PRIAM disk accepted in the industry. Only one standard product will be offered, and variations/options will be limited. The factory will be focused on that single product, and costs will be driven down to achieve the low-cost position. Strong manufacturing controls will be emphasized to allow rapid but controlled growth. Time-phased investments will be made in automatic production equipment. Class 100 clean room conditions will be established to ensure superior product reliability.

Financing PRIAM will require an equity investment of $4.1 million during the first two years. The first round of financing will be $1.5 million. Other capital will be raised via an equipment lease line, a receivables line, and inventory advances.

C. Mobile Lung Densitometer

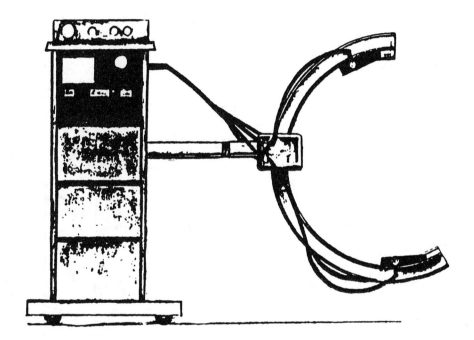

D. Sample Department Store Display

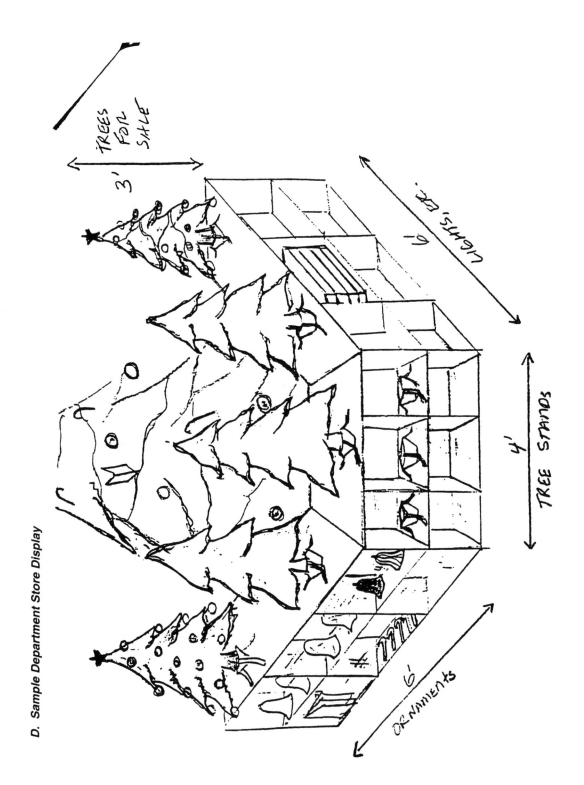

TREES FOR SALE

3'

LIGHTS, ETC.

6'

4'

TREE STANDS

6'

ORNAMENTS

4 NOTATION OF RISK FACTORS

A. Risk Analysis (FM Station)

Compared to most new venture investments, the risks associated with the proposed venture are considerably lower.

One reason for this lower risk is that the product (FM broadcasting) is a known and successful entity. Also, FM and FM/AM combinations appear to be entering the growth phase of their product life cycles and subplanting the more mature AM radio broadcasting.

A second reason for lower risk is that the entrepreneur in question is deeply familiar with the proposed business. He has direct management experience with the product, as opposed to someone with a new product but no experience managing a business built around the product.

A third reason is that the proposal calls for the acquisition of an on-going business, as opposed to a new start-up. This will maximize Mr. Merrill's strengths as quickly as possible.

Fourth, a minimum amount of capital will be exposed before an FCC licensing decision is reached. The sum in question is approximately $20-25,000* for Mr. Merrill's salary during this interim period. Also, the estimated probability of denial is extremely low given the FCC's goals.

* Assumes about six-month decision period.

B. Risk Factors (Magazine)

Projections. This Prospectus contains certain financial projections. Although no representations can be made that the circulation or advertising levels indicated by the projections will be achieved or that projected costs or cash flow will correspond even approximately to actual costs or cash flow, those projections reflect the current estimates of management of the results that are likely if circulation or advertising can be increased and the costs controlled as reflected herein. These projections are subject to the uncertainties inherent in any attempt to predict the results of operations for the next five years, especially where a new business in involved.

Additional Capital. Assuming the test projections are successful and publication of the magazine is commenced, it is estimated that at least $1 million of new capital will be required before positive cash flow is achieved. There are no commitments for any of these funds, and no assurances can be given that such funds will be available, and if available, no prediction can be made of the terms and conditions of such additional financing. Partners in the Partnership will be given the right to participate in this additional financing. To the extent this right it not exercised, a substantial dilution of the partners' interests will probably result.

Staff. To commence publication of the new magazine, it will be necessary to recruit a new staff. A full staff has not yet been recruited, and no assurance can be given that a qualified staff can be hired on reasonable terms.

Taxation. For the tax treatment of gains or losses to Limited Partners of the Partnership, see "Federal Income Tax Consequences."

General Risk. Starting a new magazine is a highly speculative undertaking and has historically involved a substantial degree of risk. The ultimate profitability of any magazine depends on its appeal to its readers and advertisers in relation to the cost of production, circulation, and distribution. Appeal to readers and advertisers is impossible to predict and depends upon the interaction of many complex factors.

Competition. The magazine business his highly competitive. In promoting the sale of *Venture*, management will be competing with many established companies having substantially greater financial resources.

5 COMPETITOR ANALYSIS DISPLAY

(Disguised due to confidentiality)

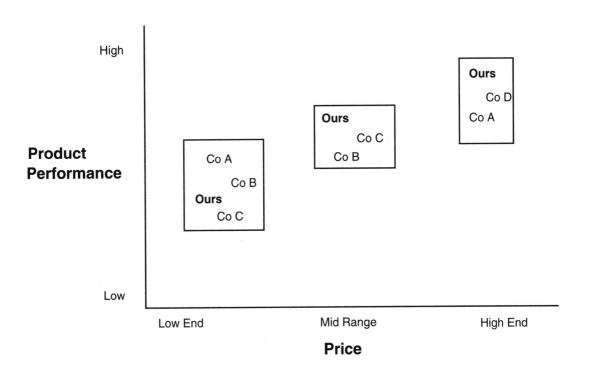

6 MARKET SURVEY RESULTS

A. Electronic Equipment Manufacturers

FIRM	Do own design	Familiar with CAD/CAM	Use CAD/ CAM	Can afford own CAD/ CAM	Are Interested in our services
Ospcon Ind.	yes	yes	no	no	yes
Eldec Corp.	yes	yes	have one	-	-
Circuits Eng. Inc.	no	-	-	-	-
Avtech Corp.	yes	yes	buying one	-	-
Solid State Syst.	no	-	-	-	-
Weico Corp.	yes	yes	no	no	yes
URS Inc.	yes	yes	have one	-	-
Universal Manuf. Corp.	no	-	-	-	-
Interface Mech.	yes	yes	no	no	no
Huntron Instru.	yes	yes	no	no	no
DDP Systems, Inc.	yes	yes	have one	-	-
Advanced Electronic App.	yes	yes	no	no	yes
Albar	yes	yes	no	no	no
Fluke John Mfg. Co.	yes	yes	yes	-	-
Micro-Mation Inc.	yes	yes	no	no	yes
Pacific Applied Electr.	no	-	-	-	-
APS Electronics Group	yes	yes	no	no	yes
DC Electronics Inc.	no	-	-	-	-

Of the ones who design:
  Familiar with CAD/CAM   100.0%
  Actual users   38.5%
  Cannot afford own CAD/CAM system   61.5%
Of the ones who design and cannot afford a CAD/CAM:
  Interested in our services   62.5%

7 MARKETING PLAN ELEMENTS SUMMARY

Plan For Distribution & Promotion of the Sperm Motility Meter

	Distribution	Promotion
Year 1	1) Seminars/Symposiums 2) Personal contacts - Dr. Lee. 3) Mail and telephone orders 4) Central Office Manager for traveling, sales and marketing efforts	1) Publish paper 2) Word of mouth 3) Brochures for seminars, mailings
Year 2	1) Seminars/Symposiums 2) 3-4 Salespeople for traveling sales and marketing efforts 3) Mail and telephone orders	1) Advertising in professional and scientific journals 2) Media 'free' promotion 3) Word of mouth 4) Brochures for seminars and mailings
Year 3	1) 10-12 Salespeople for traveling sales and marketing efforts 2) Mail and telephone orders	1) Advertising in professional & scientific journals 2) Brochures for seminars and mailings

This plan is analyzed quantitatively in the financial projections of Appendix A.

8 PRICING RATIONALE

	Labor Hours	Material
Fan Rotor		$2,500
Fan Box	80	200
Gear Box & Install	20	500
Test	20	
Box & Ship	8	50
Misc. Hardware		25
Balance	2	125
Other, Outside Service		50
	130 Hrs.	3,450
Labor Cost	$7/Hr. x 130 Hrs. =	910
Labor O/H		910
Labor & O/H Total		1,820
Total Cost		$5,270
Assume 30-percent gross profit (This amount to revenue on Operating Income Exhibit)		2,266
Selling Price		$7,536

9 SALES PROJECTIONS

A. Target Market Area: Washington State 1981, Year 1

Projected undergraduate degrees conferred in market area: 14,284

Area of Study	Number of Degrees	System Usage Rate (in %) Best /Expect/Worst			Number Using Service Best/ Expect/ Worst		
Business	2100	60	50	30	1260	1050	378
Education	1257	50	20	—	628	251	0
Social Science	1776	45	20	—	799	355	0
Public Affairs	529	45	20	—	238	106	0
Health Professions	914	40	30	10	411	274	91
Fine and Applied Arts	476	30	10	—	143	48	0
Physical Science	311	55	40	20	171	124	62
Biological Science	745	55	40	20	410	298	148
Communications	435	40	20	—	174	87	0
Engineering	714	60	50	30	428	357	214
Agriculture	568	50	15	5	284	85	28
Others	4459	25	10	5	1115	446	223
Total	14281				6061	3481	1144

Target Market Area: Washington, Oregon, Idaho & California 1984, Year 2
Projected undergraduate degrees conferred in market area: 107,582

Area of Study	Number of Degrees	System Usage Rate (in %) Best /Expect/Worst			Number Using Service Best/ Expect/ Worst		
Business	13938	60	52	30	8363	7248	4181
Education	7187	50	25	—	3594	1797	0
Social Science	17912	45	25	—	8060	4478	0
Public Affairs	3527	45	25	—	1587	882	0
Health Professions	4450	40	35	10	1780	1557	445
Fine and Applied Arts	5254	30	15	—	1576	788	0
Physical Science	1483	55	45	20	816	667	296
Biological Science	7300	55	45	20	4015	3285	1460
Communications	1928	40	25	—	771	482	0
Engineering	3618	60	50	30	2171	1809	1085
Agriculture	2859	50	25	5	1430	715	143
Others	38126	25	15	5	9311	5719	1906
Total	107582				43694	28703	9516

10 START-UP MILESTONES

| Month | 1 Mar | 2 May | 3 Jun | 4 Jul | 5 Aug | 6 Sep | 7 Oct | 8 Nov | 9 Dec | 10 Jan | 11 Feb | 12 |
| | 1982 | Apr | | | | | | | | 1983 | | |

Seek Financing
- - - - - - - 3/15/82   Complete Financing Arrangements

Negotiate Timeshare
- - - - - - - - 3/30/82   Contract Secured

Begin Database Design   Complete Database Design
- 8/1/82

Obtain Promotional Materials and Mark Sense Forms
- - - - - - - - - 7/15/82

Load Prototype Data Base
9/1/82

Complete Database Testing
9/15/82

Begin Phased Advertisements to Campuses
9/25/82 - - - - - - - - - - - - - - - - - >

Load Real Data Base;   Commence Operations with Fall Classes
10/1/82 - - - - - - - - - - - - - - - - - - >

Mass Mailings to Personnel Directors
1/15/83

11 PROJECT SCHEDULE

7/82 Clinical Traits

1/83 Publication of results

7/83 Begin Production

1/84 Delivery of first Lung Densitometer

7/84

1/85

7/85 Sustained Production

1/86

7/86

1/87

7/87

Market Research; Obtain Capital; Pro-totype Development

Marketing; Obtain Kickoff Orders

Radtech, Inc. Schedule

7/82 Commitment for Lung Densitometer

1/83

7/83

1/84 Delivery of first Lung Densitometer

7/84 Commitment for Second Project

1/85

7/85 Commitment for Third Project

1/86 First Delivery of 2nd Project

7/86 Commitment for 4th Project

1/87 First Delivery of 3rd Project

7/87 Commitment for 4th Project

12 Gantt Chart

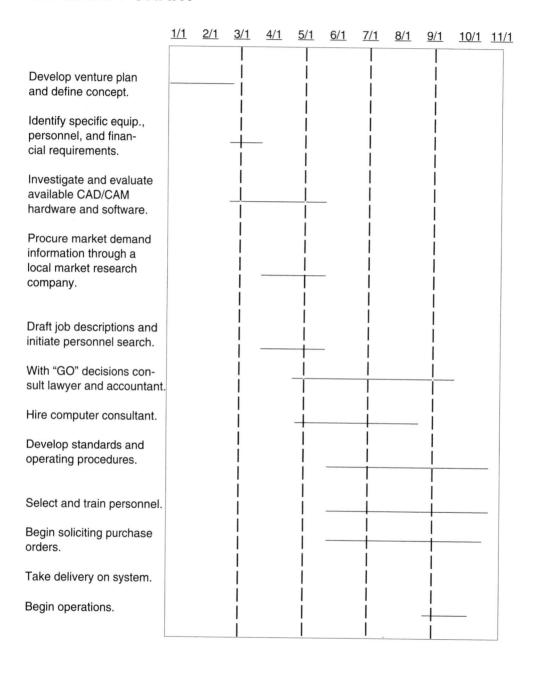

13 PERT CHART

A. Items

For VTC - For The First Year of Operations

Project	Activity	Time Required (months)	Precedence
A.	Preliminary Activities	4	-
	1. Finalize incorporation arrangements		
	2. Investigate sources of loan		
	3. Evaluate text program of product		
	4. Get legal aid - engage a lawyer		
	5. Enquire about tooling equipment		
B.	Establish contacts	3	-
	1. Contact suppliers of raw materials and equipment		
	2. Approach potential customers		
C.	Starting operations	2	A
	1. Incorporate officially		
	2. Secure loan		
	3. Set up office		
	- rent office space		
	- hire secretary		
	- arrange for utilities		
	- business insurance		
	- bank account		
	- set up accounting system		
	4. Buy tooling equipment		
D.	Place first order	1	B,C
E.	Deliver first order	1	D
F.	Aggressive marketing activities	continuous	E
G.	Evaluation of operations	2	E
	1. Product performance		
	2. Customer response		
	3. Competition's response		
	4. Level of sales		
	5. Cost and profitability		
H.	Further evaluation of expansion into manufacturing	3	E
I.	Decide on manufacturing	1	H
J.	Prepare for manufacturing operations	3	I
	1. Purchase necessary equipment		
	2. Additional employees		
	3. Additional space		
K.	Start full manufacturing operations	continuous	J

(See chart next page)

B.   Chart

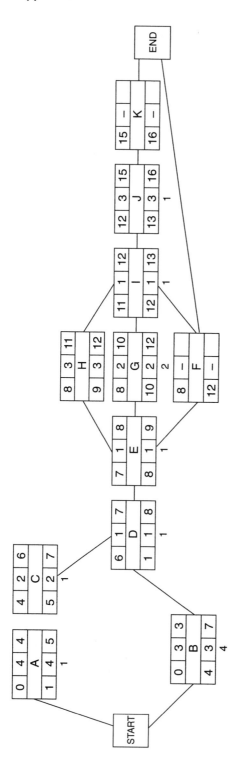

NOTE: Target for starting manufacturing is July 1990.
       Time available - 16 months.
       Time now March 1989 - period 0.
       Figures below the boxes represent the amount
       of float available - duration activity can be
       delayed without affecting operations.

KEY   D: Duration - Months
         EST: Earliest Start Time
         EFT: Earliest Finish Time
         LST: Latest Start Time
         LFT: Latest Finish Time

EST	D	EFT
Activity Code		
LST	D	LFT

14 BREAK-EVEN ANALYSIS

Radio broadcasting is a relatively high fixed-cost business. The only variable cost element that changes month-to-month with sales is commissions. These commissions include payments to agency and internal sales personnel.

Consequently, the basic costs structure of the business is:

Sales	=	100%
Variable Costs	=	27%
Contribution	=	73%

Using a contribution margin of 75 percent, we can calculate a sales (profit) break-even and a cash break-even.

As noted in Exhibit 8, the percentage of agency commissions to total sales is 12 percent. The difference between 12 percent and 27 percent (total variable costs) represents commissions paid to representatives and manager overrides. This 15 percent amounts to $75,000— which is included in operating expenses of Exhibit 8. Once removed, total fixed costs are:

$340,000 = ($305,000 - 75,000) + 20,000 + 45,000 + 45,000

Consequently, "profit" break-even is:

$$\$466,000 = \frac{\$340,000}{.73}$$

By removing non-cash expenses (depreciation and amortization of goodwill), a "cash" break-even can be calculated as:

$$\$377,000 = \frac{\$340,000 - 20,000 - 45,000}{.73}$$

These break-evens represent respectively 93 percent and 75 percent of sales.

15 COST BREAKDOWN

A. Projected Expenses

Our "Expected" case assumption (see Exhibit 1) includes first-year expenses of $924,500. The larger dollar expenses for the first year are discussed below under separate headings. We assume that during 1983, we will receive cash payment for one-third of the revenue billed, but two-thirds will remain in accounts receivable until the following year. Also, the four officers will be able to contribute approximately $5,000 each for a total of $20,000. Therefore, a total of $619,500 is required from outside sources.

Prototype Development: Based on the success of clinical trials in the fall of 1982, we expect to complete our first production model prototype by January 1983. The costs associated with this specimen are listed below:

Off-shelf equipment:	$35,000	Mobile X-ray operator
	5,000	2 X-ray tubes at $2,500 each
	3,000	X-ray detectors and counting electronics
	5,000	Data acquisition and computer
Custom Machinery and labor:	6,000	C-arm assembly
	3,000	Machinery
	3,000	Engineer assembly
Total	$60,000	

The amount of $60,000 is the expected production cost of a machine and is used as the cost of sales estimate in pro forma income statements presented in Section IX. In addition to the $60,000, we expect to spend an additional $40,000 developing this prototype.

B. Expenditure Projections

The second-year expansion in Seattle and the fourth-year expansion in Portland involves the addition of three terminal operators at each location.

Fifth-year salaries for the two locations are as follows:

SEATTLE

President	$40,000
Three Vice-Presidents at $40,000	120,000
Three Engineers at $35,000	105,000
First three Operators at $25,000	75,000
Second three Operators at $23,000	69,000
Secretary	21,000
Total	$430,000

PORTLAND

Manager	$36,000
Two Vice-Presidents at $34,000	68,000
Three Engineers at $32,000	96,000
First three Operators at $22,000	66,000
Second three Operators at $21,000	63,000
Secretary	20,000
Total	$349,000

The additional salary expense for social security, health insurance and other employee taxes and benefits is assumed to be 30 percent of the base salaries.

EQUIPMENT MAINTENANCE

This expense is based upon an established charge of 0.9 percent per month on purchase price of CAD/CAM equipment for a service contract from the vendor.

OFFICE LEASE

Both the Seattle and Portland offices are assumed rented at $15 per square foot office in each location. Rental increases are projected after the second year.

TELEPHONE AND UTILITIES

These expenses are originally projected at $1,000 per month at each location, with increases in future years.

16 APPLICATION OF FUNDS

The Partnership will be formed for the purpose of developing and conducting a mailing to test the feasibility of founding a business magazine called *"Venture* . . . the magazine for entrepreneurs."* A positive response to the test mailing in excess of 2 percent would generally be required before advancing to the next stage of the magazine's development. If the response falls below this, the project will in all probability be abandoned and no salvage value is anticipated.

If the test is successful, the next step will be to prepare for the start of regular publication of the magazine, which will involve recruiting a staff, selling advertising, establishing relations with suppliers, commencing direct mail promotion, and raising a substantial amount of additional capital (see "Prepublication Phase").

It is projected that the proceeds of the sale of interests in the Partnership will be expended approximately in the following manner.

Direct Mail test (80,000 pieces)	$24,000
Advertising Agency	4,000
Office and Travel	2,250
Magazine Design	1,750
Legal	3,000
	$35,000

Interests in the Partnership will not be registered with the Securities and Exchange Commission. The Partnership is relying on an exemption from registration for the sale of securities, which do not involve a public offering. Accordingly, each purchaser will be required to agree that his purchase was not made with any present intention to resell, distribute, or in any way transfer or dispose of his interest in the Partnership, except in compliance with applicable securities laws, and that he meets the suitability standards described herein.

No person is authorized to give any information or representation not contained in this memorandum. Any information or representation not contained herein must not be relied upon as having been authorized by the Partnership for the General Partner.

17 PRO FORMA FINANCIAL STATEMENTS

PRO FORMA INCOME STATEMENT
(Best Case Scenario)

	1990	1991	1992	1993	1994
		in thousands of dollars			
Sales Revenue	$2,000	$5,280	$5,980	$6,160	$6,390
Expenses					
Cost of Goods Sold	624	894	1,055	1,108	1,393
Gross Margin	1,376	4,386	4,925	5,052	4,997
Selling & Admin Expense	30	79	90	92	96
Depreciation Expense	1	1	2	2	3
Salaries Expense	40	68	90	100	140
R and D Expense	40	106	239	246	256
Interest Expense	12	0	0	0	0
Utilities Expense	2	3	3	3	4
Insurance Expense	8	33	60	87	114
Total Overhead Expenses	133	290	484	531	613
Net Income Before Taxes	1,243	4,096	4,441	4,521	4,384
Income Tax Expense	497	1,639	1,776	1,808	1,754
Net Income After Taxes	$746	$2,458	$2,665	$2,712	$2,631

PRO FORMA BALANCE SHEET

Assets	1990	1991	1992	1993	1994
		in thousands of dollars			
Current Assets					
Cash	$224	$1,673	$4,278	$6,931	$9,214
Accts. Receivable	250	660	748	770	799
Inventory	50	132	150	154	160
Misc.	20	53	60	62	64
Fixed Assets					
Tooling	240	580	509	641	1,068
Molding Machine	0	140	182	140	98
End Mill	0	44	57	44	31
Oven	0	11	9	7	4
Total Assets	784	3,293	5,992	8,748	11,437
Liabilities					
Current Liabilities	5	13	15	15	16
Other Liabilities	20	53	60	62	64
Total Liabilities	25	66	75	77	80
Owner's Equity					
C/S (1.8MM Shares)	12	12	12	12	12
Retained Earnings	746	3,204	5,868	8,581	11,211
Total Equity & Liabilities	$783	$3,282	$5,955	$8,670	$11,303

18 CASH FLOW PROJECTION

First Year Cash Flow Chart

Month	1	2	3	4	5	6	7	8	9	10	11	12	Yr
Cash at beginning	$0	$153,883	$125,958	$98,033	$70,108	$50,978	$31,848	$12,718	$15,574	$18,430	$21,286	$46,129	
Revenue Receipts		13,192	13,192	13,192	21,987	21,987	21,987	43,973	43,973	43,973	65,960	65,960	369,376
Cash from Outside Src	675,000	0	0	0	0	0	0	0	0	0	0	0	675,000
Tot. Cash Avail.	675,000	167,075	139,150	111,225	92,095	72,965	53,835	56,691	59,547	62,403	87,246	112,089	1,044,378
Operating Expenditures													
Salaries	28,817	28,817	28,817	28,817	28,817	28,817	28,817	28,817	28,817	28,817	28,817	28,817	
Maintenance	4,050	4,050	4,050	4,050	4,050	4,050	4,050	4,050	4,050	4,050	4,050	4,050	
Office Lease	1,250	1,250	1,250	1,250	1,250	1,250	1,250	1,250	1,250	1,250	1,250	1,250	
Tel. & Util.	1,000	1,000	1,000	1,000	1,000	1,000	1,000	1,000	1,000	1,000	1,000	1,000	
Advertising	15,000	3,000	3,000	3,000	3,000	3,000	3,000	3,000	3,000	3,000	3,000	3,000	
R&D	2,000	2,000	2,000	2,000	2,000	2,000	2,000	2,000	2,000	2,000	2,000	2,000	
Misc.	1,000	1,000	1,000	1,000	1,000	1,000	1,000	1,000	1,000	1,000	1,000	1,000	
Tot. Operating	$53,117	$41,117	$41,117	$41,117	$41,117	$41,117	$41,117	$41,117	$41,117	$41,117	$41,117	$41,117	$505,404
Other Cash Expenditures													
CAD/CAM Systm	$450,000												
Off. Site Prep.	10,000												
Furniture	5,000												
Legal & Acct.	3,000												
Total Other	$468,000												$468,000
Fed. Income Tax	0	0	0	0	0	0	0	0	0	0	0	0	0
Tot. Cash Expen.	$521,117	$41,117	$41,117	$41,117	$41,117	$41,117	$41,117	$41,117	$41,117	$41,117	$41,117	$41,117	$973,404
Cash at end	$153,883	$125,958	$98,033	$70,108	$50,978	$31,848	$12,718	$15,574	$18,430	$21,286	$46,129	$70,972	$70,972

19 FOOTNOTES TO FINANCIAL PROJECTIONS

1   Estimated at $48,000 per machine; $38,400 in lots of 10 (20-percent manufacturing discount)

2   Estimated at $12,000 per machine

3   One salesperson at $10,000 base salary plus 5-percent gross sales commission 1/83 to 1/85

Two salespeople 1985, 1986; 3 for 1987

4   Includes cost of attending annual medical equipment trade show at $8,000

5   Four officers: CEO at $30,000, others at $25,000 for 1983, 1984; CEO at $60,000, others at $50,000 for 1985, 1986, 1987

6   One salesperson 1985, 1986

Two salespeople 1987

7   One salesperson 1983

Two salespeople 1984, 1985

Three salespeople 1986

Four salespeople 1987

8   Four officers: CEO at $30,000, others at $25,000 for 1983, 1984; CEO at $100,000, others at $85,000 for 1985, 1986, 1987

9   Capital needed:

First-year expenses	($924,500.)
Expect to receive one-third gross sales, two-thirds as accounts receivable	285,000.
Capital needed	639,500.
Contributed by officer	20,000.
Required from outside funding	($619,500.)

Index